Religion Matters

AN INTRODUCTION TO THE WORLD'S RELIGIONS

Religion Matters

AN INTRODUCTION TO THE WORLD'S RELIGIONS

STEPHEN PROTHERO

BOSTON UNIVERSITY

W. W. NORTON & COMPANY

Independent Publishers Since 1923

W. W. NORTON & COMPANY has been independent since its founding in 1923, when William Warder Norton and Mary D. Herter Norton first published lectures delivered at the People's Institute, the adult education division of New York City's Cooper Union. The firm soon expanded its program beyond the Institute, publishing books by celebrated academics from America and abroad. By midcentury, the two major pillars of Norton's publishing program—trade books and college texts—were firmly established. In the 1950s, the Norton family transferred control of the company to its employees, and today—with a staff of four hundred and a comparable number of trade, college, and professional titles published each year—W. W. Norton & Company stands as the largest and oldest publishing house owned wholly by its employees.

Editor: Roby Harrington
Developmental Editor: Beth Ammerman
Project Editor: Linda Feldman
Art and Captions Editor: Kira Ganga Kieffer
Associate Editor: Gerra Goff
Assistant Editor: Chris Howard-Woods
Managing Editor, College: Marian Johnson
Managing Editor, College Digital Media: Kim Yi
Associate Director of Production, College: Benjamin Reynolds
Media Editor: Carly Fraser Doria
Associate Media Editor: Alexander Lee
Media Project Editor: Cooper Wilhelm
Media Editorial Assistant: Jessica Awad
Digital Production: Danielle Vargas
Marketing Manager: Michael Moss and Kim Bowers
Design Director: Lissi Sigillo
Photo Editor: Travis Carr
Photo Researcher: Julie Tesser
Director of College Permissions: Megan Schindel
College Permissions Assistant: Patricia Wong
Composition and Layout: Brad Walrod/Kenoza Type, Inc.
Cartography: Mapping Specialists—Fitchburg, WI
Manufacturing: Transcontinental—Beauceville, QC

Permission to use copyrighted material is included on page C-1.

Library of Congress Cataloging-in-Publication Data

Names: Prothero, Stephen R., author.
Title: Religion matters : an introduction to the world's religions/Stephen Prothero.
Description: New York : W. W. Norton & Company, 2020. | Includes bibliographical references and index.
Identifiers: LCCN 2019045009 | **ISBN 9780393912852** (paperback) | ISBN 9780393422085 (ebook)
Subjects: LCSH: Religions.
Classification: LCC BL80.3 .P765 2020 | DDC 200--dc23
LC record available at https://lccn.loc.gov/2019045009

W. W. Norton & Company, Inc., 500 Fifth Avenue, New York, NY 10110-0017

wwnorton.com

W. W. Norton & Company Ltd., 15 Carlisle Street, London W1D 3BS

1 2 3 4 5 6 7 8 9 0

To my students

Brief Contents

Contents

PART III
Religions of Reversion: China and North America   340

Preface

The public understanding of religion has never been more necessary. In the United States, Jesus, Christianity, and the Bible are regularly invoked by members of both political parties on public policy questions from abortion to immigration to economic inequality. Elsewhere in the world, religious symbols, ideas, leaders, and institutions play similarly central roles in politics, economics, and society. Unfortunately, Americans know almost nothing about their own religious traditions and even less about those of others. In the 2010 U.S. Religious Knowledge Survey by the Pew Research Center, just over half of respondents knew that the Quran was the holy book of Islam, and just under half were able to correctly identify the Dalai Lama as a Buddhist. In a 2019 follow-up survey, American adults again fared poorly, with an average score of well under 50 percent, or just 14 correct answers out of 32 very basic questions about the world's religions.

The central goal of this textbook is to cultivate religious literacy in college students in order to better equip them for participation in a public square that remains resolutely religious, both at home and abroad. A second goal is to offer students—many of whom will take no other course in religious studies—an introduction to humanistic learning and the liberal arts. As universities and their donors are increasingly emphasizing STEM disciplines, and ratings agencies are focusing more and more on quantitative outcomes such as starting salaries after graduation, the "bottom-line" thinking that used to be particular to the business world is now spreading across the world of higher education. But the skills and sensibilities learned in courses like Introduction to the World's Religions have never been more imperative than they are today. As readers of *Religion Matters* survey the world's religions from ancient China to the contemporary United States, they will have an opportunity to flex their humanistic muscles by paying close attention to scriptures and rituals, wrestling with philosophical and theological arguments, interpreting works of art, and attending to change over time.

Students will also have an opportunity to enter into conversations with the living and the dead about some of the greatest stories ever told and some of the greatest questions ever asked. These conversations can bear fruit in the world of work—in businesses where empathetic understanding of other cultures is crucial to success, and in medicine where a patient's health (or life) may hang on knowing whether a patient is taking medication during the Muslim fast of Ramadan. More important, these conversations offer students opportunities to acquire skills and sensibilities that will shape the sorts of human beings they are in the process of becoming.

A CREATION STORY

This book was not my idea. It began in the mind's eye of Roby Harrington, director of W. W. Norton's College Department, who, a decade ago, was trying to move Norton into religious studies publishing. Roby had signed on Jack Miles as general editor of *The Norton Anthology of World Religions*, and was eager to produce a textbook that might accompany it on their list. Norton history editor Steve Forman was familiar with my book *Religious Literacy* (2007) and with my primer on the world's religions, *God Is Not One* (2010). He suggested me as a possible author. When Roby approached my agent, Sandy Dijkstra, about writing the textbook, I declined. I just couldn't imagine taking it on. However, over a series of conversations, Roby won me over. I came to see *Religion Matters* as a natural next step in a career I had increasingly devoted to promoting religious literacy. I also came to conceive of the book as a team effort, with a dozen or more talented professionals at Norton working to bring my words alive in print and online and to put it in the hands of instructors at community colleges, liberal arts colleges, and private and public universities. Writing can be a solitary exercise, and I grew more and more excited about being part of such a talented and dedicated team. I was also excited about working for an employee-owned publisher with such a long and distinguished track record of commitment to the humanities.

GOALS AND THEMES

In *God Is Not One*, I argued against efforts to collapse the world's religions into one solitary "perennial" religion. In *Religion Matters*, I again emphasize the differences over the similarities among the world's religions. But here I focus on a shared human activity: storytelling.

Each chapter is organized around a series of interpenetrating stories:

- an opening journalistic story I tell from an outsider's perspective about a sacred place held dear by people inside a particular tradition
- a scriptural or mythical story paraphrased from an insider's perspective about why that sacred place matters to a particular community—why it is *the* place
- a historical story I tell about how the religious tradition started, how it changed over time, and how it produced so much internal diversity

As I tell these stories, I hope students will come to see the world's religions not as belief systems but as vast libraries of stories and the questions they ask (and attempt to answer).

Over the course of the book, a few key themes emerge. One is difference and diversity. The world's religions are not different paths up the same mountain. Their practitioners differ fundamentally from one another in their beliefs and practices—and in how they understand and respond to the human predicament. But the world's religions are also internally diverse, with Sunni and Shia Muslims and Protestant and Catholic Christians disagreeing in many cases nearly as profoundly as Confucians and Daoists do. This difference and diversity is also on display in many classrooms, including my own, where it is not at all unusual for me to welcome into a single lecture course twenty Hindus; ten Buddhists; ten Muslims; a few Jains; and many Christians, Jews, and nonbelievers.

Another theme of *Religion Matters* is change over time and from place to place. Although I do hazard generalizations about each of the religious traditions I cover, I am acutely aware of the ways that all religious traditions are historically and geographically constructed. Revelations notwithstanding, they typically come into being gradually rather than in a single flash of insight. And then they change, often dramatically, over time. They splinter. They shuffle their sacred books and rituals. They replace one set of religious professionals with another. And they refuse to stand still. As practitioners move—as immigrants or refugees or captives or missionaries or colonizers or pilgrims—they adapt their religious traditions to new places and peoples. Today, the Hinduism of Bali is very different from the Hinduism of New Delhi or Boston. Even the young Hindus who take my courses differ, profoundly in many cases, over what their gods and goddesses want them to do and to think.

A third and related theme is that these religious traditions live. Scholarship on Native nations has been bedeviled by stereotypes of the "vanishing Indian," and for far too many years scholars have similarly prophesied the withering away of religion. As a result, writing on religious traditions with ancient roots—Hinduism and Judaism and Confucianism, for example—has tended to be confined to ancient texts and the ancient world. In contrast, each chapter in *Religion Matters* begins with an account of the sacred and profane activities swirling around a place held dear by Buddhists or Sikhs or Muslims or Navajos today. Each chapter ends with a contemporary controversy.

All of these themes find expression in image as well as word. The art program underscores the fact that religion is not the exclusive province of older male clergy. Children are religious storytellers, too, as are women. And their religious histories are shaped only in part by rabbis, priests, imams, and gurus. The photographs, paintings, and sculptures reproduced in the book—and the material objects featured in each chapter—also steer away from the classical and toward the contemporary, in an effort to demonstrate that these religious traditions continue to live and breathe as surely as their adherents do.

ORGANIZATION

Religion Matters includes ten chapters organized in four parts. Part I (Chapters 2–4) explores the Religions of Release of India: Hinduism, Buddhism, and Sikhism. These religious traditions have wrestled for centuries with the problem of rebirth and redeath and the suffering that accompanies each. Rather than seeking to repair the world or to revert back to a golden age, Hindus, Buddhists, and Sikhs have sought release from the world through various forms of spiritual liberation.

Part II (Chapters 5–7) examines the Religions of Repair of the Middle East: Judaism, Christianity, and Islam. When faced with the problems of exile or sin or pride, Jews, Christians, and Muslims have sought otherworldly solace in heaven or paradise, but they have also labored to repair the world—by keeping God's commandments, by seeking justice and pursuing mercy, by acting with faith, and by submitting to the will of the divine.

Part III (Chapters 8–10) moves from China to North America as it explores the Religions of Reversion: Confucianism, Daoism, and Navajo religion. In each of these three cases, practitioners seek to fix what has gone wrong with human civilization by looking to ancient exemplars and returning to their societies of long ago: to the ordered empires of the ancient sage-kings of Confucian lore, or the state of nature idealized by Daoists, or the Navajo era of emergence from the underworld of the Holy People and the Earth Surface People they created at the beginning of time.

Part IV (Chapter 11), Rejecting Religion, brings atheists, agnostics, and other nonbelievers into the conversation. Instead of viewing religion as a solution to the human predicament, these skeptics typically view it as the problem. This part, which consists of just one chapter, attends not only to the development of critiques of God belief in the modern West, but also to the early presence of skepticism—about ritual and religion alike.

ACKNOWLEDGMENTS

As I said, I was drawn to this project by the extraordinary talents of the college book division at Norton, and I have been grateful throughout for their intelligence, creativity, hard work, and team spirit. Steve Forman, my initial editor, was a sage and steady collaborator during the first few years of this project. Roby Harrington took over those editorial duties as we worked during the last few years to bring the project to print. In addition to running an efficient meeting (something few academic departments have yet perfected), Roby brought the perfect combination of urgency and calm to the project.

Associate editor Gerra Goff juggled not only the manuscript but also the photographs, art, and maps. She brought the whole package together, syncing text and images, and keeping the team on schedule along the way. Beth Ammerman was our invaluable developmental editor and my first point of contact on the writing. She juggled as many as a half dozen outside reviews per chapter and worked hard to integrate their comments and criticisms into various drafts. I couldn't have done the revisions without her. Carly Fraser Doria was our very talented media editor who, in addition to her expertise in audio, video, and the Web, brought an upbeat spirit to all the challenges we faced. I thoroughly enjoyed working with her to tape author videos on Boston University's campus, and I continue to be amazed by Norton's adaptive quizzing tool, InQuizitive.

Other key players on *Religion Matters* include our project editor, Linda Feldman, who brought order to chaos as we worked so many different elements of the project into the page proofs, and our assistant editor, Chris Howard-Woods, who kept all sorts of different trains running behind the scenes. Ben Reynolds, associate director of production, ensured the efficient flow of manuscript and art to various outside contributors. Our photo editor, Travis Carr, worked tirelessly to track down not only beautiful photographs but also the rights to images I threw at him from left field. College permissions assistant Patricia Wong deftly handled the clearing of text permissions. Michael Moss and Kim Bowers helped shape our message as marketing managers, and Elizabeth Pieslor, Humanities specialist, led the sales effort. As those who have seen me draw are aware, I know nothing about art and design, but I love the look and feel of this book and am deeply in Lissi Sigillo's debt for her amazing design work.

I also want to acknowledge Norton's college sales team, led by director of college sales, Mike Wright. Their in-house job titles ("travelers") recall in my mind the Methodist circuit riders who went out on horseback across the American West in the nineteenth century, putting tracts and pamphlets in the hands of unsuspecting pioneers. Their enthusiastic reception of the book at a Norton sales conference in Seattle in 2019 gave me the energy to push my portion of the book to completion in 2020.

Colleagues and former colleagues in BU's Department of Religion have educated me for more than two decades now in their respective specialties. I'm especially grateful to Jonathan Klawans for fielding so many emails and phone calls about the Judaism chapter in this book, to Laura Harrington for reviewing the chapter on Buddhism, and Yair Lior for reviewing the chapters on Confucianism and Judaism. I also benefited from conversations about specific issues with David Eckel, April Hughes, Teena Purohit, Kecia Ali, David Frankfurter, Diana Lobel, Anthony Petro, and Michael Zank.

I am happy to acknowledge three other people with BU ties who contributed to the book. Kira Ganga Kieffer, a PhD student in our graduate program in Religion, began working on *Religion Matters* as my research assistant, but she quickly became an invaluable part of the broader Norton team, serving as the editor of art and captions. We had a lot to do at the end on an exceptionally tight schedule, and there just isn't any way we could have done it without her expertise and hard work. In a fit of serendipity (or providence), during a side trip to Texas State University, Roby also recruited an extraordinarily talented husband-and-wife team, Joe Laycock and Natasha Mikles, to work on this project. Joe, a former PhD advisee of mine, is a prolific writer of important articles and books in the study of American religion. Natasha is an expert on Tibetan Buddhism and Chinese religions. Both are innovative teachers who brought new ideas and energy to the table. In addition to reading and commenting on each chapter, they produced all sorts of innovative content—class activities, discussion questions, supplemental readings—for the *Religion Matters* Interactive Instructor's Guide. They also authored the InQuizitive questions and produced PowerPoint presentations and test bank questions for each chapter. I would also like to thank the students who shared their experiences on camera for the Student-to-Student video series that appear in the *Religion Matters* media program.

My thanks go out as well to the many people who met with me, toured me around, and welcomed me into their sacred places, from London to Jerusalem to Bodh Gaya to Beijing: Fei Tianhui (Sunny), who guided me so expertly (and with such unflagging cheer) around China; Professor Jiang Sheng of Sichuan University for taking a series of days out of his busy schedule to walk me up Daoist mountains outside Chengdu; Zhang Mingxin and Tang Chengqing, Daoist masters at the Jianfu Monastery on Green City Mountain outside Chengdu, China, who educated me about their traditions; Rana P. B. Singh of Banaras Hindu University for teaching me so much about the sacred geography of Varanasi; his graduate student (and my tour guide and translator in Varanasi) Ajay Pandey (Pinku); Sanderson Jones for welcoming me to a London meeting of his Sunday Assembly and agreeing to talk with me about his "atheist church"; the monks and nuns at the Temple of Supreme Purity Complex on Mount Lao outside of Qingdao, China, who graciously allowed me to stay for a time at their monastery; and Klee and Princess Benally, for orienting me to the San Francisco Peaks outside of Flagstaff, Arizona, and agreeing to reveal to me what they could about the Diné way.

Additional thanks to Todd Johnson and his staff at Boston University's World Religion Database for providing us with 2020 figures for religious adherents; Benjamin Marcus of the Religious Freedom Center for his astute criticisms of the introduction; Thomas Michael and Louis Komjathy for serving as long-standing guides to the Daoist tradition; Michael McNally for directing me to the controversy about the desecration of sacred lands on the San Francisco Peaks; Howard Shanker and his staff for opening the archives of their law office to me; Noah Silverman and Jenan Mohajir of the Interfaith Youth Core for connecting us with participant reviewers for many chapters; Andrew Henry for fact checking; and the editors of *The Norton Anthology of World Religions*, namely, Jack Miles, Wendy Doniger, Donald Lopez, James Robson, David Biale, Lawrence Cunningham, and Jane Dammen McAuliffe, for their exhaustive work on that pathbreaking project and their personal assistance to me.

This project also benefited tremendously from a series of focus groups held at American Academy of Religion meetings over the course of a few years. These meetings featured professors with on-the-ground experience teaching introductory courses on the world's religions to a wide variety of student bodies, and their comments and criticisms were extraordinarily helpful. They include:

Eliza Young Barstow, Oregon State University

Rose T. Caraway, Iowa State University

Nicole Goulet, Indiana University of Pennsylvania

Michael Graziano, University of Northern Iowa

Matthew Hotham, Ball State University

Christina Kilby, James Madison University

Evelyn Kirkley, University of San Diego

Louis Komjathy, University of San Diego

Ben Marcus, Religious Freedom Center

Kate McCarthy, California State University, Chico

Jeremy Rapport, College of Wooster

Joanne Robinson, University of North Carolina at Charlotte

William Sherman, University of North Carolina at Charlotte

Stephanie Yuhas, University of Colorado, Denver

Later in its development, *Religion Matters* also benefited from a review process far more extensive than I have experienced in my career at peer-reviewed journals and presses. The Norton team solicited a half dozen or so reviews of chapter drafts by scholars with research expertise in the religious traditions covered in the book. These extraordinarily helpful reviews saved me from numerous errors of fact and fumbling interpretations. Also, by underscoring matters of scholarly disagreement and public contention, they challenged me to attend with additional care to particularly controversial issues.

Maura Abrahamson, Morton College

Clay Bench, University of Texas at El Paso

Joseph Blankholm, University of California, Santa Barbara

Mara Brecht, St. Norbert College

Robert Campany, Vanderbilt University

Tim Chustz, Catholic High, Baton Rouge

Thomas Condry, Central Texas College

John L. Crow, Florida State University

Philip C. Dimare, Cal State Sacramento

Aaron Gale, West Virginia University

Jennifer Garvin-Sanchez, Virginia Commonwealth University—Monroe Park Campus

Marko Geslani, University of South Carolina at Columbia

Jennifer Graber, University of Texas

Greg Grieve, University of North Carolina at Greensboro

Brian Hatcher, Tufts

Susan Hill, Northern Iowa

Gregory Hillis, University of California, Santa Barbara

Pankaj Jain, University of North Texas

Lucas Johnston, Wake Forest University

Sonam Kachru, University of Virginia

Louis Komjathy, University of San Diego

Dmitri Korobeynikov, SUNY Albany

Joseph Laycock, Texas State University

Mark Leuchter, Temple University

Yair Lior, Boston University

James Lochtefeld, Carthage College

Donald S. Lopez, University of Michigan

Joanne Maguire, University of North Carolina at Charlotte

Tom Maroukis, Ohio State University

June McDaniel, College of Charleston

Michael McNally, Carleton College

Tom Michael, Beiging Normal University

Natasha Mikles, Texas State University

James Miller, Duke's China university

Sushil Mittal, James Madison University

Susan Nowak, Nazareth College

David Oughton, Saint Louis University

Grant Potts, Austin Community College

Steven Ramey, The University of Alabama

Whitney Sanford, University of Florida

Elijah Siegler, College of Charleston

Pashaura Singh, University of California, Riverside

Kenny Paul Smith, Louisiana State University and Agricultural & Mechanical College

Bin Song, Washington College

Randall Styers, University of North Carolina at Chapel Hill

Mark Thames, The Dallas County Community College District

Hugh Urban, Ohio State University

Jay Holt Valentine, Troy University

Michael S. Valle, Scottsdale Community College

Christian van Gorder, Baylor

Mark Webb, Texas Tech University

Daniel Wolne, University of New Mexico

Liz Wilson, Miami University

Stephanie Yuhas, University of Colorado, Denver

Katherine Zubko, University of North Carolina at Asheville

The Norton team also solicited reviews about their respective religious traditions by practitioners, and the book is better because of their comments and criticisms as well.

Rehan Ansari
Lily Gellman
Katie Gordon
Shivam Gosai
Jem Jebbia

Tasmiha Khan
Nicholas Price
Maneshwar Singh
Dena Trugman

Other scholars who provided additional help, from responding to queries by email to commenting on full chapters, include: Kecia Ali, Amit Basole, David Brakke, Julie Byrne, Robert Ford Campany, Wendy Doniger, Greg Epstein, Jackie Feldman, Paula Fredriksen, Menaka Guruswamy, Kate Holbrook, Hillary Kaell, Livia Kohn, Lois Lee, Donald Lopez, Gurinder Singh Mann, Peter Manseau, Joel Martin, James Miller, Robert Neville, Martyn Oliver, Greg Riley, Dana Robert, Nora Rubel, Omid Safi, Leigh Eric Schmidt, Richard Seager, Nikky-Guninder Kaur Singh, Anna Sun, Thomas Tweed, Ananya Vajpeyi, Duncan Williams, Lauren Winner, Onaje Woodbine, Fenggang Yang, and Julianne Zhou.

My literary agent, Sandy Dikstra, who has worked with Norton on other bestselling textbooks, helped me see the virtues of this project. As always, it was wonderful to work with her and with Elise Capron and others at the Sandra Dijkstra Literary Agency.

I am also grateful to my daughters, Molly and Lucy, for feigning interest in my work, and to Lucy for her meticulous fact checking. One final deep bow is also due to my talented partner and wife, Meera Subramanian. An environmental journalist and master of long-form narrative nonfiction, Meera read and commented on the entire book, accompanied me on research trips to China and India, and took many of the book's most spectacular photographs. Shukria and shabash.

About the Author

Stephen Prothero is the C. Allyn and Elizabeth V. Russell Professor of Religion at Boston University specializing in American religions. He received his BA from Yale College in American Studies and his MA and PhD from Harvard University in the Study of Religion.

A historian of American religions, Professor Prothero has written six books, including *The White Buddhist: The Asian Odyssey of Henry Steel Olcott*, which won the Best First Book award of the American Academy of Religion in 1997, and *American Jesus: How the Son of God Became a National Icon*, which was named one of the top religion books for 2003 by *Publishers Weekly*. His two most recent projects are the *New York Times* bestseller *Religious Literacy: What Every American Needs to Know—and Doesn't* and *God Is Not One: The Eight Rival Religions that Run the World and Why Their Differences Matter*.

In addition to his scholarly work, which includes peer-reviewed articles in the *Journal of the American Academy of Religion*, Prothero has written for a variety of popular magazines and newspapers, including the *New York Times, Wall Street Journal, USA Today, Newsweek, Slate, Salon, Washington Post, Los Angeles Times*, and *Boston Globe*. He has commented on religion on NPR and all the major networks, and on such television programs as *The Colbert Report, The Daily Show with Jon Stewart, The Oprah Winfrey Show, The O'Reilly Factor*, and *The Today Show*. He was the chief editorial consultant to the six-hour PBS television series *God in America* and the leading scholarly contributor to CNN's *Belief Blog*.

Visit his personal website at www.stephenprothero.com or follow him on Twitter at sprothero.

Religion Matters

AN INTRODUCTION TO THE WORLD'S RELIGIONS

Five-wicked oil lamps used during worship illuminate the interior of a small temple to the popular Hindu god Shiva in Varanasi, India.

Introduction

WHY RELIGION MATTERS

I will tell you something about stories…
They aren't just entertainment.
Don't be fooled.
They are all we have, you see,
all we have to fight off
illness and death.
—Leslie Marmon Silko, *Ceremony*

In the beginning was the story. Before *Star Wars* and *Pride and Prejudice*, before Moses and the Buddha, before the first mastodon hunt and the first crop of wheat, human beings told and listened to stories. Some of these stories concerned the size of the fish they caught. Others told of grander adventures with gods and monsters. But for nearly as long as we human beings have walked the earth, we have been telling and retelling stories.

"We tell ourselves stories in order to live," writes author Joan Didion, but we also live to tell stories.[1] We tell ourselves stories about loves lost and found, and about who we are, who we have been, and who we might become. Parents tell children folk tales about how the zebra got his stripes. Historians spin narratives that transform soldiers into presidents. Preachers tell stories about how love and justice triumph in the end. Some of these stories are true. Some are packs of lies. Most are a combination. Nonetheless, stories circulate among us as surely as the air we breathe. These stories may entertain, but they are serious stuff. They orient us in time and space, telling us where we have been and where we are going.

Fortunes rise and fall on the stories we tell. Stories determine the successes and failures of our towns and cities, political parties, and countries. Individual lives are sacrificed on the altar of a story, or snatched from certain death at the last minute by a better one. Megabrands from Alphabet to Zillow are worth billions because of the stories their founders, advertisers, and users have spun over the years. The reason you can walk into a store, pull out a dollar bill, and buy a candy bar is because you share with the person behind the counter stories about that piece of paper being a dollar and the dollar being a storehouse of value.

When we are born our parents and grandparents tell stories about us. And when we die those who remain tell stories, too—about how we will be reborn someday in another body, or how one day all the bodies buried underground will rise up and be spirited off to their afterlife appointments.

Religions are often called "belief systems." But the Christian tradition is the only major religion that puts a strong emphasis on beliefs. "We believe in one Lord, Jesus Christ, the only Son of God," Christians affirm, every Sunday in many churches, in the words of the Nicene Creed. Beliefs matter less in other religious traditions, where they are rarely pressed and processed into formal statements of belief.

So religions are not "belief systems." Are they ritual systems? ethical systems? That depends on where you are looking, since the world's religions vary widely when it comes to their relative emphases on ritual and ethics. But all religions are "story systems." To explore the world's religions is to wander up and down the aisles of a vast library housing the greatest stories ever told—stories so powerful they have lasted, in many cases, for millennia. Though adherents of the world's religions are often called believers, "storytellers" is more apt. The stories they tell inform their beliefs, practices, and ethical codes, which then double back on those stories in an infinite loop of invention. The Vedas, Hinduism's most ancient scriptures, are ritual hymnals, but they also contain stories, including one about how the world was created from the dismembered body of a primeval man. A competing creation story, about the emergence of the universe out of an egg, appears in a Hindu ethical manual called the Laws of Manu. The Upanishads, Hindu scriptures that double as philosophical dialogues, are also repositories of stories. The most translated book in the world, the Christian Bible, begins with a story of creation and ends with a story about the destruction of the world. In between, all sorts of intriguing characters engage in all sorts of messy conflicts—about fathers and mothers and brothers and daughters and murder and betrayal and famine and war. The Daodejing of the Daoists comes with its own origin story—a tantalizing tale about a sage named Laozi who quits his job and wanders off toward the mountains. As he approaches the far western reaches of Chinese civilization, a border guard familiar with his reputation for wisdom asks him for a CliffsNotes version of all that he knows. What Laozi leaves behind becomes the second most translated book in the world.

When families gather for a meal over the holidays, they tell stories, which link parents to children to sisters to brothers to cousins to aunts. Religious stories do similar work. Whether told around a kitchen table or in a car or by a Hindu kirtan singer or a Navajo sand painter, they serve as links in the chains of memory that bind members

Religious people are storytellers. Here, a monk preaches to pilgrims and tourists alike beneath the shade of the ancient Bodhi Tree in Bodh Gaya, India, where the Buddha is said to have attained enlightenment.

of religious communities to one another. To be a Jew is not to believe Jewish things. It is to tell Jewish stories. And so it goes for storytellers in each of the world's religions.

This book explores nine of the world's most influential religious traditions, plus one antireligious tradition that may or may not qualify as a tenth religion. Along the way, I attend to beliefs and practices and symbols, but I focus on stories for two reasons. The first reason is that stories animate beliefs and practices alike. The Nicene Creed doesn't just affirm core Christian doctrines and practices. It tells the story of Jesus, who took on a human body, suffered, rose from the dead, and "ascended into heaven." The Passover Seder of the Jews tells the story of a people delivered from slavery to freedom by their God's hand. In the Hindu tradition, stories serve as vehicles for philosophical and theological conversations, as in the Bhagavad Gita where, on the eve of a great battle, a soldier and a god (who just so happens to be moonlighting as a charioteer) debate the merits of doing one's duty.

The second reason I emphasize narrative is that stories are universal and easy to understand. You don't need to be a rocket scientist to understand the Buddhist story of a prince who left his palace or the Navajo story of the emergence of the first people out of the underworld. In fact, you don't even need to be literate, since stories like these originally circulated orally. Even after they were written down in books, they continued to be told in sermons, on pilgrimages, and during family reunions.

All humans—male and female, young and old, Asian and American, straight and queer, black and white and brown—tell and retell stories. Stories are what we do with our voices, and with our hopes and fears. They are the vessels in which we carry around our "priors"—the assumptions and sensibilities we use to filter new ideas and experiences. They are the nets we use to fish the world.

RELIGION MATTERS

One obvious reason to explore these stories is to cultivate religious literacy. The United States is one of the most religious countries on the planet. Politicians appeal routinely to Christianity and the Bible to justify their policies—on homosexuality and abortion, immigration and economic inequality. Yet Americans know very little about the stories and doctrines of their own traditions, and even less about the religions of others. In the *U.S. Religious Knowledge Survey* (2010), the first nationwide study of the religious literacy of American adults, the Pew Forum found that just about half of Americans could identify the Quran as the holy book of Islam and less than half knew that the Dalai Lama is a Buddhist. Results were no better in a follow-up survey in 2019, when the average person surveyed correctly answered just 14.2 out of 32 questions.[2]

So what? Why does this matter?

Religious ignorance matters because religion matters. Religion obviously matters personally to Christians who love Jesus, to Muslims who submit to Allah, and to Hindus who sing devotional songs to the goddess Durga. But religion also matters politically and economically. It moves elections in India, where the Bharatiya Janata Party (BJP) functions as a sort of "Religious Right" in defense of a "Hindu India," and in the United States, where white Christian support carried Donald Trump to the White House in 2016. Religion shapes economies in the Muslim world, where earning interest on loans is forbidden, and in America's Mountain West, where Mormons are required to tithe 10 percent of their income to the Church of Jesus Christ of Latter-day Saints. Religion also moves troops around the globe and spurs humanitarian efforts.

Religion is now associated in the United States with political conservatism, but at the 2017 Women's March religious people expressed their liberal values. Here, Gizelle Begler, an Egyptian American fashion designer, wears a hijab she designed while marching in Washington, DC.

Critics who claim that religious people have perpetrated many of the world's greatest horrors are, in my view, correct. Also correct are defenders of religion who claim that religious people have been some of the world's greatest peacemakers. Put these two facts together and what do you get? A world in which religion matters. Anyone who wants to understand that world—as a politician, an entrepreneur, a psychologist, or a citizen—needs to take account of religion's powers.

Years ago, many scholars promoted a concept called "secularization theory," which predicted that, as societies modernized, they would become less religious. So far, these scholars have been proved wrong. Today, the world remains furiously religious. You cannot understand what is going on in the Middle East without some knowledge of Judaism, Christianity, and Islam. You cannot understand what is happening in Myanmar without some knowledge of the Buddhism of the majority and the Islam of the minority. In her book *The Mighty and the Almighty* (2006), former U.S. Secretary of State Madeleine Albright wrote that, during her time in the Clinton administration, she had hundreds of economic and political advisers she could call if she had questions about the gross domestic product in Saudi Arabia or political parties in Brazil. But how many religion advisers did she have? Zero. This might make sense if human beings are motivated solely by greed and power, but we are not. The overwhelming majority of the human beings who have walked the earth have engaged intimately not only with one another but also with unseen gods and demons and ancestors and immortals. These presences have bent our human drives toward different visions of a "just society" and a "fair economy." They have shaped how we have adopted technologies from the book to the organ to the cell phone, and they have shaped those technologies in turn.

You may be an atheist, a Sikh, or an evangelical Protestant. You may be "spiritual but not religious." In any case, the world's religions—their leaders, institutions, practices, and stories—matter nonetheless. Religion may or may not make sense to you, but you cannot make sense of the world without making sense of the world's religions. But how to begin? What exactly is religious literacy and how can we cultivate it?

TWO WAYS TO TALK ABOUT RELIGION

There are two ways to talk about religion. The most common is the way of faith and devotion. This is how people talk about Judaism or Christianity in Sabbath School or Sunday School—how Buddhist teachers speak of the Buddha in dharma talks and how Hindus sing of their love of Krishna. But there is another way to talk about religion—a nondevotional and nontheological way. This is the way of the academic study of religion, also known as religious studies. Here the aim is not to *do* religion but to *study* it. Here, learning takes precedence over preaching. If the devotional way to talk about religion is like making art, this academic way of talking about religion is like doing art history.

After you have distinguished between the *religious* study of religion and the *nonreligious* study of religion, it is important to start with basic facts about the world's religions. But memorizing Buddhism's Four Noble Truths or the Five Pillars of Islam is not enough. Religious literacy, like other forms of literacy, is a skill. More specifically, it is the ability to engage in public conversations about religion. This ability requires a combination of knowledge and sensibilities:

- knowledge about the world's religions
- empathetic understanding
- critical engagement
- a comparative approach

Religious studies scholars often employ a method they call "bracketing" (or *epoché*). This method challenges us to momentarily set aside our own attitudes and beliefs in order to examine whatever we are examining in as unbiased a manner as possible. The goal of bracketing is nonjudgmental knowledge, or what Ninian Smart and other religious studies scholars have described as "empathetic understanding." The idea is that if you are able to suspend your own judgments you may be able to glimpse how a religion's symbols, beliefs, and practices look to insiders. What does it feel like to walk in their shoes? to see the world through their eyes? Of course, this is an impossible task. But to ask these questions is to call attention to your own biases and prejudices. It is to attempt to short-circuit the power of your own religious (or nonreligious) presuppositions.

This empathetic approach has led some scholars to look *only* at the sunny side of the religions they study. In his bestseller *The Religions of Man* (later retitled *The World's Religions*), Huston Smith makes this approach explicit. His goal is to write about "religions at their best," he says, showcasing their "cleaner side" rather than airing their dirty laundry.[3] This approach obviously carries biases of its own. It shields us from the evil acts that religious people do, and from the ways they draw on the resources of their religions to justify their actions. Therefore, it is important to combine empathetic understanding with *critical engagement*—to see both the good and the bad of the world's religions.

One way to balance empathy and criticism is by using a comparative approach, which seeks to understand the world's religions in light of one another. "He who knows one, knows none," said the nineteenth-century German scholar Max Muller.[4] Comparison is useful, even necessary, because we all process new information on the basis of information we already have. In fact, according to many psychologists and brain scientists, the *only* way we learn is by metaphor, analogy, and comparison. When we bite into an apple and notice its sweetness, we are comparing it to apples we have tasted in the past that were tart. When we say our favorite baseball team has better pitchers but worse hitters than its rivals, we are doing comparison again.

That said, comparison can obscure things by flattening out regional differences and change over time. If, like the pioneering religious studies scholar Mircea Eliade, we are keen to compare creation myths in different religious traditions, we may be tempted to forget how much those myths have varied from place to place and time to time. But comparison can do more than mislead. It can also be dangerous. Because we all tend to read the other in terms of the self, which is loaded with unconscious biases, comparison is freighted. In the study of religion, the freight it often carries are Protestant presuppositions. In the past, scholars concluded that Navajo religion was inferior because it does not have a written scripture like the Bible, or that all religions were progressing onward and upward from "ethnic" religions like Judaism to "universal" religions like Christianity. Edward Said and other critics of colonialism are right to observe how European and American thinkers have employed romantic images of the Middle East to justify and promote prejudice against Muslims.

The way forward is not to stop comparing, however. We could not think without comparing. We just need to avoid bad comparisons, whether we are in the kitchen, on a baseball field, or in a religious studies classroom.

In the United States, conservative Christians have invited God into the public square, while religious minorities and atheists have worked to separate church and state. Here, Christian and atheist protesters offer very different messages outside a music festival in Asheville, North Carolina, in 2013.

One final note on these two ways of talking about religion: Often the two conflict. In "He wishes for the Cloths of Heaven," the Irish poet W. B. Yeats writes of spreading his "dreams under your feet" and then asks his reader to "tread softly because you tread on my dreams."[5] When it comes to the world's religions, it is extraordinarily difficult even for the most empathetic scholars to avoid trampling on the dreams of others. The tension between the academic study of religion and the practice of religion is unavoidable, especially given the fact that practitioners of any given religion often disagree strongly with one another. This tension is heightened when advocates of one view are convinced that their intellectual opponents are distorting the facts for political purposes. No textbook can resolve these conflicts. Nor is any textbook free from their influences. Perhaps all that religious studies students and teachers can do is acknowledge the conflicts and then make every effort, as I have made here, to tread softly on the deeply held beliefs and sensibilities of others.

THE PROBLEM OF ESSENTIALISM

The study of religion has suffered in the past from overgeneralization. Many religious studies scholars assumed that religions—all religions—were, like Protestantism, largely about beliefs. They didn't account sufficiently for either change over time or internal diversity. As a result, they tended to reduce particular religious traditions to hard-and-fast "things." Scholars refer to this as **essentialism**, or essentializing something—turning it over and over in the mind until it becomes an unchanging "essence."

essentialism
ancient philosophical view that the things we see in the world express unchanging forms

After school, smartphones come out for children all over the globe, including these Muslim schoolgirls in Bali, Indonesia.

In an effort to avoid this problem of essentialism, Professor Diane Moore and Harvard Divinity School's Religious Literacy Project (RLP) have developed a useful list of principles for students of religion. After distinguishing between *doing* religion and *studying* religion—between "the devotional expression and the nonsectarian study of religion"—the RLP offers these three core assertions about the world's religions:

1. Religions are internally diverse, as opposed to uniform.
2. Religions evolve and change over time, as opposed to being ahistorical and static.
3. Religious influences are embedded in all dimensions of culture, as opposed to [functioning] in discrete, isolated, "private" contexts.[6]

As the complexity of the world's religions starts to overwhelm us, it can be tempting to distill what we are learning into quick and easy formulas. The point of this list is to remind us that many of those formulas—"Hindus are polytheists"; "Buddhists are non-violent"; "Christians oppose homosexuality"—are false. Why? Because religious traditions are *traditions*. Like all traditions, they vary over time and place and include all sorts of different people and competing ideas, including Hindu monotheists, Buddhist soldiers, and Christian lesbians.

The last RLP principle emphasizes the inseparability of religion from other aspects of life. None of the world's religions can be separated from aspects of life that influence them and are influenced by them in turn. Religious people and institutions do not exist in splendid isolation. Religion has always been intertwined in politics, economics, society, culture, art, and technology. As a result, it can be hard to distinguish religion from "the secular" and one religion from another. Just as religious traditions have always drawn on technological innovations and responded to shifting climates and cultures, they have always borrowed from one another. Every religion, like every culture, is up to its neck in debt. Buddhism has developed in conversation with Indian philosophy, Tibetan art,

Chinese ethics, and American technologies. Daoism today cannot be divorced from Chinese culture, the Chinese Communist Party, or Confucianism and Buddhism. Many Hindus today insist that Hinduism is a comprehensive "way of life" that cannot be reduced to a "religion." And many Native Americans insist that what outsiders call their "religions" cannot be understood apart from the sacred lands they inhabit or the politics of the settler empire that has confined them to reservations.

Once you are centuries downstream from any religion's source, it is easy to think of "it" as a thing—a shipment on a river conveyed from port to port, unopened and unchanged inside a rigid metal container. But religions are more like rivers themselves, rising and falling, twisting and turning, transformed over time by social, political, and economic forces. They change, and their practitioners do the changing. Hindus disagree about how many gods there are; not every Muslim prays five times a day; some Mormons take a sip of caffeinated cola now and then; and there are lots of Jewish atheists.

THE NECESSITY OF GENERALIZATION

Although it is important to avoid essentializing the world's religions, there is no way to avoid generalization, either in the study of religion or in life. Consider the forks in your kitchen. Chances are, they look very different under close inspection. Likely they are different sizes, made by different manufacturers, perhaps out of different materials. Even those that came from the same box are now nicked or bent in ways that differentiate them from one another. But we refer to them all as forks. Surely this category obscures much. But there is no way to avoid generalizing in this way. In fact, communication depends on it. We say flowers are fragrant without feeling we need to account for the odd flower that stinks like a rotting corpse.

Academic scholarship nowadays emphasizes specialization rather than synthesis because professors earn their credentials by doing specialized work. For this reason, some scholars now prefer to refer to "Christianities" rather than "Christianity," which they argue is an overgeneralized fiction. But the category of *Christians* is a useful fiction, as are the categories of Dallas Cowboys fans and Boston University students. Both specialization and synthesis are necessary to every sort of work, whether you are a taxi driver, a cook, or a professor.

In introductory courses and textbooks, generalizations are essential. The ancient Greek philosopher Heraclitus was right when he said you cannot step in the same river twice, because on your second approach the river has changed and so have you. However, it is a powerfully useful fiction to be able to refer to *the* Mississippi River and to *me*. The same goes for the term "chariot," which the Buddha famously deconstructed to prove that all things are empty of a single, unchanging essence. "Where is the essence of the chariot?" he asked, as he stripped away its wheels, its seat, and its axle, demonstrating piece by piece that the chariot is a composite thing—a figment of our overactive imaginations. And yet we use such terms, and use them we must, unless we choose to slip out of civilization into solitary silence.

One of the most influential contemporary scholars of religion, J. Z. Smith, has observed that religion is a modern Western invention, "solely the creation of the scholar's study . . . created for the scholar's analytic purposes by his imaginative acts of comparison and generalization, [and having] no independent existence apart from the academy."[7] In recent

Burning incense, either at home or in temples, is a common way to honor one's ancestors or to sacrifice to the gods. In the Quan Am Pagoda in Ho Chi Minh City, Vietnam, temple-goers participate in rituals indebted to Daoist, Buddhist, and Chinese folk-religious practices.

years, a series of books have appeared arguing that the world's religions, too, are products of the modern Western imagination.

On their own terms, these arguments are persuasive. All "isms" are fictions. The term "Buddhism" isn't a thing like an apple is a thing. Neither is "The United States of America" or "Texas." Moreover, words such as "Confucianism" and "Daoism" are English-language words, so obviously they are not native to Mandarin speakers. Arguments by J. Z. Smith and his followers are a useful corrective; they remind us, as the semanticist Alfred Korzybski reminded us in 1933, that "the word is not the object"—there is a gap between the word "religion" and the stuff to which that word attempts to point.[8] Shifting from semantics to politics, those arguments also remind us that words such as "Islam" arose in the modern West for various reasons, and that those reasons included promoting Christian missions and Western colonialism.

However, there are two problems with laying the "invention" of the world's religions at the feet of modern Europeans. The first is that human beings were praying and preaching and meditating and chanting long before Europeans came along and named them "Navajos" or "Hindoos." To pretend that the world's religions were manufactured by the European imagination is to rob religious actors of their agency *and* of their precolonial histories.

The second problem concerns scholarly authority. It is just not possible for those of us who are sitting in the "scholar's study" to create the world's religions entirely in our own images, or to control their meanings once they have been unleashed on the world. In *Through the Looking-Glass*, the sequel to *Alice's Adventures in Wonderland*, the novelist and mathematician Lewis Carroll puts these words in Humpty Dumpty's mouth: "When I use a word, it means just what I choose it to mean—neither more nor less."[9] We scholars do not have that luxury. Words such as "religion" and "Confucianism" are now well out of our control. Moreover, as abstract nouns go, they are among the realest, in the sense that they have some of the most powerful effects out there beyond the Ivory Tower. The "world religions" paradigm is literally law in many nation-states, which now use the coercive powers of their courts to enforce it. China now recognizes five official religions (Buddhism, Daoism, Catholicism, Protestantism, and Islam); Indonesia, adding Hinduism to that list, recognizes six.

In individual lives, religions calm and comfort. They move people to action. Believers (and storytellers) kill and die in the name of their religions, which are as real to them in many cases as their gods. Religions bear studying in books like these not solely as they appear in the minds of scholars but more importantly as they operate in the lives of religious people who, in the words of the historian of religions Robert Orsi, "form deep ties with saints, ancestors, demons, gods, ghosts, and other special beings in whose company [they] work on the world and themselves."[10]

The way forward here is not to stop generalizing (or to stop speaking). As we move into greater and greater specificity when it comes to religion—from "religion" to "Buddhism" to "Zen Buddhism" to "American Zen" to the San Francisco Zen Center—the problem of generalization does not go away. Every discussion of any of these topics requires massive generalizations simply to get off the ground. But there are things we can do to minimize the tendency toward essentialism.

The first is to be suspicious of the categories we use to think about the world's religions. It is important to be aware that we produce these categories through acts of the imagination—not unlike the way librarians produced the Dewey Decimal System for categorizing books. We should also be mindful that the histories of terms such as "religion" and "Sikhism" are tied up with all sorts of political, economic, and intellectual projects—nefarious, benevolent, and otherwise. With this in mind, each chapter in this book includes a genealogy box outlining how and why terms such as "Judaism," "Buddhism," and "Islam" made their way into the English language, and the ways in which the presumptions of modern Western missionaries and scholars have colored the invention of those terms. But this awareness of the genealogies and the politics of these terms should not lead us to imagine that they are more problematic than parallel terms in other academic disciplines. The term "philosophy" is an English language word and a product of the scholar's study. So is the concept of *the novel*. Each is politically freighted and fraught. The term "religion" is no different.

Religiously motivated violence is a part of all religious traditions, even Buddhism, which is famous for its commitments to nonviolence. In Myanmar, Buddhist monks have persecuted and killed members of the Rohingya Muslim community.

A second way to address the problem of essentialism in religious studies is to avoid bad generalizations. Islam does not "say" anything—that is the job of Muslims—so we should not begin any sentence with "Islam says." Neither should we allow the portion of Christians who oppose homosexuality to speak for the whole. It is now common to translate terms such as *papa* and *moksha* in Hinduism into "sin" and "salvation." But these English-language terms are too weighed down with Christian assumptions to be useful in other religious contexts. Therefore, in this textbook, *moksha* appears as "spiritual liberation," for example. For similar reasons, I avoid using the term "faiths" as a synonym for "religions."

The third and most important way to address essentialism is to acknowledge to ourselves and others that the generalizations we are making are just that: generalizations. Not all flowers smell sweet. Some forks have just two tines. Although the Dalai Lama preaches compassion and nonviolence, Buddhist monks in Myanmar in recent years have terrorized Rohingya Muslims. Repeatedly, we need to remind ourselves that religions are internally diverse and change over time.

WHAT IS RELIGION ALL ABOUT?

For as long as people have been studying religion, they have struggled to define it. As many scholars of religion have observed, "religion" is not a term religious folks have traditionally used to describe their activities. In the Navajo language, there is no word for anything like it. So it is up to scholars of religion to define and defend this key term. For more than a century, they have been trying to do just that. In 1871, the English anthropologist E. B. Tylor defined religion as "belief in Spiritual Beings."[11] This captured nicely the common-sense understanding that religion is about belief in God, but it was too narrow, as there are all sorts of religions that don't affirm "Spiritual Beings."

After Tylor, scholars of religion have come up with hundreds of other definitions of religion, some more political, some more philosophical, some more theological, some more social, and some more psychological. Here are a few of the most influential efforts to capture this admittedly slippery term:

FRIEDRICH SCHLEIERMACHER (Protestant theologian)
Religion is "the feeling of absolute dependence."[12]

KARL MARX (economic and political theorist)
"Religion is the sigh of the oppressed creature, the heart of a heartless world and the soul of soulless conditions. It is the *opium* of the people."[13]

WILLIAM JAMES (psychologist and philosopher)
"Religion . . . shall mean for us *the feelings, acts, and experiences of individual men in their solitude, so far as they apprehend themselves to stand in relation to whatever they may consider the divine.*"[14]

EMILE DURKHEIM (sociologist)
"A religion is a unified system of beliefs and practices relative to sacred things, that is to say, things set apart and forbidden—beliefs and practices which unite into one single moral community called a Church, all those who adhere to them."[15]

The ecstatic feelings of solidarity that fans get from cheering for their favorite sports teams or rock bands can be difficult to distinguish from religious ecstasy. Here, soccer fans in Accra, Ghana, support their country's team in the African Cup of Nations in 2008.

SIGMUND FREUD (psychologist)
"Religion would thus be the universal obsessional neurosis of humanity."[16]

PAUL TILLICH (Protestant theologian)
"Faith is the state of being grasped by an ultimate concern."[17]

MARY DALY (feminist theologian)
"If God is male, then male is God. The divine patriarch castrates women as long as he is allowed to live on in the human imagination."[18]

CHARLES LONG (religious studies scholar)
"Religion will mean orientation—orientation in the ultimate sense, that is, how one comes to terms with the ultimate significance of one's place in the world."[19]

TALAL ASAD (cultural anthropologist)
"There cannot be a universal definition of religion, not only because its constituent elements and relationships are historically specific, but because that definition is itself the historical product of a discursive process."[20]

The first thing to notice about these definitions is that they all include and exclude things. The sociologist focuses on society to the neglect of the individual; the psychologist focuses on the individual to the neglect of society. No one sees the whole picture.

A second observation is that some of these definitions aren't definitions at all. Daly's is a critique of patriarchal religion. And Asad rejects the possibility of any "universal definition" of religion whatsoever, preferring to uncover instead the "genealogies" of the concept of religion for clues to the ways it has been shaped by Protestant assumptions to promote the interests of Protestant missionaries and colonizers.

A third observation is that some of these definitions of religions are substantive and others are functional. Substantive definitions focus on what religion *is* while functional definitions focus on what religion *does*. Substantive definitions look at the contents and perhaps the essence of religion. Functional definitions look at how it operates in society (if they are sociological) or in the human mind (if they are psychological).

Tylor's is a substantive definition. It tells us we are looking at religion when we are looking at a particular thing, in his case "belief in Spiritual Beings." Marx's definition of religion as "the opium of the people" is functional, since it focuses on what religion *does*: it causes the oppressed to sigh and to wait patiently until justice magically materializes in the world to come. Durkheim's definition combines elements of these two types. Its description of religion as "a unified system of beliefs and practices relative to sacred things" reads like a more sophisticated version of Tylor's definition in which "belief" is expanded to "beliefs and practices" and "Spiritual Beings" is broadened to "sacred things." Yet Durkheim also tells us what this religion does: it acts like social glue, "unit[ing] into a single moral community called a Church, all those who adhere to [those beliefs and practices]."

One problem with substantive definitions is that they tend to exclude too much. For example, Tylor's definition excludes religions such as early Buddhism and Confucianism that do not affirm "Spiritual Beings." The problem with functional definitions is that they tend to include too much. If with Paul Tillich we define religion as "the state of being grasped by an ultimate concern," then some Red Sox baseball fans are doing religion when they go to Fenway Park. Some followers of Mao in China or the Castros in Cuba are practicing religion when they go to a political rally.

Lurking behind every definition of religion is a *theory* of religion. If you ask your friends, "What is religion all about?" they will respond with various theories. Religion is about believing in God or performing rituals or expressing solidarity with your grandparents, they might say. More cynical friends might say that religion is about sex: its purpose is to regulate sexuality. Or they might theorize that religion is about money: religion is a sort of reverse Robin Hoodism that steals from the poor to give to the rich. These examples tell us that to define religion is to take a stand, because there is no neutral place from which we can define religion objectively. Like facts in David Byrne's song "Stop Making Sense," each definition "has a point of view."

In recent years, many scholars have gravitated toward a family resemblance approach to the definition of religion. In a famous discussion of the category "game," the German philosopher Ludwig Wittgenstein argued that there is no single definition that can capture all the things we intuitively know to be games. Yes, most games are played for fun, but some are played to make money (professional soccer) or out of addiction (casino blackjack). Therefore, Wittgenstein proposed that categories such as "game" hold together like families do. Family members tend to resemble one another, not in every particular but in general. The best we can do is to come up with a list of overlapping family resemblances and then include inside our category those that seem to have enough of them to count as relatives.

In the case of religion, a number of lists of family traits have been offered. Ninian Smart has referred to seven dimensions of religion:

- the ritual dimension (rites and ceremonies)
- the narrative or mythic dimension (myths and other stories related to sacred things)
- the experiential or emotional dimension (experiences of awe, guilt, bliss)
- the social or institutional dimension (religious organizations)

- the ethical or legal dimension (laws and moral codes)
- the doctrinal or philosophical dimension (creeds, theologies)
- the material dimension (prayer beads, icons, temple architecture).[21]

Catherine Albanese, a historian of religions, has offered a shorter list, known as the "Four C's":

- creeds (theologies and statements of beliefs)
- codes (standards for ethical conduct)
- cultus (rituals informed by creeds and codes)
- community (groups and institutions tied together by creeds, codes, and cultus).[22]

This book takes a "family resemblances" approach to the definition of religion, referring at various times to Smart's dimensions and Albanese's Four C's. As religious studies scholar Thomas Tweed has observed, it is up to each academic discipline to trouble its central term: "culture" for anthropologists, "language" for linguistics, "music" for musicology.[23] To do so is to engage in an act of open, evolving inquiry. And the best way to do it is to investigate widely and to be open to changing your mind as you encounter new forms of culture, language, music, and religion.

RELIGIONS ARE NOT ONE

Some have looked at these lists of family traits and decided that the world's religions are akin to identical twins. When I was in college and graduate school, I was told repeatedly that the world's religions were different paths up the same mountain. Drawing on *The Perennial Philosophy* (1945) by the British novelist Aldous Huxley, these proponents of **perennialism**, as it came to be called, argued for the fundamental unity of the world's religions. No one told me that economic systems or political regimes were essentially the same—that capitalism was equivalent to socialism or that the differences between monarchy and democracy didn't amount to much. But when it came to the world's religions, it was perfectly acceptable to say a few magic words and make the differences disappear.

Today, the most popular books on religion also emphasize similarities rather than differences. The world's religions may differ when it comes to various beliefs or practices, but in essence they are one. Smith's *The World's Religions*, the bestselling book in religious studies with 3.5 million copies sold (and counting), is organized around this claim. As Smith moves from Hinduism to Buddhism to Judaism to Christianity to Islam, he highlights their fundamental unity. "It is possible to climb life's mountain from any side, but when the top is reached the trails converge," he writes. "At base, in the foothills of theology, ritual, and organizational structure, the religions are distinct. . . . But beyond these differences the same goal beckons."[24]

This is a story many of us want to hear: Once upon a time, the powers and principalities of the world's religions fought to the death, but this titanic clash was based on a tragic misunderstanding, since at their core the world's religions are fundamentally the same. Unfortunately, this story is not true. The religious people I know hold very different beliefs and perform very different practices. My Christian friends do not go on pilgrimage to Mecca or affirm the divine inspiration of the Quran. My Muslim and Jewish friends do not believe that Jesus is an incarnation of God. Most fundamentally, the religious people

perennialism
belief that there is one religion underlying what appears to be many religions—that all religions are, in essence, one

Indian spiritual leader Mohandas Gandhi (left) walks with the activist and poet Sarojini Naidu (right) during the Salt March of 1930. Their goal was to employ nonviolent civil disobedience tactics to overturn the colonial British government's monopoly over salt production in India.

I know disagree on the mathematics of divinity. Is God one? Yes, say Jews, Christians, and Muslims. But many Hindus say there is more than one God. And many Buddhists say there are fewer.

Another problem with perennialism is that those who affirm it cannot agree on who or what resides on their mountaintops. The Indian revolutionary Mohandas Gandhi was convinced it was God who awaits all the world's believers at the peak. In contrast to this doctrinal approach, Huston Smith's path was more experiential. As he saw it, the essence of all religions was to be found in mystical encounters between humans and the divine. Meanwhile, the popular religion writer Karen Armstrong and Tibet's Dalai Lama took an ethical path. What they found on their mountaintops was the universal ideal of compassion.

The fact of the matter is that adherents of the world's religions start with very different analyses of the human problem. From these varied beginnings, they naturally veer sharply away from one another, chasing after different goals. If they are "mountaineers," they are climbing very different mountains toward their respective peaks.

So it just isn't true that the beliefs and practices of the world's religions are essentially the same, and it isn't helpful either. I understand the impulse—to get along by playing along, smoothing over the rough edges of religious differences, in order to avoid a bloody rerun of the Protestant-Catholic wars of early modern Europe or the Muslim-Christian battles of the Middle Ages. A similar impulse animates many of today's "New Atheists," who lump the world's religions together in order to argue that they are equally foolish and equally dangerous. But the view that all religions are one does not make the world a safer place. In fact, it has made it more dangerous. How so? First and foremost, by making it impossible to understand global conflicts that are religiously inflected—from Myanmar to Tibet to the United States–Mexico border. If you want to understand what's happening with Israelis and Palestinians, it does not help to be told that Judaism, Christianity, and Islam are essentially the same. It does not serve diplomats working in Indonesia to be told that the Shia Islam of Iran is equivalent to the Sunni Islam of Saudi Arabia.

What we need today is not pretend pluralism. What we need is a clear-eyed look at the realities of the world's religions as they are practiced on the ground. As the Daoist studies scholar Kristofer Schipper has written, "The Tao has ten thousand gates, say the masters, and it is up to each of us to find our own."[25] To explore the world's religions is to wander through these gates. It is to tune in to Hindu/Buddhist debates over the logic of karma and rebirth and Confucian/Daoist debates over how to become fully human. It is to encounter rivalries between Hindus and Muslims in India, Jews and Muslims in Israel, and Christians and practitioners of traditional Navajo religion in the "Four Corners" region of Utah, New Mexico, Arizona, and Colorado. Perennialists see in all religions the same God, the same compassion. New Atheists see all religious folk as peddlers of the same idiocy, the same poison. What both groups miss is religious diversity; rather than ten thousand gates, they see only one.

Sacred spaces are often contested ones. Here, a coal-fired electrical plant near Page, Arizona, sends pollutants across lands the Navajo consider sacred.

A FOUR-PART MODEL OF THE WORLD'S RELIGIONS: PROBLEM, SOLUTION, TECHNIQUES, EXEMPLARS

My grandmother, Alphild Anderson, a no-nonsense daughter of late-nineteenth-century Norwegian immigrants to the United States, loved to tell a story about a cousin of hers who never spoke. Every evening the family would gather around the dinner table to share local gossip and discuss the weather rolling off of Lake Superior into Two Harbors, Minnesota. This cousin never said a word. Then, one evening, he exclaimed, "These peas are horrible!" The family was flabbergasted. He spoke! Why now, they asked him. "Until now, everything's been okay," he said.

Religions are like my grandmother's cousin. Their early utterances always include a complaint about the human condition, typically accompanied by a story about how that predicament came to be. For example:

- Humans suffer because they are desperately trying to hold on to satisfactions that are forever slipping out of their grasp.
- The world is out of balance because human beings are neglecting their relationships with each other, with the spirit world, and with the earth.
- Society is chaotic because humans have forgotten the humane values and everyday rituals that make society harmonious.

Every religion offers its own analysis of the human predicament. In fact, one way you know that you have migrated from one religion to another is because you can feel the human problem shifting under your feet. For Buddhists, this problem is suffering. For Christians, it is sin. For Muslims, it is pride. Having identified the human problem, adherents of any particular religion try to solve it. As they work toward this goal, they inevitably distinguish themselves from one another, as surely as plumbers working on leaky pipes distinguish themselves from electricians working on faulty switches.

One of the most common misconceptions about the world's religions is that they ask the same questions. They do not. Only religions that seek release from this world ask how to be liberated from it. Only religions of reversion ask how to return to our primordial harmony. There is a long tradition in Christian thought of assuming that salvation is the goal of all religions. Huston Smith, who grew up in China in a family of Methodist missionaries, once wrote that "to claim salvation as the monopoly of any one religion is like claiming that God can be found in this room and not the next, in this attire but not another."[26] In some respects, this statement is admirably empathetic. It is confused, however, because non-Christians have not traditionally affirmed sin or sought salvation from it. When the jailer in the New Testament asks the Apostle Paul, "What must I do to be saved?" (Acts 16:30), he is not asking a generic human question but a specifically Christian one.

An analogy from sports may be helpful here. Consider the following sports: baseball, basketball, soccer, and American football. Which is best at scoring touchdowns? The answer, of course, is American football, but only because it is the only sport in which a touchdown can be scored. Different sports have different goals. Baseball players try to score runs. Basketball players try to shoot baskets. Soccer players try to score goals. Therefore, if you ask which sport is best at scoring touchdowns you have answered your question by asking it. To criticize a baseball team for failing to score touchdowns is to misunderstand the game of baseball. If you see the human predicament as sin and salvation as the solution, then it makes sense to turn to Christianity. But the real question is not which of the world's religions is best at carrying us into the end zone of salvation but which of the wide variety of human problems we should be attacking, which of the religious goals we should be seeking.

Once a religious community has fixed on a problem and a solution, its adherents develop various techniques to achieve their goals. Different branches inside a given religion distinguish themselves from one another by employing different techniques to achieve their goals: the faith of Protestants and the sacraments of Catholics; or the chanting of some Buddhists and the meditation strategies of others. In Daoism alone, the techniques for achieving immortality include meditation, dietary disciplines, breathing exercises, sexual rites, and the visualization of deities residing inside human bodies or in faraway stars.

In addition to focusing on different human problems, solutions, and techniques, the world's religions offer up different exemplars—saints, gurus, immortals, medicine men—who chart the path from the religious illness to the religious cure. Again, these exemplary figures vary not only from religion to religion but also from branch to branch.

Of course, the problems, solutions, techniques, and exemplars developed in any given religious tradition are rarely confined to it. Just as the world's religions do not exist apart from cultural, political,

At a Glance

This four-part model of the world's religions examines:

1. an analysis of the human problem
2. a solution to that problem
3. techniques for achieving that goal
4. exemplars who chart the path toward the goal

social, and economic influences, they do not exist apart from one another. Like the boundaries of the cells that make up human bodies, religious traditions are permeable. The techniques they hone and the exemplars they admire slip across religious borders and change as they go. Christians in the United States learn meditation from Zen masters and make it their own. Buddhists in Japan adopt and adapt understandings of faith, grace, and salvation from Protestant theologians. In China, it has long been common for individuals to have multiple religious identities—as Buddhists, Daoists, and Confucians. But there are also Jewish Buddhists ("Jubus") who eat a kosher dinner and then go to a mindfulness meditation class. This sort of borrowing is a key mechanism for religious change.

FORMAT OF THIS BOOK

Each of the chapters that follow focuses on a particular religious tradition. I chose to organize this book around these "-isms" because, for better or for worse, they matter. They carry social, political, and legal force. They also affect individual lives. The religions I included generally have more adherents than the ones I excluded. They have exerted more influence over more time. In short, they are the ones that matter most. One exception to that rule is Navajo religion, which is included both as a useful counterpoint to the other religions in the book and as the religious tradition of the Native American tribe with the largest land mass and the second-largest population (after the Cherokees).

Each chapter in this book begins with a contemporary story set in a place held sacred by its practitioners. In almost every case, I took my body to that place and observed what the bodies of pilgrims and tourists were doing there. I listened to what they said. I watched how they prayed or meditated or napped or laughed or fiddled with their cell phones. I went to Bodh Gaya in northern India and sat with other visitors around the Bodhi Tree where the Buddha is said to have attained enlightenment. I went to Varanasi, the Indian city of Shiva, the Hindu god of destruction and recycling, and watched as mourners burned the bodies of their loved ones on the banks of the Ganges River. In southwestern China, I hiked with pilgrims and tourists up grueling mountain paths to statues and temples dedicated to Daoist immortals. In London, I sang pop songs with members of an "atheist church." In Jerusalem, I walked the Stations of the Cross with Christian pilgrims and observed Jews praying at the Western Wall.

The author, Stephen Prothero, has traveled the world taking in the sights, sounds, and senses of the world's religions. Here, in Varanasi, India, he stands in front of a street painting of the Hindu god Krishna playing in a river with the *gopis* (milkmaids).

After these journalistic stories, told from the perspective of an outside observer, each chapter offers a second story, based on the scriptures and myths of the religious tradition in question. "Our Story," as this segment is called, presents an insider account that explains why these places matter to adherents: here, on *this* hill, Jesus was crucified; here, under *this* tree, the Buddha was enlightened. I include a story of how Shiva won a bragging contest with other Hindu gods and, with it, the city of Varanasi as his prize. I also relate competing stories about where the Daoist tradition began and what its founders did on those Chinese mountains Daoists now hold dear. These stories are not direct quotations from scriptures or

Rites of passage mark life's turning points. In Judaism, the bar mitzvah (for boys) and the bat mitzvah (for girls) transform young people into adult members of the Jewish community. Here, Hillary Hass kisses her prayer shawl and touches a Torah scroll during her bat mitzvah in West Palm Beach, Florida.

oral traditions. They are my paraphrased translations into colloquial English, condensing into a few pages sacred stories that might otherwise take days or several thousand pages to tell.

After sections that offer basic demographic information about each religion (how many adherents it has and where they live) and briefly explain its key symbols, beliefs, and practices, I turn to a third mode of storytelling: history. To do history is not to list names and dates from memory. Neither is it to offer a "just the facts, ma'am" recitation of one thing after another. Every history is told from a particular perspective, in this case from that of a historian of religions on the lookout for how religious narratives intersect with political, economic, and military narratives—how the upstart Christian movement got a boost from the conversion of an emperor, how trade routes across the Arabian Peninsula helped spread Islam, how the rise of communism in China first hurt and then helped Confucianism. In each case, this historical narrative traces a religious tradition from before its founding to the present day. Along the way, it underscores the fact that religions are not unchanging essences that emerged full-born from the heads of their founders. They change over time in response to new ecologies, new economies, and new enemies. Sometimes they change profoundly, veering in directions quite unintended by founders and early followers alike.

Of course, religions cannot be reduced to their histories any more than individuals can. Each chapter also includes a section on "lived religion" that details how today's ordinary practitioners live their religious lives. This section includes a "Birth and Death" box that outlines how adherents of each religion memorialize these key life passages. Because of the influence in the modern West of Bible-driven Protestantism and the reason-driven Enlightenment, there has been a strong tendency among scholars to denigrate religion's material dimension—to see "true religion" in scriptures and ideas and to view images, idols, and objects as inconsequential. Scholars in recent years have worked to counteract that tendency by focusing on the ordinary stuff of "lived religion." With their efforts in mind, each chapter in this book also includes a "Material Religion" box that examines some particular item of clothing or devotional object or architectural feature—material objects that carry meanings for adherents. Each chapter ends by attending to a contemporary controversy in which we can see history unfolding today, setting the stage for where the religion might be heading in the future.

The book is divided into three parts, each of which tracks different types of religion in different parts of the globe. Once you have determined that the world has gone awry and the human condition is fundamentally flawed, there are only so many ways to proceed. You can try to get out. You can stay and try to fix what is broken. Or you can stay and try to restore the world to its original condition before things went so terribly wrong. In other words, you can seek release from the problems of this world. You can try to repair what is broken. Or you can try to go back to a time and place before it was broken in the first place.

In keeping with these three options, this book is divided into Religions of Release, Religions of Repair, and Religions of Reversion, with an additional section on atheism.

Religions of Release (India)
    Hinduism: The Way of Devotion
    Buddhism: The Way of Awakening
    Sikhism: The Way of the Guru

Religions of Repair (Middle East)
    Judaism: The Way of Exile and Return
    Christianity: The Way of Salvation
    Islam: The Way of Submission

Religions of Reversion (China and North America)
    Confucianism: The Way of Ritual Propriety
    Daoism: The Way of Flourishing
    Navajo Religion: The Way of Beauty

Rejecting Religion
    Atheism: The Way of No Way

India's religions of release seek to escape from a world in which we are trapped in an endless and unsatisfactory cycle of life, death, and rebirth. The religions of repair of the Middle East seek to fix what is broken through the intervention of God—through the revelation of the Torah or the Quran or through the revelation of Jesus Christ, whom Christians call the "Word of God." The religions of reversion of China seek to return to nature in the case of Daoism or to the glory days of the ancient sage-kings in the case of Confucianism. As a Native American tradition, Navajo religion is, of course, very different from these Chinese religions, but it, too, focuses on the work of reversion—in this case returning to the original beauty and balance its practitioners refer to as *hozho*. The book's final chapter is devoted to people who, in the name of reason, have rejected all of the above and either don't believe that the world has gone awry or are convinced that what ails us is religion itself.

THE POWER OF QUESTIONS

The conviction underlying the narrative approach of this book is that religions have succeeded or failed, spread or stalled, based on the power of the stories their practitioners have told. Every religion that appears in this book has been a tremendous success. It has survived for centuries or, in many cases, millennia through a long series of creative adaptations. It has gathered millions, in some cases billions, of followers. Along the way, it has shaped the stories we tell ourselves about who we are, why we are here, and where we are going after we die. To engage these stories is to learn something important about the world we inhabit. It is also to engage with some of the most profound questions that human beings have asked.

Religions are widely understood to be answer banks—ATMs of a sort where we can walk up, punch a few buttons, and get the answers to life's questions. Perhaps "Jesus is the Answer," as billboards across America's Bible Belt proclaim. But Jesus, who asks more than three hundred questions in the New Testament, is also an enigma. So are the Buddha and Laozi and other founding figures.

Naturalism is a key Daoist value. Here, a Daoist monk walks a relatively easy portion of one of the world's most difficult hikes—to the mountaintop Cui Yun Gong monastery on Hua Shan ("Flowery Mountain") in China's Shaanxi province.

Each year, I tell students in my introductory courses that there are at least three good reasons to go to college. One is to get a credential that will get you a job so you can support yourself and your family financially. A second is to answer questions you wondered about as a teenager—questions about the size of our solar system, the engineering of a bridge, or the soliloquies of Shakespeare's *Hamlet*. The third is to wrestle with questions that can take a lifetime (or more) to untangle. The study of religion offers students and professors alike the opportunity to take up that third task by entering into the imaginative worlds of some of the greatest stories ever told. Tucked inside these stories are some of the greatest questions ever asked:

Is there a self?
What must I do to be saved?
How can I become immortal?
What does it mean to be truly human?
What can I do to escape the cycle of life, death, and rebirth?
How can I eliminate my own suffering and the suffering of others?

Like every great figure in every religion, we all inhabit our own stories, which tell us who we are, what to value, and what to do. But the questions we carry around with us have the power to change those stories and to change us as well. As much as our beliefs and our values shape us, it's the questions we ask—of ourselves, our communities, and the world—that make us who we are.

QUESTIONS FOR DISCUSSION

1. In what ways is storytelling an effective approach to understanding the world's religions? How do stories affect beliefs and practices? And how do beliefs and practices affect stories?

2. How does "bracketing" help students and scholars in the academic study of religion? What might be the downsides to this approach?

3. What are the benefits and pitfalls of comparing religious traditions? What can comparison help us see? What might it obscure?

4. Which definition of religion makes the most sense to you, and why? What does your favorite definition reveal about the world's religions? What does it miss?

5. What are the components of the four-part approach to studying religion outlined here? How does this approach work to undercut perennialism? In your view, does it fall prey to essentialism?

KEY TERMS

essentialism, p. 9   perennialism, p. 17

FURTHER READING

Albanese, Catherine L. *America: Religions and Religion*. 5th ed. Belmont, CA: Wadsworth Publishing, 1981.

Herling, Bradley L. *A Beginner's Guide to the Study of Religion*. New York: Continuum, 2012.

Orsi, Robert A. *History and Presence*. Cambridge: Belknap Press, 2016.

Pals, Daniel. *Nine Theories of Religion*. New York: Oxford University Press, 2015.

Smith, Jonathan Z. "Map Is Not Territory." In *Map Is Not Territory: Studies in the History of Religions*, 289–310. Chicago: The University of Chicago Press, 1993.

I

RELIGIONS OF RELEASE
India

When faced with the realities of a broken world, human beings can try to fix it. They can work to return to a place they remember as a site of peace and harmony. Or they can look for a way to escape. The Indian religions of release take the last option.

The Indian subcontinent—which comprises India; Pakistan; Bangladesh; and smaller countries such as Nepal, Bhutan, Bangladesh, Sri Lanka, and the Maldives—is home to approximately 1.8 billion people, or close to one-quarter of the world's population. It is also the birthplace of three religions of release—Hinduism, Buddhism, and Sikhism—joined to one another like the branches on a hybrid fruit tree. As the Hindu tradition grew up in the fertile soil of North India's Ganges Plain, it gave rise to the Buddhist tradition, which originated with the fifth-century BCE religious reformer Siddhartha Gautama. Known after his enlightenment as the Buddha ("Awakened One"), he renounced not only worldly pleasures but also Hindu reverence for ancient rituals and the priestly caste that performed them. Like the Buddha, the fifteenth- and sixteenth-century Sikh founder Guru Nanak (1469–1539) retained many of his Hindu roots and rejected others. He also drew on influences from the Islamic tradition, which by his time had brought its strict monotheism to the Indian subcontinent.

Buddhists and Sikhs adopted and adapted key concepts from Hindu thought, including karma ("action"), *samsara* ("wandering through"), and *moksha* ("release"). To be human is to be trapped, all three of these religious traditions observed, and to be trapped is to yearn to breathe free. But what is it that ensnares us? According to Hindus, Buddhists, and Sikhs alike, we all find ourselves in a moral universe in which our karmic actions in past and present lives have huge consequences for who we are today. The most fateful of these consequences is that we find ourselves caught in a vicious cycle of life, death, rebirth, and redeath, known as samsara. Participants in these religions of release seek moksha, or liberation from this cycle. Instead of working to repair the world or to return to a golden age before it was broken, Hindus, Buddhists, and Sikhs seek to escape from the unsatisfactory cycle of samsara.

Each of these Indian religions has its own understanding of how life has entrapped us and how we might be liberated from its fetters. Each offers contemplative traditions of self-effort in which liberation comes through meditation, chanting, or other techniques. Each also offers devotional traditions of other-help in which liberation comes as a gift from Hindu gods, buddhas and bodhisattvas, or the singular divinity Sikhs refer to as the Timeless One and the True Name. Of the eight dimensions of religion identified by the religious studies scholar Ninian Smart, Sikhs accent the scriptural dimension, Buddhists the experiential dimension, and Hindus the ritual and narrative dimensions. These three religious traditions also differ on the god question: Sikhs pursue union with the one divine, Hindus worship a god of their choosing, and Buddhists cultivate an intriguing lack of interest in the mathematics of divinity.

Despite these differences, the stories safeguarded in the scriptures and rituals of these Indian religions chart a similar narrative arc from action (karma) to bondage (samsara) to release (moksha). Some view this world as an illusion. Others view it as a prison of sorts whose strict moral law of cause and effect makes freedom here impossible. But all seek release from its bonds into another world beyond suffering and death.

Hindu women wade into the waters near Mumbai, India, in observance of the Vedic festival of Chhath, which is dedicated to the worship of the sun god and his wife.

Hinduism

THE WAY OF DEVOTION

The sun is coming up on another day in the North Indian city of Varanasi, and already the cremation grounds along the Ganges River are alive with activity. Boats weighed down by heavy hardwood pull up to the Manikarnika Ghat, the oldest of the cremation grounds in this ancient city. Laborers hoist massive logs onto their heads and carry them up the steps along the riverbank into cramped alleyways, where they are chopped into manageable five-foot lengths and stacked as high as houses.

Members of the nearby community of Dalits, or "untouchables," who take care of this cremation ground assemble logs into open-air pyres. There are no female mourners at this all-male ritual. ("No woman, no cry," a local explains.) But cows and dogs mill about. So do pilgrims and tourists, who gawk at this ritual of transforming wood and bone into ashes and returning both to the waters from which all life comes and to which all life returns.

In Rome, another ancient pilgrimage city, not much religion takes place in the open air. Roman Catholicism seems oddly hidden away. Except for the pope, no one offers to bless you. Not so in Varanasi, where holy men offer to dot your forehead with sandalwood paste, marking your body as belonging to the divine. Death is public, too. In fact, the city itself offers a living rebuke to those who would deny the fact of death or pretty it up. Family members carry corpses on bamboo ladders, headfirst, covered in colored cloth and garlanded like gods, through the twists and turns of Varanasi's impossibly labyrinthine streets, past wood sellers and chai vendors, past boys flying kites and men playing cards, down to the sacred Ganges, through the sunlit smoke of this Varanasi day. *"Ram naam satya hai,"* chant the mourners as they dodge auto rickshaw drivers on their way to the cremation grounds: "Truth is the name of God."

It seems absurd to single out *one* anything in the Hindu world, which is renowned for its abundance of colors, tastes, smells, and sounds. The Hindu gods are also hyperabundant—numbering 330 million, according to one common estimate—as are the truths they teach and the rituals devotees employ in worshiping them. But if you had to go to one and only one place to see this religion in action, that place would be Varanasi.

In keeping with the Hindu preference for the many over the one, the name of India's holiest city is itself a compound, evoking a land between two rivers: the Varana and the Assi, both tributaries of a river that flows down from heaven and is revered as a goddess: "Mother Ganga." But Varanasi goes by many names. In the Pali language of the Buddhist scriptures, Varanasi became Baranasi, which the British turned into Banaras (or Benares). Hinduism's oldest scriptures, the Vedas, call it Kashi: "City of Light." Today this luminous city is the home, according to cultural geographer Rana P. B. Singh, of 3,000 Hindu temples and shrines, 1,388 Muslim sites, 45 Christian churches, and 15 Sikh gurdwaras. Whereas the business of New Delhi is government and the business of Mumbai is business, the business of this city is pilgrimage, not least the pilgrimage from life to death.

Where the Ganges meanders alongside Varanasi's east side, there are eighty-four ghats, or steps to the water. Pilgrims come to bathe at these ghats, to feel the river's goddess power run over their skin. They come to worship the god Shiva, whose ascetic fire supercharges this city, not least at the Kashi Vishwanath Temple (also known as the "Golden Temple"), one of the most visited shrines in the world, where Shiva's light is said to have pierced the earth at the beginning of time. They come to take in the teachings of holy men who congregate here. They come to earn karmic merit or to pay for wrongdoing. They come to complete a multiday, 55-mile circular pilgrimage to 108 temples. They come to throw a coin into the river—an offering to Mother Ganga and a plea for spiritual liberation. They come to worship at the city's thousands of *lingams* (also, *lingas*), or "marks" or "signs" of Shiva. They come to scatter the ashes of family members. Most famously they come to die, to be cremated, and to be released from *samsara*: the endlessly unsatisfactory cycle of life, death, rebirth, and redeath. "The ocean is the origin of all things," wrote the Transcendentalist and Indophile Henry David Thoreau.[1] Here that origin is the river, which is also the end of all things.

Hindus speak of certain sacred spaces as *tirthas*—"crossing places"—and for thousands of years they have come as pilgrims to holy sites where the profane crosses over into the sacred and the sacred crosses back. But all of Varanasi is a tirtha, a crossing place from life to death and from death to spiritual liberation. Here is Hindu India in microcosm, its many gods in residence and many of its most popular temples reproduced in miniature. Here, it is said, prayers are more likely to be heard and rituals are more likely to work. According to many Hindus, if you die in Varanasi, Shiva will whisper into your ear the mantra of the crossing, enabling you to achieve *moksha*, or release from rebirth and suffering. "Death in Kashi," they say, "is liberation."

There are two ancient "burning ghats" in Varanasi, plus a modern electrical crematory that few people use. The most popular of the open-air cremation grounds is the Manikarnika Ghat, which now cremates two hundred bodies a day—about what an American crematory does in a year. When you step onto this ghat, you enter the sacred center of India's most sacred city. "Just as India is said to be the 'navel' of the world, and Kashi the navel of India," writes anthropologist Jonathan Parry, "so Manikarnika is the navel of Kashi."[2] According to some Hindu myths, the universe sprang into being here, and here, at the end of time, its corpse will be purified by fire.

At this "navel of Kashi," male family members bathe their relatives' corpses one last time in the purifying waters of the now-polluted Ganges, dipping their feet in the river and splashing water in their mouths one last time. They lift the corpse onto a pyre, the feet pointed in the direction of death (south). The eldest son of the deceased, head shaven, bare chested, and dressed in two unstitched white sheets that mark him as the chief mourner, asks one of the caretakers for a bundle of reeds and a light from a flame that, according to legend, has been burning nonstop under the watch of one family for thousands of years. (In fact, it is said that Lord Shiva lit it himself.) The chief mourner circles the corpse five times clockwise, touching the mouth with the fire each time. He then lights the pyre, feet side first, until the fire engulfs the body in heat and light. When the corpse has been mostly consumed, the chief mourner cracks the skull with a bamboo stick, releasing the soul to fly off to another rebirth. He then collects water from the Ganges in a pot and splashes it onto the smoldering pyre. He does this five times, once for each of the five elements: earth, air, water, fire, ether. The fifth time, he turns his back to the pyre, throws the pot over his shoulder, and walks away.

The cremated remains are not collected here. Whereas Jews, Christians, and Muslims have traditionally seen the human person as a combination of body and soul, Hindus have classically seen the essence of the human being as a self or soul cycling through multiple bodies in multiple lifetimes. So there is no gathering of the ashes in an urn and no ceremony to come at a cemetery plot. Once the body has been burned, caretakers push most of the ashes into the Ganges. As the river rises, it will take away whatever remains.

Bathers gather along the ghats, or river steps, beside the Ganges in Varanasi, India, to perform morning prayers and cool off in the sacred water, which Hindus describe as a goddess.

OUR STORY

One of the oldest cities in the world—as old as Beijing or Athens—Varanasi was established at least as early as 800 BCE (perhaps much earlier) and was reportedly visited by the Buddha around the fifth century BCE. From that point forward, the fortunes of the city rose and fell with those of Buddhist, Muslim, and British rulers. But amid the political changes to this religious, scholarly, and commercial center, pilgrims continued to come. After returning home, they scattered travelers' tales of their experiences far and wide. Some of those stories focused on the gods. This is the most famous story recounted by Shiva devotees in various versions in Sanskrit scriptures and vernacular folktales.

Lingam of Light

Many eons ago, long before historical time, when whatever existed did so in total darkness, two gods, Brahma and Vishnu, were quarrelling about who was supreme. They called in the most ancient and venerable of Hindu scriptures, the **Vedas,** *to settle their dispute. To their shock, the Vedas said that Lord Shiva was actually supreme. As this verdict was handed down, a massive*

Vedas ("knowledge")
the oldest and most sacred Sanskrit scriptures; unauthored revelations that offer one common source of a shared Hindu identity

shaft of light pierced the ground between the quarreling gods. Brahma flew up as a gander and Vishnu dug down as a boar in an effort to determine where the light was coming from and where it was going. After thousands of years of searching, neither had found its end. When they returned to the site of their argument, neither was any wiser for the journey. What to make of this indescribable shaft of light? Neither Brahma nor Vishnu could say. But then the form of Shiva appeared out of the formless shaft, with five faces and ten arms wielding weapons. Acknowledging Shiva as supreme, Brahma and Vishnu bowed down to worship him.

There are twelve places in India where Shiva's lingam miraculously appeared as a shaft of light. The most potent of them is Kashi, the "Luminous," the "City of Light." "This is my place of utmost mystery," says Lord Shiva. "Pre-eminent among all sacred fords, the best of places, superior to all knowledge, this is my place. . . . My devotees who go there enter into me. . . . All the evil accumulated in a thousand previous lives is destroyed for one who enters [Kashi]. . . . Whether one be a sinner, a crook or a wicked person, one is wholly purified by a visit."[3]

Shiva's lingam is worshiped at the Kashi Vishwanath Temple, but all of Kashi is pierced by his light. Every square foot of it is luminous. Every mound of dirt illuminated by its lights and shadows is a lingam—a mark of Shiva's powers of creation and regeneration. And each of those marks offers an occasion to worship this god who promises liberation to all who come to this place to die with his name in their hearts and on their lips.

HINDUISM IN TODAY'S WORLD

Unlike Christians, Muslims, and Buddhists, Hindus have not traditionally attempted to attract converts. To be a Hindu is to be born into a Hindu family, and to be born into a Hindu family is to be a Hindu. Like Jews, Hindus have been content to think of theirs as

In Bali, empty chairs dedicated to Ida Sang Hyang Widhi, the high god to Balinese Hindus, are scattered across the landscape, like this one overlooking the Beratan Lake. These stone thrones represent the impossibility of describing the divine.

a religion of *a* people rather than the religion of *all* people. For that reason, it has typically been classified as an *ethnic* religion (like Judaism and Navajo religion) rather than a *missionary* religion (like Buddhism and Islam).

Today, however, Hinduism thrives in an Indian diaspora that stretches around the globe. According to the World Religion Database, there are nearly twenty million Hindus in Nepal, more than fifteen million in Bangladesh, and more than four million in Indonesia. Sri Lanka, Pakistan, Malaysia, the United States, and South Africa all boast Hindu populations in excess of one million. Hinduism is the majority religion in Nepal. It is also the leading religion on the Indonesian island of Bali, where Hinduism takes a very different shape. In many Balinese temples, there are no images of god, and from street corners to rice fields to mountaintops, there are shrines depicting the high god of Balinese Hindus in the form of an empty chair.

The overwhelming majority of Hindus in the world today still live in India. India is home to over one billion Hindus, or nearly three-quarters of the Indian population. With 13.6 percent of the world's population, Hinduism is, despite its relatively modest global footprint, the third-largest religion in the world, behind only Christianity (32.3 percent) and Islam (24.3 percent).

Hinduism developed on a subcontinent of astonishing cultural, ethnic, social, linguistic, and regional diversity. It did so in conversation with the Buddhist, Jain, Islamic, Sikh, and Christian traditions, as well as a host of other religious traditions now

Comparison of Religions Worldwide, 2020

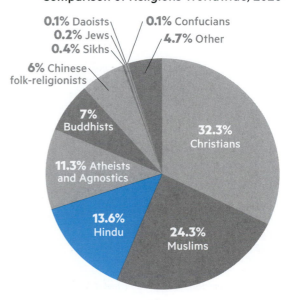

0.1% Daoists
0.2% Jews
0.4% Sikhs
6% Chinese folk-religionists
0.1% Confucians
4.7% Other
7% Buddhists
11.3% Atheists and Agnostics
13.6% Hindu
32.3% Christians
24.3% Muslims

avatar ("descent")
deity who comes to earth in human or animal form to combat evil and restore order

forgotten. As Hindus encountered people with different religious beliefs and practices, some attempted to draw sharp lines of orthodoxy ("right doctrine") or orthopraxy ("right practice"). Others welcomed religious rivals under a broad sacred canopy, refusing to banish either dissenting opinions or those who held them. As a result, what we now refer to as the Hindu tradition absorbed many outside influences. For example, the Buddha was adopted into the Hindu family—as one **avatar** (divine "descent") of Vishnu.

The upshot of this absorptive strategy was a decentralized religion with no creed or catechism, no founder, no single living religious leader such as the pope or the Dalai Lama, and no line of authority to proclaim from Rome or Salt Lake City who is "in" and who is "out." While other religions excommunicated or killed apostates, Hindus welcomed skeptics and dissenters as a vital part of what economist Amartya Sen has described as "argumentative India."[4] The result is the least dogmatic and most diverse of the world's religions. Given this multiplicity, it should not be surprising that Hindus do not agree on what to call their religion, or on whether it is a religion at all. Many modern Hindus insist that Hinduism is "a way of life" rather than a religion, referring to that way of life as *Sanatana Dharma* ("Eternal Law"), not "Hinduism." As a result, many Hindus refuse to self-identify as such. Hindus typically think of themselves as inhabitants of particular regions, speakers of particular languages, and members of particular castes.

Before going any further, it is important to address the fact that the field of Hindu studies is sharply polarized. For far too long, most scholars in this field were Europeans whose interpretations of Hinduism—as a religion with glorious ancient scriptures yet corrupted in modern times—served colonial interests by advancing Protestant assumptions about what religion really "is." In recent decades, Hindus have attempted to take control of Hindu studies scholarship. Beginning in the 1990s, Hindu nationalists attacked various books by Western scholars as offensive. As a result, some of these scholars left Hindu studies. One who persisted had eggs thrown at her in 2003 in London. In 2014,

Countries with Largest Hindu Populations, 2020
- Over 1 billion
- 10–20 million
- 1–5 million

United States
2 million

Pakistan
3 million

Nepal
20 million

Myanmar
1 million

Malaysia
2 million

India
1 billion

Sri Lanka
3 million

Bangladesh
16 million

Indonesia
4 million

South Africa
1 million

Hinduism is predominantly a Southeast Asian ethnic religion. The vast majority of Hindus live in India.

HINDUISM: A GENEALOGY

The term *Hindu* was originally a geographical marker, pointing to ancient people who occupied the valley of the river *Sindhu* (later, *Indus*) now in modern-day Pakistan and North India. During the Muslim Mughal empire (1526–1857), any non-Muslim was considered a Hindu. Into the early twentieth century, Americans used the word *Hindoo* to refer to all Indian immigrants, regardless of religion. And Article 25 of the Constitution of India counted Buddhists, Sikhs, and Jains as Hindus.

Terms akin to *Hindu* date back in English language sources to the seventeenth century. A 1662 English translation of a travelogue by the German scholar Adam Olearius describes one king as "a Hindou, or Indian, that is, a Pagan" before going on to describe his subjects as "a very ignorant people" who look in "matter[s] of religion, to their Bramans" and "believe the Immortality and Transmigration of Souls."[a] In a 1696 book, an East India Company chaplain named John Ovington compared "Hindoes" with "Mahometans" (Muslims) and observed that all "Hindoes…refrain from [eating] Bief."[b] A few years later, Englishman John Marshal used the term *Hindoo* as both an adjective and a noun, writing that "their religion consists of…the leading of a Pure Life, the Washing away of their Sins in the River Ganges, their muttering over diverse Prayets, and their doing of strange and incredible Penances."[c]

The *Oxford English Dictionary* traces "Hindooism" to 1829 and a book called *The Bengalee* by Major Henry Barkley Henderson, who offered a surprisingly sympathetic take on this religion. Henderson dressed like a Hindoo, "cooly enrobed with a dotee only," and nearly converted himself to the "goodly habits and observances of Hindooism."[d] However, there are hundreds of earlier uses going back at least to 1800. Though the scientist and clergyman Joseph Priestley does not use the term in *A Comparison of the Institutions of Moses with Those of the Hindoos* (1799), a review of that book published one year later in the New York–based *Monthly Magazine and American Review* refers to his examination of "the antiquity and history of Hindooism."[e] Also in 1800, the Irish soldier and diplomat Michael Symes contrasted the eagerness of "Musselmen" to convert others to their faith with the reluctance of adherents of "Hindooism" to do the same.[f]

This same term appears dozens of times in the first decade of the nineteenth century and hundreds of times in the 1810s. The pioneering American geographer Jedediah Morse refers to "Hindooism" in two different books. Rammohun Roy, the Indian-born founder of the reform society the Brahmo Samaj, criticizes "the theory of practice of Hindooism" for obsessing about unimportant matters such as diet.[g] However, the overwhelming majority of these early references come from the pens of Christian missionaries rejoicing over "converts from hindooism."[h]

amid lawsuits in India contending that one of her books was insulting to Hindus, her publisher agreed to destroy all remaining copies there.

Hindus themselves do not agree, however, on what Hinduism is. Some Hindus insist that Hinduism is monotheistic and that to describe it otherwise is racist. Others insist that Hinduism is polytheistic and that to describe it otherwise is to spout colonialist lies. Still others claim that both of these arguments fall prey to essentialism by assuming that Hinduism is one unchanging thing. In textbook controversies that continue today in California, Hindu groups have protested public school textbooks for failing to conform to their understanding of proper Hinduism. In all these cases, each side has accused the other of distorting history for political purposes. No textbook can resolve these controversies, but it is important for students to know that none of the work they read about Hinduism (including the words in this textbook) are free from the influences of this struggle.

HINDUISM 101

✦ How to escape from rebirth and death?

Hindus worship many gods and goddesses—from playful Krishna to fearsome Kali. They do so through many disciplines (*yogas*) and many philosophies. Their many paths (*margas*) invite believers to approach the divinities of their choosing through wisdom (**jnana**), devotion (**bhakti**), or action (**karma**). Hindus recognize different stages in life—students, householders (married folk), retirees, renouncers—each with different ethical obligations. They also recognize different aims in life: *kama*, or pleasure; *artha*, or wealth and power; **dharma**, or duty; and **moksha**, or spiritual liberation. Moreover, there are huge differences between the many local traditions scholars once described as "little," the pan-Indian traditions those same scholars once described as "great," and the regional traditions that might be described as "medium."

This expansive tradition stretches, textually, from ritual hymnals to philosophical treatises to popular epics. Linguistically, it stretches from the sacred language of Sanskrit to dozens of vernacular languages (and, in recent centuries, the English spoken by British colonizers and many Indian elites). Socially, the Hindu world has traditionally been divided into four classes, or *varnas* ("colors"):

- the priestly class (**Brahmins**)
- the warrior class (*Kshatriyas*)
- the merchant class (*Vaishyas*)
- the servant class (*Shudras*)

Outside this system of classification are the outcastes, or untouchables, now referred to as **Dalits** ("broken," "oppressed"). Since their identification at least three thousand years ago in the oldest Hindu scripture, the Rig Veda, these classes have yielded to thousands of **castes**, or *jatis* ("births"). Traditionally, these castes are hereditary, and members of different castes do not marry one another. However, today's rapidly growing Indian economy is restricting the power of caste traditions to dictate professional roles.

Hindus do not even agree on the mathematics of divinity. There are Hindu atheists and agnostics who argue either that there are no gods or that knowledge of the gods is not ours to possess. "The scriptures with their rules were invented by learned men who were clever at getting other people to give them money, tricking the simple-minded," says one Marx-style skeptic in the popular Indian epic the Ramayana.[5] Meanwhile, two of Hinduism's six classical schools of philosophy deny the existence of a personal god who intervenes in human history. The overwhelming majority of Hindus do believe in a personal god, but they disagree about whether divinity is to be described in the singular or the plural. Some Hindus are polytheists who believe in many gods. Others are monotheists who insist that there is one divine principle underlying many divine manifestations.

Today, "Hinduism" is an umbrella term for a diverse array of religious concepts, symbols, beliefs, and behaviors. Under this umbrella sit Uber drivers with images of Shiva on their dashboards, emaciated renouncers mortifying their bodies, fat-walleted businessmen with sculptures of the god Ganesha guarding the gates to their corporations, and ordinary householders worshiping Kali in their home shrines.

jnana ("wisdom")
the way of wisdom, one of the three paths to spiritual liberation, emphasized in the Upanishads and among renouncers

bhakti ("devotion")
the way of devotion, one of the three main Hindu paths to spiritual liberation and the dominant form of Hinduism today

karma
action and its consequences; ethical law of cause and effect that fuels the samsaric cycle; one of the three main Hindu paths to spiritual liberation

dharma
duty; one of the four aims of life

moksha ("freedom")
spiritual liberation; release from the cycle of birth, death, rebirth, and redeath

Brahmin
priestly social class

Dalit ("oppressed")
contemporary term for a social group previously known as "outcastes" or "untouchables"

caste (jati, or "birth group")
a signifier of social status and a definer of social boundaries that determines whom one can marry and with whom one can eat

Nonetheless, there is a Hindu tradition underlying this complex and multifaceted thing, and it is possible to make some generalizations about it. Hindus tend to affirm the authority of the Vedas and the propriety of making offerings to their deities. When it comes to their analysis of the human predicament, Hindus have traditionally fixed on the problem of **samsara** ("wandering through"), the ever-flowing cycle of birth, death, rebirth, and redeath. This vicious cycle is fueled by karma, which literally means "action" (from the Sanskrit *kri*, a cognate of "create") but refers in this case to the consequences (both positive and negative) that flow from moral and immoral words, thoughts, and actions. Among these consequences, which can take place immediately or far in the future, is a better or a worse rebirth.

Today, about one-fifth of adults in Western Europe and the United States believe in reincarnation, which they tend to interpret optimistically—one more opportunity to get the car or the spouse they always wanted, or to upgrade their profession from night security guard to astronaut. However, Hindus have not traditionally viewed the samsaric cycle this way. They have focused on redeath more than rebirth. To be born is to enter into the shadow of sickness, old age, and death. To live is to endure sorrow. To be reborn is to be strapped once again onto the hamster "wheel of re-death."[6] In short, samsara is a trap rather than an opportunity. The goal is to be liberated from it. This liberation Hindus refer to as moksha (from *muc*, "to free, release").

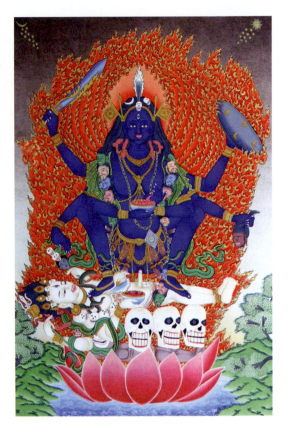

The Hindu goddess Kali is typically depicted as ferocious because of her willingness to fight for justice for her devotees. In this twentieth-century painting in the Dakshinkali Temple in Nepal, she wields a sword and tramples a corpse while blood drips from her mouth and a necklace of severed heads hangs from her neck.

But how might a person achieve this release? Here, Hindus have traditionally split into three main camps, which are often described as the three margas ("paths") or three yogas ("disciplines"). According to jnana yoga, or the discipline of wisdom, humans achieve moksha by attaining knowledge, more specifically the knowledge that the essence of the divine and the essence of the human are one and the same. This wisdom can be achieved only through self-effort—through austerity and study and mental discipline. According to bhakti yoga, or the discipline of devotion, humans achieve moksha via devotion to a god or goddess of their choosing. This is a path of other-help in which the devotee turns for assistance to a particular deity, who responds with favor in return. Finally, there is karma yoga, or the discipline of action, in which humans achieve moksha through moral and ritual action.

As in other religious traditions, Hindu exemplars vary with these techniques. Adherents of the discipline of wisdom honor renouncers adept in meditation or yogic exercises. Adherents of the discipline of devotion revere the gods themselves and their most fervent *bhaktas* ("devotees"), including poet-saints who epitomized devotion in word and worship. Adherents of the discipline of action revere moral giants such as Mohandas Gandhi, a practitioner of karma yoga and "truth force," whose techniques of nonviolent civil disobedience helped lead India to independence in 1947.

Not all Hindus take moksha as their goal, however. Like the Buddhist tradition, the Hindu tradition proceeds on two tracks. One is for people seeking the ultimate goal of moksha. The other is for those who either cannot imagine breaking away or do not want to break away from the karmic cycle. They seek thisworldly goals, including duty,

samsara ("wandering through")
unsatisfactory cycle of life, death, rebirth, and redeath and the core human problem according to the Hindu tradition

Brahma
creator God, rarely worshiped but sometimes included alongside Shiva and Vishnu in a Hindu triad of divinities

Vishnu ("The Pervader")
one of the three most popular Hindu deities (alongside Shiva and Devi), worshiped in ten avatars, including Rama and Krishna, and widely viewed as a sustainer of life

Shiva ("The Auspicious")
one of the three most popular Hindu deities (alongside Vishnu and Devi), often associated with destruction, who is worshiped in the form of the lingam and as an "erotic ascetic"

power, and pleasure, and as they approach death they hope simply for the proximate goal of a better rebirth.

Hindu Gods and Goddesses

Amidst this blooming, buzzing diversity, Hindu communities have focused on a few favorite divinities. Some Hindus today speak of a Trimurti of three gods: **Brahma** the creator, **Vishnu** the sustainer, and **Shiva** the destroyer (or recycler). This formulation has flourished in the West because of its obvious analogies to the Christian Trinity of the Father, Son, and Holy Spirit. But this "Hindu Trinity" obscures more than it illuminates. First, it overestimates the importance of Brahma who, like the aloof Almighty of Deism, has never been a popular object of worship. Second, it neglects Hinduism's many goddesses. The most popular divinities in India today are Shiva, Vishnu, the goddess Devi, and the ever-present remover of obstacles Ganesha.

Shiva ("The Auspicious") embodies the paradoxical nature of Hindu divinity, which can be both terrifying and auspicious, both destructive and creative. He is often worshiped today in the form of the lingam. He is also depicted in human form as a wandering yogi and a Himalayan meditator, his skin slathered with ashes and stretched thin over protruding bones. But this "erotic ascetic" is also a family man: the husband of Parvati and the father of the elephant-headed god Ganesha.[7] Shiva appears as well as Nataraja, a four-armed Lord of the Dance who dances inside a circle of flames and atop a dwarf demon, with one arm drumming the world into creation and another bearing the fire of destruction. None of these manifestations of Shiva, it should be noted, has power apart from the feminine principle of *shakti*, which means "power" or "energy." "Without Shakti," it is said, "Shiva is *shava*"—a corpse.[8]

A woman lights a candle offering during puja at the Dhakeswari Temple in Dhaka, Bangladesh. Originally built during the twelfth century, this is the National Temple of Bangladesh.

Vishnu ("The Pervader") is said to have ten avatars, who come to earth to make things right when the world has gone wrong. "Whenever there is a decline in *dharma*, and the absence of *dharma* increases, I create myself," Vishnu says. "I come into being from age to age."[9] These avatars are

- fish
- tortoise
- boar
- man-lion
- dwarf
- Rama with an axe
- **Rama**
- **Krishna**
- Buddha
- Kalki, the future avatar

This twenty-foot-tall relief carving of the Trimurti was fashioned out of basalt rock in the Elephanta Island caves near Mumbai, India. The Trimurti represents the divine in three forms: Shiva the destroyer (left), Vishnu the sustainer (center), and Brahma the creator (right).

The many local, regional, and pan-Indian goddesses in the Hindu tradition are sometimes categorized as manifestations of **Devi** ("Goddess") or Mahadevi ("Great Goddess"). Scholars have classified manifestations of Devi into two types: "goddesses of the tooth" and "goddesses of the breast."[10] According to folklorist A. K. Ramanujan, the goddesses of the tooth are violent, wild, and independent, whereas the goddesses of the breast are nurturing, gentle, and joined to their husbands.

Two popular tooth goddesses are **Durga** ("The Inaccessible") and **Kali** ("The Black One"). Durga was created by Brahma, Shiva, Vishnu, and other male gods. After failing to slay a buffalo demon that threatened to overrun the cosmos, they combined their powers to create a superhero of sorts to do what none of them was able to do alone. Typically depicted with eight or ten arms and riding a lion or a tiger, Durga wields the weapons of the male gods who made her. Her diet runs toward meat, blood, and alcohol. Kali is typically depicted with a skirt of severed human arms, a necklace of severed human heads, and a mouth dripping blood. Though terrifying, she uses her power to destroy evil. According to the devotional text the Devi-Mahatmya, which dates to the fifth or sixth century, she sprang forth full-born from the forehead of Durga in order to slay a demon. In the modern period, Kali has been domesticated into "Mother Kali," but she is still said to frequent cremation grounds and (like Durga) consume meat, blood, and alcohol. Kali is beloved today in Bengal and especially in Kolkata, which is named after her.

The so-called breast goddesses include Shiva's wife Parvati, Krishna's consort Radha, Vishnu's wife Lakshmi, and Brahma's wife Saraswati. Like Rama's wife Sita in the Ramayana, these women exhibit traditionally "feminine" virtues, including fidelity to husbands, and thus serve as models for all bhakti devotees (male and female), who are expected to remain faithful to their gods. However, these goddesses also rule over their own realms. (Saraswati is the goddess of learning, for example.)

Ganesha, the elephant-headed son of Shiva and Parvati, is the most ubiquitous member of the Hindu pantheon. As the fat and happy god of good fortune, guardian of thresholds, and remover of obstacles, he is the deity to worship at the beginning of any new venture, including college, marriage, or a new job. Like the mezuzah in Judaism, Ganesha is often seen near the front door of Hindu family homes. He pops up on T-shirts and tattoos and in Bollywood movies. This potbellied god is typically depicted holding an axe to destroy obstacles, a rope to rescue devotees from harm, and a sweet cake symbolizing the bliss

Rama
avatar of Vishnu, husband of Sita, and the righteous king and hero of the Ramayana epic

Krishna ("Dark One")
one of the avatars of Vishnu and one of the most celebrated gods in Hindu mythology, popularly associated with youthful play and flirtation

Devi
the great goddess, one of the three most important Hindu deities (alongside Vishnu and Shiva), and an umbrella term for all Hindu goddesses

Durga ("The Inaccessible")
fierce goddess, wife of Shiva, ten-armed warrior, slayer of demons

Kali ("The Black One")
fierce goddess and wife of Shiva, associated with death and destruction, often depicted wearing a garland of skulls and with blood dripping from her tongue

Ganesha
elephant-headed and pot-bellied god of thresholds and remover of obstacles. One of the most popular Hindu deities, he is invoked at the beginning of any new venture.

Ganesha, the elephant-headed god, is perhaps the most popular Hindu divinity. Worshiped as a remover of obstacles and blesser of new beginnings, he is often found at thresholds and doorways, including in this mural in Jaisalmer, India.

of spiritual liberation. Though equipped with four arms, he has only one tusk, since he broke off the other one to use as a pen to commit the Mahabharata to writing. Nowadays, stock and bond traders chant his 108 names each morning before the opening of the stock exchange in Mumbai.

Ways of Being Hindu

There is no Hindu equivalent of the formal divisions we see among Muslims into Sunnis and Shias, or among Christians into Roman Catholics, Protestants, and the Orthodox. However, according to the Indologist William Halfbass, Hindu worshipers can be divided into four main "religious constellations":

- Shaivas who worship Shiva as supreme. They are typically monotheistic.
- Vaishnavas who worship one of the avatars of Vishnu, especially Krishna and Rama, as their deity of choice. They are also typically monotheistic.
- Shaktas who worship as supreme the goddess Devi or some other manifestation of her goddess power (shakti). These manifestations include unmarried goddesses, who are worshiped as individuals, and spouse goddesses, who are typically worshiped in male/female pairs.
- Smartas refuse to choose among the above options because of their belief that the various manifestations of the divine are essentially the same. Though they may prefer a particular god, they regard any god in their gaze as a representation of the undivided divine.

Amarnath Ice Lingam

The **lingam** is an abstract representation of the Hindu god Shiva in the shape of a cylindrical pillar. It is worshiped in home shrines, temples, and even in natural objects, and is often embedded inside a structure called a *yoni* that serves as an abstract representation of the goddess Shakti. Long before the psychologist Sigmund Freud taught modern people to look almost everywhere for sexual symbols, visitors to India saw the lingam as a phallic symbol and the yoni as a vulva. Today, many Hindus insist that what is being represented here is simply creative power and take offense at efforts to sexualize it. Many

scholars reply that efforts by contemporary Hindus to desexualize the lingam are rooted not in ancient Hindu traditions but in the prudery of India's Victorian colonizers.

This ice stalagmite in the Amarnath cave shrine in North India is a great example of a naturally occurring lingam. Sitting nearly thirteen thousand feet above sea level in the mountains of Jammu and Kashmir, the shrine that houses it is covered with snow and inaccessible most of the year. In the summer, it opens to thousands of devotees, who trek ancient pilgrimage routes across rugged terrain to sing, chant, and perform **puja** (worship) to Shiva. The annual count of pilgrims has spiked in recent years to hundreds of thousands as the Indian government has encouraged pilgrimage here. Unfortunately, because of a combination of increased tourism and global climate change, this lingam has failed to appear in some years and melted early in others.

Hindus have also divided over philosophical matters, forming six philosophical schools, including two that denied the existence of an eternal and personal god active in human history. The dominant school is called Vedanta, meaning "the end of the Vedas," but this school is itself divided into various subschools, largely over the relationship between **brahman** (the divine) and **atman** (the self-soul). The three most influential are

- Advaita ("Nondualistic") Vedanta: The nondualists in this leading school see no essential distinction between brahman and atman. They usually understand the divine as impersonal and *nirguna* ("without attributes") and conclude that all we can affirm about ultimate reality is *neti neti* ("not this, not that"). The key figure here is the philosopher Shankara (c. 788–c. 820), who argued that spiritual liberation comes only when one realizes that multiplicity is *maya* ("illusion") and that reality is monistic ("one"). In keeping with their commitment to nondualism, members of this school today often view the world's religions as essentially one.
- Dvaita ("Dualistic") Vedanta: These "dualists" argue that brahman and atman are distinct. Humans depend on the divine for both their being and their spiritual liberation. This school, founded by the thirteenth-century philosopher Madhva, who worshiped Vishnu as supreme, conceived of brahman personally, as *saguna* ("with attributes").
- Vishishtadvaita Vedanta: Adherents of this "qualified nondualism" school argue that only one thing (brahman) exists, but that it exhibits multiplicity all the way down. Advanced most famously by the Vaishnava philosopher Ramanuja (d. 1137), this school contends that God is one yet can be described personally and with attributes.

lingam ("mark")
impersonal symbol of Shiva and a representation of creativity and regeneration, often understood to represent the male and female sex organs, though many Hindus today take offense at that understanding

puja
worship, conducted in the temple and at home

brahman
the divine principle, understood either "with attributes" (*saguna*) or "without attributes" (*nirguna*)

atman
the individual self-soul, said to migrate from life to death to rebirth to redeath

HINDU HISTORY

To make sense of this many-armed tradition, we need to start with the Indus Valley Civilization that began around 2500 BCE and trace it through to the foundation of the state of India in 1947 and beyond. We also need to transition from mythical to historical time and from ancient scripture to contemporary scholarship—to the beginning of Hinduism not as the scriptures tell it but as archaeologists, experts in ancient Sanskrit, and historians of religion understand it. To make sense of this story, we also need to move beyond India, as Hindus themselves began to do roughly two millennia ago, starting with forays into Vietnam in the second century.

It would be easy to reckon with developments inside Hinduism if the Hindu traditions presented themselves to us sequentially from one period to the next, like oddly orderly empires in which one dynasty politely succeeds the next. Unfortunately, the Hindu past is not so orderly. Instead of thinking of the Hindu tradition as a straightforward timeline of imperial succession, think of it as a series of geological strata—layers in the earth that build upon one another yet often intersect. So while it is possible to speak of older and newer layers, older layers can thrust upward through newer layers and break again onto the surface. The result is a tradition that looks something like Varanasi itself, where the ancient and the modern are forever interlocked and stone steps are layered upon one another in intersecting strata of historical and spiritual significance.

The story of the history of Hinduism told here tracks the formation and transformation of those layers. It begins with early influences on the Hindu tradition unearthed by archaeologists. It then tracks the religion of the early Hindu scriptures, the Vedas, before turning to how what we now refer to as Hinduism came to be—how thinkers identified the core human problem of rebirth and redeath and developed techniques to overcome it. The central focus of this narrative, however, is the emergence of popular devotionalism, including the stories told in the Hindu epics and the Puranas, which more than any other sources have shaped the ground on which Hindus stand today.

Indus Valley Civilization

The oldest of these layers of Hinduism was put down in the Indus Valley Civilization (IVC), which flourished from perhaps 2500 BCE to 1500 BCE. Unfortunately, the evidence regarding this Bronze Age culture, which stands alongside Mesopotamia and Egypt as one of the world's first great urban civilizations, is archaeological rather than textual, so it is difficult to say much that is definitive about IVC religion. Nonetheless, this civilization seems to offer tantalizingly early glimpses of later Hinduism, including a mother goddess, male divinities, a sacred bull, sacrificial offerings, and ritual bathing.

Indus Valley Civilization first came to be known to modern scholars in the early 1920s, when archaeologists unearthed two ancient cities, Mohenjo-daro and Harappa, in what is now Pakistan. This civilization included a uniform system of weights and measures, a written language, and multistory buildings. Geographically, it ranged widely, from today's Rajasthan and Gujarat states in western India into much of modern-day Pakistan, and wider still through

Hinduism at a Glance

Problem: samsara, the unsatisfactory cycle of life, death, rebirth, and redeath

Solution: moksha, release from this cycle

Techniques: the disciplines of karma (action), jnana (wisdom), and bhakti (devotion)

Exemplars: yogis, renouncers, and poet-saints

In short, Hinduism is a tradition in which people trapped in the unsatisfactory cycle of rebirth and redeath seek liberation from that cycle through the disciplines of action, wisdom, or devotion.

extensive trade networks that cut deep into Mesopotamia. By 1500 BCE, however, this civilization had all but vanished.

One explanation for this disappearing act is the Aryan invasion thesis, which argues that Northern European invaders calling themselves Aryans ("Noble Ones") swept across Pakistan and northern India from the west, displacing Indus Valley Civilization. Evidence for this theory is largely linguistic. What we now refer to as Indo-European languages (Sanskrit, Latin, Greek, English, Spanish, French) are not related to the Dravidian languages of South India. However, there are clear ties among these Indo-European languages. Consider these related words:

Sanskrit	Latin	Greek	English
deva	deus	theos	divine
jnana	cogno	gnosis	know

This bronze "dancing girl" statue dates back to roughly 2500 BCE. It was found in the Indus Valley Civilization city of Mohenjo-daro, located in modern-day Pakistan.

The Aryan invasion thesis explains these similarities by positing a Proto-Indo-European language that served as the mother of Sanskrit and English alike. This thesis also explains why Indus Valley Civilization went missing so suddenly: it was wiped out by Aryan invaders from the West, whose cultural DNA is still present in the Hindu tradition.

There are many variations of this controversial thesis, which is affirmed by most scholars. One contends that Proto-Indo-European speakers came not as invaders, with swords, but as settlers, in peace. They (and their horses) were welcomed by locals. Therefore, contemporary Indian civilization rests on hospitality rather than war. Many Indians today reject both of these possibilities. Many also argue that Aryans were not Northern Europeans after all but were on the Indian subcontinent from the start. Some even claim that all Indo-European languages are descended from Sanskrit, which is the mother of them all.

No matter how you make sense of the IVC's disappearance—and there is no consensus regarding the evidence—a key question remains: What sort of contributions, if any, did it make to the Hindu tradition? For decades, scholars have seen precursors aplenty: foreshadowings of Hindu goddesses in statues of buxom women and a possible forerunner of Shiva in cave paintings depicting a "lord of the beasts" comfortable in forests and among wild animals. However, we don't know enough about how these images were employed to decide if they really add up to a religion, or whether that religion (if any) contributed to Hinduism. Was the Great Bath unearthed at Mohenjo-daro a ritual site like the baths at Hindu temples today? Or was it just a public pool like one at a YMCA? Perhaps the picture will come into focus when (or if) the language of this civilization can be read. At this point, its script remains undeciphered.

Vedic Religion: Proto-Hinduism as a Way of Action

What we now call Hinduism began to speak through the Vedas, the most ancient and revered Hindu scriptures. Hindus divide their scriptures into two categories: *smriti* ("what is remembered") and *shruti* ("what is heard"). Smriti texts are lesser scriptures, made by human hands. Shruti texts are eternal and unauthored revelations merely "heard" by ancient sages and then memorized and transmitted orally. They are the more authoritative texts, and of all shruti the Vedas are the highest. In fact, one thing that binds Hindus together is a shared reverence for the Vedas. Just as to be an American is to accept the Constitution as the law of the land, to be a Hindu is to accept the Vedas (from *vid*, "to know") as true knowledge. To reject the Vedas, as Jains and Buddhists do, is to find yourself outside the Hindu fold.

The classification of the Vedas is complicated, but the basic structure is that there are (a) four Vedas and (b) four types of texts in each Veda. The four Vedas, all composed in Sanskrit, are the following:

- *Rig Veda* ("Verse Knowledge"): poems or chants praising the gods, recited by priests during sacrifices and other rituals;
- *Yajur Veda* ("Sacrificial Knowledge"): prose mantras, or sacred formulas, to recite during these rites;
- *Sama Veda* ("Musical Knowledge"): hymns;
- *Atharva Veda* ("Priestly Knowledge"): later texts, including practical prayers, charms, and incantations used to bring on success and to ward off sickness.

Upanishads
philosophical dialogues between teachers and pupils that elaborate on the Vedas and teach wisdom as a path to spiritual liberation

The four types of Vedic literature are the Samhitas, Brahmanas, Aranyakas, and **Upanishads**, and each of the Vedas just listed has each of these subclassifications. The latter three will be discussed later. The Samhitas ("collections") are the earliest Vedic texts, consisting largely of mantras and hymns chanted in Sanskrit during Vedic sacrifice. Because these texts were composed orally, they are difficult to date, but scholars estimate that they date to around 1500 BCE. Taboos on transferring this person-to-person

CHRONOLOGY OF HINDUISM

2500–1500 BCE	Indus Valley Civilization
c. 1500–1000 BCE	Rig Veda is composed
c. 800–200 BCE	Early Upanishads are composed
c. 300 BCE–300 CE	Mahabharata is composed
c. 200 BCE–200 CE	Ramayana is composed
c. 100 CE	Bhagavad Gita is composed
c. 500–1500	Puranas are composed
6th–7th centuries	Tantric texts and practices emerge
c. 788–c. 820	Life of Shankara, South Indian Advaita Vedanta philosopher
1137	Death of Ramanuja, South Indian philosopher of "qualified nondualistic" Vedanta
1206–1526	Islamic Delhi sultanate rules North India
1278 or 1317	Death of Madhva, South Indian philosopher of "dualistic" Vedanta
c. 1398–c. 1448	Life of Kabir, North Indian devotional poet
1469–1539	Life of Guru Nanak, Sikhism founder
1486–1533	Life of Chaitanya, Bengali mystic and Krishna devotee
1498	Birth of Mirabai, mystic and poet
1526–1757	Islamic Mughals rule India
1757	East India Company begins to rule large portions of India both militarily and commercially
1800	Early use of the term *Hindooism* in English
1828	Ram Mohan Roy establishes Brahmo Samaj
1836–1886	Life of Ramakrishna, Bengali mystic
1858	The British defeat both the Mughals and the East India Company and the British Raj in India begins
1863–1902	Life of Swami Vivekananda, first Hindu missionary to the United States
1869–1948	Life of Mohandas Gandhi, Indian revolutionary

knowledge into writing kept them from being written down until the ninth century CE, and they were not widely published until the late nineteenth century. These early Vedas were largely controlled by Brahmin men but wives stood by their husbands as sacrifices were performed, and women were the subjects of some verses, including a poem that describes the creation of the cosmos as a woman giving birth.

In the world according to the Vedas, the problem was chaos—cosmic, social, and domestic. The solution was order in all these realms. The technique to achieve this goal—and the central preoccupation of Vedic religion—was fire sacrifice. The exemplars were Brahmin priests tasked with performing these rites.

The hymns of the Vedas are the soundtrack to this fire sacrifice. They praise the gods for allowing the righteous to triumph over their enemies in war. They ask the gods for wealth, health, or longevity. But fire sacrifice was also accompanied by another form of speech: the **mantra**, or sacred sound. A mantra doesn't necessarily *mean* anything. It *is* something. And what it is is sacred power. **Om** (also *Aum*), the most powerful of these mantras, is said to encompass all things in sound. It is the sound of reality itself and is believed to have been reverberating from the beginning of time.

Plant offerings in Vedic religion included soma, a hallucinogenic plant (or perhaps a stimulant) offered to the gods in large-scale public rituals and small-scale domestic settings. But some Vedic priests also sacrificed animals, including bulls and horses.

mantra

sacred sound, such as Om, used to concentrate the mind in meditation and believed to unleash supernatural power or win spiritual liberation

Om (or Aum)

the most powerful mantra, employed at the beginning and end of many Hindu prayers and rituals, and said to be able to create union with the divine simply through its utterance

1875	Dayananda Sarasvati establishes the Hindu reform movement the Arya Samaj
	Helena Blavatsky and Henry Steel Olcott establish the Theosophical Society in New York City
1893	Swami Vivekananda represents Hinduism at the World's Parliament of Religions in Chicago
1918–2008	Life of Maharishi Mahesh Yogi, Transcendental Meditation guru
1920	Swami Yogananda comes to the United States to attend International Congress of Religious Liberals in Boston
1947	India wins independence from England, and Partition creates India and Pakistan as separate countries
1948	Gandhi is assassinated
1956	B. R. Ambedkar converts to Buddhism with many other Dalits in mass protest
1965	Hart-Celler Act opens up Asian immigration to the United States, beckoning ordinary Hindus and gurus alike
1966	ISKCON is founded by A. C. Bhaktivedanta Prabhupada
1977	Sri Venkateswara Temple in Pittsburgh and the Ganesh Temple in Flushing, New York, become the first Indian-style Hindu temples in the United States
1980	Hindu nationalist political party, Bharatiya Janata Party (BJP), is established
1992	Thousands die in Muslim/Hindu riots after Hindu nationalists destroy a mosque in Ayodhya
2000	Venkatachalapathi Samuldrala delivers the first Hindu prayer before the U.S. House of Representatives
2012	Representative Tulsi Gabbard of Hawaii becomes the first Hindu elected to the U.S. Congress
2014	Narendra Modi of the Hindu nationalist BJP becomes Indian prime minister

According to one story in the Rig Veda, the world came into being through the sacrifice of a primordial being. Out of this body came the entire universe, including animals and human beings, the sun and the moon, the gods, and even the verses and chants of the Vedas themselves. The social system of classes also had its origins in this account of sacrifice, as the mouth of this first person is said to have become the Brahmin or priestly class, the arms the Kshatriya or warrior class, the thighs the Vaishya or merchant class, and the feet the Shudras or the servant caste.

After this creation, fire sacrifice functioned as both a gift and an exchange. The San-skrit word for sacrifice (*yajna*) derives from *yaj* ("to offer"), so Vedic sacrifices were gifts to the gods. Worshipers offered plants or animals. Brahmin priests transformed those offerings, through proper actions, proper hymns, and proper mantras, into food the gods could consume. In exchange, the gods were said to keep the cosmos in order. Thus, Vedic people saw the entire cosmos intertwined with human actions.

Vedic fire sacrifices did more than keep the sun rising and setting, however. They also made families and societies prosperous, blessing them with health and wealth, fertility and longevity, abundant harvests and victory in war. Yajna also brought afterlife rewards, though these were not stressed in Vedic religion. In fact, the Vedas hinted only vaguely at an afterlife in the World of the Ancestors above and a House of Clay below. The emphasis in Vedic religion was practical and thisworldly; it did not yet contemplate rebirth.

Most of the Vedic gods who received these fire offerings were associated in some way with nature, including Surya the sun god, Vayu the wind god, and Rudra the mountain god (who would later develop into Shiva). There were some goddesses, most notably Vak, the goddess of sacred speech who gave power to the mantras uttered in fire sacrifices. Although many in the West think of God as all good, these Vedic divinities were, like the Greek gods, a mixture of good and bad. What made them gods was not virtue but power and they, too, coexisted in a polytheistic pantheon. As early as the Rig Veda, however, there emerged a sense of unity underlying all this diversity: "They call it Indra, Mitra,

Indra
Vedic warrior deity

Agni
Vedic god of fire and sacrifice

HINDUISM BY THE NUMBERS

Four Vedic Gods

- **Indra**, the most important Vedic deity, was a warrior god, the god of war, and the closest thing to a high god in Vedic religion. His most important role was killing a demon who had locked away the world's waters. In so doing, Indra prepared the way for agricultural civilization to come. Intriguingly, he was not known for his ethics. In fact, according to one scholar, he was "a ruffian from birth: an unfilial son, a lecherous youth, and a gluttonous, drunken, and boastful adult."[a]

- **Agni**, the second most important deity in the Vedas, was both fire itself and the god of fire, sacrifice, and the sun. He was also a messenger who shuttled between the human and heavenly realms. Offerings poured into his mouth (the sacrificial fire) were carried up as smoke to

other gods, who feasted on them. If Indra was the model warrior, Agni was the model priest. The first words of the Rig Veda are, "I pray to Agni" (1.1.1).

- Varuna was a moral god, the guardian of cosmic order and social harmony. He practiced appropriate speech, performed the proper rituals, and punished evildoers with disease while rewarding with happiness those who did good deeds.

- Soma was a hallucinogenic plant (or perhaps a stimulant—scholars are not sure), the intoxicating juice from that plant, and the god of all plants. Soma inspired priests to compose Vedic hymns and steeled warriors to go into battle.

Varuna, Agni . . . [but] the wise speak of what is One in many ways" (1.164.46). Some have referred to the worship of that one among many as "serial monotheism" or, more technically, kathenotheism: worshiping one god at a time.[11]

Like Judaism, which metamorphosed from a tradition of performing sacrifice into a tradition of reading and interpreting scripture after the destruction of the Second Temple in 70 CE, Hinduism has moved far beyond its Vedic origins. For this reason, it makes sense to think of Vedic religion as proto-Hinduism, much as the religion of the Hebrew Bible can be thought of as proto-Judaism. But the Vedic tradition lives on in the sacred fires of Hindu marriage and cremation rituals, with echoes as well in **aarti**, the fire offering of contemporary puja. Vedic religion also lives on in its gods, some of whom continue to be worshiped today.

The fire offering known as *aarti* is a central aspect of Hindu worship today. Here, devotees light a candle in a bowl of flowers before setting it afloat down the Ganges River near Rishikesh, India.

The Classical Tradition: Hinduism as a Way of Wisdom

After the composition of the Samhitas came three additional subclassifications of Vedic texts, each composed from around 800 to 100 BCE and each associated with one of the main Vedas listed earlier (Rig, Yajur, Sama, Atharva). These subclassifications were

- *Brahmanas*: prose commentary on a given Veda, explaining, often via allegorical interpretation, the meanings of Vedic sacrifice as well as the procedures for performing it.
- *Aranyakas*: more esoteric meditations on the meanings of Vedic sacrifice, rooted in secret discussions of the Vedas among forest-dwelling renouncers.
- *Upanishads*: later philosophical speculation on the Ultimate Reality to which Vedic rituals point, often presented as dialogues between teachers and students.

These Vedic texts offered mystical or philosophical reflection on the hymns and mantras of the Samhitas. It is in the Upanishads, for example, that we first hit the bedrock concepts upon which the Hindu tradition will be built: brahman and atman, karma and reincarnation. In that sense, these later Vedic texts served as bridges connecting the earlier way of ritual action in Vedic religion with a new way of wisdom that became classical Hinduism. This new religion coalesced in approximately the sixth century BCE, when wandering mystics and philosophers called **sannyasins** ("renouncers") began to challenge both the effectiveness of Vedic rituals and the power of the Brahmin priests who performed them. Focusing more on the *why* of sacrifice than on the *how*, these intellectual renegades asked hard questions about the sacred power underlying fire sacrifice. Are the divinities who respond to these rites personal or impersonal? Might there be one ultimate reality behind Agni and the other gods—some unchanging essence undergirding the ever-changing fires of human life? Is the world as it appears to be or is it an illusion?

This shift from ritual action to philosophical speculation is most pronounced in the Upanishads, which began around the middle of the first millennium BCE to give voice to the new concepts and concerns that continue to inform Hindu life. The term *Upanishad*

aarti
fire offering during Hindu worship

sannyasin
renouncer who has left behind work and family for a life of homelessness and celibacy in search of liberating wisdom

Three *sannyasins*, or renouncers, pose for a photo outside the Pashupatinath Temple in Kathmandu, Nepal. These holy men continue the Upanishadic tradition of leaving worldly life behind in order to dedicate themselves full-time to achieving *moksha*.

means "sit down near," which may refer both to students sitting at the feet of teachers and to the hard work of bringing competing ideas into connection with one another. It also carries the connotation of transferring secret teachings or making "hidden connections."[12] Among the concepts and concerns introduced in the Upanishads was the master metaphor of samsara. As has been noted, samsara literally means "wandering through," but here it refers to the flowing together of creation and destruction. The universe was created and will someday be destroyed, as will the various heavens and hells described in the Vedas. Human beings are also subject to samsara, their souls propelled from birth and death to rebirth and redeath by the fuel of karma.

In Vedic religion, karma referred to ritual action, but as classical Hinduism emerged it started to take on ethical import, referring to moral action and the consequences (good or bad) that flow from it. According to karmic theory, the circumstances of one's birth were a result of the sum of the debits and credits of one's moral actions in a prior life. Moreover, karmic logic dictated that everything one did eventually had to be rewarded or punished. Both good and bad actions produced bad karma, which needed to be experienced. If we died with a surplus of bad karma, we had to be reborn in order to be punished. If we died with a surplus of good karma, we had to be reborn in order to be rewarded. Through this endless cycle of moral recycling, the fuel of karma propelled individual souls from rebirth to redeath and back again. Doing good was not a way out. The way out was jnana, or wisdom.

Among the wandering renouncers seeking this liberating wisdom around the fifth century BCE were Siddhartha Gautama and Vardhamana Mahavira. These men, who would go on to found (or revive) what we now refer to as Buddhism and Jainism, distinguished themselves from Hindu renouncers by rejecting the authority of the Vedas. Many other renouncers remained in the Hindu fold and devised their own techniques for achieving spiritual liberation.

The word **yoga**, a cognate of the word *yoke*, means "to unite"—in this case to unite oneself with the divine. This union can be achieved only through discipline, however, so this term also connotes the discipline required to yoke with the divine. One such discipline is hatha yoga, a body posture practice that has been reborn in the modern West as "yoga." But ancient Indian renouncers used a variety of "yogas" to achieve their goal of spiritual liberation. Instead of using the soma plant of Vedic times to conjure up altered states of consciousness, they disciplined their bodies through breathing techniques, meditation strategies, fasting, and abstaining from meat. Through these "interior sacrifices," ascetics claimed to be able to generate inside their own bodies the spiritual heat that priests during the Vedic period had generated on the sacrificial fire. This achievement made spiritual power portable. So it should not be surprising that these renouncers also cultivated the yoga of wandering—leaving behind homes, jobs, and families in order to work full time to cultivate liberating wisdom.

But what was this wisdom? And how was it to be won? One of the most famous stories in the Upanishads tries to answer these questions in a convenient shorthand. A son, Svetaketu, has just come home to his father, Uddalaka, after years of hard study in Vedic texts and rituals. Svetaketu is proud of what he has learned at the feet of his **guru**, but his father wants to know whether he possesses true wisdom. He asks Svetaketu whether he has learned about subtler things, such as how that which is not heard becomes heard and how that which is not known becomes known. Confused, Svetaketu says no. So his father asks him to put some salt in water. The next day Uddalaka asks his son to give him back the salt. But the salt has dissolved into the water. So Uddalaka tells his son to taste the surface of the water. "How is it?" he asks. "Salty," Svetaketu replies. Uddalaka tells him to taste from the middle of the water. "How is it?" he asks a second time. "Salty," Svetaketu again replies. Finally, Uddalaka instructs his son to taste from the bottom of the glass. "How is it?" he asks. "Salty," the son replies again. Uddalaka concludes his lesson with one of the most famous passages in the Hindu scriptures: "Here likewise in this body of yours, my son, you do not perceive the True; but there in fact it is. In that which is the subtle essence, all that exists has its self. That is the True, that is the Self, and thou, Svetaketu, art That."[13]

The Sanskrit formula that concludes this famous lesson in the Chandogya Upanishad is "*tav tvam asi*," which has been widely translated as "That thou art."[14] In other words, the essence of the individual soul (atman) and the essence of the divine (brahman) are equivalent: You and God are one. If this sounds puzzling, that is because it is, and Hindu philosophers have puzzled for centuries over precisely what it might mean.

Inspired by the Upanishads, many Hindus came to view samsara as the human problem and moksha as the human goal. Advocates aimed not to wrest order out of chaos in this world, as Vedic priests had done, but to unlock the secrets of the next. Together they sought to cultivate, through various spiritual disciplines, the liberating wisdom that would allow them to escape samsara and reach moksha. Of that wisdom, the Chandogya Upanishad observes, "When someone knows it, bad actions do not stick to him, just as water does not stick to a lotus leaf."[15]

This way of wisdom was an extraordinary path. In Vedic religion, a patron could go to a priest and ask for a sacrifice to be performed on his behalf. Once performed, the

yoga ("union")
popular embodied posture practice loosely rooted in earlier Hindu mental and bodily disciplines designed to unite a human soul to the divine

guru
personal spiritual teacher

Yoga is an ancient Indian practice. In this eighteenth-century painting, a yogi practices a handstand upon a tiger-skin rug.

merit of that sacrifice would accrue to the patron. Classical Hinduism called for more self-reliance. Merit could not typically be transferred from one person to another. The karma you accrued was yours alone. As a result, the goal of moksha could be achieved only by full-time religious professionals.

Non-renouncers, or householders, took aim at the proximate goal of a better rebirth. Rather than seeking the wisdom that would release them from the karmic cycle of life, death, rebirth, and redeath, they tried to lead good lives in order to be born the next time around in better circumstances. In this way, they rejected the extraordinary track of release in favor of the ordinary path of rebirth. Those who did their duty on this track of rebirth would gradually work their way up. In some future lifetime, they might become renouncers themselves and achieve moksha.

Until that lifetime came, ordinary Hindus tried to enjoy the pleasures of the wheel of life. Moksha isn't the only goal of Hinduism, they insisted. There are four aims of life: *kama* (pleasure), dharma (righteousness), *artha* (wealth and power), and moksha. Until moksha was within reach, they were going to revel in the other three. They would work (and hope) for prosperity and longevity and for children and grandchildren along the way. And they would luxuriate in worldly pleasures.

There were efforts to merge these two tracks, or at least to get them to run alongside one another. One was the development of a system of four *ashramas*, or life stages, in which the high-caste men advance from students to householders to forest dwellers and then finally to renouncers. The technical term for this system is *varna-ashrama-dharma*, which refers to doing your duty (dharma) in keeping with your class (varna) and stage in life (ashrama). But this was theory more than practice, since most Hindus stayed in the householder stage and aimed simply at a better rebirth.

The Epics

The complications of the lives of these householders found expression in the Hindu epics the Ramayana and the Mahabharata, wide-ranging stories that wrestled with the challenges of ordinary life in a world in which the gods walked the earth. These stories entertained. They also redirected the Hindu tradition away from its origins in Vedic ritual and Upanishadic philosophy toward a more popular piety of devotion.

Composed between 300 BCE and 300 CE, these two narrative poems couldn't be more different from the Vedas and the Upanishads. Rather than revel in the mechanics of sacrificial rituals or the intricacies of philosophical arguments, they tell stories about gods and humans and the dramas of everyday life. Their scenes are the stuff of Shakespeare's tragedies and contemporary telenovelas, combining heroism and holiness with betrayal, lechery, murder, adultery, and lust. The heroes of these epics are neither priests nor ascetics but warriors and kings and gods. Their stories attend with care to the stuff of daily life—to duty and desire, love and loss, exile and return. While these epics are technically regarded as *smriti* (human traditions) rather than *shruti* (unauthored revelation), they have held more sway over more Hindus for more time than supposedly more authoritative texts.

It is difficult to summarize the epics because each is as vast and sprawling as India itself. In fact, their composers make the Greeks' Homer look like a short story writer. The **Mahabharata**, at some one hundred thousand verses and 1.8 million words, is longer than the Iliad, the Odyssey, and the Bible combined. Tucked inside it is the **Bhagavad Gita**, the most beloved scripture for many Hindus today—their New Testament and their Quran.

Mahabharata
one of the two major Sanskrit epics (alongside the Ramayana); a far-reaching story of duty and war that includes the popular Bhagavad Gita

Bhagavad Gita
iconic portion of the Mahabharata epic in which the warrior Arjuna and the god Krishna discuss karma and dharma and present the bhakti path as an alternative to the paths of action and wisdom

The **Ramayana**, which weighs in at twenty thousand verses, looks miniature alongside the Mahabharata, but it still is roughly three times longer than the Quran.

It is not length alone that makes it difficult to generalize about these two epics, however. They also resist generalization because, like the Hindu tradition itself, they argue against themselves and their interpretations shape-shift over time. Nevertheless, both of these stories demonstrate the power of storytelling to convey and shape cultural and religious values. Though composed in Sanskrit, each continues to be told and retold in dozens of vernacular languages and, increasingly, on television and the Internet. Their stories are beloved in Jain, Buddhist, Muslim, and Sikh communities. Those same stories serve as prompts for philosophical conversations among elites—Gandhi reportedly read the Gita, which he called his "spiritual Mother," every day for forty years—even as they thrill ordinary people in puppet shows in Bali and theatrical spectacles in Trinidad and Tobago. In 1987 and 1988, roughly eighty million Indians watched a televised *Ramayana* in seventy-eight episodes. The runaway success of that not-so-mini-series led to a 108-episode *Mahabharata*, which aired across India from 1988 to 1990.

Ramayana   The Ramayana ("Journey of Rama") tells the tale of the prince Rama and his wife Sita who is kidnapped by a demon king named Ravana. Its themes veer toward love and war but, like the Mahabharata, its preoccupation is dharma—in this case, the duties kings have to subjects, wives to husbands, sons to fathers, and brothers to brothers.

As the Ramayana opens, Rama, the eldest of three sons of the virtuous king of Ayodhya, is about to ascend to the throne. But his stepmother manages to persuade his

Ramayana ("Journey of Rama")
one of the two major Sanskrit epics (alongside the Mahabharata); a story of love and wandering in which Rama rescues his wife from the demon king Ravana

The Indian epic the Ramayana is performed across the globe and in many languages and media. Here, at a seaside Hindu temple in Uluwatu, Bali, performers reenact this epic using a traditional Indonesian dance called the *kecak*.

This animation comes from the 2008 feature film *Sita Sings the Blues*, which tells the popular Ramayana story from the perspective of Rama's loyal wife Sita. Created by the artist Nina Paley, who distributed it for free, the movie has been nicknamed "the greatest break-up story ever told."

father to promise to send Rama into exile in the forest and crown her own son instead. Faithful to this promise, the king banishes his son Rama, who is accompanied on his wanderings by his devoted wife Sita and his loyal brother Lakshmana. Learning of Sita's whereabouts, Ravana, the demon king of the island of Lanka, schemes to capture her. Thanks to a handy disguise (as a wandering ascetic), he does just that. But the monkey god Hanuman tracks Sita down on Lanka. He and Rama march to that island across a bridge built by monkeys. They kill Ravana and rescue Sita. Rama is not so sure he can take his wife back, however. After she spent so much time in Ravana's clutches, how can he be certain she has remained faithful? Sita answers this question in dramatic fashion, by walking into a fire and walking out unharmed, proving, for the moment at least, her faithfulness to her husband.

As the story draws to a close, Rama returns with Sita to his throne in Ayodhya, but his subjects continue to gossip about Sita's alleged infidelity. Putting his duty as king first, Rama banishes her. While in exile, she tells her tragic tale to Valmiki (the traditional author of the Ramayana) and gives birth to Rama's son. In the end, she disappears into the earth and Rama ascends to the sky, revealing himself to be a god as well as a king.

Or so goes Valmiki's Sanskrit Ramayana. A later (and happier) retelling in the Hindi language by the poet Tulsidas ends with Rama and Sita in each other's arms. Some low-caste versions of the Ramayana from South India take a page out of the Broadway musical *Wicked* by turning the demon Ravana into a hero and Rama into an evil interloper from the north (or, in some modern retellings, from Great Britain). *Sita Sings the Blues* (2008), an animated film by the American artist Nina Paley, narrates this epic from the perspective of Sita rather than her husband Rama. The Ramayana has also become a political tool of India's Hindu Right, which insists that there is only one true Ramayana and only one correct interpretation (their own).

Mahabharata and Bhagavad Gita The Mahabharata is a war story punctuated by an extended meditation on duty and the divine. It tells of two related clans drawn into a family feud that makes the U.S. Civil War look like a game of rock-paper-scissors. As the story opens, a righteous royal family, the Pandavas, loses its kingdom in a crooked dice game and is exiled for thirteen years. Upon their return, the not-so-righteous Kaurava family (cousins of the Pandavas) refuses to yield its crown as promised. War ensues, and the Pandavas triumph, but not until the greatest bloodletting in world literature has claimed more than a million victims.

On the eve of this apocalypse, Arjuna, of the righteous Pandava clan, experiences a crisis of conscience. As a member of the warrior class, and his clan's top fighter, it is his dharma to fight. Yet he knows that if he fights he will cause untold deaths, including the deaths of his relatives, friends, and teachers. What to do? Is ethics about doing the right thing, consequences be damned? Or does the right thing depend on the consequences? To answer these questions, Arjuna engages his charioteer (who also happens to be the god Krishna) in a lengthy discourse on karma and dharma.

This crucial portion of the Mahabharata, called the Bhagavad Gita ("Song of the Lord"), was commented upon by Shankara, who read it as a text in the way of wisdom, and Ramanuja, who read it as a text in the way of devotion. First translated into English in 1785, it rose to prominence, in India and worldwide, toward the end of the nineteenth century. S. Radhakrishnan, a philosopher and India's second president, compared its ethics to those of the German philosopher Immanuel Kant (and found Kant's wanting). The Dalit leader B. R. Ambedkar compared its ethics to the Buddha's (and found Krishna wanting). Mohandas Gandhi, who wrote a commentary on the Gita from prison, praised it as "the universal mother" and the repository of "all knowledge." Outside India, the Gita captured the imagination of the Transcendentalist Ralph Waldo Emerson, who called it "the first of books," and of the poet T. S. Eliot, who called it "the next greatest philosophical poem to the Divine Comedy" of Dante. The Gita was also praised by the scientist Albert Einstein and quoted by the physicist J. Robert Oppenheimer, who turned to its words—"Now I am become Death, the destroyer of worlds"—as he saw the first atomic bomb explode over New Mexico in 1945.[16] In recent times, the Gita has come to be widely regarded by Hindus and non-Hindus alike as the core expression of the Hindu tradition.

The question in the Gita is not really whether Arjuna is going to fight. He is a warrior, and fighting is what warriors do. The question is how he is going to fight, and this is where the Gita's core teaching about dispassionate action comes in. Each of us, Krishna says, must do our dharma—as parents, as students, as merchants, as warriors—but we must do so selflessly, without regard for outcomes. Rather than expecting that the fruits of our actions will accrue to ourselves, we must give up these fruits to the divine—as if they were a sacrificial offering.

This "karma without kama" (action without desire) approach serves as a sort of "moral Teflon" that allows an action's consequences to slide easily away from the person who did it.[17] Ordinary people no longer have to choose between life as a householder and life as a renouncer. By doing their householder duties with the dispassion of a renouncer, they can have it both ways. "All that you do, all that you take, all that you offer, all that you give, all that you strive for, in heated discipline—do that in offering to me," Krishna tells Arjuna. "You surely will be freed from the bonds of action and its fruits, the pure and the impure. With your free self, joined to the yoga of renunciation, you will come to me" (9.27–28).

The conversation about dharma ("duty") between the warrior Arjuna and the god Krishna stands at the center of the popular Hindu scripture the Bhagavad Gita. In this 1830 Indian painting, Arjuna (left) speaks about a warrior's responsibilities with Krishna (right), disguised as his charioteer.

Amidst this dialogue between Arjuna and Krishna, the Gita also outlines a new three-path model for the Hindu tradition. There is the path of jnana—of wisdom and knowledge. There is the path of bhakti—of devotion. And there is this new karma path—of offering the fruits of our action as a sacrifice to the divine. By advancing this understanding of karma, the Gita redirected the attentions of many Hindus from ritual action to moral action. And by formally dividing the Hindu journey into three paths—karma, jnana, and bhakti—it served as an early announcement for the bhakti movement to come.

The Bhakti Tradition: Hinduism as a Way of Devotion

Those who walked in this new way of devotion set aside the fire sacrifices of Vedic religion and the philosophical speculation of classical Hinduism for an easier path to spiritual liberation. Instead of simply hoping for a better rebirth, they took aim at moksha, and they didn't want to give up home, family, and employment in order to get it. They continued to do their duties as householders and hoped that the gods of their choosing would do the rest. Together these *bhaktas* ("devotees") produced a new form of Hinduism in which moksha came not through self-effort but through other-help—not through wisdom but through love.

This bhakti impulse took its stand on the recognition that love comes more naturally to most human beings than philosophy. It is hard to approach a distant and impersonal divinity. It is easier to enter into a relationship with a god or a goddess we can see with our own eyes and embrace with our own hearts. Whereas the Upanishads typically spoke of God in impersonal terms, as *nirguna brahman* ("god without attributes"), these devo- tees were more likely to speak of God in personal terms, as *saguna brahman* ("god with attributes"). In fact, they imagined the attributes of their gods in exquisite detail: Shiva's matted hair, Krishna's blue skin, Ganesha's elephant head.

Amid the supermarket of divinities available to them, bhaktas made a choice. In the Hebrew Bible, God selects the Israelites as his chosen people. Here the individual devotee selected his or her *ishtadevata* ("the god of one's choosing"). In temples and home shrines, devotees in this new religion of the heart made simple offerings of fruit and flowers to their chosen ones. They sang praise songs to them and embodied that praise in dance. They went on pilgrimages to places associated with key moments in their gods' lives.

Practitioners of bhakti yoga trusted that the gods whom they loved would use their vast storehouses of merit to transport devotees from the suffering of samsara to the bliss of moksha. Instead of performing sacrifices or engaging in meditation, bhakti Hindus sang songs of praise, chanted the names of their chosen god, and danced ecstatically—anything to conjure up the experience of intimacy with the divine that lies at the heart of this way of devotion.

Bhakti piety was deeply personal, and the relationships devotees cultivated were so intense that the word "devotion" doesn't quite do them justice. The seventeenth-century Shudra poet Tuka said devotion was like the love of a mother and a child. Others compared it to a friendship. Still other devotees, influenced perhaps by the Islamic tradition, assumed postures of submission to their chosen god or goddess. For many more, the relationship was erotic—an intense bond of lover to lover, husband to wife, in some cases adulterer to adulteress. As they wrote their verses and sang their songs, poet-saints homed in on key moments when the heart seemed to be on fire: separating from a lover, longing for a lover's return, reuniting with a lover, anticipating sexual union, and experiencing sexual release. Some poet-saints even imagined their chosen deities longing for them.

This deep emotional involvement that pulsed in bhakti poetry narrowed the gap between the human and the divine: "The pity, desire, and compassion of the bhakti gods cause them to forget that they are above it all—as metaphysics demands—and reduces them to the human level—as mythology demands."[18] In all of these relationships, devotees hoped for some measure of grace from their divine beloved—an unmerited gift of spiritual liberation, a better than expected rebirth, or healing or fertility. For some bhaktas, the bliss of this devotion was so ecstatic that intimacy (or union) with the divine began to appear not as a means to the religious goal but as the religious goal itself. What more did humans really need?

This devotional movement was an egalitarian movement whose verses were sung not only in Sanskrit and not only by high-caste men but also by women and men from all social classes. Many bhakti poets came from low-caste professions—weaver, cobbler, barber, tailor, shopkeeper, boatman—and they composed in vernacular languages rather than the elite Sanskrit of educated Brahmins. Here, gifts flowed from gods to devotees without regard to gender, caste, or language, and devotees responded in the familiar tones and amid the day-to-day realities of their own local languages.

Regarding women, A. K. Ramanujan has observed that "*bhakti* itself appears as 'feminine in nature.'" Its "chief mood," Ramanujan continues, "is the erotic . . . seen almost entirely from an Indian woman's point of view, whether in its phase of separation or union." Male bhaktas conform to this paradigm, playing the role of wife or mistress, either longing to be reunited with her lover or ecstatically lost in her lover's embrace. Or, as Ramanujan summarizes it, "The males take on female personae. . . . Before God all men are women."[19]

Bhakti's gender bending opened the doors to radical behavior by some women who left their earthly homes in order to wander in search of their divine husbands. Akka Mahadevi ("Elder Sister Goddess"), a twelfth-century South Indian poet and mystic who set aside not only her traditional roles as a wife and mother but also her cloth, wandered naked on the theory that not even the faintest strip of clothing should separate her from Shiva, whom she described as her "Husband inside."

In keeping with Hinduism's multilayered past, there were hints of this brewing bhakti movement in earlier strata of Hindu history. The Rig Veda may include at least a faint premonition of bhakti in hymns pleading with Varuna to set both justice and truth aside in order to forgive the wrongdoing of his devotees (5.85.7). Those premonitions became more insistent in the Shvetasvatara Upanishad. The first Hindu scripture to use the term *bhakti*, this text celebrated the devotee "who has the deepest love for God, and who shows the same love toward his teacher as towards God."[20] The epics were a closer and more powerful influence, but for all their heartfelt love and swashbuckling adventure, the Ramayana and Mahabharata were first and foremost about duty and remained relatively cool and intellectual when it came to divine devotion. The bhakti revolution that followed a few centuries later raised the emotional temperature.

Bhakti Hinduism sprouted in South India during the sixth to ninth centuries CE. Its vehicle was poetry. Its languages were Tamil and other regional languages.

Borrowing from local traditions of romantic love, Tamil-speaking poets created new ecstatic traditions of devotion to Vishnu and Shiva. Of all the themes of these local traditions, the most influential crossover was lovesickness, which in this context meant yearning for God as for a lost love. Gone in these love poems to God—Hinduism's answer to the Song of Songs of the Hebrew Bible—was the abstract, impersonal brahman of the Upanishads. Here brahman was unabashedly personal: father, mother, lover, bridegroom, and child. In keeping with the egalitarian spirit of the bhakti impulse, women had responsibilities in this new Hindu tradition that they had not had in classical Hinduism: "gathering flowers for the shrines, offering prayers on behalf of male members of their families, and cooking the food offered to the gods."[21]

Accompanying these new texts and ceremonies was a building boom in temples from the sixth century on and a related boom in puja, pilgrimage, and temple festivals. Visitors to temples did not have to be able to read to learn about the exploits of the gods. They could listen to recitations of poems. They could follow their stories in elaborate images carved on temple exteriors for all to see. Or they could simply make offerings to the deities at hand.

Philosophically, this bhakti path was advanced by Ramanuja, a devotee of Vishnu and his consort Sri (or Lakshmi). Mentioned above as a proponent of "qualified nondualism" and a critic of the "nondualism" of Shankara's Advaita Vedanta school, Ramanuja contended that devotional poems were scripture, too. Ramanuja is also celebrated for his contributions to a debate carried forward in many religions about self-effort and other-help. In the Hindu context, this is discussed as a debate between the Cat School (in which the mother cat carries her passive child by the scruff of its neck) and the Monkey School (in which the young monkey clings desperately to the mother). Here, Ramanuja sided with the cats, arguing that moksha comes not as a reward won by merit but as a gift delivered by grace (as in the favor bestowed by compassionate bodhisattvas in Buddhism and the plea by the Protestant icon Martin Luther for "salvation by faith alone").

The new bhakti spirit also animated Sanskrit texts called the Puranas ("Ancient Stories"). These influential collections of various genres included tales of the exploits of gods

This folio painting from a sixteenth-century version of the Bhagavata Purana depicts one of the most popular scenes in devotional Hinduism: blue-skinned Krishna cavorting with the *gopis* (milkmaids). Stranded in a river without their robes, they lock eyes with their beloved Krishna.

and goddesses that around the tenth century began to exhibit the ecstatic devotion of bhakti poets. The Puranas married pan-Indian and local piety, singing in ancient Sanskrit the glories of *our* local god, *our* village, *our* temple, *our* pilgrimage site. "Their sectarian view," observes the Indologist Wendy Doniger, "says not 'This is the whole world,' but 'This is *our* whole world.'"[22] In service of that view, each Purana served as a tourist brochure of sorts to one particular pilgrimage site, which could act as a portal either to spiritual liberation or a better rebirth.

The Puranas have been characterized as the sweetest fruit of the Vedic tree as well as the "Fifth Veda." In fact, they were more influential on the ground in India than the Vedas themselves. Widely popular, they introduced vibrant and textured stories of goddesses to many across India. One popular example is the tenth-century Bhagavata Purana. In classic bhakti form, this book features a god, Krishna, who was willing and able to wipe away the wrongdoing of those who praised him. According to the Indologist C. Mackenzie Brown, "the message is that even the worst of sinners and the ritually impure, including outcastes and Brahman-slayers, can be sanctified and redeemed through devotion to the Lord."[23] But the Bhagavata Purana's true claim to fame is its adorable rendering of the adventures of Krishna as a child and then as a mischievous youngster—a flute player and dancer who flirts with the *gopis* ("milkmaids") by, among other things, stealing their clothes. To his devotees, the message is simultaneously philosophical, religious, and fun: life is "divine play" and the point of that play is love.

Thanks to a combination of poems, prayer, puja, and pilgrimage, the bhakti impulse moved out of its South Indian home and into North India as early as the tenth century. One of the most celebrated of its northern poet-saints was a sixteenth-century woman named Mirabai. As a girl, she had a vision of Krishna and vowed to be his bride for life. After her family married her off, she struggled with her husband's family. In fact, according to legend, someone in his family tried to kill her. Eventually she left home and became a wandering pilgrim devoted to her spiritual husband Krishna. Mirabai's poems, which criticize the institutions of both marriage and renunciation, speak not only of her lifelong pursuit of Krishna—"How can I abandon the love I have loved / in life after life?"—but also of his pursuit of her.[24]

Another innovator who spread devotional Hinduism in the north was Chaitanya (1486–1533), a Brahmin-born and Sanskrit-trained Bengali now revered as a saint. After his father died, Chaitanya became in his early twenties a renouncer devoted to singing and dancing before Krishna and repeating his names. Chaitanya was confident that the path to spiritual liberation ran through trust in Krishna. But Chaitanya saw spiritual liberation as something like the Buddhist Pure Land—a paradise in which devotees would bask eternally (and passionately) in the overflowing love and grace of Krishna. Chaitanya's full name, Krishna Chaitanya, means "he whose consciousness is Krishna." That name inspired the founding in 1966 in New York City of the International Society of Krishna Consciousness (ISKCON), a Hindu movement that shares with Chaitanya a devotional piety focused on reciting the names of Krishna, singing sacred songs to him, and dancing ecstatically in his presence. Today, ISKCON members regard Chaitanya himself as divine.

As bhakti's love languages leapt from region to region and from vernacular to vernacular, they showed affinities with notions of surrender to God and striving for mystical union that were also popular in Islam. Buddhism would almost entirely disappear from India by the end of the twelfth century, but bhakti poet-saints remained conversant with Buddhist theories of how desire produced suffering. Hindu bhaktas also interacted with devotional Jains and Sikhs, leading some scholars to interpret the bhakti movement as an Indian phenomenon rather than simply a Hindu one—a tradition of the fifteenth-century Muslim-born poet Kabir and the Sikh founder Guru Nanak (1469–1539) as well as the many poet-saints of Hinduism north and south.

Because of the efforts of devotees in South and North India, this bhakti way became by the sixteenth century the primary way that Hindus practiced their religion. Today, the bhakti tradition enjoys a near monopoly over ways to be Hindu worldwide and is visible in a thinly secularized form in the sweet eroticism of Bollywood movies.

Bhakti Hinduism benefited from its absorptive sensibility—its willingness to mix elements from sacred scriptures and secular love poetry with influences from Buddhism, Jainism, and Islam. It also benefited from patrons who shifted their religious giving from supporting Vedic sacrifices to building temples devoted to specific gods. Also central to the rise of the bhakti movement were itinerant performers who moved across the subcontinent performing the popular poems and songs that created the central experience of this way of devotion: a sense of intimacy and even union between devotees and their chosen gods.

The bhakti path also benefited from its teachings about divine favor, which radically redirected the Hindu tradition from self-effort to other-help. You don't have to leave your loved ones in order to know God, bhakti poets said. You don't have to wander across the belly of India to achieve moksha. All that is required is to die in Varanasi or to take a dip in the Ganges or to chant the name of the god of your choosing. Then again, perhaps none of that is required. Perhaps all you have to do is sit still and listen for the heartbeat of God in your own body. "I, Lalla, went out far in search of Shiva, the omnipresent lord,"

Kabir (c. 1398–c. 1448)

The fifteenth-century poet and mystic Kabir is now widely viewed as a sharp-tongued champion of interreligious harmony. Facts of his life are difficult to extract from legends, however, and his own words, transmitted orally during his lifetime, have comingled over the centuries with those of his admirers. Was he born to a Brahmin widow and given up for adoption? Was he sent into exile by Muslim rulers? Who knows? Still, a few facts are clear (or, at least, probable). He was reared in Varanasi by a Muslim family of low-caste weavers. He was illiterate, composing his now-beloved poems orally, in the gruff vernacular of everyday life. At some point he was profoundly influenced by Vaishnavism, and as an adult he worshiped his god Ram without qualities.

Although Kabir is lionized today for celebrating all religions equally, he was actually an equal opportunity critic of organized religion. He satirized pilgrimage and ritual, idol worship and caste. Scriptures such as the Quran and the Vedas did more, in his view, to hide the truth than to reveal it. Mosques and temples alike distracted from the one ineffable reality, which is to be found within. Kabir's teachings, which he referred to as *sajaha-yoga*, or "simple union," drew on Hindu and Muslim themes, and Kabir himself is now claimed by Hindus, Muslims, and Sikhs as one of their own. Hundreds of his verses can be found in the Guru Granth, the principal Sikh scripture.

Skeptical of the popular superstition that all who die in Varanasi will achieve moksha, Kabir reportedly left that city as his health was failing and died in lowly Maghar, deliberately thumbing his nose at the idea that all who die in lowly Maghar will be reborn as donkeys. Today, the Kabir Panth ("Path of Kabir"), a sect that reveres him as its guru and his compositions as scripture, claims close to ten million followers, most of them Dalits who take pride in the fact that a lower-caste writer with such a salty tongue produced such lofty poetry. His popular short poems, composed in Hindi, have been translated into English by the likes of Ezra Pound and Robert Bly. Here is one poem, "His Death in Benares," translated by the contemporary Indian poet Arvind Krishna Mehrotra:

> His death in Benares
> Won't save the assassin
> From certain hell,
> Any more than a dip
> In the Ganges will send
> Frogs—or you—to paradise.
> My home, says Kabir,
> Is where there's no day, no night,
> And no holy book in sight
> To squat on our lives.[a]

writes the fourteenth-century Kashmiri poet Lalla. "Having wandered, I found him in my own body, sitting in his house."[25]

These bhakti successes have not entirely buried the early geological layers in the Hindu story. Though bhaktas have replaced Vedic priests and Upanishadic philosophers as the key actors in the Hindu drama, *pujaris* ("temple priests") still chant in Sanskrit and take the offerings devotees bring to the temples. Two minor Vedic deities—Vishnu and Rudra (who came to be identified with Shiva)—are now popular Hindu gods. And key concepts from the Upanishads—brahman and atman, karma and reincarnation—remain deeply embedded in the presuppositions of Hindu life.

Tantra

Tantra, which arose around the same time as devotional Hinduism, presented an alternative to the paths of ritual action, wisdom, and devotion. It also served as a synthesis of

Tantra
esoteric movement in Hinduism and Buddhism focused on mantras, mandalas, and transgressive behaviors designed to cultivate union with the divine (or Buddhahood)

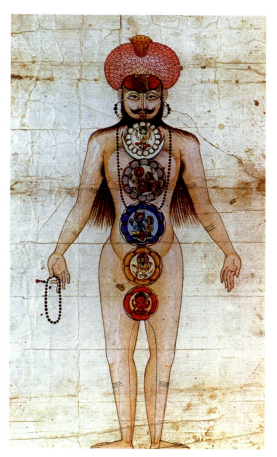

This miniature Indian painting depicts Tantrism's seven *chakras* as wheels located in the human body. Moving up from the red chakra at the bottom, these are the root, sacral, solar plexus, heart, throat, third eye, and crown chakras in today's nomenclature.

all three. This esoteric tradition, which also flourished among Buddhists and Jains, was based on transgressive rituals and secret texts, called Tantras, which emerged in the middle of the first millennium. Tantra itself flourished especially around 1000 CE. Because of its principled disregard for hierarchies of sex and caste, Tantra was, like bhakti, open to women and low-caste practitioners. Because of its emphasis on shakti, it was widespread among goddess worshipers.

Tantrikas (Tantric practitioners) recited mantras. They also used geometric maps called mandalas as aids to visualization. In kundalini yoga, a Tantric innovation, the practitioner attempted to awaken the shakti energy of the goddess said to lie coiled like a serpent at the base of the spine. Once awakened, this energy moved up through six *chakras*, or sacred centers. Ideally, the awakened shakti energy united with Shiva at the top of the skull. This union reenacted creation itself, which occurred when Shiva and Shakti united for the first time. It also demonstrated the nonduality of male and female and, more broadly, the Tantric principle of nonduality itself.

The goal of this practice, and of Tantra in general, was to realize one's unity with the divine without sacrificing worldly success in the process. More specifically (and controversially), the goal of Tantra was to transform the body into a divinity, complete with seemingly superhuman powers—levitation, invisibility, clairvoyance—called *siddhis*. In this way, Tantra offered both success in this world and release from it.

The Tantric tradition included "right-handed" and "left-handed" schools. The right-handed school was more traditional and more public, seeking to make peace with the broader Hindu tradition and downplaying transgressive rituals. The left-handed school was more radical and more secretive. It rejected many traditional ethical norms, most notably by partaking of the "Five Forbidden Things": liquor, meat, fish, parched grain, and extramarital sex. There is much controversy about Tantric sex, including to what extent it was (and is) imagined as opposed to real. In the nondualistic spirit of Tantra, many practitioners would object to this duality as well.

Hinduism in the Modern World

The most recent layer in Hinduism's geology began to form in response to Muslim and Christian critiques of Hindus as worshipers of false gods. These criticisms were conveyed during the Islamic Delhi sultanate, which ruled much of North India from the thirteenth to the sixteenth century, and during the Islamic Mughal empire, which ruled much of the Indian subcontinent from 1526 to 1720. British criticisms picked up after as the East India Company acquired its first territory in India in 1615. They swelled after the British put an end to East India Company and Mughal rule and Queen Victoria inaugurated the British Raj in 1858. Under the British, Indian intellectual circles were flooded with Western critiques of polytheism, idol worship, and child marriage. Many British thinkers followed the playbook Protestants had employed against Roman Catholics, by praising ancient scripture and denouncing devotions to "idols." As they saw it, popular Hinduism was a morally depraved and fallen faith, overly ritualized, insufficiently intellectualized, and hypersexualized. These arguments bolstered British colonists' sense of cultural and theological superiority. They also served the British colonial project by, among other things, casting Hindus as unfit for self-rule.

During the Hindu Renaissance of the nineteenth century, which took place during British colonial rule in India, Hindu intellectuals and social activists responded to these criticisms with a series of reforms. These reforms married Hindu traditions with (a) liberal Protestant ideals (a preference for scripture over ritual, for example, and an inclination toward understanding scriptural teachings in social terms) and (b) Enlightenment commitments (to science and reason, liberty and equality). Focusing more on the Upanishads than the epics, this movement accented the ethical and doctrinal dimensions of Hinduism over its ritual and narrative dimensions. In high Victorian style, its leaders downplayed Hindu eroticism. These modern Hindus also worked to undercut Christian missions to India in two ways: first, by portraying Hinduism as a "world religion" due all the respect afforded to Christianity and, second, by arguing for the unity of all religions. These reformers also had a social and political agenda. They pushed for women's education and they took on the caste system, which had swelled over time from four classes to thousands of castes. Such efforts did more than reform Hinduism, however. They helped generate support for *swaraj* ("self-rule") by fostering a common conversation among Indian intellectuals about India's place in the modern world.

Ram Mohan Roy and the Brahmo Samaj   Ram Mohan Roy (1772–1833), a Bengali Brahmin reformer, was exposed early in life to a variety of religious options, first through his father (who worshiped Vishnu) and his mother (who worshiped Shakti), and later through his teachers at the Muslim University at Patna and his Christian coworkers at the East India Company. As a Brahmin, he was steeped in a tradition that forbade travel outside India, but he was one of the first major Hindu intellectuals to travel to Europe. Sorting through multiple religious influences, including Unitarian rejections of the divinity of Jesus, he came to believe in one and only one creator God who is known through reason and worshiped in all the world's religions.

Through the institution in 1828 in Calcutta (now Kolkata) of the Brahmo Sabha (later renamed the Brahmo Samaj, or "Society of God"), Roy invoked reason to reject the authority of revelation, including the Vedas. He dismissed the epics as myths, condemned untouchability as undemocratic, and denounced polytheism, idol worship, karma, and reincarnation as superstitions. Suspicious of the femininity of the bhakti poet-saints, he opted instead for what he saw as the more masculine philosophizing of the sages of the Upanishads. Roy and the Brahmo Samaj are typically credited with launching the Hindu Renaissance.

Dayanand Sarasvati and the Arya Samaj   Dayanand Sarasvati (1824–1883) was another key figure in the Hindu Renaissance. A Gujarati Brahmin, Sarasvati was born into a Shaivite family. His misgivings about the Shiva lingam propelled him into fifteen years as a wandering ascetic. In 1875 in Bombay (now Mumbai), he founded the Arya Samaj ("Society of Nobles") in an effort to redirect Hindus away from the epics and Puranas and "back to the Vedas." Despite this conservative slogan, Sarasvati was also a Protestant-style reformer who criticized all manner of priestly "superstitions" as corruptions of an original revelation. For Sarasvati, these corruptions included pilgrimage, idol worship, bathing in the Ganges, temple offerings, untouchability, widow burning, child marriage, and arranged marriage.

Sarasvati and the Arya Samaj allied for a brief time in the late 1870s with the Theosophical Society, which was founded in New York City in 1875 by the Russian occultist Helena Blavatsky and the American social reformer Henry Olcott and worked to promote ancient Asian wisdom in the modern West. The two groups parted ways over Sarasvati's religious exclusivism. Unlike Roy, who preached religious tolerance as a first principle, Sarasvati denounced Christianity and Islam and championed Hinduism as the one true religion. In the twentieth century, his call, "India for Indians," was taken up by participants in the *Hindutva* ("Hinduness") movement, which sought to transform secular India into a Hindu nation.

Mohandas Gandhi and Indian Independence The towering figure of modern Hinduism is, of course, the diminutive Mohandas Gandhi (1869–1948), also called Mahatma, or "Great Soul." Gandhi reimagined Hinduism as a way of social action and in the process helped to win independence for India. He trained in law in London and worked as an attorney for twenty-one years in South Africa before returning in 1915 to his homeland, where he spearheaded a movement of nonviolent resistance to British rule. Many Hindus before him had argued that brahman and atman are one, but Gandhi argued for the equivalence of brahman, atman, and truth (*satya*). *Satyagraha*, or "truth force," was the name he gave to the method of nonviolent resistance that repeatedly landed him in jail. One of his most famous actions—and a major influence on the American civil rights movement—was his 240-mile march to the sea in 1930 to protest a salt tax by the British.

Gandhi is typically seen as a political figure—"the father of modern India." But he was also a deeply religious man influenced by Jain thought, the Indian epics, Advaita Vedanta philosophy, the life of the Buddha, bhakti poetry, and the Gita, which he called his daily "dictionary of conduct."[26] Born into a Gujarati family of Vaishnava merchants, Gandhi was formed as a boy by the devotional Hinduism of his father, the spiritual eclecticism of his mother (whose sect creatively combined Hinduism and Islam), and the teachings of a local Jain scholar. In London, he read the Gita for the first time even as he immersed himself in the teachings of Jesus and the writings of Theosophists.

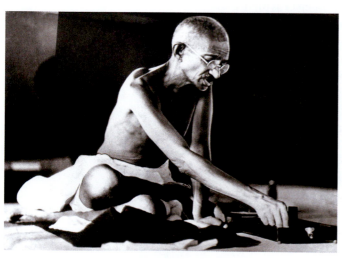

Mohandas Gandhi, pictured here in 1945, was the Hindu religious and political leader of the Indian independence movement.

Gandhi was heavily influenced by *ahimsa*, a Jain teaching usually translated as "nonviolence" or "noninjury," which also had a major impact on the Reverend Martin Luther King Jr. In fact, Gandhi seems to have read the Gita's core message—to act in the world without desire for the fruits of that action—as a commandment to act in the world without desiring to harm others. Christian pacifism and Hindu ascetic traditions of sexual renunciation also shaped Gandhi's life and thought. Like Roy and Sarasvati before him, he reimagined the Hindu project largely in ethical and political terms.

Gandhi lived to see his dream of Indian independence fulfilled when the British withdrew from India in 1947. However, that withdrawal came at a cost: the

Partition of his homeland into the Hindu-majority state of India and the Muslim-majority state of Pakistan, and the subsequent slaughter of hundreds of thousands of Muslims, Hindus, and Sikhs. Himself a victim of this violence, Gandhi was assassinated by a Hindu nationalist at a prayer meeting in Delhi on January 30, 1948. He died, according to pious legends, with the name of God on his lips.

HINDUISM IN THE UNITED STATES

Hinduism, like Buddhism, first came to the United States by way of books. In fact, Hindu texts made an earlier impact on American thinkers. Interest in textual Hinduism was sparked by pioneering English translations of Hindu sacred books, beginning with *The Bhagvat-Geeta* by the English Orientalist Charles Wilkins in 1785. One avid reader of these translations was Mary Moody Emerson, a Unitarian who rejected the divinity of Jesus and saw Ram Mohan Roy's monotheism as a modern faith akin to her own. She passed her fervor on to her nephew Ralph Waldo Emerson, who passed it along to his fellow Transcendentalists and then to a wider American audience through poems such as "Brahma" and essays such as "Oversoul." The writer and naturalist Henry David Thoreau went a step further by trying to practice what he learned from Hindu texts. Thoreau brought a translation of the Gita to his experiment in simple living at Walden Pond. Later, he wrote to a friend, "Rude and careless as I am, I would fain practise the yoga faithfully. . . . To some extent, and at rare intervals, even I am a yogin."[27]

After the Transcendentalists, the next American group to take a keen interest in Asian religions was the Theosophists. Within a few years of organizing the Theosophical Society, Blavatsky and Olcott moved to Madras (now Chennai), India, where they preached the "good news" of Asian religions. Both Blavatsky and Olcott converted to Buddhism in Ceylon (now Sri Lanka) in 1880. However, when the British socialist Annie Besant ascended to leadership in the Theosophical movement after Olcott's death in 1907, she instead championed Hinduism as the cure to the ills besetting the modern West. In 1902, one of the Theosophical Society's most illustrious members, Thomas Edison, produced a film called *Hindoo Fakir* about a magician and a levitating woman.

Missionaries and Gurus

Hinduism came to the United States in 1893 in the form of a delegate to the World's Parliament of Religions, held in Chicago in conjunction with the World's Columbian Exposition. His name was Swami Vivekananda (1863–1902), and in many respects he was ideally suited to the job. Born into a well-to-do family in Calcutta, he went to university and studied Christianity, science, and Western philosophy. He joined the Brahmo Samaj and signed on to its social reform agenda. He was also a disciple of Ramakrishna, an influential nineteenth-century Indian mystic who taught the unity of the world's religions.

The Reverend John Henry Barrows, the Presbyterian minister who organized the World's Parliament, had hoped this groundbreaking event would demonstrate the superiority of his Protestant faith. Then Vivekananda arrived. Dressed in a turban and a long, flowing robe, he spoke fluent English with an Irish brogue and captured the imaginations of American journalists. From the floor of the Parliament and in newspaper and magazine articles, he made his case for the reasonableness of Hindu thought and

SWAMI VIVEKANANDA
·The Hindoo Monk of India·

The pioneering Hindu missionary Swami Vivekananda is best known for introducing Hinduism to the United States at the World's Parliament of Religions, held in Chicago in 1893. This poster from around that time calls him "The Hindoo Monk of India."

its compatibility with modern science. In the process, he undermined the argument for Christian missions in India. Although a Kali devotee, he downplayed his bhakti sensibilities in favor of a more philosophical approach to his tradition that he thought would play better with American audiences. In 1894, while in New York City on a nationwide tour, he founded the Vedanta Society, the first Hindu organization in the United States designed to attract American converts. By the 1920s, that organization had spread to Boston, San Francisco, and Los Angeles.

Swami Yogananda (1893–1952), the next influential Hindu missionary to the United States, also came as a delegate to a global interfaith conference: the International Congress of Religious Liberals held in Boston in 1920. Like Vivekananda, he embarked on a speaking tour across the United States, but whereas Vivekananda eventually returned to India, Yogananda stayed on. One of the stated aims of his Self-Realization Fellowship (SRF), which is now based in Los Angeles, was "to reveal the complete harmony and basic oneness of original Christianity as taught by Jesus Christ and original Yoga as taught by Bhagavan Krishna."[28]

Yogananda's creative combination of Hindu and Christian teachings appealed to a wide American audience, as did his *kriya yoga* ("the scientific technique of God-realization"), which he billed as a quick-and-easy "airplane route" to God-consciousness previously employed by Jesus.[29] The SRF quickly surpassed the Vedanta Society as the largest Hindu organization in the United States. In the 1930s, it claimed 150,000 members at 150 centers in the United States, but it flagged after Yogananda's death in 1952. In 1966, the British rock group the Beatles put Yogananda alongside Gandhi on the cover of their *Sergeant Pepper's Lonely Hearts Club Band*. Yogananda lived on in print as well, thanks to his *The Autobiography of a Yogi* (1946), which became a countercultural hit in the 1960s and 1970s.

Hinduism did not again attract widespread attention in the United States until after 1965, when the U.S. Congress passed the Hart-Celler Act. By lifting earlier limits on Asian immigration, this landmark legislation led to a steady influx of Indians to the United States. It also opened the way to Indian gurus. These gurus appealed to countercultural young people who were weary of their parents' Judeo-Christian pieties and dissatisfied with post–World War II American materialism.

Two of the most popular gurus were the Transcendental Meditation (TM) founder Maharishi Mahesh Yogi (c. 1918–2008) and A. C. Bhaktivedanta Prabhupada (1896–1977) of the International Society for Krishna Consciousness (ISKCON), better known as the Hare Krishnas. Alongside other Hindu-influenced gurus, they gave the Hindu tradition its first real moment in the sun in American popular culture.

The Maharishi brought his TM technique to the United States in 1959 and in the 1960s turned himself into the "guru to the stars." Largely stripping his message of Hindu markers, he presented TM not as a religion but as a secular and scientific technique for spiritual advancement and social improvement. TM's key practice was meditating on a mantra personally chosen by one's guru. The most popular Asian religious import in 1960s and 1970s America, TM marketed itself as an easy path with "no funny clothes" and "no change of lifestyle."[30]

By contrast, Prabhupada, who came to the United States in 1965, emphasized the deep roots of his movement in Chaitanya's devotion to Krishna and made all sorts of demands on his followers. Hare Krishnas adopted Indian names, shaved their heads, wore saffron robes, and in many cases lived a communal existence devoted not only to Krishna but also to ISKCON itself. Like the Maharishi, Prabhupada emphasized mantra chanting, but he insisted that there was just one mantra suitable for this age: "Hare Krishna, Hare Krishna, Krishna Krishna, Hare, Hare Rama, Hare Rama, Rama, Hare."

These two approaches clashed in an intriguing encounter between the Beatles and Prabhupada in England in 1969. Largely through the influence of George Harrison, who had traveled to India three years earlier to take sitar lessons with Ravi Shankar, members of the Beatles had experimented with TM. When they met Prabhupada, they expected to encounter another groovy guru, but they were in for a surprise. In a discussion of the relative merits of the Hare Krishna and TM mantras, Lennon mused that it really didn't matter which mantra you picked since "all *mantras* are just the name of God." Disagreeing, Prabhupada said that for any disease you need the right prescription, and the right prescription for this age is the Hare Krishna mantra. Says who? Lennon asked. How do we know which guru to follow? Perhaps it was just a matter of taste, Harrison suggested. "Isn't it like flowers? Someone may prefer roses, and somebody may like carnations better. Isn't it really a matter for the individual devotee to decide?" No, Prabhupada persisted. A fragrant flower is better than one without a scent.[31]

Perhaps the most controversial of these new post-1965 teachers was the "sex guru" Bhagwan Shree Rajneesh (1931–1990), who established a commune called Rajneeshpuram in eastern Oregon in 1981. The subject of a widely viewed six-part documentary called *Wild Wild Country* (2018), this movement was attacked as a free love "cult" and investigated by various government authorities for drug use, weapons stockpiling, and other charges. In 1985, federal authorities arrested Rajneesh for violating immigration laws and deported him.

When the Beatles visited the Indian guru Maharishi Mahesh Yogi in India in 1968, millions of British and American youth learned about Asian religions for the first time. From left to right, George Harrison, John Lennon, Cynthia Lennon, and Jane Asher relax with the Maharishi.

Indra Nooyi (b. 1955)

When Americans think of Hinduism and the business world, they often think of information technology—Hindu leaders of Silicon Valley firms or computer programmers writing code in Bangalore in South India. For twelve years, Indra Nooyi ran a very different sort of company: PepsiCo. Born in 1955 to a devout Shaiva family in Chennai, India, she earned a BS from Madras Christian College in Chennai. Before leaving India to earn her MBA from the Yale School of Management, she played lead guitar in an all-female rock band. She joined PepsiCo in 1994, worked her way up to CEO in 2001, and retired from the company in 2019.

A vegetarian and a teetotaler, Nooyi wore a sari to work and reported that she had never tasted meat. She displayed an image of Ganesha in her PepsiCo office and maintains a shrine at her home in Greenwich, Connecticut. "Our family is so deeply religious that whenever anything goes wrong they will pray and pledge a visit to the temple," she told *Hinduism Today*. "So whenever we go to India, we spend all our time in temples, executing all the promises my mother and my mother-in-law made for the various illnesses or problems in the house." Shortly after PepsiCo announced its acquisition of Quaker Oats in 2000, Nooyi flew to Pittsburgh to give thanks at the Sri Venkateswara Temple, modeled after a famous temple in Tirupati patronized by her family. When asked what got her through tough times running one of the world's largest corporations, Nooyi said, "My family and my belief in God. If all else fails, I call my mother in India...and she listens to me...and she probably promises God a visit to Tirupati!"[a]

As Rajneesh's example suggests, one crucial part of the narrative of American Hinduism is a story of the transplantation and transformation of Hindu traditions on U.S. soil. Another is the emergence of an anticult movement that labeled new religious movements "cults" as justification for denunciation and, in many cases, litigation. As the Hare Krishnas became visible nationwide on street corners, at county fairs, and in airport terminals, many municipalities responded to growing anticult fears by passing laws banning proselytizing. In *International Society for Krishna Consciousness v. Lee* (1992), the Supreme Court upheld a ban on asking for money in airport terminals run by the Port Authority of New York and New Jersey. The purpose of airports is moving people from here to there, Chief Justice William Rehnquist wrote in the court's ruling. That interest outweighs the interests ISKCON members have in "promoting the free exchange of ideas."[32]

As controversies about Hindu-influenced movements came and went, Hindu sounds exerted a strong pull on American popular music. The Varanasi-born Ravi Shankar made a splash when he played at the Woodstock Festival in upstate New York in 1969, and for a time he was the main conduit for communicating Indian music to the West. John and Alice Coltrane played a different role, integrating Hindu mantras into the jazz tradition. A "theosophist of jazz," in the words of the music critic Nat Hentoff, John Coltrane studied with Shankar and even named his second son after him. Coltrane also read Gandhi and Yogananda and Hindu sacred texts.[33] Indian influences are obvious in his song "Om" (1965), which included this Gita-derived chant: "I am he who awards to each the fruit of his action. I make all things clean. I am Om–OM–OM–OM!"

After the death of her husband and collaborator in 1967, Alice Coltrane fell into a spiritual and psychological funk and drew ever more deeply from the Hindu well. She took Swami Satchidananda (who offered an opening address at Woodstock) as a guru, went with him to India in 1970, and one year later produced a Hindu-influenced album called *Journey in Satchidananda*. Then she abruptly withdrew from the wider world. In the mid-1970s, she took the name of Turiyasangitananda ("the bliss of God's highest song") and became a Hindu teacher. In 1983, she built an ashram in Agoura, California, in the Santa Monica Mountains. In 2017, ten years after her death, an album of her sacred music based on cassettes she made at her ashram appeared. It was her take on Indian praise songs, mixed with some of the black church sound she learned playing the church organ in her Baptist youth in Detroit.

Temple Hinduism Today, some Hindus in the United States are members of convert groups such as Transcendental Meditation and the Hare Krishnas, but most attend traditional temples that cater to immigrants and their families. After the Hart-Celler Act of 1965, immigration from India skyrocketed. The majority of these new Indian immigrants were Hindus, and as they established themselves in their adopted homeland many of them got about the business of establishing temples. The earliest gathering places were improvised in schools and churches. Next came more permanent structures in storefronts, office buildings, and decommissioned churches. In 1977, Hindus consecrated two Indian-style temples in the United States: the Ganesh Temple in Flushing, New York, and the Sri Venkateswara Temple in Pittsburgh, Pennsylvania. The 1980s and 1990s saw Hindu temples spring up in major and midsized cities across the United States. Today, according to Harvard Divinity School's Pluralism Project, there are roughly 850 Hindu centers nationwide.

Like Hinduism itself, America's Hindu temples are changing with the times. Many of the most important Americanizations of Hinduism are written into temple architecture.

The Shri Swaminarayan Mandir Temple in Atlanta, Georgia, is a place of worship devoted to the Hindu guru Sahajanand Swami (1781–1830). Swaminarayan Hindus believe that he was the incarnation of a deity, and many American temples are dedicated in his name.

In a development the religious studies scholar Joanne Punzo Waghorne has referred to as "split-level" Hinduism, many U.S. temples include basements with kitchens, meeting rooms, and classrooms where members can attend Sunday School classes or learn Indian languages or classical Indian dance. Many temples also include sanctuaries for congregational worship—a rarity in India.[34]

Hindus are the most highly educated and compensated religious group in the United States, and they have made their mark in particular on business, engineering, and computer science. Many Silicon Valley firms are run by Hindus. Hindus are also slowly making their way into the corridors of power in Washington, DC. In 2000, Venkatachalapathi Samuldrala, a priest from Parma, Ohio, delivered the first Hindu prayer before the U.S. House of Representatives. In 2012, Tulsi Gabbard of Hawaii became the first Hindu elected to the U.S. Congress (she took her oath of office on the Bhagavad Gita).

But Hinduism isn't just for Hindus anymore. Millions of Americans practice yoga every day, and an increasing portion of these practitioners understand that this practice has Hindu roots. Long gone are the days when most Americans associate Hinduism solely with Apu, the Kwik-E-Mart proprietor and Indian immigrant in *The Simpsons* television series. In fact, Apu may be gone, too. In response to criticisms that the character is racist, including a 2017 documentary called *The Problem with Apu*, his character has quietly disappeared from the show.

LIVED HINDUISM

Today, the word "Hinduism" is all but synonymous with bhakti. There are followers of Gandhi who practice karma yoga. If you travel to India you may see wandering renouncers practicing jnana yoga. But when it comes to liberation from samsara, or even a better rebirth, most Hindus prefer help. Rather than relying on their own work or their own wisdom, they fall back on the gods of their choosing and trust that they will be there to catch them. These chosen gods vary from region to region. Devotees in Maharastra tend to worship Ganesha. Devi is popular in Bengal, and Shiva in the Himalayas. But the love devotees lavish on these gods is surprisingly similar, evident not only in bhakti poetry but also in puja, festivals, and pilgrimage.

Puja

Hindu devotees have not traditionally gone to congregational worship services akin to the Catholic Mass. They worship their gods on their own time, in the temple and the home. This worship is called puja. During puja, devotees make offerings of flowers, food, water, or money to a god said to reside in an image. Because the deity does not eat anything more than the essence of this offering, the food offered in puja is offered back to worshipers as *prasada* (divine "favor"). In temples, puja may include mantras chanted by priests plus the ringing of bells. It will typically also include *aarti*—when a lamp is passed among devotees and with it the "heat" (and favor) of the god. In times before electricity, this practice also illuminated the divine image.

Unlike the Jewish tradition, which forbids approaching God through "graven images," Hinduism revels in images of the divine, which grace home shrines and city streets.

Outsiders have long criticized Hindus for bowing down to statues made by human hands. Following a visit to Varanasi, Mark Twain dismissed the city, which he dubbed "Idolville," as "a vast museum of idols—and all of them crude, misshapen and ugly."[35] But Hindus know that the images they worship are made by human hands. In many cases, they might even know the stone carvers. Nonetheless, they trust that gods can animate the inanimate. At the climax of a special ritual that tranforms dead stone into a living divinity, a priest inserts the eyes, and in that moment the god takes up residence in the image, which from that point forward requires round-the-clock attention from a priest. When Hindus go to a temple, they go to look in those eyes and to see the god of their choosing look back at them. The Indologist Diana Eck has identified this intimate encounter—**darshan**, or "sacred seeing"—as the heart and soul of bhakti worship.[36]

darshan
sacred seeing; eye-to-eye moment in Hindu worship when a god and a devotee take in one another in a visual embrace

Festivals

In India, virtually every day is a holy day. There are countless local festivals to deities. There are regional festivals celebrating gods known throughout India yet most popular in a particular state. And there are pan-Indian festivals in which gods beloved across India have their moments in the sun.

Many of these festivals feature theatrical performances rooted in episodes of the Mahabharata, the Ramayana, or popular vernacular epics. For example, the *Ramlila* ("The Play of Ram") is performed during September or October throughout India and in Nepal, Thailand, and many other countries. Typically, this performance of the battle between Lord Rama and the demon Ravana described in the Ramayana, takes place over ten days. However, across the river from Varanasi at Ramnagar, an elaborate maharaja-sponsored version that takes a full month has been staged every fall since the 1830s. The actors who play the gods in these pageants are revered as embodiments of the divine. The plays they put on function like Passover functions in the Jewish tradition—both to remember a story and to recall key values, in this case loyalty and duty.

Divali Of all the pan-Indian festivals, Divali is the most popular. In fact, it is celebrated not only by Hindus but also by Sikhs, Jains, and some Buddhists. It is an official holiday in India, Nepal, Trinidad and Tobago, Singapore, Sri Lanka, and other countries. During this five-day festival of lights, typically celebrated in late October or early November, devotees light earthenware lamps, set off firecrackers, watch fireworks, dress up in new clothes, visit friends and family members, gather around bonfires, tell stories, pray, worship, exchange presents, dance, enjoy sweets, and otherwise celebrate what they hope will be a good year to come.

Traditionally, Divali marked the last fall harvest. Today, it marks the end of one financial year and the beginning of another. Merchants buy new account books. Devotees sweep their floors to prepare for a visit from Lakshmi, the goddess of wealth. They then set out lamps (*divali* means "rows of lighted lamps") to guide her to their homes and businesses. Families also open doors and windows for Lakshmi and the good fortune she is said to bring.

In Divali celebrations in North India, devotees recall the return of Rama and Sita to the city of Ayodhya after fourteen years in exile. In South India, they celebrate Krishna's defeat of a demon who had terrorized the heavens and the earth. Sikhs on this holiday

Two young boys celebrate the colorful spring festival of Holi. During this playful celebration, people toss brightly colored powders at one another, leaving participants covered in different shades of the rainbow.

mark the liberation from prison of their sixth guru, Guru Hargobind. Jains recall the time when their last great teacher Mahavira entered into nirvana. In all these cases, celebrants mark the victory of light over darkness, good over evil, and knowledge over ignorance.

Divali was first celebrated in the White House in 2003, and Barack Obama became the first U.S. president to attend a Divali celebration there in 2009. In 2012, the Indian American astronaut Sunita Williams celebrated Divali in the International Space Station. The U.S. Postal Service issued a Divali postage stamp in 2016. Dozens of public schools on the eastern seaboard of the United States now observe Divali as an official holiday. Divali was also the subject of an episode of the hit television show *The Office.*

Holi Holi, the most photographed of Hindu festivals, also features bonfires. But here celebrants also throw colored powders and spray one another with colored water, turning their bodies into what anthropologist McKim Marriott has described as "a brilliant smear."[37] Like Divali, Holi is a harvest festival, though in this case the festival comes in late February or early March—a Thanksgiving of sorts for the start of spring. But Holi is far rowdier—a Hindu Mardi Gras in which strict social mores give way to practical jokes, raunchy songs, and intoxication. "*Holi hai!*"—"It's Holi!"—celebrants shout, in an ancient festival that may have begun as a fertility ritual before evolving into what slack-jawed British Victorians referred to as "the Hindu Saturnalia."[38]

There are many backstories to this two-day riot of colors. One tells the tale of Holika, a demoness with the power to walk into fire unscathed (thanks to the supernatural powers of a magic cloak). After an evil king ordered his son, a pious Vishnu devotee, to be put to death, the king's sister Holika picked up her nephew and marched with him into a fire in an effort to burn him alive. But the boy snatched the magic cloak from her so she died instead. An alternative backstory stresses the playfulness of the holiday. In this telling, Holi was inaugurated by Krishna, who delighted in playing practical jokes on the milkmaids of his youth. Shiva worshipers see Holi as a remembrance of the moment when Shiva, deep in meditation, was rudely interrupted by the love god Kamadeva, who was trying to wake him up so Shiva's wife-to-be Parvati could seduce him. Angrily, Shiva opened his third eye and burnt Kamadeva to a crisp. Later repenting of his rage, Shiva brought Kamadeva back to life.

In all these cases, Holi is, like Purim in Judaism, a ritual of reversal in which social taboos are relaxed and things are turned topsy-turvy. Traditional hierarchies of age, caste, and gender are suspended, and typical Indian reserve about public displays of affection is set aside. On Holi, wives ritually hit their husbands with sticks. Proper ladies and gentlemen shout obscenities and sing raunchy songs. Youngsters take pot-shots at their towns' elder statesmen. And anyone who feels like it can splatter their neighbors with cow dung or urine. All this takes place to the beat of drums that, on Holi at least, seem as capable as Mardi Gras jazz bands of seducing celebrants into otherwise illicit liaisons.

Kumbh Mela Most Hindu festivals are annual, but Kumbh Melas are held during a twelve-year cycle at four auspicious sites in India. The largest of these is the "great" Kumbh Mela held every twelve years at the confluence of the Ganges, Yamuna, and Saraswati rivers in Allahabad in North India. Here, holy men line up, led by a group of naked ascetics called the Naga Sadhus, to take a dip in the Ganges, and millions of pilgrims of all castes follow them in. This bathing is believed to earn spiritual merit and to wipe away wrongdoing because the Ganges is said to be tinctured on this occasion with the nectar of immortality. According to a popular legend, gods and demons were once fighting over a pot (*kumbh*) of this nectar. When one of the gods flew off with the pot, the demons chased after him. During this mad dash, which lasted the equivalent of twelve human years, four drops of nectar were spilled, one at each of the Kumbh Mela sites.

Visible from space, the Allahabad "Great Kumbh Mela" has been recognized by Guinness World Records as the largest gathering in human history. In January and February of 2013, it drew an estimated 120 million holy men, pilgrims, tourists, and photographers, turning Allahabad for a time into the world's largest city.

Pilgrimage

Pilgrimage (*yatra*) is another way Hindus demonstrate their devotion to the gods of their choosing. Here again, there are local, regional, and pan-Indian variants. In all these cases, pilgrims act as temporary ascetics, putting their day-to-day lives aside for a time in order to earn merit or to pay down wrongdoing. They visit places where rivers meet or places associated with a particular deity—for instance, to Ayodhya, the birthplace of Rama, or Mount Kailas, the Himalayan abode of Shiva. As much as sacred time matters in Judaism, sacred place matters here, as do the stories each of these places conjures up. "There is arguably no other major culture," writes Eck, that has such "a fundamentally locative or place-oriented worldview."[39] Today, more than half of all packaged tours in India are pilgrimages, and leading sacred sites are visited nearly as often as the iconic Taj Mahal.

Tirupati Rivaling Varanasi as the most-visited pilgrimage site in modern India is a temple in Tirupati set in the hills of Andhra Pradesh in South India. This site is famous for its *laddus*, a popular Indian sweet, but it draws upwards of twenty-five million pilgrims a year thanks to the belief that its god—Venkateswara, a local form of Vishnu who is also referred to as Balaji—is a powerful and generous giver of boons.

Pilgrims walk or ride up a steep road to approach this temple and the image within. Many shave their heads. They wait in line, often for hours, for the briefest glimpse of the divine image inside. Then they present their offerings in the hopes that Venkateswara will help them get into college, land a job, or have a child. These offerings, worth tens of millions in U.S. dollars annually, have made this temple the richest in India and one of the world's largest private holders of gold.

A mother and her sons journey home after making a pilgrimage to Venkateswara Temple, in Tirupati, India, where they shaved their heads in order to offer their hair to the god Venkateswara, a local form of Vishnu.

BIRTH AND DEATH

Hinduism accents religion's ritual dimension and is full of life-cycle ceremonies known as *samskaras*. Before birth, there are rituals of conception, of praying for a male child at the moment of quickening (now practiced only in some parts of India), and of parting the mother's hair to give the child a sharp mind or the mother an easy delivery. After birth, there are rituals for naming, for the first venture outside the home, for the first solid meal, for ear piercing, and for the first haircut. At a birth ceremony known as *jatakarma* ("birth action"), the name of the family's chosen god is whispered in the child's ear, and the father writes the sacred mantra *Om* with honey on the newborn's lips or tongue. Then prayers are offered for the baby's intelligence, strength, and long life. For practical purposes, this samskara is often combined with the naming ritual.

Hindus overwhelmingly choose cremation as a way to purify a corpse, to offer that corpse as a sacrifice to the divine, and to speed the deceased's way to a better rebirth. Typically, renouncers are not cremated, as it is believed that they have already achieved spiritual liberation and purified their bodies through their own devices. Unlike in the United States and Europe, where cremations are conducted out of sight in indoor crematories whose functions are almost entirely technological, Indian cremations are highly ritualized and usually held in the open air. Cremated remains are generally not collected if the body is burned on the banks of a sacred river. Otherwise, they are often gathered, to be scattered later in a sacred river as family members face the setting sun.

Postmortem rituals for adults last between ten and thirteen days. During this time, the deceased is said to linger as a hungry ghost (*preta*) and must be fed lest it lash out in anger at the living. The family meets this obligation with a series of daily offerings of rice, which is formed into a ball and placed in the family's home shrine beginning on the day after the cremation. Over the ensuing days of mourning, the hungry ghost is fed through the rice ball with water and sesame seeds. Gradually, a new afterlife body is said to take shape for the deceased: the head on the first day and then ears, a nose, eyes, hands, breasts, neck, feet, organs, bones, marrow, veins, nails, hair, and teeth. On the second-to-last day of this domestic

---

The governmental authorities who oversee the temple direct these funds toward various charitable activities, including extensive reforestation efforts. Money from this Tirupati temple has also been used to build new temples in the Indian diaspora, including Pittsburgh's Sri Venkateswara Temple, which has become a pilgrimage site in its own right.

Pilgrimage Circuits Although most pilgrimage routes are linear, like the ancient pilgrimage routes to a Catholic shrine in Santiago de Compostela, Spain, some are circular, leading through many destinations rather than to just one. Hindu pilgrims can travel to see the seven cities that bestow spiritual liberation or the 108 places where various parts of Shiva's wife Sati's dead body fell as her grieving husband carried her across India. The popular Ban Yatra takes Krishna devotees through several sites in North India associated with his life. The Char Dham Yatra courses through four sites that constitute the four corners of sacred India: Badrinath (associated with Vishnu) in the Himalayas in the north, Puri (another abode of Vishnu) in the east on the Bay of Bengal, Rameshvaram (an abode of Shiva) in the south, and Dvaraka (associated with Krishna) in the west. Pilgrims used to undergo this popular pilgrimage on foot, and some still do, but nowadays you can go by air-conditioned bus or train. Some of these circular pilgrimages are said to have beginning and end points, though there are rituals that can be employed to apologize to the gods for starting or ending in the wrong place. In theory, a pilgrim could travel any one of these pilgrimage circuits for a lifetime (or more).

ritual, the chief mourner shaves and bathes. On the last day, a small ball of rice representing the deceased and a large bowl of rice representing the ancestors is smooshed together and consumed by a Brahmin priest on behalf of the dead. In this way, the deceased passes into the company of the ancestors.

As for what happens next, the Hindu tradition speaks in more than one voice. Christians debate whether the soul of the deceased goes straight to heaven (or hell) or awaits judgment after Jesus returns to earth. With Hindus, parallel narratives are also at odds. According to the Vedas, the rice-ball rituals transform the hungry ghost into an ancestral spirit. After three generations in the home, that spirit moves into the world of the dead. But what about those two tracks of spiritual liberation and rebirth? What of the popular beliefs that dying in Varanasi or being scattered in the Ganges (or both) will release the deceased from the cycle of samsara? The rice-ball rituals, which were developed out of Vedic resources before the development of classical Hinduism in the Upanishads, do not fully address them. As a result, there seem to be three distinct possibilities for the deceased: moksha, rebirth, and reunion with the ancestors.

In Hindu culture, naming a baby requires consulting astrological and numerological charts to determine an auspicious name. It is customary to hold a naming ceremony one month after the birth, when the infant's name is whispered in her ear for the first time.

CONTEMPORARY CONTROVERSY: HINDU NATIONALISM

Hinduism is widely celebrated as a tolerant faith. This tolerance was enshrined in 1950 in the secular Constitution of India, which imagined India as a multireligious nation. But the temptations of membership in the tribe of the One True Way are great, and some Hindus have insisted on unity rather than diversity, confrontation rather than absorption. To these exclusivist Hindus, there is only one god, one scripture, and one correct interpretation of each. For members of today's Hindu Right in India, there is no controversy among real Hindus about vegetarianism, nonviolence, sexuality, or even politics. Critics call these "Hindu first" activists peddlers of "Brahmanical fascism."[40] They call themselves partisans of Hindutva who see India as a Hindu state that should be governed in keeping with Hindu beliefs and Hindu practices.

Like the Moral Majority, a largely Protestant group founded in the United States in 1979 and dedicated to the proposition that the United States is a Christian nation, Hindutva advocates form a "Religious Right" intent on using the levers of the state to preserve the prerogatives of their country's majority religion. As such, they oppose as non-Indian both the secular values of India's Congress Party and the Islamic values of India's Muslim minority. According to the pioneering Hindutva intellectual Vinayak Damodar Savarkar, only those who view India as both fatherland and holy land are true citizens of India.

Hindutva advocates trace their nationalist project back to Rama's reign in the Ramayana and to Dayanand Sarasvati and his Arya Samaj. In 1925, Hindutva found institutional form with the founding of the Hindu nationalist cultural organization the Rastriya Svayamsevak Sangh (RSS). "Hinduness" was later advanced by the more radical Vishwa Hindu Parishad (VHP), which was established in 1964 in an effort to ward off the encroaching "evils" of Islam, Christianity, and communism. Three key moments marked Hindu nationalism's emergence as a political force in the 1980s and 1990s. The first was the founding in 1980 of the Bharatiya Janata Party (BJP), a political party opposed to the dominant Indian National Congress, which right-wing Hindu nationalists had come to see as overly secular and insufficiently tough on Islam. The second came in 1989 when the BJP won about 20 percent of the seats in Indian parliamentary elections and established itself as a major party. The third came in 1992, when Hindu nationalist mobs destroyed a 450-year-old mosque in Ayodhya on the theory that it had been built on the ruins of a much earlier Hindu temple marking Rama's birthplace. That provocation sparked interreligious violence in India and Pakistan that left more than a thousand people dead.

Today, this marriage of nationalism and religious fundamentalism—"One Nation, One People, One Culture"—is represented most powerfully in India by the BJP, which has run India's central government in two separate stretches: between 1998 and 2004 and again beginning in 2014. The BJP is largely opposed by Muslims, by those on the left who continue to view India as a secular state, and by more cosmopolitan Hindus who affirm the essential unity of religions.

The struggle between the BJP and its opponents is a struggle for the soul of India that in many respects mirrors America's culture wars. Is India to be an inclusive nation that views Hindus, Muslims, and Christians as fellow citizens in a common project? Or is it to be an exclusive nation in which Muslims and Christians are suspect? These questions came to a head under the Hinduvta politician Narendra Modi. Modi was banned from traveling to the United States because of his role in violating the religious freedom of Muslims during his years as the governor of Gujarat. In one particularly horrific incident in 2002, a massacre started with Hindutva activists being torched on a train and then extended across Gujarat with a rash of rapes and the wholesale destruction of mosques and Muslim homes and shops. More than a thousand Muslims died, and perhaps two hundred thousand were displaced. Outsiders denounced these atrocities as genocide, but they gave Modi a national stage, which he rode to the office of prime minister in 2014 and again in 2019. Part of his support came from Hindu-firsters, but he also won votes in both elections from promises to modernize the economy, beat back corruption, and put an end to dynastic rule by the Gandhi family.

As he ascended to power, Modi did not forget his Hindutva friends. He has represented well those Hindus who, despite their majority status, feel as though they are a besieged minority in need of a muscular leader to defend them. The stories he has told resonate with their politics of nostalgia for a bygone Hindu nation. According to his critics, much of what Modi has done for the Hindutva movement he has done through silence. When mobs lynch Muslims and low-caste people they accuse of killing cattle, he has looked the other way. When Hindus rape young Muslim girls in an effort to drive their families out of their villages and towns, he has responded with promises of justice to come. Modi,

Prime Minister Narendra Modi addresses the National Council Meeting of the Bharatiya Janata Party (BJP) in 2014 in New Delhi, India. Hindu nationalists have been a key driver of Modi's electoral success.

whose BJP affirms the supremacy of upper-caste over lower-caste Hindus, has also looked the other way when it comes to atrocities against Dalits. "These developments are not a matter of uncontrollable religious hatred," argues the writer and activist Amrit Wilson, "but a systematic move towards a fascistic Hindu state"—a "republic of fear."[41]

Other critics have likened Modi's Hindu supremacy to white supremacy. Still others have slotted him alongside majoritarian strongmen such as Tayyip Erdogan in Turkey and Rodrigo Duterte in the Philippines, who draw on voters' economic anxieties to win power in a world in which consumer capitalism has left so many behind. These strongmen are also masters at conjuring up fears of immigrants, refugees, and religious outsiders. They claim that their country was originally Christian or Muslim or Hindu, and they pledge to restore it to that firm foundation. According to the Kashmiri journalist Basharat Peer, these populist leaders "share a preference for rewriting school textbooks, retelling tales of ancient glories, and reviving old wounds. They are united by their promises to make their countries great again."[42]

Although Hindu nationalism is a political movement, it is also a religious movement that raises all sorts of questions about the religion Hinduism has been and what it is becoming. Is Hinduism a fighting faith or a tolerant and pluralistic religion? Are Hindus in the process of trading in their long-standing inclusive strategy of absorption for an exclusive strategy of confrontation? Answers to those questions will depend on how this contemporary controversy plays out.

QUESTIONS FOR DISCUSSION

1. Describe the contributions the Vedic tradition made to classical Hinduism. What was lost and gained as Vedic religion gave way to Hinduism?

2. In what ways has the Hindu tradition been polytheistic? monotheistic? atheistic? Can it be all three at once?

3. What is samsara? Why do Hindus seek to escape it, and how have the techniques for that escape changed over time?

4. Describe the differences between classical and bhakti Hinduism. What are the roles of karma and the divine in each? Why might the bhakti path have developed out of the jnana path?

5. During the modern period, how did different Hindus and Hindu groups respond to the challenges of modernity and the politics of Indian independence? Consider the following: Mohandas Gandhi, Brahmo Samaj, Arya Samaj, and the Bharatiya Janata Party (BJP).

KEY TERMS

Agni, p. 46

aarti, p. 47

atman, p. 41

avatar ("descent"), p. 34

Bhagavad Gita, p. 50

bhakti ("devotion"), p. 36

Brahma, p. 38

brahman, p. 41

Brahmin, p. 36

caste (jati, or "birth group"), p. 36

Dalit ("oppressed"), p. 36

darshan, p. 69

Devi, p. 39

dharma, p. 36

Durga ("The Inaccessible"), p. 39

Ganesha, p. 39

guru, p. 49

Indra, p. 46

jnana ("wisdom"), p. 36

Kali ("Black One"), p. 39

karma, p. 36

Krishna ("Dark One"), p. 39

lingam ("mark"), p. 41

Mahabharata, p. 50

mantra, p. 45

moksha ("freedom"), p. 36

Om (or Aum), p. 45

puja, p. 41

Rama, p. 39

Ramayana ("Journey of Rama"), p. 51

samsara ("wandering through"), p. 37

sannyasin, p. 47

Shiva ("The Auspicious"), p. 38

Tantra, p. 59

Upanishads, p. 44

Vedas ("knowledge"), p. 32

Vishnu ("The Pervader"), p. 38

yoga ("union"), p. 49

FURTHER READING

Doniger, Wendy. *The Hindus: An Alternative History*. New York: Penguin, 2010.

Eck, Diana. *Darsan: Seeing the Divine Image in India*. New York: Columbia University Press, 1998.

Flood, Gavin D. *An Introduction to Hinduism*. New York: Cambridge University Press, 1996.

Knott, Kim. *Hinduism: A Very Short Introduction*. New York: Oxford University Press, 2016.

The Bhagavad Gita. Translated by Laurie L. Patton. New York: Penguin, 2008.

Williamson, Lola. *Transcendent in America: Hindu-Inspired Meditation Movements as New Religion*. New York: New York University Press, 2010.

Nestled in the cliffs of Bhutan's Upper Paro Valley is the Tiger's Nest monastery. This complex was built in 1692 around a sacred cave where the eighth-century Tantric Buddhist master Padmasambhava is said to have meditated for three years, three months, three weeks, three days, and three hours.

Buddhism

THE WAY OF AWAKENING

There is a tree in India that draws devotees by the millions. Pilgrims lay flowers beneath its limbs and splash its roots with water. They garland the fence enclosing it with prayer flags and circle it and the nearby temple as if encircling a deity. Tour groups from Vietnam, Tibet, and Sri Lanka, outfitted in color-coded baseball caps, name tags, and tour bags, smile for photographs in its shade. Hindus light incense and bow before it, like they bow before gods at their own temples. Tourists sit and observe the scene, which borders on chaos yet never seems to tilt headlong into it.

This massive Bodhi Tree marks the spot in **Bodh Gaya** in the northeastern Indian state of Bihar where, according to the Buddhist tradition, a former prince named Siddhartha Gautama was enlightened and became the Buddha ("Awakened One"). The first temple on this site was built by the Mauryan emperor and Buddhist patron **Ashoka** around 250 BCE. Although a memorial pillar from Ashoka's reign remains, the original temple is long gone. The existing Mahabodhi Temple, built of brick and rising to 180 feet, dates to the fifth or sixth century CE. In 2002, this temple complex was named a UNESCO World Heritage Site.

Between 2004 and 2014, tourism to Bodh Gaya, which UNESCO billed as "the holiest place of Buddhist pilgrimage in the world," grew tenfold, from 170,000 to 1.7 million.[1] Direct flights now run to a nearby international airport from Thailand, Sri Lanka, Myanmar, and various cities in India. Tour groups organize pilgrimage packages that include Bodh Gaya and three other sacred places intimately associated with the Buddha's life: Lumbini (where he was born), Sarnath (where he

Bodh Gaya
place of the Buddha's awakening, in modern-day Bihar in northeastern India

Ashoka (c. 304–232 BCE)
Indian emperor and Buddhist sympathizer who promoted Buddhism and interreligious understanding

gave his first sermon), and Kushinagar (where he died). But Bodh Gaya remains the main attraction—"the navel of the earth and the center of the Buddhist world."[2]

As early as 629 CE, a Chinese monk named Xuanzang left China on foot on the Silk Road and ended up in Bodh Gaya. In *The Great Tang Dynasty Record of the Western World*, which he wrote after returning to China in 645, he related a series of stories about anti-Buddhist kings and queens who hacked the Bodhi Tree from limb to limb only to see it spring miraculously back to life. Xuanzang explained how the stone walls around the site were built to ward off attackers. Every year on the anniversary of the Buddha's awakening, he wrote, "thousands and myriads" of faraway dignitaries and monks and nuns and laypeople come to "bathe the tree with scented water and milk to the accompaniment of music; with arrays of fragrant flowers and lamps burning uninterruptedly the devotees vie with each other in making offerings to the tree."[3]

Xuanzang described the shrines and statues on the site and the place north of the Bodhi Tree where the Buddha is said to have paced back and forth after his awakening, as flowers sprang up in his footprints along the way. South of the tree, Xuanzang located the shrine built by Ashoka, who visited Bodh Gaya himself. But Xuanzang begins his story with the Diamond Throne, which he traces back neither to Ashoka nor even to the Buddha, but to the beginning of human history. This carved stone seat marks the place where the Buddha-to-be became the Buddha—the place where he sat on a mat of grass and vowed not to get up until he had solved the riddle of suffering, where he meditated deep into the night, where he was tempted by offers of political power and sexual pleasures, and where he ultimately achieved awakening. But this place was not made by his enlightenment. At least according to Xuanzang, his

A pilgrim visits the Bodhi Tree at the Mahabodhi Temple in Bodh Gaya, India, which marks the spot where the Buddha is said to have attained enlightenment.

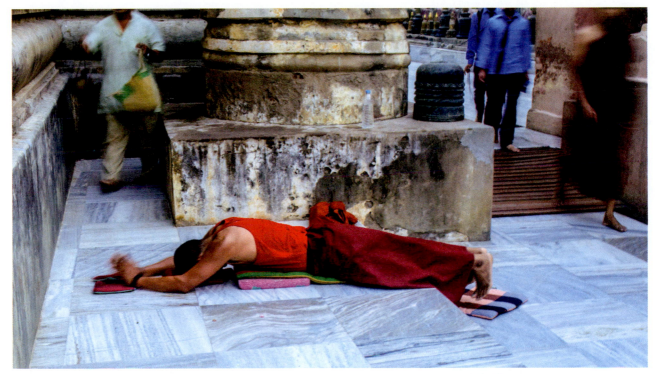

A Tibetan Buddhist monk performs full-body prostrations on the floor of the Mahabodhi Temple in Bodh Gaya, India.

enlightenment was made by this place, which is and always has been the still-point at the center of our shaken and suffering universe. "When the earth quakes, this spot alone remains stable," Xuanzang testified. As the Buddha-to-be was on the cusp of enlightenment and the whole earth shook, the Diamond Throne remained "calm and quiet, without agitation."[4]

Back under the shelter of the Bodhi Tree in modern-day Bodh Gaya, a Thai monk performs walking meditation. Tibetan monks engage in full-body prostrations, complete with body-length boards and hand cushions that allow them to glide from standing to kneeling to lying out flat (and back again). Other visitors sit quietly and alone, meditating in silence, reading from prayer books, shuffling prayer beads, or simply observing the scene. At the trunk of the tree, devotees place bills and coins in a donation box before prostrating before it. They also present the tree with flowers and monastic robes.

Pilgrims also line up and file dutifully past a gilded statue of the Buddha housed inside the temple. Signs near the Bodhi Tree guide visitors along a Buddhist analog to Jerusalem's Stations of the Cross—locations where "the Lord Buddha" supposedly spent each of the seven weeks after his awakening and before moving on to nearby Sarnath, where he delivered his first sermon and gathered his first disciples. One sign instructs pilgrims to direct their collective gaze away from the tree and toward the gilded seat described by Xuanzang over a millennium ago. "The Vajrasana or the Diamond Throne which is under this Bodhi Tree is the central place of worship," the sign reads, but this message goes largely unread and almost entirely unheeded.

A *sannyasin* ("renouncer") with prayer beads and dreadlocks checks his cell phone at Bodh Gaya's Mahabodhi Temple—a reminder that even those who have withdrawn from the world remain tied to it.

Nearby, Vietnamese pilgrims listening to a talk by a saffron-robed monk are informed that the path to the elimination of ignorance and suffering known as enlightenment lies not in the modern prayers of "religious Buddhism" but in the ancient austerities of "original Buddhism." Two Hindus approach and bow low before the teacher, asking to touch his feet. The man, who holds a PhD in Buddhist studies, seems embarrassed. There are no gods in "original Buddhism," and he does not want to play one here, he explains later, but he lets them touch his feet anyway.

Not everything here is so religious, or so original. Though the pace of life in the shadow of the Bodhi Tree is Buddha slow, signs asking pilgrims to put away their mobile phones are not always heeded. A holy man with impossibly long dreadlocks wrapped around his forehead pulls out a mobile phone and makes a call. A Tibetan monk fiddles with his iPad. Another monk dressed in a long mustard-yellow robe displays a dharma wheel tattoo on his upper right arm. A bored son quarrels with his pious father about how much longer he has to stay. Touts strike up conversations with European and American visitors. Meanwhile, everyone seems to want to pose for a photo, just to prove that, like the Buddha, they were here, too.

Like Jerusalem, whose real estate has been carved up over the centuries by Christian groups eager to claim a piece of the city where Jesus walked, Bodh Gaya has seen all manner of sacred places pop up in recent years in the footprints of the Buddha. Thanks to new temples and monasteries built by devotees from Sri Lanka, Bhutan, Nepal, Tibet, China, Taiwan, Japan, Myanmar, Vietnam, and Thailand, this once-sleepy village in North India's beleaguered Bihar state has turned into a supermarket of Buddhism—a one-stop shop for nearly every Buddhist option under the sun. But religion has long mixed commerce and piety, and so it is every day around the massive Bodhi Tree that marks the birthplace of Buddhism. Outside the Mahabodhi Temple, beggars line up for rupees, dollars, or euros. Drivers of elaborately painted horse carts offer rides. Elsewhere in Bodh Gaya, customers buy textiles in a Tibetan refugee market and patronize establishments such as "Buddha Juice Corner," "Buddha Toyota," and "Buddha Hair Cutting Sailoon." In fact, Bodh Gaya is so busy with spiritual tourism nowadays it takes a leap of faith to imagine that anyone was ever enlightened here.

In this Graceland, however, the tree is Elvis. It's a pipal tree: *Ficus religiosa.* It's not the actual tree that sheltered the Buddha, of course, but according to the faithful, it's a direct descendent. And like Elvis impersonators at Graceland, it powerfully evokes reverence for the original. Its massive lower limbs are propped up to prevent souvenir seekers from stripping them bare, but when a leaf breaks free and drifts to earth, a Thai nun seemingly deep in meditation springs to her feet to grab it. Smiling apologetically at her momentary fit of selfishness, she sheepishly makes her way back to her seat, and to her meditation, keeping this sacred relic for herself.

OUR STORY

In the Indian religions of release, trees and temples are close kin. In fact, many sacred sites in India likely got their start around a tree rather than inside a temple. Today, many Hindus see the gods in trees: Brahma (the creator) in roots; Vishnu (the sustainer) in trunks; Shiva (the destroyer) in boughs. Popular stories draw particularly close ties between the Hindu god Krishna and the banyan tree. A banyan in Jyotisar in India's Haryana state is said to be the tree under which Lord Krishna delivered to the warrior Arjuna his message on war and duty now preserved in the Hindu scripture the Bhagavad Gita. So you would not be far off if you sense something resembling nature worship operating in Bodh Gaya. But the tree is also a mnemonic device meant to stir up memories. Like the perfume of someone you knew long ago, it is a reminder. It comes with a story you might otherwise forget, like this story about how a prince woke up.

The Great Departure

Once upon a time, there was a prince who over many lifetimes of good deeds had accumulated a vast storehouse of merit. He lived a life of luxury with a beautiful wife and a beautiful son on the plains close to the Himalayas in the border zone between India and Nepal. His was a life so wondrously set apart that he knew nothing of the everyday sufferings of ordinary people.

Born into the Kshatriya, or warrior, class, this prince carried the family name of Gautama. His first name was Siddhartha, which means "he who fulfills his purpose." But what was the purpose of Siddhartha Gautama? Upon his birth, in Lumbini, likely in the sixth or fifth century BCE, a seer had predicted that he would achieve greatness either in the world of wealth and power or in the world of the spirit. His father, a practical man, tried to steer him toward wealth and power, shielding him from the troubles that have always compelled human beings to ponder spiritual things. Eventually, he grew dissatisfied with his beautiful house and his beautiful wife. He

started to ask, "How did I get here?" And he started to wonder what it might be like to wander beyond the confines of his palace and out into the wider world.

Determined to grant his son's wishes yet equally determined not to propel him toward a life as a wandering monk, the father of the Buddha-to-be organized a carefully orchestrated tour of a nearby park. He saw to it that the appointed route was swept clean of all unpleasantness. Nonetheless, Siddhartha encountered a balding man, wrinkled and stooped over a stick. "What is that?" he asked, because he had never seen old age. His charioteer

Siddhartha Gautama decided to leave his palace and seek enlightenment after encountering "Four Sights": an old person, a sick person, a corpse, and a meditating renouncer. This important Buddhist story is painted on the walls of the Vat Tai Yai Buddhist temple in Vientiane, Laos.

answered, "That is an old man. All human bodies decay and grow old. No one is exempt from old age."

On a second tour, he encountered a man hollowed out by disease. "What is that?" he asked, because he had never seen illness. His charioteer answered, "That is a sick man. All human bodies decay. No one is exempt from sickness."

On a third tour, Siddhartha saw a man who seemed too still to be merely asleep. "What is that?" he asked, because he had never seen death. His charioteer answered, "That is a corpse. All human bodies decay and grow old and expire. No one is exempt from death."

On his fourth and final tour, Siddhartha's midlife crisis deepened when he saw a holy man seated in meditation. "Who is that?" he asked. His charioteer answered, "That is a renouncer, a holy man who has left behind work and family in order to seek release from the ravages of the cycle of life, death, and rebirth."

Prompted by these "Four Sights," Siddhartha vowed that he, too, would become a renouncer. That night, at the age of twenty-nine, he said a silent goodbye to his wife and son. Then he and his charioteer sneaked away from his home under cover of darkness. The charioteer rode with him to the edge of the palace grounds. Siddhartha shaved off his hair and exchanged his princely finery for the modest robes of his charioteer. Then he wandered into the woods, homeless and alone.

The story does not end here, of course. This holy man formerly known as a prince joined a group of five fellow renouncers. Alongside them, he practiced all sorts of austerities. He slept in cemeteries. He perfected difficult breath control exercises. He hardly ever ate, and when he did, he ate hardly anything. He became famous among renouncers for his discipline. As he later told a disciple, "When I tried to touch the skin of my belly, I took hold of my backbone, and when I tried to touch my backbone I took hold of the skin of my belly."[5]

Still, he had not awakened from the illusions that give rise to human suffering. So he struck out on his own on a "Middle Path" between his old life of luxury and his new life of renunciation. He ate and slept just enough to keep his body and mind alert. After six years on the road, he

Expertly carved into a single piece of granite at Gal Vihara ("Rock Temple") in Polonnaruwa, Sri Lanka, is this forty-six-foot-long image of the Buddha, who is either simply reclining or is lying down at the end of his life and entering into *parinirvana* ("final nirvana").

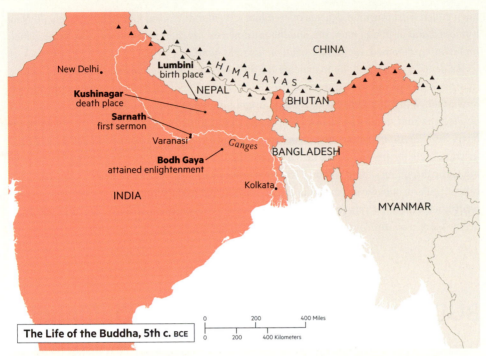

The Life of the Buddha, 5th c. BCE

Siddhartha Gautama traveled throughout what is now northern India. Today, Buddhist pilgrims travel to four sites associated with his life: Lumbini (where he was born), Bodh Gaya (where he attained enlightenment), Sarnath (where he preached his first sermon), and Kushinagar (where he passed into parinirvana and died).

made his way to Bodh Gaya, where, at the age of thirty-five, he sat beneath the Bodhi Tree and vowed not to get up until he had achieved enlightenment.

As he sat, the demon of death and desire Mara tried to distract Siddhartha with nonsense and then with fire and rain. Mara sent armies of temptations his way. Then he sent his daughters to seduce him. But Siddhartha pressed on. He touched the earth, asking nature to witness his accomplishment. "I bear witness," the earth replied. As the day gave way to his night of enlightenment, he learned how to overcome suffering by realizing the impermanence of all things. As dawn approached, he achieved enlightenment.

The Buddha ("Awakened One"), as he was now called, considered returning to a life of solitary wandering. He knew that he had achieved enlightenment by his own effort (no God involved) and through his own experience (without divine revelation). He also knew that, as soon as he tried to translate that effort and experience into words, both would evaporate into the hot, humid air. He considered resuming his wandering without speaking a word of his awakening to anyone. However, having compassion on the rest of us, mired as we are in a world of suffering, he made his way to Sarnath, outside of present-day Varanasi in northern India, where he found the group of five renouncers he had left years before. He delivered to them his first and most famous sermon—the "first turning of the wheel of dharma." There are Four Noble Truths, he said to the men who would become the first monks of this tradition: suffering exists, suffering has a cause, suffering can be eradicated, and the way to the eradication of suffering is the Noble Eightfold Path.

For decades the Buddha wandered around India, making disciples of people from all castes and weaving them together into a community of monks and nuns. At the age of eighty, in a small town called Kushinagar, a devotee offered him a meal that caused him to fall gravely ill. Now a stooped and wrinkled man, the Buddha lay down on his right side between two trees, which immediately bloomed. He laid his head on his right hand.

As death approached, he instructed his followers to cremate him and place his remains in a dome-like shrine called a stupa. He then ordained his last disciple, a wanderer named Subhadda. When his dear friend Ananda asked him how monks should remember him after he died, he said monastics and laypeople alike should make pilgrimage to the places of his birth, his enlightenment, his first sermon, and this place of his passing into parinirvana ("final nirvana"). As for his successor, he said there should be none. His teachings and his rules of monastic discipline should suffice: "You should live as islands unto yourselves, being your own refuge, with no one else as your refuge, with the dharma as an island, with the dharma as your refuge, with no other refuge." His last words were: "All conditioned things are of a nature to decay—strive on untiringly."[6]

BUDDHISM IN TODAY'S WORLD

There are an estimated one billion Buddhists in the world today. That makes Buddhism the fourth largest religion in population terms, after Christianity, Islam, and Hinduism. However, the Buddhist portion of the world's population has declined over the last century—from 31.4 percent in 1900 to 13.0 percent in 2020.[7]

Although Buddhism is a missionary religion that seeks to save all beings from suffering, it is confined largely to Asia. Particularly popular in East and Southeast Asia, it is the majority religion in Thailand, Cambodia, Taiwan, Myanmar, Hong Kong, and Japan. According to the World Religion Database, the top ten Buddhist countries in terms of

Comparison of Religions Worldwide, 2020

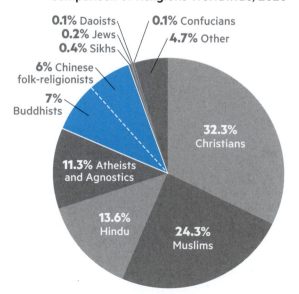

- **0.1%** Daoists
- **0.2%** Jews
- **0.4%** Sikhs
- **6%** Chinese folk-religionists
- **7%** Buddhists
- **0.1%** Confucians
- **4.7%** Other
- **32.3%** Christians
- **11.3%** Atheists and Agnostics
- **13.6%** Hindu
- **24.3%** Muslims

Types of "Wider Buddhists," 2020

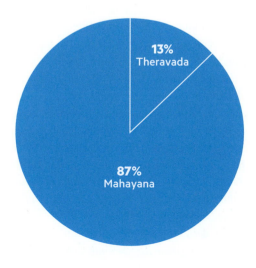

- **13%** Theravada
- **87%** Mahayana

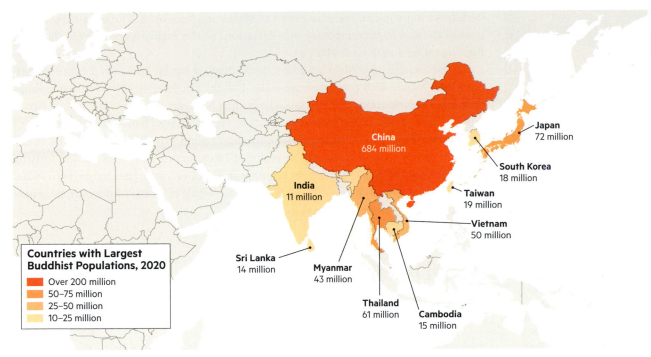

Buddhism originated in the Indian subcontinent, but few Buddhists live there today. China is now home to more than three times the number of Buddhists in Japan, the second most populous Buddhist country.

population are all in East and Southeast Asia, led by China with 684 million Buddhists, Japan (72 million), Thailand (61 million), Vietnam (50 million), and Myanmar (43 million). Buddhism, which originated in India, had almost entirely disappeared there by the thirteenth century, a victim of the popularity of devotional Hinduism and the success of Muslim conquests. Today, fewer than 1 percent of Indians are Buddhists, but given India's massive population, that still puts it in the top ten, with eleven million Buddhists.

There are only two countries outside Asia among the twenty countries with the most Buddhists: the United States at number twelve, with an estimated 4.1 million adherents, and Canada at number nineteen, with a Buddhist population of 1.4 million. According to Harvard's Pluralism Project, Los Angeles has become "the most complex Buddhist city in the entire world," with virtually every type of Buddhism on offer in a metropolitan area boasting more than two hundred Buddhist centers.[8]

Buddhists are often divided into three main branches, the **mainstream Buddhism** or **Theravada** ("Way of the Elders") Buddhism concentrated in Sri Lanka and Southeast Asia, the **Mahayana** ("Great Vehicle") Buddhism of East Asia, and the Vajrayana or Tibetan Buddhism of the Himalayan region. However, most scholars today (and most Tibetan Buddhists) view **Vajrayana** Buddhism as an expression of the Mahayana impulse that uses new strategies to arrive at classically Mahayana ends. That is the approach this book takes. Scholars use various terms to refer to pre-Mahayana Buddhism. "Theravada Buddhism" is problematic because that term refers not to all early Buddhist schools but to the one that outlasted its rivals. Other alternatives include "basic Buddhism," "conservative Buddhism," "Pali Buddhism" (after the language of early Buddhist scriptures), and "Nikaya Buddhism" (after a Pali word for a collection of scriptures). This book refers to this early Buddhism as mainstream Buddhism, because it remained the leading form of

mainstream Buddhism
early Buddhist branch, also called Vajrayana Buddhism, Theravada Buddhism, and Pali Buddhism

Theravada ("Way of the Elders")
early mainstream Buddhist branch now popular in Sri Lanka and Southeast Asia

Mahayana ("Great Vehicle")
largest Buddhist branch, based on Indian sutras that emerged a few centuries after the Buddha's death and distinguished by its doctrine that all sentient beings will eventually become buddhas

Vajrayana
Mahayana Buddhist expression popular in Tibet and focused on secretive Tantric teachings and practices

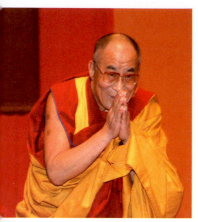

The Dalai Lama, shown here speaking in France, is the world's most widely recognizable Buddhist. He is the fourteenth in a line of Dalai Lamas ("Ocean Teachers") who have served as the spiritual and political leaders of Tibet since the fifteenth century.

Dalai Lama
political and spiritual leader of the Tibetan people and incarnation of Avalokiteshvara. Today's Dalai Lama is the fourteenth in this lineage.

dukkha ("suffering")
suffering, dissatisfaction, the first of the Four Noble Truths

arhat ("worthy one")
The exemplar in the mainstream tradition, this enlightened being will reach nirvana at death.

enlightenment
the Buddhist goal, variously understood as liberation from samsara, awakening from ignorance to insight, the attainment of Buddhahood, the realization of nirvana, and the elimination of suffering

bodhisattva ("enlightenment being")
an exemplar of compassion who vows to remain in the world to help other beings achieve enlightenment

Buddhism in its Indian homeland even as Mahayana developed. The term "Theravada" is used to refer to contemporary manifestations of the mainstream branch, the early Buddhist school that survives today.

Of the two main Buddhist branches, the Mahayana has far and away the most adherents, with nearly 86.8 percent of the wider Buddhist population. Theravada Buddhists command the remaining 13.2 percent. The leading Mahayana countries are China, Japan, and Vietnam. The leading Theravada Buddhist countries are Thailand and Myanmar.

Of all the Buddhists in the world today, the most visible is the Tibetan Buddhist icon the **Dalai Lama**. Born in 1935 in a remote region of Tibet, he fled Tibet after a failed uprising there against the Chinese government in 1959 and has lived since then in northern India. The winner of a Nobel Peace Prize for his work on behalf of Tibetan autonomy, he is now one of the most recognized people in the world.

BUDDHISM 101

✦ How can we eliminate suffering?

The religion that developed around this story of The Prince Who Woke Up was one of many new religious movements that arose in India around the fifth century BCE. Other upstarts included the Ajivikas, strict believers in fate who rejected karma, and the Jains, whose adherence to *ahimsa* ("noninjury") led them to practice strict vegetarianism. What the Buddha movement shared with these groups was a critique of popular notions of divinity and of the priestly authority of the Brahmin caste, who would play an outsized role in the development of the Hindu tradition. But Buddhists rapidly outpaced these rivals both in India and beyond, as their movement spread to Ceylon, China, Korea, Japan, and Tibet.

The problem of human existence, according to contemporary Buddhists, is suffering (**dukkha**). The goal of the Buddhist tradition is the eradication of suffering, which is accomplished through various techniques, from solitary meditation, chanting, and visualization to forms of worship that resemble deity devotion in popular Hinduism. The exemplars in the Buddhist tradition vary from branch to branch. Mainstream **arhats** ("worthy ones") are wise beings who have achieved **enlightenment**. The **bodhisattvas** ("enlightenment beings") of the Mahayana tradition are renowned for their compassion.

One typically becomes a Buddhist by taking refuge in the Three Jewels:

- I take refuge in the Buddha.
- I take refuge in the **dharma** ("Buddhist teaching").
- I take refuge in the **sangha** ("Buddhist community").

Together these Three Jewels underscore the enduring importance of the Buddha in Buddhist life and of the Buddhist community as a storehouse and guarantor of Buddhist beliefs and practices.

One function of the Buddhist tradition in the study of religion is to call into question the easy equivalence of "religion" with "belief in God." Religion has often been defined as a system of belief in God or gods. Yet early Buddhists professed no such belief. The Buddha was understood to be a pathfinder only—a human being who had woken up.

He achieved this feat by his own effort, without any miraculous assistance. One solution to this problem of classification is to banish Buddhism from the family of religions. Another is to observe that Buddhists adopted more and more of the traditional elements of religion over time. In fact, in early Buddhist texts, the Buddha is described as a miracle worker, and in early Buddhist art his miracles abound. A more useful approach is to reconsider what the term "religion" means—to wake up to the possibility that religions can exist without divine intervention.

Four Noble Truths

Buddhists don't always see eye-to-eye, of course, but most converge on a few key beliefs and practices. The Buddhist tradition emerged out of debates its practitioners were having with thinkers who both affirmed and dissented from what would come to be called Hinduism. Out of these conversations, many Indian thinkers converged on the human problem of **samsara** ("wandering through"). Like the philosophers of the Hindu scriptures the Upanishads, early Buddhists believed that humans were stuck in this ever-flowing cycle of life, death, rebirth, and redeath. This cycle was fueled by **karma**, which literally means action but in this case also refers to the positive and negative consequences of moral action. However, for these early Buddhists the root problem was the suffering that characterizes samsara. Therefore, the goal in the Buddhist tradition became the elimination of suffering, which Buddhists refer to as **nirvana**. Because this goal is difficult to achieve in any given lifetime, Buddhists, like Hindus, proceed on two tracks. While some seek the ultimate goal of nirvana through various contemplative and devotional practices, many seek the proximate goal of a better rebirth through the accumulation of karmic merit.

Most Buddhists agree on the wisdom of the Four Noble Truths, which the Buddha is said to have preached during his "first turning of the wheel of dharma" at Sarnath. This formula takes the shape of a medical case, with the Buddha playing the part of a great physician who offers, as Buddhist studies scholar Donald Lopez puts it, a list of our symptoms followed by his "diagnosis, prognosis, [and] cure."[9]

1. *Suffering.* Suffering is a fact of life. To live is to experience dissatisfaction, frustration, conflict, anxiety, stress, and sorrow. On the one hand, there is the physical suffering of birth, old age, sickness, and death. On the other hand, there is the mental anguish that comes from separation from people we like, contact with people we dislike, and not getting what we want (or getting what we want, only to find it does not satisfy). To recognize this truth of suffering is not to deny the possibility of happiness. It is simply to recognize that the moments of happiness we experience are insecure and fleeting.
2. *Arising.* Suffering has a cause, namely, craving. We thirst after sense pleasures, to become something new, and to stay who we are, but each of these desires (even if satisfied) produces more suffering. But craving is itself part of a much longer causal chain of "dependent origination," which begins with ignorance, moves through craving, and runs to the suffering of birth, sickness, old age, and death. At its root, therefore, suffering originates with ignorance of the self and illusions about the

Buddhism at a Glance

Problem: suffering

Solution: nirvana ("blowing out" suffering)

Techniques: meditation, chanting, visualization, devotion

Exemplars: arhats (in mainstream Buddhism) and bodhisattvas and buddhas (in Mahayana Buddhism)

In short, Buddhism is a tradition of monks, nuns, and ordinary people who seek to overcome suffering and reach the bliss of nirvana (or simply a better rebirth) through various contemplative and devotional practices.

dharma ("teaching")
teaching or law, one of the "Three Jewels"

sangha ("community")
the Buddhist community, one of the Three Jewels

samsara ("wandering")
unsatisfactory cycle of birth, death, rebirth, and redeath

karma
moral action and its consequences; the fuel that drives the cycle of life, death, and rebirth

nirvana ("blowing out")
the goal of the Buddhist tradition; namely, the bliss of liberation from the suffering and ignorance of *samsara*

world. We suffer because we do not see things as they really are, because we cling to false views, and because we insist on the permanence of things that are always passing away.

3. *Cessation.* Since suffering has a cause, it can be eliminated. The name for this spiritual liberation is nirvana, which refers literally to "blowing out" (a candle, for example) but in this case what is extinguished is ignorance, craving, and suffering itself. Because nirvana is said to be beyond description, it is typically described in negative terms—as release from greed, illusion, and hatred; freedom from bondage to the karmic cycle of life, death, and rebirth; and the cessation of suffering. But Buddhists also describe nirvana more positively as ultimate peace, highest happiness, stillness, and bliss.

4. *Path.* There is a path to the elimination of suffering. This path is the Middle Way between the extremes of self-indulgence and self-mortification. It is also described as the Eightfold Path, which is traditionally divided into three types of training:

BUDDHISM: A GENEALOGY

Buddhism as a concept has been widely described as a nineteenth-century invention of colonizers, missionaries, and Orientalists. However, as religious studies scholar Eva Pascal has demonstrated, Spanish Roman Catholic missionaries to Siam (now Thailand) "conceptualized Buddhism as a single religion, broad in scope across the East," as early as the sixteenth century. The Swiss historian Urs App has traced Roman Catholic constructions of Buddhism back to missionaries in sixteenth-century Japan. The view that "European Orientalists 'created' or 'invented' Buddhism in the first half of the nineteenth century," he argues, "is a problem of faulty optics."[a]

Protestants joined this conversation in the person of Robert Knox, an English sailor shipwrecked on Ceylon in 1659 and held captive there for nearly two decades. After escaping, he published in 1681 an account of his adventures that included a clearly Christianized description of the beliefs and practices of the Sinhalese (Ceylon's ethnic majority), beginning with their "great God, whom they call Buddou, unto whom the Salvation of Souls belongs." This Buddou, Knox reported, "did usually sit under a large shady Tree, called Bogahah[,] Which Trees ever since are accounted Holy."[b]

More than a century later, beginning in 1788, the Calcutta-based *Asiatick Researches* published a series of dispatches about "worshippers of Buddou" in Ceylon and Siam. Equating "Buddhou" with "the Mercury of the Greeks" and identifying the piety surrounding him as a "system of religion," William Chambers explained that the Sinhalese's holy tree was named *Bogahah*, "for *gahah*, in their language signifies a tree, and *bo* seems to be an abbreviation of *Bod* or *Buddou*." In an 1801 *Asiatick Researches* piece, the surgeon and botanist Francis Buchanan further detailed "the sect of Bouddha," which he located in China, Japan, Burma, and Cambodia.[c]

The word "Buddhism" itself appears to have entered the English language around the same time—in an 1800 translation from the French of a book by C. F. Volney, who a few years earlier had been accused of being a French spy and forced to leave the United States by President John Adams. In his *Lectures on History,* Volney referred to "the religious systems of bramism, Lamism, and Buddism."[d]

- morality (right speech, right action, right livelihood);
- concentration (right effort, right mindfulness, right concentration);
- wisdom (right view and right thought).

To agree on the importance of the Four Noble Truths, of course, is not to agree on how to interpret or live them. Buddhists do not agree on what nirvana is or how to achieve it (or whether it is an "achievement" at all). Bodh Gaya's many monasteries, each with competing understandings of the Buddha and his teachings, also testify to Buddhist diversity, leading many scholars to conclude that there is not one *Buddhism*, only multiple *Buddhisms*. Clearly, it is difficult to enforce doctrinal orthodoxy in a tradition that was born of heterodoxy ("different doctrine") and favors experience over doctrine. Is the Buddha one or many? Is nirvana achieved by self-effort or other-help? It depends on whom you ask.

BUDDHIST HISTORY

This Tibetan *Bhavachakra* ("Wheel of Life") painting features a terrifying being symbolizing impermanence who straddles the samsaric world of life, death, and rebirth. Similar images on temple and monastery walls serve as visual "dharma talks" for Buddhist visitors.

One key Buddhist doctrine is impermanence or transiency, and Buddhist history has plenty of both. The Buddha movement migrated out of North India in the wake of the Buddha's death. In the third century BCE, it made its way south into modern-day Sri Lanka. Around the time of Jesus, it moved north into China, where it mixed with the other two of China's "Three Teachings": Confucianism and Daoism. In roughly the second century CE it moved south again into Southeast Asia, and by the eighth century CE it had taken root as well in Korea, Japan, and Tibet. As Buddhists moved, they transformed their tradition, often remarkably, adopting new norms and organizational forms and adapting to new circumstances, cultures, and even climates—from the forbidding Himalayas and the Tibetan Plateau to the rich farmlands of the delta region of Burma (now Myanmar).

These changes were complicated, generated by internal conversations among Buddhist thinkers and by external interactions with people of other religious traditions and cultures. The most straightforward way to track them is to track the origins and transformations of the two main types of Buddhism: the mainstream and the Mahayana. These branches did not grow according to a simple timeline. Their stories overlap. Nonetheless, it is possible to tell a story of the afterlife of the Buddha that moves from mainstream to Mahayana and then to modern options in Asia, Australia, Europe, and the United States.

Mainstream Buddhism: The Way of Wisdom

There is much debate among experts about when the Buddha lived, with a "long chronology" of the mainstream tradition dating his birth to 556 BCE and a "short chronology," accepted by many scholars, dating it to 448 BCE. However, there is considerable consensus that either the end or the beginning of his life fell in the fifth century BCE. The period he wandered across North India looked a bit like the era of the Hundred Schools of Thought in China during that same time. Various teachers in various schools debated classical Indian conceptions such as the cycle of life, death, and rebirth and the karma (moral actions) that fuels it.

Today in China, most people practice some combination of the Three Teachings: Confucianism, Daoism, and Buddhism. The long-standing coexistence of these traditions is expressed in this painting from the Qing dynasty (1644–1911) of Confucius handing the baby Gautama Buddha to the Daoist philosopher Laozi.

sutra ("thread")
a sacred text that includes teachings of the Buddha, said to be memorized by followers and later written down

The Buddha seems to have been intriguingly uninterested in the sorts of questions often associated with theology. Like Confucius, he refused to speculate about the gods or the afterlife or the soul or about whether the world was eternal or finite (or neither or both). To him, inquiries along these lines were what the nineteenth-century translator of Buddhist texts Henry Clarke Warren called "questions which tend not to edification."[10]

In what is known as the Arrow Sermon, the Buddha is confronted by a monk, who says he will renounce his vows unless the Buddha answers a series of questions about the cosmos, the self, and the afterlife. The Buddha responds with a story about a man shot by a poisonous arrow. What would that man do? Would he ask a series of questions about the caste and skin color of the shooter? Or the type of bow or bowstring employed? Or whether the arrow flew on vulture or peacock feathers? Such a man would literally die of curiosity, the Buddha observes. And so it goes with people who demand that the Buddha answer questions about matters "not tending to edification." Life is short, the Buddha is saying. Don't spend it in fruitless speculation, especially when that speculation only multiplies your suffering. And don't expect the Buddha to join in. The purpose of his teaching is neither to affirm nor to deny dogmas. It is to pull out the arrow of suffering. Everything else is commentary.

Upon the Buddha's death, debates erupted about what he did teach. Scholars do not know precisely how these debates resolved themselves. But according to Buddhist legends, a group of about five hundred arhats gathered for the First Buddhist Council. They debated how strictly to adhere to the monastic rules taught by the Buddha, and they recited together everything they could remember him teaching. "Thus have I heard," they began, and so many Buddhist **sutras** ("threads," or sacred texts) begin that way—as written records of the oral teachings of the Buddha. After hearing these recitations, the council is said to have gathered the Buddha's teachings into the Pali canon, so named after the Pali language used in early Buddhist writings. This canon eventually coalesced into "Three Baskets":

- *Sutta Pitaka* ("basket of discourses"),
- *Vinaya Pitaka* ("basket of monastic discipline"),
- *Abhidhamma Pitaka* ("basket of higher teachings").

Many early Buddhists followed the example of the Buddha's movement from home to homelessness by living as solitary wanderers. "One should wander solitary as a rhinoceros horn," an early sutra stated, and wandering remained the ideal in the decades following the life of the Buddha.[11] Over time, these "dharma bums," as the Beat novelist Jack Kerouac would call them, began to settle down in small groups during India's monsoon season. During these "rain retreats," they constructed shelters, which became buildings, which became monasteries where Buddhist monastics would live together year-round. Royals and other patrons supported these monasteries and received spiritual

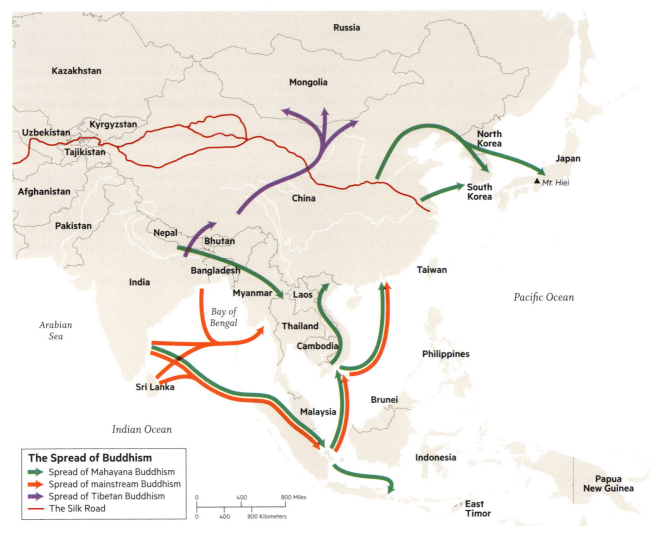

The Spread of Buddhism
- Spread of Mahayana Buddhism
- Spread of mainstream Buddhism
- Spread of Tibetan Buddhism
- The Silk Road

One of the world's most successful missionary religions, Buddhism moved northward and eastward out of the Indian subcontinent into China and Tibet and to South and Southeast Asia beginning in the third century BCE.

merit and political legitimation in exchange. Meanwhile, monastics followed strict rules and regulations about what to wear, what to eat, and how to avoid sexual improprieties. Most of these communities were for monks, but the Buddha also established during his lifetime an order of nuns that persisted after his death. According to tradition, the Buddha was reluctant to admit women into the sangha but agreed to do so in response to appeals from his close friend Ananda and his aunt and stepmother Mahaprajapati. He made nuns subservient to monks, however, by insisting that even the most junior monk be considered senior to the most senior nun, and by ensuring that nuns followed additional rules.

Monks and nuns formed a wide range of monastic groups that splintered, largely over questions of monastic discipline, into competing sects, each with its own monastic rule-books. Their competing rules were then debated at later Buddhist councils, which were also unable to produce a unified Buddhism.

About four centuries after the Buddha's death, a flurry of new scriptures began to appear, all said to come from the mouth of the Buddha himself. Those who accepted these texts as authentic took the term *Mahayana* to describe themselves. This term means "Great Vehicle," and it came with a brag: that their tradition was greater than the *Hinayana* ("Lesser Vehicle") that preceded it. And why was it greater? Because it emphasized helping others rather than attaining nirvana for oneself. And because it was able to transport more people more quickly and more easily to the far shore of nirvana. Of course, those who rejected these texts and this new branch of Buddhism did not take the pejorative name of Hinayana for themselves. Their mainstream Buddhism survives via the Theravada school, which prevails today in the southern part of the Buddhist world—in Sri Lanka and much of Southeast Asia, including Cambodia, Laos, Myanmar, and Thailand.

Like *jnana yoga*, the Hindu "discipline of wisdom," mainstream Buddhism was a wisdom path. On the road from the problem of suffering to the solution of nirvana, illusion was the roadblock. The vehicle to steer you around that roadblock was wisdom. But what was this wisdom? What was the dharma ("teaching") of the Buddha? According to mainstream Buddhists, to be wise was to understand the "three marks of existence" as a sentient being, namely:

- *dukkha* (suffering),
- *anicca* (impermanence),
- *anatta* (no soul).

The philosophers who appeared in the Upanishads at roughly the time of the Buddha said that to be wise was to experience the equivalence of *atman* ("self/soul") and *brahman* ("divinity"). It was to know in your gut that the essence of atman and brahman were one and the same. But early Buddhists rebelled against the authority of the Vedas

The Theravada Buddhist *sangha* ("community") has historically included monks and nuns. In this 1897 watercolor from Burma (modern-day Myanmar), nuns with shaved heads and simple robes carry begging bowls on their daily rounds in search of food provided by the kindness of others.

and other Hindu scriptures, refusing to recognize self, soul, or gods. There is no such thing as a solitary, unchanging soul, they argued, or, for that matter, a solitary, unchanging self. What we mistakenly call "I" or "me" is interdependent and ever-changing—an unstable flow of phenomena we mistake for the true self. Just as a chariot is composed of many parts, the illusion of a self/soul is a composite consisting of five *skandhas* ("aggregates"):

- matter
- feelings
- perception
- conditioning factors
- consciousness

It isn't just we who are ever changing, however. Anicca ("impermanence") characterizes everything we encounter. Everything is in flux. We live not on a rock by the shore but in an ever-flowing stream. Or, to put it more carefully, even the rock is in flux, on its way to being turned into finer and finer grains of sand. At Muslim funerals, participants are reminded that Allah alone determines one's life span. At Buddhist funerals, participants are reminded of anicca: "All conditioned things are impermanent."[12]

It is important to recognize that the aims of early Buddhists were practical rather than philosophical. Their goal was not to crack the metaphysical mysteries of the universe but to eliminate dukkha, which historian Ananya Vajpeyi has described as "the self's burden—its heaviness, its gravitas, its undertow."[13] The reason mainstream Buddhists taught the truth of impermanence was not simply because it is true that things change. And the reason they taught no-soul (anatta) was not simply because the self is a composite. They taught impermanence and no-soul because they observed that we suffer when we cling to changing things as if they are unchanging and to the self as if it is independent. Give up on that clinging, and the ignorance that informs it, and our suffering will melt away.

Clearlight Tara by the contemporary Tibetan American Buddhist artist Losang Gyatso illustrates not only a female bodhisattva of compassion but also the mind-bending concept of impermanence.

When it came to brahman, some mainstream Buddhists actively denied the existence of God. Others were less revolutionary. They believed that either enthusiastically affirming or enthusiastically denying the God concept aggravated our suffering. Just as we cling to the concept of "I" as if it can bring us happiness, we cling to the concept of "God" as if it can liberate us (or, in the case of some atheists, as if "no-God" can do the same). According to this Buddhist way of wisdom, however, individuals had to liberate themselves. Our suffering, and its cessation, were in our own hands.

Because of the Buddha's lack of interest in theology, Buddhism has been described as a "see for yourself" tradition that encourages us to take the prescription the Buddha offers and see if it does, in fact, cure us. There are many ways to sum up how early Buddhists understood this prescription and this cure. None is fully satisfactory. But here is one attempt: Things change, yet humans cling to things (the so-called "self" included) as if they are unchanging, and they suffer as a result. Come to see that everything is in flux, put that clinging for permanence to an end, and you will put an end to your suffering as well.

Like Hindu renouncers, Buddhist monks and nuns developed a series of techniques for winning this liberating wisdom. Following the Buddha, they meditated, and in the process they calmed and concentrated their minds and gained insight into the swirling world. They watched feelings come and go. They saw thoughts arise and fade away. And they observed their breathing—their lungs forever filling and emptying, filling and emptying, and never of their own accord.

Early Buddhism in the third century BCE benefited from the support of Emperor Ashoka. In one of the most ancient testimonies to the power of material culture, Ashoka left behind more than thirty "rock edicts" carved into stone in modern-day India, Nepal, Pakistan, and Afghanistan. One marks the spot in Sarnath where the Buddha gave his first post-enlightenment sermon. Its extraordinary sculpture of four lions is now the state emblem of India. Thanks to these objects we know not only that Ashoka lived but also how far his rule extended. It is unclear whether he actually converted to Buddhism, and he did not make Buddhism his state religion, but he was at a minimum a Buddhist sympathizer who personally visited Buddhist pilgrimage sites. According to pious legends, he contributed most powerfully to the spread of Buddhism by gathering the relics of the Buddha placed in just eight stupas after his death and scattering them in eighty-four thousand other stupas.

Like the way of wisdom of the Hindu Upanishads, mainstream Buddhism was an extraordinary tradition in which the religious goal (nirvana in this case) was accessible only to religious professionals (monks and nuns) who pursued this goal full time. Those who reached this goal were called arhats, beings who had achieved enlightenment and would never be reborn.

CHRONOLOGY OF BUDDHISM

566–486 BCE   Life of the Buddha according to the "long chronology"

486 BCE   First Buddhist Council according to the "long chronology"

448–368 BCE   Life of the Buddha according to the "short chronology"

368 BCE   First Buddhist Council according to the "short chronology"

265–232 BCE   Reign of Ashoka, Mauryan emperor and Buddhism patron

3rd century BCE   Buddhism moves into Ceylon (Sri Lanka)

200 BCE–200 CE   Rise of Mahayana Buddhism in India

67 CE   Indian Buddhist monks reportedly take Buddhism to China

c. 100   Composition of the Mahayana Buddhist Lotus Sutra

c. 150–250   Life of "Middle Way" philosopher Nagarjuna

c. 2nd century   Buddhism spreads to Southeast Asia

372   Chinese monk Shundao is said to take Buddhism to Korean Peninsula

520   Bodhidharma is credited with taking Chan Buddhism to China

552   Buddhism is adopted in Japan

629–645   Pilgrimage to India of the Chinese Buddhist monk Xuanzang

710–784   Buddhism is established in Japan in Nara period

868   Diamond Sutra is printed in China

983   Chinese Buddhist canon is printed for the first time

1133–1212   Life of Honen, Japanese founder of Jodoshu (Pure Land) Buddhism

1141–1215   Life of Eisai, Japanese founder of Rinzai Zen

In this religious system, the role of the nonmonastic householder was twofold: to support monks and nuns by feeding them, offering them robes, or supporting their monasteries financially; and to act ethically, practicing the Three Virtues (nonattachment, benevolence, understanding) rather than the Three Vices (greed, hatred, delusion). In so doing, laypeople hoped to accrue good karma and gain a better rebirth, which might allow them, after many lifetimes, to become monks or nuns and, after many lifetimes more, to become arhats and reach nirvana themselves. Over time, however, Buddhist laypeople began to hope for something more than this proximate goal. They wanted the ultimate goal: to reach nirvana. And they wanted to be able to do so quickly, in one lifetime, without renouncing spouses, children, and jobs. To do all this they would need some help.

Mahayana Buddhism

Mahayana Buddhism began around the time that Christianity and rabbinic Judaism arose. One theory claims that Mahayana emerged when lay followers of the Buddha began to make pilgrimages to stupas, which in early years were little more than large mounds of earth said to house relics of the Buddha. As these pious pilgrims gathered, they told stories about the Buddha, and as their stories became larger than life, the legends of the Buddha grew and grew until he started to look and act like the Hindu gods who were becoming popular at roughly the same time. This theory has been largely discredited, but it captures the fact that, as Mahayana Buddhism developed, the Buddhist tradition became more plainly religious. There are stories of the miraculous acts of the Buddha in

1173–1263 Life of Shinran, Japanese founder of Jodo Shinshu (True Pure Land) Buddhism

1200–1253 Life of Dogen, Japanese founder of Soto Zen Buddhism

1222–1282 Life of Nichiren, Japanese founder of Nichiren Buddhism

1357–1419 Life of the Tibetan Buddhist philosopher Tsongkhapa

1642 Dalai Lamas begin to rule politically as well as religiously in Tibet

1864–1933 Life of the Sinhalese Buddhist reformer Anagarika Dharmapala

1870–1966 Life of the Japanese Zen scholar D. T. Suzuki

1880 American Henry Steel Olcott converts to Buddhism in Ceylon and initiates a Buddhist revival there

1891 Maha Bodhi Society is established

1893 World's Parliament of Religions brings Buddhists to Chicago

1898 Japanese Buddhist missionaries first arrive in the United States, in San Francisco

1930 Soka Gakkai is founded in Japan

1942–1946 Roughly 120,000 Japanese Americans, many of them Buddhists, are forcibly relocated to internment camps as "enemy aliens"

1956 B. R. Ambedkar converts to Buddhism with more than half a million followers

1959 Dalai Lama flees from Tibet into exile in India

1989 Dalai Lama is awarded Nobel Peace Prize

1991 Aung San Suu Kyi of Myanmar is awarded Nobel Peace Prize

2001 Taliban destroys sixth-century Buddha statues at Bamiyan in Afghanistan

2002 Bodh Gaya is declared a UNESCO World Heritage Site

Among the monuments left behind by the third-century BCE emperor Ashoka were rock edicts promoting religious tolerance. This pillar of four lions in Sarnath, India, marks the location where the Buddha gave his first sermon and now serves as India's state emblem.

the early Buddhist scriptures known as the Pali canon. But in the Mahayana movement, the Buddhist tradition became more unapologetically theistic, full of supernatural figures who could perform miracles and (more importantly) transport their devotees to nirvana on their own backs.

In mainstream Buddhism, your karmic accounts were yours and yours alone. Merit could not generally be transferred, so nirvana was open only to full-time religious professionals who could achieve it by their own devices. In fact, the sangha itself was restricted to monks and nuns. In contrast, Mahayana Buddhists refused to restrict enlightenment to monks and nuns who renounced family and social obligations. They offered the religious goal and Buddhist identity to laypeople with families and jobs. In this way, the Buddhist goal of nirvana eventually came to be seen as a gift rather than an achievement—a result not of self-effort but of other-help.

Surely, this democratization of the Buddhist tradition was a huge part of the appeal of Mahayana tradition in India. But it was close to a necessity in China, which for a variety of reasons was not open to mainstream influence. In China, the begging bowls and shaved heads of monastics violated norms of ritual propriety so highly valued in the Confucian tradition, while celibacy was an affront to the Confucian virtue of filial piety, or respect for family (ancestors included). The Mahayana tradition resolved these difficulties by making it possible for householders (non-monks and non-nuns) to be full Buddhists and to achieve nirvana by reliance on the compassion of others.

Bodhisattvas and Buddhas   This Mahayana revolution offered new understandings of the Buddha, a new exemplar in the bodhisattva, and a variety of new philosophical ideas.

Like *bhakti* ("devotional") Hindus, Mahayana Buddhists prayed to beings with vast storehouses of spiritual capital, both for blessings in this life and for help in reaching the religious goal of nirvana. Some of these beings they referred to as bodhisattvas. There were bodhisattvas in mainstream Buddhism, where this term referred to a being who is on the path to reaching nirvana. In fact, a class of early texts called *jataka* ("birth") tales described in detail the past lives of Gautama Buddha when he was on this bodhisattva path. But Mahayana Buddhists underscored the importance of this figure and transformed its role. Now bodhisattvas were associated with a long list of "perfections," including generosity, moral discipline, patience, exertion, concentration, and wisdom. But their key virtue was compassion. The lofty aspirations of the bodhisattva are elegantly captured in the oft-repeated Bodhisattva Vow:

> Sentient beings are numberless; I vow to liberate them all.
> The afflictions are inexhaustible; I vow to extinguish them all.
> The Buddhist teachings are infinite; I vow to master them all.
> The Buddhist way is unsurpassed; I vow to attain it.

As this vow suggests, bodhisattvas renounced the nirvana of the mainstream arhat in order to remain in the world to alleviate the suffering and promote the awakening of other beings. According to Mahayana Buddhists, these actions demonstrated the superiority of compassionate bodhisattvas to the mainstream tradition's selfish arhats who, because of their single-minded pursuit of their own enlightenment, were always looking out for number one.

Bodhisattvas included Manjusri, the bodhisattva of wisdom, who carries a flaming sword to sever the webs of illusion. The most popular of these figures was (and is) **Avalokiteshvara** ("The Lord Who Looks Down [with compassion]"). This bodhisattva of compassion was typically depicted in India as male. As Buddhism moved into East Asia, he switched genders, taking on a female body as Guanyin in China and Kannon in Japan. Early modern visitors to China described Guanyin as a "Goddess of Mercy" akin to Christianity's Virgin Mary.[14] Some sources depicted this personification of compassion as androgynous. In Tibet, there is a male and a female bodhisattva of compassion; the male is Avalokiteshvara (Chenrezig in Tibetan) and the female aspect is Tara. During Tara's lifetime, monks asked her why she hadn't used the merit she had accumulated to be reborn in her next life as a man. Tara had no interest in that sort of magic. "For all my lifetimes along the path I vow to be born as a woman, and in my final lifetime when I attain buddhahood, I will be a woman," she said.[15]

Mahayana Buddhists did not just worship bodhisattvas, however. They also worshiped **buddhas** (in the plural). Whereas early Buddhists typically insisted that there was just one Buddha per cosmic cycle (Siddhartha Gautama for our age), Mahayana Buddhists worshiped a pantheon of different buddhas. Some even claimed there were as many buddhas as there are sentient beings.

Avalokiteshvara ("The Lord Who Looks Down") bodhisattva of compassion, also known as Guanyin (China), Kannon (Japan), and Chenrezig and Tara (Tibet)

buddha ("awakened one") a being who has achieved enlightenment. The best-known buddha is Siddhartha Gautama.

Recently restored, this elaborate statue of the bodhisattva of compassion Guanyin from the Southern Song dynasty (1127–1279) boasts one thousand hands ready to reach out to her pilgrims at the Dazu Caves in China's Chongqing province.

The fat, happy buddha is a common souvenir across the Buddhist world. These lucky buddhas await purchasers at a street-side stall in Bodh Gaya, India.

Among these buddhas is **Maitreya**, the Buddha to come. Currently a bodhisattva, Maitreya is expected to descend from heaven to earth when Buddhism has disappeared from the world in order to revive the dharma and rule over a new age of spiritual and material well-being. Revered by mainstream and Mahayana Buddhists alike, Maitreya is worshiped particularly fervently in Japan and Korea, where devotees pray, at times, for rebirth in a heavenly place known as Maitreya's Pure Land and, at other times, for rebirth in an era when Maitreya has descended to earth. Like the Coming Christ in Christendom, Maitreya has inspired peasant revolts led by figures who claim that their messiah either has come or is coming soon. Some followers of the Chinese new religious movement Falun Gong claim that their founder Master Li Hongzhi is Maitreya. Throughout East Asia, Maitreya is often depicted as the Laughing Buddha, the fat, happy character known to frequent Chinatown souvenir stands and hotel check-in counters.

Emptiness and Skillful Means Alongside new buddhas and bodhisattvas to worship, the Mahayana tradition offered new philosophical ideas. Mahayana Buddhists claimed that everyone will become a buddha. And then they claimed that all of us already have. In rejecting traditional Hindu notions of the atman, mainstream Buddhists had argued that what we conventionally refer to as the person is actually composed of five "aggregates." Mahayana thinkers took this deconstructive task further, arguing that the *skandhas*, or aggregates of matter, feelings, perception, conditioning factors, and consciousness, were themselves composites and therefore empty of "own being."

Behind this argument was the central teaching of Mahayana Buddhist philosophy: **shunyata**, or emptiness. This teaching is so crucial that some observers have referred to Mahayana as the "emptiness vehicle." Early translators of this term in the modern West rendered shunyata as "nothingness," leading commentators such as the German philosophers G. W. F. Hegel and Friedrich Nietzsche to view Buddhism as pessimistic and even nihilistic. But what emptiness actually means is that all things are interdependent and ever-changing, part of a complicated causal chain, empty of any intrinsic nature or permanent essence. Even the skandhas are empty. And as Avalokitshvara's gender switching demonstrates, so is gender. Equally lacking in permanence and independence are planes and trains and the Four Noble Truths.

Mahayana Buddhists also reconciled their seemingly irreconcilable sutras through the doctrine of "two truths." This doctrine was expounded most famously by **Nagarjuna** (c. 150–250 CE), an Indian philosopher-monk and founder of the Middle Way (Madhyamika) school. Nagarjuna argued that there are two types of truth: the relative truth of appearances and the absolute truth of ultimate reality. From the everyday perspective of relative truth, it is useful to refer to "me" and to preach the Four Noble Truths as wisdom. However, from the perspective of absolute truth, both the self and the Four Noble Truths are empty. In fact, Nagarjuna argues, even emptiness is empty. All this might sound like silly philosophizing—the Indian equivalent of counting the angels on the head of a pin— but the point of Nagarjuna's "Middle Way" was freedom. Only if everything is empty, only if things lack a fixed essence, he argued, is any change (or liberation) possible.

Maitreya
coming buddha, currently residing in a heavenly realm but destined to return to earth

shunyata ("emptiness")
core Mahayana teaching that all things are interdependent and impermanent, empty of independent or essential nature

Nagarjuna (c. 150–250 CE)
influential Indian philosopher of emptiness and founder of Buddhism's "Middle Way" school

As Mahayana Buddhists circulated new texts and new ideas that in many ways contradicted those of the mainstream Buddhists, they struggled to justify these innovations. Why would the Buddha teach one thing (the five skandhas) to early Buddhists and quite another thing (emptiness) later on? The answer they offered was the doctrine of **upaya**, or "skillful means."

Here it must be emphasized that Buddhists have classically viewed sutras as teachings, not divine revelation. The purpose of the sutras was practical, not philosophical. Rather than taking aim at abstract truth, they aimed to eliminate suffering. According to the upaya doctrine, the Buddha taught different things to different people because they needed to hear different things. He was not dogmatic. He was wise, compassionate, and flexible enough to tailor his teachings to particular times and places, even to particular listeners. By this reasoning, Mahayanists were able "both to declare a new teaching and to explain that it was in fact old."[16] By placing their words on the lips of a man who died centuries before Mahayana texts were written, their "skillful means" teaching authorized a stream of new sutras, or teachings of the Buddha, between 200 BCE and 200 CE. Many responded to this proliferation of competing texts by designating one sutra as the singular embodiment of the Buddha's teaching and then forming communities that revered that one text to the exclusion of the others. In fact, this was a defining feature of the Mahayana tradition, which simultaneously justified the endless multiplication of sutras and the choosing of one above the rest.

Competing Sutras: Heart, Diamond, Lotus Of the new sutras, the Heart Sutra and the Diamond Sutra were two of the most popular, though the Lotus Sutra ultimately emerged as the favorite, perhaps because of its emphasis on storytelling. The Heart Sutra, which consists largely of a teaching by Avalokiteshvara to a monk named Shariputra, is said to distill all Mahayana sutras into one short discourse and one key idea. "Form is empty; and emptiness is form," it reads, in one of the most commonly quoted lines in Buddhist life.[17] Among these forms are virtually every teaching anyone has ever attributed to the Buddha, including the Four Noble Truths, which are as empty as the skandhas and the self. This short text—it is just one page long—is called the Heart Sutra because it is said to offer the "heart" of the perfection of wisdom. The most often memorized of the Buddhist sutras, it is recited every day by many monks in East Asia and Tibet. It is also printed on all sorts of Buddhist swag, from teacups and bracelets to prayer wheels and prayer beads.

The Diamond Sutra explores the paradox that bodhisattvas vow to lead all beings from samsara to nirvana while, in actuality, there is no ultimate difference between samsara and nirvana. Chinese translations of this sutra were uncovered by a Daoist monk in caves in Dunhuang in western China in 1900. One of them is the world's oldest dated and printed book. Now housed in the British Museum, this book was block printed on a scroll in 868 CE, making it nearly six hundred years older than the famed Gutenberg Bible.

The Lotus Sutra, a first- or second-century CE Indian text, emerged as the favorite in China and Japan. It also played a huge role in the European and American discoveries of the Buddhist tradition and was translated into French and English in 1844.[18] One of the most radical sutras, it calls

upaya ("skillful means") Mahayana doctrine explaining why the Buddha taught different things to different people, depending on the circumstances

The Wisdom Path on Hong Kong's Lantau Island leads visitors through a winding walkway of wooden stele monuments carved with passages from Buddhism's popular Heart Sutra.

into question many of the most celebrated events in the life of the Buddha, including his enlightenment and death. The Buddha was not awakened under the Bodhi Tree because he had already been awakened long before. And he is immortal, so he only appeared to die. Therefore, there are no relics of the Buddha's corpse inside those tens of thousands of stupas, which are sanctified not by cremated remains but by the living buddhas who inhabit them.

In a famous story in the Lotus Sutra, the Buddha is likened to a father standing outside a burning house with his children inside. What to do? The house is on fire, the house is on fire, the father yells, imploring his children to come out to safety. But the children, engrossed in some ancient analogue to Fortnite or Minecraft, ignore him. So the father changes gears, promising his children that he has even more exciting toys for them outside—an ox-drawn carriage, a goat-drawn carriage, and a deer-drawn carriage. Thrilled at the prospect of these three new toys, the children run out to safety, only to see an even grander toy awaiting them—a carriage drawn by white bullocks and covered with jewels. The father had told a white lie. But that white lie had saved his children from death by fire. As Mahayana Buddhists understand this story, the Buddha is the wise and compassionate person who uses "skillful means" to save us from the burning house of samsara. But the story also has a sectarian bent to it. There are not multiple Buddhist "vehicles," it says, but one.

One of the strategies of the Lotus Sutra is to boast about itself with the swagger of the heavyweight boxing champion Muhammad Ali, who famously proclaimed, "I am the Greatest!" Schools that agreed with this boast included the Tiantai school that began to gestate in China in the sixth century and later spread to Japan (as Tendai), Korea, and Vietnam. But these schools went further than merely boasting about the Lotus Sutra. They argued that there was one and only one path to enlightenment (their own) and one and only one Buddhist scripture that led to buddhahood (the Lotus Sutra).

Mahayana Schools Mahayana Buddhism wasn't principally about texts or philosophy. It was (and is) first and foremost about devotion. Whereas early Buddhists had insisted that each of us must achieve nirvana on our own merits, Mahayana Buddhists said that help was available from others. Buddhas and bodhisattvas possessed great storehouses of merit, and out of compassion they were willing to transfer that merit to their devotees. This emphasis on other-help over self-effort meant that nirvana was made available to not only monks and nuns but also laypeople. It wasn't necessary to devote yourself 24/7 to the austerities of monastic life. All that was necessary was devotion to the buddha or bodhisattva of your choosing.

Just as bhakti ("devotion") triumphed over *jnana* ("wisdom") in Hinduism, Mahayana Buddhism proved to be more popular than mainstream Buddhism. Although it was always a minority movement in India, it dominated as it spread north from India into China and then east into Korea and Japan. It also became popular in Vietnam. As it moved, it spun off new buddhas, new bodhisattvas, new scriptures, and new techniques for the achievement of nirvana.

Chan/Zen One popular Mahayana school took its name from the word "meditation," which is *dhyana* in Sanskrit, *Chan* in Chinese, and **Zen** in Japanese. But the distinctive feature of this school isn't really meditation. It is wisdom directly transmitted.

This school began in China in the sixth century. Roughly two centuries later, it made its way to Korea as *Son* Buddhism. In the thirteenth century, it migrated to Japan as Zen.

Zen
Japanese meditation school, rooted in the Chan tradition of China, that emphasizes either "just sitting" or koan study

BUDDHISM BY THE NUMBERS

Two Buddhist Schools

Mainstream Buddhism	Mahayana Buddhism
earlier school	later school
conservative	adaptive
one Buddha	many buddhas
arhat exemplar	bodhisattva exemplar
self-effort	other-help
anatta (self is empty)	shunyata (everything is empty)
Pali canon	Pali canon plus many Mahayana sutras
popular in South and Southeast Asia	popular in East Asia

Like every Mahayana school, it traces its origins to the Buddha. Its creation story tells of the Buddha standing up to deliver a sermon before a large crowd. Instead of speaking, he holds up a flower. Everyone seems confused. When is the talk going to begin? Then one student smiles. Immediately, the Buddha recognizes that he has transmitted liberating wisdom to this student directly and without words.

The man credited with bringing Chan to China is the celebrated Indian-prince-turned-monk Bodhidharma. According to legend, he sailed from India to China in the fifth century. For nine years he reportedly sat in a cave gazing at a wall. But he was a teacher when he was not a recluse, and the four core teachings of Zen are attributed to him:

1. maintaining a special transmission outside the teachings,
2. not relying upon words and letters,
3. pointing directly at the human mind, and
4. seeing one's own nature and becoming a buddha.[19]

During Japan's Kamakura period (1185–1333), a series of military dictators known as shoguns ruled from Kamakura, a seaside city south of Tokyo that now boasts a large bronze Buddha statue that doubles as an icon of Japan itself. This period was extraordinarily creative for Japanese Buddhists, who oversaw the emergence of various schools of "New Buddhism." These schools were labeled "new" because they differed from older Tendai Buddhism, a Lotus Sutra school centered on Japan's Mount Hiei. They were also new in comparison with older Shingon ("True Word") Buddhism, an esoteric school centered on Mount Koya with affinities to Tibetan Buddhist traditions. Shingon Buddhists claimed that their key figure, the Japanese monk Kukai (744–835), had not actually died in 835 but was simply meditating as he waited for Maitreya. One key feature of Japan's New Buddhists was their exclusivism. Turning their backs on a long tradition of mixing and matching various religious influences without apology or concern, these reformers insisted that there was only one way to practice Buddhism and only one text to revere.

In the Zen tradition, Eisai (1141–1215) was one of these New Buddhists. He founded Rinzai Zen, which featured the **koan**. The term *koan*, derived from the Chinese term

koan
paradoxical word puzzle, typically utilized in the Rinzai Zen tradition, that calls forth a "solution" that eludes rational thinking

gong'an, meaning "public case," referred to an intellectual puzzle meant to open a pathway to sudden enlightenment by frustrating and exhausting the discursive mind. Koans could be questions, but more often they were brief stories or dialogues:

Two hands clap and make a sound; what is the sound of one hand?

A monk asked Ummon, "What is Buddha?" Ummon replied, "A lump of dried shit."

Sekiso asked: "How can you proceed on from the top of a hundred-foot pole?"

A monk asked Joshu, a Chinese Zen master, "Has a dog Buddha-nature or not?" Joshu answered: "Mu."

Basho said to his disciple: "When you have a staff, I will give it to you. If you have no staff, I will take it away from you."

Nansen saw the monks of the eastern and western halls fighting over a cat. He seized the cat and told the monks, "If any of you say a good word, you can save the cat." No one answered. So Nansen boldly cut the cat in two pieces. That evening, Joshu returned and Nansen told him about this. Joshu removed his sandals and, placing them on his head, walked out. Nansen said: "If you had been there, you could have saved the cat."[20]

The Amida Buddha of "Infinite Light" from the Mahayana Pure Land tradition descends from the Pure Land in this sixteenth-century painting from the Japanese Yamato School.

Dogen (1200–1253), who studied under Eisai, rejected this single-minded focus on the koan. His Soto Zen school fixed instead on **zazen**—"just sitting" in the cross-legged lotus position—as the defining Buddhist act. For Dogen, sitting meditation was not a technique to achieve enlightenment, however. It was just what you did when you realized (as he had) that enlightenment was not a *thing* to be achieved. "Practice and realization are identical," Dogen said. "There is not even the slightest gap between resolution, practice, enlightenment, and nirvana."[21]

The Pure Land Japan's two most popular Kamakura-era Buddhist schools were both of the Pure Land variety. **Pure Land Buddhism** goes back to texts and traditions revering a Buddha named **Amitabha** ("Infinite Light") who seems to have been popular in India and China at least as early as the third century. This Buddha, known as **Amida** in Japan, was famous for vowing to create out of his vast storehouse of merit a "Land of Bliss" of unimaginable beauty and power known as the Pure Land. But he vowed to do more than simply create this "buddha field." He vowed to see to it that all who called upon him at death would be reborn in his Pure Land. Classically, these Pure Lands were interpreted as halfway houses of sorts where everything—from songbirds to blades of grass—worked together to ensure that their inhabitants would reach nirvana. Over time, however, as being reborn there replaced reaching nirvana as the religious goal of many Buddhists, these Pure Lands became ends in themselves. Today, the most popular Mahayana schools are of this Pure Land variety.

Pure Land Buddhism in Kamakura Japan carried the Mahayana reliance on other-help to its logical conclusion. According to the Buddhist reformer Honen (1133–1212), since Amida Buddha had vowed to allow anyone who asked for his help to be reborn in his Pure Land, all that was

In this nineteenth-century woodcut by the Japanese artist Utagawa Kuniyoshi, the Japanese Buddhist monk Nichiren makes a snowy ascent on the island of Sado in 1271. He was exiled there by Japan's Kamakura shogunate for espousing improper Buddhist views.

required to be reborn there was to call on his name. Honen and his later Jodoshu ("Pure Land School") followers did so by chanting the *nembutsu*: *Namu Amida Butsu* ("Homage to Amida Buddha"). Convinced that this chant was the only effective practice in our degenerate age, Honen practiced it obsessively, reportedly completing as many as seventy thousand nembutsus a day.

Shinran (1173–1263), another Japanese Buddhist reformer and a student of Honen, took this view to a different logical extreme. Since the Pure Land came as a gift from the Amida Buddha, he reasoned, it was neither necessary nor desirable to repeatedly chant the nembutsu. Neither was it necessary for monks to remain celibate, as Honen's monks did. (Shinran himself married a nun and had five children.) All that was necessary was to trust in the Amida Buddha and be grateful for his help. Because this approach seems to anticipate Protestant notions of "salvation by faith through grace," Shinran has been called "the Martin Luther of Japan" (after the German Protestant reformer).[22] Shinran's Jodo Shinshu ("True Pure Land") school is the most popular form of Buddhism in Japan today. Its American incarnation, the Buddhist Churches of America, is one of the oldest and largest U.S. Buddhist organizations.

Another radical simplifier of Japanese Buddhism was Nichiren (1222–1282), a fisherman-turned-Tendai monk who, like Pure Land Buddhists, focused on chanting rather than meditation and on other-help rather than self-effort. Everyone, no matter how lowly, Nichiren said, could achieve enlightenment via devotion to the Lotus Sutra. After immersing himself in various Japanese Buddhist options, he decided they were all worthless. "The nembutsu (Amida sects) is hell; Zen is a devil; Shingon is the nation's ruin," he said.[23] Nichiren divided world history into different ages. In our modern age of degeneration, he argued, the only true Buddhist sutra was the Lotus Sutra. It alone was to be read, chanted, and worshiped. All other sutras were to be rejected as heretical, and

zazen
seated meditation in the Chan/Zen tradition

Pure Land Buddhism
Buddhist branch popular in East Asia that takes rebirth in the Pure Land of Amitabha/Amida Buddha as its goal

Amitabha/Amida ("Infinite Light")
Buddha of the Mahayana Pure Land schools

any practice other than Nichiren's *daimoku* chant—*Namu Myoho Renge Kyo* ("Homage to the Lotus Sutra")—was ineffective.

Merging nationalism with religion in an era of widespread anxiety about an impending Mongol invasion, Nichiren blamed a run of natural disasters on Zen and Pure Land Buddhism, adding that only by chanting the daimoku could Japan avoid further calamities. Because of his intolerance of other forms of Buddhism and his eagerness to take on the Japanese government, Nichiren was exiled twice and narrowly escaped a death sentence. He responded by glorying in his persecution as do the many Nichiren Buddhists who revere him today.

Tibetan Buddhism

According to legend, Buddhism ascended to "the roof of the world" in Tibet in the seventh century when two wives of King Songtsen Gampo, one Chinese and one Nepalese, convinced him to convert to Buddhism. Tibetan sources say that Songtsen's Chinese wife, Princess Wencheng, arrived in Tibet with a statue of Shakyamuni Buddha that now commands the center of the most visited shrine in Tibet, Lhasa's Jokhang Temple. Songtsen's Nepalese wife, Princess Devi, also brought icons to Tibet, but she brought craftsmen as well who later built the Red Palace in Lhasa. Both of these women would come to be revered as incarnations of the popular bodhisattva Tara. Songsten would oversee both the transformation of Tibetan into a written language and the translation of Buddhist texts.

During this "first transmission of the dharma," Buddhism superseded indigenous Bon traditions as Tibet's national religion, even as Tibetans integrated shamanistic elements from Bon into the Mahayana Buddhist tradition as part of a broader process of Tibetanization. The semilegendary eighth-century figure Padmasambhava ("Lotus-born"), popularly known as Guru Rinpoche, was credited with converting preexisting Tibetan gods and goddesses into Buddhist powers.

This first transmission era ended with King Langdarma, who came to power in 836. Siding with powerful Bon families, he persecuted Buddhists until his assassination at the hand of a Buddhist monk in 842. This ended the line of Tibetan kings and plunged Buddhism in Tibet into a difficult century and a half when political order collapsed and the only real prize for Buddhists was survival. As patronage evaporated, monasteries closed, and monastics were forced to reenter secular life.

Beginning in the tenth or eleventh century, dynamic exchanges between Indian and Tibetan thinkers stimulated the "second transmission of the dharma" and royal patronage of Buddhism resumed. This second stage in Tibetan Buddhist history was informed by traditional Buddhist sutras as well as **Tantras**, esoteric texts that originated by the eighth century in India and were then adapted to Buddhist circumstances in Tibet, China, and Japan. These texts were secret rather than public—esoteric rather than exoteric. And their truths were often transmitted directly, outside of those texts themselves, from **lamas** ("gurus" or "teachers") to students. Tantric texts and teachers emphasized the divine power of the feminine (*shakti*) that courses through the cosmos and the human body. They affirmed, in word and deed, the nonduality of seemingly opposite things even as they worked to break down conventional barriers between ritual purity and ritual pollution. They offered a variety of secretive techniques that promised a quicker path to enlightenment. Among their hidden practices, which were

Tantra
esoteric Indian texts and traditions, influential among Tibetan Buddhists, that describe and cultivate the worship of buddhas and bodhisattvas

lama
Tibetan Buddhist term for teacher or guru

often associated with indulging desires rather than renouncing them, were various sexual *yogas* ("disciplines").

One byproduct of these practices was supernatural power (*siddhi*) of the sort now associated with comic book superbeings. However, instead of having only one superpower, these superheroes had a long menu of them: "clairvoyance, clairaudience, telepathy, teleportation, the ability to fly, the ability to walk through walls, the ability to stop the movement of the sun, the ability to transmute base metals into gold, the ability to find buried treasure, the ability to attract a love, the ability to destroy an enemy, and so on."[24] According to one famous story written in India in the eleventh or twelfth century, a Tantric yogi named Virupa was drinking in a tavern and running up a massive bill. When asked to pay, he promised to do so when the sun went down. He then used his superpower to stop the sun in its tracks. It didn't move for three days. Neither did Virupa, whose excessive drinking became even more excessive. Finally, a king intervened and paid the bill. Virupa unstopped the sun and staggered away.

Tibetans who told stories like these looked back to four Tibetan schools developed in this "second transmission" era, including the Nyingma, which traced its origins back to the time of Padmasambhava. Among these newcomers, the most influential would be the *Geluk* ("System of Virtue") school of today's Dalai Lama, popularly known as the "Yellow Hats" because of their iconic tall yellow headgear. The thinker credited with founding this school is Tsongkhapa (1357–1419). His influential interpretation of Nagarjuna's "two truths" theory distinguished between "conventional" and "ultimate" truths. Conventional truths are "unreal and deceptive" yet useful in everyday life. Ultimate truths are "real and nondeceptive" yet not particularly useful in everyday life. "When an ordinary conventional mind takes a table as its object of observation, it sees a table," explains Buddhologist Guy Newland in an important passage on Tsongkhapa. "When a mind of ultimate analysis searches for the table, it finds the emptiness of the table."[25] To apply this observation to religious studies, we might say that, from the perspective of ultimate truth, terms like "Buddhism" and "religion" are empty, but for those of us who operate in the realm of conventional truths, they are useful nonetheless.

The most fascinating Tibetan Buddhist innovation was the *tulku*, or "reborn lama." The new idea here was not that lamas can be reborn. Throughout their history, Buddhists have affirmed that buddhas and bodhisattvas take on bodies and return to earth in order to help other beings. The new idea was that reincarnated lamas could be identified as children. This innovation allowed for a new sort of religious inheritance in which the successor of a lama was tapped by searching for the lama's reincarnation.

All four schools have tulkus, and there were thousands of these incarnate lamas in Tibet. The most famous was the Dalai Lama. Like the term "Christ," *Dalai Lama* ("Ocean Teacher") is a title rather than a proper name, referring to the spiritual and political leader of the Tibetan people, who is simultaneously revered as the rebirth of a prior Dalai Lama and a reincarnation of the bodhisattva Chenrezig. The first Dalai Lama was recognized in the fifteenth century. In 1642, the Fifth Dalai Lama (1617–1682), who sided with Mongol forces in their takeover of Tibet, was rewarded with political control of the region. This inaugurated a theocratic tradition that integrated spiritual and political control of Tibet under the leadership of a series of Dalai Lamas from the seventeenth to the twenty-first century.

Today's Dalai Lama, Tenzin Gyatso, is the fourteenth in this lineage. When he fled to India in 1959 to escape Chinese forces, he became the world's most famous refugee. As others fled with him, Tibetans scattered into a diaspora that brought one of the world's most secretive religions into the global spotlight. For his nonviolent struggle against Tibetan genocide, the Dalai Lama won the Nobel Peace Prize in 1989. During the 1990s, he was also a darling of Hollywood, his story retold in a series of feature films.

Amidst the ongoing controversy surrounding the Chinese occupation of Tibet, many Tibetan Buddhists today are concerned that the Chinese government might tap its own Fifteenth Dalai Lama after the bodily death of the current Dalai Lama. He has responded to these concerns by hinting that he might choose to be reborn in the United States or, perhaps, not to be reborn at all. He has also suggested that, if reborn, he might incarnate as a woman.

Today, Tibetan Buddhism is understood as an esoteric expression of Mahayana Buddhism. All religions are creoles, creative compositions of their forbears' beliefs and practices, but Tibetan Buddhism is a particularly intriguing mix, combining Tantrism with elements from mainstream and Mahayana Buddhism. Practiced in Japan (where it is known as Shingon), it is now the dominant form of Buddhism in the Himalayas and Central Asia, from Tibet through Nepal, Bhutan, and Mongolia. It goes by many names, including Vajrayana Buddhism, from the Sanskrit terma *vajra*, which means "thunderbolt" or "diamond," and *yana*, which means "vehicle." This image of an indestructible Buddhism underscores this tradition's emphasis on power—the power to help others and the power to achieve enlightenment quickly and efficiently (even in one lifetime).

Today, there are a variety of Tibetan Buddhist sects. The "Ancient Ones" (Nyingmapa), who trace their roots to Padmasambhava, are one of the groups known as "Red Hats" because of the garb favored by their lamas. The lay lamas in this Ancient Ones tradition

"Yellow Hat" Tibetan Buddhist monks from the Tashi Lhunpo monastery in India lead a procession along a beach in South Wales in the United Kingdom after completing a five-day sand mandala ceremony.

are not celibate and typically pass down their authority to their sons. The "New Ones" (Sarma) schools—of which the yellow hat "Virtuous Ones" (Geluk) group is best known—follow later teachings, including those of Tsongkhapa. Monks in these New Ones lineages, which include the Geluk Dalai Lama, practice celibacy, so new lamas are located after elaborate searches for their various reincarnations.

As in other Mahayana groups, lay practices in Vajrayana include giving alms to monks and nuns, offering *puja* ("worship") to bodhisattvas, especially to Chenrezig and his consort Tara, and turning prayer wheels with petitions to buddhas or bodhisattvas. More advanced practices (for monks and nuns and lay practitioners who have entered Tantric practice) include reciting **mantras**, especially "*Om mani padme hum*" ("Om, [Homage to You Who Hold] the Jewel in the Lotus"); mandala visualization meditation, in which one conjures up an image of oneself as a buddha at the center of a cosmic map known as a **mandala**; and partaking of the "Five Forbidden Things" (wine, meat, fish, parched grain, and sex). Together, these rites are said to be far more powerful than parallel practices in the mainstream or Mahayana traditions—so powerful that they can produce buddhahood "in this very body and in this very lifetime, not through a suppression of desire and the sensual but through the discovery of ultimate reality even there."[26] However, these rites were also aimed at thisworldly goals, including health, wealth, and power.

Derived from Indian Tantra, the sexual rites in Tibetan Buddhism are supposed to be undertaken only by advanced students under the guidance of a lama. For this reason, before one begins advanced Tantric practice, one must make an additional vow to take refuge in one's lama, not simply the Buddha, the dharma, and the sangha. Practitioners of this sexual yoga see the passions not as inherent evils but as energy that can be channeled in positive or negative directions. "Right-hand" practitioners of Tantra typically saw the union of masculine and feminine energies as symbolic, while "left-hand" practitioners actually engaged in ritual sexual intercourse. In each case, the female was seen as embodying wisdom and the male as embodying skillful means. One goal of sexual yoga was to overcome desire by indulging it ritually; another was to transcend dualistic thinking, including the dualisms of proper and improper, male and female, wisdom and compassion, nirvana and samsara, buddhas and non-buddhas, and the "objective" and "subjective" worlds.

Buddhism in the Modern World

More than any other major religion, Buddhism emphasizes the inevitability of change. So it should not be surprising that the Buddhist tradition changed as it moved around the world and adapted to modern life.

Protestant Buddhism In nineteenth-century Ceylon, a reformation of sorts produced "Protestant Buddhism," a "complex creolization" of the traditional Theravada Buddhism of that island nation and the liberal Protestantism of the United States.[27] The initial catalyst of what came to be known as the Sinhalese Buddhist revival was Henry Steel Olcott (1832–1907), the first American formally to convert to Buddhism. In 1875 in New York City, Olcott and the Russian occultist Helena Blavatsky cofounded the Theosophical Society in an effort, first, to investigate alleged spiritualist communications with the dead and, later, to spread the truths of Asian religions in the West. In 1878, Olcott and Blavatsky moved to India, later establishing the headquarters of their fledgling organization

mantra
short verbal formulation used in chanting or meditation

mandala ("circle")
map of a buddha palace used in meditation and devotion, particularly in Tibetan Buddhism

in Adyar, a suburb of Madras (now Chennai) in South India. In 1880 in Ceylon, they formally converted to Buddhism.

Almost immediately, Olcott discerned a huge gap between the textual Buddhism he had learned in books and the lived Buddhism practiced on the ground in Ceylon. Rather than deciding that there was something wrong with his Buddhism, Olcott decided that there was something wrong with theirs. He started a massive movement to reform Sinhalese Buddhism and to create an ecumenical "International Buddhist League" aimed at fostering a "United Buddhist World." Working with the Sinhalese Buddhist reformer Anagarika Dharmapala (1864–1933), "the White Buddhist," as Olcott came to be known, debated Christian missionaries on the island and started a Buddhist revival. He established Buddhist schools and colleges. He wrote a Buddhist creed and designed a Buddhist flag. His *Buddhist Catechism* (1881), which described his adopted religion as both rational and scientific, was eventually translated into twenty languages.

Although Olcott claimed to be restoring original Buddhism, he actually helped create Protestant Buddhism. Though this creole tradition was a reaction against Protestantism, it was also profoundly influenced by it. Like the gospel of the Protestant missionaries whose proselytizing he denounced, Olcott's faith was activistic, optimistic, and progressive. He, too, preached temperance, promoted the translation of scriptures into vernacular languages, and conducted revivals. As a result of his efforts, generations of Buddhists on the island were educated in Buddhist rather than Christian schools, and Protestant Buddhism became and continues to be the tradition of choice for many English-speaking, middle-class Sri Lankans.[28]

Soka Gakkai International The Meiji Restoration of 1868, which returned imperial rule to Japan after a series of Tokugawa clan shoguns from 1603 to 1867, is best known as a period of modernization and westernization. It also had major religious implications. Like modernizers in twentieth-century China who would reject Confucianism as a relic of an ancient past, the Meiji government rejected Buddhism as antimodern. However, government support for the indigenous religion of Shinto combined with the persecution of Buddhists created space for new religious movements, many inspired by Buddhist symbols and stories as well as elements from Shinto and Christianity.

A Soka Gakkai International (SGI) member chants in front of her home altar. As Nichiren Buddhists, SGI members chant *Namu Myoho Renge Kyo* ("Homage to the Lotus Sutra").

Soka Gakkai ("Value Creation Society") began in the 1930s as a lay organization within Nichiren Shoshu ("True Nichiren"). It spread rapidly after World War II, founding a university and its own political party, but it broke from Nichiren Shoshu in 1991 in an angry and public dispute over (among other things) whether the sangha should include priests only or both priests and laypeople. Today, Soka Gakkai International (SGI) is the largest "new religion" in Japan. It is also popular in Korea, Hong Kong, Taiwan, Brazil, Peru, Southeast Asia, and the United States, where it is one of the only Buddhist convert groups with a significant nonwhite population.

In the United States, Soka Gakkai gave birth to an organization of priests and laypeople called Nichiren Shoshu of America (NSA). The NSA eventually split into a priestly organization and a much larger lay organization called Soka Gakkai International-USA, which has

B. R. Ambedkar (1891–1956)

Many modern Indian leaders worked to reform the caste system, but the politician B. R. Ambedkar, himself a Dalit, or "untouchable," thought that was a lost cause. "Why do you remain in that religion which insults you at every step?" he asked.[a] The only way to leave untouchability behind was to exit Hinduism, so he vowed to find another religion.

Born in western India, Ambedkar received doctorates from New York's Columbia University and the London School of Economics after studying with the likes of the philosopher John Dewey and the historian Charles Beard. When independence came to India in 1947, he played a major role in crafting the Indian constitution, which outlawed discrimination against so-called scheduled-caste Indians and put an end to untouchability. Throughout his public career, Ambedkar weighed the merits of various religions, including Christianity and Islam, as alternatives to Hinduism, which he rejected as irrational, inhumane, and nonegalitarian. He finally settled on Buddhism because of its Indian roots and the Buddha's critique of the caste system. On October 14, 1956, just a few weeks before his death, Ambedkar and hundreds of thousands of his fellow Dalits renounced Hinduism and converted to Buddhism at a mass spectacle in Deekshabhoomi, Nagpur, India. According to Ambedkar, this conversion was also a return, since in his view Dalits were originally Buddhists, whom Brahmin elites had relegated in ancient times to untouchability.

Ambedkar's Navayana ("New Buddhism") departed from more traditional understandings of Buddhism by interpreting suffering in social rather than personal terms—as a product not of individual karma but of social injustice. His followers today gather in the Mumbai-based Buddhist Society of India (est. 1955).

attracted a diverse mix of adherents, including many African Americans and Hispanics. (Pop icon Tina Turner is one high-profile member.) Before that schism, NSA members put on a "Spirit of '76" spectacular on the American bicentennial. Gathering on July 4, 1976, at Shea Stadium in New York City, their show dramatized key moments in American history, including George Washington praying at Valley Forge (though in this case he did so in the lotus position).

Engaged Buddhism At least since the nineteenth century, Westerners have criticized Buddhists for focusing on individual suffering to the exclusion of social justice. Practitioners of **Engaged Buddhism**, a term coined in the 1960s by the Vietnamese Zen monk Thich Nhat Hanh (1926–), refute this stereotype of escapism by applying long-standing Buddhist values to the social, political, economic, and ecological problems of today. "The practice should address suffering: the suffering within yourself and the suffering around you," Thich Nhat Hanh has said. "Once there is seeing, there must be action. Otherwise, what is the use of seeing?"[29]

Thich Nhat Hanh's activism was influenced by the examples of Gandhi and Ambedkar in India, by the Reverend Martin Luther King Jr. and the civil rights movement in the United States, and by protests in his homeland and abroad against the Vietnam War. He and other Engaged Buddhists typically point to Buddhist values such as compassion and loving-kindness and to Buddhist concepts such as interdependence as key motivators for their thisworldly activism. The aim of the bodhisattva, they insist, is to help others overcome suffering.

Engaged Buddhism
modern form of Buddhism that emphasizes thisworldly activism on behalf of those who are suffering

Engaged Buddhism spread throughout Asia in the last few decades of the twentieth century, as practitioners grappled with issues such as the occupation of Tibet, genocide in Cambodia, and government repression in Burma. Sarvodaya Shramadana, a Sri Lankan NGO founded in 1958 by the high school teacher Dr. A. T. Ariyaratne, worked for peace between warring Sinhalese Buddhists and Hindu Tamils. Today, it advances a middle path between capitalism and communism that it refers to as "Buddhist economics." Meanwhile, "ecology monks" in Thailand struggle against deforestation, and a group called Tzu Chi offers free medical care in Taiwan.

Toward the end of the twentieth century, Engaged Buddhism also took off in the West. Thich Nhat Hanh's Order of Interbeing has been particularly influential in Europe and the United States. So have his "Fourteen Precepts of Engaged Buddhism," which include the following:

> Do not accumulate wealth while millions are hungry. Do not take as the aim of your life fame, profit, wealth, or sensual pleasure. . . .
>
> Do not use the Buddhist community for personal gain or profit, or transform your community into a political party. . . .
>
> Do not live with a vocation that is harmful to humans and nature. Do not invest in companies that deprive others of their chance to live. . . .
>
> Do not kill. Do not let others kill. Find whatever means possible to protect life and prevent war.[30]

Some critics have denounced Engaged Buddhism as fake Buddhism—an outgrowth of Christian rather than Buddhist values. But Thich Nhat Hanh insists that "Engaged Buddhism is just Buddhism," which has never been disengaged from worldly concerns.[31] The religious studies scholar Sallie King has similarly argued that "Engaged Buddhism is a thoroughly Buddhist phenomenon."[32] A mediating position here is to see Engaged Buddhism as a new yana, very much a part of Buddhism yet distinct from the mainstream and Mahayana vehicles. Most participants, however, see Engaged Buddhism as an impulse inside each of these schools, urging Buddhists of all sorts to act compassionately not only on themselves but also on the wider world—to bring the insights of Buddhism to prisons and homeless shelters as well as meditation halls and Zen centers.

BUDDHISM IN THE UNITED STATES

The transmission of Buddhism to the United States and its adaptation to American cultures has been textual, aesthetic, and interpersonal, driven at various times by Buddhist books, Buddhist art, and Buddhist teachers. The reception of Buddhism by Americans has also moved through various Buddhist vogues, with one focused on Zen in the 1950s and 1960s and another focused on Tibet in the 1990s.

Word of Buddhism first arrived in the United States through books. In 1844, the French Orientalist Eugene Burnouf authored the first scholarly book on Buddhism for a Western audience. That same year, Elizabeth Peabody translated a portion of the Lotus Sutra from Burnouf's French into English for the Transcendentalist periodical *The Dial*. From their home base in Concord, Massachusetts, Ralph Waldo Emerson, Henry David Thoreau, and other New England Transcendentalists read widely in Asian scriptures. In fact, theirs was the first American movement to reject missionary critiques of "heathenism" in favor of a sympathetic engagement with Asian religions. (Thoreau compared "their Christ" to "my Buddha" and found Jesus wanting.[33]) Nonetheless, there was much confusion, even in cosmopolitan Concord, about the Buddhist tradition. In an 1845 letter, Emerson referred to the Hindu scripture the Bhagavad Gita as "the much renowned book of Buddhism."[34]

These early encounters were not merely textual, however. They were interpersonal and material as well. American missionaries encountered Buddhists on the ground across Asia, and Olcott conversed with monks from Ceylon to Japan. Meanwhile, "Boston Buddhists" such as Ernest Fenollosa and William Sturgis Bigelow learned much of what they knew about the Buddhist tradition from Buddhist art in Japanese temples. But Buddhism's real coming-out party in the United States came at the World's Parliament of Religions in Chicago in 1893, when Americans came face-to-face with the Sinhalese Buddhist revivalist Anagarika Dharmapala and the Rinzai Zen monk Soyen Shaku.

As immigration from Asia picked up beginning in the mid-nineteenth century, Asian immigrants began to arrive on American shores. It now became possible for white converts and sympathizers to learn about Buddhism from living, breathing Buddhists rather than from Buddhist books or Buddhist art. More important, immigrants now began to define American Buddhism on their own terms. Pulled by the discovery of gold at John Sutter's sawmill in 1848, and pushed by war, poverty, and natural disasters, Chinese "forty-niners" came to the United States and brought their religions with them. In San Francisco in 1853, they built the first Chinese temple in America. It combined Buddhist, Daoist, Confucian, and Chinese folk influences. By the end of the nineteenth century there were roughly four hundred such temples up and down the West Coast.

As intellectuals debated the "Chinese Question," nativist groups such as the Asiatic Exclusion League made life difficult for Chinese immigrants. In 1882, the Chinese Exclusion Act halted Chinese immigration to the United States, but Japanese immigrants

Members of the Hompa Hongwanji Buddhist Temple in Los Angeles gather for worship in 1964. Established in 1905, this Japanese Buddhist community is part of the Pure Land stream of Mahayana Buddhism called Jodo Shinshu ("True Pure Land").

Manzanar Monument

Not all of the Japanese interned during World War II were Buddhists, but almost all Japanese Buddhists on the West Coast were interned. Internees made furniture and other everyday objects out of scrap lumber and the tools needed to craft them. They also made Buddhist art: paintings and sculpture and even small Buddhist shrines, despite prohibitions against Buddhist materials in the internment camps.

The first camp grew out of desert sand in Manzanar, California, on March 21, 1942, and housed more than eleven thousand Japanese Americans in military-style barracks before it closed on November 21, 1945. Since 1969, an annual Manzanar Pilgrimage has brought people to the camp, which is now a

National Historic Site. Its cemetery includes a permanent piece of Buddhist art: a modest obelisk paid for in part by families in the camp and completed with the help of the Young Buddhist Association. It is painted white, the color of death in Japan. The black Japanese Kanji characters etched into it were written by the Reverend Shinjo Nagatomi, an interned Buddhist minister. They read, on the front, "Soul Consoling Tower" and, on the back, "Erected by the Manzanar Japanese, August 1943."

In recent years, this monument has become the terminus of the annual pilgrimage commemorating the internment camp experience. People who come to this place often leave things behind: "a seashell, a Powerpuff Girl toy, a beaded bracelet, a Ganesh figurine, a rubber ball, an enameled pin, sticks of incense bound together."[a] Decorating the fence that surrounds the memorial are hundreds of origami cranes, symbolizing the ancient bird of happiness that can live for a thousand years and carry souls beyond suffering. In recent years, these cranes have also come to be symbols of healing from Hiroshima, Japan, to the World Trade Center site in New York City. As at the Vietnam Memorial in Washington, DC, National Park Service employees occasionally gather up the offerings that have been left behind and archive and store them. One note, left with a decorated teakettle, reads, "We are so sorry that this tragedy ever happened and are here to pay our respects."[b]

continued to come to Hawaii in the 1880s and to the mainland in significant numbers a decade later, prompting nativists to decry a new "Yellow Peril." The first Japanese temple in Hawaii was built by a Jodo Shinshu group in 1896. Three years later, two Japanese Buddhist monks, Shuye Sonoda and Kakuryo Nishijima, arrived in San Francisco as the first full-time Buddhist missionaries to the United States. Together they founded a True Pure Land group called the Buddhist Mission of North America (BMNA).

On February 19, 1942, during World War II, U.S. president Franklin Delano Roosevelt signed Executive Order 9066 instructing the War Department to forcibly relocate "enemy aliens" from the West Coast. As a result of this policy, nearly 120,000 Japanese Americans, including virtually every BMNA priest, were rounded up and imprisoned in ten internment camps across the United States. In an effort to demonstrate their Americanness, BMNA leaders at a camp in Topaz, Arizona, changed the name of this organization to the Buddhist Churches of America (BCA). They also learned how to survive under harsh desert circumstances. They hung American flags and images of the Buddha on their barrack walls. They called their leaders "ministers" and "bishops" and they included in their new hymnal such songs as "Onward Buddhist Soldiers."

After World War II, Zen emerged as the Asian religion of choice among non-Asian Americans. D. T. Suzuki (1870–1966), a key popularizer of Zen in the modern West, had accompanied Soyen Shaku to the World's Parliament of Religions. He published English translations of Zen texts; lectured at Harvard, Columbia, and other prestigious American universities; and was profiled in *Vogue* and *The New Yorker*. Although Suzuki devoted his life to translating and writing, he was convinced that enlightenment comes suddenly, in a flash of intuitive insight called *satori*. On the path to this experience, Zen texts and doctrines were of little use insofar as they channel our awareness into intellectual streams. The satori experience was better catalyzed instead via art forms such as haiku, brush painting, calligraphy, and the tea ceremony, which tap into the nondiscursive, nonrational parts of the human being.

Beginning with the Beat writers of the 1950s, this understanding of Zen proved quite popular in the United States. In part through the influence of Suzuki, whom the Beat writer Jack Kerouac met in Manhattan in 1957 just before a book party for the release of his novel *On the Road*, Beat writers embraced Zen as a spiritual alternative to the materialism of Eisenhower's America. Kerouac was himself more attracted to the Pure Land tradition and in the end remained committed to the Roman Catholicism of his youth. Nonetheless, Zen commitments to freedom, naturalness, and spontaneity quickly made their way into American music, dance, painting, and literature. "Zen Buddhism," *Time* magazine observed in 1958, "is growing more chic by the minute."[35] Bestselling books such as Robert Pirsig's *Zen and the Art of Motorcycle Maintenance* (1974) followed Suzuki in lauding Zen for its nonconformity and spontaneity. Contemporary Buddhist scholars, however, criticize "Suzuki Zen" as a modern construct more faithful to the romantic yearnings of countercultural Westerners (and to Suzuki's admiration for the Protestant philosopher-psychologist William James) than to the Zen tradition itself. There is plenty of ritual and doctrine in Zen, they argue, and a long history of painstaking study of Buddhist texts.

American Buddhism changed decisively with the passage of the Hart-Celler Act of 1965, which opened U.S. borders to immigration from Asia. A few Tibetan lamas and Japanese Zen masters had come earlier, including Geshe Wangyal, a Mongolian teacher who established the first Tibetan monastery in the United States in 1958, and Shunryu Suzuki, author of *Zen Mind, Beginner's Mind* (1970), who founded the San Francisco Zen Center in 1962. In the mid-1960s, however, that trickle turned to a flood, and in short order virtually every major form of Buddhism had a foothold in the United States.

Most of the immigrants who benefited from the Hart-Celler Act channeled their Buddhist energies into building and maintaining temples, which often doubled as cultural centers for Vietnamese or Tibetans or Koreans in their respective diasporas. Some Buddhist teachers reached out to converts and sympathizers, however. Soon the countercultural icon Timothy Leary was celebrating the Buddha as an avatar of his "Drop out / Turn on / Tune in" mantra; poet Gary Snyder was penning "Smokey the Bear Sutra"; and the pop philosopher Alan Watts was spreading his own hybrid faith, which he described as "between Mahayana Buddhism and Taoism, with a certain leaning towards Vedanta and Catholicism."[36] Convert groups also constructed elaborate temples, including the Hsi Lai Temple in suburban Los Angeles—the largest Buddhist temple in the Western Hemisphere.

Buddhism also made its way into popular culture via bestselling "Zen and" books, and celebrity converts such as NBA coach Phil Jackson and actor Richard Gere. Buddhism

The Hsi Lai ("Coming to the West") Temple in the Hacienda Heights neighborhood of Los Angeles is home to one of the largest Chinese Buddhist communities in North America. The architecture of the main hall depicted here reflects the style of traditional Chinese monasteries.

was a topic as well at the U.S. Supreme Court, where, in *U.S. v. Seeger* (1965), Justice William Douglas referred to the United States not as a Christian nation but "a nation of Buddhists, Confucianists, and Taoists, as well as Christians."[37] A Tibetan Buddhist vogue in the 1990s prompted a *Time* magazine cover story on "America's Fascination with Buddhism" as well as a number of Hollywood films with Buddhist themes, including *Little Buddha* (1993) starring Keanu Reeves and *Seven Years in Tibet* (1997) starring Brad Pitt.

Key trends in American Buddhism today include laicization, feminization, secularization, and social engagement. Influenced by both the Enlightenment commitment to equality and the Protestant principle of the priesthood of all believers, U.S. Buddhists have narrowed the traditional gap between monastics and laypeople. Members of the San Francisco Zen Center elect their spiritual leaders—a practice unknown in Buddhist Asia. And many U.S. laypeople engage in contemplative practices traditionally confined to monks or nuns. One institution that reflects this trend is the retreat, which offers the laity an opportunity to act like nuns or monks for a weekend at a Buddhist center while offering monastics a source of income in a society in which wealthy patrons are hard to come by.

The feminization of U.S. Buddhism is evident not only among the rank-and-file, which by most estimates is greater than 50 percent female, but also among leaders. In the United States, women author bestselling Buddhist books and occupy professorships in Buddhist studies. *Tricycle: The Buddhist Review*, the most popular Buddhist magazine in the United States, was founded in 1991 by Helen Tworkov, and the first Buddhist elected to the U.S. Congress, Rep. Mazie Hirono (D-Hawaii), is also a woman.

In one of the most significant post-1965 developments in American Buddhism, women such as Joan Halifax of the Upaya Zen Center and Sharon Salzberg of the Insight Meditation Society have ascended to leadership roles in many Buddhist communities. Born in England and raised as an Anglican, Jiyu Kennett founded Shasta Abbey, the first Soto Zen monastery in the United States, in 1970. Like many other U.S. Buddhist leaders, she Americanized Buddhism by Christianizing it. She wore a clerical collar that made her look like an Episcopal priest and introduced Gregorian-style chanting at Shasta Abbey. "The norm for religious dress in this country is a collar turned backwards and a shirt," she said. "Why have we got to go around pretending we're Japanese or Chinese or Thai?"[38]

The secularization trend, which goes back to efforts by Olcott and scholarly Orientalists to make the Buddhist tradition more "rational" and "scientific," is evident today in the writing of Stephen Batchelor. The author of *Buddhism without Beliefs* (1997), Batchelor rejects such traditional Buddhist doctrines as karma and rebirth as "religious" holdovers from ancient Indian civilization and therefore external to the Buddhist project, which he describes as secular.

Secular Buddhism is also visible in a variety of efforts to bring Buddhist practices into the public square in a society in which the separation of church and state is enshrined in the Constitution. It is much easier to bring mindfulness meditation, for example, into public schools, prisons, and hospitals if it is billed as a stress-reduction technique than if it is presented as a religious ritual. The motto of a website called Secular Buddhism sums up this approach quite neatly: "No robes. No ritual. No religion."[39]

A fourth and final trend in American Buddhism is social engagement. Many American Buddhists are Engaged Buddhists, and many leading organizations in Engaged Buddhism—such as the Buddhist Peace Fellowship (est. 1978) and Zen Peacemakers (est. 1996)—are based in the United States.

American Buddhism was rocked in the late twentieth century by a series of sex scandals that were far less visible than those of the Roman Catholic Church but every bit as earth-shaking inside the affected organizations, which run from the San Francisco Zen Center to the Zen Center of Los Angeles to the Manhattan-based Zen Studies Society. In a particularly notorious scandal, Osel Tendzin of the Vajradhatu community was charged with having unprotected sex with a variety of students while infected with HIV. Both Tendzin and one of his male students later died of AIDS.

Assessing the number of Buddhists in the United States is a tricky business. The 2010 U.S. Religious Census on Religious Congregations and Membership Study found 2,854 Buddhist centers, but estimates for the numbers of Buddhists who populate them (or simply practice Buddhism at home) vary wildly—from roughly 1 to 6 million. The 2020 estimate of the World Religion Database—4.5 million, or 1.4 percent of the overall population— seems reasonable. But adherents are only part of the story, since in the United States sympathizers abound—bookstore Buddhists who read Buddhist literature and weekend Buddhists who populate Buddhist retreats. According to one survey, one-seventh of Americans have had some significant contact with Buddhism, and one-eighth say Buddhism has influenced their religious lives.[40]

LIVED BUDDHISM

One typically becomes a Buddhist by taking refuge in the Buddha, the dharma, and the sangha (the "Three Jewels"). Lay Buddhists may vow to adhere to Five Precepts, though they are free to take one, two, three, four, or all five:

- to abstain from taking life
- to abstain from taking what is not given
- to avoid sexual misconduct
- to abstain from false speech
- to abstain from alcohol

But what else do ordinary Buddhists do?

Meditation

On American college campuses today, Asian students who describe themselves as Buddhists are often asked, "What's your practice?" The question is intended to prompt an answer that points to a particular style of meditation. But it is just as likely to prompt confusion, since meditation has generally been confined to monks and nuns. Most lay Buddhists do not meditate, and many monks and nuns engage chiefly in ritual activities, such as chanting.

Nonetheless, meditation remains a central Buddhist practice. The Buddha was enlightened while meditating, Buddhist art often depicts him in the lotus position, and the last two elements of the Eightfold Path concern techniques for training the mind. Many monks and nuns also engage in meditation of some sort, as do an increasing number of lay Buddhists, especially in Europe and the United States, where meditation is widely seen as the key Buddhist practice.

Classically, there are four postures for meditation: sitting, lying down, standing, and walking. The most popular of these is sitting, typically cross-legged, in a position that is comfortable but not so comfortable as to put you to sleep. In the classic lotus position, the body is still and the muscles relaxed. The legs are crossed, the spine is straight, the eyes are half closed, the hands lie on the lap, and the tip of the tongue touches the back of the teeth. Broadly speaking, the aim of meditation is to put an end to craving and ignorance and therefore suffering—in other words, to produce nirvana. But along the way, Buddhist meditators typically pursue two short-term aims, which have classically divided Buddhist meditation into two overlapping categories: concentration and insight.

Meditation typically starts with concentration—reining in what Buddhists refer to as the "monkey mind" by refusing to allow it to swing from one intellectual limb to another. Here the goal is to concentrate on one thing for a long time. This sort of meditation is typically not thought to produce either wisdom or nirvana, but it is a preparation for both. For beginners, attempts at concentration meditation can be frustrating, demonstrating little more than just how scattered the ordinary mind is.

The second broad type, insight meditation, offers both wisdom and nirvana. Here concentration on an object may remain a technique but the broader goal is to produce liberating insight. One common form of insight meditation—*anapanasati* ("mindfulness of inhalation and exhalation")—may seem to be simply concentration meditation.

Meditators do not necessarily have to sit still. Here, visitors to the Brahmavihara-Arama, Bali's largest Buddhist monastery, practice walking meditation.

Instructors tell practitioners to try to concentrate on the breath alone. Don't try to make your breathing shorter or longer or deeper or shallower. Just observe it as is. Feel your chest rising and falling. Watch the air pass through your nostrils and over your upper lip. Observe the inhaling and the exhaling and the short pauses in between. When your concentration wanes (as it will)—when your mind wanders to the itch on your earlobe or to what you hope to eat for dessert or to the narcissism of your friend—just observe the distraction, then redirect your focus, gently and without judgment, back to your breath. But classically the aim of this "mindfulness of inhalation and exhalation" is insight of some sort.

Other forms of insight meditation also focus on mindfulness by calling on the practitioner to observe the arising and ceasing of bodily sensations or feelings. Rather than reacting habitually to an itch, for example, or a feeling of frustration with your sibling, just observe whatever is happening—watch it arise and fade away quite of its own accord. These, too, may seem to be forms of concentration meditation, and concentration is certainly required. But there is a broader goal at play here, which is to produce insight—to learn, through direct experience, the doctrines of impermanence and the no-self.

Insight meditators can also concentrate on a concept such as karma or samsara, on a color or a shape, or on the Buddha, the dharma, or the sangha. Another classic strategy is to meditate on the impermanence of the body, imagine it getting sick, growing old, and dying. Some monks even meditate in a room with a decaying corpse. Zen practitioners attempt to meditate throughout each day, turning ordinary activities such as washing the dishes or folding the laundry into opportunities for mindfulness and insight.

Metta ("loving-kindness" or "friendliness") meditation begins with cultivating loving-kindness for oneself. It then moves on to cultivating loving-kindness for someone you love. Feel your love and affection for that person in your heart. Then direct that feeling outward:

> May you be filled with lovingkindness.
> May you be safe from inner and outer dangers.
> May you be well in body and mind.
> May you be at ease and happy.[41]

After cultivating loving-kindness for yourself or a loved one, you can move on to members of your family, your community, your nation, and then to strangers and even enemies. (The Dalai Lama has said that he practices metta meditation for Chinese rulers currently overseeing the occupation of Tibet.) Another form of metta meditation calls for meditators to look upon all sentient beings as their mothers, since in some prior lifetime all sentient beings *were* their mothers.

The ultimate fruit of meditation is nirvana, but along the way it is said to produce wisdom and compassion. Meditating on the breath, for example, teaches you the truth of impermanence, while metta meditation teaches you the truth of interdependence. Meditation can also foster a variety of altered states of consciousness. Initially, the meditator may revel in the bliss of a deep state of focused concentration or absorption known as *samadhi*. But more advanced meditators will dwell in that state dispassionately, with equanimity.

Buddhists disagree about whether the ultimate aim of meditation—enlightenment—comes suddenly or gradually. Many in the sudden enlightenment camp believe that we are all already buddhas, so all that is required is for us to wake up to the Buddha nature innate in each of us.

Some techniques for Buddhist meditation have been put to nonreligious purposes, such as stress reduction. Classically, however, the purposes of meditation were spiritual and even supernatural. In addition to producing the tranquility and insight that awakens, meditation was said to produce magical powers, including the ability to vanish, to fly, to shrink to the size of an atom, to swell to the size of the universe, to tame wild animals, to see past lives, and to walk on water or through solid objects.

Visualization

Closely related to meditation is visualization. The simplest form of visualization is meditating on an ordinary object. A flower or a soccer ball will do. Look at it. Study it. Observe its features until you can lower your eyelids and see it in your mind's eye without the object itself being present.

More advanced practitioners of this technique visualize buddhas or bodhisattvas, concentrating on the bodily form of Avalokiteshvara, for example. Begin with a painting or statue of this bodhisattva and with a spirit of gratitude and devotion. See the light emanating from his body and the crown on his head. Take in his physical features until you can close your eyes and see them in detail. The next step is to identify with Avalokiteshvara. Realize that this image is a product of your imagination. Know that you and he are equally empty. See that there is no difference between the two of you. "Such as is the Lady Prajnaparamita, even so am I," says the practitioner who visualizes this "Lady Perfect Wisdom." "Such as am I, even so is the Lady Prajnaparamita."[42] This visualization practice is said to teach a variety of Buddhist truths, including emptiness. It also endows the practitioner with the powers of the buddha or bodhisattva invoked.

Gazing at a mandala, such as this *thangka* painting from Nepal, prompts meditators to journey through a cosmic map of circles and squares with a buddha at the still point in the center.

Tibetan Buddhist practitioners also use mandalas for visualization. The term *mandala* means "circle," and mandalas do feature a series of concentric circles with squares inside each. But mandalas are also maps of the cosmos that double as maps of the mind and body. They are also understood as maps of a buddha's palace, which feature a buddha at each of the four cardinal directions, plus the main buddha, sometimes with a partner, at the center.

Again, practitioners may begin by looking at a picture of a mandala, but the goal is to eventually leave that visual representation behind by conjuring up the image in your own mind and transforming it in the process from a two-dimensional representation into a three-dimensional experience. Practitioners enter this mandala as if on a spiritual journey, entering through one of the gates and passing along the way an array of Tibetan Buddhist symbols: dharma wheel, lotus, diamond. Ultimately, the practitioner makes her way to the center of the mandala.

In keeping with the emptiness ideal, practitioners of visualization are challenged to identify with the buddhas they encounter and to claim their spiritual powers. Every buddha is empty, as is the self, so there is no ultimate difference between these buddhas and yourself. Another goal of this practice is to see the purity and perfection of the world—by visualizing the world as a mandala and everything in it as perfectly pure.

Another example of this practice is creating sand mandalas—a popular activity for traveling Tibetan Buddhist monks in the United States. Over a series of days, monks painstakingly construct an elaborate mandala out of colored sand. When they are done, in an elegant instruction on the doctrine of impermanence, they ceremonially scatter the sand into a nearby lake or river. Yet another popular mandala, the Kalachakra ("Wheel of Time") Mandala, can now be viewed online in three dimensions. A much older mandala (also three-dimensional), the ninth-century Borobudur Temple, can be visited in Central Java, Indonesia. In fact, it is one of the most-visited tourist attraction in Indonesia today.

Chanting

Outsiders often equate Buddhist practice with meditation, but chanting is more popular in most Buddhist sects. In fact, chanting of some form is practiced in virtually every Buddhist school, sometimes as a preparation for meditation and sometimes on its own. Buddhist chanting draws on ancient Indian traditions concerning the power of sacred sounds and is often conducted in ancient languages such as the Pali of early Buddhist texts.

The most widespread chants are short formulas, which can be repeated in ritual contexts or domestic devotions:

Namu Amida Butsu ("Homage to Amida Buddha") in Pure Land Buddhism;

Om mani padme hum ("Om, [Homage to You Who Hold] the Jewel in the Lotus") in Tibetan Buddhism;

Namu Myoho Renge Kyo ("Homage to the Lotus Sutra") in Nichiren Buddhism

Many Buddhists also chant the "Triple Refuge" of Buddha/dharma/sangha. A simple Theravada Buddhist mantra, *du sa ni ma*, is based on the first symbol in the ancient Pali-language terms for the Four Noble Truths: suffering, origin, cessation, path. Despite Zen's reputation for wordlessness, chanting is also popular in that tradition. In fact, the Heart Sutra is often chanted before public sessions of *zazen*. In monastic settings, monks and nuns chant much longer liturgical texts or Buddhist sutras. And all Buddhist monks chant over the dying and the dead.

Chanting is particularly popular (and controversial) in the Soka Gakkai tradition, where practitioners chant the Nichiren daimoku. Like other Buddhists, Soka Gakkai members chant in order to focus the mind, accumulate karmic merit, and realize their inner buddha nature. They also chant for material goods such as cars and houses—a practice seen by some as crass and non-Buddhistic. It should be noted, however, that there is a long tradition in the Buddhist world of casting spells for goals less lofty than nirvana—chants against snake bites, for example, or for protection against wild animals.

Devotion and Pilgrimage

The Buddha urged his followers to see him not as a god but as an ordinary man who had found a path to nirvana, but Buddhists today also engage in practices that look conspicuously like the *puja* ("worship") of devotional Hinduism. From Bodh Gaya to Boston,

BIRTH AND DEATH

Though the Buddhist tradition has devoted considerable expertise to death and dying, it has generally slighted rites of passage. Birth and naming ceremonies tend to be minimized in Buddhist families and to follow local customs. Buddhists worldwide do recruit monks to preside over births, not so much to oversee any particular rituals but out of the hope that some small measure of the monk's storehouse of merit might be transferred to the child. This transfer is enacted symbolically as monks pour water from one glass to another, symbolizing "the transfer of positive karma from the holy monk to . . . [the] newborn infant."[a]

Buddhist deathways are informed by a largely Indian worldview in which karma propels humans through a vicious cycle of life, death, and rebirth with all manner of suffering along the way. They are also informed by the quintessential Buddhist affirmation that death comes to everyone; no one is exempt. What is unclear in the Buddhist tradition, which has classically refused to affirm the soul, is precisely what it is that reincarnates. In keeping with broader Indian traditions and with Buddhist lore about the death of the Buddha, Buddhists tend to cremate their dead. Some traditions also believe that the deceased linger after death in a **bardo**, or "intermediate state," between death and rebirth. It is the job of the living to assist the recently dead in the passage to rebirth, which in

bardo
"intermediate state" between death and rebirth, important in Tibetan Buddhism

Buddhists use images of buddhas and bodhisattvas much like contemporary Hindus use images of their deities. Theravada Buddhists typically describe these devotions as reverence and Mahayana Buddhists as worship, but the mechanics of the practice—bowing, offering, chanting—are quite similar. Buddhists conduct puja in private shrines at home and in public at temples. Like devotional Hindus, Buddhists may circumambulate the temple before moving to its center and to an encounter with the buddha or bodhisattva of their choosing. In addition to taking sight of the object of their devotion (or worship), they may light a candle or offer some flowers, perhaps in concert with the recitation of some sacred verses.

One of the most popular forms of Buddhist devotion is pilgrimage. Just prior to his parinirvana, the Buddha instructed his disciples to visit four sacred places after his passing:

- Lumbini, where he was born,
- Bodh Gaya, where he was enlightened,
- Sarnath, where he preached his first sermon,
- Kushinagar, where he entered parinirvana.

Today, Buddhist pilgrims to these sites—and to other sacred places associated with miracles of the Buddha—say they are walking in the footsteps of the Buddha, but they are also retracing the steps of prior pilgrims, including Emperor Ashoka, who promoted pilgrimage by taking to the road himself; the Chinese monk Faxian, who visited Lumbini, Bodh Gaya, Sarnath, and Kushinagar on a sixteen-year sojourn in the early fifth century; and Anagarika Dharmapala, who, after visiting the ruins of Sarnath and Bodh Gaya, formed the Maha Bodhi Society in 1891 in an effort to restore Buddhist sacred sites worldwide.

Buddhists also go as pilgrims to see rock carvings of the Buddha—at Polunnaruwa in Sri Lanka, Yungang in China, and (until they were destroyed by Taliban militants in 2001) Bamiyan in Afghanistan. They also travel to encounter relics, for example, to the Temple of the Tooth in Kandy, Sri Lanka, said to house a tooth of the Buddha. In China,

some cases might last as long as forty-nine days. As at birth, Buddhist monks are called in to assist in this process, again in the hope that (among other things) they might transfer some of their abundant merit. Monks sit with the dying and read sutras or chant mantras. They do the same with the corpse. When it is time to cremate the body, they often accompany it to the cremation grounds.

Buddhists generally affirm that one's rebirth is significantly affected by one's mental state at death, so they work hard to keep those who are dying calm. After death, Tibetan lamas sit with the corpse, chanting passages from works such as the *Tibetan Book of the Dead*, which offers a play-by-play description of the bardo between death and rebirth, complete with instructions on how to respond to its various terrors and delights, including "pure luminosity" and the noise of "a thousand thunderclaps simultaneously."[b] This journey is pictured as a trek through a mandala, with different representations of buddhas (both male and female) appearing at different times. Most people will be terrified or bewildered. But if the deceased are able to recognize a given buddha as empty—a projection of their own minds (which are themselves empty)—and unite with them in heartfelt devotion, they can be liberated from the cycle of suffering. Otherwise, they will be reborn into a new body chosen by their own karma and their own lingering desires.

devotees travel to four sacred mountains, each associated with a different bodhisattva. In Japan, on the island of Shikoku, pilgrims dressed in white shirts and conical hats visit eighty-eight temples associated with the life of the Shingon founder Kukai (774–835). Traditionally, these pilgrimages were undertaken on foot, and pilgrims slept in the open air or at rustic rest houses. Now they are likely to be undertaken in air-conditioned cars and buses, with stops at five-star hotels.

In one extraordinary pilgrimage, the "marathon monks" of the Enryaku Temple atop Mount Hiei in Japan run great distances daily, leaving their temple home in the middle of the night and returning in the early morning (in order to complete their daily chores). Equipped with nothing more than a robe and homemade straw sandals, all of these monks perform this pilgrimage over 100 days, covering nearly 19 miles daily. Some continue after the 100 days, completing 1,000 days of running over a seven-year period, with daily runs as far as 52 miles, or two Olympic marathons. During the fifth year of the 1,000-day pilgrimage, which covers a course the length of the equator, monks must also endure another grueling physical challenge: nine consecutive days without food, water, or sleep.

One of the Buddhist tradition's most celebrated pilgrims is Matsuo Basho, a seventeenth-century Haiku master and radical wanderer remembered today thanks to his classic travelogue, *The Narrow Road to the Deep North*. Born into a Samurai family and trained in Zen, Basho went as a pilgrim to Mount Fuji in 1684, but when he got back home the road continued to call. So he wandered out and never came back, visiting Shinto and Buddhist sites in northern Japan on a 1,500-mile walk that did not end until he died on the road. *The Narrow Road to the Deep North*, a mixture of prose and haiku, demonstrates that pilgrimage is often as much an inner as an outer journey. And Basho himself,

The Mahaparinirvana Stupa in Kushinagar, India, marks the place where the Buddha is said to have passed into parinirvana ("final nirvana"). Here, a pilgrim presents offerings to a reclining stone buddha inside that stupa, which may date as far back as the fifth century.

Aung San Suu Kyi (b. 1945)

In 1991, Aung San Suu Kyi was awarded the Nobel Peace Prize for leading a nonviolent struggle for democracy and human rights in Myanmar (previously known as Burma). Her leadership role in this movement was something of a birthright. Her father Aung San, widely revered as the father of modern Burma, led the fight for Burma's independence from the British, only to be assassinated by a member of a rival faction in 1947, when Suu Kyi was only two years old.

Suu Kyi assumed a leadership role in Myanmar's prodemocracy movement when she delivered a speech at Rangoon's Shwedagon Pagoda to almost half a million protesters on August 26, 1988. The next month she helped to found an opposition political party called the National League for Democracy. In July 1989, she was placed under house arrest, where she remained for fifteen of her next twenty-one years. Just days after her country's 2010 elections, Suu Kyi was released. After a series of negotiations with a liberalizing government, she met with Hillary Clinton during a high-profile visit of the U.S. Secretary of State to Myanmar. In the 2012 elections, she won a seat in Parliament.

A Theravada Buddhist, Suu Kyi has insisted that "a true revolution has to be that of the spirit" and that democratic reform must come through peaceful means. Though influenced by Gandhi and the Reverend Martin Luther King Jr., she has placed Buddhist values at the heart of her activism. Meditation reportedly helped her maintain equanimity during her imprisonment, and loving-kindness kept her from hating her captors. Buddhist principles, in her view, can also serve to prevent corruption among the powerful: "As a Buddhist, I cannot help thinking that if one really understood the meaning of *anicca* [impermanence] one wouldn't chase power and wealth at the expense of one's moral being.... [M]y Buddhist background...makes me feel that everything will pass away, but my deeds and their effects will stay with me."[a]

After her party came to power in elections in 2015, Suu Kyi became Myanmar's de facto chief executive. Her refusal to denounce ongoing persecution of Rohingya Muslims—a "textbook example of ethnic cleansing," according to a United Nations human rights chief—has drawn widespread criticism, as has her refusal to defend freedom of the press.[b] In 2018, she was stripped of honors previously conferred by at least half a dozen organizations, including Amnesty International. As of 2020, however, she continued to hold her Nobel Peace Prize.

who speaks of being drawn "by windblown clouds into dreams of a lifetime of wandering," shows that not all pilgrimages come to an end. "Every day is a journey," he writes, "and the journey itself is home."[43]

Festivals

Buddhists observe a wide variety of festivals, some local, some national, some sectarian, and some global. At the Festival of the Tooth in Sri Lanka, the celebrated Buddha tooth is paraded through the streets in an ancient procession witnessed over a millennium and a half ago by the fifth-century Chinese pilgrim Faxian. Jodo Shinshu Buddhists celebrate the birthday of their founder Shinran, and Zen practitioners celebrate their first patriarch on Bodhidharma Day. In China and Japan, festivals commemorate the Lotus Sutra. Other holidays mark the birthdays of bodhisattvas, such as Avalokiteshvara, and buddhas, such as Amitabha.

Most of these festivals provide occasions for the mixing and mingling of laypeople and monastics, through visits to monasteries by the laity and public sermons by monks and nuns. But there is also a series of festivals devoted to monastic life, including one that marks the start of the three-month rains retreat, when monks gather for the monsoons, and another at the end of this retreat, when the laity offer new robes to monastics for their wanders to come.

Many pan-Buddhist festivals celebrate key events in the life of Gautama Buddha, such as his renunciation of palace life, his first sermon, and the day he organized the Buddhist community. In Myanmar, Abhidhamma Day marks the time when the Buddha went to a heavenly realm to teach his mother the Abhidhamma ("Higher Teachings"). In Thailand, the Ploughing Festival commemorates the Buddha's first meditation as a young child, while he was watching oxen plough a field.

The granddaddy of all Buddhist festivals, however, is Wesak or Vesak (from the Indian month Vaisakha), which celebrates the Buddha's birthday at the full moon in either April or May. According to legend, immediately after his birth, Siddhartha Gautama stood up, walked seven steps, and announced that this would be his last birth. In the Theravada world, Wesak is also a day to remember the Buddha's enlightenment and parinirvana—events that, according to a number of Buddhist traditions, occurred on the same date. In many Buddhist countries, Wesak is a festival of light in which devotees remember the Buddha's awakening by bathing homes, temples, and trees with light. Other Wesak traditions include bathing statues of the baby Buddha in water, setting birds free, and offering food and clothes to the needy. One of Henry Steel Olcott's signature achievements during Ceylon's Buddhist revival was the reestablishment of Wesak as a governmental holiday in 1885. Today, Wesak is an official holiday in many Southeast Asian countries, including Thailand, Myanmar, Indonesia, Malaysia, and Singapore.

CONTEMPORARY CONTROVERSY: BUDDHISM AND VIOLENCE

Buddhism is widely depicted in the modern West as a model of tolerance and nonviolence, particularly in contrast with Christianity and Islam. "Do not kill" is a Buddhist precept for monks and laypeople alike, and *ahimsa* ("nonviolence") is a key Buddhist value. But no religion survives for centuries without being able to wage both war and peace, and Buddhism is no exception.

The image of Buddhists as peacemakers is reinforced by Ashoka, who, according to legend, embraced Buddhism after winning a military campaign that claimed more than one hundred thousand lives. Horrified by the violence he had unleashed, and at the bad karma it had brought him, Ashoka allowed Buddhism to flourish. The rock edicts he inscribed across his vast Indian empire include a series enjoining religious tolerance. "Whoever praises his own religion, due to excessive devotion, and condemns others . . . only harms his own religion," one reads. "One should listen to and respect the doctrines professed by others."[44] Today, interfaith tolerance is also a hallmark of the work of Thich Nhat Hanh and the Dalai Lama. "To the unique credit of Buddhism," the Sri Lankan scholar-monk Narada Mahathera has written, "it must be said that throughout its peaceful march of 2,500 years, no drop of blood has been shed in the name of the Buddha."[45]

But Buddhism's march has not always been peaceful. According to one Buddhist scripture, the Buddha in a previous life killed a bandit who was plotting to kill five hundred merchants. According to another scripture, the Buddha killed a Hindu Brahmin who was plotting to destroy Buddhism in India. Closer to our own time, Sri Lanka's Buddhist majority engaged in a decades-long civil war against the Tamil Tigers guerilla organization that did not abate until 2009. In 2013, an American Buddhist killed twelve people in cold blood at the Washington Navy Yard.

Despite their reputation as renouncers of worldly things, monks have not stood aloof from this violence. In China in 515, a monk named Faqing led fifty thousand soldiers into a war he described as a messianic battle against the temptress Mara on behalf of the "Great Vehicle." Any soldier who killed an enemy would become a bodhisattva, he promised, and anyone who killed ten would achieve enlightenment. "Warrior monks" were also active in medieval Japan, engaging in fierce rivalries between temples and otherwise acting as the "teeth and claws of the Buddha."[46] In 1951, amidst the Cold War, a Chinese monk said, "To wipe out the American imperialist demons, who are destroying world peace, is in accordance with Buddhist doctrines; it is not only blameless, but actually will give rise to merit as well."[47] In 1959, a Buddhist monk assassinated Sri Lankan prime minister S. W. R. D. Bandaranaike. In Myanmar today, an ultranationalist Buddhist monk is called "the Buddhist bin Laden" for inciting violence against that country's Rohingya Muslim minority.

It is simply not the case that Buddhism is a "religion of peace." No religion, even that of the man who woke up under a tree in Bodh Gaya, has yet discovered an antidote to the human propensity for violence.

QUESTIONS FOR DISCUSSION

1. Describe the Four Sights that set the Buddha on his path from his palace to the road to awakening and beyond. How is the concept of impermanence related to these sights and to the Buddhist tradition more broadly?

2. Describe the Four Noble Truths. What do Buddhists mean when they say that life is suffering? What causes this suffering, and how can we escape it? Does this preoccupation with suffering make Buddhists pessimists? Why or why not?

3. Buddhist exemplars include arhats, bodhisattvas, and buddhas. How are these beings similar and different? And how are they regarded by their respective communities? Consider their various traditions (mainstream and Mahayana), as well as their purposes and goals.

4. How did the Hart-Celler Act of 1965 change the religious landscape in the United States? In particular, how did post-1965 migrations of Buddhists to the United States change American Buddhism? How did they change American culture?

5. Like Buddhist teachings, Buddhist practices are intended to reduce suffering. How do practices such as meditation, chanting, and visualization attempt to reduce suffering?

6. Shortly before he died, the Buddha refused to appoint an individual successor and appointed the Buddhist community as a whole to succeed him instead. Why do you suppose he made that decision? How, in your view, did it affect later Buddhist history?

KEY TERMS

Amitabha/Amida ("Infinite Light"), p. 104

arhat ("worthy one"), p. 88

Ashoka, p. 79

Avalokiteshvara ("The Lord Who Looks Down"), p. 99

bardo, p. 122

Bodh Gaya, p. 79

bodhisattva ("enlightenment being"), p. 88

buddha ("awakened one"), p. 99

Dalai Lama, p. 88

dharma ("teaching"), p. 88

dukkha ("suffering"), p. 88

Engaged Buddhism, p. 111

enlightenment, p. 88

karma, p. 89

koan, p. 103

lama, p. 106

Mahayana ("Great Vehicle"), p. 87

mainstream Buddhism, p. 87

Maitreya, p. 100

mandala ("circle"), p. 109

mantra, p. 109

Nagarjuna, p. 100

nirvana ("blowing out"), p. 89

Pure Land Buddhism, p. 104

samsara ("wandering"), p. 89

sangha ("community"), p. 88

shunyata ("emptiness"), p. 100

sutra ("thread"), p. 92

Tantra, p. 106

Theravada ("Way of the Elders"), p. 87

upaya ("skillful means"), p. 101

Vajrayana, p. 87

zazen, p. 104

Zen, p. 102

FURTHER READING

Gyatso, Tenzin. *Freedom in Exile: The Autobiography of the Dalai Lama*. New York: HarperCollins, 1990.

Keown, Damien. *Buddhism: A Very Short Introduction*. New York: Oxford University Press, 2013.

Lopez, Donald S., Jr. *From Stone to Flesh: A Short History of the Buddha*. Chicago: The University of Chicago Press, 2013.

Rahula, Walpola. *What the Buddha Taught*. New York: Grove Press, 1974.

Seager, Richard Hughes. *Buddhism in America*. New York: Columbia University Press, 2000.

Willis, Jan. *Dreaming Me: An African American Woman's Spiritual Journey*. New York: Riverhead Books, 2001.

The Golden Temple in Amritsar, India, sits at the sacred center of the Sikh world. Pilgrims come from far and wide to bathe in the holy waters outside the gold-plated temple that houses the Guru Granth scripture.

Sikhism

THE WAY OF THE GURU

Every day before sunrise, Sikhs gather at the Golden Temple in Amritsar, the largest city in the northwestern Indian state of Punjab, to pay their respects to their guru. They come from Delhi and Dubai, Vancouver and Sydney. They arrive on foot, on scooters, and in buses, taxicabs, rickshaws, and tractors. They wear a rainbow of turbans: some white, some blue, some yellow, some orange. In surrounding markets, they buy marigolds as offerings. Entering the temple grounds, they are greeted with hymns of praise to the grace and mercy of the one God. They lower their voices. They take off their shoes and wash their hands and feet. They bow and touch their heads to the ground.

Sikhism, the youngest of the world's major religions, was led in its infancy by a series of ten **Gurus**, beginning with founder **Guru Nanak** (1469–1539). The tenth in this lineage, Guru Gobind Singh (1666–1708), is believed to have declared that, upon his death, there would be no more human gurus. Henceforth, Sikhs would be led by their scripture and community. So as Sikhs line up to greet their guru before sunrise at the Golden Temple, they are awaiting the arrival not of a human being but of a book: the scripture they refer to as the **Guru Granth** ("Guru in Book Form") or, more formally, the Sri Guru Granth Sahib (Sri and Sahib are honorific titles, similar to "Sir").

Also known as the **Adi Granth** ("First Book"), this 1,430-page volume is the primary source for Sikh beliefs and practices. Written in multiple languages in the Gurmukhi ("from the mouth of the Guru") script, it comprises 5,871 devotional hymns, some authored by Sikh gurus and others by Hindu and Muslim holy

129

Guru
guide, teacher. Most Sikhs recognize ten human Gurus who made the divine Guru manifest. They also recognize the scriptural guru (Guru Granth) and the community as guru (Guru Panth).

Guru Nanak (1469–1539)
founder of Sikhism

Guru Granth
primary Sikh scripture, revered as a Guru

Adi Granth ("First Book")
primary Sikh scripture, revered by adherents as the Sri Guru Granth Sahib

gurdwara ("gateway to the guru")
Sikh place of worship housing the Guru Granth Sahib

granthi
gurdwara overseer charged with reading aloud from the Guru Granth Sahib

men, making it the only major scripture other than the Christian Bible to incorporate texts from other religions. This "non-denominational anthology of hymns" is read, interpreted, and contemplated.[1] Most of all, it is sung. Its words and sounds are meant to evoke the rhythms of the divine, providing the bass lines and melodies for an experiential and aesthetic religion in which the beauty and majesty of God are encountered more through the ear than through the eye.

But the Guru Granth is more than a scripture. It is a material object of veneration. What makes a Sikh temple—known as a **gurdwara** ("gateway to the guru")—holy is the presence of this holy book, which is treated like living royalty. The official who oversees a gurdwara is called a **granthi**—a keeper of the book and an authorized reader of the Guru Granth. At a Sikh wedding, the bride and groom circle the Guru Granth four times. On other special occasions, Sikhs arrange for around-the-clock recitations. The Guru Granth is treated as a person under Indian law, just as corporations are in the United States, and in this capacity, it commands vast landholdings in the Punjab. Sikhs also use the Guru Granth as an oracle or diviner, opening its pages at random in search of a timeless answer to a temporal problem. Worn copies are ritually cremated in a ceremony that recalls a human funeral. In short, the Guru Granth offers Sikhs more than the message and the sound of God. As their living and breathing Guru, it offers God's presence. Muslims refer to Judaism, Christianity, and Islam as "religions of the book," but Sikhism is the religion of the book *par excellence*.

As pilgrims enter the Golden Temple to greet this textual Guru, they do not ascend as is typical at Hindu temples. Instead, they go down a series of steps. Sikhs report that the decision to locate the Golden Temple below street level serves to remind

The head granthi of the Golden Temple, Jagat Singh, carries the Guru Granth scripture atop his head in a procession on the eve of the birthday anniversary of the Sikh founder Guru Nanak in 2017.

visitors that you must lower yourself in order to be blessed. Just as the wild ego must be tamed before we can encounter God, it is said, the Golden Temple can be accessed only via humility.

If humility is in short supply in any particular pilgrim, this site seems poised to supply the deficit. Like Sikhism itself, born five hundred years ago at the intersection of Hinduism and Islam, the Golden Temple is fluent in both Hindu and Islamic idioms, with sacred trees and a sacred pool recalling Hindu temples and two minarets and an onion dome evoking the mosques of Islam. Visitors can enter through four gates—a reminder, Sikhs say, of the openness of their religion to all Hindu castes and to religions from all four corners of the world. Inside these gates, pilgrims are greeted with white marble steps descending to white marble walkways ringing a large pool. A white marble causeway leads to the Golden Temple itself, which floats like an island in the middle of the pool—a still center to the whirl that is life on earth.

Or so says the architecture. But Amritsar, which lies near ancient trade routes linking Kabul to the northwest and Delhi and Varanasi to the southeast, has long been contested territory, caught up in the rivalries of merchants, mystics, and military men. Though the Golden Temple may feel eternal, it has been destroyed and rebuilt many times. Begun by Sikhism's fourth Guru (Ram Das), it was completed by his son, the fifth Guru (Arjan), who installed the Adi Granth there in 1604. In the mid-eighteenth century, the city was taken by Afghan armies, who burned Sikh scriptures, razed the temple, and desecrated its sacred pool with rotting cow carcasses. After the greatest of Sikh sovereigns, Maharaja Ranjit Singh (1780–1839), retook the city in 1802, the temple was rebuilt in its current magnificence. Resplendent in white marble, this **Harimandir** ("Temple of God"), as Sikhs originally called it, came to be known as the Golden Temple after it was covered with gold in the early nineteenth century.

Today, pilgrims may stop at one of three tree shrines as they circumambulate the temple grounds, or one of many shrines dedicated to Sikh martyrs. They may also bathe in the sacred tank, which they describe as a pool of nectar with miraculous healing properties. One bathing site offers devotees the equivalent karmic merit of visiting sixty-eight different Hindu temples in one dip. Another popular site is the **Akal Takht** ("Throne of the Timeless One"), Sikhism's political headquarters, whose location facing the Golden Temple symbolizes the interdependence in Sikh life of religion and politics, the timeless and the temporal.

The Guru Granth is the main attraction, however. Devotees' responses to its presence recall responses to the Virgin of Guadalupe during processions in Catholic Mexico or to the Hindu god Ganesha as he is carried through villages in India. Each evening this textual Guru is paraded from the Golden Temple to its resting place in the Akal Takht, where it is ceremonially put to bed. Each morning, in a ritual awakening, it is roused and dressed in fabric and paraded back to the Golden Temple, which volunteers have cleansed overnight with milk and water in anticipation of their Guru's arrival. In this morning rite, the granthi carries the holy book out of the Akal Takht on his head before placing it in a flower-covered palanquin befitting an earthly sovereign. As devotees jostle for the honor of carrying their Guru to the Golden Temple, an attendant continuously brushes it with a fly whisk made of white horse or yak hair. At the threshold

Harimandir ("Temple of God")
formal name for the Golden Temple at Amritsar

Akal Takht ("Throne of the Timeless One")
seat of temporal authority of the Guru Granth on the site of the Golden Temple in Amritsar

langar
community kitchen in a gurd-wara and the open-to-all meal prepared in it

amrit
nectar of immortality, sanctified water used in Khalsa initiations

of the Golden Temple, the granthi again places the Guru Granth on his head, carrying it to its seat in the inner sanctum atop a throne and under a gold canopy covered in precious gems. The granthi then opens the book to a random page and reads its daily decree. Streamed live on the Internet—the Guru Granth is now also a "digital Guru"—this decree becomes the day's lesson for Sikhs worldwide.[2]

As the day proceeds, tens of thousands of devotees file past their beloved Guru, like patriotic Americans winding through the National Archives to catch a glimpse of the Constitution. In this case, however, the faithful take *darshan* ("sacred seeing") of their Guru and leave behind offerings of food, flowers, and money. Meanwhile, devotees sing hymns around the clock to the accompaniment of harmonium, tabla, and stringed instruments.

As visitors exit the Golden Temple, they receive an edible offering made of flour, sugar, water, and clarified butter known as *karah prashad*. Before leaving the grounds, they may also partake in a free meal (**langar**) prepared in a community kitchen (also called a langar). Billed as the world's largest kitchen, the Golden Temple langar serves forty thousand or fifty thousand people daily (more than one hundred thousand on festival days). They sit side-by-side on the floor without regard to caste, gender, race, or religion.

The city that grew up around this temple is called Amritsar ("Pool of Nectar"), after the sacred pool that surrounds the Golden Temple. As this name suggests, **amrit** (literally, "not death," but typically translated as "nectar") plays an important role in Sikh piety. The Sikh founder Guru Nanak is said to have drunk this nectar of immortality during his first mystical encounter with the divine in 1499. "The Name of the Lord, Har, Har," reads the Guru Granth, "is the treasure of Ambrosial Nectar" (GG 672).[3]

OUR STORY

There is little historical data on the life of Guru Nanak, who appears in popular iconography as "a haloed, white-bearded person wearing an outfit combining Hindu and Islamic styles, his eyes . . . rapt in divine contemplation, and his right palm . . . imprinted with the symbol of the singular Divine."[4] The historian W. H. McLeod once claimed that every biographical fact we know about Sikhism's founder can fit on one page of a book. That is an exaggeration. Nonetheless, there is no scholarly consensus on Guru Nanak's birth date, his name, whether he was primarily influenced by Hinduism or Islam (or both or neither), and "the correct English label to assign to his beliefs (are they ethics, philosophy, or theology?)."[5] By contrast, the pious "birth stories" (**janamsakhis**) by Sikhs about his life are far more voluminous and self-assured. Put these popular stories together and you get something like this about the glories of Guru Nanak's life.

Guru Nanak's Vision

The man who would come to be known as Guru Nanak moved from his first breath in two religious worlds. Born into a Hindu family in 1469, he was raised in a Muslim village now called Nankana

Sahib, about forty miles west of Lahore in the Punjab in modern-day Pakistan. His father was a practical man—an accountant who wanted his son to make a good living and earn a good name. But Nanak was a solitary rather than a social type—a contemplative and a dreamer who liked to wander outdoors with his family's cattle and his own thoughts. His hometown sat on a main road from Lahore to Delhi that drew Muslim pilgrims on their way to Mecca, Hindu devotees on pilgrimages of their own, and traders of all sorts. So as a boy he was exposed to other worlds and worldviews. He was particularly drawn to questions of the spirit and to the wandering holy men who were forever passing through.

As a member of the Khatri merchant caste, he was steeped in India's upper-caste traditions, but he was also influenced by Muslim Sufi mystics, the lived Islam of his village, and Hindu ascetics, priests, and devotional poets. Five times a day he heard the call to prayer. He himself referred to God as Ram and Hari (as Hindus do) and Allah (like Muslims). However, Nanak's disagreements with these two religious traditions were at least as significant as his agreements.

Guru Nanak, the founder of Sikhism, is depicted in a mural in Kashmir, India, in the Gurdwara Pathar Sahib, which was built in 1517 to commemorate Nanak's visit to the region.

As a boy, he was already casting a suspicious eye at hollow rituals. In their rite of passage into adulthood, upper-caste Hindu boys were supposed to don a sacred thread, typically over one shoulder and under the opposing arm. Nanak refused to put his on and insisted on donning an internal thread instead, one tied together by mercy, contentment, virtue, and truth. After his marriage was arranged to a Khatri woman named Sulakhani, he refused to consult an astrologer to determine the wedding's best date. That did not prevent Nanak and Sulakhani from having two healthy sons, whom they raised in the village of Sultanpur, about one hundred miles east of his hometown, where his sister Nanaki lived with her husband. Nanak found employment there with a Muslim storekeeper, but he preferred conversing with wandering ascetics over measuring grains. Together with his close companion, a Muslim minstrel named Mardana, he bracketed his days by bathing in the river each morning and singing hymns at night.

One day in Sultanpur when he was thirty years old, Nanak went for his morning bath in the Bein River and did not return. His clothes were found by the shore. Many feared he had drowned. When he was finally discovered after three days and three nights, some thought he had lost his mind. What he had really lost was his old identity as a person wholly distinct from God. What he had gained was a new identity and a new mission.

On the morning of the day he went missing, Nanak had an uncanny experience—an ascension to the divine abode accompanied by a revelation of the singularity of God and a call to move out into the world as God's messenger. In this mystical encounter, God called Nanak into his presence and promised to remain with him. He revealed to him the truth on which the Sikh tradition today is based: "**Ik Oankar**—One Being Is," or "God Is One."[6] Then, giving his chosen messenger a

janamsakhis ("birth stories") traditional stories of the birth, life, and death of Guru Nanak

Ik Oankar (also 1 Oankar, "One Being Is") the central affirmation of Sikh monotheism and the key Sikh symbol

draught of the nectar of immortality, God charged him to devote his life to five sacred activities: remembrance of the Word, charity, ablution (ritual washing), service, and prayer.

Like Muhammad, Nanak was then told to recite. He responded with a song of praise to the divine that is now the opening composition of the Sri Guru Granth Sahib. This beloved opening chant, whose first words are taught to children as they learn about the Sri Guru Granth Sahib, distills Sikh wisdom into a few short verses:

> There is One God.
> He is the supreme truth.
> He, the Creator,
> Is without fear and without hate.
> He, the Omnipresent,
> Pervades the universe.
> He is not born,
> Nor does He die to be born again.
> By His grace shalt thou Worship Him.
>
> Before time itself
> There was truth.
> When time began to run its course
> He was the truth.
> Even now, He is the truth
> And evermore shall truth prevail.[7]

Accepting this song, which Sikhs now recite each morning as an offering, God spoke again. He promised to bless those whom Nanak blessed. He gave Nanak a robe of honor as well as a title that would resound through generations of Sikh teachers and disciples: "I am the Great God, the Supreme Creator. Thou art the Guru, the Supreme Guru of God."[8]

Following this encounter, Guru Nanak (as he was now called) quit his job, gave away his possessions, and said goodbye to his wife and children, whom he sent back to his native village. He then departed for two decades of wandering across India. In fact, he traveled in all four cardinal directions on the subcontinent. With his Muslim friend Mardana at his side, he went north to Ladakh in the Himalayas, south to Sri Lanka, and as far east and west as Assam and Mecca.

Initially, he was silent. Eventually, he spoke. "There is no Hindu, there is no Muslim," he said. "So whose path shall I follow? I shall follow God's path." In Guru Nanak's wandering years as a preacher and singer, God and nature protected him. A cobra rose high and wide to shade him as he slept. Guru Nanak spoke of divine oneness and sang of his deep love for the one and only God. He put on the garb of different religious communities. He attended various religious festivals, conversing with Sufi mystics, Hindu renouncers, and Jain and Buddhist monks. Those he encountered strained to place him in the proper religious box. To what sort of spiritual path did he belong?

In 1519, around the age of fifty, Guru Nanak put his wandering behind him. Returning home, he reunited with Sulakhani and his two sons. He settled in the village of Kartarpur, which he founded on fertile land on the banks of a river in modern-day Pakistan. As he transformed his old life of ideas into a new life of action, a community grew up around him. It was an agricultural community consisting largely of Jats, a caste that, like Guru Nanak himself, had traded in nomadic life for a settled existence in agriculture.

Sikh pilgrims gather outside the Gurdwara Darbar Sahib in Kartarpur, Pakistan, where Guru Nanak resettled with his family and initiated the Sikh community in 1519.

In response to his followers' questions and concerns, Guru Nanak began to shape the practices, ideas, and institutions of his new religious movement. He got up very early—in the "ambrosial hour"—for a bath. He composed and sang poems and hymns in the Punjabi vernacular that ordinary folks could understand. The first stage of his life had been marked by mystical encounters. An epiphany had led him to wander for two decades. In his life's second stage as a "community builder," he settled down with his family, dedicated himself to "concrete action," and built his **Panth**, or community, into a "stable institution" with its own texts and rituals.[9] He established a routine of prayers three times a day with work in between. He taught his followers to serve not only themselves but also their families and their religious community. He also shaped the office of the Guru, which would later be filled by the Guru Granth itself. Those who took him as their guru came to be called Sikhs ("learners" or "disciples"). "Together they listened to and recited the sacred hymns, together they cooked and ate the langar, and together they formed a democratic congregation without priests or ordained ministers."[10]

At Kartarpur, Guru Nanak taught the unity of God, whom he identified with truth and reality. In his distinctive form of monotheism, God was not a transcendent reality "out" or "up" there. God was inside each of us, as close as our own heartbeat, our own breath, our own song.

Although Guru Nanak did develop rituals for his own community, he believed that God was to be encountered internally—in meditation rather than through the mediation of priestly rituals. He called into question all sorts of external religious practices—from horse sacrifices and ceremonial bathing to sexual austerities and reciting the Vedas (GG 873). In fact, during his lifetime, Guru Nanak was best known as an inventive sage who spurned rules of etiquette and deliberately performed rituals incorrectly in order to call their

Panth ("path")
the Sikh community or the way of the Gurus

effectiveness into question. Just as he had done with the sacred thread ceremony of his youth, he turned popular practices inward, speaking about pilgrimage, for example, as a journey into the human heart rather than to Mecca or Varanasi (GG 468). "Let mercy be your mosque, faith your prayer-mat, and honest living your Koran," he said (GG 140).

The centerpiece of his engaged ethic was a rejection of the caste distinctions that so preoccupied the surrounding society. Disregarding powerful cultural and religious norms that required members of different castes to eat food separately, he started a tradition of community kitchens and dining halls that evolved under his successor into the langar. In the spiritual realm at least, there was no caste. The realm of the divine was open to weavers as well as priests, street sweepers, and merchants.

Guru Nanak also scoffed at the purity and pollution codes that often accompany religious rituals. Pollution issued, in his view, from moral actions, not from bodily emissions or choices of food and drink. Once, during a visit to Mecca, he fell asleep in a mosque with his feet pointing toward the mihrab, the niche that orients believers toward the Kaaba. When someone scolded him for pointing his impure feet toward that pure space, he replied, "Then turn my feet in a direction where there is no God nor the Ka'ba."[11] His critic did just that, swinging him around 180 degrees. The niche in the mosque turned miraculously with him.

In a similar moment early one morning during a pilgrimage to the Ganges River, priests were casting water toward the east and the rising sun. Guru Nanak joined them but splashed water westward instead. Mecca lies west of the Ganges, so the priests, suspecting he might be performing some strange homage to Allah, asked, "To whom are you offering water?" Guru Nanak replied, "To whom are you offering water?" The priests explained that they were offering water to their dead ancestors in the east. Guru Nanak explained that he was offering water to parched fields that lay to the west. And his destination, he added with a grin, was much, much closer.

Guru Nanak's spiritual nonconformity endured to the end of his life. When the hour of his passing was almost upon him, his Muslim friends said they would bury him and his Hindu friends said they would cremate him (each according to their own traditions). Guru Nanak responded, "Place flowers on either side. Hindus on my right. Muslims on my left. Those whose flowers remain fresh tomorrow will have their way."[12]

While his community sat around the cot of their dying Guru and recited his "Songs of Death"—"Death would not be called bad, O people, if one knew how to truly die" (GG 579)— he covered himself with a sheet. His death came very early in the morning. When his friends came to see him later that day, all the flowers were fresh but his body was gone. Rather than his corpse, the Hindus and the Muslims alike took their flowers instead. The Muslim flowers were buried, and the Hindu flowers were burned.

SIKHISM IN TODAY'S WORLD

There are roughly twenty-eight million Sikhs in the world and roughly twenty-six million live in India. However, it would be misleading to refer to India as the homeland of the Sikhs. The Punjab is their real religious homeland, the birthplace of their founder, and the site of their most sacred shrines. Amritsar is its spiritual capital and Punjabi is its language.

Historically, the Punjab ("Land of Five Rivers"), a rich agricultural region that includes one of the world's most fertile plains, spanned vast territories across what are now India and Pakistan. As an important trade crossroad, it has been a contested region, invaded by the armies of Alexander the Great and ruled by the Indian emperor Ashoka and England's Queen Victoria. The Punjab provided the setting for battles between the Kauravas and the Pandavas in the Indian epic the Mahabharata. And a million people died there in Hindu-Muslim-Sikh violence during the unprecedented relocation brought on by the Partition of India and Pakistan in 1947.

Before Partition, Sikhs were a religious minority in their homeland. As India and Pakistan were divided into separate countries, the Punjab was itself divided into an Indian and a Pakistani state. Muslims fled the Indian side and Hindus and Sikhs fled the Pakistani side. In 1966, the Indian state of Punjab was reorganized on linguistic lines—into a mostly Hindu-speaking state of Haryana and a mostly Punjabi-speaking Punjab, with the city of Chandigarh acting as the capital of both. According to India's 2011 census, India's Punjab state has a Sikh majority of 58 percent and a Hindu minority of 38 percent. Sizeable Sikh minorities exist in other Indian regions, including Chandigarh (13 percent of the population), Haryana (5 percent), and Delhi (3 percent).

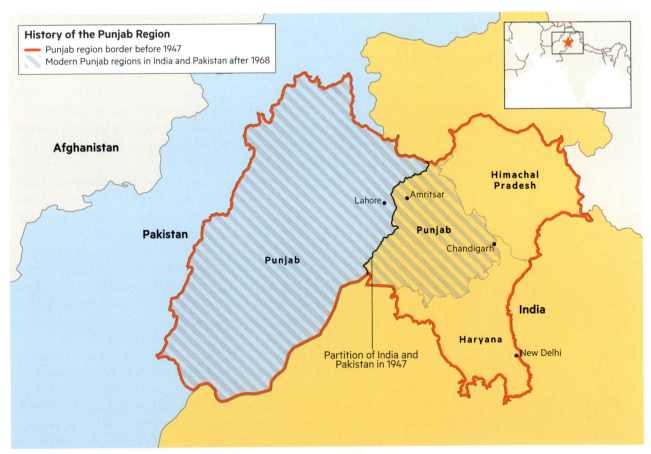

The Punjab region is the birthplace of Sikhism and, since the end of the British Raj and the Partition of India and Pakistan in 1947, a site of ongoing conflicts. This map depicts this region as it was segmented in 1947 and redefined in 1968.

"I am an American," reads the sign of a young Sikh girl attending a candlelight vigil at the Hidden Falls Gurdwara in Plymouth, Michigan, in honor of six Sikhs killed in 2012 by a white supremacist at a gurdwara in Oak Creek, Wisconsin. Her family members hold American flags to demonstrate their shared identity as American Sikhs.

Although Sikhism is often billed optimistically as the world's fifth largest religion, it isn't the majority religion in any country. In India, where it commands the allegiance of only 1.8 percent of the Indian population, it is fourth, behind Hinduism (79.8 percent), Islam (14.2 percent), and Christianity (2.3 percent).

Traditions with homelands often develop followings in the diaspora—areas outside that homeland into which their people are scattered or "dispersed." Though far smaller than the Hindu diaspora outside of India, there is a Sikh diaspora outside of the Punjab. Among Sikhs' homes away from home, the most prominent are in English-speaking countries: Canada (with 529,000 Sikhs in 2020 according to the World Religion Database), the United Kingdom (500,000), and the United States (410,000). In the Canadian province of British Columbia, Sikhs account for a higher percentage of the population (5.4 percent) than they do in India (1.8 percent). In the greater Vancouver area, where a few thousand Sikh immigrants arrived in the first decade of the twentieth century, Sikhism is the second largest religion after Christianity, with 6.8 percent of the population.

Sikhs are also taking up residence in Saudi Arabia, Kuwait, Oman, and other Arab states of the Persian Gulf region. In the United Arab Emirates (UAE), the Sikh population more than doubled (from 29,000 to 66,000) between 2005 and 2015. The UAE is also home to the largest gurdwara in the Gulf region. Built in 2012 on the outskirts of Dubai on land donated by the Ruler of the Emirate of Dubai, Sheikh Mohammed bin Rashid Al Makhtoum, the Guru Nanak Darbar is the home temple for the roughly 50,000 Sikhs who live in Dubai. Designed to echo elements in the Golden Temple, it is also a major tourist attraction—one of the highest-rated "things to do in Dubai" by TripAdvisor and a key part of a governmental campaign showcasing the UAE's commitment to religious tolerance and interfaith dialogue. The Guru Nanak Darbar's massive kitchen is designed to serve the ten thousand worshipers who attend Friday services. At a "breakfast for diversity" held in 2017, this gurdwara entered the *Guinness World Records* book by serving breakfast to people from more than a hundred different nations.

Like Muslims and Mormons, Sikhs have divided over questions of succession. Although almost all Sikhs accept ten Gurus, two groups with nineteenth-century origins—the Nirankaris ("Followers of the Formless One") and the Namdharis ("Adopters of the Divine Name")—follow additional gurus. Numerically, both of these groups are marginal, and many Sikhs who follow an orthodox Sikh Code of Conduct called the *Sikh Rehat Maryada* don't consider them to be Sikhs at all. Nonetheless, they demonstrate that, like every other major religion, Sikhism has its prominent dissenters.

Other categories Sikhs use to distinguish themselves from one another concern individual practices. For example, there are turbaned Sikhs who have been initiated into a fraternal "Order of the Pure" known as the **Khalsa**. These initiates are called **Amritdharis**, or "amrit adopters." There are also **Sehajdharis** ("slow adopters"), or unturbaned Sikhs who cut their hair and have not been initiated, and uninitiated Sikhs who look like Khalsa members because they wear the turban and do not cut their hair (Keshdharis). Another group consists of the *patit* ("lapsed"), who have been initiated into the Khalsa but have ceased to observe its precepts. Many Sikhs follow the *Sikh Rehit Maryada*, but there are competing codes of conduct, which disagree, for example, about whether to bathe in cold or hot water, whether coffee is forbidden, or whether vegetarianism is required.

Like Judaism and Hinduism, Sikhism is tied to a particular people, a particular land, and a particular language. Because Sikhs have not traditionally attempted to proselytize, almost all Sikhs are of Punjabi descent. However, there is a small but influential group of *gora* ("White") Sikhs. Many are converts (or the children of converts) of Yogi Bhajan, a Sikh who came to North America in the early 1970s. One who married into Sikhism instead, Sardar Jarnail Martin Singh, became the first gora Sikh to lead a gurdwara in 2006 when he was elected president of the Maritime Sikh Society, which is based outside Halifax, Nova Scotia.

Khalsa
"Order of the Pure" inaugurated by Guru Gobind Singh in 1699

Amritdharis
"amrit-bearing" Sikhs who have been initiated into the Khalsa

Sehajdharis ("slow adopters")
Sikhs who cut their hair and do not follow Khalsa rules

SIKHISM 101

➤ How to overcome the ego?

One of the big scholarly debates about the Sikh tradition concerns its relationship with the religions active in the Punjab during Guru Nanak's life. Sikhism has long been viewed by many as a way of being Hindu—a Nanak lane running down the Hindu highway. "In the 1891 census," writes anthropologist Richard Fox, "over a third of the people who referred to themselves as Sikhs claimed they belonged to the Hindu religion and were Sikh only by sect."[13] Obviously, these categories were neither as distinct nor as fixed as they are today. A census taker in that same 1891 census observed that "a man may be a Sikh and yet be a Hindu and return himself as such." One man he interviewed was "at a loss to describe his religion," this census taker reported. "After some hesitation he

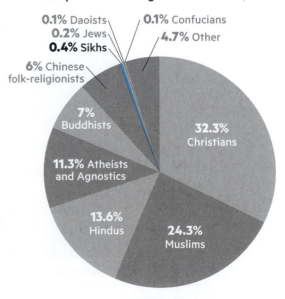

Comparison of Religions Worldwide, 2020

0.1% Daoists
0.2% Jews
0.4% Sikhs
0.1% Confucians
4.7% Other
6% Chinese folk-religionists
7% Buddhists
11.3% Atheists and Agnostics
13.6% Hindus
24.3% Muslims
32.3% Christians

said that he was not a Musalman and therefore must be a Hindu."[14] How to make sense of this situation? One way is to understand the ancestors of people we now describe as Sikhs as confused about their religious identity. A better way is to recognize that the religious boundaries we now draw, even in textbooks such as this one, were not always so firmly fixed.

Nowadays, India's census counts Sikhs separately, but the Indian Constitution does not recognize Sikhism as an independent religion. In fact, in Article 25 of India's Constitution, Buddhists, Jains, and Sikhs are all listed under the category Hindus. That fact offends the overwhelming majority of Sikhs, who now see themselves as part of a distinct religion that has little to do with either Hinduism or Islam.

For decades, scholars have described Sikhism as a Hindu-Islamic hybrid, with Hinduism providing the lion's share of its DNA. Guru Nanak was raised a Hindu, and Sikhs share with their Hindu neighbors key practices such as cremation. They also share key concepts such as karma, *samsara*, and *moksha*, though they interpret these concepts in their own way. Today, some people who identify as Hindus visit gurdwaras and read the Guru Granth Sahib as a Hindu text. The Guru Granth itself refers to many Hindu deities, including Hari, the namesake of the Harimandir. More specifically, Sikhs share with devotional (*bhakti*) Hindus an emphasis on chanting the names of the divine, singing praise songs, and doing both in the intimacy of vernacular languages. From this perspective, Guru Nanak steps onto the world stage as a devotee who worships either *nirguna Brahman* (a formless God "without attributes") in a more mystical way or *saguna Brahman* (a God "with attributes" and form) in a more ordinary way. Regardless, he had at least one foot squarely in the Hindu community of his age.

Recently, some scholars have questioned this consensus, emphasizing Sikhism's debts to Islam over its debts to Hinduism. Here, Exhibit A is the Sikh tradition's strict monotheism. Like Muslims, Sikhs reject the notion that God incarnates in human bodies. They also refuse to bow down to idols. The Sikh tradition's emphasis on the Guru Granth also echoes the Islamic tradition's emphasis on the Quran. Along with Muslim mystics of the Sufi order, Sikhs revel in an egalitarian spirituality in which caste (at least in theory) has no place and mystical encounters of the divine take precedence over priestly rituals and

A woman dips her feet into the holy pool at the Golden Temple complex in Amritsar, India. Devout Sikhs typically pray three times per day.

doctrinal formulas. According to the Sikh scholar Gurinder Singh Mann, all these factors "evoke an affinity of [Guru Nanak's] ideas with the Middle Eastern tradition rather than anything on the Hindu side."[15] Only later was the Sikh tradition Hinduized.

Of course, most Sikhs today trace their religion simply to God. They also underscore Sikh distinctiveness. Unlike Mormons, who insist on their status as Christians, most Sikhs reject the characterization of themselves as Hindus. In fact, many are offended by even the suggestion that Sikhism is an offshoot of Hinduism or Islam (or both). They point out that Sikhs from Guru Nanak forward have rejected pilgrimage, which is important in both Hinduism and Islam. They have also rejected withdrawal from the world in the manner of Hindu holy men. The Sikh tradition, they insist, is a unique religious tradition, as independent from Hinduism as Christianity is from Judaism.

No religion is self-created, of course. All draw on multiple sources as they are born and mature. Tibetan Buddhism drew not only on Indian Buddhist traditions but also on the indigenous Bon tradition of Tibet and ancient Chinese popular religion. Christianity, whose Bible contains both an Old Testament in Hebrew and a New Testament in Greek, incorporated Hebraic and Hellenistic influences. Nonetheless, Sikhism's creative adaptations of Hindu and Muslim beliefs and practices make it difficult to home in on its problem/solution dyad. Is the human predicament the cycle of life, death, and rebirth Hindus describe as samsara? Is it pride, as Muslims contend? Or something else altogether?

Sikhs have traditionally sought liberation (*moksha* in Sanskrit, **mukti** in Punjabi) from the cycle of life, death, and rebirth (**sansar** in Punjabi). "By the karma of past actions, the robe of this physical body is obtained," the Guru Granth reads. "By His Grace, the Gate of Liberation is found" (GG 2). Sikhs share with Hindus this diagnosis of our human malady and this prescription for a cure. Moreover, the title of their exemplar—the Guru, meaning "guide" or "teacher," a dispeller of darkness—is a Sanskrit term with deep roots in the Hindu tradition, though in this case (as with karma, or *karam* in Punjabi) Sikhs understand it differently. These facts would seem to offer strong evidence for viewing Sikhism as a Hindu sect rather than a distinct religion, but the human problem that preoccupies Sikhs and the solution they offer are far more complicated than a simple translation of "samsara" into "sansar" and "moksha" into "mukti."

According to the Sikh tradition, human beings are born with a divine spark. However, we are also born with a primal attachment to the self, called **haumai**. This foundational Sikh concept has been translated as self-centeredness, self-reliance, pride, and egoism. "Hau" means I and "mai" means me so haumai literally means "I, me." It has also been rendered as "I, me, mine," evoking a child who cannot stop demanding the immediate satisfaction of his desires. Sikhs do not trace this inborn egoism to Satan or a fall from paradise. It is endowed in us by God and it is not all bad. According to the Guru Granth:

> In ego [haumai] they come, and in ego they go. In ego they are born, and in ego they die. In ego they give, and in ego they take. In ego they earn, and in ego they lose. In ego they become truthful or false.... In ego they become dirty, and in ego they are washed clean.... In ego they are ignorant, and in ego they are wise. (GG 466)

Nonetheless, haumai is the source of the Five Thieves—lust, anger, greed, pride, and attachment to worldly things—that threaten to rob us of the nectar of immortality. As we age, these vices turn us into very different people from those who came into the world at birth. It is as if we are born looking toward God and then develop into adults who gaze only in the mirror. Later in this same passage, egoism is said to be a "chronic disease"

mukti
spiritual liberation; release from the cycle of birth, death, and rebirth

sansar
the unsatisfactory cycle of life, death, and rebirth, similar to *samsara* in Hinduism

haumai
egotism, self-centeredness, pride; the "I, me, mine"

Sikhism at a Glance

Problem: egotism (haumai)

Solution: union with God in the realm of truth

Techniques: hard work, service, meditation on the divine name (nam simran)

Exemplars: Gurus, who possess both temporal and spiritual authority

Therefore, Sikhism is a tradition in which "learners" seek to overcome egoism and achieve union with God through meditation on the divine name and by the guidance of the Gurus.

hukam
divine decree of the Guru Granth given each morning, but also and more generally the divine order

Akal Purakh ("Timeless One")
popular Sikh name for the divine

nam simran ("remembering the name")
meditation on the divine name

that keeps us in the karmic cycle of life, death, and rebirth. But like the predicament of pride in the Islamic tradition, this disease also separates us from God and from other human beings. Happily, for this disease there is a cure, which involves the grace of God, the wisdom of the Guru, and the willingness of humans to act. "In this way," Sikhs are told, "troubles depart" (GG 466).

Despite their close ties to the Indian tradition of release from rebirth, which can be seen in Hinduism and Buddhism alike, Sikhs are stayers rather than leavers. Their goal is not to be released from this world. Their goal is to be released from the ego in order to thrive in this world. Sikhs describe this liberation in two ways: first, as a shift in perspective; second, as union with the divine.

The typical human being is a *manmukh*—a "self-oriented" person devoted to doing the work of the Five Thieves. This work does not produce bliss. On the contrary, by causing us to forget God and others, it produces suffering. Sikhs aim to change this orientation—to turn from self to God and thus become a *gurmukh*, or "Guru-oriented" person—someone who turns her face to the divine. Therefore, the goal of Sikhism is to be delivered from haumai to **hukam** ("divine order")—from the sufferings of a life driven by the self to the peace and bliss of a life aligned with the divine will. The religious studies scholar Nikky-Guninder Kaur Singh likens the ego to a wall that separates us from God.[16] The goal is to break down this wall so you can live a more meaningful life focused on God and others. For Sikhs, this reorientation is the proximate goal. The ultimate goal is more difficult. Overcoming egoism continues to be the way forward, but in the end this path leads to union with the divine. Because the divine *is* reality, this encounter is also described as awakening or enlightenment. To enter the divine abode and unite with the Timeless One (**Akal Purakh**) is to pierce the "veil of falsehood" (GG 1) that is the ego and to realize the truth.

This ultimate goal recalls the deification pursued by Orthodox Christians but here union is stressed over likeness, and union of purpose over any union of the divine and human natures. In short, the Sikh goal is to harmonize with the divine order and thus to experience peace and bliss.

To reach this difficult-to-describe destination (which can only be attained by experience), it is not necessary to withdraw from the world. That is because God is immanent—present in the natural world and in human nature. Unlike those who worship transcendent gods (who are separate from and above ordinary life), Sikhs do not need to go far to find God. God is present in our work in the world and in family and social life. In fact, hard work and serving others are described in the Sikh tradition as key steps toward the religious goal. Just as Guru Nanak spent years as a wandering mystic only to settle down in a family, a community, and a religious institution, Sikhs are called to live here and now in this world. They do not have to wait until after death to be liberated. Theirs is a sensual tradition of the here and now—a way of song and poetry—that emphasizes the experiential and aesthetic dimensions of religion. According to the Guru Granth, eyes, ears, and lips see, hear, and speak the True Name (GG 1168).

In fact, the key technique on this worldly path to spiritual liberation is **nam simran**, or meditation on the divine name. According to Guru Nanak, this is the antidote to the problem of egoism. "I have no miracles," he said, "except the name of God."[17] Today, nam simran is the central Sikh practice. There are two ways of doing it. The first and most basic is repetition of the divine name, usually **Vahiguru** ("Wonderful Teacher"). The second and more difficult is remembrance of the divine name, which involves various meditation strategies designed to focus on God and sideline the ego.

Those who call on the divine name are said to move through five stages of spiritual development: duty, knowledge, effort, grace, and truth. The endpoint of this journey is the Realm of Truth, a state of bliss and peace in which one's essence merges with the essence of the Formless One, resides in harmony with the divine order, and is not reborn.

Sikhs offer various summaries of the things one can do to move from a self-centered to a God-centered life. In addition to reciting the divine name, these practices include giving alms, ritual bathing, hard work, love, and sharing with one's community. Given their emphasis on divine sovereignty, Sikhs do not believe that human beings can transcend egoism by self-effort alone. God's grace is also required.

God and Guru

The central utterance in the Sikh tradition, delivered by God to Guru Nanak in the divine abode and now appearing in the first line of the first page of the Guru Granth, is *Ik Oankar*. This difficult-to-translate formula is first and foremost an affirmation of monotheism. But it is much more. It begins not with a word but with a numeral: *Ik*, or 1. Next comes the first letter of the Gurmukhi script—*Oan*—a transliteration of the Sanskri *Om*, the sacred syllable that has resounded in India for millennia. The final sound, depicted by "a geometrical arc reaching away into space," connotes *kar*, or "is." Hence, "God Is One" or "One Being Is."[18]

In addition to the central affirmation of Sikh thought, Ik Oankar is the most widespread symbol in Sikh life. Like the dharma wheel for Buddhists and the Star of David for Jews, it has become an icon, appearing in gurdwaras, homes, and shops, and on the fine silk cloths that adorn the Guru Granth.

As the centrality of this symbol suggests, Sikhs prefer abstract nouns over flesh-and-blood descriptions when it comes to describing the divine. Some of the most popular include Akal Purakh ("Timeless One") and **Sat Nam** ("True Name"). Like the poet-singers from the North Indian Sant tradition, who professed their devotion to God as *nirguna*, Guru Nanak described God as indescribable. He also believed that this incomprehensible God could be comprehended through a combination of grace and guidance from a guru. As a result, Sikhs do ascribe qualities to the divine, who in their view is both personal and impersonal, both unknowable and known through the created world.

One of the more popular terms for God in the Sikh tradition is *Sahib* ("Sovereign"), which appears more than a hundred times in the Guru Granth. Alongside this transcendent understanding of the divine as creator and ruler of the world is an understanding of God as immanent—indwelling everywhere and in everyone.

Vahiguru ("Wonderful Teacher") popular Sikh name for the divine

Sat Nam ("True Name") popular Sikh name for the divine

The Ik Oankar symbol is the most important in Sikh life. Representing the oneness of God, it can be translated as "One Being Is."

This popular devotional painting depicts Sikhism's ten Gurus arrayed around an image of the Golden Temple.

The term "Sikh" is variously translated as "learner" or "follower," but in every case it is intimately paired with the guru, who teaches and leads. Although "guru" is a loan word from Sanskrit and Hinduism, Sikhs have made it their own. In the foundational moment of the Sikh tradition, God commissioned Nanak to be a Guru. And *Sat Guru* ("True Teacher") is a key Sikh name for the divine. Although Sikhs emphasize that their ten Gurus are not divine, these figures play outsized roles in their tradition. In keeping with the term "guru" itself, each of these men was a teacher and a guide. Together, they did far more. They wrote sacred texts and gathered them into sacred books. They developed rituals. They established the Golden Temple as a sacred center. Perhaps most important, they expanded the notion of guru far beyond human gurus, so that today Sikhs look to four types of gurus for spiritual authority: "the divine Guru . . . the personal Guru . . . the scriptural Guru . . . and the community as Guru."[19] Nonetheless, it is the ten historical Gurus who act as Sikh exemplars, models of human belief and practice. Sikhs have collected clothing, weapons, and other objects related to their ten Gurus and put them on display. As Asian studies scholar Anne Murphy has observed, they have also collected objects of the Gurus' wives and other women remembered for the service they offered to a Guru.[20]

The Guru—"the raft" that transports you "to the Lord's Name" (GG 17)—is also embedded in other key Sikh concepts. As previously mentioned, the script of the Guru Granth, Gurmukhi, means "from the mouth of the Guru." Holy days commemorating the birthdays of gurus are called *gurpurbs* ("guru festivals"). A gurdwara, which originally referred to a place of worship where a living guru was present, now refers to a gathering space made sacred by the presence of the Guru Granth. Gurus are so central to Sikh life that the Sikh tradition itself—its doctrines, practices, and way of life—is referred to as *Gurmat* ("The Way of the Guru"). It is to these teachers (and their teachings) that those who call themselves "learners" turn for guidance in matters of work, family, and religion alike.

SIKH HISTORY

Among the many important decisions Guru Nanak made, the most monumental was to perpetuate the office of Guru after his death. Passing over his two sons, Guru Nanak tapped a disciple named Bhai Lehna to serve as the second Sikh guru. He called him Angad, meaning "limb," to indicate that his successor should be accepted as an extension of his own body.

Over time, the lineage begun by Guru Nanak would extend to ten Gurus. In keeping with Sikhism's strict monotheism, none of them is to be worshiped as a god. Each is said to be a guide. But while Sikhs distinguish between Gurus and God, they creatively combine the identities of their Gurus. In the Guru Granth, compositions by Gurus are signed

"Nanak," as if each of these men were an extension of him. One of the most common metaphors used to describe the ten Gurus is as one light passing from lamp to lamp. Sikhs maintain that their Gurus (also referred to as Nanak 1 through Nanak 10) speak in one voice, which resounds wherever the Guru Granth is recited.

Given this view of the unity of their Gurus, it should not be surprising that Sikhs emphasize continuity over change in Sikh history. All religious traditions change over time, however. One notable Sikh change is ironic, given Guru Nanak's lack of interest in the external forms of religion and his belief in the essential unity of religions. This surprising adaptation is the gradual development of a distinctive Sikh identity rooted in identifiable Sikh dress and characteristic Sikh rituals. Religions seem to need rituals like farmers need the rain, and despite Guru Nanak's well-known wariness of external rituals and priestly mediators, the nine Gurus who succeeded him were perfectly happy to serve as Sikhism's rainmakers.

SIKHISM: A GENEALOGY

According to the *Oxford English Dictionary*, the word "Sikh" made its way into the English language via Charles Wilkins, an East India Company printer and British Orientalist who wrote the first English translation of the Hindu scripture the Bhagavad Gita. In a March 1781 letter to the Calcutta-based Asiatick Society, Wilkins referred to "that sect of people who are distinguished from the worshippers of Brahm, and the followers of Mahommed by the appellation *Seek*." In an attached account of a visit to a Sikh place of worship in Patna, India, he described members of the congregation as "very intelligent" and himself as "singularly delighted" with the man who chanted so joyously "a Hymn in praise of the unity, the omnipresence, and the omnipotence, of the Deity."[a]

There are earlier uses, however, beginning in 1768 with *The History of Hindostan* (1768) by Alexander Dow, a Scottish Orientalist and East India Company Army officer. Although "the Seiks" are described here largely in military and political terms, there is an odd reference to them as "followers of a certain philosopher of Thibet, who taught the idea of a commonwealth, and the pure doctrine of Deism, without any mixture of either the Mahomeddan or Hindu superstitions."[b] The first English-language history of the Sikhs, *An History*

of the Origin and Progress of the Sicks (1788), by the East India Company envoy James Browne, offered information on a "tribe of people called Sicks." Viewing his subject through a comparative lens, Browne wrote that their doctrine "appears to bear that kind of relation to the Hindoo religion, which the Protestant does to the Romish."[c]

The spelling *Sikhism* followed more than a half century later, in 1849, the same year the British annexed the Punjab. The source was *A History of the Sikhs*, a surprisingly sympathetic account by Joseph Davey Cunningham, another Scottish Orientalist and soldier. According to Cunningham, Sikhism was in the vanguard of global progress in both religion and society. Its modern spirit, he wrote, "rejects as vain the ancient forms and ideas" of Hindus and Muslims and "clings for present solace and future happiness to new intercessors," namely, their Gurus.[d]

Early Western interpreters of the Sikhs (variously spelled *Seiks, Seeks, Seekhs, Seikhs*, etc.) disagreed about the derivation of this term. Wilkins reported that he had heard in Patna that it was borrowed from a commandment by the Sikh founder to "learn." Later writers argued that it came from Hindu and Sanskrit terms for "disciple."

Living Gurus

The second Guru (Guru Angad) was more loyalist than innovator, but the third Guru (Guru Amar Das) developed new rites of passage for birth and death. He also established distinctive Sikh festivals to take place on Hindu festival days. The fourth Guru (Guru Ram Das) developed a Sikh marriage ceremony. Also, by founding Amritsar and ordering the digging of the sacred tank that would come to surround the Golden Temple, he gave the Sikhs a sacred center that would develop into their own mecca.

The fifth Guru (Guru Arjan) contributed more hymns (2,218) to the Guru Granth than any other guru. More important, he is remembered for compiling that scripture and enshrining it in 1604 in what would come to be called the Golden Temple. According to the Sikh tradition, the circulation of questionable compositions made this compilation necessary. By separating "fake" from "authentic" passages, Guru Arjan helped create a coherent Sikh identity (as readers and reciters of the real scripture). Because religious pluralism was part of that identity, he included in his canon not only the poems and hymns of previous gurus but also compositions by Hindu and Muslim sages. However, Guru Arjan also cautioned Sikhs against taking part in the practices of other religious communities, insisting on an exclusive Sikh identity that was increasingly divorced from Muslim and Hindu practices. In the Guru Granth, Guru Arjan writes:

> I do not keep fasts, nor do I observe the month of Ramadaan. . . . I do not make pilgrimages to Mecca, nor do I worship at Hindu sacred shrines. . . . I have taken the One Formless Lord into my heart; I humbly worship Him there. I am not a Hindu, nor am I a Muslim. (GG 1136)

Guru Arjan was also influential in his death, a watershed in Sikh history that the Sikh scholar Pashaura Singh has described as "the single most important factor for the crystallization of the Sikh Panth."[21] During his guruship, the Sikh community grew enough to catch the wary eye of the Mughal emperor Jahangir. The Mughals, who were Muslims, ruled much of northern India from the sixteenth into the eighteenth centuries, and Jahangir was their fourth emperor. In 1606, he ordered Guru Arjan's arrest and imprisonment in Lahore. After Guru Arjan refused to convert to Islam, he was tortured and died in Mughal custody. In this way, Sikhism's fifth Guru became its first martyr, and the Sikh

---

SIKHISM BY THE NUMBERS

The Ten Gurus

The ten Gurus of the Sikhs point their disciples toward the Formless One, but they themselves are also objects of reverence and remembrance. As the Asian studies professor Anne Murphy writes, "Clothing, chariots, weapons, and shoes" associated with these men "are collected and revered in private homes and in sacred sites across the Punjab, as well as in the broader Sikh diaspora in India and farther afield."[a] Here the years that follow each man's name are the years he served as a living Guru.

- Guru Nanak (1499–1539)
- Guru Angad (1539–1552)
- Guru Amar Das (1552–1574)
- Guru Ram Das (1574–1581)

- Guru Arjan (1581–1606)
- Guru Hargobind (1606–1644)
- Guru Har Rai (1644–1661)
- Guru Har Kishen (1661–1664)

- Guru Tegh Bahadur (1664–1675)
- Guru Gobind Singh (1675–1708)

tradition increasingly emphasized political and military matters alongside religious and social concerns.

In response to this turning point in Sikh history, and to wider Mughal persecution of Sikhs, Guru Arjan's son and successor Guru Hargobind reimagined the Sikh path and the role of Gurus and learners alike. He raised an army. He encouraged his followers to bear arms. Dressing like a soldier, he brandished two swords, one symbolizing his spiritual authority and the other his political authority. In another gesture toward this new union of the timeless and the temporal, Guru Hargobind also laid the foundation for the Akal Takht governmental center, now a stone's throw from the Golden Temple. Just a century after Guru Nanak heard a voice calling him from the Bein River, Sikhs were coming to see themselves as participants in a mystical *and* martial tradition that not only called on the "True Name" but also fought for justice and righteousness on God's behalf.

A Second Founder: The Tenth Guru

Guru Gobind Singh, the tenth Guru, also came to power after the martyrdom of his father (Guru Tegh Bahadur). He was a military man as well as a spiritual contemplative, and he, too, would die for his tradition. Today, he is remembered at four of the "five seats" of the Sikh tradition visited by pious pilgrims: one in Patna, where he was born; one in Anandpur, where he established the "Order of the Pure"; one in Damdama, where he compiled the final version of the Guru Granth; and one in Nander, where he died.

It was Guru Gobind Singh who declared that, upon his death, the authority of the guru would reside in Sikh scripture (Guru Granth) and the Sikh community (Guru Panth). He prepared the final version of the Guru Granth. Also attributed to him is the second most important Sikh scripture, the **Dasam Granth** ("Book of the Tenth Guru"). Guru Gobind Singh is most significant, however, for overseeing what one historian of the movement has described as "the most important event in Sikh history."[22] The story of that day—a Sikh analog to the Hebrew Bible narrative of the binding of Isaac—is now fundamental to Sikh piety. It is also historically important, because on this day the tradition added to its long-standing emphasis on interior spirituality a new emphasis on the exterior symbols of the Khalsa.

It was a crowded festival day—Baisakhi to Sikhs, celebrated at the beginning of the harvest—in Anandpur ("City of Bliss") in the Punjab in 1699. Sword in hand, Guru Gobind Rai (as he was known at the start of that day) stood before his followers and asked for a volunteer to give up his life for his Guru. After much murmuring, someone stepped forward. The tenth Guru took him inside a tent. The crowd heard metal meet flesh and a thud on the ground. The tenth Guru emerged with a bloody sword. He asked for a second volunteer, and a third, fourth, and fifth. In some versions of this story, all five men were really and truly decapitated only to be brought back to life by the power of God. In other retellings, five goats were killed inside the tent in place of these men.

Dasam Granth ("Book of the Tenth Guru")

secondary Sikh scripture, traditionally attributed to Guru Gobind Singh

This eighteenth-century illuminated frontispiece to the Dasam Granth, a Sikh scripture containing texts attributed to the tenth Guru, Guru Gobind Singh, illustrates scenes from his life.

Guru Gobind Singh, the tenth Guru, is revered as both a military leader and a mystic. He profoundly shaped the Sikh tradition by establishing the Sikh fraternity the Khalsa and, later, by naming the Sikh scripture the Adi Granth to be his successor.

The tenth Guru then conducted the first initiation ceremony for a fellowship of valor that was itself initiated that day: the Khalsa, or Order of the Pure. He and his wife, Mata Jito, transformed fresh water into the nectar of immortality (*amrit*) as he chanted Sikh verses over it while stirring it with a double-edged sword and she added some sweets to the mix. He fed this elixir to the five volunteers, each from a different caste and a different part of India, who came to be known as the Five Beloved. The tenth Guru gave each of these men a new surname, *Singh* ("lion"), as a sign of their valor and to replace their caste names. (Female initiates would later receive the surname *Kaur*, or "princess.") He instructed the initiates to leave caste distinctions behind and to see one another as brothers instead. He then received amrit himself from the Five Beloved and, adopting the name of Singh himself, was initiated as Guru Gobind Singh. Obscuring the distinctions between himself (as Guru) and them (as disciples), he proclaimed, "The Khalsa is the Guru and the Guru is the Khalsa. There is no difference between you and me."[23] Even as he blurred the lines *inside* the Khalsa, he amplified differences between Sikhs and non-Sikhs, instructing initiates not to blend into the multireligious crowd that was sixteenth-century India but to stand proudly apart from it.

Eventually Sikhs would publish detailed codes of conduct instructing learners how to dress and eat and act. On this festival day, the tenth Guru offered members of his new order a new way of being in the world. Rise at dawn with the divine name on your lips, he told them. Do not worship idols or go on pilgrimage to the Ganges. Renounce caste and see one another as family instead. Heed the Sikh scriptures rather than the Vedas or the Quran. Carry a sword and fight if necessary. Guru Gobind Singh also instructed his initiates to follow a code of conduct that today includes abstaining from smoking, from extramarital sex, and from eating meat killed in the Islamic fashion.

According to Sikh lore, the innovations of this day also extended to the distinctive form of dress called the **Five Ks**:

uncut hair and beard (*kesha*)
comb (*kangha*)
steel bracelet (*kara*)
short breeches (*kacha*)
sword (*kirpan*)

Some scholars are convinced that these Five Ks came later. But eventually Sikhs who joined the Khalsa would wear turbans to cover their long hair. They would comb their hair to distinguish themselves from unkempt Hindu holy men. And they would brandish a sword—the central symbol on the Sikh flag today—to demonstrate their willingness to fight for what is right. "When all other means have failed," Guru Gobind Singh wrote to the Mughal emperor, "it is permissible to draw the sword."[24]

Because of the Khalsa's acceptance of fighting to defend their values, it has sometimes been referred to as a military order—a Sikh analog to the Knights Templar of Catholicism

Five Ks
five symbols worn by Khalsa members, including *kesha* (uncut hair), *kangha* (comb), *kara* (steel bracelet), *kacha* (long shorts), *kirpan* (sword)

who fought Muslims in the Crusades. The sixth Guru, Hargobind, raised an army and became the first Sikh guru to fight to defend the Sikh tradition. On that pathbreaking Baisakhi day in 1699, Guru Gobind Singh advanced this trend of militarizing the Sikh tradition in the face of external dangers, bringing to fruition the ideal of the saint-soldier committed to fighting for God and righteousness. The tenth Guru now referred to this God as "All Steel" and "The Sword." The day's events also added a new goal to the Sikh tradition: creating a kingdom of righteousness on earth, a political order reflecting the justice and grace of the divine. In this way, Sikhs came to view the Punjab not only as their homeland but also as a gift they were to defend with their lives.

Guru Gobind Singh would die a martyr, as would his four sons. Most of the Khalsa members to follow would come from the Jat peasant caste, who reveled in that order's discipline, egalitarianism, and warrior ethic. For these reasons, Baisakhi in 1699 did turn "sparrows into hawks," as the title of a book on this subject affirms.[25] But the founding of the Khalsa was not simply a military action. It was a religious event that helped transform Sikhism into an organized religion. Only a minority of Sikhs would ever join this Order of the Pure (today 5 to 15 percent of all Sikhs are Khalsa initiates). Well into the modern period, it would remain largely off-limits to women. But the Khalsa norm would come to exert a strong gravitational pull on Sikh identity. In this respect, Guru Gobind Singh was Sikhism's second founder.

The Sikh flag represents the ideals of the Sikh fraternity the Khalsa, including the duty to fight for justice. The center contains a *khanda*, or double-edged sword, surrounded by a *chakram*, or throwing weapon. Both are encompassed within two single-edged swords, or *kirpans*, crossed at the bottom.

The Sikh Raj and the Sikh Renaissance

In the generations that followed the martyrdom of Guru Gobind Singh, military calculations often overrode spiritual concerns, as Sikhs and the Khalsa struggled for political as well as spiritual freedom. For much of the eighteenth century, Sikhs fought under the battle cry, "The Khalsa shall rule." But Mughals and Afghans dominated them and their homeland. In 1799, however, Sikh military campaigns produced a Sikh Raj ("rule"), led by Maharaja Ranjit Singh, who from his base in Lahore would lord over a vast territory in the Punjab and beyond until his death in 1839. This was by no means a Sikh-only kingdom. In fact, Sikhs were a minority in the lands under the maharaja's control, and "the Lion of the Punjab," as he was called, allowed for a wide variety of religious expressions among his Muslim, Hindu, and Christian subjects.

Following the maharaja's death in 1839, the Sikh Raj fell apart and, after two Anglo-Sikh wars, the Punjab became in 1849 the last part of the subcontinent to be annexed by the British. Sikhs now had a choice. They could fight the British like they had fought the Afghans and Mughals, or they could work with them. For the most part, they decided to work with them, coming to their aid in the Indian Rebellion of 1857 (also known as the Sepoy Mutiny). For a time, Sikhs were rewarded for this loyalty. The British, praising Sikhs for their "manly boldness" and "internal vigour," deployed them widely as police officers and in the military (where they were allowed to wear their turbans and were expected to follow Khalsa discipline).[26]

Before and under the British Raj, the nineteenth century was a period of religious ferment across the subcontinent, as Indians wrestled with the intellectual and social challenges of modernity. The Hindu Renaissance produced a variety of reform organizations, including the Arya Samaj, a "back to the Vedas" group that shared much with Sikhism, including monotheism and opposition to image worship and caste. Sikh reformers were also active. The political and military adventures of the Sikh Raj had, in their view, distracted Sikhs from internal spiritual pursuits. In Ranjit Singh's religiously tolerant kingdom, many Hindu and Muslim practices had flourished even among Sikhs. External threats to Sikh piety were equally troubling, as Christian missionaries, Hindu reformers, Muslims, and secularists all worked hard to influence the Sikh population.

Sikhs responded to these challenges—and to British power in India—with a Sikh Renaissance that sought to reform Sikhism by going "back to the Gurus" and by drawing ever sharper distinctions between Sikhism and Hinduism. In an era when British administrators and intellectuals were coming to view Hinduism, Islam, and Christianity as "world religions," these Sikh reformers demanded equal treatment. Sikhism was India's third religion, they argued, and increasingly the Sikh rank and file came "to think, imagine and speak in terms of a universal community of believers united by uniform rites, symbols and scripture,"[27] according to Asian studies scholar Harjot Oberoi. This growing power of the Sikh mainstream by no means drowned out Sikh dissenters, however. Much of the drama of the Sikh Renaissance concerned just how much dissent the defenders (and definers) of Sikh orthodoxy would permit.

Two nineteenth-century reform groups, the Nirankaris and the Namdharis, rejected the traditional view that the count of human gurus ended at ten. Both of these groups also sought to reform and revive Sikh spiritual practices, which in their view had sacrificed spiritual devotion to political intrigue. Each advocated for women and had its own distinctive food customs.

CHRONOLOGY OF SIKHISM

1469–1539 Life of Guru Nanak

1499 Guru Nanak's mystical encounter

1519 Guru Nanak establishes a community at Kartarpur

1577 Guru Ram Das founds a town that will come to be called Amritsar

1604 Guru Arjan installs the newly completed Adi Granth at the Harimandir (now known as the Golden Temple)

1606 Guru Arjan becomes the first Sikh martyr after being arrested by the Mughal emperor Jahangir and dying in Mughal custody

1666–1708 Life of Guru Gobind Singh, the tenth Guru

1699 Guru Gobind Singh establishes the Khalsa order

1708 Just before his death, Guru Gobind Singh appoints the Guru Granth as his successor

1799–1839 Sikh kingdom in the Punjab under Maharaja Ranjit Singh

1845–1849 First and Second Anglo-Sikh Wars

1849 British annex the Punjab

1873 Singh Sabha is organized at Amritsar in response to efforts by the Arya Samaj to win Sikhs to Hinduism and by Christian missionaries to convert Sikhs

1898 *We Are Not Hindus* emphasizes Sikh distinctiveness

1905 Singh Sabha pushes successfully to eliminate Hindu images from the Golden Temple

1907 Nativist riot in Bellingham, Washington, chases several hundred Sikhs across the Canadian border

The Nirankaris, established during the early nineteenth century when the Punjab was a Sikh state, considered their founder Dayal Das (1783–1855) to be a Guru. As their name implies, they worshiped a formless God who neither took on human bodies nor took up residence in idols. They worshiped almost exclusively through meditation on the divine name—a practice that in their founder's view had been sorely neglected as Sikhs rose to political power. Nirankaris avoided both alcohol and tobacco. Seeking to purge Sikh rituals of Hindu elements, they disposed of their dead not by cremation but by casting their corpses into a river. And they sharply criticized the ritualistic widow burning (*sati*) of the wives of the deposed leader of the Sikh Raj, Maharaja Ranjit Singh, at his funeral in 1839. Upon the Partition of India and Pakistan in 1947, the Nirankaris, who were dominated by urban merchants, split into two communities, one now centered in New Delhi and the other in Chandigarh.

The Namdharis represented a later effort to respond to what many saw as spiritual decline by following living gurus and reviving the Sikh tradition of meditating on the divine name. Founded by Balak Singh (1787–1862) in 1857 after the fall of the Sikh Raj, the Namdharis opposed British rule. Balak Singh's successor, Ram Singh, was the first Indian freedom fighter to use the business boycott as a political weapon—a nonviolent strategy later employed by both Mohandas Gandhi in India and the Reverend Martin Luther King Jr. in the United States. Namdharis, who came mostly from the carpenter caste, promoted women's rights by opposing female infanticide and holding simple weddings (sometimes with more than one couple) to avoid dowry payments to brides' families. They also insisted that the Khalsa be open to women as well as men. Today, Namdharis are readily distinguishable from other Sikhs by their white homespun garb and their distinctive turban, which is tied straight across the forehead. In foodways, they are strict vegetarians. In aesthetics, they are Shaker simple. Because their chanting can include shrieks (*kuks*), they are also known as Kuka ("Shrieking") Sikhs.

1908 Sikhs build first gurdwara in North America in Vancouver, BC

1909 Anand Marriage Act recognizes Sikh marriages performed around the Guru Granth (instead of a sacred fire)

1913 Sikhs found Ghadar Party in California

1915 The first gurdwara in the United States is built in Stockton, California

1919 Nearly four hundred Sikhs die in the Amritsar Massacre

1923 In *United States v. Bhagat Singh Thind*, the Supreme Court rules that an Indian-born Sikh man is not a "white person" and therefore cannot be a U.S. citizen

1925 Sikh Gurdwaras Act cedes administrative control of gurdwaras to the Shiromani Gurdwara Parbandhak Committee (SGPC)

1947 Partition of Pakistan and India cuts Punjab in two

1950 SGPC formulates a Sikh Code of Conduct (*Sikh Rehat Maryada*) that defines Sikh orthodoxy

1966 India creates a Sikh-majority Punjab state

1984 Operation Blue Star expels Sikh separatists from the Golden Temple

Prime Minister Indira Gandhi is assassinated by her Sikh bodyguards, prompting anti-Sikh riots

2004–2014 Manmohan Singh serves as the first Sikh prime minister of India

2018 Gursoch Kaur becomes the first turbaned woman to work for the New York Police Department

2019 550th birthday of Guru Nanak is celebrated worldwide

The Namdharis ("The Name People"), easily distinguished from other Sikhs by their all-white garb and distinctive turbans, began in the mid-nineteenth century as a reform movement emphasizing the repetition of the divine name. Unlike most Sikhs who believe that the line of human gurus ended at ten, Namdharis follow living gurus.

The most influential of the late-nineteenth-century reform efforts was the **Singh Sabha** ("Singh Society"). In 1868, India's census had shown that Sikhs constituted a small minority—less than 7 percent—of the Punjabi population. In 1873, four Sikh students at the Amritsar Mission School announced their intention to be baptized as Christians. These two developments alarmed many Sikhs. In Amritsar in 1873, reformers established the Singh Sabha in an effort to shore up support for the Sikh tradition. From the beginning, Sikhs had lived under a "big tent," with a variety of competing expressions coexisting under its sacred canopy. To the founders of the Singh Sabha, all this diversity was an embarrassment to good order and to Sikhism's good name, so they worked hard to push their tradition toward uniformity.

Though frequently described as an effort to enforce Sikh orthodoxy by sharpening the distinctions between Sikhism and Hinduism, the Singh Sabha actually served as a moderator of sorts for a vigorous debate over just how monolithic modern Sikhism should be. This organization spread to Lahore in 1879 and grew rapidly after the Hindu reform organization the Arya Samaj (once seen as a possible ally) decided to include Sikhs in its campaign to "reconvert" lapsed Hindus back to its version of Hindu orthodoxy. One particularly controversial part of that campaign was an 1897 speech by a Sikh descendant of Guru Nanak arguing that there is no essential difference between Sikhs and Hindus. That speech was later published as a tract called *Sikhs Are Hindus* (1899).

Activities and ideologies inside the Singh Sabha varied widely from chapter to chapter. Amritsar featured a more moderate approach that allowed for many ways of being Sikh and accommodated Hindu elements in the name of a broader Indian religiosity rooted in the ancient Vedic scriptures. Lahore's more radical members were keener on making Sikhism follow the "world religion" model by being more unified, more systematized, and less Hindu. Lahore reformers vigorously opposed Sikh groups that followed living gurus and worked hard to win back those who had left the tradition. They also downplayed the

Singh Sabha ("Singh Society")
late-nineteenth-century Sikh reform organization

importance of the secondary scripture the Dasam Granth, which contained extensive retellings of Hindu mythology. This stricter Tat Khalsa ("True Khalsa") approach of the Lahore Singh Sabha prevailed, spreading rapidly through institutions such as Khalsa College and the Khalsa Tract Society, both founded in Amritsar in the early 1890s.

Some scholars contend that Sikhism did not emerge out of Hinduism as a separate religion until the late nineteenth century. This is probably overstating how intertwined these traditions had been. But by 1901, when the official report on the Indian census was referring to the Singh Sabha as "the most active organization in Sikhism," a new Sikh orthodoxy had taken hold, focused on "Guru, Granth, and Gurdwara."[28] Increasingly, the term "Sikhs" referred to those who revered ten and only ten Gurus, who rejected Vedic authority in the name of the Guru Granth, who went to gurdwaras and not to Hindu temples, whose rituals were defined by their lack of Hindu features, and who honored the Khalsa as an expression of pure Sikhism. One of the signature Sikh utterances of the late nineteenth century—and a key driver of the "khalsa-fication" and "de-Hinduization" of Sikh life—was a pamphlet whose emphatic title, *We Are Not Hindus* (1898), makes any summary of its contents unnecessary. The title of this popular tract became a slogan for the assertion of a separate Sikh identity—an argument not only for Sikhism as a distinct "world religion" but also for Sikhs as a separate political community.

In 1905, the Singh Sabha and its Tat Khalsa Sikhs succeeded in eliminating Hindu images from the Golden Temple. In the Anand Marriage Act of 1909, it won the right of Sikhs to perform marriages not around a sacred fire (as in Hindu marriages) but around the Guru Granth. At the start of what came to be known as the Gurdwara Reform Movement (also the Akali Movement), Tat Khalsa Sikhs founded the Central Sikh League (CSL) in 1919 and then a political party called the Shiromani Akali Dal (SAD) in 1920.

The purpose of these activists was to take control of the Golden Temple from the British and take control of gurdwaras across the region from overseers it deemed to be either

Traditional Sikh weddings are three-day affairs, culminating in the Anand Karaj ("Blissful Union") ceremony. As part of this ritual, which is held in a gurdwara in front of the Guru Granth, the groom's father drapes his son in a scarf and gives the bride one end to hold, symbolizing their impending unity.

Shiromani Gurdwara Parbandhak Committee (SGPC)
committee that oversees the administration of the Golden Temple and other Sikh shrines

corrupt or insufficiently orthodox. Many of these overseers were monastic holy men called Udasis ("Withdrawers"), a group of renouncers that traced its origins to Guru Nanak's son Sri Chand. Though once widely regarded as Sikhs, the Udasis were marginalized in the early twentieth century as Sikhs increasingly emphasized their differences with Hinduism. Today, most Udasis, who are centered in Haridwar in northwestern India, regard themselves as Hindus.

In a struggle over the historic gurdwara at the birthplace of Guru Nanak in Nankana Sahib, more than a hundred SAD members were killed by supporters of the overseer. Before the Gurdwara Reform Movement was over, roughly four thousand were killed and thirty thousand imprisoned. Tat Khalsa Sikhs finally won control of these sites in 1925 with the passage of the Sikh Gurdwaras Act, which allowed for a democratically elected board of Sikhs, the **Shiromani Gurdwara Parbandhak Committee (SGPC)**, to oversee gurdwara administration in the Punjab. This development bolstered the authority of Tat Khalsa Sikhs. It also gave a major push to the nonviolent struggle for Indian independence by proving that the British were not immune to public pressure.

Now housed inside the Golden Temple complex, the SGPC evolved into a guardian of Tat Khalsa orthodoxy. In 1950, it put that orthodoxy in writing when it formalized the *Sikh Rehat Maryada* code of conduct that began by defining a Sikh in strikingly exclusivist terms, effectively banishing anyone who followed a living guru or interpreted Sikhism as a Hindu path:

> A Sikh is any person who believes in God (*Akal Purakh*); in the ten Gurus (Guru Nanak to Guru Gobind Singh); in Sri Guru Granth Sahib, other writings of the ten Gurus, and their teachings; in the Khalsa initiation ceremony instituted by the tenth Guru; and who does not believe in any other system of religious doctrine.[29]

The Delhi Sikh Gurdwaras Act (1971) defined Sikh even more narrowly, as someone who professes Sikhism, affirms and follows the teachings of the Guru Granth, reveres ten and only ten Gurus, and keeps unshorn hair.

Of course, Sikh leaders felt compelled to stress Sikh distinctiveness only because many Sikhs continued to participate in Hindu festivals, patronize Hindu deities, go on pilgrimage to the Ganges, and cut their hair. Similarly, Sikh leaders felt compelled to stress Sikh orthodoxy only because many Sikhs, like practitioners of all religions, followed the straight-and-narrow path irregularly, or not at all.

Indian Independence and Khalistan

Political and military events also shook the Sikh community in the early twentieth century, which saw the British Indian Army drawn into two world wars followed by the achievement of Indian independence. Many of that army's soldiers were Sikhs from the Punjab.

In 1915, during World War I, Mohandas Gandhi returned to India after a twenty-one-year legal career in South Africa. He brought with him a nonviolent tactic of civil disobedience and resistance to evil he called *satyagraha* ("holding fast to truth"). On April 6, 1919, he called for a national general strike to protest the Rowlatt Act, which had extended Britain's wartime emergency powers in India (to detain people without trial and to restrict freedom of speech and movement). British authorities responded by arresting him four days later. Protests broke out in Amritsar, and on April 13 several thousand Sikhs who

Women at the Jallianwala Bagh Memorial in Amritsar, India, look at a painting depicting the Amritsar Massacre. On April 13, 1919, British soldiers fired on unarmed Sikhs, killing hundreds and wounding many more.

had gathered for the Baisakhi festival at the Golden Temple squeezed into a nearby garden called the Jallianwala Bagh. Brigadier-General Reginald Dyer, emboldened by restrictions on freedom of assembly in the Rowlatt Act, marched his soldiers to the site and ordered them to fire. Officially, 379 unarmed civilians were killed, though that figure may have been much higher. Denounced worldwide as the Amritsar Massacre—Secretary of War Winston Churchill called it "sinister" and "monstrous"—this event played a key role in turning Sikhs against British rule and toward the cause of Indian independence.[30]

As Gandhi's campaigns went forward and independence loomed in the early 1940s, talk of splitting the subcontinent into two separate states of India and Pakistan picked up. Sikh activists agitated for a separate Sikh state—Khalistan—in central Punjab that would have the right to join either India or Pakistan. Amidst the chaos of independence and Partition, however, the Sikhs did not have the numbers or the political clout to win their own state. Muslims got Pakistan, Hindus got a supposedly secular India, and the Punjab was hacked in two. In the massive displacement that followed, the Punjab became a sea of refugees and the epicenter of post-independence violence. For the most part, Sikhs decided to cast their lot with India, so most of those with ancestral lands in newly created Pakistan moved eastward, leaving behind sacred sites such as the birthplace of their founder and the capital of Maharajah Ranjit Singh's kingdom. Meanwhile, Muslims in eastern Punjab migrated west into Pakistan and Hindus in western Punjab migrated east into India. Massive bloodshed ensued, as did a lingering longing among Sikhs for independence.

In the 1970s, that longing surfaced in the work of the Sikh scholar-turned-activist Sant Jarnail Singh Bhindranwale (1947–1984). Sikh culture was in danger of being lost to secularity, he argued, and Sikh identity was in danger of being absorbed into Hinduism. The only way to avert these dangers was Sikh separatism. In July 1982, amidst escalating

Manmohan Singh (1932–)

In 2004, when the Indian National Congress party took power in India's parliamentary elections, the Sikh economist Manmohan Singh (1932–) became India's first non-Hindu prime minister. Sikhs were still reeling at the time from the anti-Sikh riots that shook the country after Operation Blue Star two decades earlier, and Singh's ascent to power was widely hailed as a major step toward religious tolerance in India, especially because his Congress Party was displacing the Hindu nationalist Bharatiya Janata Party.

Born before Partition in Gah, a Punjabi village now in Pakistan, Singh was educated at Punjab University before moving to England, where he earned his doctorate in economics from Oxford University. Appointed India's Finance Minister in 1991, he oversaw a dramatic restructuring of the Indian economy, liberalizing its markets and opening the country to foreign investment. Though he lost his ministerial position when the Congress Party was ousted in 1996, he served as the opposition leader in the upper house of India's parliament until his party's return to power in 2004.

Singh has said little publicly about his religious identity, but his fellow Sikhs greeted the elevation of a turbaned Sikh to prime minister as an opportunity to undercut anti-Sikh bigotry and elevate the position of Sikhs in Indian society. These hopes were buoyed when, shortly after his appointment, Singh joined thousands of Sikhs in celebrating the four hundredth anniversary of the installation of the Sikh scriptures in the Golden Temple. In 2005, Singh publicly apologized on behalf of the Indian government for the anti-Sikh riots that followed Operation Blue Star in 1984. However, some Sikhs complain that Singh did little to advance Sikh rights in India. His first allegiance, they argue, was not to Sikhism but to India.

political violence in the Punjab, Bhindranwale moved into the Golden Temple complex and held forth on the duty of Sikhs to fight and die for a separate country—Khalistan—rather than live like slaves in India. He gathered supporters, who gathered weapons and occupied the Akal Takht. In June 1984, in Operation Blue Star, the Indian Army moved in and drove the separatists out, leaving hundreds of unarmed pilgrims and armed separatists dead, Bhindranwale included. The Golden Temple and the Akal Takht were severely damaged, the Sikh reference library on the premises was destroyed, and many priceless manuscripts were burned. Bhindranwale became yet another Sikh martyr.

Before Operation Blue Star, many Sikhs saw Bhindranwale as a rabble-rouser who was unduly inciting violence. In the wake of the massacre, however, even moderate Sikhs with no interest in Khalistan were outraged by the Indian Army's attack on their sacred space. On October 31, 1984, two Sikh bodyguards retaliated by assassinating Indian prime minister Indira Gandhi. The anti-Sikh riots that followed left thousands of Sikhs dead in New Delhi and other Indian cities and many more homeless or on the move. Many of these newly homeless eventually settled in the increasingly Sikh Punjab.

SIKHISM IN THE UNITED STATES

Sikhs first moved outside the Punjab in numbers after the British annexed the region in 1849. British transportation networks enabled mobility inside the subcontinent on railroads and outside it on ships. The British also dispatched Sikh men far and wide into their expanding empire in army uniforms. When these soldiers left the army, many remained in such places as Hong Kong and Singapore. Their extended families followed.

In North America in the early twentieth century, immigrants from India were referred to indiscriminately as "Hindoos," but the overwhelming majority were Punjabi Sikhs. Because Canada and India were both part of the British Empire, many Sikhs sailed to Vancouver, the site of the first Sikh gurdwara in North America (est. 1908). Some stayed in British Columbia to work on the Canadian Pacific Railway or in the lumber industry. Many more pushed south into California for agricultural work. Around six thousand such "Hindoos"—almost all of them Sikh men from the rural Punjab—came to the United States in the first decades of the twentieth century, pushed by famine in the Punjab and pulled by prospects of labor in a booming American West.

Sikhs' early years in the United States were pockmarked by intolerance and violence. Nativists denounced Sikhs as "ragheads" and sought to exclude them from the United States. In 1907, anti-Sikh riots broke out in California, Washington, and Alaska. In Bellingham, Washington, a riot led by white laborers chased several hundred Indian Americans (most of them Sikhs) across the border into Canada. Soon the anti-immigrant Asiatic Exclusion League was denouncing not only the "yellow peril" of Chinese and Japanese immigrants but also a "Tide of Turbans." In 1913, California responded with the Alien Land Act, which prevented Chinese, Japanese, Korean, and Indian farmers from owning real estate.

Rather than renouncing this nativism, the U.S. government codified it. Congress created a "barred zone" in 1917 that effectively banned immigration from India and Southeast Asia. In 1923, the court case *United States v. Bhagat Singh Thind* pitted the federal government against a Sikh veteran of the U.S. Army. The U.S. Supreme Court ruled for the government, on the theory that Asian Indians, while admittedly "Caucasian," were not "white persons" in the popular sense of that term and therefore were not eligible for naturalization. One year later, Congress passed the Oriental Exclusion Act, which cut off immigration for people not eligible for naturalization and largely terminated Asian Indian immigration.

North American Sikhs responded to this discrimination by organizing to assert their rights. However, many of the organizations they founded agitated more for self-rule in India than they did for U.S. or Canadian citizenship. Some of the most noteworthy included the Pacific Coast Hindi Association of Astoria, Oregon, and the San Francisco–based Hindustani Association of the Pacific Coast. Members of these organizations—about 90 percent Sikh along with some Hindus and Muslims—were brought together by a San Francisco–based weekly called *Ghadar* ("revolt") and by shared experiences of colonialism in India and racism in North America. In 1913, members of this Ghadar movement, as it came to be called, put out a call for Indians in the diaspora to return to their homeland, defeat the British Empire, and establish their own republic. They purchased arms with the help of German financiers and worked with the Japanese to transport a few thousand revolutionaries to India. In the short term, little came of their efforts beyond the imprisonment and execution of revolutionaries in India and a notorious trial of Indian and German conspirators in San Francisco in 1917–1918. But many of the groups' leaders later became active on the left in Punjabi politics, and their movement is now regarded as a first step toward Indian independence.

Amidst this agitation, Sikhs established a presence in the United States in the early twentieth century, building the first American gurdwara in Stockton, California, in 1912

Dr. Bhagat Singh Thind, shown here in uniform in 1918 during World War I, was one of the first Asian Indian members of the U.S. Army and its first turbaned Sikh. In *U.S. v. Thind* (1923), the U.S. Supreme Court ruled that Asian Indians like Thind were not white and therefore were ineligible for U.S. citizenship.

and officially dedicating it three years later. Almost all of the early Sikh immigrants were men, and because of a combination of racism and antimiscegenation laws preventing them from marrying white women, many wed Mexican American Catholics and blended into Catholic parishes. At death, however, Sikh traditions endured. Postmortem photographs of turbaned men in their coffins were sent home to family members in the Punjab, as were their cremated remains.

In 1946, the Luce-Celler Act reopened the door to Indian immigration. Ten years later, voters from California's 29th district elected Dalip Singh Saund to the U.S. House of Representatives, making him not only the first Sikh but also the first Asian American to serve in the U.S. Congress. In 1965, Congress cleared a path for widespread immigration from Asia via the Hart-Celler Act.

One of the early Sikhs to take advantage of this new law was Harbhajan Singh Yogi. Also known as Yogi Bhajan, he came to Canada and then the United States in 1968. One year later, he established the 3HO ("Happy, Healthy, Holy") Organization, gathering members of the counterculture who were drawn to his eclectic mix of strict vegetarianism, Kundalini yoga, and the teachings of Guru Nanak (whom he dubbed "the Guru of the Aquarian Age"). Both male and female members of this group, which is now known as Sikh Dharma International, wear white turbans. They run a popular website called SikhNet as well as an informational site called SikhiWiki.org.

Today, Sikhs remain a tiny portion of the U.S. population but, because of their turbans and uncut hair, they are a visible minority. Unfortunately, that visibility is sometimes obscured by religious illiteracy. Just days after the 9/11 attacks, Balbir Singh Sodhi, a Sikh gas station owner, was shot and killed by someone who, thanks to widespread images of a turbaned Osama bin Laden, thought he was killing a Muslim. In 2015, in a similar though less deadly case of religious illiteracy, someone posted on Facebook a racist meme of an "explosive" basketball player named "Mohammad." The player in the photo was actually the first turbaned Sikh to play NCAA basketball, Darsh Singh of Trinity University in San Antonio, Texas. After a friend came to Singh's defense, a #BeLikeDarsh hashtag went viral, with one Tweet reading, "I want to #BeLikeDarsh when I grow up because his jersey was in the Smithsonian."

In an attempt to address this religious illiteracy, the National Sikh Campaign launched a "We Are Sikhs" initiative to educate Americans about their religious tradition. According to a 2015 brochure, 60 percent of Americans admit they know very little about Sikhism. Moreover, when they see someone wearing a turban, they tend to assume he is Middle Eastern or Muslim rather than Sikh. Arguing that "Sikh values are American values," the National Sikh Campaign presented gender equality and "religious equality for all" as key Sikh tenets and the turban as a symbol of Sikh "readiness to protect all people against injustice." Its 2018 campaign of television and digital ads presented Sikhs as ordinary Americans who, like other U.S. citizens, "believe in equality, tolerance, and respect for all." The ads showed Sikh women who were PTA moms, Sikh men who loved *Star Wars* and *Game of Thrones*, and Sikh kids playing Monopoly.[31]

Antimiscegenation laws in many states in early twentieth-century America barred marriages between whites and nonwhites. Almost all early Sikh immigrants to the United States were men, so when they looked to start families, they often married Mexican women. Here, Valentina Alvarez and Rullia Singh pose for their wedding portrait in 1917.

The Turban

When Sikhs are initiated into the orthodox fraternity of Sikhs known as the Khalsa, they commit to a form of dress that marks them as members. The most obvious and visible of the Five Ks that constitute this dress is uncut hair, which is then wrapped and worn in a turban. There is no mandated color, shape, or size for Sikh turbans, and although they have been worn traditionally by men, many Sikh women now also wear them.

In the early twenty-first century, this custom clashed with an equally revered British custom when Jatinderpal Singh Bhullar joined the F Company Scots Guards. For nearly two hundred years, this company has been charged with protecting the reigning royalty at London's Buckingham Palace. Traditionally, these soldiers, famous worldwide for the Changing of the Guard, sport oversized bearskin hats. Bhullar asked to wear his turban instead. He also asked to wear a beard, which would further distinguish him from his clean-shaven coworkers. British traditionalists objected. But both of Bhullar's requests were granted, and on December 11, 2012, he became the first participant in the Changing of the Guard to march with a turban. "Conducting public duties while being a practising Sikh and wearing my turban is a great honour for me," he told London's *Telegraph*. "The regiment is full of history, as is my religion."[a]

Sikhs today are fixtures at interfaith gatherings, so much so that many such gatherings now seem insufficiently diverse without a turbaned Sikh on the dais. In 2009, President Obama hosted a White House celebration of the birthday of Guru Nanak. Sikhs can also be seen in films and on television. The 2002 British film *Bend It Like Beckham* features a Sikh girl who wants to play soccer (like the English star David Beckham) and fancies her Irish coach. This sets her on a collision course with her mother, who wants to marry her off to a proper Sikh man and otherwise act like a proper Sikh woman. Although this film identifies the family as Indian rather than Sikh, the mother can be seen praying to Guru Nanak, and the father sports a Sikh turban (though, it should be noted, he trims his beard).

Sikhism also has a strong presence in higher education, thanks to Sikh studies programs at the University of Michigan; the University of British Columbia; four campuses of the University of California, at Santa Barbara, Riverside, Santa Cruz, and Irvine; and a handful of other universities in the United States and Canada. Professorships in these programs do not come without controversy, however. In 1997, Professor Harjot Oberoi was forced out of his endowed chair in Sikh studies at the University of British Columbia by Sikhs who were angry about his scholarship, which they condemned as anti-Sikh. Oberoi told a story of fluidity across the Sikh/Hindu divide that clashed with the Tat Khalsa version of Sikh history, which accented continuity over change and took offense at the suggestion that Sikhism is or ever was a branch of Hinduism.

Like every other religion, Sikhism has changed as it has moved out of its homeland. Gurdwaras in the United States today may include screens that project English translations of the Guru Granth, and langar meals may include french fries and Lucky Charms alongside traditional *daal* (lentils) and *raita* (yogurt). While devotees typically worship and eat on the floor in the Punjab, chairs and tables have been introduced to both the langar and the gurdwara in the United States. Rituals are also being westernized, as Sikh wedding ceremonies take on non-Punjabi elements such as wedding rings and cakes, and

Thanksgiving, Christmas, and New Year's Day are added to the list of holidays in Sikh households.

Circumstances in the United States and elsewhere in the Sikh diaspora have also prompted new interpretations and uses of the *kirpan*. Like most religious symbols, this small sword carries multiple meanings. It evokes a long tradition of Sikh men serving as soldiers, but because it is supposed to be drawn solely for defense (and especially for defense of the defenseless), it also evokes Indian traditions of nonviolence. Sikhs debate as well whether the kirpan is an actual weapon or simply a symbolic object.

In recent years, Western governments have passed laws banning the kirpan in a variety of venues, and Sikhs have gone to court to secure the right to wear it. Lawsuits have gone both ways. In 2006 in Canada, which has a large Sikh presence in its legislature, the Supreme Court overturned, on religious freedom grounds, a Quebec school authority order outlawing kirpans in schools. However, in a 2011 case, the National Assembly of Quebec prohibited people from entering its legislative buildings with a kirpan. Sikhs contested the ruling in the name of tolerance and multiculturalism, while defenders of the restriction argued for it on security grounds. In 2018, Canada's Supreme Court upheld this ban. Similar debates have arisen concerning kirpans in prisons, in movies, and in the Olympics. In response, Sikhs have agreed to limit the size and sharpness of kirpans. They have also reinterpreted the kirpan itself by arguing that it is not intended to be a weapon but rather a "ceremonial" object, an "article of faith," or part of a uniform.[32]

LIVED SIKHISM

Guru Nanak was a critic of empty rituals and insisted that, since God is as close as the Sat Nam ("True Name") on your lips, there is no reason to celebrate God on any particular holy day or to go on pilgrimage to any particular place. But religions do not live on the inner life alone. Like other religions begun by mystics who were skeptical of "empty" rituals and the priestly class overseeing them, Sikhism witnessed the development of many rites of its own. Its most popular practices, however, seem designed to cultivate in ordinary folk the interiority Guru Nanak so highly prized.

Given the importance of the Guru Granth in this "religion of the book," it should not be surprising that many Sikh rituals focus on scripture. When Sikhs come into the presence of the Guru Granth, they bow, often pressing their foreheads to the floor. Most families conduct their daily prayers with the aid of an abridged scripture known as a *Gutka*. If a family home has a Guru Granth, then it is officially a gurdwara and family members are obliged ritually to awaken the book in the early morning and to put it to rest at night. In more public gurdwaras, these rituals are typically performed by male granthis, but in the home they are often performed by women.

Observant Sikhs recite five prayers three times during the day: Three prayers are offered in the early morning, one at sunset, and one at bedtime. These prayers begin with Guru Nanak's *Japji* ("Revered Recitation") hymn, which opens the Guru Granth and is recited before dawn (ideally after a meditative bath). They conclude with the *Kirtan Sohila* ("Hymn of Praise"), which is a suite of five hymns recited at bedtime as the Guru Granth is put into its "posture of contentment." These end-of-day hymns are also sung at cremation services. There is no set pattern for how to embody these prayers, as there is

A Sikh woman reads from the Guru Granth in a gurdwara in Queens, New York.

in the Muslim tradition, for example. Devotees can stand or sit. They can sing or recite the prayers or simply listen to them.

Whereas Hindus do not typically gather for congregational worship, Sikhs do. Together they sing **kirtans**, praise songs from Sikh scripture typically accompanied by musicians playing traditional Indian instruments (harmonium, tabla, and a stringed instrument). These hymns are sung with the *rag* ("musical composition") indicated in the Guru Granth and are effective only if sung and pronounced correctly and performed in the appropriate mood. After kirtan, the granthi opens the Guru Granth at random and receives the day's divine decree. Prayers are offered and the sacred sweet, the *karah prashad*, is received. Then the congregation typically discusses practical matters of politics and society before the granthi brings the service to a close with a concluding prayer.

Following the service, participants gather for the langar meal. Although Sikhs have not traditionally prohibited meat eating, langar is vegetarian out of respect to the many Sikhs (and non-Sikhs, who are welcome at this meal) who do not eat meat.

Like marriages throughout the Indian subcontinent, Sikh marriages have traditionally been arranged, though increasingly (and especially in the diaspora) they are love matches. The "bliss ceremony," as Sikh weddings are called, incorporates many Hindu elements, though it takes place around the Guru Granth rather than around a traditional Hindu fire. The couple holds opposite ends of a scarf, and the groom leads the bride around the Guru Granth four times clockwise while the *Lavan* ("Circling") is recited. This scriptural composition by Guru Ram Das lauds married life and then draws parallels between the union of husband and wife and the union of the devotee and the divine.

Another important rite of passage in the Sikh tradition is initiation into the Khalsa, though it is important to restate that only a small minority of Sikhs choose to join this order. There are no Sikh clergy—nothing equivalent to Jewish rabbis or Hindu priests—so this ceremony, sometimes described as a Sikh baptism, is officiated by five Khalsa

kirtan
singing of praise songs and those songs themselves

Mata Khivi (1506–1582)

Mata Khivi was the wife of Guru Angad, the second Guru, with whom she had three or four children. She is also the only woman mentioned in the Guru Granth, where she is praised for her generosity and for offering "ambrosial" langar meals. There were hints under Guru Nanak of what would become the langar, but this signature Sikh institution really came into its own under Guru Angad and Mata Khivi. Perhaps derived in part from medieval Sufi traditions of commensuality, or eating together in social groups, the langar became, in Mata Khivi's hands, not just a symbolic meal, like the Christian Eucharist, but a square meal, including a dessert of rice pudding. The langar is now widely understood as a repudiation of the codes of purity and pollution within India's caste system. Meals are prepared by volunteers without regard to caste, and they are eaten by participants who sit on the floor together to enjoy the meal without regard to distinctions of caste, sex, age, or social standing. The passage in the Guru Granth that mentions Mata Khivi praises her contributions to this langar tradition. It reads:

> Khivi, the Guru's wife, is a noble woman, who gives soothing, leafy shade to all. She distributes the bounty of the Guru's Langar; the kheer—the rice pudding and ghee, is like sweet ambrosia. (GG 967)

members who act as the Five Beloved. They create the amrit by mixing fresh water and sugar with a double-edged sword in an iron bowl. Initiates then sip the amrit five times from cupped hands. The Five Beloved sprinkle it five more times on the initiates' hair and eyes. Initiates are then charged to follow Khalsa rules, which include displaying the Five Ks and observing four prohibitions: not to cut one's hair, not to commit adultery, not to eat meat slaughtered in the Muslim fashion, and not to smoke tobacco. In this way, initiates are reborn as members of the Khalsa order.

Nam Simran

The central practice for Sikhs is *nam simran*, or calling on the divine name. This practice takes a variety of forms. Singing praise songs is a form of nam simran insofar as it puts God on worshipers' lips and in their ears. But nam simran is more often an individual discipline. Devotees typically sit on the floor with their legs crossed and repeat the divine name, typically Vahiguru, often with a rosary of some sort. More advanced practitioners seek to meditate continuously on the divine name. This practice of remembrance assumes that we once knew God, as in the Greek philosophical tradition all learning is said to be remembering. In this sense, nam simran is a technique of repair that aims to fix a broken chain of memory. We innately know God. God is inside each of us. But our ego has caused us to forget what we have always known. By breaking down the ego, nam simran refamiliarizes us with the divine and leads us to the divine abode. More expansively, to engage in nam simran, according to religious studies scholar James Lochtefeld, is to bear in mind the being and activity of the divine—"to reflect on and be conscious of the whole sweep of the divine presence in this world."[33]

To outsiders, repeating God's name might appear to be precisely the sort of rote ritual condemned by Guru Nanak. "By merely saying it with the tongue, one's bonds are not broken, and egotism and doubt do not depart from within," he said (GG 353). Sikhs insist, however, that the repetition is simply an aid to meditation, which is the real pathway to transcendence. "Of all religions the best religion, the purest deed, is repeating the Name," writes Guru Arjan. "Of all efforts, the best effort is to chant the Name of the Lord in the heart, forever" (GG 266).

According to the Sikh gurus, nam simran can release practitioners from the cycle of life, death, and rebirth. It reacquaints them with truth and reality by bringing them into union with God. It also teaches humility, transforming humans from self-centered to God-centered beings. One theory here is that the ego constructs and maintains itself through language. We say "I" and "me" so often that the self becomes the center of our universe. However, just as language programs us, it can deprogram and reprogram us, first by undercutting our egoism and then by replacing our self-orientation with a God orientation. This is accomplished by calling on the name of God.

In one rapturous passage from the *Sukhmani* ("Jewel of Peace"), a series of hymns by Guru Arjan that appears in the Guru Granth, the many fruits of this discipline are described like this:

Through remembrance of the Lord one is freed from rebirth.
Through remembrance of the Lord death's messenger flees.
Through remembrance of the Lord death itself succumbs.
Through remembrance of the Lord all enemies are scattered.
Through remembrance of the Lord all barriers fall.
Through remembrance of the Lord one remains alert.
Through remembrance of the Lord our fears are dispelled.
Through remembrance of the Lord all pain is relieved.
Through remembrance of the Lord one is numbered with the devout.
Steeped in remembrance of God's divine Name, we gather all the treasures which
    His grace supplies. (GG 2.1)[34]

Initiation into the Khalsa recalls the day Guru Gobind Singh welcomed the first five members into this Sikh fraternity. Here, five men play the parts of these "Five Beloved" in a Khalsa initiation.

BIRTH AND DEATH

Upon the birth of a son or daughter, Sikh parents bring their child to the gurdwara for a naming ceremony. The granthi opens the Guru Granth to a random page, locates the start of the chosen passage, and then announces the first letter of that passage, which becomes the first letter of the child's name. Many Sikhs then add the name "Singh" for boys and "Kaur" for girls, plus a family name. At this name-giving ceremony, the child is also often given its first *kara* (steel bracelet)—a foretaste of the Five Ks.

After death, Sikhs follow the Indian custom of cremation. Family and friends bathe and dress the corpse and then carry it to the cremation grounds. After the eldest son (or the oldest male relative) lights the pyre, mourners sing a traditional evening praise song. They then return home and sit in silence with their grief. On the fourth day, the family places the ashes in a river (most auspiciously, the Sutlej in Kiratpur, where Guru Hargobind's ashes were scattered). A full reading of the Guru Granth, completed on the tenth day, marks the passing of the deceased. On the one-year death anniversary, the family hosts a langar at the gurdwara, marking the end of the mourning period.

As Sikhs have migrated from the Punjab into the diaspora, they have adapted these traditional death rites to new circumstances and new laws. Given restrictions on funeral pyres in

seva
service, the key Sikh practice of selfless action

Of all these treasures, perhaps the most important is humility. As forgetfulness of the divine name falls away and devotees draw closer and closer to God, they feel drawn to action, including service on behalf of their community and the poor.

Service

Fauja Singh, a Punjabi British centenarian marathon runner, has set many running records. His nicknames include the "Turbaned Tornado" and the "Sikh Superman."

Meditation on the divine name is not enough. Neither is heartfelt devotion. Although Nanak was a wanderer for many years, he ultimately rejected the fasting, begging, and celibacy of Hindu renouncers. He became convinced that there is more to life than soaking up the bliss of the divine and expelling it in joyful song. We humans cannot abide in the realm of the divine forever. We must return, as Guru Nanak did, to the ordinary world of family and community and work and service. Whereas many mystics have seen the world as a distraction from their real work (and often as an illusion), the Guru Granth teaches an engaged ethic in which "spiritual liberation is attained in the midst of laughing, playing, dressing up and eating" (GG 522).[35] In addition to contemplating the truth, we need "truthful living" (GG 62), not least acts of service (**seva**) on behalf of our community and the poor. Many Sikhs describe nam simran and seva as brother and sister disciplines, comparing them to the right and the left hand or to two wings of a bird. In this way, the Sikh tradition dissents from other religions of release. It presents the world as Guru Nanak did: not as a place that must be escaped but as a fragrant garden in which the glory of the divine dwells.

Sikhs can serve others by offering their talents or money to worthy causes. One example is Fauja Singh,

the United States and the United Kingdom plus long-standing legal requirements that cremations be performed indoors, Sikhs have in many cases turned over the cleaning and cremating of the corpse to funeral directors. Lobbying by Sikhs and others for outdoor funeral pyres has been largely unsuccessful, though efforts to secure an open-air cremation of a Sikh immigrant drowned in London in 2007 led UK courts to allow that cremation to proceed. Three years later, UK courts declared funeral pyres lawful as long as they took place inside a walled structure of some sort with a roof open to the sky. In Colorado, the Crestone End-of-Life Project offers open-air cremations in what its website describes as an "ecumenical open-air cremation site."

a centenarian marathon runner from London who has raised thousands of pounds for various charities while setting multiple records for runners in his age bracket. But the most important form of service is old-fashioned manual labor, accomplished with one's own hands and feet. This service includes the sort of work that in traditional Indian society was done only by lower castes, such as mopping floors or cleaning toilets. "Shoe seva," or cleaning and sorting the shoes left at the entrance to a gurdwara, is said to be particularly auspicious for fostering humility. Seva is also practiced at the Golden Temple, where volunteers clean silt from the sacred pool or scrub the floors to prepare for another day of visitors. "One who performs selfless service, without thought of reward," reads the Guru Granth, "shall attain his Lord and Master" (GG 286).

Happily, we do not need to do all this by our own devices, because God is immanent in nature, in human beings, and in social life. God can be found at work, in marriage, and in family. There are echoes here of the Buddha, who taught a "middle way" between asceticism and hedonism, though for Guru Nanak this path bent back home—to a wife and children and an ethic of "moderate living and disciplined worldliness."[36]

Holy Days

Gurpurbs commemorate key dates in Sikh history, including the birthdays of Guru Nanak and Guru Gobind Singh, the installation of the Guru Granth in the Golden Temple, and the martyrdoms of Guru Arjan and Guru Tegh Bahadur. These occasions typically feature the singing of hymns, langar, displays of Sikh relics, distribution of sweets, and parades of the Guru Granth through the streets. They also include unbroken recitations of the Guru Granth, which typically take around forty-eight hours.

Three additional holy days represent adaptations of preexisting Hindu festivals. In Hinduism, Vaisakhi is a spring harvest festival focused on ritual bathing. For Sikhs, Baisakhi, as they call it, is the first day of the year and a day to remember the founding of the Khalsa in 1699. On this day of new beginnings, Sikhs place new flags atop their gurdwaras. Baisakhi is also a good day for Khalsa initiations. Over the last century, this day has also been a time to remember those who died in the Amritsar Massacre, which took place on Baisakhi in 1919.

A festival of lights called Diwali ("string of lighted lamps") is celebrated across India in the fall. For Hindus, it is a day to remember the goddess of prosperity Lakshmi and to recall the return from exile of heroes in the Ramayana and Mahabharata epics. For Sikhs, this day commemorates the release of Guru Hargobind from prison. As Sikhs tell it, the sixth Guru was imprisoned alongside fifty-two Hindus under Mughal emperor Jahangir. Jahangir ordered his release, but Guru Hargobind refused to go until the Hindu prisoners with him were released also. When the emperor said he would release only as many prisoners as could hold onto the guru's clothes, Guru Hargobind arranged for the creation of a multi-tassled cloak that bore them all to safety. When he returned to Amritsar on Diwali, his followers lit up the Golden Temple with lamps to greet him. Today, Sikhs celebrate this day of freedom by shooting off fireworks and decorating their homes and gurdwaras with elaborate light displays. The Golden Temple is particularly spectacularly illuminated.

CONTEMPORARY CONTROVERSY: WOMEN AND SIKHISM

Many Sikhs are proud of their egalitarianism. Guru Nanak defied caste distinctions, Sikhs observe, pointing to the langar as an example of cross-caste eating that is hard to find among Hindus. "There are no classes or castes in the world hereafter," reads the Guru Granth, which includes compositions by low-caste authors, including a tanner, a weaver, and a tailor (GG 349). Nonetheless, caste has never ceased to be a force inside the Sikh community. All ten Gurus were of the Khatri merchant caste. None of them married out, and neither did their children. Today, many gurdwaras in both the Punjab and the diaspora are split along caste lines.

This gap between ideals and reality is also visible in relation to gender, where it has occasioned a spirited debate over the role of women in the Sikh tradition. The langar has no use for gender distinctions, and Guru Nanak is now widely understood as a pioneer for gender equality who opposed Muslim veiling and Hindu widow burning. In a famous passage from the Guru Granth, Guru Nanak seems to push back against sexism. "From woman, man is born. . . . So why call her bad?" he asks. "From her, kings are born. From woman, woman is born; without woman, there would be no one at all" (GG 473). Today, Sikh feminists point out that the first person to recognize Guru Nanak as God's messenger was his sister Bibi Nanaki, so a woman was the first Sikh. Gurus after Guru Nanak also spoke out against dowries and female infanticide.

Famously linking male conceptions of God to patriarchy, the American feminist theologian Mary Daly wrote, "If God is male, then the male is God."[37] In the Guru Granth, God is portrayed as Father and Mother (GG 103). "You Yourself are the male, and You Yourself are the female," reads one passage. "Your form cannot be known" (GG 1020). In a "bold rejection of sexism," in the words of the leading Sikh feminist scholar Nikky-Guninder Kaur Singh, God in the Guru Granth is said to conceive, gestate, lactate, and give birth.[38]

But these ideals have not always translated into action. Every one of Sikhism's ten Gurus was a man, as were all the authors of Guru Granth compositions and each of the

Following in the tradition set by Mata Khivi, the beloved wife of Sikhism's second Guru, the langar meal is a central Sikh practice. Here, three women in Kolkata, India, prepare roti, a traditional bread, for a langar memorializing the five hundredth anniversary of Guru Nanak's birth.

Five Beloved who established the Khalsa. Four of the Gurus practiced polygamy. Despite Sikh prohibitions of such practices as veiling in Islam and widow burning in Hinduism, Sikhs have practiced both during their history. Guru Nanak's repeated criticisms of purity and pollution taboos have not prevented contemporary Sikhs from barring menstruating women from the daily rituals of waking the Guru Granth and putting it to rest. Despite the tradition's emphasis on family life, gurdwaras today generally split up families during congregational worship, with fathers and sons sitting on one side and mothers and daughters on the other. And though in theory there is no prohibition against women acting as granthis, men enjoy a near monopoly over that vocation.

Perhaps most disturbingly, the birth of a girl is often considered a burden instead of a gift. In the 2011 Indian census, the two states with the lowest child sex ratios (number of girls aged zero to six per 1,000 boys of the same age) were also the two states with the highest percentage of Sikhs. In the Sikh-majority Punjab in 2011, there were just 895 girls to 1,000 boys, and that figure was even lower in the city of Amritsar (826). In other words, although sex-selective abortion is banned in India, more than one out of every ten girls "goes missing" in the Punjab through abortion, infanticide, or neglect before reaching the age of seven.[39] "Sikhs like to talk a big game about gender equality," writes Amardeep Singh of Lehigh University, "but most of the time it's just talk."[40]

How to make sense of this gap between early ideals and later realities? According to Kaur Singh, Sikh history is a straightforward story of decline in which a feminist founding succumbs to a patriarchal culture. As she tells this story, Guru Nanak opposed "'isms' like casteism, classism, creedism, and sexism." Moreover, his "pattern of inclusivity" persisted throughout the Guru period, which included "excellent paradigms of women leading Sikh institutions, . . . reciting sacred poetry, fighting boldly against oppression and injustice, and generating liberating new rituals." The early period also saw female heroes, such as

Keeping the Golden Temple complex clean is a way to fulfill the Sikh duty of *seva*, or service. Here, women and children volunteers sweep the grounds prior to evening prayers.

Mai Bhago, who fought bravely for the tenth Guru against imperial forces. After she was injured in battle in 1705, she became his bodyguard.

So what happened? According to Kaur Singh, there was a "clear reversal" in which the egalitarian origins of the Sikh tradition were buried under centuries of "macho Sikh culture" and "strangled by the age-old habits and customs of the Punjab."[41]

Sikhs are not unique here, of course. The further you get away from the visions of religious founders or the practices of early religious communities, the harder it becomes to leverage them against the pressures of contemporary circumstances. One response, employed as well by Protestants during the sixteenth-century Reformation, is to try to leap backward over centuries of tradition to the first texts and institutions. This is Kaur Singh's strategy, which she refers to as the "refeminization" of the Sikh tradition.

Louis Fenech has criticized Kaur Singh for lapsing into "Orientalist essentialism"—"Sikhism as a 'pure' religion prior to the Sikh kingdom . . . but 'decadent' in the late nineteenth century and in need of reform." But Fenech concedes that "Guru Nanak championed the equality of both men and women and vehemently denounced ideas of female pollution."[42] Guru Nanak's call for equality has not been forgotten, as the work of contemporary Sikh feminists attests. In 1996, Sikh women from the United States agitated for and won the privilege of participating in the ritual washing of the floor that takes place every night at the Golden Temple. Previously, this responsibility had been reserved exclusively for men. In 2003, two British women who had been initiated into the Khalsa insisted on participating in the nightly parade of the Guru Granth back from the Golden Temple to its resting place in the Akal Takht. Two years later, the SGPC ruled that Sikh women could participate in that ritual and in kirtan singing as well. Finally, in 2018, Gursoch Kaur became the first woman to wear a turban on duty for the New York Police Department. So there is at least some evidence that a "refeminization" of the Sikh tradition is taking place.

QUESTIONS FOR DISCUSSION

1. How do Sikhs venerate the Guru Granth? Why do they refer to this sacred text as a "guru," a term commonly used to refer to a spiritual teacher?

2. Scholars debate the influences of Hindu and Islamic beliefs and practices on the Sikh tradition. Discuss the ways in which Sikhism converges on and diverges from these two traditions. Why might Sikhs reject these comparisons?

3. How do Sikhs negotiate between the "proximate" and the "ultimate" goals of their tradition? What are the practices that allow for unification with the divine?

4. In what ways does the Punjab region function as a homeland for Sikhs? How has the Sikh tradition changed as Sikhs have moved outside of that homeland into the wider world?

5. Clothing is one way that many religious people express their identities. What articles of clothing make a Sikh a Sikh? How do Sikhs differ from one another in terms of how they dress? How is Sikh clothing misunderstood in modern Western countries?

KEY TERMS

Adi Granth ("First Book"), p. 129

Akal Purakh ("Timeless One"), p. 142

Akal Takht ("Timeless Throne"), p. 131

amrit, p. 132

Amritdharis, p. 139

Dasam Granth ("Book of the Tenth Guru"), p. 147

Five Ks, p. 148

granthi, p. 130

gurdwara ("gateway to the guru"), p. 130

Guru, p. 129

Guru Granth, p. 129

Guru Nanak, p. 129

Harimandir ("Temple of God"), p. 131

haumai, p. 141

hukam, p. 142

Ik Oankar ("One Being Is"), p. 133

janamsakhis ("birth stories") , p. 133

Khalsa, p. 139

kirtan, p. 161

langar, p. 132

mukti, p. 141

nam simran ("remembering the name"), p. 142

Panth ("path"), p. 135

sansar, p. 141

Sat Nam ("True Name"), p. 143

Sehajdharis ("slow adopters"), p. 139

seva, p. 164

Shiromani Gurdwara Parbandhak Committee (SGPC), p. 154

Singh Sabha ("Singh Society"), p. 152

Vahiguru ("Wonderful Teacher"), p. 143

FURTHER READING

Leonard, Karen Isaksen. *Making Ethnic Choices: California's Punjabi Mexican Americans.* Philadelphia: Temple University Press, 1992.

McCleod, Hew. *Sikhism.* New York: Penguin Books, 1998.

Singh, Khushwant. *History of the Sikhs.* Vols. 1 and 2. New York: Oxford University Press, 2005.

Singh, Nikky-Guninder Kaur. *Sikhism: An Introduction.* New York: I.B. Tauris, 2011.

Singh, Pashaura, and Louis E. Fenech, eds. *The Oxford Handbook of Sikh Studies.* New York: Oxford University Press, 2014.

RELIGIONS OF REPAIR
Middle East

The most distinctive feature of the desert religions that emerged a few millennia ago between hot sand and big sky in the Middle East is their insistence on worshiping one and only one God. This monotheism varies from strict for Jews and Muslims to more lenient for Christians, who affirm three persons in one Godhead (the Trinity). But Jews, Christians, and Muslims all affirm an *ethical* monotheism in which one God is said to be good—a wise lawgiver and a fair judge. This "big god" upholds a moral universe through a combination of revelation, judgment, and punishment.[1]

In recent decades, Judaism, Christianity, and Islam have been categorized as the Abrahamic religions in recognition of their shared reverence for the prophet Abraham and their shared commitment to a singular divinity who speaks to prophets whose words are written down in scriptures. Because of this shared focus on a God who speaks, it is tempting to categorize Christianity, Judaism, and Islam as religions of revelation, and then to proceed by exploring the scriptures they gave to the world: the Torah, the Bible, the Quran. But scripture is neither the alpha nor the omega of these desert religions. In the lived religion of their practitioners, scripture is just one tool among many in a repertoire that extends to rituals, sermons, laws, myths, icons, relics, and holy days.

When faced with a world that has gone awry, human beings can seek to escape to a world beyond pain and suffering. Or they can try to go back to a primordial place of happiness and peace—to return to a blissful state of nature or a harmonious empire ruled by the wise and the just. Judaism, Christianity, and Islam all incorporate parts of these two strategies. But all three are preeminently religions of repair, in which adherents work to fix what is broken in human life. Jews refer to this work as *tikkun olam*, or "repairing the world."

Of course, adherents of these religions do not agree precisely how this work should go forth. More traditional Jews emphasize the importance of observing Jewish law by performing Jewish commandments. More progressive Jews emphasize working for social justice as a means to this end. But this notion of world repair is not confined to Judaism. The Christian story begins with an account of a world shattered by sin. Into this fallen world, the god-man Jesus Christ was born and was crucified. Through his saving death, he repaired broken humanity by wiping away sins. The Islamic story begins not with a fall but with a great forgetting. Though created to worship God, humans forget who they are and who God is. Into this world of forgetting comes the Quran, the Islamic analog to the god-man described in the New Testament Gospel of John as the Word of God. God speaks to an angel, who tells the prophet Muhammad to recite. As those recitations are spoken and heard, forgetting yields to remembering, and a broken world is repaired.

Over the last few decades, Jews, Christians, and Muslims have sometimes been described as participants in one overarching Judeo-Christian-Islamic tradition. This image of interfaith harmony has been shattered by the events of recent years, which have increasingly pitted Muslims against Christians against Jews. In short, there is much to repair, not least the antagonism arising from competing views about what is broken and how to fix it. For all these differences, however, there is a shared analysis among Jews, Christians, and Muslims that the world lies in pieces at their feet, and that it is their work to pick up those pieces and to put the world right.

A bar or bat mitzvah, which marks a child's coming-of-age into the adult Jewish community, includes reading a Torah portion in Hebrew in front of family and friends. Here, a bar mitzvah boy wears a traditional *kippa* and prayer shawl while using a pointer to keep his place in the text.

5

Judaism

THE WAY OF EXILE AND RETURN

At the Western Wall in **Jerusalem**'s Old City, at almost every hour of the day or night, the whole Jewish world seems to gather: modestly dressed strictly Orthodox women and their black-hatted husbands, newly grown-up Jewish girls celebrating recent bat mitzvahs with their families, modern Orthodox guys with knotted fringes hanging over their cargo pants, and American college students snapping selfies on Birthright tours. But it isn't just Jews who congregate here. Tourists abound. So do Christian pilgrims from Korea and Nigeria and the United States, identifiable not so much by their headgear or clothing as by their tour buses and nametags.

The ways and means of official Jewish life in **Israel** are overseen by Orthodox rabbis, so as the prayerful move down from an adjacent plaza toward the Western Wall, men are ushered to the left and women to a smaller area on the right. Many men pick up and don courtesy *kippot* (plural for *kippa*, or yarmulke), which sit uncomfortably on their heads or fly off in the wind. At the Kotel, as Israelis refer to the Western Wall, men with more substantial head coverings, typically secured with a hair clip, read from prayer books, rocking back and forth on white plastic chairs. The bobbing and weaving of this "people of the book"—the intimate orchestration of one group here and another there, each moving to similar rhythms—creates a ritual symphony of sorts. But there are solos too: Israeli soldiers, American pilgrims, and Ethiopian Israelis singing their own private hymns to the divine.

On the wall itself, every crack seems to be preoccupied with a prayer—petitions and thanksgivings in

Jerusalem
capital of Israel; sacred city for Jews, Christians, and Muslims; and the site of the First and Second Temples and the Western Wall

Israel
people of God and nation-state founded in 1948

Shabbat (Sabbath)
day of rest observed on the seventh day of the week, between Friday and Saturday at sundown

Hebrew and Hindi and scripts of all sorts, bearing to this place stories that might otherwise be unbearable, fleeting glimpses of the sacred burrowed between mortar and stone. Twice a year, these notes are cleared out. But every day prayers are expelled from the wall by wind or rain or the unrelenting impress of gravity. Then they are swept into clear plastic bags and reverently buried on the nearby Mount of Olives.

Judaism is carved up by time as well as territory, however, and the Sabbath (**Shabbat** or Shabbos) runs from shortly before sundown on Friday to shortly after sundown on Saturday. So if the Kotel is, as many believe, the holiest place on earth, Shabbat is the holiest time to be there. Driving is forbidden on this day of rest and, as it approaches, observant families race toward their cars lest they arrive home after it begins. Other observant Jews, including an African American man with four sons in matching black suits and sidelocks, walk toward the wall with the easy calm that befits the day. After a siren announces the start of Shabbat, men sing and dance in a circle that momentarily ignores the sectarian divisions among Israel's Jews. Across a makeshift metal fence dividing the sexes, women embody joy in their own ways, with youngsters on both sides standing tip-toe on chairs, straining to glimpse the revelry beyond. Farther down the wall, a new egalitarian prayer space inaugurated in 2016 allows men and women to pray together.

As tourists take out cameras and a scholar takes up a notepad, officials remind them that neither photography nor writing is permitted here on Shabbat. Harsher realities loom above, in the form of the Al Aqsa mosque and the Dome of the Rock, where Jewish-Muslim antagonisms simmer and sometimes boil over, and to the side, where Israeli soldiers, armed and vigilant, patrol this flashpoint 24/7.

The Western Wall in Jerusalem attracts people from all walks of life, from the devout Jew to the spectating tourist. Because use of the wall is overseen by Orthodox Jews, there is a partition between men and women, with men shown here on the left and women on the right.

The Kippa

Clothing is a distinguishing mark of many religious people, but the head is the most common place to express one's religiosity in cloth. There are turbans for Sikh men, habits for Roman Catholic nuns, and hijabs for Muslim women. The skullcap referred to as a yarmulke in Yiddish and a kippa in Hebrew is worn by Orthodox and many Conservative Jewish men, plus some observant women.

Wearing a kippa is not a biblical commandment, but the Talmud describes men covering their heads, including one Rabbi Huna, who would not walk four cubits (about two yards) bare-headed. The mystical text the Zohar is stricter, warning that a man who dares to walk that distance without a head covering could be struck dead. Today, observance is more a matter of personal choice. Some Jews who wear kippot don't wear them at work or wear them only to eat or while attending services or studying Torah.

The kippot worn by the boys in this photograph are among millions made available to visitors to Jerusalem's Western Wall. For roughly forty years, cardboard kippot were given out for free, but they flew off far too easily, leading many to pray with one hand awkwardly fixed on their heads. In 2010, the Israeli Russian industrialist Michael Mirilashvili donated a million nylon versions to the Western Wall Heritage Foundation, an Israeli governmental organization established in 1988 "to cultivate, develop and preserve the Kotel." Since that time, this foundation has given away similar cloth kippot, complete with a logo of the Western Wall surrounded by other iconic sites in Jerusalem.

If you visit the Western Wall for a few days running, you will meet pious Jews who see Israel as their sacred homeland, Jerusalem as their sacred city, and the Kotel as the place where all Jewish belief and practice converge. Not everyone stands in reverence before this wall, however. A feminist criticizes the sex segregation. A skeptic mutters, "It's just a wall." A theologian asks how she can pray there with a clear conscience given the fact that to walk to the Kotel is to be "treading on the foundations of someone's destroyed home."[1] And a Boston University undergraduate, whose synagogue back home boasts a replica of the Western Wall, says he feels like an "intruder" here because the "super Orthodox" dominate the site.

Rabbi Jeremy Milgrom, an American-born activist who has devoted his professional life to Jewish-Muslim interfaith work, rejects the notion that a wall could stand as the central symbol of any religious tradition. In his view, there is almost nothing Jewish about this political symbol of Israeli power cordoned off by security checkpoints and manned by armed soldiers. Judaism is not about taking land and holding it, forever dividing Jews from their neighbors, he says. It is about study and learning, "talking to texts together."

According to the Hebrew Bible, a collection of sacred texts roughly equivalent (though not identical) to the Christian Old Testament, Jerusalem's First Temple was built by King Solomon roughly three thousand years ago. His father, King **David**, is said to have killed Goliath, lusted over Bathsheba, and written the Psalms, but he is largely remembered for ruling a nation centered in Jerusalem. It was here, according to Jewish tradition, that Solomon built the First Temple, which housed the Ark of the Covenant, which contained the two stone tablets engraved with the Ten Commandments. One of

David
king who united Israel's northern and southern kingdoms

these commandments forbids "graven images," so at the heart of Solomon's temple was a chamber empty of everything but the presence of God. Cube-shaped like the Kaba shrine at Mecca, this Holy of Holies could be entered only by the high priest and only on Yom Kippur, the Day of Atonement. Elsewhere in the temple, lesser priests offered sacrifices, which were the centerpiece of the proto-Jewish religion out of which today's Judaism would grow.

Tensions inside the kingdom united under King David gave way to civil war and then splintered into the northern kingdom of Israel and the southern kingdom of Judah, which would later lend *Judaism* and *Jews* their names. In 722 BCE, the Assyrians conquered Israel in the north, scattering its people and obscuring their stories from future historians. In 586 BCE, the neo-Babylonians sacked Jerusalem and destroyed the First Temple, sending inhabitants of Judah in the south into exile and captivity in Babylon (in modern-day Iraq). Or, as the Book of Isaiah puts it:

> The holy cities are become a wilderness, Zion is become a wilderness, Jerusalem a desolation. Our holy and beautiful house, where our fathers praised Thee, is burned with fire; and all our pleasant things are laid waste. (Isaiah 64:9–10)[2]

During this Babylonian exile, the Israelites (as the Judeans were now also called) were cut off from their temple's rites and its Holy of Holies. This experience of exile spurred the development of a portable religion the Israelites could take with them as circumstances pushed and pulled them hither and yon. It would eventually contribute to the development of the synagogue as an alternative to the temple—a place of prayer and study in lieu of ritual and sacrifice.

In 539 BCE, the neo-Babylonians were defeated by the Persian king Cyrus, who allowed the Israelites to return to Jerusalem and rebuild their temple, which was dedicated around 515 BCE. In the fifth century BCE, the stories of these returners were codified into the Hebrew Bible and read by the priest and scribe Ezra in the newly constructed Second Temple.

JUDAISM BY THE NUMBERS

Ten Commandments

The laws given by God to Moses on Mount Sinai and inscribed on two stone tablets are known as the Ten Commandments, the Decalogue, or the Ten Words. The Jewish tradition actually speaks of 613 commandments, and the Hebrew Bible, which contains two of these lists, never numbers them. Jews, Catholics, and Protestants use different versions of the Ten Commandments. This one is widely used in Jewish circles:

1. I the Lord am your God who brought you out of the land of Egypt, the house of bondage.
2. You shall have no other gods besides Me.
3. You shall not swear falsely by the name of the Lord your God.
4. Remember the Sabbath day and keep it holy.
5. Honor your father and your mother.
6. You shall not murder.
7. You shall not commit adultery.
8. You shall not steal.
9. You shall not bear false witness against your neighbor.
10. You shall not covet your neighbor's house; you shall not covet your neighbor's wife, or … anything that is your neighbor's.

During this Second Temple period (515 BCE to 70 CE), control over Jerusalem passed first to the Greeks, who under Alexander the Great defeated the Persian Empire in 332 BCE and provided considerable latitude for Jewish worship. As Jews came to speak and read Greek, they produced a Greek version of the Hebrew Bible, called the Septuagint, in the third and second centuries BCE.

After Alexander's death, things got worse for Jews under the rule of the Ptolemies of Egypt and the Seleucids of Syria. The Maccabean revolt (167–160 BCE), sparked by Jewish resistance to efforts to impose Greek culture and pagan religion on Jews, won Jerusalem back momentarily,

This second-century CE depiction of the biblical figure Ezekiel's prophecy of the Babylonian exile comes from a mural in the Dura-Europos Synagogue, whose ruins are in modern-day Syria. It illustrates a maelstrom of dismemberment, abduction, and destructive chaos that evokes the losses felt by the Israelites shut off from their homeland and temple.

but power passed more permanently to Jews during the Second Commonwealth of the Hasmonean dynasty, which ruled from 142 BCE until the Romans rose to power in 63 BCE.

The relatively modest Second Temple was lavishly rebuilt by the Roman ruler Herod, whose much more ornate structure, also called the Second Temple, arose in 20 BCE. It was here that Jesus, according to the Christian New Testament, debated the rabbis as a boy. Herod's temple stood atop a huge platform now referred to as the Temple Mount (by Jews) and the Haram al-Sharif, or Noble Sanctuary (by Muslims). This platform was held up by four limestone retaining walls so massive that the Jewish historian Josephus described them as "the greatest walls ever heard of by man."[3] In 66 CE, Jews rebelling against Roman rule took Jerusalem. In 70, Roman soldiers retook the city and destroyed Herod's short-lived temple. Leaders of the revolt went into exile, though most Judeans remained until after the failed Bar-Kokhba Revolt of 132–135 sent them into the diaspora once again.

Today's Kotel is one of those retaining walls. It was not originally a religious site. No prayers were offered there, no rituals performed. When pilgrims came to Jerusalem to offer a goat or a dove for sacrifice in the temple, they would have walked by without giving it a moment's notice. In the eighteenth century, during the Ottoman Empire, when the Muslims who controlled Jerusalem forbade Jews from entering their Noble Sanctuary, some Jews started to pray in what was then a narrow alley at the Western Wall—as close as they could get to their Holy of Holies. Lithographs and photographs of Jews weeping at this wall over their exile and the loss of their temple were popularized in the nineteenth century by Christian pilgrims traveling to the Holy Land, turning this "Wailing Wall," writes the classicist Simon Goldhill, into "the dominant icon of Jerusalem for the Jewish imagination."[4]

Today, the Western Wall is a repository of stories as much as prayers. Yes, it is a tourist trap, but it is a key link in the chain of memory Jews use to pass their stories down from generation to generation. Like the bricks of the Mahabodhi Temple in Bodh Gaya or the steps into the Ganges at Varanasi, these stones speak.

Precisely what they might say is up for grabs. Jewish studies scholars have long disagreed over whether Jews and Judaism should be understood as a people, a religion, a culture, an ethnicity, or all of the above. Some have drawn a sharp distinction between Jewishness and Judaism. From this perspective, Jewishness is a broader category that focuses on peoplehood and includes secular Jews, while Judaism is a narrower category that focuses on rituals and theological beliefs and excludes secular Jews. But this distinction is hard to maintain. As the historian David Biale observes, "Only in the modern period can one make a distinction between Judaism and Jewishness…and between Judaism and Jewish peoplehood." Today, even antireligious Jews celebrate holidays informed by religious stories and otherwise fail to separate their Jewishness from the Judaism they reject. As the religious studies scholar Yair Lior observes, "Even a radical denial of religious Jewish symbols takes place in contradistinction to religion."[5]

This chapter focuses on Judaism as a religion. However, in keeping with the widespread understanding in religious studies that religion is embedded in culture and is never experienced apart from social and political realities, it attends as well to Jewishness. Alongside theological beliefs, religious rituals, and sacred stories, this chapter explores matters of morality, law, society, and peoplehood, which are also mixed together at the Western Wall and in the lives of Jewish communities worldwide.

OUR STORY

Jewish communities have told the story of their connection as a people to Jerusalem and their promised land in countless ways. One of the tales they tell is how a Third Temple will someday rise again, and with it the sacrificial rites of the ancient Israelites. A far more common story looks to the past instead, explaining how the one God called a people to be his own and then summoned them to a new life in a new place. Here is one version of that story, as it might be told on the basis of Jewish texts and traditions. It begins with the exile of two people out of a garden paradise. It ends with a search for the return of God's people to a land of promise, with all manner of adventures and misadventures in between.

Exile and Return

*In the beginning, **God** created the heavens and the earth. And animals. And a man and a woman, **Adam and Eve**. And a garden home called Eden. In this garden, God made a deal—a covenant—with the first human beings. They would live happily ever after in this garden of delights, and God would supply their every need. But they must not, under any circumstances, eat from the tree of knowledge of good and evil. Adam and Eve were seduced by a wily serpent to eat the forbidden fruit. As punishment, God exiled them from the garden. Henceforth, God announced, men would have to toil to meet their needs, women would agonize in childbirth, and all human beings would die. But in addition to suffering and death, knowledge now entered the world, and human history started to move toward learning and wisdom.*

Later, after God had all but ended life on earth with a great flood, he entered into another covenant, this time with Noah,

God
the one true divinity, referred to by Jews as Hashem, Adonai, or Elohim

Adam and Eve
first biblical characters, exiled from the Garden of Eden after they defied God's commandment by eating the fruit of the tree of knowledge

The biblical book of Genesis includes a story about the beginnings of human life. Woven into this nineteenth-century Jewish rug from Turkey are the first two humans, Adam and Eve, in the Garden of Eden in the shade of the Tree of the Knowledge of Good and Evil. The frame surrounding them depicts other biblical stories.

his descendants, and even the animals sheltered two by two in Noah's ark. Under the symbol of the rainbow, God promised that he would never again destroy the world by flood.

These universal covenants with Adam and Noah later gave way to more particular covenants made no longer with all of humanity but with a portion of it: God's chosen people. In the earliest of these covenants, symbolized by male **circumcision***, God instructed* **Abraham** *and his descendants not to engage in idol worship and to obey the one true God instead. God promised to bless Abraham and his descendants, to make them as numerous as the stars in the sky. God would also make them a great nation and give them "the whole land of Canaan" (Genesis 17:8). In turn, Abraham was called to wander west from his home in Ur in Mesopotamia toward an unknown promise. "Go out of your land, and away from your kin, and out of your father's house, and into the land that I will show you," God told Abraham (Genesis 12:1).*

This theme of exile and wandering surfaced again in the **Exodus** *story of bondage and freedom. During their long wanderings, God's people were enslaved in Egypt. The Egyptian ruler the Pharaoh ordered the murder of all the first-born sons*

circumcision (bris)
ritual cutting of the male foreskin and sign of the covenant between God and Abraham

Abraham
Hebrew Bible patriarch and father of the so-called Abrahamic religions: Judaism, Christianity, and Islam

Exodus
influential biblical story narrating the escape of Moses and the Israelites from slavery in Egypt to freedom in the promised land

Moses
the most important figure in the history of Judaism, who led the Exodus of the Israelites out of slavery in Egypt and received the Torah on Mount Sinai

*of the Israelites. The mother of a baby boy named **Moses** hid him in a basket in the reeds along the Nile River in an effort to save him from the slaughter. Found and adopted by Pharaoh's daughter, he was raised as royalty. As a man, Moses went to Pharaoh and demanded that he let the Israelites go. God hardened Pharaoh's heart and Pharaoh refused, so God visited the Egyptians with plagues of locusts and lice and frogs and boils—ten in all.*

Pharaoh relented, and agreed to release the Israelites, but as they were leaving he changed his mind and sent his Egyptian armies after them. As Moses and the Israelites were trapped at the Red Sea shore, with water ahead and Pharaoh's armies behind, God miraculously parted the waters so the Israelites could pass into freedom but then allowed the waters to flood back, drowning Pharaoh's armies. Moses then led the Israelites through the desert toward the promised land.

After God appeared to the Israelites on Mount Sinai, Moses went up that mountain and stayed for forty days and forty nights. He returned with God's commandments written on stone tablets and began to teach God's people the Torah. For forty more years, Moses and the Israelites made their way through the desert to the edge of the promised land. But Moses, like Abraham before him, did not live to see that land. He died at the age of 120 before entering it. God then "buried him in the valley in the land of Moab near Beth-Peor; and no one knows his burial place to this day" (Deuteronomy 34:6).

For much of their later history, a remnant of Abraham's descendants lived in Canaan, and they controlled that land at times. But for most of their history and, therefore, for most of their formation as a people, they were, like Abraham and Moses, exiles and wanderers in the lands of others. As such, they were repeatedly subject to persecution and even death, which made them long even more for their land of promise. The biblical book of Psalms gives voice to this longing, recalling a people who laid down by the rivers of Babylon and wept as they remembered Zion—a people who asked, "How shall we sing the Lord's song in a foreign land?" (Psalms 137:4).

JUDAISM IN TODAY'S WORLD

Today, Judaism is the leading religion in one country, Israel, which has roughly 6.2 million Jews, according to 2020 data from the World Religion Database. There are almost as many Jews in the United States: 5.6 million. Together Israel and the United States are home to 80 percent of the world's Jews. Other notable Jewish populations (more than 100,000) can be found in France, Canada, the United Kingdom, Argentina, Russia, Germany, and Australia. There are also 675,000 Jews living under the rule of the Palestinian Authority.

In the United States, Judaism is divided into three main groups, often referred to as branches or denominations: Orthodox, Conservative, and Reform. Some Jews also align themselves with the much smaller denominations of Reconstructionist Judaism or Humanistic Judaism, and an increasing number of Jews affiliate with no denomination at all.

In keeping with the emphasis in Judaism on orthopraxy (right action) over orthodoxy (right belief), these groups distinguish themselves from one another more in practice than in doctrine. More specifically, they differ over whether and how to follow the 613

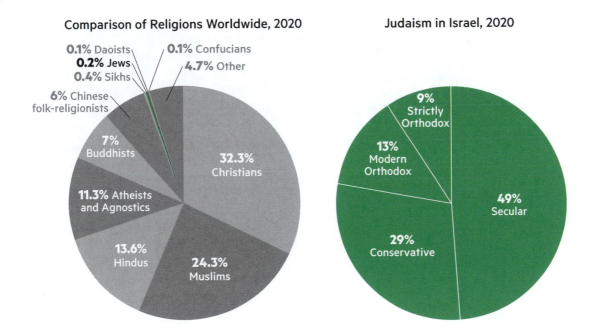

Comparison of Religions Worldwide, 2020

- **0.1%** Daoists
- **0.2% Jews**
- **0.4%** Sikhs
- **6%** Chinese folk-religionists
- **7%** Buddhists
- **11.3%** Atheists and Agnostics
- **13.6%** Hindus
- **24.3%** Muslims
- **32.3%** Christians
- **0.1%** Confucians
- **4.7%** Other

Judaism in Israel, 2020

- **9%** Strictly Orthodox
- **13%** Modern Orthodox
- **49%** Secular
- **29%** Conservative

Jewish commandments. Orthodox Jews, who view all these commandments as divine revelation, work to follow them without asking why. Reform Jews view these commandments more symbolically and emphasize the ethical over the ritual laws. When it comes to specific legal matters, Conservative and Orthodox congregations insist on the observance of kosher dietary laws (**kashrut**), for example, and Reform and Conservative congregations defy older traditions of gender segregation by seating men and women together during worship.

Only about half of American Jews are members of a synagogue, however, and in both Israel and the United States many identify as secular. Whereas it is unimaginable to call oneself a Christian and deny the existence of God, the term "Jewish atheist" is not an oxymoron. Classically, Judaism has been more about belonging than believing.

European Jewry has long included two main ethnic groups with distinctive customs: the Ashkenazi Jews of Germany and Eastern Europe and the Sephardic Jews of the Iberian Peninsula and North Africa. Ashkenazim traditionally spoke Yiddish, a largely Germanic language with elements of Hebrew, and Sephardim spoke a Judeo-Spanish language called Ladino. Two other important Jewish ethnic groups are Mizrahi Jews, from the Middle East, and Ethiopian Jews, who lived for centuries in East Africa before migrating in large numbers to Israel beginning in the 1980s.

Judaism is a very small religion in population terms. There are only about fifteen million Jews worldwide, or roughly the population of metropolitan Los Angeles. Most people in the world have never met a Jew. But Judaism is significant for its place at the head of the table in the family of Western religions. It was Jews who started a monotheistic revolution that gave the world both Christianity and Islam. Judaism also gave the world the prophetic voice, which inspired the Reverend Martin Luther King Jr. and the U.S. civil rights movement and continues to demand justice for the poor and the oppressed. An endless stream of everyday phrases—"bite the dust"; "a drop in the bucket"; "a broken heart"; "eat, drink, and be merry"; "to the ends of the earth"; "Amen!"—have flowed out of the Hebrew Bible, which also produced some of the great stories in world literature:

kashrut
Jewish dietary laws

The Exodus story has been reinterpreted throughout American history, including by civil rights activists. Here, the Reverend Martin Luther King Jr. links arms with fellow religious leaders, including Rabbi Abraham Joshua Heschel (second from right), on March 21, 1965, in a march from Selma to Montgomery, Alabama, on behalf of voting rights.

Adam and Eve in the Garden of Eden, Noah and the Flood, David and Goliath, Daniel in the Lion's Den, Jonah and the Whale. When it comes to deciding which is the greatest story ever told, reasonable people will disagree, but Judaism's Exodus narrative of slavery and freedom, exile and return, surely stands among them.

This Exodus story belongs to Jews, of course, but it has been told and retold by the wider world. In fact, no story has tugged harder on the American imagination. Seventeenth-century Puritans saw England as Egypt, its king as Pharaoh, the Atlantic as the Red Sea, Native Americans as the Canaanites, themselves as God's New Israel, and the New World as a howling wilderness in the process of becoming a New Zion. When Benjamin Franklin and Thomas Jefferson were tasked with designing a seal for the United States, each turned to the Exodus story. Franklin suggested an image of Moses standing by the shore of the Red Sea, and Jefferson the cloud by day and pillar of fire by night that led the Israelites through the wilderness. Later generations of Americans also wrote themselves into this story, which became a map of sorts for the northward migration of slaves to their own Canaans via the Underground Railroad, the westward trek of Mormons into their own Zion of Utah, and the marching of the civil rights pioneers across the Edmund Pettis Bridge, over their own Red Sea, into Selma, Alabama. Even *Moby-Dick* author Herman Melville called Americans "the peculiar, chosen people—the Israel of our time."[6]

In "Chanukah Song," comedian Adam Sandler celebrates Jewish celebrities, including "Captain Kirk and Mr. Spock" (the actors William Shatner and Leonard Nimoy). Unmentioned in Sandler's song are such world transformers as the psychologist Sigmund Freud and the physicist Albert Einstein. Though widely regarded as secular thinkers, each of these men harbored keen religious interests. Freud wrote widely on religion, which he reduced to neurosis, infantile wish fulfillment, and illusion. Einstein was friendlier to religion, describing himself not as an atheist (as did Freud) but as an agnostic and a "religious nonbeliever." Convinced that "God does not play dice with the universe," Einstein rejected not only miracles and other forms of supernaturalism but also the whimsy introduced into modern physics by new theories of quantum mechanics.[7]

Although Americans have not yet elected a Jewish president, Jews have won seats in the House, the Senate, and the Supreme Court (where as of 2019 there were three Jewish justices). The same is true of CEO seats at Fortune 500 companies. But Jews made their deepest impression on American popular culture—on Broadway and in the Hollywood Walk of Fame. Judaism gave the United States some of its most celebrated writers—from poet Allen Ginsberg to novelist Philip Roth—and some of its most celebrated buildings, thanks to architects Louis Kahn and Frank Gehry. More than any other American art form, comedy has been shaped by Jewish sensibilities. In fact, the history of American comedy is unimaginable without the Marx Brothers, the Three Stooges, Milton Berle, Jack Benny, Mel Brooks, Woody Allen, Lenny Bruce, Jerry Lewis, Joan Rivers, Jerry Seinfeld, Jon Stewart, and Sarah Silverman. This celebrity is not limited to the United States, however. Fourteen of *Time* magazine's 100 most influential people of the twentieth century were Jewish.

These successes have taken place against a backdrop of persistent anti-Semitism. In a 2011 survey, the Pew Research Center found that only 2 to 4 percent of respondents in Egypt, Jordan, Pakistan, Lebanon, Turkey, and the Palestinian territories had favorable views of Jews. Although that number was 82 percent among Americans, anti-Semitism lingers in the United States, too.[8] In 2018, the Jewish community in the United States experienced its deadliest attack ever when a gunman killed eleven people and injured seven during Shabbat services at the Tree of Life congregation in Pittsburgh, Pennsylvania.

According to a 2016 Pew survey, 35 percent of American Jews in the United States identify with the Reform movement, 18 percent with Conservative, and 10 percent with Orthodoxy. Another 30 percent are secular Jews, identifying with no denomination, and 6 percent identify with "other" groups. In Israel, the categories are quite different, and the Jewish population is divided roughly equally into secular and observant Jews. According to a 2016 Pew survey, 49 percent identify as secular, 29 percent as Conservative, 13 percent as Modern Orthodox, and 9 percent as strictly Orthodox (also known as ultra-Orthodox, though many take offense at that term).[9] There are very few Reform Jews in Israel, where an Orthodox institution called the Chief Rabbinate of Israel controls official interpretations of such vital matters as conversion, life-cycle rituals, and the question of who is and who is not a Jew. Progressive Judaism, as it is known there, has been growing in recent years under the banner of the Israel Movement for Reform and Progressive Judaism.

JUDAISM 101

➴ How to return to God and repair the world?

It is difficult to generalize about any religion because each contains multitudes. Generalization is particularly difficult when it comes to Judaism, not least because Jews have always welcomed dissent. The Indian economist Amartya Sen has referred to his

bar mitzvah ("son of the commandment") coming-of-age ritual for Jewish boys

bat mitzvah ("daughter of the commandment") coming-of-age ritual for Jewish girls

messiah figure who will come at the end of times, restore the Jews to the promised land, rebuild the temple, and inaugurate a peaceful and just world to come

homeland, which has long valued diverse viewpoints, as "argumentative India." To be a Jew is to participate in "argumentative Israel." If you go to a **bar mitzvah** ("son of the commandment") or **bat mitzvah** ("daughter of the commandment"), the rites of passage that transform Jewish boys and girls into Jewish men and women, you may well hear a young person first reading and then critically commenting on the Torah portion read aloud that day. The point is not to agree meekly but to engage fiercely. The term "Israel" itself derives from the Hebrew term *Yisra'el*, meaning "he who struggles with God." It originated in the biblical book of Genesis with the patriarch Jacob, who was renamed Israel after he wrestled all night with a mysterious angel. It was then also given to Jacob's descendants, the Israelites. So Jews are those who wrestle with God—arguing with God, one another, and even themselves. (If there are two Jews in the room, an old joke goes, there are likely to be three opinions.) To be a Jew is not to agree on a common creed. It is to participate in an ongoing conversation.

Why does Judaism, which affirms one God, abide so many different interpretations? First, Judaism is not a missionary religion. Although there have been times when Jews missionized, for the most part they have not. In fact, rabbis historically discouraged conversions. There is a traditional teaching that one should rebuff potential converts three times before agreeing to begin the conversion process, in order to ensure their commitment to joining the community. So there has rarely been a compelling reason for Jews either to define a unified message to outsiders or to stay on that message. In this way, Judaism, unlike Christianity, has no real creed. For most of its history it has been a minority religion struggling for survival, so excommunications have been rare, as have efforts to root out heretics through Inquisitions. For two millennia, Jews have emphasized behavior over belief, orthopraxy over orthodoxy.

Another reason that repelling heretics has never been a Jewish preoccupation is that Jews have traditionally seen themselves as a people as well as a religious community, and not only as a people but as a people under threat. Other religions have founders who, by diagnosing the human problem in a novel way and offering a novel solution, gather communities around them. With Judaism, the starting point was a people and its story. Although Judaism, like other religions, offers its own diagnosis of the human condition, the central purpose of the tradition as it emerged more than two millennia ago was to keep a particular community together. And that job was best performed by collective action.

Nonetheless, Jews have converged on a problem and its solution. Not surprisingly, for a tradition so focused on peoplehood, the predicament in this case centers on "us" rather than "me." This problem is exile—distance from God and from one's true home. For most of their history, Israelites lived in exile from the homeland promised to them by God through Abraham. They also lived in exile from God. According to some Jewish mystics, part of the Godhead—the feminine Shekinah—is in exile from the world, leaving it incomplete and in need of repair.

The solution to this predicament is return—return to God and to one's true home. The epic journey of God's people from garden paradise to desert wilderness to Zion is not without triumphs. Yes, Joshua entered the promised land. Yes, the state of Israel exists. But the problem of exile is chronic. And return, like the goals of other religious traditions, always lies tantalizingly out of reach. Even those who live in Israel today live betwixt and between, with hope for the place they are going and lamentations over the places they have left behind. Many Jews do not hope for a coming **messiah** (literally, "the anointed," which is to say the king), but even those who do hope, recognize that he has not yet come to reign over a new era of justice and peace. As anyone who reads the news can attest, neither has that new era.

In this awkward in-between time, otherwise known as human history, it is the job of the Jewish people to make things right—to "repair the world" (**tikkun olam**) and put an end to exile. Until they complete that task (or the messiah returns to do it for them), Jews abide in that awkward middle space of almost and not yet. They are a people of both exile and return—a pattern that provides, according to the Jewish studies scholar Jacob Neusner, "the structure of all Judaism(s)," not to mention the central turn of much Jewish literature and film.[10]

Whereas Christianity highlights the doctrinal dimension of religion, Judaism highlights narrative and law, which in this tradition are inseparable. The anthropologist Mary Douglas once called the biblical book of Numbers "a law and story sandwich," and the same can be said of Judaism itself. If the central Jewish story speaks of exile and return, the way of that return—to God, to one's community, to one's true self, and to the promised land—runs through remembrance and obedience: the telling of their story and the observance of God's law. That law itself directs Jews toward the ethical and ritual dimensions of religion, instructing the Jewish community how to act morally and how to worship. But how do Jews follow their laws and tell their stories? Almost always through rituals, which themselves are commanded by the law and provide occasions to tell the stories. In this tradition of remembrance and observance, the central symbols are God, Torah, and Israel. Together these symbols point to religion and to peoplehood—to Judaism and Jewishness.

The Hebrew saying *tikkun olam*, "repair the world," is a powerful directive for Jews. This lithograph by the Jewish artist Judy Sirota Rosenthal illustrates the concept of being "in the middle" of repairing the world. The message reads: "You are not obligated to complete the work but neither are you free to abandon it."

God

For those who locate the Jewish tradition at or near the birth of **monotheism**, the Hebrew Bible is shot through with fascinating hints of polytheism. Its common epithet for God, *Elohim*, is likely the plural for *El*, meaning "gods." God is also addressed as *Adonai* ("my Lords"), which is likewise a plural noun. The Hebrew Bible also contains multiple references to Yahweh (another name for the divine, traditionally not written out or spoken aloud) as "above all gods." This seems suggestive not of monotheism but of henotheism: the worship of one "high god" among many. Over time, however, Jews developed an emphatically monotheistic worldview that underscored the unity and uniqueness of God. Rather than accepting the ancient commonplace that different tribes serve different gods, the Israelites rejected the polytheism that surrounded them and affirmed the existence of only one divinity. There may appear to be competing forces underlying birth and death, the sun and the moon, but all are underwritten by the one true God.

Like Muslims, Jews today are strict monotheists who have rejected the incarnation of the divine in human form and the soft monotheism of the Christian Trinity. This commitment to the oneness of God is even stronger among Jews nowadays than is the

tikkun olam ("repair the world")
mandate to work to heal what is broken in the world

monotheism
belief that there is only one god

Shema
Jewish creed, beginning, "Hear, O Israel"

ethical monotheism
form of single-god belief that describes God as lawgiver and judge and emphasizes religion's ethical dimension

commitment to God's existence. As Rabbi Stephen Wylen observes, "One could deny God and still be a Jew, but to deny the unity of God would be to remove oneself from the Jewish fold."[11] The **Shema**, the closest Judaism gets to a creed, begins with a staunch affirmation of monotheism:

"Hear (*Shema*), O Israel! The Lord is our God. The Lord is One!"

In the Jewish tradition, God is said to be above and beyond human comprehension, and Jewish philosophers have repeatedly warned against describing this transcendent divinity in human terms. Nonetheless, this God has been widely described as a merciful being who heeds our prayers, acts in human history, and maintains a covenantal relationship with his people. "He" has been depicted largely in masculine terms—as a patriarch of "his" people—though the feminine image of God as the Shekinah ("Indwelling") has long been popular in Jewish mystical circles, and in Genesis 49:25 God is said to offer "blessings of the breast and womb." Today some Jewish communities are beginning to use feminine language for God in communal prayer.

Because its God is said to be good—both lawgiver and judge—Judaism has also been described as **ethical monotheism**. This perspective offers a simple logic in which one God creates and rules one universe according to one law. But it also produces the so-called theodicy problem, which Jewish, Christian, and Muslim thinkers have never quite been able to shake: If there is one all-powerful, all-knowing, and good God, why is there evil in the world? And doesn't the presence of evil—in humans and in nature itself—demonstrate that God is either not omnipotent or not omniscient or not good?

The Torah scroll is kept in a special cabinet, known as an ark, in Jewish places of worship. At the start of weekly services, a congregational leader removes the Torah from the ark and carries it throughout the sanctuary. Here, a man holds the Torah, which is commonly clad in silver, at his synagogue in Brooklyn, New York.

Torah

A second central symbol in the Jewish tradition is **Torah**, which means "teaching" or "instruction." According to this tradition, one of the most important ways that the God of Israel acted in human history was by delivering the Torah to his people through Moses on Mount Sinai. Remembered on the Jewish holiday Shavuot ("The Feast of Weeks"), this moment of divine revelation is, according to many Jews, the foundational event in human history. Like temple sacrifice in Israelite religion, reading, interpreting, and debating the Torah are the central acts in Judaism today.

Torah refers most basically to the Five Books of Moses (the Pentateuch): Genesis, Exodus, Leviticus, Numbers, and Deuteronomy. It refers more broadly to the Written Torah, or the Hebrew Bible, a collection of sacred texts that Christians call the Old Testament and Jews refer to as the **Tanakh** or TaNaKh, after its three parts: Torah, or the Five Books of Moses; Neviim, or the prophetic books; and Ketuvim, or assorted writings (including two, Ruth and Esther, named after women). The Tanakh, which influenced both the Christian Bible and the Quran, may be the most influential book in Western civilization. It is certainly one of the most intriguing, overflowing with stories not only of divine creation and revelation but also of love, lust, loyalty, and

The Tanakh

Jews refer to their Bible as the Tanakh, an acronym derived from its three parts: Torah, Neviim, and Ketuvim.

Torah in this context refers to the Five Books of Moses, or the Pentateuch:

- **Genesis:** the first biblical book, beginning with creation and including stories about the expulsion of Adam and Eve from the Garden of Eden, Cain's murder of his brother Abel, and Noah's Ark. Other narratives cover the adventures of the matriarchs and patriarchs and their covenant with God. As the book ends, the Israelites are on the move from Canaan into Egypt.

- **Exodus:** an account of the mass escape of the Israelites, under the leadership of the prophet Moses, from enslavement by Pharaoh in Egypt

- **Leviticus:** a book of laws concerning sacrifice, diet, and purity and impurity

- **Numbers:** a narrative book of the suffering and rebelliousness of the Israelites as they wander in the wilderness with the promised land still out ahead of them

- **Deuteronomy:** a collection of speeches delivered by Moses as the Israelites are about to enter the promised land. Moses recalls their past and reminds them of God's commandments.

Neviim includes eight prophetic works divided into two parts:

- **The Former Prophets,** which are actually historical books: Joshua, Judges, Samuel, and Kings

- **The Latter Prophets,** namely, Isaiah, Jeremiah, Ezekiel, and a book devoted to the twelve "minor" prophets (Hosea, Joel, Amos, Obadiah, Jonah, Micah, Nahum, Habakkuk, Zephaniah, Haggai, Zechariah, and Malachi)

Ketuvim is a catchall category that includes eleven books spanning genres from apocalyptic literature (Daniel) to love poetry (Song of Songs) to songs (Psalms) to history (Chronicles) to wisdom literature (Proverbs and Ecclesiastes) to short stories (Ruth and Esther).

---

betrayal. This sprawling anthology of twenty-four books includes poetry and songs and prophecy and proverbs and law and chronicles and apocalyptic visions. In keeping with Judaism's emphasis on ritual, it includes a book of ritual laws of purity and impurity. It also includes multiple narrative books. Its Exodus story narrates the enslavement and liberation of the Israelites and their reception of the Torah through Moses on Mount Sinai. It also tells of plagues and war, brothers killing brothers, philandering kings, a queen who saves her people from destruction, and a man swallowed up by a fish.

But the term "Torah" does not refer solely to this Written Torah. It can also refer to the Oral Torah, which was eventually written down in the **Talmud** ("learning"), a vast collection of rabbinic commentary on virtually every aspect of Jewish life that appeared between 400 and 500 CE. Also viewed as Torah is the whole corpus of later Jewish teachings, including various legal codes and a vast body of responses that provide answers to contemporary legal questions about such matters as artificial insemination, the use of hearing aids on the Sabbath, the hybridization of oranges and grapefruits, and even whether Torah legislation applies on the moon. Studying and debating the Torah can also be seen as Torah. Some even regard everyday conversations in Israel as Torah.

In devotional contexts, the Written Torah is reverently recorded on handwritten scrolls and reverently stored in arks in synagogues worldwide. It is then lifted, carried, unrolled, and read each week in services. The words of the Torah also metamorphose into material culture, including the *mezuzah*, a ritual object placed at the doorposts of many Jewish homes, and *tefillin*, leather straps that attach black boxes to the arm and forehead and are worn during prayer, both containing tiny scrolls of biblical passages.

Torah ("teaching")
the written law of the Tanakh and the oral law of the Talmud

Tanakh (also TaNaKh)
Written Torah; acronym for its three parts: Torah ("Teaching"), Neviim ("Prophets"), and Ketuvim ("Writings")

Talmud ("learning")
authoritative collection of Torah interpretations

Israel

The word "Israel" today refers to a nation-state created in 1948, but it originally referred to a people. As has been noted, this term is used in Genesis in relation to Jacob, who was renamed Israel ("he who struggles with God"). Later, the term came to refer to the descendants of the patriarchs Abraham, Isaac, and Jacob and the matriarchs Sarah, Rebecca, Rachel, and Leah. To be Jewish today is not to believe in God or even to observe the commandments. To be Jewish is to belong to a people. It is said that Judaism is about ethnicity as much as religion, but that is not quite right, since there are Ashkenazi Jews of Eastern European descent, Sephardic Jews of Spanish and North African descent, Mizrahi Jews of Arab descent, and Jews of East African descent. Contrary to the claims of Nazis, Jews are not a race but a people made up of many peoples. Like Hindus, Jews are bound together not so much by a common ancestry or even a common creed as by shared stories and a shared conversation about them.

But how did this people come to be? According to the Jewish tradition, God selected the people of Israel to enter into a special relationship with God and play a central role in the divine-human drama. "For you are a people consecrated to the Lord your God," reads the classic biblical passage in Deuteronomy 7:6, "of all the peoples on earth the Lord your God chose you to be His treasured people." This concept of the Jews as a "chosen people" is a vexed one. Many Jews have emphasized that biblical references to their election do not imply any sort of superiority—that this relationship is a responsibility rather than a boast. In the modern period, many Jews have downplayed chosenness, and Reconstructionist

Among the many marvels of the Exodus story is the parting of the Red Sea as Moses leads the Israelites out of bondage in Egypt and across to freedom in the promised land. In this illustration from the Sarajevo Haggadah, which dates to fourteenth-century Spain, Moses (on the left) wears a crown while leading the Israelites through a thin band of red, symbolizing the Red Sea.

Jews have rejected it altogether. Nonetheless, it remains a formative component of the Jewish tradition, linking religion and theology with group identity and sociology.

To be a member of the Jewish people today is to live not only between exile and return but also between law and liberation. The Exodus story celebrated on **Passover** (Pesach), which tells how Moses led the Israelites out of bondage in Egypt, does not end on the far side of the Red Sea. The freedom delivered in this Exodus was not the freedom to do whatever the Israelites wanted but the freedom to follow God's commandments. As their Exodus continued, the Israelites made their way through the wilderness to the base of Mount Sinai. On that mountain, Moses the liberator became Moses the lawgiver. (In fact, Moses became such a central symbol of law that his image appears, Ten Commandments in hand, at the center point of the East pediment of the U.S. Supreme Court building.) Some Mosaic law is about morals and how to act toward others. Other Mosaic law is about ritual and how to act toward God.

In the Jewish calendar, the festival of Shavuot, which celebrates the giving of the Torah on Sinai, comes right after the festival of Passover, which celebrates the Exodus. So after you have turned the last page of the book of liberation, Exodus, you begin the book of law, Leviticus. In this way, liberation yields to law—to legislation regarding agriculture, menstruation, animal husbandry, sacrificial offerings, ritual purity and pollution, holy days, oaths, haircuts, and clothing; and to prohibitions against idolatry, lying, tattoos, astrology, eating vultures, incest, and male homosexuality (though not lesbianism). As this litany of Levitical codes demonstrates, **halacha**, which is often translated as "law" but really means "way" or "path"—the Dao of Judaism—is not only about morality. It is also about ritual and the practice of daily life.

JEWISH HISTORY

Historians of Judaism cannot look back with much clarity into the lives of Abraham and Moses. In fact, they cannot be sure that these men even existed. If they did, they surely lived more in legend than in the archives of history. There is no hard evidence for the Exodus either, at least not of the sort that might convince archaeologists or historians. In Judaism, as in so many other religions, there are insider traditions that scholars must sift through with care as they create their own reconstructions. One fact this sifting uncovers is a large gap between what is now called "Judaism" and its precursors.

From Israelite Religion to Second Temple Judaism to Rabbinic Judaism

Plainly, there are major differences between the **Israelite religion** of the kingdoms of Israel and Judah (sometimes also called Israelite-Judean religion) and later developments now referred to as **Second Temple Judaism** and **rabbinic Judaism**. The Israelite religion described in the Tanakh (and the temple around which it revolved) was a tradition of priestly sacrifice closely integrated into the surrounding rural and agricultural economy and society. Like the Vedic religion of ancient China and the Confucianism of ancient China, its core technique was ritual sacrifice. Unlike Vedic religion and Confucianism, which sought to ward off social chaos and produce social harmony, its goals had to do with

Passover (Pesach)
holiday commemorating the Exodus story

halacha
Jewish law

Israelite religion
proto-Jewish religious tradition focused on priestly sacrifice in the Jerusalem Temple

Second Temple Judaism
religious tradition that followed Israelite religion and developed while the Second Temple was standing from 515 BCE to 70 CE; it helped produce rabbinic Judaism

rabbinic Judaism
textually oriented religious tradition of Jews today that developed around the time of the destruction of the Second Temple in 70 CE

repairing the covenant of a people with their God. As participants in Israelite religion saw it, God's chosen people had broken their covenantal relationship with God by committing various sins. The way to repair that covenant was for priests to perform sacrifices in the Jerusalem Temple in order to draw God near and for prophets to listen for divine instruction and then relay it to God's people so that they might mend their ways. Ordinary people also sought God's favor by coming to the Jerusalem Temple as pilgrims during festivals.

The destruction of the First Temple in 586 BCE put an end to this place-based Israelite religion by taking away the place where it was practiced. It also stimulated the development of a more portable religion, by spurring the development of places for prayer and the study of sacred texts, as well as early efforts to gather those texts into a canon. The construction of the Second Temple around 515 BCE led to what scholars now refer to as Second Temple Judaism, but the shift away from sacrifices at a singular site to texts that could be studied and taught anywhere continued. Second Temple Judaism saw the development of the Hebrew Bible canon and the emergence of the synagogue as a place of prayer and worship. The end of this period also saw increased interest in the fate of the individual human being in the afterlife and with it belief in the bodily resurrection. Out of Second Temple Judaism grew a number of religious groups, including the Pharisees, who helped produce rabbinic Judaism around the first century CE.

Christians often identify Judaism with the Hebrew Bible, and just as Hinduism is rooted in scriptures called the Vedas, Judaism is rooted in the stories and commandments of the Tanakh. But the Tanakh never details how exactly its commandments are to be observed. Precisely what sort of labor does the Sabbath prohibit? What sorts of fish and

The destruction of the Israelites' Second Temple in 70 CE by Roman soldiers is carved into stone on the Arch of Titus at the Roman Forum in Italy. Roman artists carved this relief, which dates to 81, to celebrate the "Spoils of Jerusalem," including a seven-branched candelabra, which they looted from the temple.

grains and locusts are kosher? As rabbis answered these and other questions about working and eating and speaking and money and sex, they built up an oral tradition of legal and textual interpretation that later made its way into the Talmud. The new religion we now know as rabbinic Judaism focused on studying and interpreting this text.

With this transformation from Israelite religion to Second Temple Judaism to rabbinic Judaism, Judaism became a textual rather than a sacrificial religion. Its key site shifted from the Jerusalem temple to the synagogue and its exemplars from priests and prophets to rabbis.

Judaism is often described as the mother of the so-called Abrahamic religions, and Christianity and Islam do borrow from it a host of characters, themes, and doctrines. These "religions of the book" all affirm one God who speaks to humans through prophets who write down these revelations in scriptures. Christianity also began as a movement of Jews following a Jewish leader and, like rabbinic Judaism, it was born out of Second Temple Judaism. But the rabbinic Judaism we see around the world today itself emerged around the time of the Jesus movement and in tandem with it. The Christian religion proper would come later, but the simultaneous development of the Jesus movement and rabbinic Judaism make today's Jews and Christians fraternal twins as well as parent and child. As strange as it might seem, neither Abraham nor Moses was, strictly speaking, a Jew. Each became a Jew by adoption, accepted into a religion born long after they had passed away.

> ## Judaism at a Glance
>
> | | Israelite Religion | Rabbinic Judaism |
> |---|---|---|
> | **Problem:** | exile | exile |
> | **Solution:** | return | return |
> | **Techniques:** | ritual sacrifice | narrative and law |
> | **Exemplars:** | priests and prophets | rabbis |
>
> In short, Judaism is the religious tradition of the people of God, led by interpreters of the words of God, who seek to return from exile by telling their story and following God's law.

Sadducees, Essenes, Zealots, and Pharisees

In keeping with their long-standing tradition of debate, Jews formed different schools as rabbinic Judaism emerged. These schools converged on a few key matters, including belief in one God, a refusal to use images of the divine in worship, an identity as God's chosen people, a fidelity to the Torah, and the practice of male circumcision. They also looked to the Jerusalem Temple as a key institution and idealized it even after it was gone. Nonetheless, these competing Judaisms were rooted in different interpretations of law and scripture.

The Sadducees were a priestly party of legal and theological conservatives friendly to Roman rule but suspicious of efforts to accommodate Judaism to Greek culture. They rejected the Oral Torah and the doctrine of the bodily resurrection, which they could not find in the Tanakh. They also rejected postmortem rewards and punishments. As a priestly party, the Sadducees lost their power base after the destruction of the Second Temple in 70 CE. But their priestly lineage continued for centuries, and their legacy continues today in the lives of contemporary priests and in rituals such as the "Blessing of the Priests" conducted once a year at the Western Wall.

Rejecting the authority of the Sadducees and Rome alike, the Essenes established their own monastic communities quite apart from the Jerusalem Temple and Roman society. Members were supposed to be celibate and follow a strict diet. Classic sectarians, they drew sharp distinctions between insiders and outsiders. They pooled their resources. They looked forward to a coming apocalypse in which they would fight on God's side in an epic battle between the forces of light and the forces of darkness. In the meantime, they were strict interpreters of the law and deeply concerned with ritual purity. Our contemporary understanding of the Essenes owes much to the discovery, beginning in the winter of 1946–1947, of a vast library known as the Dead Sea Scrolls, which was likely hidden right around the time of the Roman destruction of Jerusalem in 68 CE. Essenes may well have constituted the ancient community at Qumran (about a mile from the Dead Sea) that left this library behind. Like the Sadducees, this group disappeared after the temple's destruction in 70.

Unlike the Essenes, who waited for God to initiate the coming cataclysm, Zealots were political revolutionaries. Convinced that their people should be governed by God alone, they took it as their sacred duty to overthrow Rome by force. They rose up in a popular rebellion in 66, and many perished in Jerusalem when the Romans took that city and destroyed the Second Temple in 70. Others escaped to Masada, a fortress on a mountain plateau not far from the Dead Sea. When the Romans breached their barricades, they committed suicide en masse in 74.

Of these four early groups—the Sadducees, Essenes, Zealots, and Pharisees—only the Pharisees survived, thanks in part to their willingness to accommodate to Roman rule and

CHRONOLOGY OF JUDAISM

10th c. BCE King David rules a nation centered in Jerusalem; his son and successor, King Solomon, builds the First Temple

c. 928 Division into the northern kingdom of Israel and the southern kingdom of Judah

722 Assyrians conquer the northern kingdom of Israel and its ten "lost tribes"

586 Babylonians conquer the southern kingdom of Judah and destroy the First Temple, sending the Judeans into exile in Babylon

539 Persian king Cyrus conquers Babylonians and allows Judeans (now called Israelites) to return to Jerusalem and rebuild their temple, and for more than two centuries, Judeans live under Persian rule

515 Second Temple is dedicated and Second Temple Judaism begins

332 After defeating the Persian Empire, Alexander the Great takes control of the land of Israel and the Hellenistic period begins

167–160 Maccabean revolt against efforts by Seleucids of Syria to impose Greek culture and pagan religion

142–63 Hasmoneans rule in a Second Commonwealth of Judean independence recalling David's reign

63 Rome annexes Israel

c. 4 BCE Birth of Jesus

c. 10 CE Death of Rabbi Hillel

70 After defeating a Jewish revolt, Romans retake Jerusalem and destroy the Second Temple, putting an end to Second Temple Judaism

132–135 Bar-Kokhba rebellion

306–337 Constantine rules the Roman Empire and legalizes Christianity after his conversion in 312

380 Christianity becomes the official religion of the Roman Empire, and Jews suffer under anti-Jewish legislation

c. 400 Jerusalem Talmud is completed

c. 500 Babylonian Talmud is completed

1040–1105 Life of Rashi, the medieval French rabbi and commentator

1096 Amidst the First Crusade, anti-Jewish pogroms claim thousands of Jewish lives in France and the Rhineland

1138–1204 Life of Maimonides, medieval philosopher

1290s Zohar appears

1492 Jews are expelled from Spain

1654 Jews arrive in New Amsterdam (now New York City)

Greek culture. Instead of focusing on military and political adventures like the Maccabees, they focused on more obviously religious matters. Simultaneously, they adapted to Hellenistic norms, turning the rabbi, for example, into something resembling a Greek sage. The New Testament Book of Acts describes Paul as a Pharisee who came to follow Jesus. Elsewhere in the New Testament, the Pharisees are disparaged as obsessive-compulsive legalists, but this school actually offered progressive readings of the Oral Torah. Like early Christians, they affirmed life after death and the bodily resurrection, both of which the Sadducees rejected. Pharisees also hoped for a messiah who would usher in a new world of peace and justice. Unlike early Christians, they did not believe that Jesus fulfilled that role. Although scholars cannot quite connect the dots between the Pharisees and the emergence of rabbinic Judaism, the Pharisees are now widely remembered, because of their emphasis on the Oral Torah, as "the fathers of rabbinic Judaism."

One other group of ancient Jews were the Jewish members of the Jesus movement. As that movement opened itself up to non-Jews and as the Roman emperor Constantine made Christianity the dominant religion in his empire, the gap between these religions widened.

1729–1786 Life of the German Jewish philosopher Moses Mendelssohn

1760 Death of Baal Shem Tov, founder of Hasidism

1791 French Jews are emancipated, paving the way for Jewish emancipation in Prussia (1812), Italy (1861), Austria-Hungary (1867), and Germany (1871)

1817 First Reform temple opens in Hamburg, Germany

1824 First Reform temple in the United States opens in Charleston, South Carolina

1840s Germans immigrate in large numbers to the United States

1880s Massive immigration to the United States by Eastern European Jews

1890s Theodor Herzl argues that the only real response to persistent anti-Semitism is a Jewish state

1917 Balfour Declaration affirms the need for a Jewish homeland in Palestine

1920s Reconstructionist movement founded by Mordecai Kaplan

1933–1945 During the Third Reich in Germany, led by Adolf Hitler and the Nazi Party, Jews are systematically persecuted; approximately six million are murdered by Nazis in the Holocaust (Shoah)

1935 Berlin-born Regina Jonas becomes the first female rabbi

1938 *Kristallnacht* ("The Night of Broken Glass"); attacks on Jews turn violent on November 9–10, as Jews are murdered, Jewish homes, businesses, and synagogues are destroyed, and thirty thousand men are shipped to concentration camps

1946–1956 Dead Sea Scrolls, discovered near the Dead Sea, revolutionize the study of early Christianity and Second Temple Judaism

1948 State of Israel is established

1967 Six-Day War between Arabs and Israelis

1972 Sally Priesand becomes the first American woman rabbi

1974 Sandy Eisenberg Sasso becomes the first woman Reconstructionist rabbi

1985 Amy Eilberg becomes the first woman Conservative rabbi

1990–1991 Persian Gulf War

2009 Sara Hurwitz becomes the first Orthodox "rabba"

2017 On behalf of the United States, Donald Trump recognizes Jerusalem as the capital of Israel

2018 The Pittsburgh synagogue shooting becomes the deadliest attack on Jews in the United States

The Talmud is the main source of Jewish law, or *halacha*. Its pages include arguments by different rabbis literally circling around texts at the center of the page. This page is from a nineteenth-century copy of the Babylonian Talmud, which was compiled in the fifth century CE.

The Talmud

After a series of ill-fated rebellions against the Romans, including one that led to the destruction of the Second Temple in 70, rabbis decided to put the Oral Torah so central to rabbinic Judaism into writing, lest it be forgotten among a dwindling people. This writing began around the year 200 with the Mishna, sixty-three tractates on agriculture, holy days, civil and criminal law, marriage and other relations between the sexes, temple sacrifices, and ritual purity and pollution. In the spirit of "argumentative Israel," these tractates recorded both majority and minority opinions. Next came commentaries on the Mishna known as the Talmud. The Jerusalem Talmud appeared around 400 in Jerusalem. A more extensive and authoritative collection appeared around 500 in Babylon. This exhaustive collection, considerably longer than the Jerusalem Talmud, came to be known as the Babylonian Talmud and is now the most widely used.

The Nobel Laureate Elie Wiesel called the Talmud "a masterwork, unequalled in Jewish memory," and today it is the defining text of the Jewish tradition.[12] This text reproduces the Mishna alongside rabbinic discussions known as the Gemara. In keeping with Judaism's dual emphasis on law and storytelling, the Talmud includes both. Its discussions of legal matters are referred to as *halacha*. Nonlegal discussions about folklore and ethics are called *aggadah*.

A vast tangle of competing lines of argumentation, the Talmud's two and a half million words do not just contain contradictions, they revel in them. In fact, they are designed around them, with a passage at the center of each page literally surrounded by competing interpretations. In one of the great intellectual contests of all time, two rabbis, **Hillel** and Shammai, joust in this anthology of arguments about three hundred different issues. Hillel, a contemporary of Jesus, is perhaps best known for his pithy summary of Jewish teaching: "That which is hateful to you, do not do to another: This is the whole Torah. The rest is commentary. Now go study." In his duels with Shammai, he almost always gets the upper hand. But the Talmud records Shammai's dissents alongside Hillel's rulings. So Shammai's words, too, are scripture. Or, as the Talmud itself puts it, "Both are the words of the living God, but the law is in accordance with the view of the house of Hillel."

With the emergence of rabbinic Judaism and the Talmud, the sacrificial rites of the temple were domesticated and internalized. Jews continued to pray for the rebuilding of the temple, but the way back to communion with God was now observing the commandments rather than performing sacrifices. Holy days that once centered on the temple now migrated to the home.

Today, Judaism is rabbinic. Its exemplars are rabbis, not priests. It centers on books, not altars. It sanctifies the world through words and deeds rather than ritual sacrifice. These words and deeds make not just a religion but a way of being in the world—a way of cooking and eating and washing and having sex and speaking and working. This way can be lived in Israel or outside it, and by rabbis and ordinary Jews.

Hillel
early rabbi whose debates with Shammai play a central role in the Talmud

The Convivencia and Medieval Jewish Thought

For many Jews in the Middle Ages, as in many other periods in their history, mere survival was a victory. During this period, Jews lived largely under either Christian or Muslim control: Sephardic Jews (from *Sepharad*, a biblical place name associated with Spain) populated the Iberian Peninsula, and Ashkenazi Jews (from *Ashkenaz*, a biblical place name associated with Germany) lived in northern France and Germany. Because Jews did not have the territory that nations typically had, their experiences in this time were punctuated by expulsions and massacres and their responses to the same.

A year after Pope Urban II announced the First Crusade in 1095, thousands of Jews died at the hands of crusaders and mobs in Europe's first recorded pogroms in France and the Rhineland. According to the historian Arno Mayer, these anti-Semitic attacks "set a disastrous precedent, depositing a fatal poison in the European psyche and imagination."[13] When crusaders took Jerusalem in 1099, they slaughtered Muslims and Jews alike, banning both from the city. Later crusades saw more persecution and murders of Jews. In 1215, Pope Innocent III decreed that all Jews were to wear clothes that distinguished them from Christians. In 1240, in a show trial in Paris, the Talmud itself was convicted

JUDAISM: A GENEALOGY

The English term "Judaism" derives from the Greek term *Ioudaismos*, which appears twice in the second century BCE in 2 Maccabees, a noncanonical Jewish text later included in Roman Catholic and Orthodox Christian Bibles. This term might have referred to what we would now call a religion. However, it might have pointed instead, as the Jewish studies scholar Shaye Cohen argues, to "the aggregate of all those characteristics that makes Judaeans Judaean"—to a people rather than a religion: "Judaeanness."[a] At any rate, most scholars now believe that what we now refer to as Judaism emerged gradually at some point between the construction of the Second Temple around 515 BCE and the destruction of that temple in 70 CE.

The earliest known use of "Judaism" in a European language can be found in a manuscript from roughly 1400 now held at Corpus Christi College in Cambridge, England. There, in a translation of the Pauline Epistles, the beginning of Galatians 1:13 is rendered, "For ȝee hafe herde my conuersacyoun sum tyme in Iudaisme." A 1516 chronicle by the London-based author Robert Fabyan speaks of a man who "renouncyd his Iudaisme or Moysen lawe, and was cristenyd." Thirty years later, in a Protestant Reformation debate about the sacraments, the English Bible translator George Joye refers to "the very Judaisme & ryte of religion of the Iewes."[b]

Some scholars have argued that what we call "Judaism" did not emerge until roughly the time of Jesus or even until the fourth century CE. Stretching this argument to its breaking point, the historian of religion Daniel Boyarin contends that the concept of Judaism as a religion is a modern invention. "There is no 'native' term with this meaning in antiquity or the Middle Ages," he writes.[c] That may be true, but, as Jewish studies scholar Jonathan Klawans observes, there are no "native" terms for any of the concepts—from ethnicity to nationalism to race to religion itself—that scholars use to analyze ancient religions. All these terms are anachronistic. It is up to scholars to choose their terms wisely, define them carefully, and avoid bias creep as best as possible along the way. By these lights, if we are looking for the origins of "Judaism," we can certainly find them at least by the first century BCE.[d]

This statue of Moses Maimonides (1138–1204), executed by Amadeo Ruiz Olmos in 1964, is located in Cordoba, Spain. Maimonides was a Jewish philosopher who approached Jewish law through the rationalist lens of ancient Greek philosophy.

of blasphemy and publicly burned two years later. Jews were expelled from England in 1290 and from France in 1306 and 1394. In many European cities where they were allowed to settle, they were cordoned off in ghettos—a term that likely originated in 1516 in Venice where Jews were restricted to an area next to a *giotto* (iron foundry).

As a rule, life was better under Muslims, who saw Jews as fellow "people of the book," and it was best in Spain under relatively tolerant Muslim rulers from the tenth through the twelfth centuries. During this time of interfaith collaboration, also known as the Convivencia ("coexistence"), Jews, Christians, and Muslims collaborated in astronomy, mathematics, art, architecture, and philosophy. In 1492, however, King Ferdinand and Queen Isabella captured the entire Iberian peninsula except for Portugal and ordered all Jews to leave. Some Jews became *conversos*—converts to Catholicism. Others, whom the Spanish dubbed *marranos* ("pigs" or "deviants"), became fake converts who practiced Judaism in hiding. Some Jewish refugees from Spain were crew members under Christopher Columbus, who famously sailed with his Niña, Pinta, and Santa Maria to the New World in 1492. A few historians have suggested that Columbus, who signed letters to his son Diego in the Hebrew characters for "with God's help," may have been a secret Jew himself who crossed the Atlantic in search of safe haven for his fellow Jews.

Conversos were persecuted by the Spanish Inquisition, which had begun in 1478. Inquisitors accused many of being marranos. Inquisitors eventually tortured and killed thousands of Jews. This dragnet even caught up the dead, whose bones were dug up and committed to the flames. But Catholics were not the only persecutors of Jews in this period. Martin Luther, the German Catholic monk and Protestant provocateur, authored some of the vilest anti-Semitic literature in world history, arguing for the destruction of Jewish homes and synagogues, the confiscation of Jewish scriptures and other property, and the banishing of Jews from his homeland. Luther's *On the Jews and Their Lies* (1543) blasted "these Jews" as a "thoroughly evil, poisonous, and devilish lot . . . who for these fourteen hundred years have been and still are our plague, our pestilence, and our misfortune."[14]

As Jews struggled to survive this poison during the Middle Ages, they also produced some of Judaism's greatest thinkers, beginning with Rashi and Moses Maimonides. Rashi, an acronym for Rabbi Shlomo ben Isaac (1040–1105), is renowned as Judaism's foremost interpreter of sacred texts. His commentary on the Torah was the first book ever printed in Hebrew. Virtually every Talmud published today includes Rashi's commentaries plus those of his students. Born in 1040 in Troyes in the Champagne district of France, Rashi was an Ashkenazi Jew who studied with leading teachers in Mainz and Worms (in modern-day Germany) before returning to his hometown to found an academy of Jewish learning known as a yeshiva. There he taught his now-famous method of seeking first after the literal meaning of a scriptural passage and only then turning to the meanings read into it by later rabbis. Today, Rashi's followers are known as Tosafists ("those who add on"), because they added on to their teacher's thinking, just as he himself added on to the Torah and Talmud.

Whereas Rashi is the great Jewish commentator, Moses Maimonides (1138–1204) is the great Jewish philosopher. But Maimonides (also known by the acronym Rambam) was also a Renaissance man before the Renaissance, who worked as a medical doctor, commanded Hebrew and Arabic, and wrote both a commentary on the Mishna and a code of Jewish law. When his Iberian hometown of Cordoba was taken over by an intolerant Muslim group that destroyed synagogues and forced Jews to convert, he and his family escaped to Morocco, Palestine, and finally Cairo, where Maimonides lived out the rest of his life as a Jew.

Maimonides' legal code is a model of rationalism, dismissing laws based, in his view, on magic or superstition and arguing against astrology and for the natural sciences. Regarding the messiah, Maimonides presented a wholly naturalistic explanation of a political figure who would win control over Zion and reestablish the sacrificial cult in a rebuilt temple without resorting to a single miracle. This skepticism got Maimonides in trouble in some quarters. Nonetheless, he was (and is) widely praised for his classic, *Guide for the Perplexed* (c. 1190), which offers a rationalist's interpretation of Judaism rooted in the ancient Greek philosophy of Aristotle. In this book and elsewhere, Maimonides taught a "negative theology" that depicted God as utterly transcendent and beyond human understanding. Echoing the teaching in the Hindu Upanishads that describes the divine as *neti neti* ("not this, not that"), he argued that only negative statements can be made about God. Anything we might affirm about God presumes too much. So while we can say that God is not many, we cannot affirm that God is one.

JUDAISM BY THE NUMBERS

Thirteen Principles by Maimonides (1160)

In addition to his *Guide for the Perplexed*, Maimonides is remembered for crafting Judaism's "Thirteen Principles," a creed of sorts for a conspicuously noncreedal tradition. This list, now recited in many synagogue services, first appears in his *Commentary on the Mishnah* (1160), where Maimonides refers to these beliefs as "the fundamental truths of our religion and its very foundations."[a]

1. Belief in the existence of the Creator, be He Blessed, who is perfect in every manner of existence and is the Primary Cause of all that exists.

2. The belief in G-d's absolute and unparalleled unity.

3. The belief in G-d's noncorporeality, nor that He will be affected by any physical occurrences, such as movement, or rest, or dwelling.

4. The belief in G-d's eternity.

5. The imperative to worship Him exclusively and no foreign false gods.

6. The belief that G-d communicates with man through prophecy.

7. The belief that the prophecy of Moses our teacher has priority.

8. The belief in the divine origin of the Torah.

9. The belief in the immutability of the Torah.

10. The belief in divine omniscience and providence.

11. The belief in divine reward and retribution.

12. The belief in the arrival of the Messiah and the messianic era.

13. The belief in the resurrection of the dead.

Jewish Mysticism and the Kabbalah

The historian of Jewish mysticism Moshe Idel has argued that the commandments of the Bible are the "what?" of Judaism, and the Talmud is its "how?" The "why?" he says, is philosophy and Kabbalah. **Kabbalah** is a mystical branch of Judaism that, like other forms of esotericism, offered its initiates secret wisdom. That wisdom came not by doing philosophy but by contemplating God, the human being, and the relationship between them.

There were mystics in early Jewish history, including the "chariot" mystics of first-century Palestine who meditated on visionary ascents to heavenly realms akin to the prophet Ezekiel's sci-fi-like vision of a chariot with sixteen faces and sixteen wings. The core text in this mystical tradition is the Sefer Ha-Zohar ("Book of Splendor"), a commentary on the Hebrew Bible that, according to the faithful, contains secret wisdom that goes back to Moses and Mount Sinai and even creation itself. Though the Zohar was written largely in invented Aramaic, set in Roman Palestine, and attributed to a second-century BCE rabbi, most scholars believe it was actually compiled toward the end of the thirteenth century in Castile, Spain, by the rabbi who claimed to have discovered it in a Galilean cave: Moses de Leon (1250–1305).

"The jewel in the crown of Jewish mystical literature," the Zohar searches after the mystical significance of a scriptural passage rather than its literal or allegorical meanings.[15] Another book of books that includes not only Torah commentary but also sermons, parables, and conversations among ancient sages, the Zohar reads a bit like an autobiographical novel featuring its alleged author Rabbi Shimon bar Yochai and his followers, who see him as a holy man revealing mystical secrets to a small circle of disciples as they wander across the Galilean landscape.

While Maimonides and other Jewish philosophers wrote into a yawning gap between an abstract God and human beings, the Zohar hosted its conversations in a space where the two could enter into intimate conversation. Its key term for God is *Ein Sof* ("Endless One")—that which is beyond the limits of time and space and therefore beyond human knowing.

At the heart of the Zohar is a story of descent and ascent between heaven and earth derived from a mystical outgrowth of ancient Greek philosophy called Neoplatonism. In this story, God as Ein Sof sounds a lot like the god of the philosophers—distant and aloof, stubbornly silent. But God does not remain "up there," hidden and alone. In a grand unmasking, God makes Godself known through the ten *sefirot*, or divine manifestations. These ten emanations of the names, faces, powers, and qualities of God have been depicted as a tree and as a human body.

As the Ein Sof manifests, divinity changes, shape-shifting from unity to multiplicity, rest to action, distance to proximity. Paradoxically, this divinity is both merciful and just, both good and evil. In the yin/yang symbolism of China, the one gives rise to the two (the feminine yin and the masculine yang). In the erotic imaginings of the Zohar, the one (Ein Sof) gives rise to the ten (sefirot), who together testify to an androgynous divinity who is both male and female. Particularly crucial here is the tenth sefira, Shekinah, this god's indwelling feminine aspect. By meditating on these emanations, Kabbalists can acquire secret wisdom and experience the ecstasies of this Book of Splendor.

The ultimate goal of the Zohar's take on Judaism's exile-and-return myth is to transform our world of separation into a world of unity—to unite the ten sefirot with the one Ein Sof

Kabbalah
Jewish mystical tradition rooted in the Zohar

and in the process to unite humans with one another and with the divine. All this happens in a world of correspondences between the visible and the invisible—a reciprocal world in which what humans do "down here" affects God "up there" (and vice versa).

The Spanish expulsion that scattered Jews across Europe after 1492 also dispersed Kabbalism, which over the course of the Middle Ages had come, in the analysis of historian Yaacob Dweck, to refer to "a mode of reading, a library of texts, a series of concepts, and a range of practices."[16] By unveiling in books the secret truths that previously had been passed directly from teacher to disciple, this dispersion also democratized a tradition that had previously been reserved for a few elites. As reinterpreted by Isaac Luria of Palestine (1534–1572), Kabbalah was now unhidden, like God himself at the creation. Along the way it picked up a more urgent emphasis on messianism, greater attention to the sexual union of the Kabbalist with Shekinah, a tighter focus on evil and redemption, and a preoccupation with tikkun olam ("repairing the world"), which for many modern Jews has become the emphasis of Jewish life. Like the Hindu who first said that there were 330 million gods (one, perhaps, for every Hindu), Luria said there were six hundred thousand faces of the Torah (one, perhaps, for every Jew). More daringly, Kabbalists claimed that God was damaged, and only through the actions of God's chosen people could that damage be repaired.

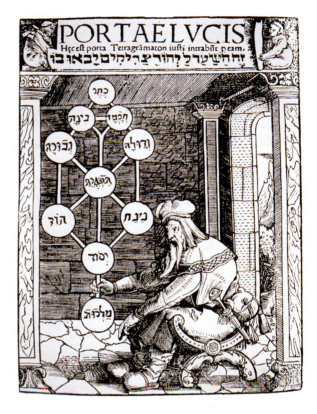

A Jewish kabbalist holds a *sefirot* "tree" in this cover page from *Portae Lucis* (1516), a translation of the Kabbalah by Paolo Riccio from Augsburg, Germany. This tree portrays ten ways the Infinite reveals itself in this mystical text.

According to Luria's complex mythology, before creation all was one. After creation, multiplicity was the rule. In a spiritual version of the Big Bang, everything exploded out into the cosmos in fragments of the original unity but with a spark of the divine secreted inside. How to fix this brokenness and "repair the world"? Through prayer and Torah study and by observing other commandments. Each of these acts of redemption was said to liberate divine sparks, allowing them to return to their Creator and bringing us all a bit closer to unity with one another and with God.

Like the Sufis in the Islamic tradition, Kabbalists were criticized for trading in reason for unheavenly nonsense. Critics called them out for substituting experience for law and for flirting too heavily with dualism (because of their understanding of the battle between good and evil) and pantheism (because of their close identification of God with the world). Others denounced the ten sefirot teaching as uncomfortably akin to the Christian Trinity and were scandalized by efforts to align these ten emanations with parts of God's body. Critics also worried about the Kabbalists' flirtation with reincarnation and the transmigration of souls. Wasn't Judaism committed to the bodily resurrection?

Nonetheless, as the center of world Jewry shifted after 1492 from Western to Eastern Europe, Kabbalism arose as a potent challenge to the rationalism of Maimonides and the legalism of Talmud study. For many seventeenth-century Jews, it became *the* way of being Jewish. The Kabbalah also influenced Western occultism, showing up in Renaissance humanism thanks to Pico della Mirandola (1463–1494), who studied with Jewish Kabbalists, and later in Mormonism thanks to its founder Joseph Smith, whose God was,

Hasidism
Orthodox school of the "pious," which emphasizes prayer over study and the heart over the head

in the words of the literary critic Harold Bloom, "a daring revival of the God of some of the Kabbalists and Gnostics."[17] Although Kabbalah may sound like the sort of thing only a philosophy major could love, it remains popular today, and not just among Jews. In recent years, it has attracted a litany of celebrities—Madonna, Britney Spears, Lindsay Lohan, David Beckham, Ariana Grande—to the Kabbalah Centre in Los Angeles long associated with the controversial pop Kabbalist Philip Berg.

One concept from Kabbalah that particularly resonates today is tikkun olam. This concept enjoins Jews not to wait for the messiah to repair the world but to engage actively and persistently in that task themselves. From this perspective, exile is not just historical and political. It is cosmic. We are in exile from our true selves, from one another, and from God. But part of God is in exile, too. To "repair the world" is to return, spark by spark, to God's original unity.

Judaism as Joy: Hasidism

After the expulsions of Jews that propelled Maimonides out of Spain and uprooted millions of others from Western Europe, Judaism's center of gravity shifted to Poland, whose nobles had given Jews legal autonomy and personal freedoms as early as the thirteenth century. By the mid-sixteenth century, four out of every five Jews lived in this region. Many lived in shtetls (villages) but were not allowed to own land. Many among these villagers worked as peddlers or ran stores. During the eighteenth century, as Poland came under the control of Russians, Austrians, and Prussians, Jewish life there became even harder.

In late-eighteenth-century Poland, a new form of Jewish piety, **Hasidism**, flourished. However, the Hasidim ("Pious Ones") traced their roots to an earlier figure: Rabbi Israel

A group of Orthodox Jewish men wear traditional dress as they walk to synagogue on Shabbat in Williamsburg, Brooklyn.

Temple Emanu-El of New York, located on Manhattan's Upper East Side, was founded in 1845 as the first Reform Jewish congregation in New York City. Like other nineteenth-century American Reform synagogues, Temple Emanu-El features architectural elements, including stained glass and an organ, patterned after Christian churches.

ben Eliezer (d. 1760), who under the title of the Baal Shem Tov ("Master of the Good Name") personified the life of the pious Hasid. Hasidim engaged in serious study, but they emphasized the heart over the head, prayer over knowledge.

Though once celebrated as an itinerant wanderer, the Baal Shem Tov (also known by the acronym the Besht) was actually a well-respected employee of the Jewish community of Mezhbizh in modern-day Ukraine. According to the many legends that have sprung up around his life, the Besht lost almost all interest in ordinary things after being initiated into the mysteries of Jewish mysticism. At the age of thirty-three, he became a teacher and miracle worker who used God's "good name" to heal his townspeople, Christians included. Upon his death in 1760, Polish Jews were sharply divided between Hasidim and their opponents. By the mid-nineteenth century, Hasidism had won the hearts of most Jews in Poland.

Hasids revered a new Jewish exemplar, the *zaddik* ("righteous one"), who was distinguished by charisma, not education. Like Hindu gurus, these zaddikim, also known as *rebbes*, did not restrict themselves to spiritual matters. They weighed in on business concerns and matters of the heart. Their fervent prayers turned not infrequently into singing and dancing—Judaism as joy. Like Zen masters, these "righteous ones" ran roughshod over traditional distinctions between the sacred and the profane. By treating cutting wood and cleaning laundry as joyful service to a loving God, they sought to sanctify every nook and cranny of the mundane world.

During World War II, as the Nazis invaded Poland, most Hasidic communities there were destroyed. Some Hasidim fled to the United States, which they had previously regarded as an "unkosher nation." By this time, the role of the zaddik had become hereditary, and Hasidic dynasties had formed. One of these family dynasties is the

Brooklyn-based Lubavitchers, best known for reaching out to unaffiliated Jews through their organization, Chabad.

Today, the Hasidic movement is especially strong in three Brooklyn neighborhoods, where on the Sabbath passersby can see tens of thousands of Hasidic men in large black hats and long black coats walking to and from services in Williamsburg, Crown Heights, and Borough Park. Here, Yiddish-speaking Hasidim maintain their own ambulance services as well as a gender-segregated bus line that relegates women to the back and men to the front. As hipsters and young professionals have gentrified these previously closed communities, they have clashed with Hasidim over efforts to impose dress codes for stores (banning "low-cut necklines") and to shut down bike lanes (and their "scantily clad" female riders)—all in the name of modesty.

Modern Judaism and Jewish Denominationalism

Modern Jewish history is often dated from the emancipation of European Jews from legal inequality in revolutionary France in 1791. During this period, new ideas (equality, liberty) and social circumstances (industrialization, immigration) challenged traditional forms of religion, and Jews developed new ways of being Jewish. Ghettos collapsed under the weight of increasing commitments to civil rights, individual liberty, and religious toleration. So Jews had to decide whether their Jewish religion was inherited or chosen.

As emancipation dawned, Jews also had to decide whether they were for or against the Enlightenment, just as Pharisees and Essenes once had to decide whether they were for or against Rome. Were they willing to pay the prices countries were demanding in exchange for emancipation, not least their identity as a chosen people? Was it possible to modernize without bowing down to modernity? Was it possible to belong simultaneously to the people of Israel and the nation-states of France or Germany? Different Jews had different answers to these questions.

Some Jews responded to modernity with an "amen" to Enlightenment ideals. In Germany, Moses Mendelssohn (1729–1786) the founder of the Jewish Enlightenment (Haskalah) and the first great modern Jewish intellectual, pushed for Jewish emancipation and assimilation. An advocate of religious tolerance and the separation of church and state, Mendelssohn was convinced that Jews could be both modern people and traditionalists. He himself held on to his Jewish identity and to halacha by reimagining Judaism not as a revealed religion but as a "revealed legislation." A believer in a natural religion common to all, Mendelssohn rejected the notion that God revealed new truths at Sinai. As an observant Jew, however, he affirmed that God had revealed new laws binding for Jews.

Mendelssohn played a key role in transforming Judaism into a modern religion along Protestant lines. According to the religious studies scholar Leora Batnitzky, he paved the way for viewing Judaism as a religion that was private rather than public, voluntary rather than compulsory, focused on personal faith rather than community rituals, and independent from politics and other supposedly secular spheres of life.[18]

Other Enlightenment enthusiasts advanced a series of reforms that would make Jewish worship look and feel more like Protestant services, including the introduction of organ music and an emphasis on the Bible (over the Talmud) and ethics (over ritual). Four of Mendelssohn's six children, along with his grandson, the composer Felix Mendelssohn, went further, deciding that converting to Christianity was a faster route to social

Samson Raphael Hirsch (1808–1888)

Samson Raphael Hirsch was a German rabbi whose commitments to preserving traditional Judaism while engaging with the modern world gave rise to Neo-Orthodoxy and earned him the title the "father of modern Orthodox Judaism."

Born in Hamburg, Germany, Hirsch studied the Talmud under leading scholars and served as a rabbi in various places beginning in his early twenties in Oldenburg. In 1851, a small Orthodox community hired him to come to Frankfurt-on-Main. There he built that congregation into a thriving community of five hundred families.

Hirsch affirmed the divine origins of the Torah and was skeptical of new social scientific study of Judaism, but he allowed some Jewish customs to change. As a rabbi, he opposed the emerging Reform movement, insisting on using the Hebrew language for prayers. But he followed many Reform rabbis by shaving his beard, wearing robes, and delivering sermons in German. Because of his loyalty to his fellow Germans, he too was ambivalent about Zionism.

Hirsch understood "genuine Judaism," as he called it, in terms clearly influenced by modern Protestants—as a community of free individuals brought together by their individual choices to follow a particular religious tradition. In keeping with that vision, he was instrumental in convincing the Prussian government in 1876 to give Jews like himself the freedom to choose to separate from state-sponsored Judaism and to form their own congregations.

Hirsch is remembered for affirming both Torah and "the way of the land," and he understood that way to include not only earning a living but also engaging with modern culture and society. For him that engagement meant stressing secular education alongside Torah study. Hirsch also idealized the "Israel-Mensch": a Jew who was both religious and enlightened, both observant and cultured, who belonged fully to his people and to the modern world.

acceptance, and taking it. This cautionary tale convinced many Jews that the Enlightenment needed to be met with something other than a warm embrace.

Those who did not wade into the waters of Christian baptism had three main options: to liberalize and modernize Judaism, to reject modernity in the name of tradition, or to forge a middle path. Out of these choices came Judaism's three main branches: Reform Judaism, Orthodox Judaism, and Conservative Judaism. Members of these branches tell the quintessentially Jewish story of exile and return in different ways. They differ especially over the observance of Jewish law and the 613 commandments. They also disagree over whether and to what extent Jews should remain a people set apart or whether they should mingle with non-Jews. While Christian denominations distinguish themselves largely on the basis of doctrine, these denominations differ more on practice.

Zionism and the Holocaust

As nationalism spread across the globe in the late nineteenth century, another option for Jews began to find favor: a movement in central and eastern Europe calling for a Jewish state. That movement was called **Zionism**, after Zion, the ancient name of one of Jerusalem's hills and later a term used to refer to the promised land itself. Like all movements, it evolved, but by the early 1940s the goal of most Zionists was to create a nation-state where Jews would be full citizens, free from the persecution that had followed them elsewhere.

Zionism is now both widely accepted among Jews and extraordinarily controversial. When a Jewish state was first proposed in the late nineteenth century, many Jews opposed

Zionism
movement to create a Jewish nation-state, which resulted in the creation of Israel in 1948

David Ben-Gurion, Israel's first prime minister, publicly declares the formation of the state of Israel on May 14, 1948.

it. Most Orthodox Jews believed it was up to God and the messiah to create a Jewish homeland. Also wary were Reform Jews. Why push for your own state when you are working so hard to assimilate into Germany or the United States?

A key figure on the "yes" side of this debate was Theodor Herzl, an Austro-Hungarian lawyer, playwright, and literary critic from Vienna who argued beginning in 1896 that the only real solution to persistent anti-Semitism was a Jewish state. Many early Zionists were secular Jews, moved more by power politics than by biblical stories of exile and return. Herzl himself was by no means a religious man. He refused to circumcise his son, he displayed Christmas trees in his home, and he spoke neither Hebrew nor Yiddish. During a visit to Jerusalem in 1898, he described the Western Wall as a site of "hideous, miserable, scrambling beggary" and Jerusalem itself as a "musty" repository of "2,000 years of inhumanity, intolerance and foulness."[19] Nonetheless, he was appalled by anti-Jewish riots in Russia in 1881 and by the persecution of Jews elsewhere. A Jewish state was, in his view, the only real answer to the "Jewish question." "We are one people," he wrote, who deserve a state where "we shall live at last as free men on our own soil, and die peacefully in our own home."[20]

There was talk of establishing this home in Argentina or Uganda or upstate New York, but the world's eyes focused on the Middle East when the United Kingdom's Foreign Secretary Arthur James Balfour declared in 1917 that his government supported "the establishment in Palestine of a national home for the Jewish people."[21] Establishing this state became more urgent during the **Holocaust**.

Also known as the Shoah ("Catastrophe" in Hebrew), the Holocaust saw the murders of six million Jews, including 1.5 million children—about two of every three Jews in Europe—at the hands of Nazi Germany before and during World War II. The Nazis also murdered unknown numbers of Soviets, Poles, Serbs, Roma, Jehovah's Witnesses, gays and lesbians, and the disabled. As this evil was revealed to the world, Jews wrestled with

Holocaust (also Shoah, or "Catastrophe")
systematic persecution and mass murder of Jews in concentration camps by Nazi Germany and its collaborators before and during World War II

how to hold on to their understanding of God as an ethical power who acts in human history. If God is both good and all-powerful, where was God in the concentration camps? Some tried to make sense of this conundrum by viewing it through biblical events of individual suffering or mass death in which God tested Job, Noah, and other righteous ones. Others dispensed with belief in God or described God as lost in exile. Still others drew on the Talmudic traditions of argumentation, shaking their fists and calling God to task.

Anne Frank's *The Diary of a Young Girl* (1947), written during the Nazi occupation of the Netherlands, introduced the world to the intimate terror of the Holocaust. "I still believe, in spite of everything," Frank wrote before dying of typhus in a concentration camp, "that people are truly good at heart."[22] Elie Wiesel, a Holocaust survivor who won the Nobel Peace Prize in 1986, was not so sure. His bestseller, *Night*, published in Yiddish in 1956, French in 1958, and English in 1960, is a searing indictment of God and the human condition. After describing a hanging of young boys in the Nazi death camp at Buna, Wiesel asks, "Where is God?" Then he hears a voice within: "Where is He? This is where—hanging here from this gallows." But more than a Death of God treatise, *Night* is a call to remember that resounds across the globe in Holocaust memorials dedicated to the proposition that the Nazis' killing machine should never be forgotten. "Never shall I forget that night, the first night in camp, that turned my life into one long night seven times sealed," Wiesel wrote. "Never shall I forget that smoke. Never shall I forget the small faces of the children whose bodies I saw transformed into smoke under a silent sky. Never shall I forget those flames that consumed my faith forever."[23]

Wiesel has been criticized for turning the Holocaust into a singular event in Jewish history—"Auschwitz is as important as Sinai," he has said—and for turning the millions of Roma, gays, Polish Christians, and other non-Jews who died at the hands of the Nazis into "second-class victims."[24] But perhaps more than anyone else, he must be credited with keeping the world's eyes on an event many would prefer to forget.

As news of the "final solution" of the Nazis spread and the horrors of death camps at Auschwitz and elsewhere became plain around the globe, the community of nations echoed Herzl's call for a Jewish state. Efforts focused on Palestine. In 1947, the United Nations General Assembly passed a resolution calling for the partition of British-ruled Palestine into a Jewish state of Israel and an Arab state of Palestine. According to this resolution, Jerusalem would be a neutral, demilitarized city. On May 14, 1948, the state of Israel was formed. Its Declaration of Independence spoke of a people "forcibly exiled from their land" yet never ceasing to "pray and hope for their return to it."[25]

Peace was, unfortunately, elusive. For Israel's first two decades, Jerusalem was divided, with Jordan controlling the Western Wall and prohibiting Jews from praying there. In 1967, when Israel took Jerusalem during the Six-Day War, Israeli soldiers seized the Western Wall. There they wept as they said the prayer for the dead for their family members and fellow soldiers. The Israeli government leveled nearby buildings in the Moroccan Quarter in order to create the plaza that now stands in front of the Western Wall. However, it

Anne Frank (shown here at school in 1940), was thirteen years old when she began writing the diary that detailed her family's harrowing experience hiding from the Nazis during the Holocaust. Published in 1948 as *The Diary of a Young Girl*, this book gave the world a poignant, firsthand account of the life of a child before she was killed in a concentration camp.

agreed to allow Jordan to control the Temple Mount and to prohibit Jews from praying there, even as the area remained under Israeli security control.

This unstable status quo seems to be challenged almost every year, as strictly Orthodox Jews press for the right to pray on the Temple Mount and some Arabs claim that there was never a Jewish temple anywhere near the Noble Sanctuary. So peace can feel like an increasingly distant dream. Failed peace proposals, swelling Jewish settlements, and Arab uprisings known as intifadas remain pressure points in an ongoing political, military, economic, cultural, and religious struggle.

Today, some messianic Orthodox Jews continue to look forward to the rebuilding of the Jerusalem Temple and the restoration of the sacrificial rites of its priests. Possessed of a similar hope, evangelical Christian Zionists believe that a new temple must be standing before Christ will return to earth in glory. These were once fringe positions, but as of 2020 the Israeli government was funding some messianic groups, and evangelical Christians were key government partners. Nonetheless, Jews remain, for the most part, a "people of the book" rather than a "people of the temple." Their exemplars are rabbis rather than priests, their focus is on reading and interpreting texts, and they understand Judaism to be a religion that neither needs nor looks forward to another temple to come. Many Jews have moved to Israel. Many others have chosen to live in the United States or elsewhere in the diaspora.

JUDAISM IN THE UNITED STATES

The demographics of Judaism make it difficult to discuss the history of Judaism apart from the history of Judaism in the United States. There are almost as many Jewish Americans today as there are Jewish Israelis, and the history discussed previously made repeated forays into the United States. Similarly, the discussion of Judaism in the United States that follows looks back to developments in Europe because of the close connections between American Jews and Jews in Germany and Eastern Europe as American Judaism began and developed.

Jews first settled in what is now the United States in 1654 in New Amsterdam (now New York City) and established the first Jewish community in North America there. The first synagogue in North America was built, also in New York City, in 1730. Many of these early settlers came via Brazil and were Sephardic Jews, so American Judaism in colonial times was heavily influenced by the Sephardic tradition. Following the American Revolution, Jews were given full rights as citizens under the Constitution, which was ratified in 1788. When the Bill of Rights was ratified in 1791, the First Amendment guaranteed all Americans freedom of religion.

American Judaism changed dramatically through the next two periods of immigration and became overwhelmingly Ashkenazi. In the 1840s, large numbers of Reform-minded Jews immigrated to the United States from Germany, and in the wake of the 1880s pogroms large numbers of more traditional Eastern European Jews arrived. There are many ways to tell their story. Here we focus on the emergence of the pattern that came to define American Judaism as it divided that community into denominations such as Reform Judaism, Conservative Judaism, and Orthodox Judaism. Though this is a story of American Judaism, it is by no means confined to the United States, as key developments took place elsewhere.

Reform Judaism

When Christianity splintered during the Protestant Reformation, the burning issues were theological, including whether salvation came by faith alone or by faith and good works. When Reform Judaism emerged in Germany in the early nineteenth century, its distinguishing features were largely related to worship. Reform Jews said prayers and sang hymns in German rather than Hebrew, and their rabbis delivered sermons in the vernacular, too. They brought organs into their places of worship, despite traditional prohibitions against playing musical instruments on Shabbat. They often referred to these meeting places as temples because they no longer yearned for a rebuilt Jerusalem Temple and saw their own places of worship as taking its place. In these temples, they sat together as families rather than segregating the sexes. Reform services were shorter, and some congregations even shifted services to Sunday in keeping with Christian norms. To further signal that they were at home in Germany and among their Protestant friends, Reform Jews eliminated prayers for a return to Israel.

As this last example suggests, ideas also mattered. Some Reform communities cut professions of belief in the messiah and bodily resurrection out of Maimonides' Thirteen Principles. In keeping with the Enlightenment emphasis on universalism over nationalism, Reform Jews also downplayed the chosenness of the Jewish people—a view criticized during the nineteenth century as parochial and racist. Reform Jews also embraced biblical criticism—efforts to understand through various historical and literary methods the sources of the Tanakh. They averted their collective gaze away from the Talmud toward the Bible. Reform Jews also drew a sharp distinction between ethical and ritual laws, adhering more strictly to the former than to the latter. In fact, they abandoned many ritual laws, including the dietary laws of *kashrut*. Some even eliminated the traditional practice of circumcising Jewish boys.

As emancipation dawned, Reform Jews wanted to be both Jewish and German (or Austrian or French). Some gave up entirely the long hope for a Jewish homeland; others transformed Canaan into a distant country reachable only at the end of times. Increasingly, Reform Jews viewed exile not as a punishment for sin but as part of the divine plan for scattering Jewish wisdom into the diaspora. All this amounted to a new vision of Judaism no longer as a people or a way of life but as a world religion. The hallmark of this religion was a universal ethic, not parochial foodways or nationalist dress. Accompanying this transformation was a shift of emphasis from the Talmud and its debates over Jewish law to the biblical books of the prophets and their emphasis on justice and mercy. In this way, Judaism increasingly signaled not just monotheism but ethical monotheism.

Reform Jews also reinterpreted Jesus, whom they increasingly saw not as the progenitor of a rival religion but as a tragically misunderstood Jew. During the closing years of the nineteenth century, virtually every leading Reform rabbi in the United States wrote a book or major article about Jesus. He was, in their view, not a messiah but an exemplary Jewish rabbi—"one of the best and truest sons of the synagogue" and "a religious genius of the first rank."[26]

Though the Reform movement gestated among Germans, most notably at a Reform temple in Hamburg built in 1818, it spread rapidly across Europe. It also spurred the Reform Society of Israelites in Charleston, South Carolina (est. 1824), and the West London Synagogue (est. 1842). In 1841 in Charleston, at the dedication of a new building for the Congregation Beth Elohim, the Polish-born rabbi Gustavus Poznanski gave voice to

Rabbi Isaac Mayer Wise (1819–1900) was a leader of American Reform Judaism who helped to found three key Reform institutions in the United States.

the Reform Jewish determination to dig in and put down roots wherever they might be. "America is our Zion," he said, and "this synagogue is our temple, this city our Jerusalem."[27] The key figure in the Reform movement in the United States, however, was Rabbi Isaac Mayer Wise (1819–1900). Born in Bohemia, Wise immigrated to the United States in 1846 and became the rabbi at Congregation Beth El in Albany, New York, later that year. After moving farther into the frontier to Cincinnati, Wise became the driving force behind the founding of three key Reform institutions: the Union of American Hebrew Congregations (established in 1873 in Cincinnati), Hebrew Union College (established in 1875, also in Cincinnati), and the Central Conference of American Rabbis (established in 1889 in Detroit).

Innovations in Reform Judaism in the United States have traditionally been interpreted largely as efforts to assimilate by adopting and adapting American Protestant norms and organizational forms. But as historian Shari Rabin has demonstrated, many of these innovations are better understood as practical adaptations to unsettled life on the frontier. When Wise's Albany congregation moved into a former church that had not segregated seating by sex, he decided it made sense to keep the pews as is. That was how his congregation became the first in the United States to institute family seating. Later, while traveling through Lafayette, Indiana, Wise heard of a small congregation that was having trouble gathering the quorum (**minyan**) of ten men required for worship. Again his response was more practical than theological: "Count the ladies" in the minyan, he said.[28]

Another Wise brainchild was the Pittsburgh Platform, the classic expression of Reform Judaism, drafted at a gathering of Reform rabbis in Pittsburgh in 1885. Part manifesto, part creed, this document described Judaism as a "progressive religion, ever striving to be in accord with the postulates of reason." It rejected miracles, the bodily resurrection, and heaven and hell, and described the Bible as reflecting "the primitive ideas of its own age." In a clear affirmation of religious tolerance, it recognized all religions as attempts "to grasp the Infinite" and Christianity and Islam as "daughter religions of Judaism," though it insisted that Judaism offered "the highest conception of the God-idea." Crucially, the Pittsburgh Platform divided the law into its ethical and ritual components, declaring only the ethical laws to be binding. Laws concerning "diet, priestly purity, and dress" may have been appropriate in ancient times, it observed, but they are "apt rather to obstruct than to further modern spiritual elevation."[29] The Pittsburgh Platform also rejected peoplehood, Zionism, and the restoration of the Jerusalem Temple. It reimagined messianism not as the miraculous return of an individual but as the hard and very human work of repairing the world by establishing justice and peace on earth. In short, this document aimed to reverse two millennia of efforts to cast Jews as a people set apart and to mainstream them instead by tearing down the walls that prevented Jews from integrating into non-Jewish societies. To put this in the terms of the sociology of religion, Reform Jews were reimagining their religion not as a sect (with high boundaries between insiders and outsiders) but as a church (which blurs the distinction between members of a religion and citizens of a country).

During the twentieth century, the Reform movement began to ordain female rabbis, starting with Regina Jones in Germany in 1935. In recent years, Reform Jews, alongside many liberal Protestants and Catholics, have also gravitated toward the acceptance of homosexuality, same-sex marriage, and LGBTQ rights. But there is also a countervailing trend in this movement to return to practices perhaps too hastily abandoned by earlier Reform Jews. Many Reform temples now include some prayers in Hebrew, and many

minyan
quorum of ten adult Jews, traditionally men, required for group prayer

Reform Jews keep kosher in some fashion. With the recent rise of multiculturalism and identity politics, the notion of Jews as a special people is also making a comeback. Opposition to Zionism, which nineteenth-century Reform Jews had seen as a barrier to assimilation, weakened in the aftermath of World War II, when the horrors of the Holocaust made plain to many the necessity of a Jewish state. That opposition has ramped up in recent years because of the ongoing occupation of territories taken by Israel in 1967 in the Six-Day War and the ongoing development of Jewish settlements on that land, which some Jews condemn. In a recent Pew survey, only 35 percent of Reform Jews in the United States said they believed that Israel was given by God to the Jewish people.[30] Nonetheless, the Reform movement remains committed to Zionism, even as many Reform Jews criticize the Israeli government and its policies.

Orthodox Judaism

Like Protestant fundamentalism, Orthodox Judaism is a modern invention—a reaction to efforts by Reform Jews to modernize Judaism. And its response to modernity is a resounding "No." Orthodox Jews argued, as the Hungarian rabbi Moses Sofer did in the early nineteenth century, that "innovation is prohibited by the Torah." Nonetheless, they took the Jewish tradition in new directions.

In the United States, Reform Judaism predominated into the 1880s. In fact, it was so dominant that Wise had reason to hope that American Jewry would unite behind it. Beginning in 1881, however, large numbers of more traditional Jews emigrated from Eastern Europe. Ethnic and religious tensions ensued with earlier Jewish immigrants, who were far less traditional and largely of German descent. These tensions bubbled up and boiled over at a notorious banquet in Cincinnati in 1883. The occasion was the graduation of the first rabbinical class of Wise's Hebrew Union College. When the rabbis sat down to eat, the first course was littleneck clams. Then came soft shell crabs and shrimp and frogs' legs. None of this was kosher. Two rabbis walked out in disgust. When more traditional Jews on the East Coast heard of this "*trefa* ['unkosher'] banquet," as they called it, they were outraged. Some began organizing their own institutions, including the Union of Orthodox Jewish Congregations of America (est. 1898), as an alternative to Wise's Union of American Hebrew Congregations.

Orthodox Jews defined themselves more in legal than theological terms—as strict followers of Jewish law. They rejected efforts by Reform Jews to divide halacha into required ethical precepts and voluntary ritual precepts. Because both the Written and Oral Torah were given by God on Mount Sinai, they believed, the eternal and unchanging commandments conveyed in the Tanakh and the Talmud were binding on all Jews. Orthodox Jews also affirmed all the traditional doctrines of Maimonides, including the bodily resurrection and the coming messiah. They opposed intermarriage. Any changes they made in their tradition typically widened the gap between themselves and non-Jews.

Today, the differences between Orthodox and Reform Jews are particularly plain when it comes to gender and sexuality. Men and women worship separately in Orthodox services, while in Reform services women, men, girls, boys, and nonbinary and transgender people worship together as families. Orthodox prayers to "God of our fathers, Abraham, Isaac, and Jacob" are recast in Reform temples as: "God of our ancestors: of Abraham, Isaac, and Jacob; of Sarah, Rebekah, Rachel, and Leah." The Orthodox do not count women among the ten Jews required for a minyan. Reform Jews do, though many have relaxed the traditional rule of ten altogether. Finally, for Orthodox Jews, Jewish identity is passed down through the mother, so you are Jewish only if your mother was Jewish. For Reform Jews, either parent being Jewish is sufficient.

The Orthodox also remain formally opposed to homosexuality, while Reform Jews celebrate same-sex marriages and have ordained gay and lesbian rabbis since the 1990s. However, there is a group of Orthodox lesbians—"Orthodykes," as some playfully refer to themselves—who contend for lesbianism on the grounds that, while male-male sex is clearly denounced in the biblical book of Leviticus, female-female sex is never mentioned. There are also Modern Orthodox Jews who advocate for open inclusion of LGBTQ Jews, and Modern Orthodox women are increasingly studying the Talmud.

The Varieties of Orthodox Experience

Though they speak of preserving one ancient tradition, Orthodox Jews are a house divided. The spectrum of groups spans from the more accommodative Modern Orthodox to the strictly Orthodox Haredim. These groups disagree first and foremost over how vigorously they as a "peculiar people" (Deuteronomy 14:2) must separate from the outside world.

Modern Orthodox Jews are more open to the wider world, wearing modern dress and studying in secular universities. "Torah with the way of the land" is their ideal. Their intellectual home in the United States is Yeshiva University in New York, where it is common to see young men wearing fashionable blue jeans with traditional *tzitzit* ("knotted fringes") overhanging them.

The **Haredim**—"Tremblers" before God (also known as the ultra-Orthodox)—distance themselves as much as possible not only from modern life but also from other Jews. Strict sectarians, they reinforce the walls surrounding their "fortress Judaism" by living

A Haredi Jewish family enjoys a day at an amusement park in Coney Island in Brooklyn, New York.

JUDAISM BY THE NUMBERS

Three Jewish Movements

	Reform	Orthodox	Conservative
keep kosher?	personal choice	yes	yes
worship language	mostly vernacular	Hebrew	mix of languages
Jewish identity	through father or mother	through mother	through mother
Torah	record of Jewish people	revealed by God to Moses on Mt. Sinai	divinely inspired
name for place of worship	temple	shul (Yiddish for school)	synagogue

in separate neighborhoods modeled after early modern Eastern European settlements and by wearing distinctive clothing (often black hats and black suits for men and modest clothing that covers the ankles and wrists for women). Some Haredim also refuse to read newspapers or watch television. Many restrict themselves to rabbi-approved cellphones that either offer a "Koshernet" filtered for modesty or block the Internet altogether. Some speak Yiddish, a German dialect spoken historically by Ashkenazi Jews. Because of their extraordinarily high birth rates (six to eight children per couple), the Haredi population is skyrocketing. Now one out of every eleven Jews in Israel, Haredim are projected to constitute a majority of UK Jews by 2031 and of U.S. Jews by 2050.

Unlike religious Zionists, who are the driving force behind the settler movement, the Haredim generally argue that the creation of the state of Israel by secular Jews was illegitimate because it usurped the roles of God and the messiah. So even those who live in Israel live as exiles there. Not all Haredim shun the outside world, however. Though many Haredi men in Israel devote themselves full-time to Torah study in the yeshiva, most in the United States are employed, including hundreds at B&H Photo and other electronics stores in New York City. Recent news stories about Haredi men refusing to sit next to women on airplane flights (for fear of violating a prohibition against touching any women who are not their wives) simultaneously demonstrate their disengagement from modern norms and their engagement with modern technology and modern life.

The Hasidim are the best known of Haredi Jews, but they differ from other strictly Orthodox Jews in many respects—in the organization of their communities around rebbes and in their emphases on piety over learning and on God's immanence over God's transcendence. Hasidim testify to the presence inside Judaism of the sort of ecstatic experiences also visible in Pentecostal churches.

Many Orthodox Jews take a page out of the book of Protestant fundamentalists (who often refuse to recognize liberal Protestants as Christians) by refusing to recognize Reform Jews as Jews: There is only one Judaism, and Reform Jews are not practicing it. In turn, some Reform Jews dismiss the obsession of the Orthodox with kosher laws as "kitchen Judaism." Judaism is not about what you eat, they argue. It is about how you act toward your fellow human beings. Other Reform Jews observe that, while the Orthodox claim simply to be following ancient traditions, Orthodoxy nowadays is actually stricter than it was before the Enlightenment. In this sense, Orthodoxy is itself an innovation, even though the Orthodox are explicitly opposed to innovation.

Conservative Judaism

Tracking a middle path between Reform and Orthodoxy, Conservative Jews affirm the necessity of both tradition and adaptation. Like the Orthodox, they determine Jewish identity by matrilineal descent (through the mother). They, too, affirm that all of Jewish law is binding on all Jews in all times. Like Reform Jews, they insist that this law has always evolved and must continue to adapt to new circumstances. Conservative Jews also more closely resemble the Reform movement in their openness to modern society and secular education. Orthodox inflexibility, they claim, is not in keeping with the Jewish tradition, which has traditionally been open to change.

As a rule, Conservative Jews are more progressive when it comes to theology and more traditional when it comes to ritual. They embrace historical criticism of the Bible, for example, but observe dietary laws with care. They also observe Shabbat but, unlike the Orthodox, typically allow both driving and the use of electricity on that day of rest. When it comes to worship, Conservative Jews share elements with both Orthodox and Reform Jews. Like Reform Jews, they have female rabbis and cantors (who lead the congregation in song during worship). They also ordain both gays and lesbians. They have mixed-gender seating at their services and allow women to be counted among the ten adult Jews making up a minyan. However, most prayers in a Conservative service are in Hebrew.

The Conservative movement is often traced to the principles of "positive historical Judaism" articulated in the mid-nineteenth century by the German rabbi and scholar Zecharias Frankel. But its real founder was Rabbi Solomon Schechter, who moved in 1902 from England's Cambridge University to New York City to serve as president of the Jewish Theological Seminary, which to this day serves as Conservative Judaism's intellectual home. Conservative Judaism remains strongest in the United States, where it has long vied with Reform Judaism for the loyalty of American Jews.

Reconstructionist Judaism

Reconstructionism is both more and less traditional than Reform Judaism. An American invention, it originated with a Jewish Theological Seminary professor, Rabbi Mordecai Kaplan (1881–1983), and takes its cues from his book *Judaism as a Civilization* (1934). Drawing on the Jewish sociologist Emile Durkheim, who viewed religion as a symbolic expression of society, Kaplan argued that Judaism is more social than spiritual—an evolving civilization rather than a supernatural religion. As such it wanted neither reforming nor conserving. It simply needed to be reconstructed.

Kaplan demystified God, Torah, and Israel alike. God, whom he understood as a power and a process rather than a supernatural person, was an expression of the highest ethical ideals of human beings. Torah was a living document rooted not in divine revelation but in the people of Israel, and its commandments were the "folkways" of that people rather than the voice of God. Though a nationalist, Kaplan rejected the chosen people idea, which he viewed as arrogant, intolerant, and offensive to modern notions of equality. However, in keeping with his roots in the Conservative movement (Kaplan taught for more than half a century at Jewish Theological Seminary), Reconstructionists created a movement that is more traditional, ritually, than the Reform movement, observing a full range of Jewish holidays and drawing heavily on Hebrew in worship services.

Ruth Bader Ginsburg (1933–)

The first Jewish woman appointed to the U.S. Supreme Court, Ruth Bader Ginsburg was born in Brooklyn in 1933 to a Jewish father who emigrated from Russia when he was thirteen and a Jewish mother who was conceived in Poland and born in the United States. Ginsburg excelled as a student at two high schools in Brooklyn; at Cornell, where she majored in government; and at Harvard Law School, where in 1956 she was one of nine women in her incoming class. After her husband, Martin Ginsburg, graduated from Harvard Law and took a job with a New York City law firm in 1958, she transferred to Columbia Law School, where she graduated in 1959 as the covaledictorian of her class. Few law firms were hiring Jews and fewer still Jewish women. But she managed to land a clerkship, which she later leveraged into a position as a law professor at Rutgers, where she taught through the tumult of the years from 1963 to 1972.

Ginsburg was the lead author on a brief in *Reed v. Reed*. In its 1971 decision in this case, the Supreme Court overturned an Idaho law that had discriminated against women in the administration of the estates of the dead. The next year, Ginsburg became the codirector of the ACLU's new Women's Rights Project and was hired onto the faculty of law at Columbia. She made her national reputation in *Weinberger v. Wiesenfeld* (1975), a landmark women's rights case that she cleverly chose in part because her client was a man. After Mr. Wiesenfeld's wife died in childbirth, he applied for the survivor's Social Security benefit traditionally paid to women whose husbands had passed away. The Supreme Court agreed unanimously with Ginsburg that this regulation was discriminatory and unconstitutional. In 1993, Ginsburg was nominated by President Bill Clinton and confirmed by the Senate to serve as the second woman (after Sandra Day O'Connor) on the Supreme Court.

As Ginsburg became an octogenarian, and especially after the election of President Donald Trump in 2016, she became an unlikely American icon, particularly among girls and young women. At the nationwide Women's March in 2017, fans wore "Notorious RBG" T-shirts and drank out of coffee mugs that read, "The Ruth Will Set You Free." It is tempting to say the 2018 documentary *RBG* burnished her image, but it was that unlikely image—as a slight superhero for justice—that made this film a surprise box-office hit. Ginsburg has credited her parents and her Jewish heritage with the "love of learning" that carried her to a seat on her nation's highest court. She has also said that growing up "in the shadow of World War II" with a "sense of being an outsider" made her "more empathetic" to minorities and outsiders.[a]

Reconstructionists pushed early for gender equality. One of the reasons Kaplan left his Orthodox congregation in New York City was its refusal to allow men and women to sit together. In 1922, he founded the Society for the Advancement of Judaism (SAJ) as an alternative. That same year, his twelve-year-old daughter Judith Kaplan became the first Jewish girl to celebrate her bat mitzvah in the United States. In 1984, the Reconstructionist Rabbinical College (est. 1968) became the first Jewish seminary to admit openly gay and lesbian students, and today its rabbis perform same-sex marriages. In 2018, this movement renamed its central organization "Reconstructing Judaism."

Humanistic Judaism

Most secular Jews do not attend synagogue, but they have an institutional home in Humanistic Judaism, which began in 1963 in suburban Detroit when the "atheist rabbi" Sherwin Wine (1928–2007) began writing God out of his new liturgies. An empiricist who believed that Judaism's power derived from human beings, Wine was not exactly an atheist, however. Calling himself an "ignostic," he argued (along with many analytic philosophers) that the God proposition was meaningless and therefore neither true nor false. His Birmingham Temple, which kept the Torah scrolls in the library rather than the sanctuary, expanded from 8 to 145 families in its first two years.

Today, Humanistic Jews reject the *bris*, or circumcision ritual, as sexist, preferring naming ceremonies alone for boys and girls alike. Their nontheistic congregations neither pray to God nor read from the Torah. For them, the ethical dimension of religion is paramount. Many are influenced by the early modern thinker Baruch Spinoza (1632–1677), whom Israel's first prime minister, David Ben-Gurion, himself a secular Jew, described as "the deepest, most original thinker to emerge [from our people] from the end of the Bible to the birth of Einstein."[31] Spinoza challenged virtually every classic belief in Jewish life, including a God who created and acts in the world, a Torah that reveals his teachings, and an Israel whom God has chosen as his people.

One current spokesperson for Humanistic Judaism is Greg Epstein, a Wine protégé ordained by the International Institute for Secular Humanist Judaism (IISHJ) (est. 1985) in 2005. A Harvard University chaplain, Epstein is the author of *Good Without God* (2009), which offers a vision of atheism that is both socially active and friendly to religion. Today, the Society for Humanistic Judaism (SHJ) (est. 1969) claims ten thousand members in thirty congregations in North America. Both the IISHJ and the SHJ define Judaism as a "human creation" and Jewish identity as an "ethnic reality."[32]

Jewish Renewal

Another recent innovation, Jewish Renewal, is often traced to the arrival in December 1949 of Zalman Schachter-Shalomi and Shlomo Carlebach at a Hanukkah party at Brandeis University, a predominantly Jewish institution in suburban Boston. Old World Jews who had escaped from Europe during the Nazi scourge, these young men were eager to share their love of Hasidism with American youth. At the party they told stories, talked mysticism, and wrapped willing students in *tefillin*. They also learned that American Jews lived in a world apart. They vowed to investigate that world and use what they learned to renew Jewish life.

Carlebach went on to become a professional musician—"The Singing Rabbi"— and the founder of a San Francisco commune called the House of Love and Prayer. Schachter-Shalomi, or Reb Zalman as he is popularly known, went on to drop acid with Timothy Leary, pray with Sufi sheikhs, and teach at the Buddha-friendly Naropa Institute in Boulder, Colorado. He also cultivated friendships with the Trappist monk Thomas Merton, the Jesuit antiwar activist Daniel Berrigan, and the Buddhist icon the Dalai Lama. Reb Zalman also served as the founder and leader of Jewish Renewal, a rebellion against suburban Judaism in post–World War II America that combined Hasidic traditions and countercultural impulses to create a new spirituality featuring storytelling, music, dance, prayer, chanting, yoga, and meditation. Along with this experiential and embodied spirituality came a commitment to tikkun olam that in Jewish Renewal meant working for peace, social justice, women's rights, LGBTQ rights, environmental justice, and interfaith understanding. The result was a spiritual mix that included not only Hasidism and Kabbalah but also Tibetan Buddhism, feminism, and environmentalism. According to Reb

Shlomo Carlebach was an important figure in the Jewish Renewal movement, which aimed to bring new forms of contemporary spirituality and social engagement into Jewish life. Known as "The Singing Rabbi," he is shown here performing in 1964 in New York City.

Zalman's ideal of "eco-kashrut," kosher food needs to do more than meet the requirements of Jewish law; it needs to be environmentally sustainable and ethically grown.

Renewal Jews came together in informal worship groups called *havurot*. In addition to "fellowship," the term *havurah* connotes "friend," so these were fellowships of friends that shared much with meetings of the Society of Friends (Quakers), including informal worship, casual dress, and an egalitarian spirit wary of authority. This "paradigm shift Judaism" found broader institutional form in Philadelphia in 1969 with the founding of B'nai Or Religious Fellowship, which evolved in 1993 into ALEPH: the Alliance for Jewish Renewal.

Traditionalists disparaged Jewish Renewal as "new age Judaism" and "Judaism lite." Did not God say, "I have set you apart from other peoples to be Mine" (Leviticus 20:26)? If so, who are we to confuse Jews with non-Jews? And why combine Jewish and Buddhist identities into "Jubus"? Jewish Renewal advocates respond by pointing out that Hasidism is also a modern invention and Judaism itself has always been a dance between the old and the new.

Reb Zalman's death in 2014 meant growing pains for Jewish Renewal, but ALEPH lives on in a network of forty-four communities extending from the United States to Australia, Peru, Israel, and Germany. Its influence—in liturgical music, meditation, yoga, ritual innovation, eco-kashrut, social activism, and havurah groups—is much broader, pulsing in virtually every form of Judaism except strict Orthodoxy. In fact, some scholars now argue that the Jewish Renewal impulse is as mainstream in the United States as Kabbalah was in early modern Europe. "Even if Jewish Americans are not explicitly followers" of Reb Zalman, writes the Jewish studies scholar Martin Kavka, "their postethnic lives entail a theology that is functionally equivalent to that of Jewish Renewal."[33]

LIVED JUDAISM

As practiced by ordinary people, lived Judaism refutes the widespread assumption that religion is largely about scriptures and beliefs. The emphasis among Jews on the narrative, legal, ethical, and ritual dimensions of religion is plain—in the celebration of Shabbat and other holy days, and in the observation of Jewish law.

The Sabbath and Other Holy Days

Jews carve up their experiences more by time than by place. Their three main pilgrim festivals are holy days that once drew Jews by the thousands to the Jerusalem Temple. Each commemorates a key moment in Jewish history. Shavuot recalls the day God gave the Ten Commandments to Moses on Mount Sinai. Sukkot ("Feast of Tabernacles") recalls the wanderings of the Israelites in desert camps. The most widely observed of these three festival holidays is Passover (Pesach), which recalls the Exodus of the Israelites from slavery in Egypt to freedom in the Promised Land.

Every spring before Passover, Jewish families sweep their homes clean of leavened bread and other fermented grain products (bread, pasta, whiskey). Then they gather for the Passover **Seder**, a domestic meal that includes, in addition to the holiday's trademark matzah (unleavened bread), both bitter herbs (to commemorate the harshness of life under

Seder
Passover meal

Every spring, Jews celebrate Passover with a ritual meal called a Seder. The Seder commemorates the Exodus story by combining stories, prayers, and music with foods, including matzah, wine, and bitter herbs, that symbolize key moments in this story of bondage and freedom.

Egypt's Pharaoh) and wine (to celebrate liberation). At this meal, children ask questions, most famously, "Why is this night different from other nights?" Adults answer by telling the Exodus story.

The term "Passover" refers to the last of the ten plagues God is said to have sent to the Egyptians in this story, in which the Angel of Death kills the first son in every Egyptian household but "passes over" the homes of Israelites who had followed the instruction of Moses to mark their doors with lamb blood. Observing the Seder fulfills the commandment to "tell thy son in that day, saying: It is because of that which the Lord did for me when I came forth out of Egypt" (Exodus 13:8). Therefore, like Judaism itself, the Seder is about both telling and doing, story and law.

Just as there are different sorts of Jews, there are thousands of Haggadahs ("tellings") of the Exodus story used at Seders. These include the popular "Maxwell House Haggadah" distributed by the coffee manufacturer starting in 1932, as well as contemporary Haggadahs inspired by the civil rights and feminist movements. As a Haggadah is read, the meal stops here and there for reflection and debate. One contemporary version, by the mystic and activist Alice Frank, speaks of the journey of Passover as a passage not only from slavery to freedom but also from duality to unity, likening "the narrow place" of Pharaoh's Egypt to the ego and the Exodus to liberation from the discursive mind.

Two other important Jewish holidays—the New Year (**Rosh Hashanah**) and the Day of Atonement (**Yom Kippur**) are "days of awe" that mark the beginning of the Jewish year as a time of reflection, repentance, and return to God. Together these two commemorations constitute Judaism's High Holidays.

Hanukkah, which falls near Christmas, is the only Jewish holiday many non-Jewish Americans can name. In fact, many public school winter concerts now include songs

Rosh Hashanah
Jewish New Year

Yom Kippur
Day of Atonement; a major Jewish holiday

Hanukkah
Jewish festival of lights, which lasts for eight days

referring to the dreidel or the menorah, both symbols of this holiday. But Hanukkah is a relatively minor day in the Jewish calendar, commemorating the purification and rededication of the Second Temple after enemies defiled it in the second century BCE.

Purim, another relatively minor Jewish holiday, is a raucous celebration that recalls both Halloween and the Hindu celebration of Holi. Purim celebrates the heroine Esther, who in the biblical book of the same name works with her cousin Mordecai to foil a plot to destroy the Jews by the villain Haman. Purim traditionally includes a lot of drinking and satirical skits called *spiels*.

Judaism is the only major religion whose most important holy day occurs every week. Shabbat runs from just before sundown on Friday to an hour after sundown on Saturday. It recalls and reenacts God's rest on the seventh day after creation. It also commemorates the freedom from slavery celebrated on Passover. As the only holy day prescribed in the Ten Commandments, Shabbat is debated exhaustively in the Talmud, which prohibits thirty-nine kinds of labor on this day, from cooking and sewing to lighting a fire and putting one out.

The Sabbath is typically thought of as a day when work and other acts of creation are prohibited, but many Jews prefer to think of this holy day in more positive terms. Colloquially, Jews speak of entering into this sacred time. On Shabbat everything slows down. Families gather around the dinner table, lighting candles, saying special prayers, drinking wine, and eating a special kind of bread known as challah, often shaped into braided loaves.

Lighting candles is an important ritual for Jews who observe the Sabbath. Women traditionally light these candles before covering their eyes to recite a blessing for this day of rest.

613 Commandments

In addition to observing holy days, observant Jews strive to follow 613 commandments, in stark contrast to the 10 listed by Christians. **Mitzvah** is often translated as "good deed," but it is more literally translated as "commandment." The commandments derived from the Torah and enumerated in the Talmud include ethical as well as ritual requirements, with some now moot as they concern temple sacrifice. Among these commandments are the following: love God, study Torah, circumcise newborn boys, leave crops behind for the poor, love strangers, honor your father and mother, do not commit sodomy with a male, do not covet, do not murder, do not destroy fruit trees, do not worship an idol, and rest on Shabbat and other holy days.

Jewish law can seem irrational to outsiders who do not understand how it works. For example, Jewish law prohibits carrying things outside the home on Shabbat. To allow parents to carry their babies across the street to grandmother's house and otherwise knit Jewish communities together across generations, however, rabbis devised a creative solution employed by some Jews: a boundary called an *eruv*, which uses wires strung from house to house to create a symbolic fence that expands the territory of the "home." Since 2007, an eruv has covered most of Manhattan, complete with an "eruvitect" who makes sure it remains intact and offers regular online updates on its status.

mitzvah
religious obligation; good deed; commandment

BIRTH AND DEATH

Jews traditionally mark the birth of sons by circumcising and naming them on the eighth day. Until recently, there was no parallel to this bris for daughters, but in the synagogue on the Sabbath after a girl's birth, the father was called up to bless the Torah and she was formally named (in absentia). Since the 1970s, Reform, Reconstructionist, and some Conservative congregations have named and welcomed newborn girls into the Jewish community through a variety of rituals under various names, including *Simchat Bat* ("the joy of a daughter") and *Shalom Bat* ("Hello, daughter").

When a Jew dies, the corpse is stripped and washed and covered in a simple white shroud, traditionally by a nonprofit Jewish funeral society. Burial follows quickly, ideally within a day. At the cemetery, the shrouded body is placed directly into the ground. Where coffins are required, a plain wooden box is used. At the graveside, an ancient funeral prayer praising God—the Kaddish—is said. Mourners reckon with the hard fact of death by throwing dirt into the grave, taking on the responsibility of burying the dead as an act of kindness that cannot be repaid. They tear their clothing as a sign of loss. In the name of equality in death, Jews typically forgo the elaborate tombstones and funerary structures marking many other cemeteries. Cremation has traditionally been prohibited as a desecration of the body, and the death by fire of millions of Jews in the Holocaust made cremation abhorrent to many Jews, though some Jews do cremate.

In keeping with their focus on sacred time, Jews define the stages of mourning more clearly than do adherents of most other religions. After burial, the family returns home for seven days of mourning called sitting **shiva** (literally, "seven"). A candle burns for twenty-four hours each day. Mirrors are covered. Mourners sit low to the ground. Those in mourning refrain from sex, bathing, shaving, haircutting, and work (unless economic deprivation requires it). During these seven days

shiva
seven days of mourning after burial

The Jewish concern for law, accompanied by efforts to follow it in the modern world, has left its mark even on the lowly elevator. Orthodox Jews do not use elevators on Shabbat, since pressing a button to call an elevator creates an electrical circuit akin to the creation of fire outlawed on that day of rest. Here the work-around is the Shabbat elevator, which stops automatically at every floor on the Sabbath, enabling observant Jews to move up and down their apartment buildings without pressing any buttons.

To outsiders this may look like a simple case of circumventing religious law. But a far simpler way to get around a law is to ignore it. In the case of both the eruv and the Shabbat elevator (which Jews themselves recognize as legal loopholes, and some Orthodox Jews will not use), there is respect for the law, including a commitment to observing it. That deep bow, however, is accompanied by some flexibility in interpretation.

Keeping Kosher

It is common for religious communities to distinguish themselves from their neighbors by what they will and will not eat. Observant Mormons shun coffee, many Muslims do not drink alcohol, and many Hindus are vegetarians. Observant Jews are also strict about their diets and believe that following the laws of kashrut make them mindful throughout the day that all food comes from God. According to these laws, sheep and cattle can be eaten, but pork is forbidden, as is the flesh of camels and birds of prey. Fish can be eaten if they have both scales and fins, but lobsters, shrimp, and clams (lacking both) are prohibited. Fruits and vegetables are kosher, but they must be free of bugs, which are not kosher. Because meat and dairy cannot be mixed (in a cheeseburger, for example), some

of mourning—a reversal of the seven days of creation—the front door remains unlocked as friends come by with food and condolences. In keeping with the biblical teaching that there is "a time for being born and a time for dying" (Ecclesiastes 3:2), Jewish tradition discourages euphemisms for death and looks askance at premature consolations of a better life to come. Corpses are not embalmed for viewing. No flowers beautify the shiva house.

For the immediate family, some ritual obligations continue into a thirty-day period of less intensive mourning. Observant children mourn parents for eleven months, refusing simple pleasures such as listening to live music. They gather to say Kaddish. One reason Jews traditionally hoped for sons was so that someone could say Kaddish for them when they died, but today most Jewish women join these prayer quorums and say Kaddish.

Each year, observant families gather at the Yahrzeit (anniversary of a death) to light a candle, recite the Kaddish, and remember the life of the deceased. But according to a

Tombstones in Jewish cemeteries are typically inscribed in Hebrew and positioned so that the feet of the deceased point toward Jerusalem, such as at the Jewish Montefiore Cemetery in Queens, New York.

medieval Jewish law book, "one should not grieve too much for the dead," so after a year of mourning it is time for sons and daughters to return to ordinary life.[a]

Jews have two separate sets of plates and flatware and, in some cases, even two separate kitchens: one for meat and another for dairy.

Theories about the origins of these dietary laws are legion. One, of course, is that they came from the mouth of God. Another is that kosher eating was sanitary eating, an early form of hygiene that saved Jews from trichinosis carried by pigs. A social theory sees Jewish food prohibitions as a way to distinguish Jews from non-Jews. An ethical theory contends that the animals that can be eaten, such as cattle, represent virtues, and those that cannot be eaten, such as hawks, represent vices.

The anthropologist Mary Douglas has advanced an intriguing symbolic interpretation. What drove kosher food prohibitions were notions of purity and pollution, she argues, and what made things impure and polluted in the symbolic world of the biblical book of Leviticus (where many of these laws appear) was their ambiguity—their stubborn refusal to fit into the neat three-part division in the Bible of animals of earth, water, and air. Lobsters, who crawl like land animals yet live in the sea, are obvious category busters that, by their very existence, call our neat categories into question. Genetically modified plants might also be nonkosher from this perspective, since they confuse conceptual categories. According to Douglas, male homosexuality is outlawed for the same reason; it too was, at least in the worldview of Leviticus, a conceptual anomaly.

Arguing for the Sake of God

Many human beings find ambiguity intolerable. Chasing after certainty and running away from contradictions, they squint when testing their eyes, determined to bring what is blurry into focus, as if wanting could make it so. Jews are trained not just to abide in this ambiguity but also to glory in it. If, as the Irish writer and bon vivant Oscar Wilde wrote, "the well-bred contradict other people" while "the wise contradict themselves," Judaism is wisdom personified.[34]

The Jewish community includes scrupulous observers of halacha and secular Jews who don't know what that word means. Jews also differ when it comes to keeping kosher and observing Shabbat. According to a 2016 Pew Forum study, 93 percent of Israel's Jews participated in a Passover Seder the prior year, but only 63 percent kept kosher at home and only 60 percent fasted on Yom Kippur. In the United States, observance rates were lower: only 70 percent participated in the most recent Passover Seder, 40 percent fasted on Yom Kippur, and 22 percent kept kosher at home. In another recent Pew study, just over half of American Jews reported that they had a bar mitzvah or a bat mitzvah.[35]

The Jewish tradition of argument may be one reason for the gap between the lived Judaism of ordinary folks and the prescribed Judaism of elites. For millennia, Jews have wrestled with their scriptures and with one another. The Talmud includes arguments between Hillel and Shammai and other rabbis, who rarely agree about much other than the value of study itself. The most authoritative collection of halacha after the Talmud, the *Shulchan Aruch* (literally, "Set Table") closely follows this model of "argumentative Israel." Its main text was written by a Sephardic Jew from a Sephardic perspective, but the glosses, which serve as the "tablecloth" to the "table" set by the Sephardim, were written by an Ashkenazi scholar.

No religion speaks with one voice, of course, but Judaism is unusually contested. Should you ever stumble on a traditional yeshiva, a Jewish school for Torah study, the first thing you would notice is the spirited debate. Students study in pairs in large halls and rarely in hushed tones. They read aloud from a text and argue about its meanings. "If you are proved right, you accomplish little," goes a Hasidic saying. "But if you are proved wrong you gain much: you learn the truth."[36]

Jews have long distinguished between two types of arguments: arguing for the sake of ego and arguing for the sake of heaven. The goal in one is victory. In the other it is truth. We are all familiar with arguments for the sake of ego. You start arguing for this theory (or this politician) or that, and pretty soon all you can think about is winning. Arguments for the sake of heaven are different. Here the assumption is that only God has the full truth. All we can do is try to approximate it. So you attempt to listen to and learn from your opponent and in the process move a little closer to the truth.

What is required in Judaism is not to agree but to engage. According to Elie Wiesel, "If a Jew has no one to quarrel with, he quarrels with God, and we call it theology; or he quarrels with himself, and we call it psychology."[37] It was a Jew (Sigmund Freud) who founded psychoanalysis, which is based on the insight that there are competing voices not only among individuals but also inside them. Albert Einstein's theory of relativity turns on the strange fact that even scientific observations depend on one person's perspective. Another Jewish thinker, the philosopher Horace Kallen, coined the phrase "cultural pluralism" and with it introduced the metaphor of a civilization as an orchestra in which differences in religion, language, and art enhance rather than undermine social harmony. In what might seem like a cacophony of yeshiva training, Jews hear a symphony.

CONTEMPORARY CONTROVERSY: WOMEN IN JUDAISM

Just as Jewish women—*Ms.* magazine founder Gloria Steinem and *The Feminine Mystique* author Betty Friedan, for example—played a major role in the feminist movement in the United States, the feminist movement had a profound effect on American Judaism. In her pathbreaking article, "The Jew Who Wasn't There" (1971), Rachel Adler, an Orthodox Jew, observed that Jewish law cast women as "peripheral Jews" who are "excused and sometimes barred from the acts and symbols which are the lifeblood of the believing community." Learning and teaching were closed off to Jewish women. Like children and slaves, their testimony was not allowed in legal proceedings. Stereotypes of men as spiritual and women as physical kept them in exile from their community and their fuller selves. Images of women as "semidemonic" in the Talmud further alienated them from their own people.[38]

The theologian Judith Plaskow argued that even in non-Orthodox congregations, women remain "Other," akin to the Jew as "Other" in non-Jewish societies. One source of this alienation is patriarchal language. "The images we use to describe God, the qualities we attribute to God, draw on male pronouns and male experience and convey a sense of power and authority that is clearly male in character," Plaskow wrote. "The hand

Members of the activist group Women of the Wall pray at the Western Wall in Jerusalem. These women are pushing the gendered boundaries of the Jewish tradition by asserting their right to wear prayer shawls and tefillin, and to pray aloud there.

that takes us out of Egypt is a male hand—both in the Bible and in our contemporary imaginations." Echoing the post-Catholic feminist Mary Daly, who famously wrote, "If God is male, then the male is God," Plaskow concluded that "the Otherness of women" is inextricably connected to "the maleness of God." For this reason, Plaskow and others called for Judaism to move beyond the restructuring of Jewish law to a reimagining of Jewish theology—"a new understanding of Torah, God, and Israel."[39]

Amidst these debates, Jewish women became more visible and more vocal, especially in the United States. In 1972 in Cincinnati, the Reform movement ordained Sally Jane Priesand as its first American woman rabbi. The Reconstructionist and Conservative movements followed with their own ordinations of women in 1974 and 1985. Orthodox leaders, arguing that God's laws were eternal and unchangeable, were appalled.

Amidst these milestones, Jewish feminists challenged a series of traditions, some legal and others merely customary, including the exclusion of women from the minyan, the inadmissibility of women as legal witnesses, the inability of women to petition for divorce, and the exclusion of women from Torah study and from reading the Torah aloud during worship. Their critiques produced changes in prayer books, including an option in Conservative prayers to refer to the matriarchs alongside the patriarchs.

The Orthodox resisted. But they, too, were divided. When faced with Orthodox women who wanted to pray wearing the prayer shawls and tefillin, which were traditionally worn only by men, Orthodox authorities responded, "Do not make a comedy out of Torah."[40] Some Orthodox women wear them regardless.

Still, changes came, even among the Orthodox, and particularly in the area of women's education. In 2009, Sara Hurwitz was ordained by two Orthodox rabbis. Among the non-Orthodox, innovations continued to spread by word of mouth, including feminist Passover Seders and new ceremonies for births, menopause, weddings, and divorces.

QUESTIONS FOR DISCUSSION

1. Think about the differences between Jewishness (and peoplehood), on the one hand, and Judaism (and religion), on the other. How does viewing the subject of this chapter as a people differ from viewing its subject as a religion? What does each perspective see, and what does it miss?

2. Judaism is described in this chapter as "strict monotheism" and "ethical monotheism." What do these two terms mean? How do they point to differences in the way monotheism functions in Judaism and other religions?

3. What were some of the key turning points in the shift from Israelite religion to rabbinic Judaism? Consider the role of sacred places, religious authorities, and political and military battles.

4. How do the themes of exile, return, and diaspora operate throughout Jewish history and tradition? How have these themes been utilized by non-Jewish groups over time?

5. How do the Orthodox, Conservative, and Reform branches of Judaism differ today? How do practitioners of each view the Torah, observe halacha, and imagine Jewish identity?

KEY TERMS

FURTHER READING

Heschel, Abraham Joshua. *The Sabbath: Its Meaning for Modern Man*. New York: Farrar, Straus & Giroux, 2005.

Lawrence Fine, ed. *Judaism in Practice: From the Middle Ages through the Early Modern Period*. Princeton, NJ: Princeton University Press, 2001.

Plaskow, Judith. *Standing Again at Sinai: Judaism from a Feminist Perspective*. New York: HarperOne, 1991.

Sarna, Jonathan D. *American Judaism: A History*. 2nd ed. New Haven, CT: Yale University Press, 2019.

Solomon, Norman. *Judaism: A Very Short Introduction*. New York: Oxford University Press, 2014.

Wiesel, Elie. *Night*. Translated by Marion Wiesel. New York: Hill and Wang, 2006.

The cross is the central symbol of the Christian tradition, and the suffering and crucifixion of Jesus is one of its central stories. Here, a statue of Jesus carrying a cross to his death stands guard in a vineyard overlooking the town of Escherndorf, Germany.

Christianity
THE WAY OF SALVATION

It is a bit before 4 p.m. on a Friday afternoon in the Old City of Jerusalem, and Franciscan friars are gathering to lead a pilgrimage down the Via Dolorosa, Latin for "Way of Sorrows." There are about thirty of them: all male, all dressed in the signature brown robe of their Roman Catholic order, which traces its origins to St. Francis of Assisi, the iconic twelfth-century namesake of the twenty-first century pope. Joining them are more than a hundred souls ready to walk where Jesus is said to have walked in roughly 30 CE to his death by crucifixion. At the head of the line is an elderly friar. At the rear is a Muslim attendant in a trademark red fez. In between are tourists and pilgrims from across the globe. Three friars sport wearable microphones and another lugs a wireless amplifier on his back so everyone can hear what these guides have to say about the fourteen Stations of the Cross walked by Jesus on his last day.

"Station One," the friars announce in Latin, English, and Portuguese at the first stop. "Jesus is condemned to death." As this multinational assembly winds its way through the impossibly narrow roads of the Muslim Quarter, it starts to feel less like a tour group and more like a congregation. Some heads are bowed and some eyes are closed as all pause to remember the central figure in the Christian story—where he fell, where Veronica wiped his brow, and where Simon of Cyrene carried his cross. Between stops, the friars chant prayers in Latin. When pilgrims respond in kind, that ancient tongue starts to sound like a universal language, sent from heaven to earth and back again by Koreans, Brazilians, Americans, and Russians, all made in the image of a Latinate God.

225

Toward the end of the Stations of the Cross, the friars take a sharp right turn up a pair of stone steps and onto a monastery roof. The walk slows to a crawl as pilgrims duck and wiggle through a small stone opening into one chapel and then another before finding themselves in a plaza in front of the Church of the Holy Sepulchre.

Jerusalem is a majority Jewish city and Israel a Jewish state, but it is home to more holy sites for Christians than for Jews. This church is their Holy of Holies. Like most everything else in Jerusalem's Old City, it has been built and destroyed and built again. It has also been subject to the shifting fortunes of life in a place won and lost by Christians, Muslims, and Jews alike. The Church of the Holy Sepulchre dates to the fourth-century Roman emperor Constantine, but much of the current structure was constructed by eleventh- and twelfth-century crusaders. Today this building, which Orthodox Christians call the Church of the Resurrection, is controlled by six different Christian groups: Roman Catholics, the Greek Orthodox, and the Oriental Orthodox from Armenia, Egypt, Syria, and Ethiopia. Every day, these groups perform a complex choreography of rituals along and across each other's borders in a place as territorial as the Middle East itself. The ground rules are set by a "Status Quo" from the early 1850s that dictates how every square inch of the building is to be used for every second of every day. Weaving in and out of this dangerous dance—priestly fisticuffs have been known to break out upon violations (real or perceived)—are tour guides (most of them Jewish), who initiate visitors (most of them Christian) into the legends of this place, including how Jesus's blood on the cross dripped through a crack in the stone of the skull-like hill where he was executed and dribbled down to the tomb of Adam himself. Such solemn stories do not entirely overwhelm human desires, however. In a dark corner of the Armenian chapel, uniformed schoolgirls and schoolboys flirt on cold stone benches.

Meanwhile, the friars guide their impromptu congregation up a steep stone staircase to the site where Jesus is said to have been nailed to the cross. Down on the main floor and just past representatives of the Muslim family charged with opening the church's ancient doors each morning, the tour stops at a flat red stone. "The thirteenth station," the friars say. "Jesus is taken down from the cross." Long an afterthought, this "Stone of Anointing" is now a TripAdvisor attraction, brought to life in recent years by Russians who rub scarves into its cracks in an effort to come into contact with the body of Christ itself, which is said to have been prepared for burial upon it. Every day thousands of visitors make souvenirs sacred by laying them on this stone and praying over them.

The Stations of the Cross end where Jesus was laid in the tomb, only to be resurrected three days later. Momentarily, the Greek Orthodox priests who control this shrine yield to the Franciscans, who enter it. Minutes later, the friars leave and a long line of gawkers and devotees resumes its march of memory toward the place where the god who became human is said to have become the man who defeated death.

Noticeably absent from the Church of the Holy Sepulchre, especially for visitors from the United States and United Kingdom, is any hint of Protestant sensibilities. To them, this place, with its smells and bells, its dark and dilapidated corners, its peeling paintings blackened by smoke, is a world apart from their Methodist or Baptist congregations. Many feel let down by the site, offended by the ugly veneer its overseers have

Tourists and pilgrims from all over the world visit the Church of the Holy Sepulchre in Jerusalem as they wind their way along the Stations of the Cross that commemorate the events of Jesus's final hours.

pasted over the places once walked by their Lord and Savior. Is this land really holy? Or is it a showcase, as Mark Twain once put it, of "clap-trap side-shows and unseemly impostures of every kind"?[1] To commune with *their* Jesus, Protestant pilgrims must wind their way through the Muslim Quarter, past shops with stacks of spices and whole lambs awaiting butchering, then exit the Old City at the Damascus Gate and walk north a few blocks through East Jerusalem to the Garden Tomb. This site was unearthed in 1867 and purchased in 1894 by British Protestants as a place to remember and retell their Jesus story.

At the Garden Tomb, the aesthetic is bright and quiet, as clean as a megachurch lobby. And it is open to the sky. Volunteer tour guides make a case for the possibility that Jesus was buried and raised here, but they are careful not to overreach. "We cannot say for sure," a tour guide says. "Nobody knows." What really matters is that Jesus was raised from the dead, and this place, even if it is not *the* place, is a reminder of that fact. Jesus was "not killable," another tour guide says. "That's the message of the Garden Tomb."

But the "browning" of Christianity—its growing strength in Africa, Asia, and Latin America—is turning this site into something more than a place of reserved Anglo-American remembrance. As conservative Protestantism spreads around the world, evangelicals from Korea, fundamentalists from Nigeria, and Pentecostals from Brazil are transforming the Garden Tomb into a devotional site, weeping, praying, speaking in tongues, and crying out, "He is risen! Our Lord is risen indeed!" "It used to be Americans and Europeans here," a British tour guide explains. "Now it's Indians and Indonesians."

OUR STORY

Muslims refer to Jews and Christians as "people of the book," because they, too, worship a God who speaks through prophets, whose revelations are recorded in scripture, which is read with all the reverence of a face-to-face encounter with the divine. But Christians distinguish themselves from the strict monotheism of Jews and Muslims by ascribing divinity to a human being. In Judaism, God buries Moses in an unknown place, perhaps to ward off the temptation to turn his plot into a tomb and his tomb into a place of worship. In Islam, it is idolatry to ascribe divinity to any human being, Muhammad included. Christians, who worship Jesus as God in the flesh, practice **soft monotheism**. Yes, Jesus is their **Christ** (Greek for the "messiah" long awaited by the Jews), but he is also divine. In Mark, the earliest of the Christian New Testament's **Four Gospels**, everyone seems confused about Jesus until the big reveal at the end, when a Roman soldier standing guard at the foot of the cross says, "Truly this was the Son of God" (Mark 27:54).

In the Apostles' Creed, which circulated in different versions in the early church and is still recited today, Jesus is said to be "conceived of the Holy Spirit, born of the Virgin **Mary**, suffered under Pontius Pilate, was crucified, died and was buried." But Christians typically set Jesus's Passion narrative inside a broader story that runs from the creation of the world "in the beginning" to the coming apocalypse at the end of times. Like all religious people, Christians tell their stories selectively, forgetting this and remembering that, in keeping with their personal and societal preferences and the cultural and political preoccupations of their times. However, the most popular versions of the Christian story, such as the one that follows here, focus on the problem of **sin** and the solution of **salvation**.

soft monotheism
belief in one God who appears in human form, as distinct from the strict monotheism of Muslims and Jews, who reject the descent of the divine into a human body

Christ
Greek term for messiah in Hebrew and the title Christians give to Jesus

Four Gospels
New Testament books that tell stories of Jesus's life, namely, Matthew, Mark, Luke, and John

Mary
virgin mother of Jesus and the most revered of Christian saints

sin
both a state of separation from God and an act of wrongdoing; said by Christians to be wiped away by the death of Jesus on the cross

salvation
liberation from sin, the Christian religious goal

Sin and Salvation

In the beginning, God created the first man (Adam) and the first woman (Eve) and set them up in a blissful paradise called the Garden of Eden. Life was good. Then Adam and Eve ate fruit from a tree God had forbidden to them. As punishment for this "original sin," Adam and Eve were banished from Eden, and sin, suffering, and death entered the world. God reached out to the descendants of this first family by entering into a series of new covenants—with Noah, Abraham, and Moses—which were again broken by human beings. Sin and suffering continued to spread. Humans remained alienated from God and from one another. The door to heaven, that blissful paradise beyond death, was barred to them. Eventually, God sent his son Jesus to Earth to save us from our sins.

Born to a virgin named Mary in a lowly manger in Bethlehem, Jesus was raised as a Jew and apprenticed as a carpenter under Mary's husband Joseph. He left home as a young man and took up a life of wandering, which began with baptism at the hands of another itinerant preacher, John the Baptist. As a rabbi (which means "teacher" in Hebrew), Jesus's trademark genre was the parable, a short yet confounding tale about the stuff of ordinary life in his Galilean homeland—neighbors, farmers, sheep, seeds, moneylenders, coins, fathers, sons—meant to illustrate the surprising nature of the coming "kingdom of God."

Jesus, who called himself the Son of Man, preached repentance but expected his Jewish followers both to observe the law and to internalize it. His radical ethic included criticizing the rich, blessing the poor, and loving one's enemies in whatever time is left before the arrival of God's kingdom, which is right around the corner. Jesus was more than just a rabbi, however. He was also a miracle worker who turned water into wine at a wedding, calmed a raging storm, walked on water, fed vast crowds with meager portions of food, healed the sick, exorcised demons, and raised the dead.

After three years of teaching and healing, Jesus had gathered a core group of twelve disciples, or fol-

This fifth-century mosaic, located on the ceiling of the nave at the Arian Baptistry in Ravenna, Italy, depicts Jesus being baptized in the Jordan River by the itinerant preacher and prophet John the Baptist (right).

lowers. With them, he went to Jerusalem for the Jewish festival of Passover. As he entered the city on a donkey, many cheered, shouting, "Hosanna! Blessed is he who comes in the name of the Lord!" In the days that followed, he gathered his disciples for a simple meal now referred to as the Last Supper. Betrayed by his disciple Judas, he was arrested and beaten almost to death. He appeared before a Jewish tribunal and before Pontius Pilate, the Roman governor who sentenced him to death by crucifixion. His crime? Pretending to be "The King of the Jews." As he was nailed to a cross, he took all human sin on his own sinless frame. After he breathed his last, he was taken down from the cross, prepared for burial, and laid in a tomb.

Three days later, early in the morning, some of his female followers went to the tomb. The rock covering it had been rolled away, and when these women walked into the tomb it was empty. They left and told their friends, "He is not here, but has risen" (Luke 24:6). Later, Jesus appeared, alive, multiple times, to his followers before ascending to heaven. His followers spread the good news that Jesus, the messiah long awaited by the Jews, had been raised from the dead. Today, Christians affirm that their bodies, too, will be resurrected when Jesus, the Second Adam, returns in his Second Coming at the end of days.

CHRISTIANITY IN TODAY'S WORLD

Christianity is now the religion with the most adherents, accounting in 2020 for 32 percent of the world's population, according to the World Religion Database. The United States is not by law a Christian nation, but it boasts more Christians than any country in

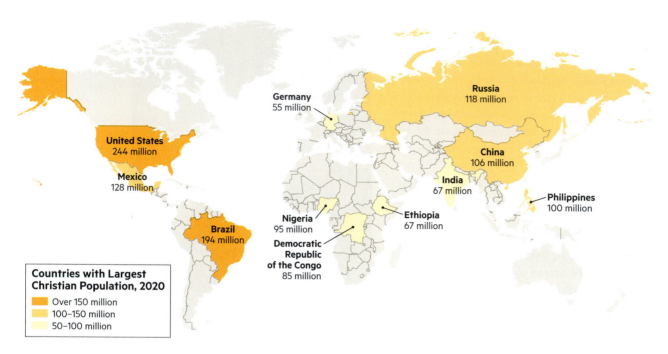

Countries with Largest Christian Population, 2020

- Over 150 million
- 100–150 million
- 50–100 million

Germany 55 million
Russia 118 million
China 106 million
India 67 million
Philippines 100 million
Ethiopia 67 million
Nigeria 95 million
Democratic Republic of the Congo 85 million
Brazil 194 million
Mexico 128 million
United States 244 million

The United States has more Christians than any other country on earth, but in recent decades the Christian population has boomed in the Global South while Europe's Christian population has declined.

Roman Catholicism
one of the three main Christian branches, particularly strong in Latin America, which looks to the authority of the pope in Rome

Protestantism
one of the three main branches of Christianity, which grew out of the Reformation and traditionally emphasizes faith over works and biblical authority over church tradition

Eastern Orthodoxy
one of the three main branches of Christianity, particularly strong in Eastern Europe, which honors the Patriarch of Constantinople (Istanbul)

the world, followed (in order) by Brazil, Mexico, Russia, and China. In recent decades, Christianity has seen massive gains in the Global South (Asia, Africa, and Latin America), accompanied by losses in its former strongholds of Europe, which is rapidly secularizing, and the United States, where the religiously unaffiliated ("nones") are on the rise. As a result, the Christian share of the world's population has remained surprisingly steady over the last century or so, declining slightly from 34.5 percent in 1900 to 32.3 percent in 2020.

Although many Christians speak of one universal church, that church is divided into three main branches—**Roman Catholicism** (49 percent of the world's Christians), **Protestantism** (23 percent), and **Eastern Orthodoxy** (12 percent). The remaining 16 percent of Christians are independent. The countries with the largest Roman Catholic populations are Brazil (roughly 150 million members), followed by Mexico (116 million), the Philippines (83 million), the United States (74 million), and the Democratic Republic of the Congo (49 million). Although numerically strongest in the Americas, Roman Catholicism is a global tradition, with Catholic majorities in Poland, Spain, Portugal, Ireland, and, of course, Vatican City.

Russia has the world's largest Eastern Orthodox population, estimated at close to 114 million. Eastern Orthodoxy is also the largest faith in Greece and roughly a dozen other European countries. It has a strong presence in the United States, which has roughly seven million Orthodox Christians.

Although Protestantism tends to be associated with Europe, where it began, all of the leading Protestant countries today in terms of population lie outside Europe. The United States heads this list with 118 million Protestants, or about 35 percent of its population. Next come China with 96 million, Nigeria with 90 million, and Brazil with 58 million. Protestants have also produced a dizzying array of options, with thousands of **denominations** splintering over such matters as original sin, infant baptism, slavery, women's ordination, and gay marriage. In recent decades, denominational differences have become less important, as battles between Christians and secularists or Christians and Muslims have taken precedence over earlier battles between Catholics and Protestants or Lutherans and Episcopalians. In the United States, the key religious divisions now cut across political lines, with liberal Catholics, for example, having more in common with liberal Protestants than they do with conservative Catholics.

Still, the most striking feature of Christianity today may be its diversity. Bible and creed remain two hallmarks of Christian life, so much so that it is commonplace for Christians to imagine that all religions are "belief systems" articulated first and foremost in sacred texts. But Christianity is now so elastic that it seems a stretch to use a single term to refer to the beliefs and practices of silent Quakers in Kenya, megachurch preachers in Korea, Mormons in Utah, liberation theologians in Colombia, and Coptic Christians in Egypt. Some Christian services feature sixteenth-century hymns played on nineteenth-century organs. Others feature Christian rock performed by live bands while lyrics are projected onto Jumbotrons. Unlike Muslims, who have resisted translating the Quran out of its original Arabic, Christians have eagerly translated **Old Testament** Hebrew and **New Testament** Greek into almost every spoken language. The film *Jesus*, by the evangelical student group Campus Crusade for Christ International, has been translated into more than seventeen hundred languages and shown in every country. As the gospel has been read and heard in local tongues, it has also taken on local beliefs and practices—from Confucianism in China to spirit possession in West Africa. Members of the popular Kimbanguist Church of the Congo celebrate Holy Communion with sweet potatoes and honey rather than bread and wine. In Appalachia, at the Church of God With Signs Following, true believers drink poison and handle rattlesnakes.

But Christian diversity is nothing new. According to an extraordinary story told in the biblical book of Acts, when the disciples of Jesus came together not long after his death, on the Jewish holy day of Shavuot (Pentecost), they began to speak in unknown languages

denomination
a religious subgroup of organizations that operate under a common name, such as Methodism or Episcopalianism

Old Testament
portion of the Christian Bible written in Hebrew and borrowed from the Jewish tradition, which refers to its books as the Hebrew Bible

New Testament
portion of the Christian Bible written in Greek and focused on the life of Jesus and the history of the Jesus movement, including the Four Gospels, Acts, various epistles (or letters), and Revelation

Comparison of Religions Worldwide, 2020

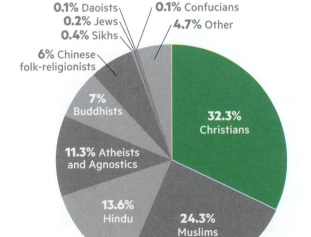

Major Christian Branches, 2020

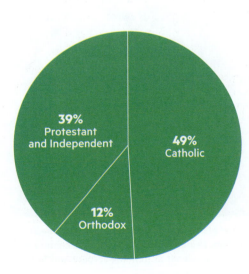

from around the world. Early Christians saw this as a sign that they should take the gospel to every corner of the globe. It was also a sign of Christian diversity. The first followers of Jesus did not speak many languages, but they had different views about their Jesus, about how Hebraic and how Greek their movement should be, about which rituals to practice (and how), and about the relative importance of Jesus's death versus his teachings. Did Jesus have a body? Was the Hebrew Bible inspired by God? It depended on whom you asked.

CHRISTIANITY 101

➥ What must I do to be saved?

Given the diversity within Christianity, it is tempting to observe that there are as many varieties of Christianity as there are Christians and leave it at that. But Christians do converge on some key symbols, beliefs, and practices, so it is possible to hazard some generalizations about the stories Christians live by.

Christians follow a man who died a brutal death by crucifixion, a common and shameful form of capital punishment in ancient Rome, so it should not be surprising to learn that they believe the world is broken and in need of repair. They trace that brokenness back to the very first human beings. Jews, in their own readings of the Garden of Eden story, have typically emphasized the dawning of knowledge that came with the violation of God's commandment not to eat from the fruit of the Tree of Knowledge. Christians, by contrast, have described this story as "The Fall"—a descent not so much from innocence to knowledge as from innocence to sin.

In the Christian tradition, the human problem is not exile as Jews describe it or pride as Muslims claim. The problem is sin. This term means different things to different

Michelangelo's *The Fall of Man* is the most iconic painting of the story of Adam and Eve's expulsion from the Garden of Eden in the biblical book of Genesis. Painted during the sixteenth century on the ceiling of the Sistine Chapel in Vatican City, this section illustrates Eve taking the forbidden fruit from the serpent and Adam reaching for it, followed by their exile.

Christians, but typically it refers to violations of God's commandments—wrong thoughts and evil deeds. Theologians distinguish between these "actual sins" (what we do) and "original sin" (what is inherited). Original sin is a fallen state or condition passed down via Adam and Eve to all of humanity like some genetic mutation. What follows from these sins and this sinfulness is all manner of suffering here and in the hereafter. Sin distances us from God, from our fellow human beings, and from our true selves. And because heaven is by definition a place without sin, we are barred from heaven as well, unless we can find a cure. Christians describe that cure as salvation, which is to say salvation from sin. But they have largely agreed that there is little to nothing we can do to attain it ourselves. There is something God can do, however. According to the Christian tradition, God responded to the human epidemic of sin by sending his son Jesus Christ into the world. Born to the Virgin Mary and therefore without sin himself, he grew up in our midst. He taught, he healed, and then he died a brutal death on a cross. In that death, something important happened. Sin was overcome. Salvation became possible.

Christians describe how this all happened in various ways. One common way to describe the gateway from sin to salvation is **atonement**—the reconciliation of a human being with God. Atonement also points to how this reconciliation takes place—how human beings and God are made "at one." This is where the crucifixion comes in: According to the Christian tradition, something astonishing took place when Jesus died on the cross. Jesus was to Christians a God/man who was born without original sin and never sinned himself. He didn't deserve to die. As a God, he certainly could have escaped death. But he chose to die anyway. In so doing, he became, according to the New Testament, a sacrificial lamb "who takes away the sins of the world" (John 1:29).

Christians disagree about the mechanics of this atonement and the best metaphors to describe it. Perhaps it is like a payment of ransom to liberate captives—"a ransom for many" (Matthew 20:28). Perhaps it is more like a payment for a debt owed or like a friend serving a prison term in your stead. Others argue that Jesus died on the cross in order to provide a moral example of self-giving love. This view is particularly influential among liberal Protestants and in Eastern Orthodoxy, where the moral transformation of human beings made possible by the crucifixion opens up a path not only to salvation but also to deification, in which the faithful are increasingly transformed into the likeness and image of God.

Whereas Christians disagree about how the sacrificial death of Jesus did what it did, for the most part they agree on what it accomplished. It took away human sins, reconciling humans to God and to one another. For the first time since the exile of Adam and Eve from Eden, it enabled human beings to live free from the threat of afterlife punishments to come. Saved from their sin, Christians were able to rise to a new life in heaven. Today, Christians disagree on how to interpret Christian teachings about the pleasures of heaven and the horrors of hell. Some take classical descriptions literally. Others take them metaphorically. But Christians largely agree on the goal of salvation from sin. Classically, Christians have seen sin as an individual problem and salvation as an individual goal. However, many contemporary Christians see both as social. Sin is not just about an individual transgression, they argue. It is also about vast institutions that perpetuate

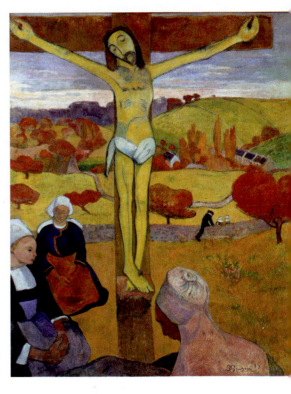

The Bible says that Jesus is "the same yesterday, today, and forever" (Hebrews 13:8), but images of Jesus have always reflected local circumstances. In *The Yellow Christ* (1889) by the postimpressionist artist Paul Gauguin, Jesus is crucified in the nineteenth-century French countryside.

atonement
reconciliation of human beings with God, made possible by the sacrificial death of Jesus on the cross

The Virgin Mary is said to have appeared to the peasant Juan Diego in Mexico City in 1531. Now known as Our Lady of Guadalupe, this popular saint appears in home shrines as well as public statues, like this one at the San Fernando Cathedral in San Antonio, Texas.

injustice. From this perspective, salvation is social, too. It is about repairing the world—making it more like the kingdom of God.

While adherents of any religion tend to agree on the problem and the goal, they often disagree on the techniques to achieve that goal. Here Christianity is no exception. Roman Catholic and Orthodox Christians typically affirm that the gift of salvation offered by Jesus on the cross has to be accepted by human beings, and that this acceptance involves both **faith** and works. Christians need to trust in Jesus. But the faithful also need to act—to do good deeds in the world and to participate in Christian sacraments such as the initiation ritual of baptism and the **Eucharist**, referred to by Roman Catholics as the Mass. Protestants disagree. According to a formula popularized during the Protestant **Reformation** in sixteenth-century Europe, salvation comes "by faith alone" and not by "works."

The exemplars held up as models vary similarly. Protestants admire "knights of faith," a term coined by the Danish theologian Soren Kierkegaard to describe the mind-boggling faithfulness of Abraham but now applied to anyone whose life centers around faith in God. These exemplars of faithfulness are heroes and some have their own holidays—the Reverend Dr. Martin Luther King Jr. comes to mind—but Protestants do not revere them on feast days.

The Orthodox and Roman Catholics, by contrast, revere saints as models of good works. Orthodox Christians revere their saints via two-dimensional **icons** made of paint or mosaics lest they violate the biblical prohibition against "graven images." Many Roman Catholics carry prayer cards depicting their favorite saints, which include the Blessed Virgin Mary, the mother of Jesus; St. Peter, the fisherman friend of Jesus and the first **pope**, whose remains are said to lie in the Vatican basilica that bears his name; and, more recently, Saint Theresa of Calcutta (Mother Theresa), proclaimed a saint in 2016 for her unflagging service to the poor. Most Roman Catholic saints are more local and particular, however, remembered for their specific and even idiosyncratic virtues: St. Francis of Assisi, who cares for the poor and for animals; St. Jude, the patron saint of lost causes; and Saint Kateri Tekakwitha, the first Native American saint, remembered for her vow of virginity. Perhaps the most popular Catholic saint today is **Our Lady of Guadalupe**, a dark-skinned representation of the Blessed Virgin Mary particularly revered by Mexican Catholics. Her Basilica of Our Lady of Guadalupe in Mexico City is the most visited Christian pilgrimage site in the world. It draws twenty million people a year to remember the life of the "Lady from Heaven" who miraculously appeared in 1531 to a poor Native American in what is now Mexico City, leaving behind a cactus-cloth image of herself enshrined today in the basilica. Now a pop icon, she appears on taxicabs, T-shirts, key chains, and bumper stickers that read, "In Guad We Trust."

Another popular icon in the contemporary world is Jesus. According to the New Testament book of Hebrews, Jesus is "the same yesterday, and today, and forever" (Hebrews 13:8). But understandings of Jesus have changed remarkably over time, shifting with the cultural

Christianity at a Glance

Problem: sin

Solution: salvation from sin

Techniques: faith and good works (for Roman Catholics); faith alone (for Protestants)

Exemplars: saints (for Roman Catholics); knights of faith (for Protestants)

Christianity is a tradition in which followers of Jesus Christ are saved from their sins by faith in Jesus Christ or some combination of faith and good works.

and political winds. Jesus art also varies considerably from continent to continent and country to country, with Jesus taking on distinctive facial and bodily characteristics as he moves out from Galilee to Brazil and Nigeria and Vietnam. In the United States, Jesus has been particularly chameleonic, with Americans depicting him as a pacifist and a warrior, black and white, gay and straight, liberal and conservative, a socialist and a capitalist, a Ku Klux Klansman and a civil rights agitator. The result is a profusion of Jesuses that Christians have used to adapt their tradition to changing circumstances. His image can now be found on posters and bobble head dolls and "I'll Be Back" T-shirts. Most of this merchandise is faithful, some is satirical, and it is often difficult to discern the difference. Is a "Jesus Saves" T-shirt depicting its subject with both a sacred heart and the stick and pads of a hockey goalie trying to get unbelievers to chuckle or to convert unbelievers to Christ?

CHRISTIAN HISTORY

Christians have described the life of Jesus as "the greatest story ever told," but the story of the emergence and growth of Christianity is equally intriguing. That narrative moves, as the scholar of ancient Christianity Paula Fredriksen has observed, "from Jesus to Christ," as devout Christians increasingly ratcheted up the reputation of their tradition's central symbol.[2] In a parallel development, a ragtag group of a few dozen followers of Jesus somehow turned into a Jesus movement with many different theologies, many different gospels, and many different teachers. That movement then consolidated into a church, which allied with an empire, which propelled this new religion around the ancient Mediterranean and then across the globe. How did this happen? How did Jesus escape the fate of the hundreds of other failed prophets of his time? Why was he not just buried in the annals of forgotten history? And how did the movement he started turn into the most popular religion today? To answer those questions, we need to look at two other men who, perhaps more than Jesus himself, turned Christianity into what it is today, and then at the ways that Christians of all sorts—mystics and monks, patriarchs and popes, and ordinary folks of various spiritual and religious persuasions—bent the arc of Christian history toward the modern world.

Unlike Muhammad, who died surrounded by a vast empire of his own creation, Jesus left behind little more than a small group of followers and a radical vision of the kingdom of God. These followers turned their memories of him into a gospel and then spread that "good news" far and wide across the ancient Mediterranean. Within a century of Jesus's death, the Jesus movement had separated itself from its Jewish origins and become a religion of its own, with its own leaders, its own rituals, its own sacred texts, and its own formulas of faith. During the fourth century, this new religious movement became the official religion of the Roman Empire, supported and spread through imperial power. None of this would have been imaginable to Jesus's earliest followers. And none of it would have been possible without Christianity's two other founders: Paul and Constantine.

Paul

Saul (c. 5–c. 67) was a Jewish tentmaker and Roman citizen of Tarsus (in modern-day Turkey). Upon his conversion to the faith that would become Christianity, he took the name Paul. Today, he is famous principally as a letter writer. The Christian New Testament includes fourteen epistles attributed to him or his followers. But these letters also

faith
a central Christian term that originally referred to "trust" but is now typically understood to refer to "belief." Protestants affirm that salvation comes by "faith alone" and not by works.

Eucharist
worship service consisting of the consumption of bread and wine and commemorating both the Last Supper of Jesus with his followers and the death of Jesus by crucifixion; also called the Mass, Divine Liturgy, and Holy Communion

Reformation
sixteenth-century movement that, by challenging the authority of priests, popes, and the Roman Catholic Church, ultimately created Protestantism as its own Christian branch

icon ("image")
sacred image of Christ or a saint believed by Eastern Orthodox Christians to facilitate contact with the subject of the image

pope
bishop of Rome and, according to Roman Catholics, the leader of the Christian church on earth

Our Lady of Guadalupe
popular Catholic saint in the Spanish-speaking world. Her basilica in Mexico City is the world's most visited Christian pilgrimage site.

Paul's conversion marks a crucial beginning to the transition of Christianity from a small movement to a regional religion in the ancient Mediterranean. This miniature painting from a fifteenth-century illuminated Catholic missal, or prayer book, by Fra Angelico depicts Paul falling to the ground after being blinded by a light from heaven.

testify to Paul's missionary work—his efforts to spread the gospel of Jesus Christ among Jews and non-Jews alike, and to put out all sorts of theological fires in the process.

In his pre-Christian life, Paul aligned himself with the Pharisees, a Jewish school that affirmed the doctrine of bodily resurrection. He was said to be a zealous persecutor of Christians and even witnessed the stoning of Stephen, the first Christian martyr, in roughly 35. In a moment that would provide a model for Christian conversions to come, Paul's life took a new turn on the road from Jerusalem to Damascus. He saw a blinding light. He heard a voice asking, "Why do you persecute me?" Soon this convert became the Jesus movement's foremost missionary and thousand-mile traveler, preaching from Jerusalem in the east to Rome in the west, and in Corinth, Philippi, Thessalonica, and Ephesus in between.

The earliest followers of Jesus had no intention of starting a new religion. They gathered in private homes to pray, to tell stories about their teacher, to mourn his death, to celebrate his resurrection, and to share an informal common meal that would evolve into the ritual now known as the Divine Liturgy, Mass, or Holy Communion. They also went to synagogue and (until the Romans destroyed it in 70) the Jerusalem Temple. As their movement spread among non-Jews, tensions arose regarding just how Jewish it should be. Did they need to follow kosher dietary rules? Did male converts need to be circumcised? No and no, they decided around 50 at the Council of Jerusalem described in the New Testament book of Acts. The good news of Jesus offered salvation from sin, Paul argued, and that goal did not require adherence to Jewish law. In an era with many rival understandings of this enigmatic figure now called Jesus Christ, Greek-influenced Gnostics (literally, "knowers") embraced Jesus as a disembodied teacher of secret wisdom. But Paul, who downplayed Jesus's role as rabbi and miracle worker, preached "nothing except Christ crucified" (1 Corinthians 2:2).

Arrested in Jerusalem for disturbing the peace, Paul was imprisoned for two years before being transferred to Rome for two more. In 64, a massive fire overran Rome. Emperor Nero blamed the Christians, and in 70 the Romans destroyed Jerusalem's Second Temple. It is not known how Paul died, though ancient writers report that he was beheaded in Rome during Nero's bloody reign. Paul did not live to see the sort of success Muhammad would later have with Islam, but within three generations of Paul's conversion, the Jesus movement had spread west into Spain, east into Persia, and south into North Africa.

Today, Paul is rightly remembered as Christianity's second founder. The spread of Christianity owed much to easy travel across Roman roads and ease of communication in the colloquial *Koine* Greek spoken empire-wide. It was also indebted to long forgotten Christian missionaries, and to the authors of the four New Testament Gospels, likely written between 70 and 100 and accepted as canonical around the end of the second century. But Paul was the key shaper of what came to be known as Christianity.

It was Paul who worked so hard to harmonize the Hebraic and Greek influences surrounding the early Christian movement. In the process, he imagined into being a salvation religion focused on the death and resurrection of Jesus. Paul's teaching that this salvation comes by other-help rather than self-effort influenced Augustine of Hippo (354–430) and Martin Luther (1483–1546) and, through them, both Roman Catholic and Protestant thought. His preference for chastity over marriage also left a long legacy, not only in Catholic traditions of celibate priests and Orthodox traditions of celibate bishops but also in Western ideas about women and bodies. Paul worked hard to cultivate uniformity in the Christian movement, both by his travels and through letters to far-flung churches, but the letters themselves testify to the diversity he confronted.

Paul was a controversial figure in his lifetime and remains one today. While some praise him for his spiritual egalitarianism—"There is neither Jew nor Greek, there is neither slave nor free, there is neither male nor female; for you are all one in Christ Jesus" (Galatians 3:28)—others criticize him as the man who told slaves to obey their masters. (In some black churches, the letters of Paul are never read.) Critics denounce Paul as a fomenter of sexism, anti-Semitism, and antigay bigotry. To Thomas Jefferson, who loved Jesus's moral teachings as fiercely as he hated "the speculations of crazy theologists," Paul was the "first corrupter of the doctrines of Jesus."[3] Today, Paul remains a popular scapegoat for those (Christian and otherwise) who want to love Jesus while hating organized Christianity.

CHRISTIANITY: A GENEALOGY

The Greek term *christianismos*, the root of the English word "Christianity," first appears in the early second-century letters of Ignatius of Antioch. It takes its first steps into the English language in the very early fourteenth century, in a few Middle English texts that refer variously to *cristiante*, *cristentie*, and *cristianite*. Later in that same century, the English poet Geoffrey Chaucer, in a passage of his *Canterbury Tales* describing how "Jesus hath converted thurgh his grace" a pagan, also observed that paganism had at that time largely pushed Christianity out from England to Wales: "To Walys fledde the Christyanytee / Of olde Britons, dwellynge in this ile." In the sixteenth century, amidst the theological arguments of the Protestant Reformation and aided by book publishing and increased literacy, the term "Christian" went mainstream. "Ye lyfe of euery christian, is as a pilgrimage," read one book in 1526. Later books referenced "the Christian fayth" in 1553 and lamented "the waine and declination of Christian pietie" in 1597. In a telling later adaptation, the term "Christian" came in Shakespeare and other early seventeenth-century sources to serve as a generic term for human being. "Shee hath more qualities then a Water-Spaniell, which is much in a bare Christian,"[a] Lance says in *The Two Gentlemen of Verona* (1623).[b]

The earliest writers who tried to compare the world's religions did so largely in binary terms (Christianity versus others) and often as Christian missionaries and for the purpose of spreading Christianity. Even after more objective scholars of the world's religions emerged in the nineteenth century, the category of Christian continued to stand in, as it had in Shakespeare's works, for human in general. As a result, many came to expect Christian features—a God, a founder, scriptures, creeds—to be mirrored in other religions, and they judged as inferior religions that did not have them. Today, scholars of the world's religions are struggling to overcome these inherited biases and to see Christianity as one religious animal among many, rather than the only proper human being in the group.

Constantine

As Paul's story suggests, some Christians were already being persecuted in the first century. But as Christians defiantly insisted on following an executed criminal over the emperor himself, and as rumors of cannibalism ("take, eat, this is my body," Mark 14:22) spread, Roman authorities clamped down on a foreign group they increasingly saw as both atheistic (because of its refusal to worship Roman gods) and a political threat. Christians from the first century to the present have exaggerated the extent of this anti-Christian violence, so much so that some scholars now speak of a "myth of persecution."[4] In reality, this persecution was largely local and sporadic until Emperor Decius made it imperial policy in 250 CE.

Decius decided that his empire's troubles—inflation, unemployment, threats of barbarian invasions—were punishment for the demise of Greco-Roman religion, and he decreed that all Roman subjects must sacrifice to the Roman gods. When some Christians,

CHRONOLOGY OF CHRISTIANITY

c. 4 BCE–30 CE   Life of Jesus

c. 46–62   Paul's letters written

c. 50   Council of Jerusalem opens Jesus movement to non-Jews

70   Jerusalem destroyed and the Jerusalem Temple with it

c. 70–100   Four New Testament gospels written

303   "Great Persecution" of Christians by Roman emperor Diocletian begins

312   Roman emperor Constantine's conversion

313   Edict of Milan ends widespread persecution of Christians in Roman Empire

325   Council of Nicaea drafts the Nicene Creed

354–430   Life of Augustine of Hippo

380   Christianity becomes the official religion of the Roman Empire

451   Council of Chalcedon declares that Jesus is one person with two natures (divine and human)

1054   Great Schism splits Christendom into Roman Catholicism in the West and Orthodoxy in the East

1095   Pope Urban II proclaims First Crusade

1099   Crusaders conquer Jerusalem

1187   Saladin takes Jerusalem for Muslims

1225–1274   Life of Saint Thomas Aquinas

1380s   Wycliffe and his followers produce the first English-language Bible

1483–1546   Life of Martin Luther

1492   Christopher Columbus explores the West Indies

1509–1564   Life of John Calvin

1517   Martin Luther publishes his Ninety-Five Theses on indulgences

1521   Luther is excommunicated

1531   Our Lady of Guadalupe appears in Mexico

1534   King Henry VIII breaks with Catholic Church and takes control of the Church of England

1545–1563   Council of Trent gives voice to the Counter-Reformation

1555   Peace of Augsburg declares principle of one religion per realm in Europe

1562–1598   French Wars of Religion

1611   King James Version of Bible is published

1618–1648   Thirty Years' War, which ends with Peace of Westphalia

1619   African slaves arrive in Jamestown, Virginia

1620   Separatist Pilgrims sail from England on the *Mayflower* and arrive in Plymouth, Massachusetts

including bishops in Jerusalem, Antioch, and Rome, refused, they were executed as "atheists" hostile to the state. Other Christians responded by turning the pious dead into Christ-like martyrs (literally, "witnesses"). Gathering their relics, telling their stories, and praying for their help, Christians flocked to the shrines of such martyrs as Perpetua, a twenty-two-year-old noblewoman who left behind a prison diary that ends just as she is being led with the slave Felicitas to her death.

In the "Great Persecution" that began in 303, the emperor Diocletian oversaw the burning of churches, the destruction of sacred texts, and more executions. But stories of these horrors did little to kill the movement. In fact, Christianity continued to expand its footprint as believers once again turned brutal deaths into paradoxical victories—testimony to the life-giving power of the one true God and guarantees of afterlife rewards in heaven (for the martyrs) and punishments in hell (for the perpetrators). Through this upside-down theology, "the blood of the martyrs" became, as the North African theologian Tertullian famously put it, "the seed of the church."

1636	Roger Williams founds Providence Plantation on the principle of religious freedom
1730s–1740s	First Great Awakening in Europe and North America
1738	The Wesley brothers (Charles and John) found Methodism in England
1776	American Revolution begins when North American colonies declare their independence from England
1789–1799	French Revolution separates the French Republic from Roman Catholicism
1799	Friedrich Schleiermacher publishes *On Religion*
1801	Cane Ridge Revival begins Second Great Awakening in North America
1816	Richard Allen establishes African Methodist Episcopal Church in Philadelphia
1830	The Book of Mormon appears
1859	Charles Darwin publishes *On the Origin of Species*
1861–1865	American Civil War
1869–1870	First Vatican Council declares papal infallibility
1895–1898	*The Woman's Bible* critiques biblical teachings on the subjugation of women
1906	Azusa Street Revival in Los Angeles introduces Pentecostalism
1910–1915	*The Fundamentals* proclaims biblical infallibility
1925	Scopes "Monkey Trial" in Dayton, Tennessee, upholds state ban on teaching evolution in the public schools
1938–1945	Holocaust claims the lives of six million Jews plus millions more Soviets, Poles, Serbs, Roma, Jehovah's Witnesses, gays and lesbians, and the disabled
1962–1965	Second Vatican Council defines the Church as "the people of God"
1969	James Cone authors *Black Theology and Black Power*
1971	Feminist theologian Mary Daly stages an "exodus" out of Harvard's Memorial Church and out of Christianity itself
1979	Founding of Moral Majority signals arrival of the New Religious Right in the United States
1980	Archbishop Oscar Romero of El Salvador is assassinated
2003	Gene Robinson of New Hampshire becomes the first openly gay priest to become an Episcopal bishop
2013	Pope Francis becomes the first Latin American pope

The Roman emperor Constantine and his mother, Empress Helena, stand with the True Cross of Jesus that Helena is said to have discovered in Jerusalem. While Constantine played the crucial role in making Christianity a global religion, Helena's piety and Holy Land pilgrimages were key influences on her son.

That seed germinated across the Roman Empire thanks to a vision as spectacular and consequential as the blinding of Paul on the Road to Damascus. In 312, on the eve of the battle at Milvian Bridge (outside Rome), the Roman emperor Constantine reported a miraculous vision that would set him on a course to full control of the Roman Empire. In the midday sky, floating above the sun, he saw, according to church historian Eusebius, "a cross of light in the heavens . . . bearing the inscription, 'CONQUER BY THIS.'"[5] With shields emblazoned with the Chi-Rho (the first two Greek letters for *Christ*), Constantine's soldiers won the battle. In 313, the Edict of Milan put an end to Roman persecution of Christians, and under Constantine's reign Christianity became the de facto religion of the Roman Empire.

This account of Constantine's conversion may be more story than fact. The narrative fits perhaps too neatly into a global pattern of rulers conscripting gods to legitimate their power. What is undeniable in this case is that Constantine and Christianity grew up together, their names and symbols intertwined. Whereas Paul helped transform the Jesus movement into Christianity, Constantine set Christianity on the course to becoming a global religion.

As Christian martyrs gave way to Christian rulers, it became increasingly difficult to distinguish between what the North African theologian Augustine of Hippo called the heavenly "city of God" and the earthly city of human beings. Though Constantine would not be baptized until he was on his deathbed, he referred to himself as a "bishop among bishops." The capital he built at Constantinople (now Istanbul) was a Christian capital—a Rome of his own. Constantine also oversaw the construction of the Church of the Holy Sepulchre as part of the rebuilding of Jerusalem. During that project, Constantine's Christian mother Helena discovered (again, according to legend) the True Cross used in the crucifixion of Jesus. Sunday became an official holiday in the Roman Empire in 321, and worship conducted on that day moved progressively from modest homes to freestanding church buildings to lavish basilicas. In 380, Christianity became the empire's official religion, and in 391 pagan worship was forbidden. In this way, a countercultural rebellion of carpenters, fishermen, women, and the poor ascended from powerlessness to power. Instead of occupying a world where their faith could cost them their lives, Christians now benefited socially and politically from their Christian identity. Martyrdom became a pagan occupation, and Christianity an imperial religion, itself conquering under the sign of the cross.

Councils, Creeds, Canons, and Clergy

Before Constantine and his imperial church, Christians had no official creeds and no official Bible. Whatever control bishops and other church authorities exerted over their movement was exercised locally. So even as the term "Christian" came into vogue, there were many ways to be one. Beliefs and practices among Greek-speaking gentiles in Rome differed from those in Hebrew-speaking communities in Galilee. Some emphasized the Greek soil in which their Judeo-Greco hybrid was blooming. Others emphasized its Jewish roots. On the Greek side, the ship owner Marcion of Sinope (in modern-day Turkey) and others distinguished sharply between the supposedly inferior angry god of the Jews and the supposedly superior loving god of the Christians. Meanwhile, "Judaizers" insisted that all followers of Jesus also follow Mosaic law.

But what sort of person was this Christ? Christians could not converge on an answer, and a proliferation of gospels about his life complicated the matter. At the time, proponents of the different viewpoints in this intellectual contest did not think of themselves as being on one "team" or another, but after the fact scholars have pieced together the various players. There were Docetics (from the Greek *docet*, "to seem") who believed Jesus was a god who only *seemed* to have a human body. There were Arians (named after the fourth-century Egyptian thinker Arius) who saw Jesus as a created being rather than an eternal god. Various Gnostic groups saw ignorance, not sin, as the fundamental human problem, and Jesus as a disembodied revealer of the sort of secret wisdom that could cure that disease. But the Jesus story told by Paul and the later church turned on crucifixion and the resurrection of Jesus as the Son of God.

Some religions get along just fine without settling such disputes. Buddhists had no creed until a nineteenth-century American Protestant convert decided that every self-respecting religion needed one. Closer to home, rabbinic Judaism, which emerged around the same time as Christianity, happily included competing voices in the debates that would come to constitute its Talmud. But Constantine was keen to maintain order in his church, lest it disorder his empire. So as the unwieldy Jesus movement became Christianity, its leaders started to draw sharp lines between **orthodoxy** ("right doctrine") and heterodoxy ("wrong doctrine"). They policed these borders through councils, creeds, canons, and clergy—by convening councils to rule on orthodoxy, by crafting creeds that articulated that orthodoxy, by gathering into their own sacred book the writings that conformed to that orthodoxy, and by recognizing bishops as the authoritative teachers of that orthodoxy. The aim of these efforts was to create one universal church. Instead, they further revealed the diversity of Christians, who were increasingly divided between orthodox winners and heretical losers.

Something like today's Apostles' Creed had circulated as early as the second century as a quick-and-easy profession of faith for use at baptisms and the communal meal. But its vague language did not settle disputes regarding the nature of Jesus and his relationship with God the Father. So in 325, Constantine convened Christianity's first church council in Nicaea in present-day Turkey. Bishops who had once been tortured by Roman authorities were now welcomed like dignitaries before Constantine himself. At Nicaea, they ruled on such matters as whether Easter Day should be set by the Jewish lunar calendar (no) and whether to kneel on Sundays (no again). Their main work was to draft what would come to be called the Nicene Creed—a formula now accepted by most Roman Catholic, Orthodox, and Protestant churches.

This creed (from *credo*, "I believe," in Latin), which took its current form in 381, played a major role in bending the Christian tradition toward orthodoxy ("right doctrine") over orthopraxy ("right practice"). It described Jesus as fully human *and* fully divine—"born of the Virgin Mary" *and* "of one substance with the Father." While this solved one problem (by rejecting both Docetism and Arianism), it created another: it opened up Christians to accusations of polytheism, or believing in more than one god. In their response to this

orthodoxy ("right doctrine") belief accepted as correct by church leaders, as contrasted with heresy, or unacceptable belief

Trinity
Christian doctrine that there are three persons (Father, Son, and Holy Spirit) in one Godhead

problem, the bishops at Nicaea made things even more confusing—by adding to their already crowded pantheon a third entity: the Holy Spirit. According to the mysterious doctrine of the **Trinity** they proclaimed in the Nicene Creed, the Father, Son, and Holy Spirit were three persons in one Godhead.

At Nicaea, the transformation of the Jesus movement into a religious institution (under Paul) and then an imperial force (under Constantine) produced a religious tradition unusually focused on doctrine. It also produced a new binary—between orthodoxy and heresy. Already, to be a Christian was to say "*credo*": "I believe." To believe in something else—that Jesus was spirit only, or that the Father was superior to the Son—was now to out yourself as a heretical proponent of false doctrine and a danger to social order.

The making of a Christian canon, or list of authoritative scriptures, goes back to the second-century anti-Judaizer Marcion, whose Bible included ten letters of Paul and a version of the Gospel of Luke but no Jewish scriptures. Christians later decided to include Jewish books in their canon, referring to the Hebrew Bible as the Old Testament and to their own texts as the New Testament. There was little controversy about Paul's letters or about Acts, a book written by the author of the Gospel of Luke that narrates the founding and spread of the early church. Regarding the Gospels, Christians settled on the current number during the second century thanks to their first great theologian, Irenaeus, who reasoned that just as there are four winds and four corners of the earth, so should there be four Gospels (Matthew, Mark, Luke, and John). Texts left on the cutting room floor included the Gnostic Gospel of Thomas, a collection of the secret sayings of Jesus with no Passion narrative; the topsy-turvy Gospel of Judas, in which the title character is a hero and Jesus is prone to fits of uncomfortable laughter; and the Gospel of Mary (Magdalene), who even better than Peter understands her savior's secret teachings.

The mystery of three persons in one godhead called the Trinity is one of the most difficult Christian doctrines to explain. In this 1938 painting by Lou Mohr on the ceiling of the Oslo Cathedral in Norway, Jesus the Son (left), God the Father (center), and the Holy Spirit (right) all appear in human form.

Augustine of Hippo (354–430)

Who is the most influential Christian of African descent? That title belongs to Augustine of Hippo, who was born in Thagaste in what is now Algeria. Augustine is also the most original Christian thinker after Paul, whom most Christians today read through the thick monocle of Augustine's work.

For a Church Father, Augustine is a curiously modern figure. He was born into an interfaith household, with a pagan father and a Christian mother (Monica, now a Catholic saint). He himself was a religious switcher: a Christian, then a Manichaean (who affirmed two dueling cosmic principles), then a Neoplatonist philosopher, and then a Christian again. He even wrote his own memoir. For a man who implicated sex in original sin, Augustine enjoyed a surprisingly saucy sex life. "Make me chaste," he famously prayed in his youth, "but not yet."[a] In this interim, he had a lover for fifteen years who bore him a son, but he abandoned her (at his mother's urging) for a proper wife, whom he in turn cheated on and then left before the wedding.

Like the Christian story itself, Augustine's autobiographical *Confessions* arcs from sin to redemption. The climax comes in 386 in a garden in Milan, where Augustine, then in his early thirties, has been working as a rhetoric professor. He is weeping under a fig tree, perhaps over his inability to wrestle the problem of evil to the ground, perhaps over a "broken heart."

He hears a child's voice. "Pick it up and read," it says. Obediently, he opens up the book at hand to Romans 13:13-14: "Let us walk honestly, as in the day; not in rioting and drunkenness, not in chambering and wantonness, not in strife and envying. Put ye on the Lord Jesus Christ, and make not provision for the flesh, to fulfill the lusts thereof." Emboldened by a "light of certainty," Augustine backs out of his engagement and commits himself to celibacy. He is baptized on Easter in 387. Eight years later he becomes Bishop of Hippo, a post he would hold until his death in 430.[b]

Augustine wrote voraciously, shaping Christian thought by contrasting it with what he saw as the errors of the dualistic Manichaeans, the hyper-ritualistic Donatists, and the free-will Pelagians. His theory that God predestines each of us before birth to heaven or hell was taken up by John Calvin during the Protestant Reformation and carried to North America by the Puritans. His view, developed in *City of God*, that humans are aliens on earth—that this is our "temporary home" (to quote the country star Carrie Underwood)—is another major contribution to lived Christianity. Augustine shaped the Christian world even more profoundly via his preoccupations with sex. Long after he rejected the Manichaean teaching that the cosmos is a battleground between the forces of light and darkness, he remained a dualist when it came to spirit and matter, viewing sex as shameful, women as temptresses, and original sin as a sexually transmitted disease.

If Augustine were subtracted from Christianity's long and winding road, Christian culture would be unrecognizable today—lacking, perhaps, its emphasis on conversion, its preoccupation with sexual sin, its uneasiness with the human body, and its world-denying desire to fly away to another world.

Today, seven Old Testament books included in Roman Catholic Bibles are not in Protestant Bibles, and Orthodox Bibles include books that Protestants and Catholics reject. However, as early as 200, many Christian communities were already using lists of authoritative writings, and by the second half of the fourth century there was widespread consensus about the canonization of the twenty-seven New Testament books used in most modern Bible translations.

As the distinction between the church and the world was increasingly blurred—as the trappings of imperial protocol (incense, processions, choirs, ministerial garb) bled into Christian worship and Jesus was depicted in a golden toga befitting an emperor—many came to see the imperial church as sinful, more interested in power than prayer.

In an effort to reconstruct the countercultural lifestyle of Christ the wanderer, some took to the roads and then to the desert, absenting themselves from worldly pleasures and social obligations in order to abide in the divine presence. Drawing on the classic Greek distinction between spirit and body, they disciplined the body for the sake of the spirit. Monasticism became the new martyrdom. The desert monk became a "martyr every day of his life."[6]

The term "monk" is rooted in the Greek word for "solitary," but early Christians were drawn to monks as surely as nineteenth-century American city dwellers who had not quite yet adjusted to the clamor of city life were drawn to the quiet beauty of rural cemeteries. So monastic life quickly became communal, paving the way for medieval monastic orders, including the Franciscans, whose friars now lead pilgrims down Jerusalem's Via Dolorosa.

Eastern Orthodoxy and the Great Schism

The Nicene Creed spoke of "one holy catholic and apostolic Church"—"catholic" in this case meaning "universal." But Constantine's decision to build a "New Rome" in Constantinople in present-day Turkey and then to convene the first church council across the Bosphorus in Nicaea meant that early Christianity was developing two sacred centers, which mirrored the political division of the Roman Empire into east and west. One of these centers was in Western Europe in Latin-speaking Rome. The other was on the cusp of Asia in Greek-speaking Constantinople.

At a series of church councils—Nicaea (325), Constantinople (381), Ephesus (431), Chalcedon (451), Constantinople II (553), Constantinople III (680), and Nicaea II (787)—bishops juggled the competing demands of these very different centers. The goal was always unity, but every time they identified any particular belief as central to "right doctrine" they ended up banishing another group of "heretics." In this way, these councils acted like forks in a river, splitting the early church into its various streams, not unlike the way early Islamic leaders—caliphs and imams—split the early Islamic movement into the Sunni and the Shia.

In Christianity's first major schism, what is now referred to as Oriental Orthodoxy was carved off from the rest of Christendom after the Council of Chalcedon (451) deemed Jesus to be one person in two natures (divine and human). Those who came to be known as the Oriental Orthodox rejected this view, insisting that Jesus had only one nature. Today, four of the six churches active at the Church of the Holy Sepulchre—the Armenian, Coptic, Ethiopian, and Syriac Orthodox—are part of this communion, which accepts as authoritative only the first three church councils.

More monumental was Christianity's second schism, which split Christianity into Eastern Orthodoxy in the Greek East and Roman Catholicism in the Latin West. This separation began after the 787 ecumenical council, but the divorce was not finalized until the last efforts at reconciliation failed at the councils in Lyons (1274) and Florence (1439). The intertwined causes of this schism are hard to disentangle, extending to questions of authority, theological and liturgical disagreements, political intrigue, military maneuvers, and cultural and linguistic differences.

Since 451, Christendom had been divided into five geographical areas, each overseen by its own patriarch. Rome, Constantinople, Alexandria, Antioch, and Jerusalem all saw the church as ecumenical ("one"), but tensions simmered between Rome and

Constantinople, and those tensions came to a head in Constantine's city in 1054. One problem was the objection of Constantinople to Rome's insertion into the Nicene Creed of a single Latin word (*filoque*: "and the Son") which, by affirming that the Holy Spirit proceeded from the Father "and the Son" seemingly demoted the Holy Spirit. The broader issue was the authority of the pope of Rome. Though honored as "first among equals" in the patriarchate, he had no authority (according to officials at Constantinople) outside of his Roman region. And he certainly had no authority (again, according to Constantinople) to change unilaterally the words of the Nicene Creed that had been agreed upon at prior councils. Church leaders in Constantinople objected to the filoque, and Rome responded by objecting to the use of the title "Ecumenical Patriarch" for Constantinople's overseer. Into this volatile situation, Pope Leo IX sent Cardinal Humbert to Constantinople to meet with representatives of Patriarch Michael Cerularius. It was important that this meeting go well, because Arab Muslims, who already controlled the lands of three patriarchates (Antioch, Jerusalem, and Alexandria), were poised at Christendom's borders, and Normans, who had recently invaded southern Italy, posed an even more immediate military threat to Christians west and east.

The meeting did not go well. Instead of insisting on the supremacy of the pope and leaving it at that, Humbert (who by most accounts possessed the tact of a sledgehammer) played the aggressor. The outraged Greeks responded by charging their Roman counterparts with trying to impose unilaterally a series of innovations, including priestly celibacy, the use of unleavened wafers (instead of real bread) in the Eucharist, and the dreaded filoque. This high drama concluded with Humbert marching into the glorious Hagia Sophia cathedral just as the Divine Liturgy was starting and placing on its altar a papal bull excommunicating Cerularius (who excommunicated Humbert in turn). Not until the intervention of Pope Paul VI and Patriarch Athenagoras I in 1965 would these dueling excommunications be lifted. In 1054, the damage had been done.

More damage was inflicted by the Crusades, beginning in 1096, which escalated these theological and liturgical disputes into armed conflict. Ironically, the impetus for the first of these four holy wars was an appeal from Constantinople to Pope Urban II for military aid against the Turks. But the pope did more than say yes. In what is now known as the First Crusade (1096–1099), he called on Catholics to take the Holy Land back from Muslims, who had seized it in 638, held it for centuries, and destroyed the Church of the Holy Sepulchre in the process. In exchange for answering his call to "destroy that vile race from their lands," the pope offered Crusaders spiritual benefits known as indulgences for the "immediate remission of sins."[7] Inspired by this offer, not to mention the spoils of war, crusaders captured Jerusalem in 1099 and rebuilt the Church of the Holy Sepulchre, only to see the Sultan Saladin reclaim both in 1187.

The Crusades might have united Eastern and Western Christians against their common enemies (which included Jews, who were killed by the tens of thousands in Europe's first officially recorded anti-Jewish pogroms in the Rhineland in 1096), but in 1204 during the Fourth Crusade, Rome's holy warriors captured and sacked Constantinople, briefly setting up a Latin empire in the East and driving a fatal wedge into Orthodox-Catholic relations. In Constantinople, crusaders raped and murdered Orthodox Christians, whom they regarded as "enemies of God." They desecrated the Hagia Sophia, destroying its icons and turning its altar into a stage for dancing prostitutes, prompting even Pope Innocent III to denounce his crusaders for violating "matrons and virgins" and "holy places" alike.[8]

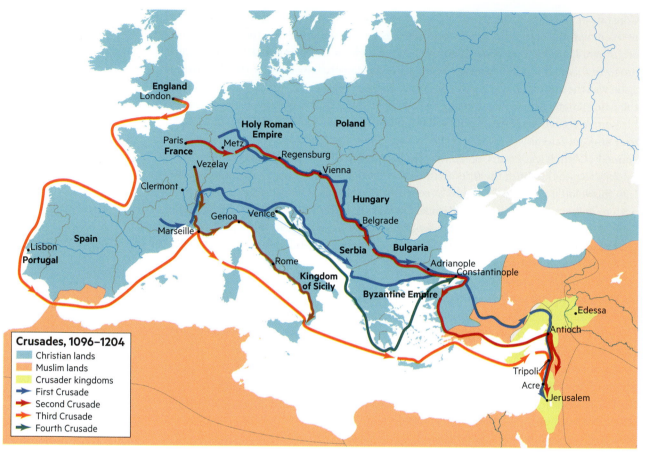

Crusades, 1096–1204
- Christian lands
- Muslim lands
- Crusader kingdoms
- → First Crusade
- → Second Crusade
- → Third Crusade
- → Fourth Crusade

Over roughly 150 years, four major Christian crusades attempted to capture Jerusalem. By land and by sea, Christian soldiers set out to seize control of their "Holy Land" from Muslim powers.

More than the row over papal supremacy in 1054, this siege of Constantinople drove a wedge between Roman Catholic and Eastern Orthodox Christians. Today, it is bitterly remembered by the Eastern Orthodox as if it happened yesterday.

As their name implies, the Orthodox pride themselves on preserving the "right doctrines" and practices of the apostles as formulated in the Bible, the writings of the Church Fathers, the creeds of the first seven ecumenical councils, and the liturgies, hymns, and icons of their tradition. Often referred to as Eastern Orthodoxy because of its roots in the eastern part of the Roman Empire, this Christian branch includes more than a dozen "autocephalous" ("self-headed") churches run by patriarchs, metropolitans, or archbishops empowered to appoint their own bishops and oversee their respective domains. The Patriarch of Constantinople, also known as the Ecumenical Patriarch, is honored but is emphatically not to be seen as an infallible pope. That is because Eastern Orthodoxy is a conciliar church, which settles disputes not by papal decree but by the consensus of bishops gathered at councils. Bishops are selected from the ranks of celibate monastics, while priests are usually married men.

The heart and soul of Orthodox Christian life is the Divine Liturgy, just as the Sabbath is to Orthodox Jews. Unlike Roman Catholics, who until recent decades insisted on the Latin Mass, the Orthodox have typically performed their Eucharist in local languages.

Traditionally, this service is sung a capella amidst a congregation that is standing (and sometimes informally milling about), though some congregations in North America have recently introduced organs and pews. In keeping with their focus on the ritual dimension of religion, the Orthodox celebrate their Divine Liturgy in high style—with incense, candles, chanting, and much crossing of themselves and bowing.

Of all the senses, sight is primary for the Orthodox, who venerate the divine through icons—images of Christ, Mary, and other saints—whose power relies on the willingness of the divine to take up residence in matter, as in the **Incarnation** of Jesus. Lest they run afoul of the prohibition in the Ten Commandments against "graven images," Orthodox icons are typically two-dimensional objects painted on wood.

The Orthodox generally recognize seven sacraments, just as Roman Catholics do. These "holy mysteries," as the Orthodox describe them, are baptism, "christmation" (or confirmation), Eucharist, confession, holy unction (healing), marriage, and ordination. Baptism is typically done by triple immersion, and infant baptism is the norm. Chrismation, or anointing with oil to confer the Holy Spirit, occurs right after baptism, so it is common to see babies participating in the Divine Liturgy. In Greek Orthodox marriage, many of the rituals—exchanging rings, exchanging crowns, and circling the altar—are performed three times, in recognition of the Trinity. Another distinctive feature of Orthodox practice is the recitation of the popular Jesus prayer: "Lord Jesus Christ, Son of God, have mercy on me, the sinner"—which has been safeguarded over the centuries at Mount Athos in Greece, where twenty self-governing monasteries reside.

Of all the Christian doctrines, the Orthodox emphasize the Trinity and the Incarnation. It is important to them that God exists in a communion of three persons and that Jesus is fully human *and* fully divine. The Christian mystery of the Incarnation begins with the Almighty God coming into the world as a helpless baby, born to a frightened young woman and cradled in the rough hands of a carpenter. This story mixes up the

Incarnation
Christian doctrine that Jesus is a god who was embodied in human form and lived and died as a human being

Russian Orthodox churches are known for their pageantry, pomp, and circumstance. Here, Patriarch Kirill leads the Easter service at the Cathedral of Christ the Savior in Moscow, Russia, in 2017.

categories of divinity and humanity, investing the mundane comings and goings of everyday life with sacred import. It also affirms the power of God, who took on human form in a manger whose only fragrance was animal dung, to make anything holy. In the Orthodox tradition, the doctrine of the Incarnation is reinforced by an emphasis on sacraments and icons, both of which also intermingle spirit and matter, the divine and the human.

Although the Orthodox believe in original sin, they understand it less as a punishment passed down naturally through Adam than as our unnatural separation from God. They seek to overcome this separation through mystical union with the divine and, ultimately, "deification." Or, as the Orthodox put it: God became human so that humans might become divine. In taking aim at this goal, theology, worship, and prayer alike bend toward the mystical. The "negative theology" of Orthodoxy emphasizes what we do not know about God over what we know. Their sacraments are referred to as the "mysteries," since they, too, are ultimately incomprehensible to mere mortals.

Mystics and Philosophers

As battles raged between Eastern Orthodox and Roman Catholic leaders, medieval philosophers and mystics were struggling to know and feel God through reason and experience. The Middle Ages are generally dated from the fall of Rome to the dawn of the Renaissance (400 to 1400)—a period when Christendom was largely on the run, invaded by Arabs and Vikings in the seventh through ninth centuries and by Mongols in the thirteenth. But the key era in Christian thought was the High Middle Ages, beginning in the eleventh century. This was a period of scholasticism, in which academics ("scholastics") tried to reconcile philosophy and Christian theology. It saw the development of European universities (Oxford University and the University of Paris) and new religious orders (the Dominicans and the Franciscans), plus the construction of great cathedrals. An explosion of new translations and commentaries led to the rediscovery of ancient Greek and Roman authorities, most notably Aristotle. Islamic philosophers such as Averroes and Jewish philosophers such as Maimonides also influenced the scholastics, who struggled to create one integrated body of knowledge that was indisputably Christian yet responsive to insights gathered from ancient philosophy and other religions. These scholastics pondered the problems of evil and free will but also the ways and means of logic and science. They offered proofs for the existence of God, including the famous ontological argument of Anselm of Canterbury: humans conceive of a God who is so great you can conceive of nothing greater; it is greater to exist in the world than merely in the mind; therefore, this conception of God must exist in reality.

The intellectual giant of this period of Christian thought was Thomas Aquinas (1225–1274). Though teased by fellow students as "the dumb ox," he came to be called "The Philosopher" in the way New Yorkers today refer to "The City." He gave the Catholic world not only a saint but also a school: Thomism. A friar of the Dominican order on the theology faculty at the University of Paris, he refused to choose between faith and reason, between Jesus and Aristotle. Best known for his *Summa Theologica* (1265–1274), Aquinas offered five arguments for the existence of God rooted not in logic but in our experience of the world. These "five ways" affirmed:

1. God as the first or unmoved mover.
2. God as the first or uncaused cause.

3. God as the necessary being that is the source of the existence of all else.
4. God as the perfect being (as opposed to everything else that is good by degrees).
5. God as the source of the direction of the universe.

Aquinas stopped work on this never-completed magnum opus after he had a mystical experience while celebrating Mass in 1273. "I cannot go on," Aquinas explained. "All that I have written seems to me like straw compared with what has now been revealed to me."[9]

Other medieval Christians came to mysticism earlier in life and with a less impressive résumé, approaching God through a *via negativa* ("negative way") that was skeptical about any positive statements about divinity. As do many modern believers, these mystics reveled in experience rather than doctrine, in this case direct experience of the divine. The German mystic Meister Eckhart (1260–1328) evoked a divine reality beyond space and time and therefore beyond description. Theresa of Avila (1515–1582) worked to contemplate God without the distortion of images and to cultivate experiences of union with divinity that were beyond words and concepts alike. Even Aquinas said that it is harder to say what God is than what God is not.

Though they could not describe Him (or Her or It), medieval mystics sought union with God—something like the deification long sought by Orthodox Christians such as Athanasius, the fourth-century founder of the Mount Athos monastery, who wrote that humans "become by grace what God is by nature."[10] Saint Francis of Assisi (1182–1226), a wealthy playboy and soldier who traded in his family wealth for a life of poverty and contemplation, sought communion with God in nature. Julian of Norwich (1342–1416) reveled in the feminine aspect of God as mother.

Catholic officials were generally wary of mystics, much as they are wary today of those who report visitations from the Virgin Mary. But these medieval mystics added an important element to a faith often criticized (from within and without) for its tendency to attribute human thinking to God. Experience matters, they insisted, including the experience of doubt. The mysteries of the Christian life can never be captured in simple formulas about sin and salvation (including the formulas presented in this textbook). Every answer contains inside it the seed of a question. So, the big questions of death and birth and the space in between, far from being answered by philosophy or theology, abide.

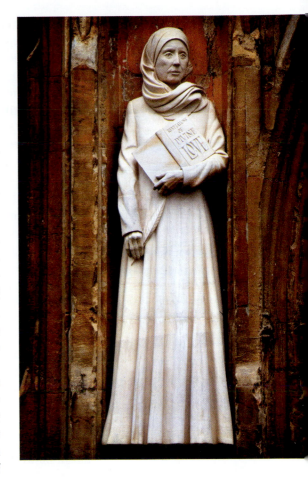

Julian of Norwich, a medieval Roman Catholic mystic, was the first woman to write a book in English: *Revelations of Divine Love* (1373), which records her visions of God. This statue welcomes visitors to Norwich Cathedral in Norwich, England.

The Protestant Reformation

Like the Great Schism between Orthodoxy and Roman Catholicism, the next great split in Christendom dates to a dramatic event. Some start the clock of the Reformation at the moment on October 31, 1517, that German professor Martin Luther reportedly nailed his famed Ninety-Five Theses against indulgences to the door of the Castle Church in the university town of Wittenberg. However, scholars now observe that these supposedly revolutionary theses, which prompted debate about salvation among peasants and professors alike, were not all that revolutionary. They addressed an obscure Catholic practice. They

Martin Luther was a German monk whose desire to reform the Roman Catholic Church set off the Protestant Reformation. This sixteenth-century portrait by Lucas Cranach the Elder has become the iconic image of this iconic reformer.

did not challenge papal authority. And they dropped none of the bombshells about the authority of scripture or the ways and means of salvation that would come to characterize the Reformation.

Others date the Reformation to the moment when Luther appeared before the Holy Roman emperor at the Diet of Worms, a council held to decide his fate in Worms, Germany, on April 17, 1521. Just as Luther probably never actually nailed his theses to a church door (he may have simply circulated them among friends), he probably did not say, "Here I stand. I cannot do otherwise." But he was resolute. "Unless I am convinced by Scripture and plain reason—I do not accept the authority of the popes and councils, for they have contradicted each other—my conscience is captive to the Word of God," he said (in Latin). "I cannot and I will not recant anything for to go against conscience is neither right nor safe."[11] The Scottish writer Thomas Carlyle later described this bold assertion of private conscience over imperial power as "the greatest moment in . . . modern history."[12] Had Luther stood down, Carlyle concluded, there would have been no fight for American independence and no French Revolution.

But the Protestant-Catholic schism cannot be seen as an absolute break from medieval Catholicism, which was full of reform efforts. Neither can it be reduced to the actions of one individual. A century and a half before Luther, John Wycliffe (c. 1331–1384), who believed that the church comprised not just popes and priests but all whom God had elected for salvation, had criticized the practice of selling indulgences. He found no warrant for papal authority in the Bible, which he regarded as the sole source of right doctrine. The Lollards, who drew considerable lower-class support, interpreted Wycliffe's call for biblical authority as a mandate for all Christians to interpret scripture for themselves. They worked with Wycliffe to produce the first full Bible translation into English in the early 1380s.

Wycliffe and other medieval reformers paved the way for the Protestant Reformation by imagining a church in which power shifted decidedly from religious professionals (popes, priests, monks) to ordinary Christians, or laypeople. But as far reaching as their reforms were—from popular piety to the Eucharist to priestly ethics to biblical authority—they did not attend to the matters of grace, faith, and salvation that would preoccupy Martin Luther and his fellow Reformers. And they did not create the new branches of Christianity now known as Protestant denominations.

Luther (1483–1546) was a Bible professor as well as a Roman Catholic monk who had no designs on creating a new branch of Christianity. But he managed to do just that, thanks to the help of other reformers, princes, and millions of peasants across the European countryside, who sang his hymns, read his pamphlets, and said a collective "Amen" to his insistence that salvation was a gift. Luther was also indebted to the recent invention of printing presses that used movable metal type to print the pioneering Gutenberg Bible in 1456. Luther would use this new technology to create a mass medium: short, easy-to-read, German-language pamphlets addressed to the ordinary reader. These pamphlets—"an instant publishing sensation," according to *Brand Luther* author Andrew Pettegree—transported his ideas with unparalleled speed across Europe.[13]

There are many ways to read Luther's contributions to the Reformation (a term, unknown to Luther, that did not come into widespread use until the eighteenth century). One is to read him as a pastor—a critic of the indulgences flooding into his parish and exploiting his parishioners. Inaugurated during the Crusades and sold by church agents, indulgences were complicated religious and financial instruments: the believer paid a fee or provided a service in exchange for a reduction in the punishment owed for

In this 1617 cartoon marking the centennial of Martin Luther's posting of his Ninety-Five Theses against Roman Catholic corruption, Luther wields a torch "set alight by God's word" against a devil pope spouting water as he tries to extinguish the Protestant flame. On the left, a Catholic priest is shown as a court jester selling indulgences.

a given sin. These products were likely understood differently by the different popes who authorized them, but many of the agents who sold them made wild claims for the benefits they offered, and many of the folk who bought them believed they were purchasing an express ticket out of purgatory for deceased family members.

The doctrine of purgatory had arisen in the medieval church as a way to explain what happened to people who were not quite ready for heaven when they died. Underlying this doctrine was a transactional understanding of sin as incurring a "debt" to be "paid." Though Christians could pay off their sins in this life through penance, all but the most saintly died in spiritual debt. Purgatory—literally a place of "cleansing"—was where they paid for their sins in suffering before being admitted to heaven. Crucially, this debt could also be paid by living loved ones who gave to the poor, arranged for masses, and purchased indulgences—all on behalf of the dead.

The particular indulgences in question in Luther's Germany were issued in 1515, allegedly to pay for the Basilica of St. Peter in Rome. But much of the proceeds went to an archbishop to repay a huge debt he had run up in purchasing his appointment. The agents who sold these indulgences routinely claimed that loved ones would be released from purgatory as soon as a payment was made. Luther's Ninety-Five Theses protested against this robbing from the poor to pay the rich. So did the forty-five pamphlets he had produced in three hundred different editions by 1519.

A second way to interpret Luther's contributions to the Reformation is to read him not as a pastor but as an anxious believer "continually vexed" by his sins and "miserably tormented" about his own salvation.[14] Was he "justified" in the eyes of God? Luther's parents were strict, and as a young man Luther joined one of the strictest monastic orders:

the Augustinians. As a monk he prayed, fasted, and confessed obsessively. But his strict performance of Roman Catholic piety—"If ever a monk got into heaven through monkery, I, too, would have gotten in," he wrote—failed to convince him that he was saved.[15]

In order to find deliverance from this "monster of uncertainty," Luther turned from fasting and confessing to Paul and Augustine, who together convinced him that salvation came not by self-effort but by other-help.[16] Christians were not saved in cooperation with God. They were saved, quite apart from human work and individual merit, by a gift from God—by grace. Or, as Paul put it: "the just shall live by faith" (Romans 1:17). In this "eureka" moment, Luther writes, "I felt that I had been born again and entered into paradise itself through open gates."[17] And those who said eureka with him started to bring into being a tradition in which, like *bhakti* Hinduism and Mahayana Buddhism, the religious goal of salvation came not by works but by mercy—not by payment but as a gift.

In this idea lay the destruction not only of indulgences but of most of the spiritual transactions long brokered by the priesthood, since what priests had to offer (the sacraments) were, from Luther's new vantage point, "works" that had no place in the drama of salvation. Also undermined were the institutions of monasticism and the papacy itself. Before the Reformation, only popes and priests enjoyed a sacred calling. After the Reformation, every Protestant did.

Over the centuries, Luther's understanding of salvation by faith through grace has been obscured by the shifting meaning of the term "faith," which, since the powerful emergence of skepticism during the early modern period, has come to mean something akin to "belief." For Luther, however, faith was trust—"a living, bold trust in God's grace."[18] When he said that Christians were saved by grace through faith he meant that all we needed to do was trust in God and God would do the rest. Lest faith itself devolve into "work," and salvation into yet another transaction, Luther emphasized that faith itself was a gift.

Luther's genius lay in his synthetic imagination—his reduction of an ancient religious tradition, replete with complicated and contradictory theological formulas and liturgical rites, to a simple slogan: "justification by faith." Where did Luther get his big idea about salvation? Not from any pope or church council, but from his own reading of the Bible. So Luther's revolt went far beyond new understandings of faith, grace, and salvation. It also extended to the questions of papal authority and church tradition. This is where Luther really got himself into trouble.

If, as some scholars argue, the Reformation gave birth to the modern West, it did not do so by criticizing indulgences, praising the Bible, or rejecting "salvation by works." It did so by proclaiming "Christian liberty"—by criticizing priests and popes and thereby calling into question the hierarchies that in the medieval world seemed not just divinely ordained but natural. In this new world order, even the distinction between the religious and the secular started to evaporate—as reformers found the profane in the priesthood, monasticism, and virginity and the sacred in marriage, family, work, and other staples of everyday life. As clergy were cut down to size and the laity elevated, a calling to ministry became increasingly difficult to distinguish from a calling to farming or commerce or banking. That was the bombshell. That is what turned Luther into a bestselling author in the first age of the bestseller. That is what attracted townspeople and peasants alike to his side. And that is what eventually called down the condemnations of pope and emperor alike.

One year after Luther declared in a public debate in 1519 that scripture alone was an infallible guide to Christian belief and practice, and that the pope did not have any special authority to interpret it, Pope Leo X sent Luther a bull of excommunication blasting him as a "wild boar" who is "seeking to destroy the vineyard" and ordering his books to be burned.[19] Luther, who now saw the pope as the Antichrist, burned the bull instead. One year later, at the Diet of Worms, he took on the emperor, who denounced him as a "devil in the habit of a monk" and ordered his books "to be eradicated from the memory of man"—a tall task given the fact that Luther had authored roughly one in five of the ten thousand or so pamphlets published in Germany during the height of the Reformation.[20]

John Calvin and the Second Reformation

The Reformation French theologian John Calvin profoundly shaped Protestant thought by emphasizing the sovereignty of God and the sinfulness of humans. In 1964, the French government released this postage stamp commemorating the four-hundred-year anniversary of his death.

Luther was not the only midwife of the modern West, however, and his was not the only Reformation. The French lawyer and theologian John Calvin (1509–1564) reimagined Christian theology in his *Institutes of the Christian Religion* (1536–1559) and then put his vision to the test in Geneva. Calvin's theology, now referred to as Reformed theology or, more simply, Calvinism, profoundly influenced Puritans in England and New England alike and played a major role in the development of American political life.

Calvin's thought rested on two core principles: the absolute sovereignty of God and the total depravity of human beings. For centuries, Christian theologians had struggled to figure out just how close divinity and humanity were in a universe in which God took on flesh and bones. Focusing on the Old Testament over the New and on God's power and glory over his love and mercy, Calvin maximized the difference between God and humanity. Humans were abject sinners, he argued, and God was totally, absolutely, unarguably in charge. These presuppositions led Calvin to his signature theological position, double predestination, which says that there is nothing humans can do to affect their salvation or damnation, which has been determined before birth by God alone.

Today, Calvinism is often summed up under the acronym TULIP, after the five points of Calvinism articulated at the Calvinist Synod of Dort (1618–1619):

Total depravity
Unconditional election
Limited atonement
Irresistible grace
Perseverance of the saints

Though forced out of his adopted home of Geneva, in modern-day Switzerland, in 1538, Calvin was invited back in 1541 by a town council willing to turn his adopted hometown into a theocracy of sorts run by pastors, lay leaders, and Calvin himself. In an effort to make Geneva's citizens holy, Calvin pursued a wave of reforms that, depending on your point of view, turned Geneva into either a holy city or a police state. In an effort to wipe away any vestige of Roman Catholicism, crucifixes were outlawed, as were fasting, prayers for the dead, and prayers in Latin. Parents were required to give their children biblical names.

This zeal devolved into zealotry, including the burning for heresy in 1553 of the Spanish physician-theologian Michael Servetus who, in an effort at improving relations with Jews and Muslims, had rejected the Trinity. This event came to symbolize the tyranny of Calvin's Geneva even as it consolidated his power over his adopted home.

Legacy of Calvin

Calvin's influence ran deep in the Reformed, Presbyterian, Congregational, and Baptist churches of Switzerland, France, Germany, the Netherlands, England, and Scotland. In England, Calvin inspired the **Puritans**, separatists who left behind the Church of England as insufficiently anti-Roman. Calvinism also had a huge influence on many giants of modern Protestant theology, including the German theologian Karl Barth and President Obama's favorite theologian, the German American Reinhold Niebuhr.

In *The Protestant Ethic and the Spirit of Capitalism* (1904), the German sociologist Max Weber famously argued that Calvinism was characterized by an "inner-worldly asceticism" that pushed believers to discipline themselves through hard work and to see their professions as sacred "callings."[21] This orientation was, according to Weber, a major factor in the rise of capitalism. Although, strictly speaking, there is nothing for human beings to do in Calvin's thinking to achieve salvation, there are things they can do to *convince* themselves of their election. Calvinists believed that God favored those he chose to be saved (the elect) with thisworldly as well as otherworldly rewards. Therefore, earning money through hard work and then saving it diligently might produce some measure of assurance that you were among that elect. The funds saved for that purpose became the accumulations of capital needed to fund capitalist enterprises in such Calvinist strongholds as the Netherlands.

Calvin's ideas sailed to North America with English Puritans, who worked to "purify" their Church of England of Roman Catholic influences. They dedicated their "errand into the wilderness" of the New World to creating an exemplary "city upon a hill" for all the world to see. In Plymouth, Massachusetts Bay, Connecticut, and New Haven, they established "Holy Commonwealths" purified of what they considered Catholic abominations. For roughly two hundred years, beginning with the arrival of the Pilgrims in 1620, Puritanism was the most powerful religious influence among Europeans who resided in the land that would become the United States. As Calvinists, early Americans focused on the Old Testament rather than the New, interpreting their own experiences through the biblical story of the Exodus, reading themselves as God's "New Israel" who had been "enslaved" by the British and liberated from bondage by a New Moses: George Washington. In American literature, Calvinism profoundly influenced such classics as Nathaniel Hawthorne's *The Scarlet Letter* and Herman Melville's *Moby-Dick*, as well as more recent fiction, including Marilynne Robinson's *Gilead*. Calvin lurks in American politics, too—in Abraham Lincoln's brooding second inaugural address, which reads the Civil War as a scourge brought on the nation by an inscrutable Almighty who "has His own purposes."[22] Calvin is also present in spirit wherever schoolchildren pledge their allegiance to "one nation under God" and presidents place their hands on a Bible and promise to uphold the Constitution.

Henry VIII and the Church of England

The Reformation famously leapt the English Channel thanks to the domestic troubles of King Henry VIII (1491–1547). After his marriage to Catherine of Aragon failed to produce a male heir, Henry asked the Vatican for an annulment so he could marry Anne Boleyn, the daughter of a prominent courtier who had been reading up on Protestant thought. Pope Clement VII refused. Henry, whose attacks on Luther's writings had previously won him the title Defender of the Faith (the Roman Catholic faith, that is), started his own church, the Church of England. One year after his secret marriage to Anne Boleyn in 1533, Parliament effectively annulled his first marriage and declared him Supreme Head of the Church of England.

Henry VIII did not go wholly over to the Protestant side, however. In fact, his thinking remained largely medieval. He was thoroughly modern in his liberality toward divorce, however. When he set his sights on his sixth wife, Luther sneered that "Squire Henry means to be God, and do as he pleases."[23] Later British sovereigns did the same and, despite a brief return to Roman Catholicism under Mary Tudor between 1553 and 1558, England became a Protestant stronghold. During Elizabeth I's reign, "Puritans" influenced by Calvin worked to "purify" the Church of England (and, later, New England's churches) from all vestiges of "popery," surging to power under the English political leader Oliver Cromwell from 1649 to 1658.

Nonetheless, Anglicanism (or Episcopalianism as it is known in the United States) is, of all the major forms of Protestantism, the closest to Roman Catholicism. **Anglicans** place authority in scripture, tradition, and reason. Anglican churches celebrate Holy Communion every Sunday. Their *Book of Common Prayer* (1548), one of the classics of English prose, has had a major impact on British and American literature.

Radical Reformers

Luther, Calvin, and Henry VIII were all reformers, but none was truly radical. In Geneva, some wanted to outlaw Christmas (as New England Puritans later did), but Calvin allowed it. Luther's gradualism led him to oppose celebrating Mass in German, and Latin also remained the language of worship in England during Henry VIII's lifetime. But one feature of the Reformation (and later of Protestantism itself) was its tendency to spin out radicals.

In Zurich in 1522, the founder of Swiss Protestantism Ulrich Zwingli (1484–1531) defended friends who ate sausages during Lent (when they were supposed to be abstaining from meat). But Zwingli's radicalism, rooted in notions of Christian liberty, went well beyond thumbing his nose at fasting. While other reformers insisted that Christians should simply purge themselves of practices forbidden in the Bible, he said that Christians should practice only what is specifically taught in the Bible. Therefore, he stripped his churches of religious images and organs alike.

Soon Zwingli's critics outdid him. They celebrated Holy Communion in the vernacular. Finding no biblical warrant for infant baptism, they started rebaptizing adults. And finding no biblical warrant for Constantine's marriage of church and state, they pressed for more countercultural Christian communities, called out of and distinct from the state. Soon runaway Protestants were even claiming direct personal revelations from the Holy Spirit, and at times prophesying that the end of the world was around the corner.

As if intent on proving that anarchy was the only sure fruit of the Reformation, Thomas Muntzer marched a peasant army toward the apocalypse, taking on Europe's biggest landowner, the Roman Catholic Church, in Germany in 1524, in what came to be known as the Peasants' War. In a response that demonstrates a conservative strain in the Reformation, Luther published a pamphlet, *Against the Murderous, Thieving Hordes of Peasants* (1525), which in high medieval style sided with the princes and proved in the process that "Christian liberty" would not necessarily translate into political liberty.

Of all the Reformation's radicals, the most enduring and influential were the Anabaptists ("rebaptizers"), who emerged in Zurich in opposition to Zwingli in 1523. Although

Anglicans
Christians, including Episcopalians in the United States, who trace their roots to the founding of the Church of England by King Henry VIII

the Anabaptists were best known for recognizing only the baptisms of adults who made a public confession of faith, it was their insistence on the total separation of church and state that distinguished them from other reformers. As the Anabaptists saw it, Christianity had taken a wrong turn when it became an imperial religion under Constantine. Luther and Calvin had continued down that road by refusing to draw any sharp line between church and state. Many Anabaptists refused to swear oaths, pay tithes, or engage in war. Persecuted by Catholics and Protestants alike and tried by both civil and church courts for sedition and heresy, Anabaptists were executed in both Germany and Switzerland, often (ironically) by drowning.

One group that emerged out of this Anabaptist branch of the Reformation was the Mennonites, followers of the Dutch priest Menno Simons (1496–1561), who along with their Anabaptist kin, the Amish, are visible today in the United States, primarily in rural Ohio, Pennsylvania, and Indiana, where they stand out for their distrust of modern technologies and their commitments to a communal life of simplicity. Another Anabaptist group was the Quakers, who are best known today for their pacifism and for their protests against nuclear arms.

The Reformation and Its Reformations

This splintering of Christianity into Catholics and Protestants, followed by the splintering of Protestants into Lutherans and Calvinists and Anglicans and Anabaptists of all sorts seemed to offer quick proof of the Catholic claim that, once you give up on tradition, it is just anarchy all the way down.

In keeping with Christianity's preoccupation with the doctrinal dimension of religion, these Protestant groups articulated their distinctive theologies through statements such as the Lutherans' Augsburg Confession (1530) and the Calvinists' Westminster Confession (1646), though some heirs of the Radical Reformation, including the Quakers, refused all creeds. These statements of faith revealed fault lines in the emerging Protestant landscape that recalled the radical diversity of the Jesus movement. Protestants disagreed about infant and believer baptism, for example. On the Eucharist, they rejected the Catholic doctrine of **transubstantiation**, which held that this sacrament was a sacrifice in which the priest mysteriously transformed the bread and wine into the body and blood of Christ. Protestants held on to a spectrum of views about what was actually happening to the bread and wine, from Luther's rather conservative affirmation of the "real presence" of Christ's body and blood in the bread and wine to Calvin's view that Christ, while absent from the bread and wine, is "spiritually present" in the Eucharist to Zwingli's insistence that this ritual was a commemoration only. The radically egalitarian Quakers alone took the Protestant principle of the "priesthood of all believers" to its logical conclusion, reducing Catholicism's **seven sacraments** to zero, refusing hierarchical titles of any sort, and running their meetings without any officiant whatsoever.

There were also similarities among the Reformers—enough to justify speaking of *a* Reformation amidst the *Reformations*. Most held on to two sacraments: baptism, because of the example of Jesus's baptism in the Jordan River; and Holy Communion, after Jesus's celebration of the Last Supper. They stressed the sermon over the Eucharist—an emphasis apparent in their church architecture, which drew the eye to the pulpit rather than the altar.

transubstantiation
Roman Catholic doctrine that the bread and wine used in the Mass are ritually transformed into the actual body and blood of Jesus Christ

seven sacraments
central rituals for Roman Catholics and Orthodox Christians, namely, baptism, confirmation (or christmation for the Orthodox), Eucharist (or the Divine Liturgy), confession, anointing of the sick (or holy unction), marriage, and ordination

Protestants have long distinguished themselves from Roman Catholics by emphasizing Bible reading and sermons rather than the Mass during worship. They articulated this preference in church architecture, including at the Old First Church of Bennington, Vermont. Built in 1763, its massive pulpit elevates its preachers up toward its balcony.

Reformers also agreed on a few simple slogans: **sola scriptura** ("scripture alone"), *sola gratia* ("grace alone"), *sola fide* ("faith alone"), and the "priesthood of all believers." They relied on the Bible as the sole authority in matters of doctrine and practice, in contrast to Roman Catholics, who relied on a combination of scripture and church tradition. Because of their belief that all could read the Bible for themselves, reformers championed translations into local languages over the Latin Vulgate Bible of the Roman Catholics. They affirmed that salvation came by grace through faith (and not by works). And they had a democratic understanding of the church that elevated the importance of the laity and undercut the authority of popes and priests alike.

Before the Reformation, the cosmos of Catholics was filled with sacred beings and sacred things. These intermediaries between divinity and humanity—the Virgin Mary and other saints, popes and priests, monks and nuns—had charged lived Catholicism with the stuff of the superhuman. But Protestants emptied the Catholic cosmos, leaving the individual standing alone before God, who now interacted with his people almost exclusively via the Bible and prayer. In doing so, Protestants contributed to the secularization of the modern West, even though they were not secular people. Once you had learned to sneer at Catholic priests, it was easy to sneer at Protestant pastors. And in a world in which relics were for fools, it was not a far leap to seeing the Bible as foolish, too.

Catholic Counter-Reformation

The Roman Catholic response to Luther, Calvin, and company has been understood both as part of the Reformation (the "Catholic Reformation") and as a repudiation of it (the

sola scriptura ("scripture alone")
Protestant Reformation slogan affirming the sole authority of the Bible

The late-sixteenth-century Italian Jesuit priest Matteo Ricci (left) was the first European to enter the Forbidden City in Beijing, China, at the invitation of the emperor. He stands alongside the Chinese Christian convert Paulus Li in this engraving by Athanasius Kircher (1667).

"Counter-Reformation"), perhaps because it was a combination of the two. Since the eighteenth century, however, this movement has been widely known as the Counter-Reformation, since many of its signature moves were designed to "counter" Reformation reforms.

The pivotal moment of the Counter-Reformation was a gathering of Catholic bishops and theologians in northern Italy between 1545 and 1563 at the Council of Trent. This council sought to redefine Catholicism and to reorganize its institutions in a world in which Protestantism was not going away. In a nod to Luther, the council allowed for sermons in vernacular languages and rejected the sale of indulgences. But rather than attempting to co-opt the Protestant Reformation by simply inaugurating reforms of their own, Catholic authorities sharply distinguished Roman Catholicism from its rivals. They reaffirmed the seven sacraments and the Latin Vulgate Bible. Rejecting sola fide and sola gratia, they traced salvation to a combination of works and faith. Rejecting sola scriptura, they reaffirmed the power of the papacy and the importance of tradition in both producing and interpreting scripture. In a schismatic world in which the dream of one church was fading, Catholic leaders tried to project an image of one Catholicism. They also tried to enforce it.

In 1542, the Roman Catholic Church had established a Roman Inquisition (based on the Spanish Inquisition a century earlier). In 1559, this Inquisition published the Index of Forbidden Books, which branded works by Luther and Calvin, and many Bible translations, as heretical.

The Counter-Reformation also produced new religious orders that served as proving grounds for renewed piety, centers of research and education, and launching pads for global missionary activity. The Society of Jesus (or Jesuits, as they are popularly known) epitomized this assertive style of the Counter-Reformation. Established in 1534 by the Basque soldier-saint Ignatius Loyola (1491–1556), the Jesuits devoted themselves to education and preaching. Their quasi-military discipline also put them in the vanguard of global missions.

Roman Catholic efforts to counter the Reformation were only partly successful. In Europe, they regained some lands, though much of that success was due to military rather than missionary effort. As the West lurched toward modernity, the religious landscape on the continent took the shape it still exhibits today, with Catholics controlling much of southern Europe and Protestants dominating in the north.

But the Age of Reformation was also the Age of Discovery, so more than Europe was being divided up. Although Vikings had come to the Americas earlier, Spaniards were the first to leave their mark, via the arrival of Columbus in the Bahamas (which he mistook for East Asia) in 1492. Colonists later split North America into New France and New Spain (both Catholic) and New England (Protestant). Catholics also dominated Central and South America and the Caribbean. Before the Counter-Reformation had come to an end, orders such as the Jesuits, Franciscans, Augustinians, and Dominicans were working with the Spanish and Portuguese governments to establish trade and mission outposts in Asia and Africa as well.

Race-based slavery followed these missionaries almost wherever they went. Colonizers enslaved Native Americans up and down the Americas. In 1501, Spanish settlers brought the first African slaves to the island of Hispanola, which now comprises Haiti and the Dominican Republic. This island soon became a central port in the Atlantic slave trade and, in 1522, the first site of a slave rebellion, over two and a half centuries before the more celebrated Haitian Revolution began in 1791. In the lands that would become the United States, African slavery began with the arrival of nineteen African slaves in Jamestown, Virginia, in 1619. Among slaveholders, views were mixed about the utility of converting slaves to Christianity. Missionaries argued that converted slaves would be more obedient, but slaveholders feared that Christian slaves would demand their freedom and revolt. Slaveholders won this argument, and slave conversions were rare into the nineteenth century.

Wars of Religion and Religious Freedom

Among the tragic effects of the Reformations were the wars of religion that ravaged sixteenth- and seventeenth-century Europe as Roman Catholics and Protestants alike fought and died to impose religious uniformity on the lands they controlled. This carnage included the French Wars of Religion (1562–1598) between Catholics and Protestants, the Thirty Years' War (1618–1648) between Catholics and Protestants in Central Europe, and the English Civil War (1642–1651) between Anglicans and Puritans.

The most obvious effects of these wars were corpses. Germany alone lost a third of its population, and England and Ireland lost more people than they did in World War I. But this bloodshed also produced early inklings of the principle of religious freedom that would come to characterize the modern West. The Edict of Nantes (1598), which ended the French Wars of Religion, gave some measure of religious and civil liberty to the Huguenots in Catholic France. The Peace of Westphalia (1648) that ended the Thirty Years' War harked back to the *cuius regio, eius religio* principle first articulated at the Peace of Augsburg in 1555. Literally translated as "whose realm, his religion," this principle carved Europe up into Catholic, Lutheran, and Calvinist areas of influence. But even as it gave states the power to determine which religion its subjects would observe in public, it also recognized limited religious liberty rights for minorities to worship in the privacy of their own homes. This germ of religious freedom would leap the Atlantic in the seventeenth century and take root in places like Providence Plantation (now Rhode Island), which Baptist Roger Williams (c. 1603–1683) established in 1636 as a safe harbor for religious minorities.

Modern (and Anti-Modern) Christianities

In the monsoon of modernity that followed the Reformation and the wars of religion, Protestants and Catholics alike were buffeted about by the winds of social and intellectual change. The eighteenth-century Enlightenment forced Christians of all sorts to decide whether to ally with science and reason or with the Bible and church tradition. As work shifted from farms to factories, and as young people moved from rural to urban areas, the social solidarity commonplace in villages and small towns (including the solidarity of the local church) also began to erode. Scientific advances in geology and evolutionary biology undercut biblical and clerical authority. These intellectual and social changes divided modern Western Christianity into three camps:

- skeptics, who rejected Christianity in the name of reason;
- anti-modernists, who rejected skepticism in the name of orthodoxy and tradition;
- liberals, who tried to steer a middle path between skepticism and anti-modernism by adapting Christian symbols, beliefs, and practices to modern circumstances.

There was no quick-and-easy split into these camps, however, since the modernity that was being rejected or embraced or mediated shifted with the times and individuals involved. The fact that many vehemently anti-modern religious groups eagerly embraced certain aspects of modernity—think fundamentalist radio shows and Pentecostals "searching for Eden with a satellite dish"—further complicated things.[24] So did the rise of nationalism and the nation-state. In theory, nationalism posed a challenge to the primacy of Christianity in Europe. But any tensions that might have arisen between God and monarch were soothed by the fact that church and state worked hand in glove there: to be French was to be Catholic; to be German was to be Lutheran. So Europe's new nations were legitimized by the same denominations that legitimized them.

The boldest critique of modernism was the *Syllabus of Errors*, issued in 1864 by Pius IX, Roman Catholicism's longest-running pope. A rhetorical blast against the high crimes and misdemeanors of the modern world, this document can be confusing to read. Instead of cataloging propositions the Catholic hierarchy holds to be true, it lists modernity's errors from 1 to 80, concluding with an unapologetic condemnation of the view that "the Roman pontiff can and should be reconciled with, and agree to, progress, liberalism, and modern civilization."[25]

The *Syllabus of Errors* defended miracles and divine revelation. It refused to bow down to rationalism or to privilege matter over spirit. It dismissed communism and socialism as "pests." It asserted the primacy of theology over philosophy and the primacy of Roman Catholicism—"the only true religion"—over Protestantism. Unlike Protestant anti-modernists who focused on the authority of the Bible, it focused largely on the authority of the church—its temporal power, its right to property, its right to oversee marriage. To that end, the *Syllabus* rejected religious freedom, freedom of the press, public schools, and the separation of church and state.

Pius IX later convened the First Vatican Council of 1869–1870, which pronounced papal infallibility to be "a divinely revealed dogma." This dogma did not mean that everything a pope said was true. But it did allow a pope to speak infallibly under certain rare circumstances, namely, when he "speaks EX CATHEDRA, that is, when, in the exercise of his office as shepherd and teacher of all Christians, in virtue of his supreme apostolic authority, he defines a doctrine regarding faith or morals to be held by the whole church."[26]

CHRISTIANITY IN THE UNITED STATES

The American Revolution overthrew not only England's King George III but also this long-standing model of church-state establishment. According to the terms of the First Amendment to the U.S. Constitution, the federal government was not to interfere with the religious liberty of its citizens; neither was it to establish any one religion as the nation's own. Many antidisestablishmentarians (those who said "no" to separating church and state) feared that this new model would kill religion in America. Instead, it made for a fiercely faithful population pursuing an ever-increasing number of religious (and spiritual) options.

Deists, Unitarians, and Other Skeptics

Although favored by many of America's founders, **Deists** emerged in sixteenth-century England, offering an alternative to the dogmas of Christianity and other religions of revelation. All we need to know about God and the afterlife, Deists argued, comes to us naturally, by reason alone. As reason is common to all human beings, religion is universal. Revelation is unnecessary and no one religion enjoys a monopoly on truth. Deists did not always practice the religious tolerance they preached, however. The French Deist Voltaire (1694–1778) described his hateful play *Mahomet* (1736) as written "against the founder of a religion false and barbarous." Elsewhere, he accused Jews of peddling "impertinent fables" and engaging in "bad conduct and in barbarism."[27]

Though Deists rejected the Trinity and described Jesus as simply a great moral teacher, they were not atheists. Inspired by the English physicist Isaac Newton, who saw the universe as a machine, they imagined God as a watchmaker who created the universe and wound it up, only to let it run on its own, without the interference of miracles. Deists affirmed that this distant deity should be worshiped. They also affirmed afterlife rewards and punishments.

One great Deist thinker was the English writer and American hero Thomas Paine (1737–1809). His *Common Sense* (1776) spurred North American colonists to declare their independence from England. As if to prove he could provoke in both politics and religion, Paine also wrote *Age of Reason* (1794), a Deist broadside against Christianity (a "strange fable"), theology ("the study of nothing"), and the Bible ("the word of a demon"). Like Voltaire, Paine was an equal-opportunity skeptic who saw all religions as "human inventions set up to terrify and enslave mankind, and monopolize power and profit."[28]

This culture of religious doubt made deep inroads in the late eighteenth century among intellectuals in England, France, Germany, and the United States. In fact, the first three U.S. presidents—George Washington, John Adams, and Thomas Jefferson—were either card-carrying Deists or sympathetic to the movement. In France, beginning in 1789, a more radical doubt fueled the French Revolution, in which the thought of Voltaire and other philosophes combined with more popular calls for *liberté, égalité,* and *fraternité* (liberty, equality, and brotherhood) to end monarchy and upend Roman Catholicism. The French republic did not stop at withdrawing support from Catholic priests and parishes, however. In a massive push toward de-Christianization, it seized land from the Roman Catholic Church, which was at the time France's largest landowner. It destroyed crucifixes, statues, and other Church property. In the name of a secular public square, France's revolutionaries pushed Catholicism out of earshot and out of sight, forbidding the ringing of church bells and public processions of saints. In the bloody chaos of the Reign of Terror that brought the guillotine down on the necks of King Louis XVI and Marie Antoinette, hundreds of priests and nuns were executed by the state or murdered by mobs.

Far less radical than these French revolutionaries were the **Unitarians**, whose creed has been described as "the fatherhood of God, the brotherhood of man, and the neighborhood

Deists
people who believe that God is like a watchmaker who creates the world and then simply observes its activities without intervening

Unitarians
Christians who reject the doctrines of original sin, the Trinity, and the divinity of Jesus; the Unitarian Universalist Association now includes both Christians and non-Christians

During the French Revolution, anti-Catholic revolutionaries sought to eliminate all vestiges of religion from their new republic. This 1871 engraving depicts the execution of Monsignor Carboy, the bishop of Paris, by a revolutionary mob.

of Boston." Though Unitarians are now associated with early-nineteenth-century Boston, they drew on sixteenth-century criticisms of the Trinity by radical Protestant reformers such as Michael Servetus of Spain and Faustus Socinus of Italy. Their rejection of the divinity of Jesus in the name of the unity of God lent the Unitarians their name. But their defining feature was their rejection of original sin, and with it the theory that Jesus's death on the cross was a ransom paid to an angry God.

A protracted "Unitarian Controversy" roiled New England Protestants beginning in 1805, splitting the Congregationalist denomination into **Congregationalists** who continued to affirm the Trinity and Unitarians who did not. That controversy ended in 1825 with Harvard firmly in the Unitarian camp and the newly formed American Unitarian Association emerging in 1825 under the leadership of William Ellery Channing (1780–1842). The "Luther of Boston," Channing combined liberal theology with work for social justice (in his case, antislavery reform), as many Unitarians do today.

Finding even Channing's theology insufficiently radical, some Unitarians followed Ralph Waldo Emerson and Henry David Thoreau into Transcendentalism, a post-Protestant spiritual, literary, and political movement influenced by German Romanticism and Asian religions. Transcendentalists found God less in church than in nature—on morning walks in the woods and during dips in Walden Pond. In his famous "Divinity School Address," delivered at Harvard in 1838, Emerson called for a new form of religion that harkened less to the secondhand authority of bibles and ministers and more to the God within: "Yourself

Congregationalists
Protestants who insisted on the independence of each congregation. Dominant in New England beginning in the colonial period, they are now active in the United States in the United Church of Christ.

a newborn bard of the Holy Ghost—cast behind you all conformity, and acquaint men at first hand with Deity."[29]

The Evangelical Century

In 1822, in the midst of the Unitarian Controversy, President Thomas Jefferson prophesied that Unitarianism would sweep the nation. "There is not a young man now living in the U.S.," he wrote a friend, "who will not die a Unitarian."[30] Jefferson was wrong. By the time Jefferson himself died—on July 4, 1826, the same day that claimed the life of his rival, President John Adams—American Christians were becoming more conservative, not more liberal. Evangelicalism was replacing Puritanism as America's dominant religious impulse and was spreading rapidly in England as well.

The historian David Bebbington has defined evangelicalism in terms of four distinguishing marks:

- the conversion experience (conversionism)
- the divine inspiration of the Bible (biblicism)
- the doctrine of Jesus's atoning death on the cross (crucicentrism)
- the missionary and evangelistic effort (activism)[31]

During the early nineteenth century, this retort to Deism and Unitarianism flowered into a powerful grassroots movement that spread throughout North America and the British Isles.

Evangelicals trace their roots to the "Grand Itinerant" George Whitefield, an Anglican clergyman (and former actor) from England, who made seven trips to the colonies between 1739 and 1770. Whitefield's booming voice enabled him to preach to crowds as large as twenty or thirty thousand, prompting conversions up and down North America's eastern seaboard. The reach of this eighteenth-century "Great Awakening," as it came to be called, provided a sense of a collective "us" among colonists, preparing the way, according to many historians, for the American Revolution. It also produced Jonathan Edwards, a Congregationalist minister from Northampton, Massachusetts, and one of America's most influential thinkers, as well as many of the techniques of revivalism, which emphasizes heartfelt preaching, urgent calls to repentance, and emotional conversions.

Participants in the first Great Awakening interpreted their revivals as (in Edwards's words) "surprising work[s] of God."[32] In keeping with the Puritan emphasis on divine sovereignty, they saw God as the author of the Great Awakening and its conversions. The Second Great Awakening of the early nineteenth century was different. Evangelicals read its revivals as the not-so-surprising works of human beings who had rejected the predestination theology of the Puritans in favor of a theology more in keeping with the aspirations of a rising middle class. Arminianism, as this theology was called (after Calvin's Dutch critic Jacobus Arminius), granted to all sinners the free will to determine their own destinies by accepting or rejecting the saving grace of Jesus.

Nineteenth-century revivalism also diverged sharply from the heartfelt but orderly piety of colonial revivals, which had typically featured ministerial elites reading learned sermons from carefully prepared texts. In keeping with the rebelliousness of the American Revolution and the egalitarian age of Andrew Jackson, who served as president from 1829 to 1837, the firebrand evangelists of the Second Great Awakening defied authority, aristocracy, and tradition. Glorying in their lack of formal education, they made up their soulful

evangelicals
Protestants who emphasize conversion, biblical inspiration, the atoning death of Jesus, and Christian activism

Methodists
Protestants, classically evangelicals, who trace their roots to John and Charles Wesley and emphasize the power of the Holy Spirit to change lives

sermons on the spot and gesticulated wildly. ("When I hear a man preach," Abraham Lincoln said, "I like to see him act as if he were fighting bees."[33]) But the entertainments of these "divine dramatists" were more than matched by the spiritual ecstasies of their audiences—orgies of sobbing, shouting, laughing, singing, dancing, and in some cases falling to the ground like the dead and jerking spasmodically—that seemed to augur not only a "new birth" but also a new America. "Increasingly assertive common people wanted their leaders unpretentious, their doctrines self-evident and down-to-earth, their music lively and singable, and their churches in local hands," writes church historian Nathan Hatch.[34] The "religious entrepreneurs" of the Second Great Awakening met that demand.

In its earliest phases, this "transatlantic revivalism" was exported from England to the United States by Methodists. Led by the Anglican clergymen John and Charles Wesley, who founded this movement in 1738, **Methodists** began as Church of England reformers but in the 1790s became their own denomination. They pushed for a more devotional faith focused on prayer, Bible study, and a personal relationship with Jesus Christ. Upsetting traditional hierarchies of race, class, and gender, they sent uneducated traveling preachers known as "circuit riders" out on horseback to win souls. They also encouraged slaves and women to win people to Christ. Though often dated from an 1801 Cane Ridge, Kentucky, revival that Methodist evangelist Peter Cartwright termed the greatest outpouring of the Holy Spirit since the Day of Pentecost, America's Second Great Awakening had precursors in rural revivals in Connecticut and New Hampshire in the late 1790s. It burned hottest at camp meetings in the South and West, but wherever it went it reflected the rough-and-tumble society of the expanding frontier.

The camp meeting revivals of the Second Great Awakening of the mid-nineteenth century combined open-air locales with passionate and lively preaching. This lively lithograph by Alexander Rider portrays women fainting and falling down in response to a preacher's rousing sermon.

Methodists did not have a monopoly on revivalism, however. It was also practiced by **Baptists** and Presbyterians and a host of new denominations including the Disciples of Christ. Charles Finney (1792–1875), a country lawyer turned Presbyterian minister who perfected new techniques for winning souls, viewed the revival as a human technique rather than a divine gift. As he argued his case for Christ, Finney developed several "new measures." He allowed women to pray in public. And he used the protracted meeting (measured in days, not hours), the altar call, and the "anxious bench" (where potential converts could agonize over the state of their souls) to spark the emotional crises that would inspire conversions. While his ability to light spiritual fires under citizens in central and western New York gave that region the nickname the "Burned-Over District," Finney led revivals in eastern cities as well, including Philadelphia, New York, and Boston.

Baptists
Protestants, classically evangelicals, who insist on adult baptism by immersion and the independence of local congregations

The Second Great Awakening was perfectly suited to circumstances in a new nation where authority was suspect, equality was valued over order, and the First Amendment had made religion a matter of individual choice. But it also transformed American society. It shuffled the denominational pecking order of the United States, vaulting Methodists and Baptists to the top and pushing the more reserved Episcopalians and Congregationalists down. It spurred the development of a wide variety of nondenominational voluntary associations dedicated to making America Christian again. Some of the groups in this "benevolent empire," including the American Bible Society, the American Tract Society, and the American Sunday School Union, focused on spreading the gospel. Others, such as the American Anti-Slavery Society, focused on social questions, almost always taking the progressive side. The new revivalism also rapidly expanded church membership, which doubled from 17 percent at the start of the Revolution to 34 percent in 1850. And it diversified American Christianity, chiefly by bringing huge numbers of African American converts into the fold.

Earlier, Americans had taken the gospel to Native Americans—a fact attested in paper and glue by the Algonquian Indian Bible published by the English missionary John Eliot in 1663, the first Bible to be printed in North America. And there were fitful early efforts to convert slaves in the colonial and early national periods, with one black preacher, freeman Harry Hosier, being lauded by founding father Benjamin Rush as "the greatest orator in America."[35] But African Americans did not convert in large numbers until the Second Great Awakening, whose "new measures" echoed some West African religious traditions and did not require the ability to read, which was typically withheld from slaves. Initially, black converts often worshiped with whites. Eventually, they formed their churches and even their own denominations, beginning with the African Methodist Episcopal Church, founded by Richard Allen in Philadelphia in 1816. Among the members of Allen's Philadelphia congregation was Jarena Lee, the first African American woman to write her biography and one of the first American women to become a preacher.

Ironically, the Second Great Awakening also contributed to Americans' religious illiteracy, by shifting the focus of Protestantism from doctrine and intellect to experience and the emotions. Though more Americans came to see the Bible as the inspired word of God, fewer and fewer seemed interested in knowing what God had to say. Increasingly anti-intellectual, evangelicals boasted of their homespun ignorance, turning American Protestantism into a faith that emphasized the heart over the brain. In this way, a nation of evangelicals became a "nation of forgetters"—an outcome the bookish Puritans would have found devilish.[36]

This "evangelical century" was by no means confined to the United States. British revivalists preached in the United States, and American revivalists preached in the British Isles. Also crisscrossing the Atlantic were evangelical books such as Finney's *Lectures on Revivals* (1835), which threw fuel on the fire of a Welsh revival in the early 1840s. Evangelicalism also took Canada by storm. Between 1815 and 1915, the Christian portion of the U.S. population jumped from about 25 percent to roughly 40 percent, but growth in Canada was even more dramatic—from about one-fifth of all Canadians to roughly one-half.

The enthusiasm of the revivals in the United States, Canada, and the British Isles also spilled over into a vast missionary movement that took evangelicalism to Asia and Africa and beyond. As early as 1812, the American Board of Commissioners for Foreign Missions (est. 1810) dispatched missionaries to India. British missionaries followed their colonial administrators wherever the sun rose on the British empire. Later in the nineteenth century, as an increasingly muscular America took territory of its own overseas, Americans redoubled their missionary efforts, leading the Methodist layman John Mott in 1900 to prophesy (overly optimistically) "the evangelism of the world in this generation."[37]

Mormonism and Other Communitarian Experiments

The Second Great Awakening made the nation not only more evangelical but also more religiously diverse. Among the flowers in the "antebellum spiritual hothouse" were a series of communitarian experiments.[38] The Millerites, so named after their leader William Miller, attempted to forecast the return of Jesus down to the precise day. After the "Great Disappointment" of October 22, 1844 (the day Miller predicted the world would end), many Millerites shrugged their shoulders and went on with their lives. Others argued that Jesus *had* returned . . . spiritually. Their Adventist movement (from "advent," or the Second Coming of Jesus Christ) produced a long list of new denominations, including the Seventh-Day Adventist Church, founded by the visionary Ellen White in 1863 and now best known for practicing the Sabbath on Saturday.

The Restorationists, in contrast, aspired to re-create the "pure, primitive Christianity" of the early church. The most prominent Restorationist group was the Christian Church (Disciples of Christ), now one of America's mainline Protestant denominations. Like other Restorationists, the Disciples of Christ (who preferred to call themselves, simply, "Christians") tried to stop the multiplication of competing Christianities by uniting all Christians under one banner tied to the Bible and the model of the early church. Alas, America's Christians could not agree on how to read the Bible or reanimate the early church, so they ended up adding yet another denomination to the mix.

Mormons, the most successful new religious group in U.S. history, also began their movement as a response to the problem of religious diversity. As a teenager living in Manchester, New York, in the "Burned-Over District," Joseph Smith Jr. (1805–1844) was, in his own words, "exceedingly distressed" by all the religious possibilities swirling around him. Methodists, Baptists, and Presbyterians had stirred up "an unusual excitement on the subject of religion," accompanied by "great confusion and bad feeling" all around, but Smith had no way to determine "who was right and who was wrong."[39]

One day he went into the woods and knelt down in prayer, begging God to show him "which of all the sects was right, that I might know which to join."[40] None of the above, God replied, and soon Smith was on a hill in upstate New York digging up ancient tablets that, when translated, would become the Book of Mormon. This "new testament of Jesus

Mormons
members of the Church of Jesus Christ of Latter-day Saints, founded by Joseph Smith Jr. and now headquartered in Salt Lake City, Utah

Christ," which recounts how Jesus founded his true church in North America shortly after his resurrection, became the calling card of the Church of Jesus Christ of Latter-day Saints (popularly known as the Mormons), which now claims sixteen million followers worldwide.

The most persecuted religious group in American history, Mormons were driven by critics from New York to Ohio to Missouri to Illinois, where their founder and his brother, Hyrum Smith, were dragged from prison and murdered by an anti-Mormon mob. Their second president, the "American Moses" Brigham Young (1801–1877), then led the Mormons on a long exodus to the wilderness of the western territory of Utah, where the Church of Jesus Christ of Latter-day Saints now maintains its international headquarters in Salt Lake City.

Anti-Mormons objected first to Smith as a fake and the Book of Mormon as a forgery. Later, they fixated on the Mormon practices of polygamy and theocracy, a system of governance in which religious leaders and political leaders are one and the same. Critics likened Mormons to Catholics with their own pope, and to Muslims with their own Quran. They also likened Brigham Young, who had fifty-five wives, to Muhammad because of their shared practice of polygamy. State and federal governments also mobilized against them. Presidents attacked them in state-of-the-union addresses. Missouri's governor issued an order to exterminate them. The U.S. Army was dispatched to Utah to subdue them. The Supreme Court decided that their religious liberty was guaranteed when it came to beliefs but not to actions. And both the Senate and the House refused to seat duly elected Mormon members of Congress.

In 1890, a Mormon manifesto banned polygamy and theocracy, paving the way for Utah statehood six years later. In the 1920s, movies and magazine articles started to depict Mormons more favorably, and today they are widely described as "quintessential Americans" who run for president, serve in Congress, captain football teams, write bestselling novels, wear the Miss America crown, and win on *Jeopardy!*, *American Idol*, and *Dancing with the Stars*.[41]

Located in Salt Lake City, Utah, the Salt Lake Temple is the largest temple of the Church of Jesus Christ of Latter-day Saints. Dedicated in 1893, it is a site for baptisms, marriages, and other rituals.

Liberal Protestantism

The world the revivals made gave way in the late nineteenth century to what is known as liberal Christianity. In both Europe and North America, Christians had been in conflict since the eighteenth-century Enlightenment. More rational "Old Lights" criticized the emotional revivals of the "New Lights" as threats to traditional churchgoing, disturbers of social order, dangerous anti-intellectualism, and triumphs of popular entertainment over genuine faith. But liberal Protestantism came into its own in Germany, beginning with "the father of modern Protestant theology" Friedrich Schleiermacher (1768–1834). Many of his friends had left the church because they could no longer believe in the Bible or recite the creeds. Schleiermacher responded by shifting the focus of Protestant theology from dogma to experience—from teachings about God to how the divine manifests in our daily lives. Drawing on German Romanticism, which had seasoned Enlightenment rationalism with a heavy dose of emotion, intuition, and the imagination, he emphasized the experiential dimension of Christianity. Religion was not fundamentally about doctrine or philosophy or ethics, Schleiermacher argued in *On Religion: Speeches to Its Cultured Despisers* (1799). The essence of religion is subjective and emotional—"the feeling of an absolute dependence." Out of that feeling, the "opinions, dogmas, and usages" of all religions proceed. But these secondhand formulations are external to genuine religion. So if you despise them, he told the "cultured despisers," what you despise is not religion itself.[42]

These early voices swelled in the late-nineteenth-century United States when liberal Protestantism displaced evangelicalism as the dominant impulse in American religion. Drawing on both the scientific and rationalist philosophies of the eighteenth-century Enlightenment and the valuing of individual experience associated in the early nineteenth century with Romanticism, Christians in the United States increasingly found truth in reason and experience as well as scripture and doctrine. Convinced that the new cry for freedom in things political must echo in things religious, they worked to adapt their faith to new discoveries in science and new social circumstances. Too traditional for skeptics and too radical for evangelicals, liberals found a middle way. Or, as historian Gary Dorrien put it, they cut "a faithful, but critical path between the literalistic dogmatism of Christian orthodoxy and the antireligious dogmatism of modern rationalism."[43]

Liberal Protestants did not always agree on how to adapt, or even on what they were supposed to be adapting *to*. Nonetheless, a few generalizations can be made. Liberals dismantled both the church authority of Catholics and the biblical authority of evangelicals, heeding instead the inner authority of reason and experience. They read the Bible more metaphorically than literally, emphasizing "the spirit" of a passage over the letter of the law. Cringing at dogma, they saw the divine as immanent (down here) rather than transcendent (up there), and human beings as basically good. Like evangelicals, they set their eyes on Jesus, but they emphasized his career as a rabbi over the Passion, his moral teachings over his crucifixion. Liberals also focused on this world rather than the next, aiming at the improvement of society over the salvation of the individual. And they were doggedly optimistic that those improvements would lead to social progress.

Liberal religion was not confined to Protestantism, however. Liberal Catholics in the United States pushed back against papal infallibility just as liberal Protestants pushed back against biblical infallibility. Liberal religion was not limited to Christianity either. Reform Judaism is a form of religious liberalism, as are the many metaphysical movements that offer healing and therapy by harmonizing the energies of the individual and the cosmos. Still, liberal religion was strongest, most visible, and most influential among liberal Protestants in the United States and Europe.

Evangelical Protestantism lost ground to liberal Protestantism in the late-nineteenth-century United States for intellectual and social reasons. In the realm of ideas, the "acids of modernity" eating away at the old evangelical orthodoxy included biblical criticism, the new sciences (geology and evolutionary biology), and comparative religion.[44] Biblical critics called into question Moses's authorship of the biblical books of the Pentateuch (Genesis, Exodus, Leviticus, Numbers, and Deuteronomy). More important, they demonstrated to many that the words of the Bible issued not from the mind of one God but from different humans with contradictory viewpoints. The new geology, which dated fossils by the billions of years, challenged biblical accounts of the creation of the universe in just six days (plus one of rest). *On the Origin of Species* (1859) and *The Descent of Man* (1871) by

Charles Darwin (1809–1882) called into question the Adam and Eve story by presenting an alternative narrative in which *homo sapiens* gradually evolved out of apes. Meanwhile, pioneers in comparative religion undercut traditional divisions of the world's religions into two categories—the true religion of Christians and the false religions of everyone else—by finding beauty and truth in the Daodejing and other "Sacred Books of the East."

The massive changes brought on by industrialization, urbanization, and immigration were also unsettling. As laborers moved from farms to cities and from milking cows to milling cotton, the norms, values, and habits once inculcated in small towns and local churches rarely moved with them intact. Increasingly, the values of consumer capitalism—of spending and self-expression rather than saving and self-denial—stepped in to fill the void. Rapid immigration further complicated matters, by bringing Catholics and Jews into the country in massive numbers and threatening to reduce Protestant beliefs and practices to local folkways.

The American Civil War also liberalized American religion. Long before this war broke out in 1861, many Protestant denominations had split North/South over the issue of slavery. As citizens continued to debate this question, both sides turned to scripture for an answer. By most commonsense readings, the Bible seemed to be pro-slavery. The Old Testament regulates it, and in his letters Paul writes, "Slaves obey your masters" (Eph. 6:5; Col. 3:22). Thanks to Harriet Beecher Stowe's *Uncle Tom's Cabin* (1852), which rivals *Common Sense* as the most influential book in U.S. history, Northerners increasingly came to see slavery as America's original sin. In the end, the Bible was unable to provide

Eliza escaping across the Ohio

In one of the most climactic scenes in Harriet Beecher Stowe's novel, *Uncle Tom's Cabin* (1852), Eliza, a slave, is cheered on by her family as she flees to freedom by crossing the Ohio River with her newborn baby. This illustration by Florence Maplestone appears in the 1891 publication of the book.

Social Gospel
liberal Protestant movement that saw sin and salvation as social and worked to address structural injustice

an answer to the slavery question, which was settled only by force of arms. According to historian Mark Noll, the Civil War precipitated a "theological crisis" that undermined the authority of the Bible and of evangelical ways of reading it.[45] Americans increasingly came to see this "Book of Books" as one book among many.

One way out of this mess was to give up on religion altogether. Liberal Protestants adapted their faith instead, starting with a more metaphorical approach to the Bible that sought after the "spirit" rather than the "letter" of its words. Perhaps the Genesis account of creation in six days was not supposed to be read literally. Perhaps, as the American historian John Fiske put it, evolution is God's way of doing things. Liberal Protestants accommodated themselves to new socioeconomic realities by casting Jesus as a progressive and pushing for social reforms. In his bestseller *In His Steps* (1897), the Congregationalist pastor Charles Sheldon described how society would change radically for the better if only people would stop and ask, "What would Jesus do?" The gospel of this carpenter Christ, he argued, was as relevant to textile workers in the mills of Lowell, Massachusetts, as it was to fishermen in ancient Galilee.

A movement now referred to as the **Social Gospel** brought ethics to the fore in liberal Protestant theology. Rooted in the Salvation Army founded by William and Catherine Booth in East London in 1865, it flowered in the United States thanks to Social Gospel ministers such as Congregationalist Washington Gladden (1836–1918) of Columbus, Ohio, and Walter Rauschenbusch (1861–1918), who served as a Baptist pastor on the rough streets of Manhattan's Hell's Kitchen neighborhood. Taking cues from the Hebrew Bible prophets—"the beating heart of the Old Testament," according to Rauschenbusch—and from Jesus as he appears in the Gospel of Luke (which shows a decided preference for the poor over the rich), Social Gospelers argued that sin and salvation were social. The human predicament was not original sin. It was injustice and oppression, whose ill effects were expanding with the economic inequalities of the Gilded Age. Setting aside the goal of "personal religion" (to save souls) for "social religion" (the "kingdom of God on earth"), these progressive Protestants pushed for a living wage, a six-day work week, and an end to child labor. "Religion and ethics are inseparable," wrote Rauschenbusch, and "ethical conduct is the supreme and sufficient religious act."[46]

The Social Gospel movement found institutional expression with the founding of the Federal Council of Churches (later renamed the National Council of Churches) in 1908. Some scholars credit the success of the New Deal of the 1930s to the pathbreaking work done by Social Gospelers decades earlier.

Roman Catholicism's Americanist Controversy

Many American Catholics also said yes to modernity, though their affirmation pushed up against the authority of the church rather than the authority of the Bible. The aggressive anti-modernism of the late-nineteenth-century Roman Catholic hierarchy meant trouble for liberal Catholics, who were struggling after the Civil War to prove, in the face of fierce anti-Catholicism, that good Catholics could also be good Americans. From the colonial period forward, Protestant nativists had argued that the United States was and ought to remain a Protestant Christian nation. And they had focused their ire primarily on Roman Catholics, whom they saw as immoral and antidemocratic purveyors of false doctrine. Now, thanks to the *Syllabus of Errors* and the First Vatican Council, the papacy seemed to be going out of its way to prove, as nativists had argued for decades, that Catholicism and Americanism were incompatible. But as Irish and German Catholic immigrants were settling in American cities and striving to demonstrate their allegiance to their new nation, liberal Catholics in the United States pushed for an understanding of their faith consistent with such American ideals as religious tolerance and church/state separation.

A cadre of progressive priests—led by Cardinal James Gibbons of Baltimore; Archbishop John Ireland of Saint Paul, Minnesota; and John Keane, rector of Catholic University of America—came to be called "Americanists" for their efforts to assimilate these new immigrants into public schools and trade unions and to create one English-speaking Catholic culture in the United States. "The Church in America must be, of course, as Catholic as in Jerusalem or Rome; but so far as her garments may be colored to suit environment, she must be American," Ireland said. Keane added, "This is the era of democracy, the day of absolute government is over."[47]

In *Testem Benevolentiae* (1899), Pope Leo XIII condemned "Americanism" without pointing the finger at any particular Americanists. Insofar as there were American Catholics who thought that the Roman Catholic Church should adapt its essential beliefs and practices to American Protestant norms, or to American democracy, they should abandon such thinking, he proclaimed. Instead of joining this fight, Cardinal Gibbons took the out that the Vatican was obviously offering him, reassuring Leo XIII that no Catholics in America held such views. Americanism today is thus referred to as a "phantom heresy."

Fundamentalism

Protestant **fundamentalists** are often confused with evangelicals, and these two groups do have much in common. Both emphasize the Bible, conversion, atonement, and missionizing. Both criticize efforts to modernize Christianity. But the two groups are different. While evangelicalism was an early-nineteenth-century transatlantic response to the culture of doubt spreading across Europe and the United States, fundamentalism was a twentieth-century American response to the rise of liberal Protestantism. Fundamentalists claimed simply to be holding fast to the eternal truths of an ancient faith, but they, too, employed modern technologies such as radio and television to serve their cause.

The birth announcement for fundamentalism came in the form of a series of books on Christianity's fundamental truths called *The Fundamentals*. Published between 1910 and 1915, these twelve paperback volumes were conceived in Los Angeles by the oil tycoon Lyman Stewart and authored in Chicago by a group of writers assembled by the newspaper columnist A. C. Dixon. Thanks to Stewart, three million free copies were sent to ministers, missionaries, and theology students and professors.

The Fundamentals defended fundamentalist Christianity against its liberal despisers. Individual essays defended the "five fundamentals":

1. biblical infallibility
2. the virgin birth
3. the atonement
4. the resurrection of Jesus
5. the miracles of Jesus

The Fundamentals also attacked a host of secular and heretical "isms," including "Romanism," Darwinism, Mormonism, Spiritualism, and Modernism. In a not-so-subtle effort to distinguish themselves from Social Gospel advocates, the authors barely mentioned ethics

fundamentalists
modern Protestants who reject biblical criticism and evolutionary theory and interpret the Bible literally. Though fervently opposed to modernity, they have creatively employed modern technologies, including radio, television, and the Internet.

or politics. The overarching goal was to assert the perfection of scripture, which fundamentalists referred to as "inerrancy." The Bible, one author proclaimed, is "a Book dropped out of heaven," and science had erred by dismissing the possibility of the miraculous.[48]

To evangelical ears, none of this news was earth shattering. But the fundamentalists did differ significantly yet subtly from their evangelical elders. For example, fundamentalists gravitated toward "dispensational premillennialism," a perplexing theology that (1) explained historical change by carving time up into different "dispensations" in the human/divine drama and (2) predicted that Jesus would return before lording over the world for a thousand years. Whereas evangelicals typically called the Bible divinely inspired, fundamentalists asserted its inerrancy and insisted that even its poetry should be interpreted literally.

The most important differences between evangelicals and fundamentalists came down to style and temperament. Evangelicalism had emerged in a Puritan world already sympathetic to many of its beliefs and practices, and in the aftermath of the Second Great Awakening the voluntary associations led by evangelicals were able to steer American society in its direction. Fundamentalists, who came along roughly a century later, saw themselves as a besieged religious minority in an increasingly secular society. America was never theirs as it had been for their evangelical kin. As a result, fundamentalists tended to draw sharper boundaries between themselves and the rest of American society. Their intolerance was unconcealed, and their anti-Catholicism sharper than that of evangelicals. Like strictly Orthodox Jews, they typically refused to attend secular colleges. (Evangelicals, by contrast, were more like modern Orthodox Jews, whose model was to engage rather than withdraw from secular society.) Fundamentalists also refused to extend a hand of fellowship to liberal Christians. In *Christianity and Liberalism* (1923), the Princeton theologian J. Gresham Machen drew a sharp line between authentic Christianity and "un-Christian" liberalism. "Despite the liberal use of traditional phraseology, modern liberalism not only is a different religion from Christianity but belongs in a totally different class of religions," Machen wrote.[49] In other words, while modern liberals were free to believe whatever they wanted, they ought to have the decency not to try to pawn themselves off as Christians.

Both evangelicals and fundamentalists saw Christianity as a body of doctrine that had to be defended against unbelievers, but evangelical rhetoric tended to be more measured and the temperaments of evangelicals more calm. An evangelical, it is sometimes said, is a fundamentalist who plays well with others. A fundamentalist, as church historian George Marsden put it, is "an evangelical who is angry about something"—a culture warrior in the making.[50]

Of Monkeys and Modernists

The Fundamentals did not go unanswered, of course. In 1922, the Baptist pastor and activist Harry Emerson Fosdick (1878–1969) ascended his pulpit at Manhattan's First Presbyterian Church and preached a sermon against fundamentalism called "Shall the Fundamentalists Win?" His answer was no and his reasons were many. According to Fosdick, fundamentalism was an "illiberal and intolerant" ideology whose dogmas were incredible or antiquated or both. But Fosdick's main objection was to fundamentalist attempts to banish liberals like himself from the Christian community. Real Christianity, he insisted, was "intellectually hospitable, open-minded, liberty-loving, fair, tolerant."[51]

A Christian protest sign points back at the statue of lawyer Clarence Darrow outside the Rhea County Courthouse in Dayton, Tennessee, the site of the controversial Scopes "Monkey Trial" in 1925.

In a countermove to Lyman Stewart's backing of *The Fundamentals*, the businessman and philanthropist John D. Rockefeller paid to print and distribute 130,000 copies of Fosdick's classic sermon. Then he did Stewart one better, by building Fosdick a gothic cathedral, Manhattan's Riverside Church, which to this day serves as a national center for liberal Protestantism and the Social Gospel.

In 1925, the fundamentalist/modernist controversy shifted from Princeton and New York City to Dayton, Tennessee, where a judge and a jury were considering whether John Scopes had violated state law by teaching evolution in Rhea County High School. The first of many "trials of the century," this "Monkey Trial" pitted the Democratic icon and fundamentalist William Jennings Bryan against the crusader for secularism Clarence Darrow. In the trial's surprise climax, Darrow called Bryan to the witness stand and seemed to best him in a barrage of questions about Genesis. (Was Eve literally created out of Adam's rib? Where did their son Cain get his wife?) It is often forgotten that the fundamentalists won this case—it took the jury just nine minutes to find Scopes guilty—but they lost in the court of public opinion, where they continue to be stereotyped as anti-intellectual country bumpkins.

Neo-Orthodoxy

You didn't have to be a fundamentalist to find Protestant liberalism wanting, of course. The horrors of World War I, the Great Depression, and the totalitarianism that followed exposed liberal Protestantism and liberalism itself as hopelessly naïve about both human nature and social progress.

Neo-orthodox theologians, led by the Swiss Reformed thinker Karl Barth (1886–1968), reemphasized God's sovereignty and human sinfulness, underscoring the "infinite qualitative distinction" between humanity and divinity. Refusing both facile fundamentalism and easy liberalism, they reaffirmed the fact of revelation without lapsing into simplistic interpretations of the Bible. As the principal author of the Barmen Declaration (1934), Barth joined other anti-Nazi Christians in denouncing both Nazi theology and the German Christians who pledged their allegiance to Adolf Hitler. Together they paved the way for Christians who later joined the resistance to the Nazi regime.

Neo-orthodox theology exerted a strong influence on American Protestant thought through the German American ethicists Reinhold Niebuhr (1892–1971) and his younger brother H. Richard Niebuhr (1894–1962). In his widely quoted summary of liberal Protestantism—"A God without wrath brought men without sin into a kingdom without judgment through the ministrations of a Christ without a cross"—H. Richard made plain how far that tradition had fallen short in his view of Bible teachings about divinity, Christ, sin, and salvation.[52] Reinhold's "Christian realism," which attended with care to human sin and unintended consequences, had a profound impact on American foreign policy realism, so much so that President Barack Obama called him "one of my favorite philosophers."[53]

Theologies of Liberation and the Religious Right

The ongoing struggle between the Christian left and the Christian right took a new turn in the 1960s and 1970s in response to various liberation movements. On the left were theologies of liberation that presented Jesus as a prophet on the side of the poor and the oppressed. Among these thisworldly theologies of social justice were **Latin American liberation theology** in South America and black liberation theology and feminist theology in the United States.

A chief architect of liberation theology, Gustavo Gutierrez (b. 1928), a Peruvian theologian and Dominican priest, joined other Latin American liberation theologians in an effort to rewrite Christian theology "from below." These thinkers homed in on the social problems of poverty and oppression endemic in developing countries. Inspired by Karl Marx (1818–1883) and by the Second Vatican Council (1962–1965), which had called for *aggorniamento* ("updating") of the Roman Catholic tradition and redefined the church as the "people of God," liberation theologians viewed Jesus as a revolutionary who sided with the poor over the rich. Like Social Gospel theologians, they drew on socioeconomic analysis, though they often read their data through a Marxist lens, which saw ideas as the products of socioeconomic circumstances (rather than vice versa). Like Marx, their focus was praxis, a coming together of theory and practice in a particular time and place.

This theology was endorsed in 1968 at a conference of Catholic bishops held in Medellin, Colombia, that articulated a "preferential option for the poor." It spread quickly through "base communities," small groups dedicated to prayer, Bible study, and reflection on the meaning and power of the gospel in their local contexts. The military dictatorships across Latin America were not friendly to priests who were friendly to the poor, however. Many of these priests, including Archbishop Oscar Romero of San Salvador, were brutally murdered because of their theological beliefs and practices.

Worried for other reasons about slippage of Catholic theology into Marxist dogma, Catholic authorities, including Cardinal Joseph Ratzinger (later Pope Benedict XVI),

Latin American liberation theology theological school that depicts Jesus as a prophet on the side of the oppressed and emphasizes action over theory

denounced liberation theologians in the mid-1980s for bowing lower to Marx than to Christ. But Benedict, who censored and excommunicated liberation theologians, was succeeded by Pope Francis, the first pontiff from Argentina, who brought liberation theology back into Roman Catholicism's good graces. In 2013, he hosted Gutierrez at the Vatican, and in 2018 he oversaw the canonization of Archbishop Romero as a Catholic saint.

Black liberation theology grew out of the civil rights and black power movements of the 1950s and 1960s. It borrowed from the writing of Frederick Douglass, the influential abolitionist and former slave who drew the sharpest possible distinctions between "the Christianity of Christ" and "the corrupt, slaveholding, women-whipping, cradle-plundering, partial and hypocritical Christianity of this land."[54] It focused on the experiences of African Americans of slavery and segregation, on the Exodus as a story of liberation, and on Jesus as a liberator.

In 1967, the year of a deadly Detroit race riot, Albert Cleage installed an eighteen-foot-high painting of a black Mary and Jesus in a church he was pastoring in Detroit and renamed that church the Shrine of the Black Madonna. A friend of Nation of Islam convert Malcolm X, Cleage was deeply influenced by the NOI's black nationalism and its argument that the civil rights movement had been overly cautious. In his book *The Black Messiah* (1968), he called for the crucifixion of the "white Christ" and the resurrection of a "Black Messiah" who, Moses-like, would lead the "Black Nation" from slavery to freedom.[55] Union Theological Seminary professor James Cone, the most celebrated early black liberation theologian, spoke of blacks as God's chosen people. For him, blackness was more about solidarity than genetics, however. "Being black in America has little to do with skin color," he wrote in his *Black Theology and Black Power* (1969). "Being black means that your heart, your soul, your mind, and your body are where the dispossessed are."[56]

While Cleage, Cone, and others worked to empower blacks to fight racism, feminist theologians worked to empower women to fight sexism. The key figure in this movement, which dates back at least to *The Woman's Bible* (1895–1898) and nineteenth-century evangelical efforts to win women the right to vote, was Mary Daly (1928–2010), a Roman Catholic theologian who eventually rejected Christianity altogether. In *The Church and the Second Sex* (1968), Daly criticized sexism in Catholicism with an eye on reforming it. Three years later, Daly stepped up to the pulpit in Harvard's Memorial Church to deliver its first sermon ever by a woman. Instead, she called for an "exodus from sexist religion" to a post-Christian "Sisterhood."[57] She then embodied that exodus by walking out of the building and urging parishioners to join her. In *After the Death of God the Father* (1974), Daly decried a sexist cycle in which patriarchal cultures created patriarchal divinities who then sanctified the patriarchal cultures that had given them birth. "If God is male," she wrote, "then the male is God."[58]

Feminist theology has followed two paths since the late 1960s. Those who were convinced that Christianity was essentially sexist moved into post-Christian thought, with some "thealogians" influenced by neopagan and other goddess traditions. Others

A woman kneels before a portrait of the martyred Roman Catholic archbishop and liberation theologian Oscar Romero in Metropolitan Cathedral of the Holy Savior in San Salvador, El Salvador.

black liberation theology
theological school that draws on the civil rights and black power movements and focuses on Jesus as a "Black Messiah" of liberation

feminist theology
theological school that critiques patriarchal god language and develops resources for women's liberation in Christianity and other religions

Before a capacity crowd in Yankee Stadium on July 20, 1957, "America's Pastor" Billy Graham, bows his head in prayer alongside Vice President Richard M. Nixon on the last night of Graham's famed New York Crusade.

Pentecostals
participants in a twentieth-century American Protestant movement distinguished by its affirmation of both the baptism of the Holy Spirit as a second experience of grace (after conversion) and the gifts that comes with that experience, including speaking in tongues

worked to reform Christianity from within, arguing for the ordination of women, for example, and reinterpreting the creation stories and other biblical texts to undermine long-standing views of women as the "lesser sex."

Wary of the racism they saw in feminist theologies and the sexism they saw in black liberation theologies, a new group of thinkers worked, beginning in the 1980s, to write the experiences of black women into Christianity. Drawing on the novelist Alice Walker, who had defined the term "womanish" as "referring to outrageous, audacious, courageous or willful behavior," these black female thinkers called themselves womanist theologians.[59] In recent years, a series of related "contextual theologies" has extended the insights of these pioneering thinkers to gay and lesbian liberation theologies, and to Dalit ("untouchables") theology in India and Minjung ("poor people") theology in Korea.

Of course, not every Christian was convinced that Jesus was a revolutionary. In response to what they saw as the radicalism and moral relativism of the 1960s and the counterculture, American evangelicals and fundamentalists joined hands with political conservatives to form the "New Religious Right." For decades after the Scopes trial of the 1920s, evangelicals and fundamentalists had concentrated their energies on building their own institutions, including their own radio and television stations. As the success of the telegenic evangelist Billy Graham attests, they never quite disappeared from public view. In fact, Graham met with every U.S. president from Harry Truman to Barack Obama. But evangelicalism reemerged powerfully in the late 1970s in the televangelist Jerry Falwell, who oversaw the rise of the modern Religious Right as a powerhouse for "family values" and Republican politics.

Through groups such as the Moral Majority (est. 1979) and the Christian Coalition (est. 1989), these "cultural conservatives" helped send a series of Republican politicians—Ronald Reagan, George H. W. Bush, George W. Bush—to the White House. However, none of those presidents quite delivered on their promises to outlaw abortion or to bring prayer back into the public schools. In 2020, abortion remained legal, and same-sex marriage was the law of the land. In fact, the Religious Right lost virtually all of the culture wars it waged, leading some Christian conservatives to withdraw from electoral politics and others to back the decidedly un-evangelical businessman Donald Trump in the presidential election of 2016.

Religion plays a much smaller role in European politics, where the public square is far more secularized, but there are analogs to America's Christian nationalism in India, for example, where conflicts between Hindu nationalists and Muslims mirror the conflict between America's cultural conservatives and secular humanists.

The Pentecostal Age

The most successful Christian movement of the twentieth century spread because of its intriguing mix of primitivism and pragmatism. A distant heir of the Methodist revivals of the nineteenth century, Pentecostalism mixed a "primitive" emphasis on the apostolic faith of early Christians with a "pragmatic" style open to whatever modern technologies might serve its purpose. **Pentecostals**, writes church historian Grant Wacker, seized on the "timeless formula" of pious Mary and practical Martha "and brilliantly put it to modern use."[60] Unlike fundamentalism, which focused on doctrine, Pentecostalism focused on experience, and especially on the experience of "speaking in tongues" (glossolalia).

One distinctive feature of Methodism was its affirmation of a second work of grace called sanctification. Among evangelicals, the defining moment in a Christian's life comes at conversion. Because this moment makes the new Christian just, or righteous, in God's eyes, it is called justification. But Methodists added a second key moment, called sanctification, when God empowers believers to live lives of "perfect love," free from the power of sin. This new doctrine led to a quest for individual and social perfection—"Be ye therefore perfect, even as your Father which is in heaven is perfect" (Matthew 5:48)—that fueled both revivals and social activism. It also produced new offshoots of Methodism focused on the "second blessing" of sanctification. These offshoots included the Holiness movement, which saw this "second blessing" as an instantaneous experience of grace that could produce "entire sanctification."

Pentecostalism grew out of the Holiness movement but added to the sanctification experience the "baptism of the Holy Spirit" experienced by the disciples in Jerusalem on the day of Pentecost:

> And suddenly there came a sound from heaven as of a rushing mighty wind, and it filled all the house where they were sitting. And there appeared unto them cloven tongues like as of fire, and it sat upon each of them. And they were all filled with the Holy Ghost, and began to speak with other tongues, as the Spirit gave them utterance (Acts 2:1-4).

The miracles that shook the early church did not die with the apostles, Pentecostals argued. All were still available in the modern world, including glossolalia.

In a rebuke of the notion that every story of American religion must start in New England and move westward, Pentecostalism was born in Los Angeles on April 9, 1906, days before the Great Earthquake shook San Francisco and the same year ancient fossils were first excavated from the La Brea Tar Pits, not far from Beverly Hills. The film industry had not yet come to the city, so it was still rather sleepy. But there was plenty of drama once William J. Seymour (1870–1922), a Holiness minister and the son of slaves, started preaching in a private home and worshipers responded by speaking in unknown tongues.

The Apostolic Faith Mission, located at 312 Azusa Street in Los Angeles, California, is the birthplace of the Azusa Street Revival that began in 1906. Originally an African Methodist Episcopal church, the building was later used as a warehouse before becoming a Pentecostal church.

As more and more people gathered to gawk or worship (or both), Seymour moved his base of operations to an abandoned building in a black neighborhood at 312 Azusa Street. His makeshift altar was a plank suspended over two chairs; two shoeboxes formed his pulpit.

Among the miraculous signs of this revival, which ran nonstop from 10 a.m. to around midnight every day for three years, was divine healing. Another was the racial mixing, scandalous at the time, of blacks, whites, Asian Americans, and Mexican Americans. In a classic demonstration of what anthropologist Victor Turner has dubbed *communitas*, hierarchies crumbled at Azusa Street as different languages melted into the universal language of the Holy Spirit. "Everybody was just the same," said the African American worshiper Mattie Cummings.

Aimee Semple McPherson (1890–1944)

The controversial Pentecostal evangelist and faith healer Aimee Semple McPherson was born in 1890 on a small farm in Ontario, Canada, to a Methodist father and a Salvation Army mother. She converted to Pentecostalism in 1907 after listening to the preaching of Robert James Semple, who became her first husband one year later. In 1915, decades before the Beat writer Jack Kerouac turned "on the road" into a metaphor, "Sister Aimee" barnstormed across the United States in a "Gospel Car" whose slogans alone ("Jesus Is Coming Soon—Get Ready") were capable of drawing a crowd. Deftly steering clear of the doctrinal disputes dogging fundamentalists and modernists after World War I, she focused instead on the Pentecostal experience of Spirit baptism.

McPherson settled in 1918 in Los Angeles, where she started KFSG, the first Christian radio station in the country. Her 5,300-seat Angelus Temple, dedicated in 1923, was the headquarters for her Church of the Foursquare Gospel, which preached Jesus as savior, baptizer, healer, and coming king. But thanks to McPherson's charismatic gifts, spiritual and otherwise, it also became the home to the country's first celebrity evangelist.

Angelus Temple featured a giant cross that could be seen from miles away, and Jesus was clearly on offer. But McPherson was the star attraction, playing the feminine evangelist one moment and the Hollywood starlet the next. She was by all accounts a beautiful woman, with thick hair tinted blond and flowing over long white robes. But she was also a farm girl who would marry (unsuccessfully) three times, so her audiences could identify with her even as they put her on a pedestal. McPherson's "illustrated sermons," complete with elaborate sets and fancy costumes, were part Bible, part Vaudeville, and part Hollywood. In one, she cross-dressed as George Washington at Valley Forge as fake snow descended from the rafters. In another, she dressed as a cop and hopped on a motorcycle, warning listeners to stop speeding toward hell. Her act, *Harper's* wrote, was "the most perennially successful show in the United States."[a]

But celebrity gives and celebrity takes away. On May 18, 1926, less than a month after she had returned from a highly publicized trip to the Holy Land, McPherson disappeared. Her mother said she had gone out for a swim and drowned. Not everyone was so sure. Had she been kidnapped by "underworld characters"? Had she snapped? Meanwhile, her rumored lover, a former KFSG engineer, was also reported missing. When McPherson resurfaced in late June, she claimed she had been kidnapped and held for ransom in a shack in Mexico. Many suspected that she had faked the whole thing and run off with her alleged lover, who was also located around the same time (and without any alibi). Charges were filed, and dropped, and McPherson went on preaching.

In 1944, in a hotel room in Oakland, she died, like so many Hollywood celebrities would in decades to follow, of an overdose. But if McPherson's personal life was largely a failure, her professional life was not. One of the most influential preachers in American history, she pioneered radio evangelism and founded a new Pentecostal denomination, the International Church of the Foursquare Gospel, that now boasts almost 3.6 million members worldwide. She also helped to move Pentecostals from the margins of American culture, paving the way for future female stars of a different sort, including Alaska governor Sarah Palin.

"It didn't matter if you were black, white, green. . . . Nobody ever thought of race."[61] Seymour himself referred to the revival as a "melting time" in which "God is melting all races and nations together."[62] Sociologically speaking, Azusa Street demonstrated the egalitarian effects of a shift from "bureaucratic" to "charismatic" authority. Here, whomever the Spirit inspired to speak commanded the room.

Seymour's teacher, the itinerant Methodist layman Charles Parham, had brought Pentecostalism into the world in a revival in Topeka, Kansas, in 1901. Parham also provided the intellectual foundation for Pentecostalism by turning baptism of the Holy Spirit into a third stage in the Christian life, after justification and sanctification. Speaking in unknown tongues was, in his view, proof positive that an individual had in fact been sanctified, and the return of this gift of the Holy Spirit to earth was an equally sure sign of the Second Coming of Jesus. Parham, a white supremacist who believed that Anglo-Saxons were descended from the Ten Lost Tribes of Israel, had allowed Seymour to sit in on classes at his Houston Bible School, but only if he listened from outside the classroom. During a visit to Los Angeles, Parham denounced the Azusa Street revivals as "Holy Ghost Bedlam" in which worshipers "pulled all of the stunts common in old camp meetings among colored folks."[63]

After the fuel that fired up Azusa Street had burned out in Southern California, the Pentecostal movement followed the Protestant pattern by splintering repeatedly. It also followed the American practice of racial segregation, dividing along racial lines into two leading denominations: the largely white Assemblies of God and the largely black Church of God in Christ. Although Pentecostalism has been widely interpreted through the lens of "deprivation theory" as a salve for poor folk set adrift after migrating from rural to urban areas, the target audience was actually far broader than the uneducated and the dispossessed. The typical Pentecostal was a member of "the stable working class," and the typical Pentecostal leader enjoyed a social profile roughly equal to the average Southern Methodist or Southern Baptist leader.[64]

One way of tracking the story from Puritanism to evangelicalism to Pentecostalism is to think of their different readings of the Trinity. Like Calvinism, Puritanism was an Old Testament faith focused on the mystery and majesty of God the father. In this theological system, which gloried in the gap between God and human beings, a God/man like Jesus made little sense. Therefore, Puritan ministers preached largely from the Old Testament, interpreting colonial governors and American presidents as Hebraic patriarchs of a sort. Around the time of the Second Great Awakening, evangelicals shifted the focus of American Christianity to the New Testament and to the Son of God. Pentecostals, too, sang "What a Friend We Have in Jesus" and gloried in their personal relationships with him. Theirs remained a Jesus faith in which "Jesus offers salvation ... Jesus heals ... Jesus baptizes with the Holy Spirit ... [and] Jesus is coming again."[65] But more than earlier forms of Protestantism, Pentecostalism shined a spotlight on the power of the Holy Spirit.

The Pentecostal Boom

During the 1970s, a "charismatic" movement (from *charism*, meaning "gift" in Greek) propelled speaking in tongues and other spiritual gifts far outside the orbits of Pentecostal denominations into Roman Catholic and mainline Protestant churches. In recent years, these "gifts" have also been on display in megachurches with thousands and even hundreds of thousands of members. But the most important legacy of the Pentecostal movement is its explosion worldwide. "The Pentecostal wine, fermented in America, and bottled on the mission field, has been uncorked with dazzling success in the third World," Grant Wacker writes.[66] As shrewdly pragmatic in adapting to the twenty-first-century Global South as it was to adapting to the early twentieth century, Pentecostalism has become a huge engine of church growth in Latin America, Africa, and Asia.

The Yoido Full Gospel Church in Seoul, South Korea, is the world's largest Pentecostal megachurch. Founded in 1958, it now boasts more than eight hundred thousand members.

Today roughly a quarter of the world's two billion Christians are Pentecostals or charismatics—up from just 6 percent in 1980. In fact, roughly 8 percent of human beings on earth are now Pentecostals or charismatics. This category comprises

- "classic Pentecostal" denominations such as the Assemblies of God
- charismatic churches affiliated with non-Pentecostal denominations
- independent churches that follow Pentecostal beliefs and practices (including many megachurches)

Together, these groups are growing four times faster than other forms of Christianity. In Latin America, nearly two-thirds (65 percent) of all Protestants identify as Pentecostals or charismatics. But these "spirit-filled" Christians are also growing in that old home-land of Christianity, Europe, often at the expense of mainline Protestant denominations. Between 2010 and 2016, 168 Church of England churches closed their doors, but for every one of these churches, three Pentecostal or charismatic churches popped up, appealing in many cases to younger and more diverse populations. The Pentecostal spirit has also caught fire inside the Roman Catholic Church; more than half of Brazil's Catholics are charismatics.

With a membership exceeding eight hundred thousand, the largest megachurch in the world is Yoido Full Gospel Church of Seoul, South Korea. Affiliated with the Assemblies of God, it boasts more than five hundred pastors and draws more than two hundred thousand souls per weekend. It also sits on a prime piece of real estate facing the National Assembly—a material reminder of the rising political power of Christianity in the Global South. The Deeper Christian Life Ministry of Lagos, Nigeria, an independent church, is one of the largest churches in Africa. El Salvador's Mision Cristiana Elim International, also independent, is one of the largest churches in Latin America. It holds many of its events in sports stadiums.

Why this amazing growth? Pentecostals attribute it to Holy Spirit power. But there are more mundane reasons to explain why we are living in a Pentecostal age. First, Pentecostalism is growing because Pentecostals are trying to make it grow. Unlike Shakers, who forbid sex, or Jews, who frown on proselytizing, Pentecostals are growing both through childbearing and evangelism.

Second, Pentecostals continue to adapt to new languages and new cultures. But they are also crafting a global movement, as much a part of the ongoing process of globalization as brands like Apple and Oprah. They borrow unapologetically from corporate culture and from the therapeutic culture of self-help and self-fulfillment that can now be found from Santa Barbara to Shanghai. They also adapt to consumer culture via the prosperity gospel, which affirms that God desires, in addition to our salvation in the next world, our health and wealth here and now. To believe in Holy Spirit power, it seems, is to believe in the power of contextualization—that God can appear not only in the ancient Mediterranean but also in contemporary South Korea and on Instagram and WeChat. The prosperity gospel has even worked its way into the White House, according to journalist Jeff Sharlet, who sees this "religion of winning" as an animating force behind Trumpism.[67]

Third, Pentecostalism is egalitarian, offering the gifts of the Holy Spirit without regard to education, race, class, or gender. Latin American Pentecostalism has enjoyed huge growth, as tens of millions of Catholics have left their parishes for tongue-speaking churches in recent decades. One reason for this religious switching is that, unlike the Roman Catholic Church, which is led by elites, Pentecostal churches are frequently led by ordinary folks—by indigenous people in Guatemala and Mexico and by Afro-Brazilians in Brazil. Moreover, the gifts, spiritual and otherwise, offered by these churches are largely spread orally, making them readily available even to people who cannot read or write. But Pentecostalism is not a religion of the dispossessed alone. One huge engine of its global growth is its popularity with the new middle classes, who gravitate to its promises of health and wealth (and its endorsement of both).

Fourth, not unlike Islam, which is rivaling Pentecostalism in global growth, this movement refuses to restrict its reach to one day a week or to the privacy of the home. It offers a comprehensive way of life in which God is deeply invested not only in our salvation but also in our families, our jobs, our love lives, our sickness, and our health.

Finally, it is important not to underestimate the draw of supernatural experiences. Some readers of this textbook may lead largely secular lives, but the vast majority of human beings throughout world history have walked and talked with wonder-working gods. Pentecostalism offers immediate, personal access to that mystery. It offers a life shot through with divine energy and purpose, where ecstasy can always erupt amidst the tedium of everyday life. The core message? We are not alone.

LIVED CHRISTIANITY

Christians seek salvation. Classically, Roman Catholics affirm that salvation comes through a combination of faith and works, so to borrow from the Hindu tradition, their techniques for attaining the religious goal are *bhakti* (devotion) and *karma* (action).

The Seven Sacraments

Roman Catholics traditionally recognize seven sacraments. These rituals, which employ words, gestures, and some earthly material (oil, water, bread, wine) as vehicles for divine grace, are:

1. baptism
2. confirmation
3. Eucharist
4. penance (or reconciliation)
5. anointing of the sick (or last rites)
6. holy orders (or ordination)
7. matrimony

Protestants affirm that salvation comes through faith by grace—as a gift of God. In this regard, they stand with bhakti Hindus in emphasizing the role of other-help over self-effort in attaining their religious goal.

Whereas Roman Catholics recognize seven sacraments, Protestants cut this list down to two, baptism and the Eucharist. The Eucharist (or Mass, Holy Communion, or the Divine Liturgy) commemorates Jesus's Last Supper with his disciples. The desert-born initiation rite of baptism also goes back to the early Christians, who also met regularly to pray and to share a ritual meal. Also like baptism, the Eucharist is practiced differently by different Christian groups. For Roman Catholics and liturgically minded Protestants such as Lutherans and Episcopalians, virtually every Sunday service includes the Eucharist. But less ritualistic "low church" Protestants celebrate it infrequently or not at all. In most churches, wine and a flat wafer of unleavened bread are the standard fare. Some churches use grape juice rather than wine, however, and Orthodox churches typically use leavened bread. Increasingly, churches also offer worshipers a choice of elements—wine or grape juice, or a gluten-free wafer, perhaps—as well as a choice of how to consume them (by drinking from or dipping into a common cup, for example, or by drinking from an individual cup). Interpretations of this rite were a major sticking point during the Reformation: Catholics insisted on the transubstantiation, or physical transformation, of the bread and wine into the body and blood of Christ, but Protestants typically believed that the Eucharist was not an actual sacrifice but rather a commemoration.

Worship is another practice central to Christianity. Whereas Hindus generally go to temple on their own schedules, the norm in the Christian world is congregational worship at set times of the week, typically at 10:00 or 11:00 a.m. on Sunday morning. In Orthodox services, parishioners often stand. Protestants and Catholics usually sit in pews, though many megachurches now offer plush, theater-style seating. At Roman Catholic worship, the key moment comes when the priest transforms the bread and wine into Christ's body and blood, but in Protestant worship the climax comes when the Bible is read aloud and the minister (who in this case can be a woman) offers the sermon.

Prayer, Saints, and Icons

Virtually all Christians engage in some sort of prayer, from blessings over meals to bedtime prayers to the around-the-clock prayer vigil of the International House of Prayer of Kansas City that began on September 19, 1999, and continues to this day. Mormons address prayers to God the Father. Evangelicals typically address Jesus. Catholics also pray to various saints. The "Ave Maria" ("Hail, Mary") is so popular among Catholics that it has become the name for an end-of-the-game football play where the ball is hurled into the end zone on a wing and a prayer.

Saints play an important part in Catholic and Orthodox piety, where the cosmos is filled with people and objects saturated with the sacred. There are statues and paintings of the saints to remember them by, and candles sitting before them to light. There are also relics, including the controversial Shroud of Turin (said to be the burial shroud of Jesus) and the full body of St. Peter interred in St. Peter's Basilica in Vatican City. So powerful was the allure of these relics, in medieval times, that saintly bodies were boiled or butchered, in order to maximize the relics produced—a practice banned by Pope Boniface VIII in 1299.

Saints are remembered on their feast days and on pilgrimages to holy sites associated with their births, lives, or deaths. St. Jude, the patron saint of lost causes, is popular. So is St. Francis of Assisi, the founder of the Franciscan order (and namesake of the twenty-first-century Pope Francis), who sought God in nature and among the poor. Popes, bishops, and priests are not saints unless they are officially canonized as such, but they also embody sacred power in the Catholic world.

Officially, Mary is one among many Catholic saints. But in much of the Catholic world, she is the central object of devotion. In fact, one recurring conflict between "lived" and "prescribed" Catholicism concerns the many and varied appearances of the Virgin Mary—in Lourdes, France, and Fatima, Portugal, most famously. Someone sees her. Someone hears her speaking. Witnesses claim to be cured. Priests are conflicted. They are grateful for the conversions Marian apparitions produce, the church pews they fill, the devotions

Roman Catholic gift shops all over the world feature devotional items, including prayer cards, icons, statuettes, and rosary beads, to be kept close at hand for prayer and guidance.

This painting, *Jesus of the People* (2000) by the Vermont artist Janet McKenzie, won an art contest in search of "Jesus 2000" sponsored by the *National Catholic Reporter*. It features an intriguingly androgynous Jesus figure surrounded by a yin/yang symbol and a feather.

they popularize, and the pilgrims they summon. (The basilica of the Virgin of Guadalupe in Tepeyac, Mexico, the most visited Catholic site in the world, draws three times more visitors annually than St. Peter's in Rome.) Yet priests are wary that a particular apparition of Mary may be heard to say something contrary to official Roman Catholic doctrine. Catholic authorities have investigated some of these apparitions and declared them invalid. Other apparitions, from Tepeyac to Lourdes to Fatima, have been officially approved.

Protestants empty this Catholic cosmos of saints and sacred objects, which they often dismiss as superstitious. As "people of the book," Protestants access the divine directly, through the revealed Word of God, instead of sending their prayers through intermediaries. Protestants criticize Catholics for bowing down to "graven images" and for their "Mariolatry." The exemplars in Protestantism are not saints but ordinary "knights of faith," who do not have supernatural powers.

Or do they? As a group, Protestants do focus more than Catholics on the Bible. And they do not generally accumulate the religious stuff— crucifixes and prayer cards and rosaries—that many Catholics do. But to quote from a different Madonna, Protestants, too, "are living in a material world."[68] The Reverend Dr. Martin Luther King Jr. may not be a saint, but his relics are scattered in museums throughout the world. There is a national holiday for him in the United States, and a memorial in Washington, DC, with a thirty-foot-tall statue—a "stone of hope" carved out of granite. Warner Sallman's 1940 painting *Head of Christ* has been reproduced roughly half a billion times, and it is almost entirely Protestants who use this image of a not-too-masculine, not-too-feminine Jesus on lithographs framed in their homes, key chains for their cars, and magnets on their refrigerators. Evangelicals turn to the Bible as the Word of God, but they also wear "What Would Jesus Do?" bracelets and "Keep Calm and Pray On" T-shirts. They tattoo their limbs with Bible verses and their cars with bumper stickers ("God Answers Knee-Mail").

Meanwhile, as if to poke a finger in the eye of the notion that Jesus never changes, all sorts of alternative images of Jesus continue to spring up. As the year 2000 approached, the *National Catholic Reporter* sponsored an art contest in search of "Jesus 2000." The winning entry—an oil painting called *Jesus of the People* by the Vermont-based artist Janet McKenzie—depicted an androgynous savior with African features framed by a yin/yang symbol and a feather that seemed to gesture toward Native American spirituality.

Holy Days

Christianity's most important holy days are Christmas and Easter. Christmas recalls the birth of Jesus—his incarnation in human form. On Easter, Christians celebrate the resurrection of Jesus—the triumph of life over death. Christmas is preceded by an Advent period of thirty days dedicated to awaiting Christ's birth. Easter is preceded by Lent, forty days of prayer and asceticism, when observant Christians give up something they love as a reminder of the forty days and nights Jesus spent fasting in the wilderness. (In a humorous take on this practice on *The Colbert Report*, the Catholic comedian Stephen Colbert once gave up Catholicism for Lent.)

The Ground Zero Cross

Amidst the rubble of Lower Manhattan's World Trade Center flattened two days earlier by 9/11 terrorists, construction worker Frank Silecchia spied a sign of God's presence in the form of a two-ton, seventeen-foot-long crossbeam. Two days later, he brought Father Brian Jordan, a Franciscan priest, to see it. Jordan convinced city officials to remove this object and place it on nearby Church Street, where Jordan said Mass and grieving family members came to pray. Replicas of the Ground Zero Cross, as it came to be called, were handcrafted from the rubble as relics and then manufactured as souvenirs. One nearby body artist personally tattooed the cross onto a thousand laborers working on "The Pile." Years later, the Ground Zero Cross itself was installed at the National September 11 Memorial and Museum, which was dedicated on September 11, 2011.

The American Atheist Association filed a lawsuit to have the cross removed. The cross is a Christian symbol, it argued, and as such has no place in a memorial overseen by a nation committed to the separation of church and state. Partisans of the cross argued for legal reasons that the object in question was a historical artifact rather than a religious relic—a "symbol of hope and optimism for first responders, families of the victims, and America at large."[a]

In July 2014, the U.S. Court of Appeals for the Second Circuit agreed, ruling that "as a matter of law" the "actual purpose in displaying The Cross at Ground Zero has always been secular." Like the cross itself, the controversy surrounding this particular cross carries multiple meanings. It testifies to the enduring public power of Christian symbols in the modern West and to the usefulness, in certain cases, of attempting to turn them into generic or universal symbols. It demonstrates the difficulty of locating any line that supposedly separates the religious from the secular. And, it suggests that the Christian tradition of finding relics among the dead is alive and well even in the supposedly "secular city" of New York.

Holy Week, the last week in Lent, is particularly important to Christians worldwide. It includes Palm Sunday, when Jesus was said to ride humbly yet triumphantly on a donkey into Jerusalem as his followers shouted "Hosannah"; Maundy Thursday, when Jesus celebrated the Last Supper with his disciples; and Good Friday, when Jesus died by crucifixion (yet saved humans from their sins, hence the "Good"). Holy Week processions are widespread throughout the Catholic world, and the last days of Jesus have been reenacted for centuries in "passion plays" worldwide, most notably in Oberammergau in Bavaria, where townspeople asked God in 1633 to spare them from the bubonic plague and vowed to perform a passion play every ten years if only that plague passed over them. First performed in 1634, the Oberammergau play is now put on every year ending with a zero.

On Christmas—December 25 in most of the world and January 7 among Orthodox Christians—families attend church services, where they listen to the story of the manger-born Christ child and sing Christmas carols such as "Silent Night" and "O Little Town of Bethlehem." At home, families gather to sing "Jingle Bells," decorate Christmas trees with lights and ornaments, and bake Christmas cookies. Meanwhile, children wait expectantly for Santa Claus and his reindeer to show up with toys and stocking stuffers.

Christmas is an example of a practice that is both religious and secular. If you miss out on either Jesus or Santa Claus, you miss out on the "spirit of Christmas," which, for better or for worse, is about both the birthday of the Son of God and the buying and selling of stuff upon stuff. Every year seems to bring new efforts to "put Christ back into Christmas."

BIRTH AND DEATH

Many Christians welcome their children into the world by baptism, a ritual that recalls the immersion of Jesus in the Jordan River by John the Baptist. Historically, Christians have understood baptism as a cleansing of sin, a descent of the Holy Spirit, and a symbolic death and resurrection. Some groups baptize by full immersion; others sprinkle water on the head. Although infant baptism remains the norm among Catholics and liturgical Protestants such as Lutherans and Episcopalians, many Protestant groups reject infant baptism as unscriptural, insisting on adult baptism accompanied by a profession of the Christian faith.

Like Jews and Muslims, Christians have traditionally disposed of the dead via burial. All three of these groups describe the self as a psychosomatic unity: human = body + soul. So it makes sense for the body to rest underground until it is resurrected at the end of time and reunited with its immortal soul. The examples of Hebrew patriarchs and of Jesus (all buried) play a part in inclining Christians toward burial, which also served in the ancient Mediterranean as a way for the Jesus movement to distinguish itself from its Roman overseers (who traditionally cremated).

Some of the most memorable words of mourning in the English language can be found in the Book of Common Prayer, originally published by the Church of England in 1549. At the burial site, as earth is covering the coffin, the minister says:

In sure and certain hope of the resurrection to eternal life through our Lord Jesus Christ, we commend to Almighty God our *brother/sister N.*; and we commit *his/her* body to the ground; earth to earth, ashes to ashes, dust to dust. The Lord bless *him/her* and keep *him/her*, the Lord make

---

In Venezuela, many parents tell their children that it is Jesus who delivers the toys made by Santa's elves in the North Pole. The Three Wise Men did offer gold, frankincense, and myrrh to the baby Jesus, after all. And the lords of the religion of consumerism show no signs that they are willing to stop selling what the faithful remain eager to buy. Ironically, even Donald Trump's 2016 promise that, if he were elected president, shoppers would be saying "Merry Christmas" rather than "Happy Holidays" assumed that this holiday is observed as much in Macy's and Walmart as in the home and the church.

Easter also mixes the sacred and the profane, even as it joins the resurrection story of Jesus with ancient festivals of a coming spring. In addition to an Easter sunrise service to attend, there are Easter hats to buy and eggs to color and Easter baskets to fill with jelly beans and chocolate bunnies.

CONTEMPORARY CONTROVERSY: THE BROWNING OF CHRISTIANITY

Christian faith and churchgoing are declining rapidly in Europe, where today half of all adults no longer believe in God. They are also stagnating in North America, which is experiencing a rapid rise in the religiously unaffiliated ("nones") and those who are "spiritual but not religious." But Christianity is booming in Africa and Asia and South America. As a result, Christianity is rapidly "browning." Roughly a century ago, four times as many Christians lived in the Global North (North America, Europe, Australia, Japan, and New Zealand) as in the Global South (Africa, Asia, Latin America). Christianity was largely a

his face to shine upon *him/her* and be gracious unto *him/her*, the Lord lift up his countenance upon *him/her* and give *him/her* peace. Amen.

Cremation remained a scandal to almost all Christians into the late nineteenth century, and it was effectively banned by the Roman Catholic Church in 1884. That ban was lifted in 1963, and since the 1970s cremation has boomed in many Christian countries, where the old view of the self as body-plus-soul is yielding to a more Greek (and Hindu) view, more compatible with cremation and reincarnation, of the self as spirit only. Today roughly three out of every four people are cremated in the United Kingdom and seven out of ten in Canada. In the United States, cremations exceeded burials for the first time in 2016, though cremation rates continued to vary widely from state to state—from 24 percent in Mississippi to 80 percent in Nevada in 2018.

Baptism is an important Christian rite of passage. While Roman Catholics, the Orthodox, and many Protestant denominations prefer infant baptism in a church, Baptists and some other Protestant groups baptize adults by full-body immersion. Here, a member of the London-based Mount Zion Spiritual Baptist Church is baptized in the sea in Felixstowe, England.

religion of white Europeans and Americans, and its color was white. Today, the color of Christianity is various shades of brown, with the overwhelming majority (61 percent) of the world's Christians calling Africa, Latin America, or Asia home. The rise of Christianity in sub-Saharan Africa is particularly dramatic: from 9 percent of the overall population in 1910 to 59 percent a century later. Today, one out of every four Christians lives in Africa. There are more than twice as many Protestants in Nigeria as in Germany (the home of the Protestant Reformation), and more than twice as many Catholics in Brazil as in Italy (the homeland of Roman Catholicism).

This combination of steady decline in the Global North and rapid growth in the Global South have caused Christianity's geographical center of gravity to track steadily south. After leaping over the straits of Gibraltar from Spain into North Africa in 1970, that center of gravity sits today near Timbuktu, Mali, in central Africa. Increasingly, then, the face of Christianity looks less like the American evangelist Franklin Graham and more like the black Christian rapper Lecrae. Or, more precisely, like a less famous Argentinian or Nigerian woman, since, as church historian Dana Robert has observed, the typical Christian today is "no longer a European man, but a Latin American or African woman."[69]

American megachurches, such as Joel Osteen's Lakewood Church in Houston, often feature jumbotrons, live bands, espresso bars, and architecture that evokes your local shopping mall more than your grandmother's sanctuary. But the United States doesn't even crack the top twenty when it comes to the world's leading megachurches. The biggest of these big congregations—all Protestant and Pentecostal—are found in countries such as South Korea, Chile, Colombia, El Salvador, Nigeria, and the Ivory Coast. In fact, Seoul, South Korea, alone has seventeen megachurches. But not all megachurches are Pentecostal, or even Protestant. The Cave Cathedral, carved out of rock near a garbage dump in Cairo, Egypt, blasts praise songs and preaching over its massive sound system every Sunday to about twenty thousand Coptic Orthodox believers.

The browning of Christianity may seem to be a departure, but it is actually a homecoming. In the beginning, Christianity was nearly as multicultural as Los Angeles is today. As it broke beyond the boundaries of the Roman Empire, it quickly spread as far as Ethiopia and India. When Constantine endorsed it, only one of its five major centers (Rome) was in Europe. The others were in Asia (Constantinople, Antioch, Jerusalem) and Africa (Alexandria). Many of the greatest thinkers in the early church, including Augustine, were Africans. In 500, two-thirds of the world's Christians lived in either Africa or Asia. Not until the Middle Ages would Christianity become largely European.

As Christianity is relocating, it is also "glocalizing," adjusting to local circumstances even as its networks extend across the globe. And as the color of Christians is shifting, so is the shape of Christianity itself. Christians in the Global South are poorer than those in the Global North. They are also more conservative, both theologically and socially. They are more likely to take the Bible at face value, to assign traditional roles to women, and to condemn homosexuality as a sin. They are also more likely to speak in tongues than to preach liberation theology. Their faith is "Spirit-filled"—supercharged with the Holy Spirit. And though they emphasize the experiential dimension of religion over its ethical dimension, they do see Jesus as a partisan of the poor as well as an exorcist and a healer. Supernaturalism, chased out of many European and American churches by scientific data and philosophical arguments, is also back in vogue in the Global South. Crucially,

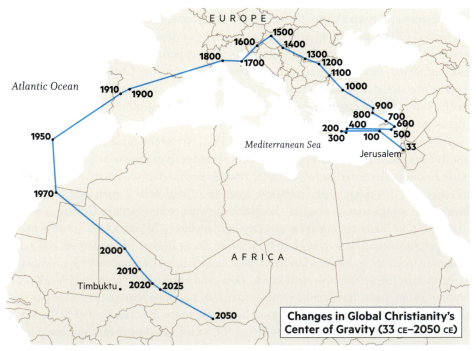

Changes in Global Christianity's Center of Gravity (33 CE–2050 CE)

Over the past two thousand years, the "center of gravity" of the world Christian population has moved north and west from Jerusalem into Europe before moving sharply south in 1900 and jumping into North Africa. Since 1970, as Christianity has boomed in Africa and Asia, it has been moving sharply south and east.

Christianity is a global religion with untold local and regional variations. Here, members of a small Roman Catholic church in Escoma, Bolivia, celebrate the Mass in their native language of Aymaran.

Christians here are in conversation not so much with British and American atheists as with Muslims next door in Nigeria or their Hindu neighbors in India. As a result, they are not just crafting different understandings of the Bible than did Aquinas or Luther, they are remaking evangelicalism, fundamentalism, and Pentecostalism in their own image. For example, these new Christians are more entrepreneurial and inventive, and their Christianity, says church historian Mark Noll, is "self-starting, self-financing and self-spreading."[70]

Tension in this tale of two churches is on display in the Anglican Communion, a global gathering of churches in 160 countries that grew out of the Church of England, including the Episcopal Church in the United States. This group has been rocked in recent decades by a culture war over homosexuality. Whereas liberals in Canada and the United States bless same-sex unions and have elected an openly gay bishop, conservatives in the Global South insist that the Bible denounces homosexuality as a sin. According to church historian Philip Jenkins, this battle is a harbinger of a broader clash of Christianities to come.

In a process known as "reverse missions," the formerly colonized are now evangelizing Europe and North America. One of Western Europe's largest congregations, the London-based Kingsway International Christian Centre (KICC), is run by a senior pastor of Nigerian descent who attracts up to twelve thousand people each Sunday. The Universal Church of the Kingdom of God, a Brazilian "prosperity gospel" church with origins in a funeral home, has temples in the United Kingdom, the United States, India, and several African countries. This dynamic of the South coming North and the East coming West—"everywhere to everywhere" is the new mission's mantra—is also visible in American universities, where many evangelical student groups long dominated by white Americans are rapidly browning. For example, Yale's Campus Crusade for Christ was all white twenty years ago; today it is 90 percent Asian and Asian American.

QUESTIONS FOR DISCUSSION

1. When it comes to beliefs and practices, how are Roman Catholics, Orthodox Christians, and Protestants similar? How are they different? Consider creeds, sacraments, worship styles, and the concepts of "faith" and "works."

2. Who were the key figures responsible for transforming Christianity from a small movement into a global religion? What were their contributions, both religiously and politically?

3. How did religious, social, political, and technological factors contribute to the Protestant Reformation? Why did the Reformation set off a new pattern of rapidly splintering Christian groups?

4. What is evangelicalism? How did it spread in the United States and Great Britain during the early nineteenth century? How did it differ from the Puritanism that preceded it?

5. During the late nineteenth and early twentieth centuries, liberals and fundamentalists fought for the right to define Christianity. How did their views of modernity and Christianity differ?

KEY TERMS

Anglicans, p. 255

atonement, p. 233

Baptists, p. 265

black liberation theology, p. 275

Christ, p. 228

Congregationalists, p. 262

Deists, p. 261

denomination, p. 231

Eastern Orthodoxy, p. 230

Eucharist, p. 234

evangelicals, p. 263

faith, p. 234

feminist theology, p. 275

Four Gospels, p. 228

fundamentalists, p. 271

icon ("image"), p. 234

Incarnation, p. 247

Latin American liberation theology, p. 274

Mary, p. 228

Methodists, p. 264

Mormons, p. 266

New Testament, p. 231

Old Testament, p. 231

orthodoxy ("right doctrine"), p. 241

Our Lady of Guadalupe, p. 234

Pentecostals, p. 277

pope, p. 234

Puritans, p. 254

Protestantism, p. 230

Reformation, p. 234

Roman Catholicism, p. 230

salvation, p. 228

seven sacraments, p. 256

sin, p. 228

Social Gospel, p. 270

soft monotheism, p. 228

sola scriptura ("scripture alone"), p. 257

transubstantiation, p. 256

Trinity, p. 242

Unitarians, p. 261

FURTHER READING

Butler, John, et al. *Religion in American Life: A Short History.* New York: Oxford University Press, 2007.

Fredriksen, Paula. *From Jesus to Christ: The Origins of the New Testament Images of Jesus.* New Haven: Yale University Press, 1988.

Glaude, Jr., Eddie S. *African American Religion: A Very Short Introduction.* New York: Oxford University Press, 2014.

Kim, Sebastian, and Kirsten Kim. *Christianity as a World Religion: An Introduction.* London: Bloomsbury Publishing, 2016.

Pelikan, Jaroslaw. *Jesus Through the Centuries: His Place in the History of Culture.* New Haven: Yale University Press, 1985.

Beneath this dome of the Sultan Ahmed Mosque in Istanbul, Turkey, Muslims answer the call to prayer five times a day. This "Blue Mosque" is famous for its geometric and calligraphic ornamentations, both hallmarks of Islamic architecture.

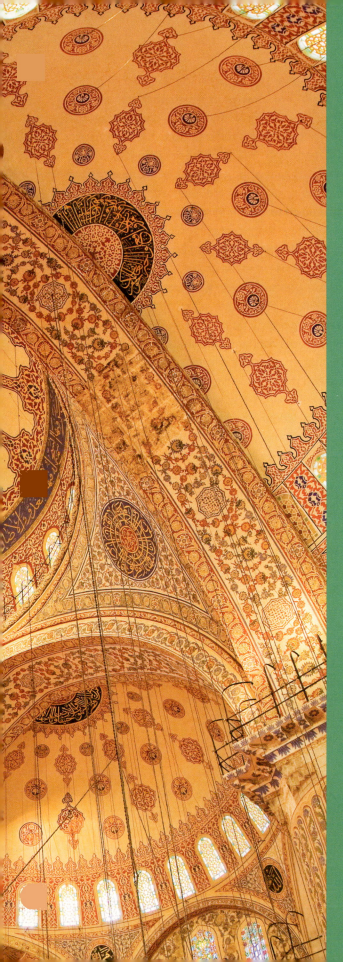

7

Islam

THE WAY OF SUBMISSION

It is hot and dry and impossibly crowded on the Mount of Mercy, which rises out of the desert plain of Arafat twelve miles southeast of Mecca in Saudi Arabia. Today, more than two million Muslims have converged on this hill for the central ritual of the annual pilgrimage known as the **hajj**. This ritual is called "standing at Arafat" and many do stand under the hot sun from noon till sunset. Others take shade in tents or under umbrellas, reading a book or chatting with friends. Most give themselves over to the appointed task of the day: contemplating their shortcomings and praying to God for forgiveness.

Mecca (or Makkah, as the Saudis officially spell it) is the birthplace of the prophet Muhammad and the place he was living when he received the revelations that became the Quran. It is also the geographic center of the Muslim world—a place so sacred it has become a generic term, as in "Wimbledon is the mecca of tennis" or "Wall Street is the mecca of finance." The "Mother of Cities" according to the Quran (6:92), this ancient desert town was transformed by oil and air conditioning into a shining city with a population roughly that of Dallas, Texas. Cranes and skyscrapers hover over the minarets of Mecca's Grand Mosque, the world's largest **mosque**. The famed Kaaba shrine, which believers acclaim as the House of God on earth, is literally shadowed by the Royal Mecca Clock Tower complex, one of the world's biggest buildings, which tempts tourists and pilgrims with its five-star hotel rooms and five-story shopping mall.[1]

hajj
annual pilgrimage to Mecca and one of the Five Pillars of Islam

Mecca
Saudi Arabian city, the sacred center of the Muslim world, and the home of the Kaaba shrine around which the annual hajj revolves

mosque
place of community prayer that includes a niche in the wall marking the direction to Mecca, toward which that prayer is directed

martyr
literally a "witness" (*shahid*), someone who dies in the struggle for Islam

Kaaba
the cubic House of God in Mecca toward which observant Muslims pray every day and around which pilgrims walk during the hajj. Typically covered in an ornate black cloth, it includes a sacred black stone said to have fallen from heaven.

In and around Mecca, pilgrims will perform a series of rituals that make up the five-day hajj, one of the Five Pillars of Islam and traditionally an obligation for all Muslims who are able to meet its costs and physical exertions. To fail to perform any of these rituals (or to perform them at the wrong time) is to fail to complete the hajj.

Classically, pilgrims traveled to Mecca by foot or on camel via dangerous caravan routes from Damascus or Baghdad in the north, or on arduous overseas trips from Southeast Asia that might take years to complete. Storms at sea, desert marauders, epidemics, and extreme temperatures made these journeys perilous. In 1361, a winter chill claimed one hundred Syrian lives, and in 1430, three thousand Egyptians succumbed to the heat. No wonder Muslims recognize those who die on the hajj as **martyrs**, with all the afterlife rewards accorded to those who suffer and die defending their religion.

The Quran, the holy book of Islam, speaks of pilgrims traveling "on foot and upon all [manner of] lean beast, coming from all deep and distant mountain highways" (22:27), and some Muslims continue to travel to Mecca overland by train, bus, or car, sleeping in homemade tents along busy highways. In 2016, one pilgrim came by bicycle from China—a trek of more than five thousand miles. Nowadays most pilgrims fly on jets that complete in hours trips that once took years. After touching down in a specially designed Hajj Terminal in the port city of Jeddah, they board air-conditioned buses that whisk them toward Mecca.

Officially, the hajj begins each year on the eighth day of the lunar month of Dhu-al-Hijjah (literally, "the month of the pilgrimage"). But the start of the hajj is one thing and the start of an individual's pilgrimage is another. There are day-to-day preparations, including obtaining a difficult-to-procure visa and paying for the costly trip. But the key moment comes just outside Mecca at one of six official thresholds marking the crossing of pilgrims from the profane world of everyday life into the sacred precinct of the hajj. To mark this crossing into the sacred condition of *ihram*, pilgrims cut their nails, comb their hair, and bathe. They put on special hajj clothing (also called ihram): for men, two plain white cotton sheets in which many will one day be buried; for women, equally loose and simple clothing (often also white) that cloaks them in modesty. Pilgrims do not officially enter ihram, however, until they formally announce their intention to perform the hajj and ask God to accept it. Then they chant the prayer that can be heard on the lips of pilgrims throughout the hajj:

Here I am, God, here I am!
Here I am, You have no partner, here I am!
All praise, grace, and sovereignty belong to You.
You have no partner.

After moving into ihram, pilgrims are supposed to refrain from sex, quarreling, killing animals, using perfumes, shaving or cutting their hair, and (for men) covering the head and (for women) covering the face. Only then do they enter Mecca itself, typically through a checkpoint marked by a massive sculpture of the Quran, beyond which only Muslims are allowed.

Once inside the city, the pilgrims proceed to the Grand Mosque. After entering its octagonal courtyard they move over gray and white marble toward the **Kaaba**

Millions of Muslim pilgrims circumambulate the Kaaba shrine each year in Mecca, Saudi Arabia, as part of the *hajj*, which is one of the Five Pillars of Islam.

("Cube"), which marks the direction in which observant Muslims pray. Covered in black silk embroidered in gold with Quranic sayings, this shrine is said to have been established by Adam, circled by Noah's Ark during the Great Flood, rebuilt after that disaster by **Abraham** and his son Ishmael, defiled by idol worshipers, and later reconsecrated by Muhammad on behalf of the One True God.

In the first and most iconic rite of the hajj, pilgrims stream around the Kaaba counterclockwise in spirals of human bodies. The Grand Mosque is the only major mosque where members of both sexes worship together, so men and women, boys and girls move as one as they circle the Kaaba seven times. The elderly and infirm are pushed in wheelchairs or carried overhead. Family members lock arms in an effort to stay together. Meanwhile, people of all ages and abilities snap selfies, adding a new, arm-outstretched bodily posture to this ancient ritual. Some brave souls press through the widening gyre of human bodies to kiss the silver-clad black cornerstone, possibly a meteorite, believed to be the only remnant from Abraham's renovation. But here the assembly looks more like a mosh pit than a religious congregation, so it is mostly sturdy men who venture near.

After circling the Kaaba, pilgrims perform "The Run," which reenacts the episode when Abraham left his infant son, Ishmael, and his Egyptian wife, Hagar, alone in the desert. When their water ran out, Hagar ran back and forth between two hills seven times, desperately seeking water for her thirsty son. As she was about to give up hope, Ishmael kicked at the sand and water bubbled up in a torrent. Pilgrims used to reenact this story by running back and forth between these two hills in the open air. Today, they walk indoors in long air-conditioned halls. Another element in this remembrance (a rare moment in the world's religions when men imitate the actions of a woman) is drinking from a well, supposedly at the very site that Hagar and Ishmael discovered,

Abraham (or Ibrahim)
major Islamic prophet and champion of monotheism

hadith
Islamic scripture, second in authority only to the Quran, consisting of the exemplary sayings and actions of Muhammad and his companions

which is near the Kaaba. Nowadays this holy water is piped in through a purification plant that also bottles water for purchase.

Although Mecca and the hajj are inseparable in the popular imagination, this five-day event occurs mainly outside Mecca. In fact, it does not really get going until pilgrims leave Mecca on the first day of the hajj after performing the first rite at the Kaaba. Together they move—on foot, on tens of thousands of buses, and via high-speed rail—five miles east to Mina, which each year shape-shifts from a largely uninhabited village to a massive tent city. There they spend the night, as their prophet Muhammad himself is said to have done on his own pilgrimage.

At dawn on the second day, guides usher pilgrims from Mina to Arafat for the central act of the hajj. Here the pilgrimage downshifts from movement to stillness in the noon-to-sunset ritual of standing at Arafat. Like so many other events of the hajj, this is a ritual of remembrance—in this case, of the time Muhammad, during his hajj, sat on his camel and delivered his farewell sermon on the Mount of Mercy. But to stand at Arafat and gaze up at the obelisk marking the spot where Muhammad spoke is not merely to recall that day. It is to look back to the moment when Adam and Eve were reunited at Arafat and to look forward to the Day of Judgment, when all will be called to account.

At Arafat, the prayers of pilgrims fill the air like incense in a traditional Catholic Mass. Meanwhile, God draws near, lowering himself to hear the pleas of believers. According to a saying of Muhammad known as a **hadith**, "There is no day on which God frees people from the Fire more so than on the Day of Arafat." This day ends at sunset with a cannon shot that signals it is time for pilgrims to proceed to Muzdalifah, midway between Arafat and Mecca, where they stay overnight. During this "halt at Muzdalifah," they gather forty-nine small stones that they will later throw at pillars representing Satan.

Much is made of the equality of believers at the hajj, as men and women of all skin colors in their indistinguishable white outfits pray together in the open air. In fact, equality is the theme of a chapter titled "Mecca" in *The Autobiography of Malcolm X* (1964), which speaks of "all races, all colors—blue-eyed blonds to black-skinned Africans" living "as one" in "true brotherhood." One night, Malcolm X writes of his hajj, "with nothing but the sky overhead I lay awake amid sleeping Muslim brothers and I learned that pilgrims from every land—every color, and class, and rank; high officials and the beggar alike—all snored in the same language."[2]

But this equality is more dream than reality. Tensions abide between Sunni and Shia Muslims, who represent Islam's two main branches, and particularly between Saudis (who are mostly Sunnis) and Iranians (who are mostly Shia). In 2016, the Iranian government boycotted the hajj, refusing to allow any of its citizens to participate. Gender distinctions also persist. All women must be accompanied by a male guardian or be part of an authorized group, in which case they need a letter of permission from a husband, brother, or son. In *Standing Alone at Mecca* (2005), journalist Asra Nomani describes the loneliness she felt as an unmarried mother making her hajj in a patriarchal society, even as she was comforted along the way by a "spiritual umbilical cord" that connected her to Muslim matriarchs from Eve to modern feminists.[3]

As the Kashmiri journalist Basharat Peer has argued, the most visible affront to the egalitarian ideal of the hajj is economic. Though water is sprayed on perspiring pilgrims without regard to their incomes, only the well-to-do sport solar-powered umbrellas with built-in fans, flashlights, and GPS systems. And while everyone sleeps under the stars at Muzdalifah, at Mina and Arafat the poor bake under the hot sun, nibble biscuits, and sleep on bridges while the wealthy lounge in air-conditioned tents boasting flat-screen televisions and sumptuous buffets.

On the third day of the hajj, still miles away from Mecca, pilgrims return to Mina. They recall the story, known to many Christians and Jews, of Abraham's near-sacrifice of his beloved son. Satan tries to convince Abraham to ignore God's command to sacrifice his son (Ishmael in the Quranic telling), but Abraham is faithful. Each time Satan tempts him to disobey God, he throws stones at Satan to chase him away. Just as Abraham is about to kill Ishmael, an animal is substituted instead. On this day, the Festival of Sacrifice known as Eid al-Adha, Muslims worldwide participate in the hajj from a distance, slaughtering animals as offerings themselves. Meanwhile, back in Mina, pilgrims cast stones at Satan as Abraham had done.

After casting these stones, pilgrims start to transition from the state of ihram back to everyday life. Men stand in long lines to have their heads shaved. Women trim their hair. Pilgrims of both sexes bathe and put on normal clothes—a sign that the central rituals of the hajj are over and it will soon be time to return home.

On days four and five of the hajj, after again throwing stones at the pillars in Mina, pilgrims return to Mecca to circle the Kaaba one last time. Afterward, many travel two hundred miles north to **Medina** to visit the mosque and tomb of Muhammad, though that journey is not officially part of the hajj. When they return home, pilgrims will be lauded as *hajjis* (men) or *hajjas* (women). In some countries, folk art of the journeys, complete with images of jets and the Kaaba itself, will be painted on their homes.

Medina
Islam's second holiest city, the place where Muhammad and his followers migrated in 622 and established the Muslim community and calendar

When Muslims return from the hajj, it is customary in some regions to depict their journeys on the exteriors of their homes, like this one in Egypt.

OUR STORY

The hajj is said by pilgrims to incorporate virtually every key element of Muslim life, including prayer, submission, divine unity, and the unity of the Muslim community. The importance of the sacred places in and around Mecca through which pilgrims move each year is reinforced by the stories pilgrims tell. These stories are personal. They are also collective, drawing on the Quran and other Islamic texts that place Mecca at the center of the world. To tell the story of Mecca is to revisit the story of creation, the biography of Muhammad, and the coming Day of Judgment. This is one way Muslims have told that story among themselves.

Adam and Abraham in Mecca

*In the beginning, Allah the Creator, the Maker, the Shaper of Forms brought the cosmos into being. He created the sun and the moon, separating day from night. He placed the heavens above and the earth below and called each to himself in submission. Into this creation, God crafted Adam, the first human being and the first **prophet**, out of dust gathered from the house of God known as the Kaaba, from Jerusalem, and from other points around the globe. God then brought Adam to life by blowing his spirit into him and appointed him his viceregent on earth.*

In the Garden of Eden, God told Adam and Eve not to eat from the Tree of Immortality. But Satan tempted Adam to eat from the tree, and he did. This did not make human beings sinful, but it did demonstrate their ability to forget their true nature and to neglect God. Adam and Eve were then cast out of Eden. They were also separated from one another: Adam was banished to the Indian subcontinent and Eve to Jeddah.

Eventually, Adam repented and asked for forgiveness and God appointed him as his first prophet. God then dispatched him to Mecca with an angel as his guide. There, at the site where angels worshiped God before human creation, Adam built the Kaaba shrine, complete with its iconic black stone sent from the heavens. He then performed (again with an angel's help) the first pilgrimage, circling the Kaaba, standing at Arafat, and casting stones at the devil. At Arafat, Adam and Eve were reunited. The children of these original humans were not born with original sin. Therefore there was no effort at salvation, no atonement by Jesus, no incarnation of God in a human body, and no crucified Christ. But humans are a forgetful and ungrateful lot. They turned away from their innate understanding of God and became selfish instead. God in his mercy sent reminders in the form of prophets and scriptures warning them to return to the true path.

Adam and Eve had children in and around Mecca. Out from that sacred center, human civilization spread. Later heroes from the Hebrew Bible were drawn to Mecca much as pilgrims are drawn today. Noah circled the Kaaba in his Ark as it is destroyed during the Great Flood. Abraham and Ishmael rebuilt it. But the central figure in our story, and the

prophets
human beings through whom God brings his revelations into the world, including Adam, Abraham, Moses, Jesus, and finally Muhammad, "the seal of the prophets"

Muhammad (570–632)
founder, lawmaker, jurist, politician, general, family man, the human exemplar of the Islamic way, the source of the sayings and actions in the hadith, and the final prophet of Islam

Quran
the Arabic words of God brought into the world through the prophet Muhammad; a short book of 114 chapters, the Quran's key teachings include the unity of God, the prophethood of Muhammad, the Day of Judgment, and afterlife rewards and punishments

Jesus
Islamic prophet and messenger and a key figure in the Quran, where he appears as Isa

final prophet in a line that runs from Adam to Abraham to Ishmael to Jesus, is **Muhammad**. Through this illiterate man, the **Quran** came into the world as the perfect and eternal Word of God. This text is both a warning and a reminder. No, humans are not self-sufficient. Yes, they are meant to submit to God. And, yes, a final reckoning is coming on the Day of Judgment, when God will dispatch unbelievers to hell and believers to paradise, depending on their actions in this world.

"There is no God but God," God says repeatedly in the Quran, so Muhammad is obviously not divine. That does not mean, however, that his life is not as miraculous as the life of the prophet **Jesus**. Before Muhammad was born, angels appeared to his mother Amina to inform her that she is to give birth to a prophet whom she should call Muhammad, which means "highly praised." Later in his life, after his miraculous Night Journey from Mecca to Jerusalem, this "highly praised" man went to heaven with Gabriel by his side. In heaven, he met Adam, Moses, and Jesus, and God taught him how to perform the five daily prayers required of all who truly submit.

But Muhammad is more than a prophet bringing God's words to earth. He is the exemplar for Muslims today. He models the submission required for entry to Paradise. He is Islam's model lawgiver, judge, ruler, statesman, general,

This Persian illustration of Muhammad's Night Journey appears in the *Khamsa of Nizami*, a twelfth-century book of Islamic poetry. During medieval times, it was common for devotional paintings to show Muhammad's face. Later, many Muslims declared it forbidden to depict prophets' faces.

and family man. Finally, Muhammad is also a spiritual geographer of sorts. This "seal of the prophets" (the last in a line from Adam through Moses and Jesus) is also the man who seals the fate of Mecca as the most sacred place on earth.

ISLAM IN TODAY'S WORLD

Today, Islam is the world's second-largest religion, and it is steadily gaining on Christianity. Nearly 1.9 billion people call themselves Muslims. While the global percentage of Christians has declined slightly since 1900—from 34.4 to 32.3 percent—Islam's share of the world's population has nearly doubled over that same period—from 12.4 to 24.3 percent. Thanks to high birth rates in Muslim-majority countries, this gap is rapidly narrowing, though it should be noted that high birth rates are more closely tied to economic factors than to religious ones. According to the World Religion Database, Muslims are expected to account in 2050 for 28.7 percent of the world's population compared with 35 percent for Christians.

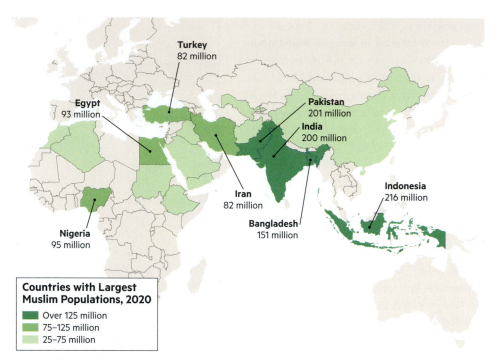

As the global Muslim population grows, Islam is moving out from its origins on the Arabian Peninsula and becoming an "Asian religion," thanks to large numbers of Muslims in countries such as Indonesia and India.

Although Islam is widely associated with its birthplace on the Arabian Peninsula, it is now a religion of Asia. The overwhelming majority of Muslims reside in Asia. Indonesia is the country with the largest number of adherents: 216 million. The next three countries with the largest Muslim populations—India, Pakistan, and Bangladesh—are also in Asia. Three more countries in the top ten— Nigeria, Egypt, and Algeria—are in Africa, and the remaining three are Turkey, Iran, and Iraq. The Central Asian republics of Kazakhstan, Kyrgyzstan, Uzbekistan, Turkmenistan, and Tajikistan all have Muslim majorities. In Eastern Europe, Islam is the leading religion in Kosovo and Albania, and there are rapidly growing Muslim populations in many Western European countries, led by France with 9.4 percent, Sweden and Belgium with over 8 percent, and Austria and the Netherlands with over 7 percent. In Canada, about 3.7 percent are Muslims, and in the United States, where roughly a million Muslims support about a thousand mosques, that figure is only 1.5 percent.

Muslims are often depicted in popular Western movies and television shows as terrorists or taxi drivers, but in the real world this religious community contains multitudes. Muslims are rich and poor, gay and straight. They speak Arabic and Urdu, English and French. They play professional basketball, football, soccer, and hockey. There are traditionalist Muslims, progressive Muslims, and secular Muslims. Terrorists chanting "Allahu Akbar" ("God is great") perpetrated the attacks on the World Trade Center on 9/11, but twenty-eight Muslims—janitors and bond traders and police cadets—were killed in those attacks, which were widely denounced by Muslims worldwide.

Muslims also differ in how they live their religion. The Quran speaks of God as closer to believers than their own jugular veins (50:16). Many Muslims feel that closeness. Others do not. Religions are lived by human beings whose beliefs and experiences do not always match those prescribed by religious authorities. Just as some Jews eat cheeseburgers, some Muslims drink alcohol and eat pork (both generally forbidden by the traditional tenets of Islam). Many Muslims perform the prescribed five prayers a day, others pray only once a week (during Friday prayers in the mosque), and some never pray at all. Many Muslim women wear no head covering at all. Others wear a burka in public, a veil that covers the head and face entirely, with just a mesh over the eyes to see.

The most fundamental dividing line in Muslim identity runs between Sunni and Shia traditions. After the death of Muhammad, these two main Islamic groups split over who should lead their communities, what role their leaders should play, and how Islamic law and theology should be interpreted. Among **Sunni** Muslims (from *sunna*, or established custom), the term **imam** ("leader") refers simply to the person who leads congregational worship services on Fridays. Sunnis select these leaders from among their community as a whole and invest them with social and political authority, but they invest religious authority in the **umma**, or Muslim community. The **Shia**, by contrast, select their Imams from descendants of Muhammad and invest them with social, political, and religious authority. Among Shia Muslims, the Imam leads the entire Shia community and is widely regarded as infallible. Today roughly 89 percent of Muslims are Sunnis and 10 percent are Shia. The remaining 1 percent fall into smaller groupings that either reject both the Sunni and Shia traditions or attempt to bridge them. Iran, Azerbaijan, Bahrain, Yemen, and Iraq all have Shia-majority populations, but Iran is the largest and most influential. The countries with the largest Sunni-majority populations are Indonesia, Pakistan, and Bangladesh.

Sunni
majority branch of Islam that predominates in most Muslim-majority countries

imam/Imam
among Sunnis, the local leader who oversees congregational prayers; among the Shia, the community leader and a blood relative of Muhammad

umma
literally "community," more specifically the worldwide community of Muslims

Shia
minority branch of Islam now dominant in Iran

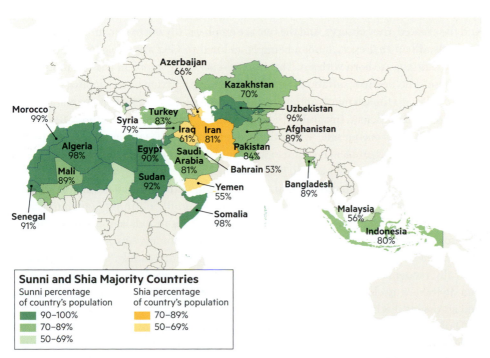

Among the world's Muslim-majority countries, Shia Islam predominates in Iran while Sunni Islam predominates from Morocco to Saudi Arabia to Pakistan.

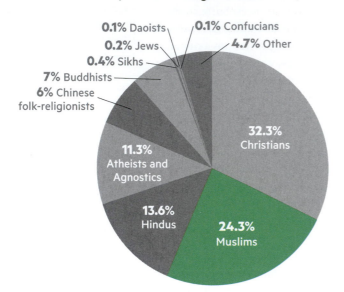

Comparison of Religions Worldwide, 2020

0.1% Daoists
0.2% Jews
0.4% Sikhs
7% Buddhists
6% Chinese folk-religionists
0.1% Confucians
4.7% Other
32.3% Christians
11.3% Atheists and Agnostics
13.6% Hindus
24.3% Muslims

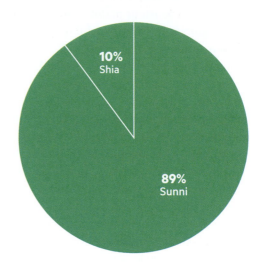

Major Islam Branches, 2020

10% Shia
89% Sunni

ISLAM 101

➔ How to succeed in this life and the life to come?

When it comes to the key categories of divinity and humanity, some religions, such as Hinduism, blur the line. Muslims underscore it. There is a vast gap between the creator and the created, they observe, and the two are emphatically not to be confused. However, Muslims affirm that every human being is inclined to God and the good. They do not believe humans are born with sin. Therefore, sin is not the problem Islam is designed to fix. There is no need for salvation from sin, or for a crucifixion to accomplish it.

According to the Islamic tradition, the human problem is pride. Human beings act as if they are self-sufficient, imagining that they can get along just fine without God or one another. "The idol of your self," writes the Sufi mystic Rumi, "is the mother of (all) idols."[4] The solution to this problem is submission to God, who alone is self-sufficient. But to submit is not just to bow to divine will. It is to follow Islamic law. **Sharia** is the Arabic word for this law, so strictly speaking "Sharia law" is redundant. But this term also conjures up related concepts such as *religion* and *way of life*. Literally meaning "a path to water," Sharia marks the route to God and paradise. Like Torah in Judaism, Sharia points not only to the law but also to the broader process of legal reasoning. Again like Torah, Sharia is comprehensive, attending to worship, food, war, sex, and family. However, Muslims typically recognize a significant gap between the law as we know it via jurisprudence and divine law itself—a gap that allows for a wide variety of competing opinions inside and across legal schools.

Daily prayers literally put Muslim bodies into a posture of submission, with their knees, hands, foreheads, and noses pressed to the ground. "Are you prostrate or are you proud?" the Islamic tradition asks, and observant Muslims respond by lowering themselves in prayer. *Masjid*, the Arabic term for mosque, means "place of prostration," and

Sharia ("path to water")
Islamic law and, more broadly, the Islamic way of life

the truly devout who surrender to this practice for a lifetime often develop a mark on their forehead that the Quran calls the mark or "effect of prostration" (48:29). In addition to an open space for prayer, mosques typically include a niche in the wall marking the direction to Mecca and therefore the direction of prayer. Mosques also have a place for ritual washing, a stand for the Quran, and a pulpit where the congregational leader delivers the Friday sermon.

Submission to God leads to the goal of Islam: success here and in the hereafter. This success includes health and happiness. It also includes an afterlife of rivers and gardens and other delights, whether those rewards are taken literally or metaphorically.

The techniques for achieving this goal—for turning the proud into the successful—are belief and works, and submission of the entire person, both mind and body, to the divine will and purpose. "Those who believe and perform righteous deeds," reads the Quran, "theirs shall be . . . the supreme triumph" (85:11). Some passages in the Quran seem to emphasize belief over practice. "It is not piety to turn your faces toward the east and west," reads one. "Rather, piety is he who believes in God, the Last Day, the angels, the Book, and the prophets." But after this nod to belief, this passage returns to practice, defining "the reverent" as the person "who gives wealth, despite loving it, to kinsfolk, orphans, the indigent, the traveler, beggars, and for [the ransom of] slaves; and performs the prayer and gives the alms" (2:177). Given this emphasis on submission—"The Bedouin say, 'We believe.'. . . Rather, say, 'We have submitted'" (49:14)—scholars often describe Islam as "orthopraxy" ("right practice") rather than "orthodoxy" ("right doctrine"). Whereas early Christians came together around statements of belief known as creeds, early Muslims (like Jews) coalesced more around practices. Muslims have classically affirmed **Six Articles of Faith**—namely, one God; angels; holy books; prophets, including Muhammad; the Day of Judgment; and predestination, which refers in this case to God's knowledge, before we are even born, of our eternal destiny. But to be a Muslim has typically been more about action than belief.

Central to this orthopraxy today are the so-called **Five Pillars** of Islam: reciting the Shahada ("There is no god but God, and Muhammad is the prophet of God"), praying

Six Articles of Faith
six key Islamic beliefs, namely one God; angels; holy books; prophets, including Muhammad; the Day of Judgment; and predestination

Five Pillars
five key Islamic practices, namely Shahada, or "witnessing" that "there is no God but God and Muhammad is the Messenger of God"; five daily prayers; almsgiving; fasting during the month of Ramadan; hajj

Upon hearing the call to prayer, Muslims unfurl their prayer mats and prepare to pray, whether at home, at work, or even in a crowded Malaysian shopping center.

Written in the sacred language of Arabic, the Shahada, or "testimony" to the unity of God and the prophethood of Muhammad, frames the entrance to a mosque in Istanbul, Turkey.

five daily prayers, giving alms to the poor, fasting during Ramadan, and going on the hajj. Each of these Five Pillars is a technique of surrender and, as such, a pathway to worldly and otherworldly success. Visible in each of these Five Pillars, and indeed in all of Muslim life, are the three key symbols of Islam: God, Muhammad, and the Quran.

God

Like Jews, Muslims are strict monotheists who reject the Christian and Hindu notions that God can incarnate in human form. **Tawhid**, usually translated as "divine unity," is the central concept in this strict monotheism. The standard formula for praising God in Islam is *Allahu Akbar*: "God is great" (or "God is most great"). The term **Allah** here is the Arabic term for God, also used by Arabic-speaking Christians and other theists. The greatness of God in this formula means that he is eternal, omniscient, omnipotent, and singular. According to the Islamic tradition, God's number is one, not three. God is not engaged in a duel of equals with some demonic force. God is unique, without partners, and without worthy antagonists. To mistake a human being for God or to make a god of wealth or power is to commit **shirk**, or ascribing partners to God.

God is traditionally said to have ninety-nine "beautiful names," including The Merciful, The Powerful, The Creator, The Just, The Loving, The Wise, The Nourisher, The Friend, The Guide, The First, and The Last. These names might seem to anthropomorphize God—by reducing the divine to human terms. But one purpose of this list is to suggest that God is beyond our understanding—that God's nature cannot be captured even in these ninety-nine names.

Islam's strict monotheism has made Muslims wary of the sort of paintings and sculptures of God or Muhammad that Christians produced in the Sistine Chapel or the Pietà. As a result, Muslims do not typically produce the "graven images" also prohibited in the Hebrew Bible. Though some Muslims have produced figurative art, including paintings of Muhammad, their sacred art of choice is calligraphy, beautiful renderings of the words and letters of the Quran. These are widely viewed, according to the Metropolitan Museum of Art, as "the most highly regarded and most fundamental element of Islamic art."[5] This judgment is not confined to museum curators, however. Islamic calligraphers also had a major influence on modern Western artists, including the great cubist painter Pablo Picasso, who once remarked, "If I had known there was such a thing as Islamic Calligraphy, I would never have started to paint."[6]

Muhammad

Although in Islam God is all-powerful, he is also merciful. When humans forget him, he sends prophets to call us back to himself and to our true nature. Muhammad is the final messenger and the "seal" (last) of the prophets. He conveyed the message of God's unity to the Arab people and, through them, to the wider world. Therefore, Muhammad is often referred to as "the Prophet," with the epithet "Peace be upon him" appended to his name. Muhammad is emphatically not God. He is the exemplary human being, but he *is* a human being and, as such, is not to be worshiped. Neither is Islam "Mohammedanism," an antiquated word for the tradition once used by non-Muslims. Even so, Muslims glory in stories about Muhammad's heroic life, which make it plain that he is an extraordinary figure not only in religion but also in law, politics, and military and family affairs. After twenty-four years of monogamous marriage to his first wife, a businesswoman named Khadija, he entered into a series of marriages in keeping with a custom of polygamy widespread among not only Arabs but also Jews. One of the earliest sources for personal Muslim piety, a gravestone for an Egyptian woman that dates to 690–691, speaks of "being bereft of the Prophet Muhammad" as "the greatest calamity of the People of Islam."[7]

To determine how to imitate this exemplary man, Muslims have gathered vast collections of hadith (literally "happenings"): accounts of things Muhammad and his companions said or did, which are second in authority only to the Quran. For example, one hadith states, "Seeking knowledge is a duty of every Muslim, man or woman."[8] Hadith are the key source for determining how to follow Muhammad's "beautiful example" (33:21) and for ruling on Islamic law, since many legal questions are not addressed in the Quran. Each individual hadith includes a chain of transmission and the content itself, and no hadith is authoritative unless the chain of transmission (from Muhammad or his companion to the person reporting it) is sound and the content of the text accords with the Quran.

In the ninth and tenth centuries, Sunni scholars gathered hadith into six main collections, each deeply influenced by the debates of the time. The Shia produced parallel collections, which also include the sayings and actions of their Imams. One of these collections, Muhammad Baqir Majlisi's *Oceans of Lights*, runs to 110 volumes and is Islam's longest book. The hadith give Muslims insights into many mundane matters, such as how their prophet slept (on his right side), whether he trimmed his mustache (yes) or his beard (no), and whether he thought it was acceptable for a man to eat with a menstruating woman (yes).

Together with the Quran, the hadith provide the basis for the **Sunna**, or customary practice of Muslims. One crucial way to determine the Sunna of something is to ask "What Would Muhammad Do?" Thus there is in Islam a tradition of the imitation of Muhammad that parallels in some respects the *Imitatio Christi* ("What Would Jesus Do?") tradition in Christianity. In this case, however, the imitation goes as far as putting your right shoe on first and preferring cats to dogs.

Quran

A third central symbol in Islam is the Quran, which Muslims regard as the very words of God spoken in perfect Arabic. *Quran* means "recitation." The first words revealed to Muhammad were "Recite in the Name of thy Lord Who created, created man from a blood clot" (96:1–2). According to Muslims, the Jewish and Christian scriptures were also revealed by God through his prophets but

tawhid
divine unity: God is not three but one and God is unique, unequalled, and without partners; this is the central teaching in Islam

Allah ("The God")
Arabic term for the singular divine and the central symbol in the Islamic tradition

shirk
idolatry; ascribing partners to God or otherwise bowing down to anyone or anything other than the one, true God

Sunna
authoritative custom and therefore a key source of Islamic law, typically rooted in the Quran and the *hadith* but also complementing both

Islam at a Glance

Problem: pride

Solution: submission

Techniques: daily prayer, fasting, almsgiving, pilgrimage, and affirming the unity of God and the prophethood of Muhammad

Exemplar: Muhammad, who in addition to being the final prophet is also the exemplary human being; also (for the Shia) Imams and (for Sufis) sheikhs

Therefore, Islam is a tradition of Muslims ("submitters") who give up their pride and achieve thisworldly and otherworldly success by bowing down to the one true God.

were later corrupted. The Quran, by contrast, is the pure and perfect word of God, who gave his words to an angel, who recited them to Muhammad, who recited them to his companions. While the voice of the Christian Bible varies from God to Jesus to Paul, it is God alone who speaks in the Quran. Because God spoke Arabic for this final revelation, the Quran is only the Quran in Arabic. Translations are just interpretations, not the Quran itself.

It is tempting to compare the Quran to other scriptures, but according to the British historian Michael Cook, "Nothing resembling the Koran as such is to be found in any other tradition; . . . and if it had predecessors, we know nothing of them."[9] Religious studies scholar Wilfred Cantwell Smith has compared the Quran to Jesus, because each is viewed as the Word of God. As Christians "take and eat" the gift of Christ in the Eucharist, Muslims take the gift of the Quran into their bodies by reciting it, inhaling its words into their lungs and expressing them out over their lips. From this perspective, the Christian analog to Muhammad is the Virgin Mary, since both are pure vehicles (one illiterate, one a virgin) through whom the gift of God comes into the world.

Today, the Islamic gift is, of course, a book, but only one in five of the world's Muslims understand its Arabic. Even for those who can, the Quran is, like the sacred syllable *Om* to Hindus, more about the sound than the meaning. Its words are recited more than read. In fact, it is not unusual for children to memorize the whole thing. Those who do are revered as *hafiz* (for boys and men) or *hafiza* (for girls and women). Qurans themselves are also treated as sacred objects, protected on special stands above the polluting floor. Favorite passages are secreted into amulets and lovingly painted on mosques and tombs across the Muslim world.

Though originally transmitted orally, the Quran was written down perhaps twenty years after Muhammad's death. The current text, about the length of the Christian New Testament, is divided into verses called *ayas* and chapters called *suras*, which are roughly arranged longest to shortest. Suras come with easy-to-remember titles, such as "The Cow," "The Unbelievers," and "The Earthquake."

Scholars distinguish between earlier suras revealed in Mecca and later suras revealed in Medina. The Meccan suras (often shorter) tend to focus on spirituality and theology, while the Medinan suras (often longer) typically focus on the legal and practical concerns of a growing community. Like Hinduism, Islam is considered an all-encompassing way of life by many adherents. The Quran tells Muslims how to worship, but it also tells them how to divide estates, hunt, punish criminals, wage war, draft contracts, and marry and divorce.

The main purpose of the Quran, however, is to provide a warning. Its core doctrine is God's oneness. The core fact of human existence is that we all turn away from this singular God, and we must turn back—or suffer the consequences here and in the afterlife. There is only one God, *the* God, and to him all human beings must submit.

Jewish and Christian readers who pick up the Quran for the first time are often surprised to see that its cast of characters extends to biblical figures such as Abraham, Adam, Abel, Cain, David, Goliath, Isaac, Ishmael, Israel,

Quranic recitation competitions are the spelling bees of the Muslim world. Here, Abdullah Dhabi, age eight, recites at a competition in Australia in 2005.

Jacob, Jesus, John the Baptist, Joseph, Mary, Moses, Noah, Pharaoh, and Satan. **Mary**, the virgin mother of Jesus and the only woman named in the Quran, actually plays a much bigger role here than she does in her New Testament cameo. The only woman to command her own sura, she is presented as a model Muslim with strong and enduring faith.

One of the great themes of the Quran, and a major reason for Islam's success, is its emphasis on social justice. The Quran articulates a "preferential option for the weak" that some have compared to the "preferential option for the poor" that is the hallmark of liberation theology in Catholic Latin America. The pious, says the Quran, "give food, despite loving it, to the indigent, the orphan, and the captive" (76:8). Muslims follow this injunction by giving alms to the poor. Another consequence of this commitment is a prohibition on charging interest for loans of money, which has produced in the modern world a specialized Islamic banking industry with total assets approaching $3 billion.

The Quran is preoccupied, however, with the world to come. In fact, it is difficult to find a sura that does not address the afterlife. Hundreds of verses spell out the horrors of hell, the splendors of paradise, the rewards awaiting martyrs, the mechanics of bodily resurrection, and the events of the Day of Judgment. Muslims disagree on how these verses are to be read—literally? allegorically?—but hell and paradise are described here in far greater detail than in the Christian Bible.

Mary is the only woman with her own dedicated *sura* in the Quran. In this miniature painting from the Safavid dynasty, Mary holds the baby Jesus, whom Muslims recognize as a prophet.

ISLAMIC HISTORY

Muslims trace their tradition back to Abraham, whom they regard as the father of monotheism. Beyond Abraham, that tradition goes back to Noah and the Flood. It goes back even to Adam and Eve and the creation of the universe. From a historical perspective, what came to be known as Islam began with an Arab trader who became, arguably, the most influential figure in world history. But religions do not spring, full born, from the heads of their founders. Like human beings, they develop over time, in fits and starts, in response to internal cues and external pressures. The Jesus movement took centuries to evolve into Christianity. Islam developed more quickly, but it took many decades after the first whispers of an angel in the ear of Muhammad to develop into a religion of its own, and its current Sunni/Shia structure was not constructed until centuries later.

Muhammad and Proto-Islam

According to Islamic traditions, Muhammad was born in Mecca around 570 CE and died in Medina sixty-two years later, in 632. Today, he is remembered as the founder of a religion expected to surpass Christianity in followers sometime before the end of this century. But he was also a missionary and commander-in-chief who spread his movement far and wide across the Arabian Peninsula. For this reason, he can be credited with playing in early Islam the roles that Jesus (the founder), Paul (the missionary), and Constantine (the ruler) played in early Christianity. Nonetheless, the historical Muhammad, like the historical Jesus, is an elusive and controversial character, who is both praised by Muslims

Mary
mother of Jesus and the subject of a full *sura* in the Quran

as God's final messenger and criticized by his opponents as a false prophet, a heretic, and an Arabian imposter.

Resolving these disagreements may be impossible, because evidence from Muhammad's life is scant and later sources carry the biases of either insiders or outsiders. About the only thing regarding Muhammad's life that historians now agree on is that he had one. He is named early on in a Syriac and a Greek source, and an Armenian's account from the 660s describes him as a merchant who preached about Abraham. In the absence of in-depth secular sources, most historians rely heavily on traditional Muslim narratives, even as they try to cut from these narratives obvious references to miracles or God's providence.

According to traditional accounts, Muhammad was born into the influential Quraysh tribe of Arab merchants. His father died before he was born. His mother's death orphaned him when he was very young, so he was raised by his paternal grandfather (who also died shortly thereafter) and then by an uncle. As a boy, he worked as

CHRONOLOGY OF ISLAM

c. 570 Muhammad's birth

610 First revelations of the Quran

622 Muhammad and his followers move from Mecca to Medina (the hijra), where they establish their community and begin the Islamic calendar

630 Muhammad takes Mecca

632 Muhammad performs the hajj and dies shortly thereafter; he is succeeded by Abu Bakr, who becomes the first caliph

638 Muslims take Jerusalem

661–750 Umayyad dynasty, centered in Damascus

c. 653 The text of the Quran is fixed under the third caliph Uthman

680 Muhammad's grandson Husain is martyred at Karbala, precipitating the split between Sunni and Shia Muslims

692 Dome of the Rock is completed in Jerusalem

711 Muslims expand their footprint west into Spain and east onto the Indian subcontinent

750–1258 Abbasid dynasty, centered in Baghdad

874 "Occultation" of the twelfth Shia Imam, who goes into hiding

909–1171 Shia Fatamid dynasty of North Africa

1058–1111 Life of the philosopher, wanderer, and Sufi mystic al-Ghazali

1099 Crusaders capture Jerusalem in Pope Urban II's First Crusade

1187 Saladin retakes Jerusalem

1200 Muslims move into Southeast Asia

1207–1273 Life of Rumi, Persian mystic, poet, and inspiration for Mevlevi Sufi order

1238 Construction begins on the Alhambra in modern-day Granada, Spain

1258 Mongols take Baghdad, ending Abbasid dynasty

1281–1922 Ottoman empire

1441–1888 Transatlantic slave trade captures and transports millions of Africans to Europe and then the Americas; at least 10 percent are Muslims

1492 Christians take Granada, the last stronghold of Muslim Spain, expelling Jews and Muslims

1501–1722 Safavid empire spreads Shiism throughout Persia

1526–1858 Mughal empire in India

1556–1605 Reign of the Mughal emperor Akbar, now known for his early efforts at religious pluralism

1627 Construction begins on the Taj Mahal, Shah Jahan's tomb to his wife in modern-day Agra, India

1649 *The Alcoran of Mahomet* becomes the first translation of the Quran into English

1703–1792 Life of Muhammad ibn 'Abd al-Wahhab, antimodern reformer

a shepherd. As a young man, he worked on a caravan for an accomplished older widow and wealthy businesswoman named Khadija, who around 595 became his wife. Khadija's thriving business introduced him to the wider world, including the religious worlds of Jews and Christians.

It also launched him on a life of contemplation that included retreats to the mountains outside Mecca. In 610, in a cave on Mount Hira, when he was roughly forty years old, he encountered an angel who appeared to him, commanding that he recite. Like prophets in other religions, Muhammad was at first reluctant to accept the role. Perhaps he had been possessed by an evil spirit. Or perhaps he was a budding poet. But Khadija believed in him and became the first Muslim. Encouraged by his faithful wife, Muhammad returned to the cave, where he continued to receive revelations for the next twenty-three years. The words he received he transmitted to followers, who later wrote them down. This divine dictation was in Arabic, so just as the early Christian movement was initially for Jews, the early Islamic movement was initially for Arabs. It affirmed strict monotheism

1848 *The Life of Omar ibn Said, Written by Himself*, the first book written in Arabic by an American Muslim slave

1857 After a failed mutiny, the British expel the last Mughal emperor from India and wrest control of the country from the British East India Company

1906–1966 Life of Sayyid Qutb, Egyptian thinker, makes takfir a centerpiece of radical Islamist thought

1922 Ottoman caliphate becomes the last of the great Islamic dynasties to fall

1925–1965 Life of Nation of Islam leader and black nationalist Malcolm X

1930 W. D. Fard establishes the Nation of Islam in Detroit, Michigan

1947 British rule ends in India, and the subcontinent is partitioned into largely Hindu India and largely Muslim Pakistan

1948 State of Israel is founded

1957–2011 Life of Osama bin Laden, Saudi Islamist and al-Qaeda terrorist

1963 Muslims in Dearborn, Michigan, construct the largest mosque in North America

1964 Heavyweight boxing champion Cassius Clay announces his conversion to Islam and takes the name Muhammad Ali

1967 Israeli victory over Egypt, Jordan, and Syria in the Six-Day War brings one million Palestinians under Israeli rule

1978–1979 The Iranian Revolution leads to the founding of the Republic of Iran as an Islamic state

1988 Prime Minister Benazir Bhutto of Pakistan becomes the first Muslim woman elected head of state

1996 First Lady Hillary Clinton hosts the first Eid al-Fitr celebration at the White House

2001 Al-Qaeda terrorists hijack planes and kill roughly three thousand people in New York City; Washington, DC; and Pennsylvania

2005 Feminist Amina Wadud leads a pathbreaking mixed-gender prayer service in New York City

2007 Keith Ellison (D-MN) becomes the first Muslim in the U.S. Congress when he is sworn in on a Quran once owned by President Thomas Jefferson

2010–2012 Arab Spring

2017 Donald Trump becomes U.S. president after pledging to ban Muslims from entry into the United States

2019 Representatives Rashida Tlaib of Michigan and Ilhan Omar of Minnesota become the first Muslim women in the U.S. Congress

hijra
migration of Muhammad and his followers from Mecca to Medina in 622

versus Meccan paganism. It sided with the poor over wealthy merchants. And it looked forward to a Day of Judgment in which God would separate believers worthy of paradise from unbelievers worthy of hell.

By the time Muhammad began to preach, around 613, he had not just rejected polytheism (many gods). He had rejected Christian Trinitarianism (one god but three persons) and dualism (two warring spiritual entities). Muhammad was also convinced that "The God" (*Allah*) worshiped alongside his daughters at the Kaaba shrine was the one and only divinity, who had spoken earlier through Jewish and Christian prophets.

Many of the themes Muhammad taught—divine unity, prophecy, prayer, care for the poor, the coming judgment, the horrors of hell, and the splendors of paradise—echoed Jewish or Christian themes. So Muhammad had reason to hope that Jews and Christians would recognize that the God who had spoken through Abraham and Jesus was now speaking through him. But support came more slowly than he might have hoped. Muhammad's recitations sided with the poor and urged listeners to turn away from paganism toward the "straight path" of monotheism. These teachings angered Mecca's power brokers, whose livelihoods depended on spiritual tourism to Mecca's Kaaba shrine, where pilgrims came to worship various gods for a few months each year. Among those power brokers were his own Quraysh tribespeople, whose rituals endowed caves and stones with sacred power, including the black stone of the Kaaba. Muhammad won the allegiance of some members of his tribe, who for a time provided him with protection. But for the most part his converts—women, slaves, the poor, and working classes—lacked social power.

The deaths in 619 of Khadija and of the uncle who had raised and protected Muhammad led to even greater tensions with Mecca's elites. To escape persecution, some of Muhammad's followers moved to Christian Ethiopia. Others migrated 275 miles north to Yathrib, an oasis town whose feuding tribes asked Muhammad to mediate their disputes in return for safe haven for his followers. Muhammad and his trusted friend Abu Bakr went to Yathrib, a journey that Muslims now refer to as the **hijra** ("migration"). When they arrived in this town in 622—a date so dear to Muslims that the Islamic calendar begins from this "year of the hijra" (AH)—they established an *umma* (community). With Muhammad as their leader, this ragtag refugee community soon gained control of Yathrib, which was renamed Madinat al Nabi ("The City of the Prophet"), or Medina for short. Quranic revelations gradually shifted from theological to practical matters. Muhammad set down the rituals—of washing, praying, almsgiving, fasting, and pilgrimage—that would come to define this community.

This early Medinan community was complicated. It included "emigrants" from Mecca and "helpers" from Medina. It included former Arab polytheists who had come to believe in Muhammad's recitations, as well as Jews, Christians, and perhaps Zoroastrians. According to the Islam scholar Fred Donner, what the members of this diverse community shared was not yet Islam. It was a common commitment to strict monotheism, to intense piety, and to belief in a coming Day of Judgment. Participants in this community of pious monotheists, Donner contends, understood themselves not as "Muslims" but as "Believers"—a term that occurs nearly a thousand times in the Quran (versus less than seventy-five times for the term "Muslim").

The movement that Muhammad led to Medina and then out into the wider world also operated within a broader Arabian culture in which individuals and groups were linked by blood ties in a complex network of competing tribes. To hold this community together took economic, social, and political savvy. Unlike Mecca, which was a commercial town,

Medina was agricultural. So Muhammad had to redirect the economy of his community from trading to raiding Meccan caravans. This transition did not go smoothly. Muhammad fought with some Jewish tribes. He also fought with Meccan tribes, who finally ceded to him in 630.

Not long after his migration to Medina, Muhammad changed the direction in which his followers prayed from Jerusalem to Mecca. He also took control of the Kaaba itself. In an event that recalls the biblical story of Jesus chasing money changers out of the Jerusalem temple, Muhammad destroyed the Kaaba's 360 idols (though he supposedly spared images of Jesus and Mary). In 632, he returned, triumphant, to Mecca and performed the hajj. Back in Medina, he grew sick and died later that same year. Mourning him were four surviving children (all daughters), nine widows, and one Egyptian concubine. Again, according to tradition, his body was interred next to his mosque in a tomb that is now visited each year by millions.

For centuries, early Christians had struggled simply to survive in a hostile Roman empire. By contrast, Muhammad had spread his empire and his strict monotheism across much of the Arabian Peninsula in just two decades. Through a combination of political savvy, legal acumen, military might, and missionary zeal, he replaced what had been a stateless society with what was, in effect, the first Islamic empire.

The Sunni/Shia Split

Religions often experience a succession crisis after a founder dies. The Mormons splintered after a mob assassinated their founder Joseph Smith Jr. Muslims went through a similar crisis after Muhammad's death in 632. During Muhammad's lifetime, his followers were by no means one people. There were Meccans and Medinans and Jews. There were fellow fighters in his military campaigns, coworkers in his economic enterprises, collaborators in his political work. Muhammad kept these factions together through the force of his charismatic personality. After he died, three questions loomed: *Who* was going to lead the community? *How* was that leader to be chosen? *What* sort of authority was that leader going to have?

One group pushed for **Ali** (Muhammad's cousin and the husband of his daughter Fatima), whom they believed Muhammad had personally tapped as his **caliph** ("successor") shortly before his death. This group, convinced that Muhammad's successors should come from his extended family, later came to be known as the *shiat Ali* ("partisans of Ali"), or Shia for short. Another group, which came to be known as Sunnis, or people of the Sunna, believed that Muhammad's successor should be the best available person, regardless of lineage.

Out of this unresolved struggle, Abu Bakr, the father of Muhammad's beloved wife Aisha, emerged as Muhammad's first caliph in 632. But not everyone agreed to follow Abu Bakr. Some of Muhammad's followers returned to their pagan religions. Others continued to submit to God but not to Abu Bakr. As a result, Muslims were launched into "wars of apostasy." These wars were won by Abu Bakr and his men, who then pushed their military conquests (and their caravan raids) farther and farther afield, spreading their new religion and his caliphate in the process.

Abu Bakr, who ruled from 632 until his death two years later, was succeeded as caliph by Umar (634–644), Uthman (644–656), and then Ali (656–661). Then the real battle for succession occurred in a period Muslims now call their "First Civil War" (656–661).

Ali
son-in-law of Muhammad, fourth of the Sunnis' "right-guided" caliphs, and the person who, according to the Shia, should have succeeded Muhammad after his death

caliph
"successor" to Muhammad who governs the Muslim community

Husain

early Shia figure martyred in 680 on the Karbala battlefield and remembered especially on Ashura, the day of mourning

As Ali tried to broker a cessation of hostilities, a group of purists known as Kharijites ("seceders") objected to both sides. In fact, they objected so strongly that in 661 one of these seceders assassinated Ali—an act justified by the argument that those who disagreed with the Kharijites were apostates from Islam who deserved death.

In the wake of Ali's death, Mu'awiya, a nephew of the third caliph Uthman, consolidated power and began the Umayyad dynasty (661–750). He also moved the headquarters of the Islamic movement to Damascus in modern-day Syria and established Arabic as its official language. Thanks to victories in the early eighth century over Roman and Persian troops, the Umayyads extended their reach from Spain into the Indian subcontinent. They minted Islamic coins. They also built Jerusalem's Dome of the Rock, which contains some of the earliest existing verses from the Quran.

One of the defining events in this period—and one of the most monumental in Islamic history—came on the battlefield at Karbala in modern-day Iraq in 680. There Ali's son (and Muhammad's grandson) **Husain** led a failed uprising against the Umayyads. And there he was killed and beheaded. This event would produce the first sectarian split in the proto-Islamic movement, which permanently divided the Muslim community into a Sunni majority (which accepted the first three caliphs as "rightly guided") and a Shia minority (which rejected them as mere usurpers of Ali's rightful role). To the Shahada of the Sunnis—"There is no God but God, and Muhammad is the messenger of God"—the Shia added one more phrase: "and Ali is the friend of God."

The death of Husain at Karbala in 680 also seared into Shia consciousness a tradition of martyrdom that continues to this day. Each year during the opening days of the month of Muharram, Shia Muslims recall Husain's death in performances reminiscent of U.S. Civil War reenactments and Christian passion plays. They also recall Husain's devotion

Completed in the seventh century under the Umayyad caliphate, the golden-topped Dome of the Rock shines over the Old City of Jerusalem. One of Islam's holiest places, it stands on contested ground, atop the Western Wall on the site of the Israelites' Second Temple.

ISLAM BY THE NUMBERS

Four "Rightly Guided" Caliphs

Sunni Muslims regard four early caliphs as "rightly guided." They revere these men both for carrying on Muhammad's work and for expanding the "abode of submission" in the early age of conquest. The Shia, who believe that Muhammad had personally tapped Ali as his successor, reject the authority of all these men except Ali. They regard Islam's first three decades not as a golden age of expansion but as a dark era of sharp and sudden decline. Of these four caliphs, only Abu Bakr died of natural causes. The rest were assassinated.

- Abu Bakr (632–634), who won the "wars of apostasy" against those who had left the community after Muhammad's death.

- Umar (634–644), who skillfully united warring Arab tribes into an army that, in battles with Romans and Persians, took Jerusalem and transformed Islam into a world power that reached from Libya in the west to Persia in the east.

- Uthman (644–656), who produced a standard text of the Quran still in use today.

- Ali (656–661), son-in-law and cousin of Muhammad whom the Shia ("partisans of Ali") believe should have been proclaimed their prophet's successor from the start.

---

to God. The climax comes on Ashura ("ten"), the tenth day of this month, as men parade through the streets, flagellating themselves in imitation of Husain's redemptive suffering. During the rest of the year, some Shia perform daily prayers with their foreheads pressed to a piece of clay from Karbala. During the Iranian Revolution of 1978–1979, which brought theocracy to Shia-majority Iran, rebels chanted, "Every day is Ashura and every place is Karbala."

One of the puzzles of early Islam is why it expanded so far so rapidly. One answer, of course, is God's providence. Another, favored by many historians, is that it spread largely by the sword. The problem with this argument is that there is scant archaeological evidence testifying to the sorts of battles this thesis necessitates. Donner's counterargument is that religion drove this expansion. Why did so many convert so quickly? Because they did not really have to convert. Islam was not yet a distinct religion. What was spreading across the Arabian Peninsula was a "Believers' movement." To join it, one did not have to submit to a new religion. One simply had to sign on to an inclusive community of pious monotheists committed to deepening their piety. This revision is likely overstated. Donner himself admits that the surprisingly rapid expansion of this "community of Believers" was "driven by [both] religious and material motives." Nonetheless, there seems to be every reason to believe that, like virtually every other religion, the religion we now think of as Islam was not born in a single moment. It emerged gradually and changed over time.[10]

In fact, it was not until the Umayyad dynasty that Islam became a religion wholly distinct from Judaism and Christianity. One of the most important signs of this shift was the gradual elevation in the importance of Muhammad. This elevation is clear in inscriptions on the Dome of the Rock in Jerusalem, which date to 691—nearly six decades after Muhammad's death. These inscriptions include a clear rejection of the divinity of Jesus and equally clear affirmations of the beliefs in God's unity and Muhammad's prophethood that make up the Shahada today. A few years later, in coins dated 696–697, we again find this "double Shahada," with the affirmations that "There is no god but God alone" and "Muhammad is the messenger of God."[11] Only in this period, around the turn of the eighth century, do we see Islam emerge as a separate religious tradition. "Muslim"

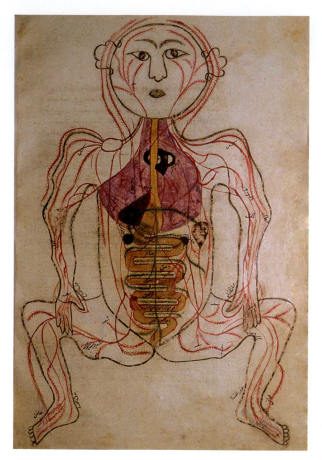

Among Muslims pushing the boundaries of scientific knowledge in medieval times was Persian physician Mansur ibn Ilyas, who wrote the first colored atlas of the human body. This fourteenth-century image from *Mansur's Anatomy* depicts the human circulatory system.

replaced "believer" in common parlance. Proto-Islam's fuzzy boundaries were replaced by sharper ones. Muslim thinkers became more antagonistic to Christianity, and Christian theologians attacked Muslim teachings. Memories of the sayings and actions of Muhammad began to circulate widely in the hadith. And the earlier "community of Believers" morphed into what we now know as the religion of Islam.

Classical Islam

In 750, the Umayyads fell to a new caliphate called the Abbasids, who pushed the center of the Muslim world eastward, from Damascus to Baghdad, and ruled until the Mongols overran them five centuries later in 1258. During this long classical period, Islamic civilization flourished in law, art, architecture, literature, mathematics, astronomy, philosophy, and medicine. Theologians argued against Trinitarians and dualists as their geographical footprint expanded into the Christian-dominated West and Zoroastrian-dominated Persia. Philosophers such as al-Farabi (c. 870–950) worked alongside their Jewish and Christian counterparts to reconcile revelation with reason. Meanwhile, the Abbasids integrated Persian language and culture into Islam, which until this period had been both linguistically and culturally Arabic. *The Arabian Nights*, a collection of stories providing glimpses of Muslim life during this period, would become one of the key sources of European and American understandings (and misunderstandings) of Islam from the eighteenth century forward.

"Twelver" and "Sevener" Shiism During this classical period in Islamic history, the Shia themselves split, into "Twelvers" (about 90 percent of the Shia today) and "Seveners" (about 10 percent). After the sixth Imam died in 765, some Shia Muslims followed his son Musa and then a line of successors concluding with a twelfth Imam, who by their account did not die but went into hiding ("occultation") in the late ninth or early tenth century. Today, this group is referred to as Twelvers. They are most popular in Iran, where they came to power under the Safavids in 1501 and again during the Iranian Revolution of 1979. Their distinctive doctrine is a belief in a still living yet hidden Imam—a perfect interpreter of the Quran who oversees the Muslim community from unseen realms. In the last days before the Day of Judgment, this hidden Imam will reveal himself as a long-awaited messianic figure known as the *madhi* ("guided one"), who will return to establish peace and justice on earth. In Twelver Shiism, legal rulings are channeled from this hidden Imam through religious scholars, such as the Ayatollah Ali Khamenei, now the Supreme Leader of Iran. Here the emphasis on community consensus so dear to Sunni Muslims is not in play. What matters are the rulings of clerical elites.

The Seveners did not accept Musa as their seventh Imam. Instead, they embraced his older brother Ismail. Some Seveners believe that this lineage ended with seven Imams. Others, known as Ismailis, believe that it continues today. One group of Ismailis known as Nizaris thrived on the Indian subcontinent, in part because of their willingness to adapt Shia ideas to Indian circumstances (for example, by representing their first Imam Ali as an incarnation of the Hindu god Vishnu). Since the early nineteenth century, the largest group of Nizaris has recognized a series of living Imams they refer to as Aga Khans. Their current leader, Aga Khan IV, was born in Switzerland in 1939 and graduated from Harvard in 1959. Today he is a successful businessman and racehorse owner who has used his money and influence to promote religious pluralism and advance the status of women.

Despite their divisions, the Shia as a whole continued to insist that, before his death, Muhammad had tapped Ali to succeed him. They also continued in their deep devotion to the "People of the House" (33:33) of Muhammad, including his daughter Fatimah, her husband Ali, and their sons Husain and Hasan, who live on in the stories told and retold by the Shia today.

As Shiism developed, Sunni Islam changed in turn. In the process, Sunni and Shia Muslims replayed what the first Muslims had done at the turn of the eighth century with Jews and Christians. In law schools and libraries, Sunni and Shia thinkers drew sharper boundary lines between themselves and policed them vigorously.

The Shia experienced a golden age of sorts in the tenth and eleventh centuries in Baghdad and Iran, where Shia legal thinking matured and Shia hadith were collected. It was during this period in Baghdad that the Ashura commemorations of the martyrdom of Husain began, alongside another Shia festival celebrating the day Muhammad selected Ali to succeed him. Shrines to Imams were built and pilgrims flocked to them. The Shia Fatimid dynasty (909–1171), which spanned a vast area across North Africa into the Middle East, systematized the Ismaili strain of Sevener Shiism.

Four Sunni legal schools emerged during this classical period. Although the Quran and hadith covered many topics, they did not cover them all, so jurists developed a vast

Ismaili Muslims dress in silk robes and crowns to celebrate Didar, the "sighting" of the Aga Khan in the remote, mountainous village of Alichur, Tajikistan, in 2016. This festival commemorates the anniversary of the Aga Khan's visit to the region in 1995.

Sufis

members of Islamic mystical tradition focused on direct experience of the love of God; key practices include the remembrance of God (*dhikr*) via techniques such as repeating his names and ecstatic music and dancing

body of Islamic law, which sorted human actions on a spectrum from obligatory to recommended to permitted to disliked to forbidden. These four legal schools disagreed over how the teachings of the Quran and the hadith should be interpreted and to what extent the Quran and Sunna could be augmented by secondary sources, community consensus, and analogical reasoning. Shia schools rely on the first two of these three sources but substitute intellect for analogical reasoning.

Sufism Not long after the emergence of the four Sunni legal schools in the classical period, Sufism also began to develop, offering a mystical alternative to an Islam driven by legal, theological, and political considerations. **Sufis** get their name from *suf*, which means "wool" in Arabic. This name points to Sufism's origins in asceticism—the tendency of early Sufis "to put on wool" like other ascetics and more broadly to reject, in the name of a simpler existence, the lavish lifestyles of the Islamic rulers of their age. Sufism is not a third Islamic branch alongside the Sunni and the Shia. It is instead an impulse toward mystical experience that can be found among both Sunni and Shia Muslims.

Sufi practitioners used metaphors of locomotion to describe their tradition as a way or path to absolute reality. Some took this metaphor literally, taking to the road as bedraggled wanderers and referring to themselves as strangers both in this world and in the societies through which they were vagabonding. Sufis worked to cultivate the higher self of acceptance and gratitude—acceptance of the world as it is and gratitude for their place in it. Simultaneously, they engaged in the "inner jihad" against the lower or disobedient self, by fasting and otherwise living in solidarity with the poor. But they did not just struggle against indulgence, greed, and selfishness. They also resisted the back-patting, holier-than-thou performance of piety itself. "The [lower self] has a Koran and a rosary in the one hand and a dagger in the sleeve," said the beloved Persian Sufi poet Rumi.[12] Other Sufis insisted that what really mattered in a life of submission to God was not the Five Pillars but love.

ISLAM BY THE NUMBERS

Four Sunni Legal Schools

The Shia have their own schools of law, which distinguish themselves by relying heavily on legal reasoning, but for more than one thousand years there have been four main Sunni schools, each founded on the Quran and the example of Muhammad.

- Hanafi School: The most liberal and speculative school, because of its openness to weighing the preferences of jurists and the public interest in interpreting Islamic law, this school is now prominent in Central and South Asia. Its founder is Abu Hanifa (c. 699–767).

- Malaki School: Founded in Medina, this earliest Islamic legal school is influential today in North Africa, West Africa, and Upper Egypt. It leans heavily on Muhammad's example, but it views the practice of the Medinan Muslim community of the prophet's time as better evidence of that example than individual hadith. Its founder is Malik ibn Anas (d. 796).

- Shafi School: Established by Muhammad ibn Idris al-Shafii (767–820), this school is rooted in the Sunna of

Muhammad as it is found in hadith, analogical reason, and community consensus. It is prominent today in Egypt, East Africa, Indonesia, and other parts of Southeast Asia.

- Hanbali School: This socially conservative legal school, founded by Ahmad ibn Hanbal (780–855), is committed to adhering to the Quran and hadith alone and to reading both via a "rigid literalism," without relying on analogical reasoning. It is hugely influential in the modern period, especially among Wahhabis and other antimoderns who denounce all "innovations" as illicit. Many Hanbalis today are not Wahhabis, but Wahhabism predominates in Saudi Arabia and the many madrasas it funds worldwide.

At first glance, this simple lifestyle would not seem to be particularly Islamic, since Muslims had long rejected the asceticism of the Christian apostle Paul and early Christian monastics. In fact, the Quran rejects monasticism as a Christian invention and not an ordinance of God (57:27). But as Sufis walked their spiritual path, they evoked Muhammad's own fasting and self-denial as well as his mystical flights into the presence of the divine. Among the practices they employed to bring themselves closer to God were silence, night vigils, fasting, and wandering. Sufis also cultivated techniques such as breath control and the contemplative visualization of saints or Sufi masters.

Sufis learned these practices in the context of a master-student relationship in which the Sufi master (*sheikh* in Arabic or *pir* in Persian) served as the transmitter of secret wisdom from the divine to the devotee. It should not be surprising, therefore, that Sufis turned to Sufi masters (both alive and dead) as exemplars alongside Muhammad, consulting the masters' pious biographies and lauding them at their homes and tombs. In doing so, they drew the ire of traditionalists who saw such veneration as *shirk*.

Over time, however, the Sufi tradition shifted its attention from asceticism to mysticism. Sufis spoke of the day-to-day practices of ordinary Muslims as external rites and of the Sufi way as the inner path to the reality of God. They spoke of that reality as immanent rather than transcendent—something "in here" rather than "up there." Along the way they engaged in dialogue with mystics who were not Muslims, turning Sufism into a form of Islam committed to interreligious understanding.

The goal of Islam, as these mystics saw it, was less to submit to God than to encounter (or even unite with) him. In a gesture toward this ultimately indescribable experience—"ineffable" in the language of mysticism theorists—many Sufis wrote poetry. Taking their cue from Sura 5:59—"He loves them and they love Him"—their poetry returned repeatedly to the theme of the ecstatic union of God and human beings. For some Sufis, the distinction between self and God dropped away, leaving love itself. Other Sufis turned to a sort of performance art. Rabia of Basra (714–801), for example, was renowned for carrying a bucket of water in one hand and a torch in the other. When asked why, she said, "I want to pour water into Hell and set fire to Paradise so that these two veils disappear and nobody worships God out of fear of Hell or hope for Paradise, but only for the sake of His eternal beauty."[13]

In an effort to evoke the divine/human union in words, Sufis gravitated toward language of drunkenness and intoxication, metaphors that had the added benefit of explaining why some Sufis seemed to act like "wise fools" gleefully ignoring social norms and religious duties. The most radical of these renegades resorted to language that many regarded as shirk. "Glory be to me, how great is my majesty!" said the ninth-century Persian Bayazid Bistami.[14] More famously (and notoriously), another early Persian master, al-Hallaj, said, "I am the Absolute Truth," or "I am God."[15] Sufis defended these exclamations as the words of God channeled through the body of an annihilated ego. But to literal interpreters, they were blasphemy, and in 922 al-Hallaj paid for his ecstasies with his life.

After al-Hallaj, Sufis increasingly distinguished between "drunk" and "sober" mystics. The "sober" type were those who had two feet firmly planted in everyday reality and in Islamic traditions. In his *Deliverance from Error*, the "sober Sufi" al-Ghazali (1058–1111) plays the philosopher, taking on Shia and Sunni theology before withdrawing from his family and his Baghdad professorship in order to wander for more than a decade as a solitary Sufi mystic. Real insight, he decides, comes not from words and theory but from actions and the experiences they produce, especially the mystical experiences brought on by Sufi practices of self-denial.

In the twelfth and thirteenth centuries, Sufis gave up their wanderlust and settled into brotherhoods and orders, typically centered on a Sufi master. But Sufism gradually spread beyond the confines of these groups into wider networks of friends and supporters. The mystical practices cultivated in these early Sufi orders and still alive today include various breathing techniques and meditative practices as well as the dancing of the now-famous Whirling Dervishes. The most widespread Sufi practice is recalling, silently or aloud, the names of God—an activity known as *dhikr* ("recollection") that brings to mind various forms of chanting in the Hindu and Buddhist traditions. Like Quranic recitation, which internalizes the words of God, dhikr is supposed to internalize the reality of God by focusing the believer's heart on God alone. One treatise on dhikr instructs the practitioner to use the negation, "There is no god," to push everything other than God out of the heart, followed by the affirmation, "but God," to flood the heart with God alone.

Sufi orders also developed strong traditions of the veneration of saints, which extended to veneration of living Sufi masters. As these orders gathered support from local rulers, the roots of Sufism deepened and spread. Devotees went as pilgrims to shrines and tombs of these masters who, like Catholic saints, typically specialized in miraculous cures of specific human problems.

In the modern period, more militant Muslims have attacked Sufis for importing into their tradition an unholy host of foreign religious beliefs and practices, including

Whirling Dervishes of the Mevlevi order of Sufis in Cappadocia, Turkey, practice twirling as a form of embodied meditation aimed at union with God.

Rumi (1207–1273)

More than 750 years after his death, the Persian Sufi master Jalal al-Din Rumi is the bestselling poet in the United States. He was born in modern-day Afghanistan and died in Konya, Turkey, where his tomb is now a popular pilgrimage site for Muslims and non-Muslims. As a young man, Rumi was initiated into a Sufi order. He also inherited the mantle of his father, a theologian and jurist renowned as "King of the Scholars." However, the most transformative event in Rumi's life was his encounter in 1244 with Shams al-din Tabrizi, a wandering mystic who changed the course of Rumi's life and work.

After this fateful meeting, the two men went into seclusion for a year and a half, composing spontaneous poetry and plumbing the depths of Sufi mysticism. Rumi's family was scandalized by the tight bond between these men, so Shams left Rumi for a time and, after a brief reunion, disappeared forever. (Some claimed he was assassinated by a member of Rumi's family.) Rumi then spent the rest of his career as a mystical poet reflecting on longing and loss through the lens of the Sufi teaching that God is the only reality and that this reality is love. Like the biblical Song of Songs, which has been read as both a love song to God and a song to a lover, Rumi's poems can be read as songs to God, to his lost friend, or to both. "When kept from their true origin all yearn," writes Rumi, "for union on the day they can return."[a]

Among scholars, Rumi is best known for the Masnavi, an epic poem of twenty-five thousand verses that has been lauded as the Persian Quran. In the United States, he is mostly known via popular poets such as Robert Bly and Coleman Barks who have freely translated his poetry into bestsellers. But Rumi does not live in words alone. He is embodied in the Mevlevi Sufi order, founded by his son at the close of the thirteenth century, which specialized in setting Rumi's poetry to music and dance. Out of this order developed the now famous Whirling Dervishes, who twirl in a meditative dance as a way to recall the names of Allah.

Christian saint worship and pantheistic Greek philosophy. For this reason, one of the main objectives of the Wahhabis and other modern-day antimoderns has been to destroy the "idolatrous" tombs of Sufi saints (as well as Shia Imams). Even Sufism's critics must acknowledge, however, that it was through these "intimate enemies" that Islam spread into sub-Saharan Africa and South and Southeast Asia. Like other mystics, Sufis emphasized religion's experiential rather than its doctrinal dimension, so they were able to accommodate themselves more than more orthodox Muslims to the local circumstances they encountered. This emphasis on experience also made them more open than others to finding truths in other religions.

Islamic and European Empires

Like Christianity and Buddhism, Islam is a missionary religion with a message intended not just for one tribe or language group but for every human being. During its first century—under Muhammad and the first four caliphs and during the reign of the Umayyads—it spread through military as well as missionary expeditions. Later, it expanded through the subtler influence of traders, philosophers, and mystics. In recent years, it has spread through the power of television and the Internet.

In 711, under the Abbasid dynasty, a group of Umayyads moved into Andalusia in modern-day Spain. Muslims then ruled much of the Iberian Peninsula until the late fifteenth century. This period has been widely described as a time of mutual

The fourteenth-century Patio de los Leones (Court of the Lions) at the Alhambra Palace in Granada, Spain, features Moorish architecture that reflects a melding of Spanish and Islamic styles.

"coexistence"—the *Convivencia*—in which Muslims, Christians, and Jews lived together in relative harmony, especially in Cordoba. Here, these "people of the book" cooperated via a shared Arabic language in philosophy, mathematics, medicine, architecture, poetry, and other intellectual endeavors. Through these interactions, words such as "algebra," "average," and "algorithm" made their way from Arabic into Spanish and English. Another product of this peaceful coexistence was the architectural masterpiece in Granada, Spain, known as the Alhambra.

Jews, who suffered under anti-Semitic regimes in northern Europe, fared better in Muslim Spain, where the long-standing representation of Jews as a "protected people" offered them security in exchange for a poll tax owed by non-Muslims. Though they were second-class citizens, Jews also enjoyed some political influence and a relative free hand in economic matters, thanks to positive Islamic attitudes toward trade that went back to Muhammad's career as a merchant. But this era was no interfaith paradise, and there were periodic outbreaks of mob violence. The *Convivencia* eventually yielded to a gradual *Reconquista* ("reconquest") by Christians of the Iberian Peninsula, including the recapture of Toledo by Roman Catholics in 1085 and the subsequent persecution of Jews.

Farther east, the second Christian millennium brought on the First Crusade, ordered by Pope Urban II in 1095 in an attempt to capture the Holy Land (and the Holy Cross) from Muslims. In this holy war, the Christians captured Jerusalem in 1099, only to lose it to the Sunni Muslim warrior Saladin in 1187. In the 1250s, on Islam's eastern front, Genghis Khan and the Mongols took Iran and Iraq, leveling Baghdad in 1258 and putting the Abbasid caliphate to rest.

Back on the Iberian Peninsula, the Catholic monarchs Ferdinand and Isabella did more than dispatch Columbus across "the ocean blue" in 1492. They took Granada that same year and brought the curtain down on the Convivencia. The restoration of Spain to Christian rule began a long period of colonialism in which European powers, impelled by capitalism and Christian missionary imperatives, pushed into virtually every corner of the globe. Muslims pushed back. In fact, as the medieval age began to turn modern, Islam was ascendant. By 1492, the Ottomans had taken Constantinople, which they renamed Istanbul and held for four decades. The next few centuries were an age of empire for Islam, which expanded so rapidly that by 1700 its footprint extended from Timbuktu, in present-day Mali, up into Eastern Europe, down through much of India, and into Java and other parts of Southeast Asia. This expanding Muslim world was ruled in the east by Ottomans (1300–1922), in Persia by the Safavids (1501–1722), and in India by the Mughals (1526–1858). Of these dynasties, the Ottomans and Mughals were Sunnis and the Safavids were Shia.

The sixteenth-century Mughal emperor Akbar, who reigned from 1556 to 1605, came to control most of the Indian subcontinent, in part because of a policy of religious tolerance that encouraged what we now refer to as interfaith conversations among Muslims, Hindus, Christians, and Zoroastrians. The seventeenth-century Mughal prince and Sufi student Dara Shikoh went even further in the direction of religious pluralism. Anticipating twentieth-century arguments for the unity of all religions (and borrowing from Hindu philosophers as well), he argued in *Confluence of Two Oceans* (1655) for the essential unity of Hinduism and Islam. The ancient Indian sound *Om* was, in his view, equivalent to the name of God.

By the early seventeenth century, Muslims outnumbered Christians worldwide. As Muslims spread across the globe, Islam became something very different from the Arab-centric tradition of its foundational period. In fact, it became so varied that it was a challenge to refer to it as any one thing at all.

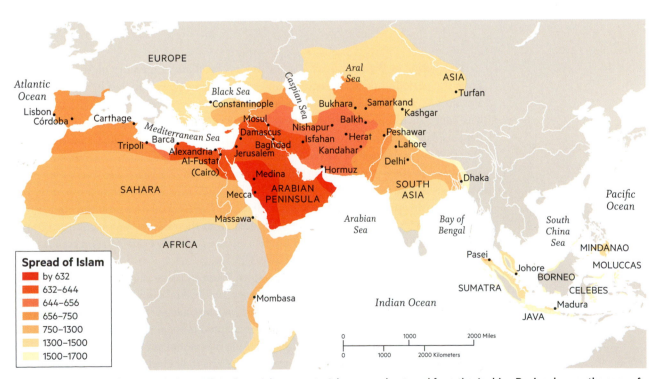

From Muhammad's military campaigns to later imperial conquests, Islam spread outward from the Arabian Peninsula over the span of roughly one thousand years, reaching as far west as modern-day Spain and as far east as Indonesia.

ISLAM: A GENEALOGY

Every student of Islam must reckon with the word "Islam," which is related to the term *salaam*, which means peace. Muslims greet each other with *Salaam alaykum*, ("Peace be upon you") and respond with *Wa alaykum as salaam* ("And upon you be peace"). But the word "Islam," which appears seven times in the Quran, means surrender or submission. In the medieval period, Western thinkers referred to these submitters as Turks, Saracens, Ishmaelites, and (after Hagar) Hagarenes. But the presumption that religions are defined by their founders led many in the West to refer to Islam by some variant of Mohammedanism or Mahometanism. Around 1390, Chaucer's "The Man of Law's Tale" referred to the Alkoron (Quran), Makomete (Muhammad), and Makometes lawe (Muhammad's law). *Godeffroy of Boloyne*, a book from 1481 about "the siege and conqueste of Jherusalem," speaks of "theyr mahometry and fowle lawe of machomet."[a] In 1529,

an author described "the Machometanys" as "a sensual sect" that "dyd in fewe yeres draw the great part of the world unto it." Later sixteenth-century books referred to "supersticious mahometrie" (1531), "Mahometicall… wickednes and tiranny" (1561), and "Their detestable Mahumetisme" (1597).[b] Obviously, these were not terms of praise. As late as 1949, a respected book on Islam by the Harvard professor H. A. R. Gibb was titled *Mohammedanism*. Since the 1950s, that term has fallen into disfavor, as writers have come to understand that Muslims worship God alone and that nothing is less Islamic than to mistake a human being for the one true God. Today, the term for the topic of this chapter is "Islam," a word that first appeared in English in 1613. Adherents of this religion are called "Muslims," meaning "submitters," who seek peace in this life and the next by surrendering themselves to God.[c]

This period of Islamic power is a key link in the chain of memory of Muslims today. So is the period of decline that followed, as European power, fueled by the Industrial Revolution, was cast far and wide by trade ships, naval power, and missionary energy. The Mughals fell to the British in India in 1857. The Ottoman Empire came apart by degrees, losing southeastern Europe and North Africa before fighting on the losing side in World War I and forfeiting to the French and British its Middle Eastern lands, including Palestine. In 1922, the Ottoman Empire collapsed, and one year later Turkey emerged as a post-Islamic secular state. Meanwhile, the Dutch moved into lands previously controlled by Muslims in India, the Russians into Muslim Central Asia, and the French into Muslim Africa. As one scholar has observed, "From the time of Napoleon's invasion of Egypt in 1793 to the breakup of the Ottoman empire … nearly every Muslim country was conquered and colonized by foreign powers."[16]

It is in this historical context that modern Islam must be understood. By the nineteenth century it had moved far beyond its roots on the Arabian Peninsula, in the Arabic language, and among Arab peoples. In fact, it had become, according to historian Teena Purohit, a "global formation" that creatively adapted to local circumstances.[17] In India, for example, it was strongly influenced by Hindu devotionalism. But it was also engulfed worldwide by colonialism. All these transformations took place under the legal and cultural regimes of colonial powers, which directly influenced this religious tradition, not least by classifying it as a "world religion."

Islam in the Modern World

As Muslims responded to the rise of European Christian power, they diverged on whether to say yes or no to modernity, and which "modernity" they were giving their assent to or withholding it from.

In Muslim-majority Turkey, citizens opted for strict secularism, effectively banning religious expression from the public square. Their republic's founder, Mustafa Ataturk, adopted the Roman alphabet and bent Turkish law more toward Swiss than Islamic models. Elsewhere, Muslim modernists engaged in a give-and-take with European and American thinkers and values, defending their tradition against Western attacks even as they adopted and adapted certain Western ideas and practices. In the Arab Cultural Renaissance, nineteenth-century writers and intellectuals in Syria and Egypt embraced modern science as well as new ways of interpreting the Quran. Together they laid the groundwork for the powerful emergence of Arab nationalism after World War I.

As Christian powers pushed back the boundaries of earlier Islamic empires, the Pakistani poet, lawyer, and philosopher Muhammad Iqbal (1877–1938) wondered whether God had abandoned Muslims. Iqbal, who studied in Cambridge and Munich, integrated into his thinking not only Sufi luminaries such as Rumi but also Friedrich Nietzsche and other Western European philosophers. In the process, he developed a philosophy of God as "immanent, not transcendent" and produced, in the words of religious studies scholar W. C. Smith, "the most important and the most necessary revolution of modern times."[18] Despite his argument that "the modern Muslim . . . has to rethink the whole system of Islam without completely breaking with the past," Iqbal rejected both capitalism and materialism, arguing that any rethinking of Islam must begin with a creative reconstruction of its past.[19]

A modern group known as the Ahmadiyya community was founded by Mirza Ghulam Ahmad (1835–1908) in the Punjab in British India in 1889. Ahmad integrated Hindu and Christian ideas into his worldview, styling himself as both an incarnation of the Hindu god Krishna and a Christlike messiah. Ahmad also claimed that holy war had become un-Islamic—that struggles against unbelievers now had to go forward nonviolently via debate. The Ahmadis split in 1914, chiefly over their founder's title. Was he simply a "renewer" of Islam? Or was he a new prophet sent by God? Today, some Ahmadis consider other Muslims to be apostates. Many other Muslims return the favor. In 1974, the Muslim World League declared that the Ahmadi movement was not authentically Islamic, and, in 1984, Pakistan declared the Ahmadis infidels, causing many to flee in order to escape persecution.

Opposing this "House of Acceptance" of Western modernity was, to borrow from Quranic scholar Jane Dammen McAuliffe, a "House of Rejection."[20] One group, sometimes referred to as fundamentalists, sought to revitalize Islam by reemphasizing its glorious past. Like Protestants in Europe's Reformation, these reformers worked to ward off creeping secularity by returning Islam to what they saw as its pristine origins—by purifying it of unwanted "innovations." These revitalization movements took aim both at external enemies of Islam and at internal "innovators," whom they saw as Muslims in name only. But for all their emphasis on returning Islam to its fundamentals, these reformers also drank deep from modern thought.

The most influential of these figures was Muhammad ibn 'Abd al-Wahhab (1703–1792), whose name survives in **Wahhabism**, now the official theology of Saudi Arabia and of the

Wahhabism
antimodern theology emphasizing God's unity and strictly opposing *shirk,* now the official theology of Saudi Arabia and the guiding ideology of many radical Islamist groups

Ultra-conservative Wahhabism is the state-sponsored religious orientation in Saudi Arabia. Here, students at an all-male Wahhabi school in Riyadh, Saudi Arabia, take an annual governmental exam.

many schools and mosques the nation's oil revenues have bankrolled worldwide. Calling themselves "Unitarians," Wahhabis joined other Muslims in emphasizing divine unity (*tawhid*), but they were more aggressive in identifying and rooting out transgressions of strict monotheism. Wahhab gained political power through a loyalty oath he struck in 1744 with Muhammad ibn Saud, the founder of the Saudi dynasty. After the Saudi family established the Kingdom of Saudi Arabia in 1932 and discovered vast quantities of oil in 1938, Wahhabism became an international force, influencing the thought of the Taliban, al-Qaeda, ISIS, and other Islamist groups.

Closely associated with the Wahhabis are the **Salafis** ("pious ancestors"), who, in the fourteenth century, emphasized returning to the pure, primitive Islam of the earliest generations of Muslims. Among the things the Salafis reject as illicit innovations are Islam's legal schools and Sufism. Although some terrorist groups have drawn on various manifestations of Salafi thought, most Salafists reject ISIS-style violence.

The most controversial Wahhabi practice was the destruction of shrines and tombs of saints, on the theory that so-called Muslims seeking intercession there were committing shirk. But the most fateful Wahhabi innovation was the belief that those who did not share their understanding of Islam were not really Muslims at all. As such, they could be targeted and killed. Throughout most of Islam's history, Muslims greeted one another with a spirit of inclusion rather than with accusations of unbelief. Whether you were Sunni or Shia, if you submitted to God by uttering the Shahada, you were a Muslim. In the modern period, Wahhabis paved the way for far more stringent rules regarding who is and who is not an authentic Muslim.

Building on Wahhabi beliefs, the Egyptian scholar Sayyid Qutb (1906–1966) made *takfir* a centerpiece of his thought. Takfir refers to the accusation that someone who claims to be a Muslim is actually not a Muslim. It likely derives from a fourteenth-century

Salafis
members of a Sunni movement calling Muslims back to the pure, primitive Islam of their "pious forebears" (*salaf al-salih*). Salafis reject as illicit "innovations" Islam's legal schools, its philosophical and theological traditions, and Shiism and Sufism.

thinker who refused to accept Mughals who converted to Islam as real Muslims. Qutb took this notion further, excommunicating by the force of his imagination virtually all Muslims who did not agree with his views. "The Muslim community," he argued in his book *Milestones* (1964), "has been extinct for a few centuries" and was now alive only among a small group of followers.[21] This idea had deadly consequences, since in Islamic law Muslims are not allowed to kill a fellow Muslim unless they are convinced that the person is not actually Muslim. Qutb also called on his followers to go to war against their Muslim and non-Muslim opponents.

Qutb's battle cry has been taken up in recent decades by various Islamists. Scholars have used the term "Islamism" to refer to new social and political movements and ideologies ("isms") fueled by Islamic concepts and ideas. Some restrict this term to the efforts of militant Muslims whose politics call for establishing an Islamic state under Islamic law that is at war with Israel, the United States, and the West, broadly construed. Others argue for a more expansive understanding of the term as an "antimodern ideology of reform in Muslim countries" or "a form of social and political activism, grounded in an idea that public and political life should be guided by a set of Islamic principles."[22] From this more inclusive perspective, the heirs of Qutb and likeminded revolutionaries would be classified as "radical Islamists" while the category of "moderate Islamists" would include less militant yet still politicized Muslim reformers. Scholars who prefer to use "Islamism" to point more narrowly to radical groups and ideologies argue that more inclusive definitions reduce Islamism to political Islam or even to Islam itself, since almost every Muslim believes that one's social and political life should follow Islamic principles.

Definitions aside, it is plain to see that, particularly since the 1980s and 1990s, the Muslim world has seen an uptick in political ideologies, activists, and movements that have sought to return to various visions of an "original" and therefore "authentic" Islamic state. These movements were responding to modernity in general and to the rise of European Christian nation-states and the decline of Muslim power in particular. But they were also motivated by political successes in the Muslim world. After World War II, many Muslim-majority countries—Pakistan and Bangladesh, Egypt and Iran, Indonesia and Algeria—gained their independence. Some of these new countries followed Turkey in attempting to construct secular states. But the failure of Marxism and communism led many in the Muslim world to lean on religious models in their postcolonial struggles.

The years immediately following World War II delivered two shocks that continue to reverberate among Muslims worldwide: the creation of India and Pakistan, largely along Hindu/Muslim lines, in 1947, and the creation of the state of Israel via a partition of Palestine. In the Six-Day War of June 1967, Israel took lands in the Golan Heights, the West Bank, the Gaza Strip, and the Sinai Peninsula and displaced roughly three hundred thousand Palestinians. Over ensuing decades, Israel embarked on an ambitious program of building settlements in these areas. Much of this area remains contested, and this seemingly insolvable Arab-Israeli conflict remains a flashpoint for violence worldwide. The Partition of India and Pakistan was more immediately catastrophic, displacing some fourteen million people and claiming the lives of perhaps a million in horrific Hindu/Muslim violence. Stories of these events continue to inform Muslim lives in the modern world as well as the politics of secularists, Muslim activists, and Islamicists alike.

ISLAM IN THE UNITED STATES

Islam initially made its way into the consciousness of Europeans and Americans through books. The Quran first appeared in English in 1649 in *The Alcoran of Mahomet*, a translation from the Arabic via French published in London. Islam made an even more powerful impression through a series of translations of the popular tale *The Arabian Nights*, a story within a story of a woman betrothed to a murderous king who spins tales night after night in order to save her own life. Also known as *One Thousand and One Nights*, this ever-evolving anthology of folk tales—including "Ali Baba and the Forty Thieves" and "Aladdin's Lamp"—was translated into Western languages beginning with a French version by the orientalist Antoine Galland in 1704. According to American University professor Martyn Oliver, *The Arabian Nights* has been a crucial source for the construction of Islam as a "lived religion," not only in the popular imagination but also in academic circles.[23]

Muslims first came to North America as slaves. Estimates vary, but between 10 and 30 percent of the slaves stolen and transported to what is now the United States between the seventeenth and nineteenth centuries were Muslims. The conditions for sustaining their religious traditions on plantations were dismal, however. Only whispers of Islam survived on those plantations in the shackled bodies of the half-million souls forcibly transported on slave ships.

The earliest known Muslim slave in North America was Ayuba Suleiman Diallo (1701–1773) of modern-day Angola. He is known to us because of his capture as a runaway, his imprisonment, and his appearance in 1731 before a judge in Annapolis, Maryland, who later told his story. According to that story, Diallo was captured in West Africa in 1730 shortly after he had himself sold two slaves belonging to his family. Shipped across the Atlantic, he tended tobacco and livestock on a Virginia plantation before his escape and recapture. After observing that Diallo could not speak English but could write the words "Allah and Mahommed" in a foreign script, the judge "perceived he was a Mahometan" and "no common Slave."[24] James Oglethorpe, who would later go on to establish the state of Georgia, purchased his freedom and sent him to London, where he was lionized in the press and sat for an oil painting that now hangs in the National Portrait Gallery there.

The only known book authored in Arabic by an American Muslim slave was *The Life of Omar ibn Said, Written by Himself*, which was handwritten in 1831 and then translated into English and published in 1848. Though marketed as a Christian conversion narrative, ibn Said's story began with the opening lines of the Quran—"In the name of God, the merciful, the compassionate"—and quoted Quranic passages along the way. Ibn Said referred to his slavemaster as a *kafir* (infidel) and wrote on the walls of his jail cell in Arabic. Many scholars believe he never fully converted to Christianity and remained in some meaningful sense a Muslim until his death in 1864.

Muslims arrived as free people in the United States after the Civil War. They came from Syria, Jordan, Lebanon, and Palestine. Many settled in the Midwest. Though they did not come in large numbers, they left their mark. One was the Moslem Temple, now known as the Mother Mosque of America, which was built during the Great Depression through the donations and manual labor of a small Lebanese and Syrian Muslim community in Cedar Rapids, Iowa. Upon its completion in 1934, this structure became

This 1733 portrait of Ayuba Suleiman Diallo by William Hoare of Bath portrays the subject of one of the earliest slave narratives. Diallo appears in traditional West African Muslim dress, an ironic contrast between his high social standing in Senegambia as the son of religious leaders and his slave status in North America.

"the first place of worship specifically designed and built as a Mosque in North America."[25] Today, it is the country's oldest surviving mosque.

The **Nation of Islam** (NOI), established in Detroit in 1930 by W. D. Fard and led, beginning in 1934, by Elijah Muhammad, gave public prominence to both black nationalism and Islam. More traditional Muslims observed that the NOI, which consisted almost entirely of African American converts, departed notably from more traditional Islamic beliefs and practices. NOI members fasted in December (rather than Ramadan), prayed in English (rather than Arabic), and met on Sundays (rather than Fridays). They also embraced Fard as an incarnation of God. Critics of NOI also rejected this group's racial and political views—its categorization of whites as a race of devils and its call for a separate black nation.

The NOI expanded rapidly following the prison conversion in 1948 of Malcolm X, who became its most charismatic spokesperson and the most outspoken black critic of the Reverend Dr. Martin Luther King Jr.'s emphasis on desegregation and nonviolence. After a pilgrimage to Mecca in 1964, Malcolm X embraced Sunni Islam. After Elijah Muhammad died in 1975, his son and successor Warith Deen Muhammad also steered the NOI in the direction of Sunni Islam. "There will be no such category as a white Muslim or a black Muslim," W. D. Muhammad said. "All will be Muslims. All children of God."[26] W. D. Muhammad also renamed and dissolved the NOI at various times. Many groups later claimed the mantle of the NOI. The most visible is now led by the controversial Louis Farrakhan, who has attempted to revive the group's original spirit by emphasizing Elijah Muhammad's racial teachings. In recent years, however, Farrakhan has made his NOI more Sunni, by holding congregational prayers on Fridays, fasting during the traditional month of Ramadan, and observing five-times-a-day prayers.

The black nationalist and convert to Islam Malcolm X (second from the left) sits in prayer in a mosque in 1964, the same year that he went on hajj to Mecca.

The composition of the American Muslim community changed dramatically after the U.S. Congress opened up immigration from Asia in 1965. Muslims in the United States are far more racially diverse than many other religious groups, with a mix of 41 percent white adherents, 28 percent Asian, 20 percent black, 8 percent Hispanic, and 3 percent other or mixed. Of American Muslim adults, 42 percent were born in the United States, while the remaining 58 percent are immigrants. Of the foreign-born, well over half (57 percent) came from Asia (Iran included), followed by 24 percent from the Middle East and North Africa, 10 percent from sub-Saharan Africa, and 9 percent from elsewhere.[27]

Today, American Muslims are increasingly visible—as neighbors, coworkers, and media personalities. Muslim comedians such as Dave Chappelle and Aasif Mandvi alert their fans to the ordinariness of Muslim life. A network of "progressive Muslims" pushes against both Islamist radicalism and corporate capitalism, arguing for a form of Islam that is committed to justice for all. One of these progressive Muslims, the political activist Linda Sarsour, cochaired the 2017 Women's March. The Chicago-based Interfaith Youth Core, the country's most dynamic and influential interfaith organization, is run by an Ismaili Muslim, Eboo Patel. In 2007, Keith Ellison of Minnesota's 5th District became the first

Nation of Islam
religious movement drawing on both black separatism and Islam that was established in 1930 in Detroit and later popularized by Malcolm X and Muhammad Ali

Muhammad Ali (1942–2016)

Today, the world's most famous Muslim is likely the late al-Qaeda leader Osama bin-Laden, but before him that title belonged to the Olympic gold medalist and heavyweight boxing champion Muhammad Ali. In fact, for a time Ali may have been the most recognized person in the world.

Born Cassius Clay in Louisville, Kentucky, and raised a Baptist, he publicly joined the Nation of Islam (NOI) and changed his name to Muhammad Ali shortly after seizing the heavyweight title from the seemingly invincible Sonny Liston in 1964. When asked if he was a Black Muslim, Ali said, "The real name is Islam. That means peace. Islam is a religion and there are 750 million people all over the world who believe in it, and I'm one of them. I ain't no Christian."[a] For a man who proclaimed himself "The Greatest," it was an intriguing choice—to embrace a religion that bestows that title upon God alone. But it would prove to be a lifelong fit.

A consummate entertainer and, according to some, the first real hip-hop artist (he was sometimes called the "Louisville Lip"), Ali used his gifts as a wordsmith not only to promote himself but also to push for social justice and against white supremacy. The media pushed back, with *Sports Illustrated* denouncing him as "a member of the Black Muslim cult, a twisted form of Islam that advocates racial separation."[b] Ali's refusal to be drafted in the midst of the Vietnam War—"Man, I ain't got no quarrel with them Vietcong," he told reporters in 1966—led boxing commissions to strip him of his many titles and his license to fight.[c] Although he won back his license in a Supreme Court case in 1971, he lost three of his peak years in the ring. When Ali announced his return to boxing, the NOI disowned him. He competed nonetheless in a series of classic bouts with Joe Frazier and George Foreman. When the NOI under W. D. Muhammad moved in the direction of Sunni Islam, Ali moved with it.

Diagnosed with Parkinson's disease in 1984, Ali devoted his postretirement years to humanitarian efforts. By the end of the century, the man once widely feared in White America had become one of the most beloved human beings on earth. At the 1996 Olympic Games in Atlanta, Ali lit the Olympic Torch. In 2005, President George W. Bush bestowed on him the Presidential Medal of Freedom. And upon his death in 2016, obituaries echoed President Barack Obama in lionizing Ali as "The Champ." Meanwhile, black athletes who joined Black Lives Matter protesters in addressing implicit bias in American life, and particularly in police forces, invoked Ali as a pathbreaking activist for racial justice.

Muslim in the U.S. Congress when he put his hand on a Quran owned by Thomas Jefferson and swore to uphold the U.S. Constitution. In 2019, Rashida Tlaib of Michigan and Ilhan Omar of Minnesota became the first Muslim women in the U.S. Congress.

The proportions of Muslims in European countries are much higher than in the United States. Tensions are higher as well, as countries that once had racially and religiously homogeneous populations have struggled to reimagine themselves amidst the new racial and religious diversity. One result has been the rise of ultraconservative political groups that have called for sharp limits on immigration and the settlement of refugees. In Europe and the United States today, Muslims are increasingly threatened by hate crimes, and Islam is increasingly viewed through the distorting lenses of terrorism and Islamophobia.

The Iranian Revolution and 9/11

Two important events of the last half century catapulted Islam (and religion more broadly) into U.S. news: the Iranian Revolution and the September 11, 2001, terrorist attacks on various targets in the United States, including the World Trade Center towers in New

Demonstrators hold up a poster in support of Ayatollah Khomeini, soon to become Iran's head of state, during the Iranian Revolution, which overthrew the secular Shah of Iran in favor of an Islamic Republic run by Shia clerics.

York City. Each was a plain rebuke to the secularization thesis, which had predicted that societies would become less religious as they became more modern and technological.

The Iranian Revolution of 1978–1979, which took place in a highly westernized country with a highly educated population, replaced a secular Shah, Mohammad Reza Pahlavi (1919–1980), with a clerical theocrat, the Ayatollah Khomeini (1902–1989). Khomeini had been deported in 1964 because of his criticism of the Shah, who had been installed by the Americans after a CIA-led coup in 1953. While living in exile, Khomeini spread through cassette tapes his belief that true Islam required an Islamic state governed by jurists such as himself. In this way, Khomeini joined a long line of antimoderns who spread their views through modern technologies. Returning to Iran in 1979 amidst a grassroots uprising that led the Shah to seek refuge in the United States, Khomeini became the Supreme Leader of a new Islamic state led by clerical elites.

On November 4, 1979, a group of Iranian students responded to the anti-American sentiment of their new nation by storming the U.S. embassy in Tehran and taking sixty American hostages. The Iranian hostage crisis that followed played out on live television and helped Ronald Reagan win the 1980 election in a landslide over President Jimmy Carter. (Iran released the hostages just after Reagan's inauguration in January 1981.)

If the Iranian Revolution sounded an alarm in the West, 9/11 woke people up to the public power of religion. The mastermind behind the 9/11 terrorist attacks was Osama bin Laden (1957–2011), the Saudi-born leader of the radical Sunni Islamist organization **al-Qaeda**, which he founded in 1988. Along with other militant Islamists, he was engaged in global warfare against not only Israel, the United States, and "the West" but also the vast majority of the world's Muslims, who did not share his ideology or approve of his tactics. (Twenty-eight innocent Muslim employees died in the Twin Towers of the World Trade Center.)

al-Qaeda ("the base") organization once led by Osama bin Laden that carried out the September 11, 2001, attacks that killed nearly three thousand people in Pennsylvania, New York City, and Washington, DC

Six days after the terrorist attacks of September 11, 2001, President George W. Bush visited the Islamic Center of Washington, DC, to demonstrate that the United States was at war with terrorists, not with Muslims.

After 9/11, U.S. president George W. Bush was careful to describe Islam as a religion of peace. Like his successor President Barack Obama, he repeatedly emphasized that the United States was at war not with Muslims but with terrorists. This approach shifted sharply under the administration of President Donald Trump, who as a candidate called for "a total and complete shutdown of Muslims entering the United States" and has issued executive orders blocking immigration from certain Muslim-majority nations.[28]

After the U.S. military killed bin Laden in Pakistan in 2011, global attention shifted to the so-called Islamic State (also known as ISIS or ISIL and by the Arabic term *Daesh*), an Islamist group that in 2014 proclaimed itself a caliphate with authority over every Muslim on earth. This group advanced its goals through videos of beheadings on social media and more traditional warfare in Iraq and Syria.

The impact that Islamic extremists in al-Qaeda and ISIS have had on contemporary life is incalculable. In addition to terrorizing their primary antagonists, they have redirected trillions of dollars into airport security, counterterrorism campaigns, and military operations in Iraq, Afghanistan, Syria, and elsewhere. Their actions have also transformed the way many in Europe and the United States think about Muslims, turning Islam into the globe's most frequently discussed religion and transforming Islamophobia into the new normal in many European countries and American states.

However, there are likely far fewer radical Islamists than many in the West imagine. The sociologist Charles Kurzman asks in his book *The Missing Martyrs* (2011), "If terrorist methods are as widely available as automobiles, why are there so few Islamist terrorists?" One answer is that Islamic liberalism is far more popular than many analysts imagine. "Given a choice between Islamist revolution and democratic elections," Kurzman observes, "Muslims overwhelmingly prefer democracy." According to a 2017 survey, Muslims worldwide have "overwhelmingly negative" views of ISIS, with only 9 percent in Pakistan, 4 percent in Indonesia, and 1 percent in Lebanon reporting positive views. Moreover, "sympathy for Islamist terrorism rarely translates into Islamist terrorist activities." The minority who tell pollsters they view ISIS or al-Qaeda favorably are not lining up to lay their lives on the line, Kurzman argues. They are making a symbolic protest against imperialism and the modern West, similar to the way the Black Panthers of the United States in the 1970s argued for the legitimacy of violence while committing hardly any.[29]

But Islamists and Islamophobes are not the only people propelling Islam onto the nightly news. The Arab Spring protests of the early 2010s, democratic uprisings that overthrew regimes in Tunisia and Egypt, led not to secular democracies but to regimes backed by Islamic legitimation, leading some to assert that we are entering a postsecular world in which religion plainly matters once again. As these protests illustrate, new social media technologies are also fostering increasing interactions between Muslims and non-Muslims, even as new transportation technologies are fostering increasing interactions in neighborhoods, workplaces, and schools. Christians and atheists live and work in Qatar, and Muslims and agnostics live and work in Brazil. Non-Muslims are divided about what to think of taxi drivers who stop to pray on sidewalks in Paris and Manhattan. In the United States and Europe, many welcome Muslim immigrants as important contributors to their societies. Others are convinced that unless immigration is stopped, their societies are going to lose what has in the past made the United States, France, or the Netherlands distinctive. Meanwhile, Muslims have responded to our increasingly interconnected world both by preaching against "infidels" and by establishing nonprofits devoted to interfaith dialogue. At the governmental level, the state of Saudi Arabia forbids both churches and synagogues. But Indonesia has adopted an official policy of religious pluralism that recognizes and protects Hinduism, Buddhism, Confucianism, Catholicism, and Protestantism alongside Islam.

Surely, there is evidence to support the "clash of civilizations" narrative associated with the political scientist Samuel Huntington, who argued that a fierce battle between the Islamic world and the Christian West was all but inevitable.[30] Huntington is right that cultural and religious identities are alive and well and motivating all sorts of people to do all sorts of things. But neither the "Islamic world" nor the "Christian West" speaks or acts in one voice. At least for now, whatever clashing is going on seems more like a mismatched outfit than a global conflagration.

LIVED ISLAM

The core techniques for cultivating submission and achieving success are the Five Pillars of Islam. The metaphor is architectural, and the image we are supposed to conjure up is of a building with supports on four corners and one at the center. The central pillar is the Shahada, the closest Islam comes to a creed. To become a Muslim, you do not need to be baptized. In fact, the Quran explicitly rejects baptism. To convert to Islam, you need only to say the Shahada, bearing witness, out loud and ideally in the presence of witnesses, to the singularity of God and the prophethood of Muhammad.

The pillars supporting the four corners of Islamic life are prayer, almsgiving, fasting, and hajj. To fulfill these obligations, Muslims must perform the rituals at the right time and in the right way. They must also declare in advance their intention to complete each obligation, just as those who go on the hajj begin that journey with a statement of intention.

Five times a day, 365 days a year, a call to prayer goes out in Arabic from Sunni mosques and minarets from Mecca to Minnesota. (The Shia normally combine prayers and pray three times daily.) Prayers vary a bit over the course of the day and from region to region, and nowadays they are also broadcast on television, online, and via mobile apps. But this is the most common formula:

God is great
God is great
God is great
God is great
I bear witness that there is no God but God
I bear witness that there is no God but God
I bear witness that Muhammad is the messenger of God
I bear witness that Muhammad is the messenger of God
Make haste toward prayer
Make haste toward prayer
Make haste toward success
Make haste toward success

God is great
God is great
There is no god but God

Some ignore this call to prayer. Some heed it when the mood strikes. But the observant step out of their ordinary lives each day to pray. They prepare by ritually washing their feet, hands, and face. They turn toward Mecca and declare their intention to pray. Muslims stop to pray at home, at work, and in mosques. They also put down prayer rugs in New York City's LaGuardia Airport and in office buildings in Montreal.

These prayers are spoken in Arabic, accompanied by a tight choreography of standing, sitting, kneeling, and prostrating. Beginning with *Allahu Akbar* ("God is great"), submitters move their hands from behind their ears to their torsos. They bow forward at the waist, hands on knees, back flat. They stand up straight again. They prostrate themselves into a posture of submission to God, pressing their knees, hands, foreheads, and noses into the ground. Then they alternate between sitting and prostration as the prayer proceeds.

As part of this ritual, Muslims recite the most common of Islamic prayers, which comes from the first *sura* of the Quran, known as "The Opening":

In the Name of God, the Compassionate, the Merciful.
Praise be to God, Lord of the worlds,
the Compassionate, the Merciful,
Master of the Day of Judgment.
Thee we worship and from Thee we seek help.
Guide us upon the straight path,
the path of those whom Thou hast blessed,
not of those who incur wrath, nor of those who are astray (1:1–7)

Muslims are also obliged to give alms (*zakat*) to the poor. Different Muslims calculate this obligation in different ways, but unlike the Christian practice of tithing, which involves giving 10 percent of your income to the church, the amount Muslims owe in alms is typically calculated based on their assets. The percentage varies (from 2.5 to 10 percent).

Fasting occurs during the ninth month of the Islamic year known as Ramadan. During this month, which commemorates the revelations that became the Quran, observant Muslims abstain from eating, drinking, smoking, and sex from dawn until sunset. As with the hajj, some Muslims are exempt. This class includes the sick and the elderly, travelers, mothers who are breastfeeding, and women who are menstruating. Ramadan ends with the fast-breaking festival of Eid al-Fitr.

The hajj incorporates each of the other four pillars, offering Muslims an opportunity to come together once a year to pray, fast, give alms to the poor, and testify to the uniqueness of God and the prophetic mission of Muhammad.

Jihad

jihad ("struggle")
external struggle against enemies of Islam and internal struggle to submit fully and completely to the divine

Jihad is not typically classified among the Five Pillars of Islam, but it is a key term in the Islamic tradition. Though often mistranslated as "holy war," jihad literally means "struggle." Muslims have long understood jihad to include armed struggles in defense of Islam. From the ninth and tenth centuries forward, many have divided jihad into two types: the "inner struggle" against pride and self-sufficiency (the higher jihad) and the "outer

Mihrab

When Muslims gather to pray, they do so in the direction of Mecca, more specifically in the direction of the Kaaba shrine in Mecca's Grand Mosque. In almost every mosque, a mihrab, an arched niche in the Mecca-facing wall, marks the direction in which believers are to bow in prayer. The earliest mihrabs were simple lines of paint or bricks on a wall. In the early eighth century, the mosque of the prophet Muhammad in Medina included a niche mihrab, and that has been the style ever since. Mihrabs can be ornate like the famous horseshoe-shaped niche covered in gold and glass mosaics in the Great Mosque of Cordoba, Spain. They can be plain, like the simple wooden one tucked in a corner of the Mosque of Aylmer in Quebec, Canada. In any style, a mihrab is said to point not only toward Mecca but also toward the unseen realities of the world beyond. Some also interpret the arches of the mihrabs as lingering signs of the now absent Prophet, and as gestures toward the cave where Muhammad received the recitations that became the Quran. The mihrab pictured here is in the Sakirin Mosque in Uskudar, Turkey, just outside of Istanbul. Opened in 2009, this was the first mosque designed by a woman, the Turkish interior designer Zeynep Fadillioglu. Evoking the future more than the past, Fadillioglu's striking, shell-shaped mihrab is brilliant turquoise. She calls it "an opening to God."[a]

struggle" against enemies of Islam (the lower jihad). Those who submit to the rigors of the hajj are engaged in the first of these struggles. The second calls for a variety of tactics, including preaching and teaching, but it can also include, in some cases and under specific circumstances, the waging of war. So while it is incorrect to translate jihad simply as "holy war," the sort of struggle to which this term points can be either spiritual or military.

Since 9/11, there has been much public debate over whether Islam is a peaceful or a warlike religion. This question goes much further back—to anticolonial Islamic movements that fought the British, French, and Russians, and further still to Christian-Muslim clashes during the Crusades. Both characterizations are valid, however, since no religion can survive for more than a millennium without knowing how to wage war and make peace. Nonetheless, it is worth examining what Muslims have said about violence. Are Islamists who kill in the name of God really Muslims? Are they really extremists? Is a "clash of civilizations" between the Islamic world and the Christian West inevitable?

Reasonable people can disagree about whether it is better for scriptures largely to ignore war (like the Christian New Testament) or to regulate war (like the Quran), but there is no debating the importance of the themes of fighting and killing in the Quran and Islamic law. Like the Jewish and Christian bibles, the Quran contains both "peace verses" and "sword verses." One controversial passage commands Muslims to "fight," "slay," and "expel" in the course of just two sentences (2:190–191), while another says that fighting is "prescribed . . . though it is hateful to you" (2:216). Another "sword verse" instructs the reader to "slay the idolaters wheresover you find them" (9:5–6). But the Quran also contains "peace verses":

BIRTH AND DEATH

In Islam there is no set rite of passage at birth, perhaps because of a popular hadith stating that all children are born Muslims. One widespread practice is to recite the Shahada into the right ear of the newly washed and swaddled newborn. Another is to recite the call to prayer. In keeping with a hadith about Muhammad chewing a date and offering a bit of its fruit to a newborn, Muslims often give babies something sweet to eat before breastfeeding begins, and the child is usually given a name a week after birth. Like Jews, Muslims typically circumcise boys. In the United States and Europe, this is often done in a hospital before the newborn comes home. In the wider Muslim world, circumcision is done years later, roughly between the ages of four and twelve. Jurists disagree about whether male circumcision is obligatory, but it is required for males making the pilgrimage to Mecca. Far more controversial and less widely practiced, female circumcision—or "female genital mutilation," as critics call it—is performed in some Muslim-majority societies, but it is more of a cultural rather than a specifically Islamic practice, undertaken as well by some Central African Christians and Ethiopian Jews.

At death, Muslims regard the Shahada as the ideal last words. If the dying person cannot speak, someone may whisper these words in the dying person's ear, like a Tibetan Buddhist monk chanting *sutras* on one's deathbed. As with Jews, Muslims bury their dead quickly. The corpse is laid bare and ritually washed,

- "There is no coercion in religion" (2:256).
- "Say, "O disbelievers! . . . Unto you your religion, and unto me my religion" (109:1–6).
- "Whosoever slays a soul . . . it is as though he slew mankind altogether, and whosoever saves the life of one, it is as though he saved the life of mankind altogether" (5:32).

The Quran is not the only authority here, however. There are also community consensus and Islamic law. Nonetheless, jurists have almost always converged on the view that it is impermissible in war to kill women, children, noncombatants, and other Muslims.

Suicide bombing began in 1983 in Beirut with the Shia organization Hezbollah. It then spread to some Sunni Islamists and, outside Islam, to the Tamil Tigers in Sri Lanka. Some Muslims (both Shia and Sunni) have justified suicide missions as acts of martyrdom, though Muslim jurists have almost universally rejected them.

However, recent polls among Muslims show both widespread opposition to suicide bombing and disquieting support for it. According to a 2014 Pew survey, most Muslims in Indonesia, Pakistan, and Nigeria believe that suicide bombings of civilians can never be justified. However, in each of these countries, significant minorities believe that suicide bombing can be justified in rare situations (22 percent in Indonesia, 7 percent in Pakistan, and 26 percent in Nigeria). In the Palestinian Territories, only one in three say that suicide bombing is never justifiable.[31]

Practitioners of every religion wrestle with elements in their tradition that have been used to justify evil, and then try to bend those elements back toward the good. Many Christians simply ignore New Testament passages that blame Jews for the crucifixion of Jesus. They also ignore how these passages have been used to justify anti-Semitism and genocide. Other Christians take it as their responsibility to attend to these words with care and to drain them of anti-Semitic connotations. Similarly, many Muslims today see it as their responsibility to scrutinize and argue for more peaceful readings of passages in the Quran that extremists have used to justify the killing of innocents.

an echo of the ablutions Muslims perform before prayer. After it is wrapped in a simple burial shroud, the body is then carried to the cemetery without a casket—though where coffins are required by law, Muslims use them. At the graveside, witnesses are reminded that everyone dies, that the time and manner of our deaths is controlled by God alone, and that death is a homecoming: "Truly we are God's, and unto Him we return" (2:156). For all these reasons, emotional demonstrations of grief, such as tearing clothes or wailing, are discouraged. Next, the corpse is placed into the ground, with the believer on his or her right side, facing Mecca and awaiting resurrection on the Day of Judgment. Then comes a period of mourning (three days, in contrast to Judaism's seven days of sitting *shiva*), in which friends bring food to the mourners' home.

Topkapi Palace in Istanbul houses relics of the lives of Muhammad and other prophets. Kept under lock and key in the palace's Chamber of the Blessed Mantle is a garment believed to have been worn by Muhammad himself.

Holy Days

The most important holy days for Muslims are two celebrations known as **Eids**, or "festivals." Eid al-Fitr ("Festival of Fast Breaking") begins on the day after Ramadan. For three days, observant Muslims exchange gifts and eat with families and friends. Eid al-Adha ("Festival of the Sacrifice"), which lasts for four days, begins at the end of the hajj. Many Muslims sacrifice animals and offer meat to the poor to commemorate Abraham's faithfulness to God. First Lady Hillary Clinton hosted the first Eid al-Fitr celebration in the White House in 1996, and that tradition continued throughout the George W. Bush and Barack Obama administrations. In 2001, the U.S. Postal Service released a postage stamp commemorating Eid al-Fitr. Today in Dearborn, Michigan, the first U.S. city with a Muslim majority, there is one public school holiday for each Eid.

Muslims celebrate their new year on the first day of their first month, known as Muharram. Because Muslims follow a lunar rather than a solar cycle, this holy day and others migrate across the calendar typically used in the West. During Muharram, on the day of Ashura, the Shia commemorate Husain's death in Karbala. This is part of a broader ten-day holiday of mourning their beloved martyr. Shia Muslims also celebrate the birthdays and death days of their Imams. The devout make pilgrimages to the Imams' tombs, circling them seven times, similar to the circling of the Kaaba during the hajj. Some Muslims also commemorate the birth and death of their Prophet.

Veneration of Saints

One of the most controversial practices in the Islamic tradition is the veneration of the saints. Because of their strong commitment to strict monotheism, Muslim thinkers have, from the start, insisted that God alone is to be worshiped. This commitment to divine unity is plain in the story of Muhammad's stripping the Kaaba of idols. It is also evident

Eid
Muslim holiday feast, including Eid al-Fitr, which ends the month-long Ramadan fast, and Eid al-Adha, which falls each year during the hajj

On September 1, 2001, the U.S. Postal Service issued the first postage stamp featuring a Muslim holiday. The stamp reads "Eid Mubarak" ("Blessed Festival") and commemorates the fast-breaking festival at the end of Ramadan.

in the opposition of jurists to large or lavish markers to memorialize the dead. But pre-scribed religion and lived religion are often at odds. Some of the most visited sites in the Islamic world are tombs of Sufi and Shia saints. And some of the most magnificent examples of Islamic architecture are royal tombs, including the Taj Majal in India, which was constructed in the early seventeenth century by the Mughal emperor Shah Jahan in loving memory of his wife.

Veneration of saints mirrors the veneration of gods in devotional Hinduism and of *bodhisattvas* in Mahayana Buddhism. In Islam, devotees patronize the shrines of saints by bringing offerings and making vows. They come away with talismans meant to shield them from evil forces and with amulets supercharged by the sacred power of their saints and intended to safeguard pregnancies. Believers also wear miniature Qurans or jewelry with the ninety-nine names of God—as charms. Even Muhammad is venerated: His hair, a tooth, and pieces of his clothing are admired as relics.

CONTEMPORARY CONTROVERSY: WOMEN AND ISLAM

For centuries, one of the main criticisms of Islam in the West has been that it denigrates women. "New Atheists" such as the British philosopher Richard Dawkins point to sexism and misogyny in Muslim countries as evidence that Islam is "one of the great evils in the world."[32] On this question of women and Islam, it is important to note that, like the Christian Bible and Judaism's Talmud, the Quran and Islamic law are a mixed bag. Like almost every religion on the planet, Muslims have traditionally espoused patriarchal values. Although Muslims insist that the divine transcends human attributes such as gender, they almost always use masculine pronouns for God. Muhammad was a man. Most mosques are segregated by gender and are attended more by men than by women (who are not required to attend and in some cases are not even permitted). There is also a troubling passage in the Quran (4:34) that seems to give a husband license to beat his wife in certain circumstances.

Muslim feminists counter that Islam improved the lives of women in seventh-century Arabia—by outlawing infanticide, by recognizing marriage as a contract between hus-band and wife, by giving wives ownership of dowries, and by allowing women to inherit property (though at only half the rate of men). In early Islam, women were key links in the chain of hadith transmission. They founded mosques and taught Islamic law. Some of the leading Sufi poets and teachers were women, and leading Sufis of both sexes explored the depths of the feminine divine. Muslim women have served as prime ministers, notably Benazir Bhutto in Pakistan and Shaykh Hasina in Bangladesh. Yemen, Egypt, Morocco, Spain, India, and Indonesia have also had political rulers who were women.

Classically, Muslim men and women have followed the same route to paradise. All are obliged to observe the Five Pillars of Islam. Nonetheless, Muslim feminists have for some time protested the secondary status of women in many Islamic societies, calling for reforms in such areas as education, polygyny, concubinage, seclusion, and veiling. They view Islam as an egalitarian religion of justice that has been contorted by men to serve their purposes. To support this view, Muslim feminists offer new interpretations of the

| Hijab | Chador | Niqab | Burka |

Many Muslims have interpreted a Quranic mandate for modest dressing as a mandate for women to cover themselves in public, but types of veiling vary widely—from the *hijab* that covers head and neck only to the *burka*, a full-body covering that also veils the eyes.

Quran and new approaches to hadith. In some cases, they have also altered Islamic rituals and other practices. On March 18, 2005, Dr. Amina Wadud, an Islamic studies professor at Virginia Commonwealth University, broke a glass ceiling when she led a mixed-gender congregation prayer service in New York City.

One key contemporary debate concerning women in Islam has swirled around the **hijab**. Is veiling required by Islamic law? Is unveiling required by modern Western values? Seven times the Quran speaks of a hijab, though the term in Muhammad's time referred simply to a "partition" or "screen." The more relevant Quranic mandate is that men and women dress modestly (24:30–31). Nonetheless, many Muslim societies went on to adopt from surrounding cultures what we now refer to as the hijab. Veiling varies considerably, however, from person to person and society to society—from women who wear no head covering of any sort to those who wear a *niqab*, *burka*, or *chador*. Muslims also differ on whether women have the right to choose whether to cover or not to cover: nine out of ten adults in Turkey say women have that right, but fewer than one in three in Afghanistan say they do.

In 1999 in secular Turkey, Merve Kavakci was prevented from taking the National Assembly seat she had won at the ballot box because she insisted on wearing a headscarf, which had been banned in government buildings. In Iran, the hijab has been both forbidden (in 1936 under Reza Shah Pahlavi) and mandated (in 1983 under the Ayatollah Khomeini). In December 2017, an Iranian protester named Viva Movahed climbed on top of a large box on a busy street in Tehran, took off her white hijab, and waved it in protest. When other young women did the same in cities across Iran, dozens were arrested, including Movahed, who was sentenced to one year in jail in 2019.

For more than a century, Western critics have pointed to the veil as evidence of the backwardness of Islam and as an argument for the necessity of "civilizing" Muslims through colonization. During the twentieth century, many Muslim women took off their veils to symbolize their solidarity with a women's rights movement that had advocated for their right to vote, to work, and to receive an education. But not all Muslim women see the hijab as a sign of inferiority. Some wear it as a rebuke to colonial powers and a sign of Muslim pride. A woman in a hijab is more free than an American or European woman who is forced by the examples of Kim Kardashian and other celebrities to bare her body in public, they argue.

hijab
head covering for Muslim women

QUESTIONS FOR DISCUSSION

1. What was Muhammad's role in the founding of Islam, and how is he remembered by Muslims today?

2. What are the Five Pillars of Islam? How does each of these pillars contribute to Muslim identity?

3. What differentiates Sunni and Shia Muslims? Consider both beliefs and practices. Also, discuss internal diversity within each of these branches.

4. What differentiates Sufis from other Muslims? Why do you think poetry and dancing are so important in the Sufi tradition?

5. Islam is, in one sense, a Middle Eastern religion and, in another sense, an Asian one. How so?

KEY TERMS

Abraham (or Ibrahim), p. 295	Mecca, p. 293
al-Qaeda ("the base"), p. 329	Medina, p. 297
Ali, p. 311	mosque, p. 293
Allah ("The God"), p. 304	Muhammad, p. 299
caliph, p. 311	Nation of Islam, p. 327
Eid, p. 335	prophets, p. 298
Five Pillars, p. 303	Quran, p. 299
hadith, p. 296	Salafis, p. 324
hajj, p. 293	Sharia ("path to water"), p. 302
hijab, p. 337	Shia, p. 301
hijra, p. 310	shirk, p. 304
Husain, p. 312	Six Articles of Faith, p. 303
imam/Imam, p. 301	Sufis, p. 316
Jesus, p. 299	Sunna, p. 305
jihad ("struggle"), p. 332	Sunni, p. 301
Kaaba, p. 294	tawhid, p. 304
martyr, p. 294	umma, p. 301
Mary, p. 307	Wahhabism, p. 323

FURTHER READING

Ali, Kecia. *The Lives of Muhammad*. Cambridge: Harvard University Press, 2014.

Curtis, Edward E., IV. *Muslims in America: A Short History*. New York: Oxford University Press, 2009.

Ernst, Carl W. *Following Muhammad: Rethinking Islam in the Contemporary World*. Chapel Hill: The University of North Carolina Press, 2003.

Esposito, John L. *Islam: The Straight Path*, 4th ed. New York: Oxford University Press, 2010.

Malcolm X, Alex Haley. *The Autobiography of Malcolm X*. New York: Ballantine Books, 1992.

Sells, Michael. *Approaching the Qu'ran: The Early Revelations*, 2nd ed. Ashland, OR: White Cloud Press, 2007.

RELIGIONS OF REVERSION
China and North America

If you look around, see the mess the world is in, and decide to stay and make it better, you have two choices. You can pick up the pieces in the world around you and try to repair it, or you can reengineer the world in keeping with some prior model. Reversion to a primordial past is particularly visible in the religions of ancient China and the traditions of Native nations of North America.

According to Chinese religious traditions, yin and yang are complementary and interpenetrating, so things tend to move toward one extreme and then revert back to the mean before moving on toward the opposite extreme. In this way, the flow of everyday life can be seen as part of a broader pattern. The Daoist classic the Daodejing speaks of "reversion" as "the movement of the Dao" ("Way") from which all things came and to which all will return.[1] Daoist practitioners seek to break away from the fetters of the workaday world to revel in the freedom of the Dao. More philosophically minded Daoists seek to act spontaneously—to revert to the state of nature that preceded human civilization. But Daoists have also developed a series of religious practices in which this reversion to the Dao happens both mentally and physically: "quiet sitting," which empties the heart-mind of distinctions and judgments, and internal alchemy, which cultivates immortality by revitalizing one's vital energies.

Like Daoism, Confucianism is a religion of reversion, though the state to which Confucians seek to return is the early civilization of China's culture heroes and sage-kings. Rather than acting naturally, Confucians imitate the Duke of Zhou, the ancient sage-king revered by Confucius for his ritual propriety and his humaneness. Both Daoists and Confucians find the contemporary world wanting, but they do not seek to escape from that world. Instead, they seek to revert to an earlier time when the way of the world was the natural way of the Dao or the civilizational way of the culture heroes and sage-kings.

A similar narrative arc is visible in Navajo religion, which speaks of a primordial state of harmony that was present shortly after the Diné (as the Navajo call themselves) emerged from a series of underworlds and became the Earth Surface People. Since that time, life on earth has been a struggle between the principle of *hozho* (harmony) and the principle of *hocho* (disharmony).

The Diné seek to live in harmony with a natural world that orients them in time and place, and particularly in harmony with the four sacred mountains that define the bounds of their sacred land. When things go awry—in an individual life, in Diné society, or in the cosmos—medicine people perform ceremonies intended to restore the balance that existed at the beginning of time.

What these three religions of reversion have in common is a commitment to life here and now, on this earth and in this place. Because of a Western bias in both the academic study of religion and in popular understandings of religion, there is a widespread tendency to classify both the religions of China and the religions of Native nations of North America as something other than religions—as ways of life or philosophies. This book presents them instead as *thisworldly* religions whose stories begin and end here and now on earth rather than returning to some past paradise or seeking release from this world altogether.

The spirit of these religions is conservative insofar as their practitioners are always looking backward in time for their exemplars. But these religions have revolutions in them, too. They challenge practitioners to make this world a way of harmony and order, a way that has been lost to all but those who remember their elders and a shared and glorious past.

In South Korea, Confucius is honored twice a year with a ceremony that includes sacrificial offerings of food and alcohol as well as an elaborate music and dance performance. Here, students take part in this ceremony at Seoul's Sungkyunkwan University.

Confucianism

THE WAY OF RITUAL PROPRIETY

In Qufu in China's Shandong province, about 350 miles south of Beijing, busloads of tourists wedge through turnstiles to enter the Temple of Confucius, or *Kongzi* ("Master Kong"), as he is known throughout China. The Chinese government brought bullet trains to this "Holy City of the Orient" in 2011, and the investment is paying off to the tune of some five million visitors a year. Inside the walls encircling the temple complex, tour guides with bullhorns broadcast facts and figures about the height and breadth of its gates, arches, courtyards, and pavilions. Ancient cypress trees (including one said to have been planted by Confucius himself) provide more natural attractions, with some thousand-year-old specimens standing stock straight while others tilt precariously, propped up by massive metal hoists. Here in Qufu, even wood and metal embody the ethics of care for the elderly and the deceased for which Confucius is celebrated.

"How delightful it is to have friends come from afar," reads a line from the opening verse of the **Analects**, the collection of the sayings and actions of Confucius known in China as the Lunyu. True to this message, there are visitors here from Europe and the Americas as well as various Chinese provinces. Tour guides take them past the Apricot Platform, where Confucius is said to have taught his students in the cooling shade of an apricot tree. At the central temple, called the Hall of Great Achievement (*Dacheng dian*), visitors learn that there was a temple here in the fifth century BCE and that the structure that stands before them was built in 1730 after lightning set an earlier one ablaze.

Analects
collection of the sayings and
actions of Confucius

For some, the highlight of this visit is snapping a selfie before moving along to Confucius Six Arts City, a theme park celebrating Confucius's alleged mastery of archery, calligraphy, charioteering, mathematics, music, and ritual. However, there are also pilgrims who view this city where Confucius was born and buried as holy ground. After ascending the thirteen steps up the two-tiered platform surrounding the Hall of Great Achievement, these pilgrims get down on their knees in prayer. Placing both feet on a soft brown pad facing the statue of Confucius inside this sacrificial hall, they cup one open hand over the other and bow three times. They put coins or a bill in a red donation box. Some perform full-body prostrations with a confidence born from practice. Others seem out of place and embarrassed, giggling as if trying to remember a game they learned as children.

Next comes a sequence of choreographed moves repeated by thousands of visitors per day. They walk to the left side of the temple platform to buy three long incense candles colorfully inscribed with prayers they will soon recite. They return to the center line of the temple complex, which runs from the entrance in the south through a series of buildings to the north. After orienting their own bodies toward the statue of Confucius, they make the offering they have come from near and far to make.

There is no priest to instruct them, but the incense vendors, sharply dressed in button-down shirts and dark blue or black sport coats, show pilgrims how to hold and light their three offerings properly. They direct worshipers to stand facing a massive antique incense burner decorated with dragons, which are symbols of imperial power. Peering through the burner and then through the temple's front door, worshipers can see the statue of Confucius ahead of them. Holding the three burning incense candles to their foreheads, they follow the instructions of the vendor, who also acts as a makeshift priest. "Hands together," he says. "Hands up. Bow." The pilgrims repeat this three-part sequence three times: first, for a safe and healthy family; second, so their children will enjoy successful careers; third, for their children to study hard and pass their examinations. "Send my prayers to Confucius," they say, "who will give us happiness and imperial protection."

Vendors place the incense in the burner and direct worshipers back to the kiosk where they may purchase a wooden tablet, adorned with a tassel and tied in a knot, all colored Chinese red, which symbolizes happiness and good luck. On this tablet they write prayer requests and sign their names. They vow to return to offer thanks if their prayer is answered. They hang the tablet on a wooden structure that looks something like a coat rack. As these tablets accumulate, the effect is a miniature Western Wall, although in this case the prayers are the wall itself.

Pilgrims do not come to Qufu for cures to cancer or infertility. Prayers concerning marriage, sickness, and health are tasks for other temples and other gods, as rare here as old-school Marxists in contemporary China. Another translation for *Dacheng dian* is "Great Success Hall," and prayers here are for just that, though the success requested is typically of the nerdy sort for which Confucius is revered: success in studies, in exams, and in jobs requiring book learning. On one tablet, a student writes, "Please protect me, bless me so I can get into university." Other tablets beg for help on standardized entrance exams such as the TOEFL and the GRE.

In earlier times, in a grand ceremony held each year in Beijing's Forbidden City, the emperor announced the names of those who had proved their knowledge of Confucian classics by passing imperial examinations. Their names resounded throughout China, further honoring those whose success also yielded them prestigious jobs in the Chinese bureaucracy. That tradition was buried more than a century ago with the last Chinese dynasty. But the close connection between Confucius, scholarship, and professional success endures.

After offering their prayers and sacrifices, the pious proceed to the front door of the Hall of Great Achievement itself. Surrounded by temple grounds rivaling those of the Forbidden City, this exquisite wooden structure is held up by ten fourteenth-century limestone pillars exquisitely carved with dragons. The roof overhead is imperial yellow. Wooden plaques attributed to various Chinese emperors proclaim Confucius to be a teacher for a thousand generations and praise him for his gentle manner and his deep learning in literature, culture, and the arts. Visitors are barred from approaching the altar, but as you make your way through the crowd to the front door, there is another chance to leave a donation or to offer a prayer (or both). Most visitors just take a quick photo and walk away. Others pause to take the measure of the man who gave Confucianism its name.

In front of them, in the center of the altar, is a wooden ancestral tablet said to house the spirit of *Kong Fuzi* ("Great Master Kong"), who was given the Western name Confucius by sixteenth-century Roman Catholic missionaries to China. Directly behind this tablet is a statue of a seated Confucius flanked by some of his closest disciples. Instantly recognizable because of his homely face and bucktoothed grin, he is crowned and adorned in imperial robes. But his hands are cupped in on themselves in a gesture that suggests humility.

A short motorbike ride north of the Temple of Confucius sits the Kong family cemetery. The resting place of some one hundred thousand descendants of Confucius, this hauntingly beautiful forest of the dead is more than two thousand years old. Ancient tombstones are scattered among stone carvings of spirit animals, but the most striking feature of this landscape is the undulating land, which rises and falls like a mad sea, swelling with burial mounds commemorating in dirt and grass individual lives come and gone. Unlike most Western cemeteries, this one is heavily forested. After the death of Confucius, it is said, his students brought trees from their hometowns. Today, more than a thousand trees from across China enliven this deathscape. Paths meander under the canopy, and you can walk for miles without encountering a living soul.

From the parking lot, it is a short walk to Confucius's grave. Here the mood is

The Kong family cemetery in Confucius's hometown of Qufu, China, is a rolling landscape of the dead that contains the tomb of Confucius and the graves of more than one hundred thousand of his descendants.

more somber than at the Temple of Confucius. Visitors slow down and grow quiet as they approach his burial mound, which is some twenty feet high and forty feet across. To the southeast is the tomb of Confucius's son, Kong Li. To the south is the tomb of his grandson, Kong Ji. The grave of Confucius himself is marked by two large stone slabs, or stelae. One, which dates to 1244, identifies the site as the Tomb of the Exalted Sage. The other, from 1443, proclaims Confucius the Exalted King of Culture.

As visitors come to pay their respects, vendors again show them how to hold their hands in prayer, how to bow, and what to say as they offer incense and flowers. Here, too, visitors can leave a red wooden prayer tablet. These prayers also are related to education and worldly success. One student asks for help on exams and university admissions, and a teacher asks Confucius to make her a proper example to her students.

Most people in China today view Confucianism not as a religion but as a philosophy or a way of life. How you evaluate that claim depends not only on what Confucians do and think, but also on what you mean by "philosophy" and "religion." But in Qufu there seems to be plenty of religion to go around, and far more religion than philosophizing. As you walk in the footsteps of Confucius, it is hard not to see his temple and tomb—these places of bowing and prayer and sacrifice and reverence—as sacred spaces.

A visitor hangs a prayer tablet among thousands of others at the Temple of Confucius in Qufu, China. Requests on these tablets typically focus on educational rewards such as a high SAT score or entrance into a prestigious university.

OUR STORY

During his long afterlife in China and around the world, **Confucius** has been remembered as a communist and a capitalist, a political reformer and a law-and-order conservative, a humble sage and a pretentious know-it-all. He has been hated and loved as an autocrat and a democrat, a misogynist and a feminist, an elitist and a man of the people, a royal and a commoner, an obsessive-compulsive ritualist and one of those losers who taught because he could not do. The Confucian scholar Tu Weiming has described his thinking as a sweet elixir that stands ready to cure what ails the modern world. The Chinese dissident Wang Xiaobo likens it to "2000-year-old chewing gum" that under no circumstances should be chewed for a second time.[1] Amid this cacophony of Confuciuses, the founder of Confucianism stands shoulder to shoulder with the founders of other religions, who have been repeatedly reinvented over the centuries in keeping with shifts in the political and cultural winds.

Here in his hometown, Confucius is widely revered. He is remembered as China's premier teacher and philosopher, an author and editor of the Confucian scriptures known as the Five Classics, and the single most important person in Chinese history. But he is also remembered as a superhuman spirit to whom the devout address their prayers and send up their sacrifices. Here, at least, that spirit resists efforts to reduce Confucianism to either morality or philosophy. This is one way his pious followers have told the story of his life and his efforts to redirect human history back to the golden age of social harmony.

Culture Heroes and Sage-Kings

In the beginning, before history itself, humans ran with the animals. We would still be running with them today if it were not for the **Three Sovereigns** *who came down from heaven to inaugurate civilization.*

Fuxi, the "Ox Tamer," domesticated animals, making husbandry possible. An expert cook, he also invented trapping, fishing with nets, and hunting with iron weapons. He figured out how to raise silkworms and how to make clothing out of their silk. He taught these arts of civilization to the Chinese people.

Shennong, the "Divine Farmer," made agriculture possible by inventing the hoe, the plough, and the sickle and by figuring out how to grow five grains. He also taught humans how to set up markets to trade the food they grew. The father of traditional Chinese medicine, he ate all the plants he could find and studied their healing properties—a task made easier by his see-through stomach. Shennong was also the father of tea. One day, while napping under a tree, leaves fell into water he was boiling. Ever curious, he stirred and sipped the mixture, and the art of tea was born.

Huangdi, "the Yellow Emperor," made civilization richer by inventing boats, the bow and arrow, and writing. He also invented warfare, defeating the barbarians at the gates of civilization and giving birth to China as a great nation.

With the advances made possible by these Three Sovereigns came the necessity of securing those advances through government—a task taken up by three great sage-kings. First

Confucius
the key figure in classical Confucianism, credited as the author of the Analects and later divinized

Three Sovereigns
rulers who together inaugurated Chinese civilization: Fuxi the Ox Tamer, Shennong the Divine Farmer, and Huangdi the Yellow Emperor

came Yao who, after observing the sun and the moon, created a calendar that allowed humans to harmonize their activities with the seasons. Yao is most important for establishing centralized government and for harmonizing its ways and means with the needs of the people. When Yao was close to death, everyone assumed he would name his son his successor. However, knowing his son lacked virtue, he found a virtuous peasant to succeed him instead. In this way, he bequeathed to China a tradition of meritorious rule by the worthy.

The worthy man Yao chose to succeed him was Shun. Shun came from a family with a hateful father and an evil stepmother, yet he remained fiercely loyal to them. Aside from this remarkable filial piety, Shun's major accomplishment was creating rituals and ceremonies. He understood that politics and society were intertwined—that political order was possible only with social harmony. He understood as well that appropriate rites secured them both.

There are sculptures of Confucius at temples and parks around the globe, including this one at Tokyo's Yushima Seido Temple, which was constructed during Japan's Edo period at the end of the seventeenth century.

During his reign, China was beset by devastating floods that washed away roads and cut off neighboring regions from one another. Shun called in a man named Yu to help. After traveling far and wide to investigate, Yu defied nature by digging canals and channeling the rivers to the sea. Shun rewarded Yu by making him his successor. Yu is now remembered as both the last of the great sage-kings of antiquity and the first emperor of China's first dynasty, the Xia.

These culture heroes and sage-kings presided over a golden age when rulers were moral, when the people practiced appropriate rituals, and when social harmony was the order of the day. But with the arrival of the first three Chinese dynasties—the Xia, the Shang, and the Zhou—a pattern emerged as certain as the patterns of the sun and the moon. A sage-king would establish an empire that would bring peace and harmony to the people. The wise and virtuous rulers who followed him would maintain that empire. Inevitably, a foolish and unethical ruler would emerge. The people would suffer. Harmony would give way to chaos and strife. Then another sage-king would arise to establish a new dynasty.

Duke of Zhou
eleventh-century BCE culture hero glorified by Confucius as the exemplar of Confucian virtues

Not long after the Shang dynasty fell to the Zhou, the founder of the Zhou dynasty died. His son was not old enough to assume power so his brother, the **Duke of Zhou**, stepped in to rule on his behalf. The Duke's advisers, possessed by the not-so-virtuous spirit of dirty politics, urged him to kill his nephew and take the crown himself, but the Duke of Zhou was a good man as well as a good ruler. When his nephew grew up, he stepped down, devoting the rest of his life to scholarly pursuits, including writing portions of the beloved Confucian classic the Book of Changes.

One of the big ideas of the Zhou dynasty was the **mandate of heaven**. According to this idea, heaven communicated with rulers by sending them signs. If a ruler was good, peace and prosperity would follow. If a ruler was evil, heaven would dispatch natural disasters. If a bad ruler ignored the message and refused to change his ways, heaven would withdraw its mandate and replace him with someone else.

In 771 BCE, the Western Zhou dynasty lost its heavenly mandate and collapsed. After shifting the capital eastward, the Eastern Zhou continued to rule until 256 BCE. These long centuries of decline saw unending feuding and bloodshed between warring states. Virtue seemed to go into hiding. Wealth and fame were the new gods. Into this chaos was born a child who would go on to become the most influential philosopher in world history.

Kongzi's father, Kong Shu Lianghe, was a strong man and a brave soldier descended from the royal house of the Shang dynasty. His first wife had given him nine daughters. A concubine had given him a disabled son. So, when he was sixty years old, he and his second wife, the twenty-year-old Yan Zhengzai, traveled to Mount Ni, about twenty miles outside of Qufu, to pray for a healthy son. Before that son came, his mother-to-be heard celestial music lauding a coming sage. Most auspicious of all, a unicorn appeared to her, announcing that her child was destined to become an "uncrowned king."

Upon his birth, two dragons flew around the Kong home in the small feudal state of Lu. The boy's body, which possessed the forty-nine birthmarks of a sage (seventeen more than the Buddha), was another sign. He had the forehead of Yao, the eyes of Shun, the neck of Yu, and the facial features of the Yellow Emperor. In fact, his forehead was so prominent it reminded his parents of a hill (qiu), so they named him Kong Qiu. His father died when he was three, and his mother while he was still a teenager, so Kongzi, as he would come to be called, had to make his way toward adulthood without his parents. Perhaps this

Although Confucius has been widely described as a humble philosopher, legends about his supernatural origins abound. This painting, from a 1918 book on Chinese religions compiled by Jesuit missionary Henri Doré, depicts the appearance of a mysterious unicorn heralding Confucius's birth as an "uncrowned king."

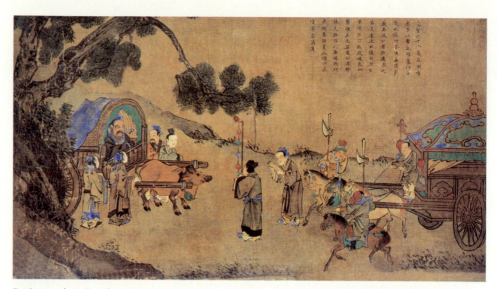

Dating to the Ming dynasty (1368–1644), this painting comes from a book about the life of Confucius. Here, he is shown in a carriage pulled by an ox (left) surrounded by disciples and followers.

loss explains why he was obsessed with rituals as a child, his favorite toys the vessels used in performing traditional rites.

Kongzi married young, and the marriage produced a son and a daughter. Their father kept accounts in a grain storehouse and oversaw livestock. He also embarked on a modest bureaucratic career, working for a time as a police commissioner. But government work never offered him the political influence he sought. In his fifties, he left his job. For thirteen years, he wandered China, offering advice to any ruler who would listen.

Kongzi's solution to the tumult of his times was to revert to the rituals and values of the golden age of the early Zhou, when the people flourished under the benevolent rule of sage-kings. Unfortunately, the rulers Kongzi encountered met his advice with indifference bordering on contempt. They failed to see that the man before them carried the mandate of heaven. The few appointments he received were short-lived. In addition, the road was a dangerous place back then, with battles breaking out among feudal lords. Kongzi and the students who traveled with him were threatened and beaten. Kongzi was even targeted for assassination.

In his sixties, Kongzi returned to his home state of Lu and took up a career as a teacher and scholar that shaped him into the world's greatest sage. He studied poetry, music, history, and rites. Regardless of their economic or social standing, he accepted students who valued learning, and some three thousand students gathered around him. Kongzi described himself not as an innovator but as a transmitter of ancient wisdom. He gloried in the exemplary lives of the great culture heroes of antiquity who invented Chinese civilization, and he longed for a renewal of leadership like that of the great sage-kings who founded and maintained China's earliest dynasties. Among the ancient values he emphasized were humaneness, ritual propriety, and filial piety. When he was not teaching, he was writing and editing. In fact, he either wrote or edited portions of each of the **Five Classics***: the Book of History, the Book of Poetry, the Book of Rites, the Book of Changes, and*

Five Classics

the fundamental texts for classical Confucianism: Book of History, Book of Poetry, Book of Rites, Book of Changes, and Spring and Autumn Annals

*Spring and Autumn Annals. Through this work, he took his place among the **ru** ("scholars") who studied the great books of Chinese antiquity. "Be a gentleman ru, not a vulgar ru," Kongzi says in his Analects, and in his life, he was just that.*[2]

Toward the end of his time on earth, hunters carried a rare animal back to his hometown. Recognizing it as a unicorn, Kongzi read its death as a sign of his own impending end and as the death rattle of his state of Lu. After his passing in 479 BCE *in his early seventies, Kongzi was buried in Qufu. His students, who respected him as a father, mourned him for the three years that dutiful children mourn for their parents. Through Kongzi, his students learned to love the ancients. They loved Kongzi, too—as a culture hero and an "uncrowned king" who, like the sovereigns and sage-kings of old, taught the arts of civilization and government. Through these arts, he pointed the way toward both self-cultivation and social and political harmony. After he was gone, and even to this day, his disciples and their disciples' disciples have attempted to walk in his way of ritual propriety.*

ru
Chinese word for scholar and the source for the term *Ruism*, a popular Confucian alternative to "Confucianism"

CONFUCIANISM IN TODAY'S WORLD

When it comes to religions that are not our own, stereotypes rule. Europeans and Americans probably know less about Confucianism than they do about any of the world's major religions, and much of what they think they know they do not like. In the minds of many Westerners, Confucianism is about empty rituals, stodgy etiquette, strict social roles, and otherwise maintaining a hierarchical status quo: wives obeying husbands, workers bowing and scraping before bosses, and the masses blindly following the great and powerful Chinese Communist Party (CCP). Could anything be more antimodern and antidemocratic than that? Thanks to revolutionaries from Alexander Hamilton to Elon Musk, Americans famously celebrate the new and the young, while Confucius, a loyal lover of antiquity, commands us to revere our elders and commemorate the dead. In a time of Emmas and Emilys, Confucianism lauds Mildreds and Myrtles. Most of all, Confucius is identified with broken syntax and fortune-cookie aphorisms. Google "Confucius," and you will be dispatched to page after page of "Confucius says" jokes, many off-color and most with grammatical errors.

If we take a longer and less biased view, it is hard to dismiss Confucius as anything less than one of the most influential people in world history. The Analects, a collection of his words and deeds, is doubtless one of the world's most influential books. In fact, it likely has had a greater effect on more people over more time than any other scripture, with the possible exception of the Bible. While debate persists regarding whether Confucianism is a religion, there is no denying the enduring global impact of Confucian ideas, symbols, ethics, sayings, and stories.

Confucianism is, of course, most consequential in China, where it provides much of the scaffolding for the

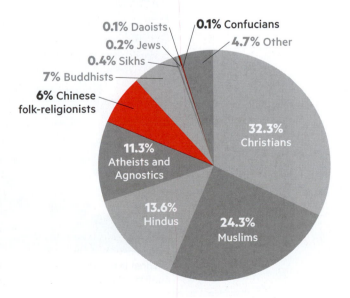

Comparison of Religions Worldwide, 2020

- **0.1%** Daoists
- **0.2%** Jews
- **0.4%** Sikhs
- **7%** Buddhists
- **6% Chinese folk-religionists**
- **0.1% Confucians**
- **4.7%** Other
- **32.3%** Christians
- **24.3%** Muslims
- **13.6%** Hindus
- **11.3%** Atheists and Agnostics

beliefs and practices of a human population of nearly 1.4 billion, or roughly one in five of all humans on earth. However, this influence extends far beyond mainland China into Taiwan, Hong Kong, Japan, Korea, and Vietnam, where Confucianism provides the ritual framework for practices such as ancestor veneration and the basic model for relationships between parents and children, husbands and wives. It teaches respect for authority useful to political elites even as it justifies resisting those elites under certain circumstances. Its emphasis on morals and etiquette provides a foundation for everyday conduct in the workplace and at home.

Confucianism also informs the rhythms of day-to-day life in large Chinese communities in New York City, San Francisco, Vancouver, Toronto, London, Sydney, Melbourne, Johannesburg, Bangkok, and Singapore. Its impact extends among non-Chinese throughout East Asia, especially in Japan and Korea, where Confucian rituals and values continue to influence family life, small businesses, and educational institutions.

Over the last century, Confucianism has been dismissed not only by Americans obsessed with the new and the now but also by Chinese Communists and Nationalists who have denounced it as a backward-looking ideology designed to provide cover for economic and political oppression. The German sociologist Max Weber, who lauded "the Protestant ethic" as a boon to capitalism, was convinced that Confucianism hurt economic development. Nowadays, capitalism is booming in East Asia, and many see the invisible hand of Confucius guiding both the rise of China as an economic power and the seemingly miraculous economic growth of the four Asian Tigers: Hong Kong, Taiwan, Singapore, and South Korea. Yes, Confucius sneered at people who valued wealth and fame over learning, but his love of education is driving East Asian economies forward in an era when what we need to know seems to shift daily.

But how many Confucians are there? Unfortunately, there is no easy answer to that question. The Chinese government does not count this "ism" as a religion. In its five

Children in Qufu, China, recite excerpts from the Analects to commemorate the 2,568th birthday of Confucius in 2017.

religions policy, only Catholicism, Protestantism, Islam, Daoism, and Buddhism are officially recognized. Therefore, if asked to name their religion, most Chinese adults would not even consider Confucianism an option. Moreover, the very notion of religion is vexed in China. The Western concept of religion did not gain a widespread equivalent in Chinese until the late nineteenth and early twentieth centuries, when the term *zongjiao* ("sect teaching") began to take hold. This Mandarin term was first used in China in the sixth century to describe various Buddhist sects. After migrating to Japan, it returned, more than a century ago, to China. So even those who might in theory consider Confucianism to be their religion would likely trip over the term "religion" itself.

Another obstacle to a proper count of Confucians is China's long-standing Three Teachings doctrine, which views Confucianism, Daoism, and Buddhism as distinct yet complementary. The West's three teachings—Judaism, Christianity, and Islam—have traditionally been seen as exclusive my-way-or-the-highway projects that demand a believer's sole allegiance. China's big three have long been polyamorous. According to a popular Chinese saying, "Every Chinese wears a Confucian cap, a Daoist robe, and Buddhist sandals." According to another saying, the Chinese are Confucians during the day, Daoists at night, and Buddhists at death. This long-standing refusal to draw sharp boundaries between Confucianism, Daoism, and Buddhism—all English words coined in the modern West—makes it impossible to count with any accuracy the numbers of Confucians, Daoists, or Buddhists in China. When a Western pollster calls random telephones in China asking, "What is your religion, if any?" almost everyone who picks up is hard-pressed to pick just one.

Sculpted by Hermon A. MacNeil, the East Pediment of the U.S. Supreme Court building in Washington, DC, interprets Confucius (left of center) as a lawgiver alongside Moses (center).

More than a century ago, two scholars tried separately to count China's Confucians. One fixed on 256 million; another on 240 million.[3] Both figures were based on the assumption that virtually everyone in China was a Confucian. Today social scientists counting religious folks typically focus on self-identification or group membership, and by either metric the numbers of Confucians in the world is miniscule. The World Religion Database (WRD) found only 9 million Confucianists worldwide in 2020. However, virtually all of the 468 million "Chinese folk religionists" counted by the WRD blend the beliefs and behaviors of Buddhists, Daoists, and Confucians. Combining Confucians and Chinese folk religionists into a category the WRD refers to as "wider Confucians" yields a total approaching half a billion, or 6 percent of the world's population.

Numbers aside, Confucianism was China's official orthodoxy for more than two millennia, taught in Chinese schools and tested on Chinese civil service examinations. Its lessons on how to become human through education, ritual, music, and ethics were also taught and learned for much of that time in East and Southeast Asia. Nowadays you don't need to know what Confucius says to work for the Chinese government, but Confucian values such as reverence for the past, respect for education, deference to elders, and filial piety continue to influence profoundly how ordinary people in China and the Chinese diaspora act politically, conduct business, interact socially, mourn and grieve, teach and learn, and seek to harmonize with the impersonal heaven known as *tian*. Confucian commitments also course through almost every Buddhist, Daoist, Christian, and atheist in East and Southeast Asia. More than Buddhism, Daoism, or Communism, Confucianism has shaped Chinese minds and Chinese ways of life. But it is also impossible to understand contemporary life in Taiwan, Hong Kong, Japan, North and South Korea, Singapore, or Vietnam without reckoning with the long shadow of Confucius and his followers. Even in the United States, the economic success of many Chinese Americans is born of a reverence, bordering on faith itself, for Confucian values such as learning, hard work, and family.

The recent restoration of Confucius's reputation among leaders of the CCP also testifies to the power and persistence of his legacy. Whether Confucianism is to China a boon or a burden—the secret ingredient that gives Chinese civilization today its special flavor or the stench seeping out of China's decaying feudal past—is still debated. What is indisputable is the key role Confucianism has played in shaping the lives of billions of Chinese, both home and abroad. Given the massive populations in China, Korea, Japan, Vietnam, and the wider Chinese diaspora, where this tradition holds sway, Confucianism surely stands with Islam, Christianity, Buddhism, and Hinduism among the most influential of the world's religions.

CONFUCIANISM 101

➜ How can we become truly human?

Unlike religions that focus on an individual religious goal, Confucianism is a community-focused tradition that still bears the marks of its origins during China's tumultuous Spring and Autumn (770–476 BCE) and Warring States (475–221 BCE) periods. The urgent predicament during this time was the social chaos brought on first by the breakdown of the Zhou dynasty and then by the jockeying for power among small feudal states. The solution Confucius and his followers offered to this problem focused on the moral and ritual dimensions of religion, and more specifically on the cultivation of three interrelated values: humaneness (**ren**), ritual propriety (**li**), and **filial piety** (*xiao*).

ren
the key Confucian virtue of humaneness, or benevolence

li
the key Confucian virtue of ritual propriety; also "principle" or "pattern," a central concept in the Neo-Confucian School of Principle

filial piety (xiao)
respect for and deference to one's parents

junzi
profound person, an exemplar of virtue emphasized by classical Confucians

sage (shengren)
wise person, the Confucian exemplar emphasized after the rise of Neo-Confucianism

The person who embodies these values—the exemplar in the classical Confucian tradition—was called a "**junzi**," a key Confucian term that appears more than one hundred times in the Analects. This term has been variously translated as "true gentleman," "superior man," "perfected person," "exemplary person." Here, it is rendered as "profound person." Profound persons are first and foremost virtuous persons. They are concerned with righteousness rather than wealth or fame. Committed to the well-being of others, the junzi, according to the Analects, is someone who has mastered himself. As a result, he is always virtuous. He "does not, even for a single meal, act contrary to *ren*" (4.5).[4]

In the Chinese language of the time of Confucius, junzi meant "ruler's son." It was a title conferred at birth. For Confucius, this title was an achievement instead, and one did not need to be a noble to aspire to it. Even a commoner could become a junzi through his own self-effort.

Roughly a millennium and a half after Confucius, a reform movement called Neo-Confucianism took aim at an even more ambitious goal: becoming a **sage** (**shengren**). By any name, however, the Confucian goal was (and is) extraordinarily difficult to attain. Human beings do not become either sages or profound persons easily. They have to work at it, and the work borders on impossible. In fact, in the Analects, Confucius refuses to call himself either a junzi or a sage. Consequently, the Confucian goal is, like becoming a Catholic saint, out of reach for almost everyone.

That said, it is possible in the Confucian tradition for everyone to aspire to a more proximate goal: becoming more truly human through self-cultivation. In keeping with their focus on community, Confucians insist that we become ourselves and transform society through others. The path to social harmony runs through human flourishing, and human flourishing is made possible through right relations with other human beings. But Confucians are by no means opposed to individual spiritual practices. In fact, meditative strategies such as "quiet sitting" have long been essential components of the Confucian project. As the Confucian tradition developed, it focused more and more on these sorts of contemplative practices, without ever losing sight of the close connection between self-cultivation and social harmony. Like Protestant evangelicals, Confucians were convinced that individual transformation would produce social change. In their view, however, the self was part of a vast web of relationships that includes both the living and the dead.

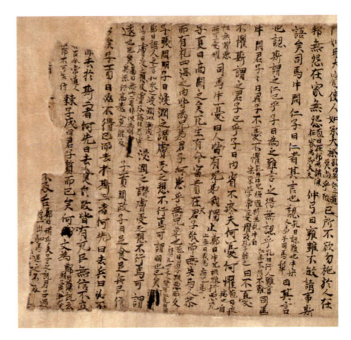

This portion of a scroll from the Analects was found in the early twentieth century by archaeologists digging in the Mogao caves at Dunhuang in northwestern China. With noticeable cross-outs that mark it as a practice copy, the scroll, which dates to 890, was probably written by a student.

Inside this web, Confucians have traditionally fixed on what they call the Five Relationships:

- father and son
- elder brother and younger brother
- husband and wife
- older friend and younger friend
- ruler and subject

These relationships reflect the age and gender hierarchies of ancient China. Each is characterized by deference—of the junior to the senior or the female to the male. The son is to revere the father. The younger brother is to respect the older brother. The wife is to be loyal to her husband. The subject is to serve the ruler. But these relationships are all marked by reciprocity as well: the father is supposed to show love to his son, the elder brother is supposed to be gentle toward his younger brother, the husband is supposed to be good to his wife, and the ruler is supposed to be benevolent toward his subject. Without this vast complex of overlapping networks of mutual obligations, there may be an ego but there is no self.

There is no self apart from these relationships because we are social beings who become more fully ourselves by engaging with others. As more of us become more truly human, the families, communities, and societies in which we live become more ordered and harmonious. In this way, the individual goal of becoming more truly human aligns with the collective goal of social harmony.

How do we accomplish these goals? What are the techniques of self-transformation that promote human flourishing and social harmony? First and foremost, learning. This emphasis on learning is plain in a term many Confucians now use for their tradition:

Confucianism at a Glance

Problem: social chaos

Solution: social harmony

Techniques: humaneness, ritual propriety, and various methods of self-cultivation

Exemplar: junzi ("profound person") and shengren ("sage")

In short, Confucianism is a tradition in which individuals seek to cultivate social harmony by reverting to the humaneness and ritual propriety of the sage-kings of ancient China.

Ruism (rujiao), or the tradition of the *ru* ("scholar"). In fact, "learning" is the very first word in the Analects. Later in the Analects, Confucius offers a short biography of his life, which begins at the age of fifteen when, in his words, "my heart-mind was set upon learning" (2.4).[5] One of the only times he ever forgets his trademark humility comes when he brags that "there will be no one who can compare with me in the love of learning" (5.28).[6] Today, education is increasingly seen in the West largely as a means to the end of employment. Confucius commends learning for its own sake. The purpose of education is not to turn out workers who can turn out widgets but to empower students to become truly human beings— people who both understand and enact the virtues.

But what are we supposed to learn? First and foremost, the Five Classics. The task of learning is not simply to memorize Confucian scriptures or recite the sayings of Confucius, however. It is to emulate the sages by paying attention to what they did, including their morals, their manners, how they performed rituals, and how they cultivated themselves.

Classically, Confucians have affirmed Five Virtues that emerge from the long and difficult process of self-cultivation and self-realization:

- humaneness
- righteousness
- ritual propriety
- wisdom
- integrity

Of these virtues, the two that are most emphasized are humaneness (ren) and ritual propriety (li). Another absolutely essential virtue in the Confucian tradition is filial piety, which calls for proper relations inside the family, and in particular for children of all ages

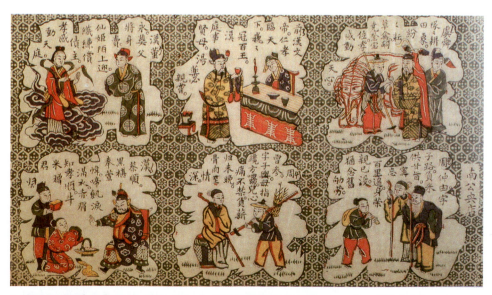

A Chinese woodcut from the Qing dynasty (1644–1911) depicts six examples of filial piety, a Confucian virtue that enjoins respect for one's parents and ancestors.

CONFUCIANISM: A GENEALOGY

Like the term "Confucius," a transliteration of Kong Fuzi by sixteenth-century members of the Roman Catholic Society of Jesus (Jesuits), the term "Confucianism" is a Western invention. Undergirding this word are a long train of assumptions, including that Confucianism is a religion akin to Buddhism and Christianity and that Confucius is its founder.

Many scholars have used the *Oxford English Dictionary* to date to 1862 the first appearance of "Confucianism" in English, but there are hundreds of earlier usages. China scholar T. H. Barrett traced this term to the British diplomat Sir John Francis Davis, who describes Confucianism in *The Chinese* (1836) as "the orthodoxy, or state religion of China."[a] The earliest usage seems to occur in a November 1825 article in *The Evangelical Magazine and Missionary Chronicle* by Robert Morrison, an Anglo-Scottish Presbyterian missionary to China. His "Remarks on the Language, History, Religions, and Government of China" lists China's "three religions" as "Confucianism, Laoukeunism [Daoism], and Budhism."[b]

The word "Confucius" is far older. A 1599 book by the English writer and champion of North American colonization Richard Hakluyt includes not only a reference to "one Confucius a notable philosopher" but also an extensive discussion of how he was "worshipped with burning of incense and with tapers" and on bended knees with heads bowed "downe to the ground."[c]

to respect their parents. To be filial is to respect your parents when they are alive and to worship them as ancestors after they have passed away. Filial piety can even be seen in the facial expressions of children, who should refrain from sneering or rolling their eyes when upset by a parent. Because filial piety is taught from birth, it is understood by Confucians to serve as the schoolhouse of all virtues.

CONFUCIAN HISTORY

What we now call Confucianism emerged during the Axial Age, which dates between the eighth and third centuries BCE, when religious thinkers from Socrates in ancient Greece to the Buddha in North India to Confucius in China walked the earth. As Bronze Age societies melted down and the Iron Age emerged, wars broke out in Greece, India, and China. Amid the fear and chaos, thinkers pondered how to administer a state. They also inquired after the meanings and ends of individual lives. Should we withdraw from society into smaller experimental communities or into nature itself? Should we seek release from this lost world into a realm above? As these questions resounded, followers of many of these thinkers transformed their ideas and practices into new religions.

In Chinese history, this was the time of the decline of the Eastern Zhou dynasty (770–256 BCE), which spanned the Spring and Autumn and Warring States periods. This chaotic time uprooted many lives, but it was fertile intellectually—the period of One Hundred Schools of Thought, which tried to make sense of it all. The central human predicament, as these thinkers saw it, was the same problem that had vexed the authors of India's Vedas: social chaos. China's old feudal order was breaking down, and with it the authority of the aristocratic class. Old religious solutions to this problem had lost their power, as the ancient gods of the Xia, Shang, and Zhou dynasties seemed unable or unwilling to staunch the bloodshed.

Confucius (551–479 BCE) lived during this tumultuous time. Setting aside questions regarding divinity and the supernatural, he and his rivals focused their energies on this-worldly matters. Together they envisioned a harmonious society guided no longer by aristocrats but by scholars like themselves. But what should this harmonious society look like? And how would it come to be?

The Life of Confucius

The life of Confucius has been told by billions of people, but facts about his life are hard to come by. Much of the evidence comes from pious tales intended to elevate him into a hero or a god (or both). Even his own words passed on in the Analects are problematic, as they were written by his followers and then collected over centuries. Though some of its passages were found in a fourth century BCE tomb, the Analects as we now know it does not seem to have circulated much until the first century BCE. The earliest excavations of anything like today's text come from a 50 BCE tomb. Images of Confucius have also shifted over time, so much so that Confucius has proven to be as much of a chameleon as Jesus, and as much an icon of Chinese nationalism as Jesus is of American nationalism. Nonetheless, there is some scholarly consensus about key aspects of his life.

According to scholarly accounts, which both differ and overlap with Confucian traditions that informed the "Our Story" narrative, Confucius was born in a village in the state of Lu near modern-day Qufu in China's Shangdong province. The year was 551 BCE, making him a rough contemporary of the Daoist sage Laozi. Confucius's father may have been a soldier. About his mother, who died when he was young, almost nothing is known, in part because there is no record of Confucius ever discussing her. Perhaps there was something illegitimate about his birth. She may have been a concubine. She may not have been married to his father. Or perhaps they married and then separated. At any rate, his father died when Confucius was very young, and his mother before he was an adult, so, like many heroes in world history and literature, he entered adulthood as an orphan.

In the Analects, Confucius reports that as a boy he was "of humble status" (9.6).[7] Scholars agree that his family was of modest means. Many suspect he was a noble because he was able to obtain an education, including training in the six arts: archery, calligraphy, charioteering, mathematics, music, and ritual. If so, he was a lowly noble, perhaps from a class of scholar-bureaucrats. Oddly, for a man who emphasized filial piety, as little is known about his wife and children as about his parents, but he married young and appears to have had a son and a daughter. As for Confucius himself, he seems to have enjoyed a good drink and a good meal. He was not attracted to the strict asceticism of a buddha or a Daoist recluse. Neither a denier of the world nor a discipliner of the body, he liked to sing, fish, and hunt.

In his early fifties, after an on-again-off-again career in low-level government jobs, Confucius resigned from an appointment as police commissioner in the state of Lu and left home. For the next thirteen years he wandered around China, looking for a ruler who would pay for his advice and heed it. With those hopes dashed, he returned home in his

Confucius understood music to be one of the most valuable of the "six arts" because of its power to create harmony. This Song dynasty (960–1279) mural at Holy Mother Hall in Jinci Temple in Shanxi, China, depicts women playing music.

sixties, setting himself up as a teacher. Confucius took on students of all social classes. Few seem to have come from wealth. Today the maxims that China's "First Teacher" taught them resound in the Analects.

Confucius died in or around Qufu in 479 BCE at the age of seventy-one or seventy-two. By all accounts, he died a failure, an adviser to rulers without a single ruler to advise. So it is hard not to read the words he left behind as a literature of complaint. He probably never said the last words popularized by the nineteenth-century Scottish missionary and China scholar James Legge—"No intelligent monarch arises; there is not one in the kingdom that will make me his master. My time has come to die"—but they sum up his complaint nicely.[8]

What Confucius Taught

What did Confucius teach? Nothing new, according to the man himself. "I do not forge new paths," he says in the Analects. "I cherish the ancients" (7.1). But Confucius was a transformer as well as a transmitter. Yes, he derived his thinking from the Three Sovereigns who invented Chinese civilization and the sage-kings who later presided over it. But it was Confucius who redirected Chinese culture from a hierarchy of birth to a hierarchy of merit. He insisted that it was possible for commoners and nobles alike to ascend to become profound persons.

Like others in the Hundred Schools of Thought, Confucius was preoccupied with the problem of social chaos brought on by the Zhou dynasty's demise. However, he understood chaos as a general rather than a specific problem—the fundamental human predicament—and he took aim at social harmony as his goal. Reaching this collective goal was possible only if individuals took life's ethical and ritual dimensions seriously, by transforming themselves into profound persons who exhibited the virtues, performed rituals appropriately, and otherwise walked in the way of heaven.

Scholars disagree about whether Confucius was a conservative or a revolutionary. They agree that his thinking began by looking backward. He believed that human beings could achieve moral perfection and that individual moral perfection would lead to social harmony. But the only way to accomplish these goals was to revert to the time-honored ways of the ancient sage-kings. To that end, he taught his students the Five Classics of China's golden age of peace and prosperity, and he infused in them a reverence for the culture heroes and sage-kings of Chinese antiquity, especially the Duke of Zhou. Study the history, rituals, and songs of these great men, he said, and then go and do likewise. Cultivating the wisdom and virtue of these exemplars was, in his view, the way to become truly human. It was also the way toward social harmony. For social life to become harmonious again, humans needed to cultivate and act on the virtue of humaneness. They also needed to act in accordance with ritual propriety. For Confucius, these were the values that had made ancient China great and would make it great again.

Duke of Zhou

CHRONOLOGY OF CONFUCIANISM

1600–1046 BCE Shang dynasty develops bronze technology, written language, and the calendar

1046–256 Zhou dynasty invents the notion of the mandate of heaven and provides a blueprint for Confucius's ideal society

770 to 221 Hundred Schools of Thought era spanning the Spring and Autumn period (770–476) and the Warring States period (475–221)

551–479 Traditional dates for Confucius

470–391 Life of Mozi, founder of the Mohists

371–289 Life of Mencius, Confucianism's Second Sage

221–206 Qin dynasty briefly unites China under the Legalist ideology

206 BCE–220 CE Han dynasty establishes Confucianism as China's state ideology

136 BCE Canonization of Confucianism's Five Books, which will soon form the basis for the Chinese government's civil service examination

1st century CE Buddhists first arrive in China

220–581 Six Dynasties period of disunity includes the Three Kingdoms (220–265), the Jin dynasty (265–420), and the Northern and Southern dynasties (386–581)

581–618 Sui dynasty sees the arrival of New Buddhist schools as Confucianism loses ground

618–907 Tang dynasty favors Buddhism under Empress Wu and Daoism under Emperor Wuzong

907–960 Five Dynasties period

960–1127 Northern Song dynasty returns Confucianism to dominance

1127–1279 Southern Song dynasty sees the maturation of Neo-Confucianism

1130–1200 Life of Zhu Xi, Neo-Confucian thinker associated with the rationalistic School of Principle

1279–1368 Yuan dynasty brings foreign rule to China under the Mongols

1313 Four Books replace the Five Classics on the curriculum for China's civil service examinations, making Neo-Confucianism the official Confucianism until the end of the imperial era

1392–1910 Korea's Joseon dynasty promotes Neo-Confucianism as its state ideology

1368–1644 Ming dynasty reestablishes Chinese rule

1472–1529 Life of Wang Yangming, Neo-Confucian thinker associated with the idealistic School of Mind

Ren, or Humaneness Confucius's central teaching was ren—a term that appears more than one hundred times in the Analects. This cardinal Confucian virtue is traditionally translated as "benevolence," but it is also rendered as humaneness, goodness, kindness, human-heartedness, humanity, altruism, and fellow-feeling.

Ren is typically used to point to the particular virtue of humaneness and the allied virtue of non-harm articulated in the Analects' negative Golden Rule: "Do not impose upon others what you yourself do not want" (12.2, 15.24). But ren can also refer to a wider array of virtues, encompassing, for example, the Five Virtues of humaneness, justice, ritual propriety, wisdom, and integrity, or the "five attitudes" of deference, tolerance, making good on one's word, diligence, and generosity (17.6). Finally, ren can refer to a person who exhibits these qualities—a truly humane person.

The Chinese character for ren includes two images: a human being and the number two. Someone who possesses the virtue of ren understands that human beings do not stand alone. We are social creatures, living and moving in what the Reverend Martin Luther King Jr. once called "an inescapable network of mutuality."[9] Therefore, we can become neither humane nor human in isolation. Or, as the philosopher Herbert Fingarette

1644–1911 Qing dynasty, China's last imperial dynasty

1825 First use of the term "Confucianism," by the British missionary Robert Morrison

1843 Henry David Thoreau edits two groups of sayings from Neo-Confucianism's Four Books in the Transcendentalist periodical *The Dial*

1848 Discovery of gold in California sparks a Gold Rush that lures Chinese immigrants to the West Coast of the United States

1853 First Chinese temple in the United States opens in San Francisco's Chinatown

1882 Chinese Exclusion Act bans Chinese immigration and naturalization

1893 World's Parliament of Religions brings representatives of many religions, including the Confucian Pung Kwang Yu, to Chicago's World's Fair

1905 Civil service examination era comes to an end in China

1911 The fall of the Qing dynasty brings an end to China's long imperial history

1912 Republic of China is established

1924 U.S. Congress passes Asian Exclusion Act, which imposes a national origins quota system that severely restricts immigration from Asia

1928 Nationalists come to power in China under Chiang Kai-shek

1949 People's Republic of China (PRC) is established as Chinese Civil War ends with a Communist victory over the Nationalists, who flee to Taiwan

1965 The landmark Hart-Celler Act reopens the United States to immigration from Asia, including China

1966–1976 Cultural Revolution attacks the "Four Olds," Confucianism included

1980s Confucian revival begins on mainland China

2004 State-sponsored sacrifices are resumed at Qufu

2006 *Confucius from the Heart* by the media professor Yu Dan sells four million copies in its first three months

2008 Opening Ceremonies of Beijing Olympics showcase Confucianism

2014 President Xi becomes the Chinese Communist Party's first chief to attend a Confucius birthday celebration

put it, "For Confucius, unless there are at least two human beings, there can be no human being."[10]

Broadly speaking, ren is a type of self-mastery. Mastery over selfish desires is the hallmark of the profound person. But ren is not for Confucius a subjective reality. It is an objective reality, readily observable in one's actions. When Confucius says in the Analects that ren is about loving others (12.22), he is not talking about something we feel. He is talking about something we do. The exemplary person "takes the high road" and brings out the best in others, we read in the Analects, whereas the "petty person takes the low" road and brings out the worst in others (14.23, 12.16). In the world according to Confucius, virtue is the foundation of civilization, and the foundational virtue is ren. It is ren in action that makes people truly human and society harmonious.

Closely related to ren is filial piety. The Jewish commandment to honor your father and mother is a call to filial piety, but this virtue is emphasized even more in the Confucian tradition. Whereas the Mohists argued that humans should love all human beings equally without regard to familial relations, Confucius was a staunch defender of family values. In fact, the opening chapter of the Analects refers to filial piety as the "root" of ren. It is in the family that we take our first baby steps toward humaneness. Here our self-centeredness begins to be tempered as we learn how to act with reverence for heaven and respect for others.

Li, or Ritual Propriety How do the lessons of humaneness learned among parents, children, siblings, and spouses move out into the wider world? In a word, li. Li is often translated as "ritual," and before Confucius this term referred fairly narrowly to religious activities such as ancestral rites. With Confucius, it acquired broader associations, referring to everyday manners, courtesies, customs, ceremonies, etiquette, civility, and propriety. In addition to telling people what to do at births, weddings, and funerals, li came to govern everyday human-to-human interactions such as how to eat, how to give gifts, how to dress, and how to carry one's body. In short, ritual propriety came to refer to doing the right thing in the right way under a given set of circumstances—the ancient Chinese equivalent of holding doors open for the elderly and saying "please" and "thank you."

When you meet new coworkers, there are appropriate and inappropriate ways to do so. In the United States, ritual propriety might dictate that you look them in the eye, shake their hand firmly, and offer some customary comment, such as "Nice to meet you." An appropriate response might be "Nice to meet you, too." Either holding your new acquaintance's hand too limply or squeezing it too tightly would be inappropriate. A hug would likely be weird in a workplace setting. So would a detailed response to the pleasantry "How are you?"

As these examples suggest, li is most evident to us while it is breaking down—when someone introduces herself and fails to give her name, or when a man in the quiet car on the train talks way too loudly about things that are way too personal, or when (as in a *Seinfeld* television episode) a close-talker rears his ugly head. When President Barack Obama met Queen Elizabeth II at Buckingham Palace in 2009, his gift—an iPod—was widely criticized as a faux pas. In 2018, President Trump arrived late for his meeting with Queen Elizabeth II—a gaffe made worse by his later claim that the queen had kept *him* waiting. Both the tardiness and the blaming violated li.

In the Islamic scripture known as the *hadith*, Muslims look to Muhammad to learn how to act appropriately. In the Analects, Confucians look to Confucius, just as Confucius himself looked to the Duke of Zhou. Here, Confucians learn that Confucius did not talk while eating; when fishing, he used a line rather than a net; and when sleeping, he did not lie flat on his back like a corpse. In answering a question about filial piety, Confucius seems more concerned with the facial expressions we use than with what we otherwise say or do. "It all lies in showing the proper countenance," he says (2.8). All this might seem like fussy formalism, the sort of starchy behavior a grandfather might insist on merely to feel himself superior to his less inhibited grandchild. But just as words can sting, so can expressions of annoyance or disdain.

Ancestor worship is an important ritual in many Asian cultures, thanks in part to the emphasis of Confucius on filial piety. Here, a child examines ancestral tablets in Malacca, Malaysia, on Chinese New Year in 2010.

Here we bump up against a fundamental distinction between values of the Confucian tradition and those of the modern West. Since the Enlightenment, it has been a doctrine of popular faith in the West that human beings are and ought to be independent free agents. In the United States, where individual freedom is so highly prized, many Americans insist on shaping their own identities and destinies. They resist being slotted into cookie-cutter roles or conventional identities. Therefore, ritual propriety is to many Americans wildly inappropriate. It violates their autonomy. It demands that they bow to the king.

Confucius had a different understanding of the human being. He saw ritual propriety as the social glue holding society together and as a social lubricant allowing human interactions to operate more smoothly. Human beings were, in his view, networks of social relations that could not be understood apart from their connections to members of their families and communities. Confucius believed that morals and social harmony had decayed in his time largely because of the degradation of manners and rituals, which taught people how to respect others as surely as ancient rites of sacrifice taught them how to revere the gods.

In the modern West, there is also resistance to ritual, so much so that the phrase "empty rituals" seems to many to be redundant. For Confucius, acting in keeping with li was not simply a matter of blindly following the rules. As he put it, ritual propriety is not just about "jade and silk" or "bells and drums" (17.11). Those who possessed li were said to know intuitively what to do in any situation, but the right action in any given case was not always carved in stone. For example, at the time of Confucius's father's death, ritual propriety dictated that children should bury their parents together and that, prior to burial, the deceased should be placed in a coffin outside the home for a few days. When his mother died, Confucius had no idea where his father had been buried. So he placed his mother's coffin conspicuously in a busy street to stir up chatter about his father's burial site. The gambit worked. By violating the less important ritual of displaying his mother's coffin in her yard, Confucius was able to follow the more important ritual of burying his parents at the same gravesite.

When it comes to ren and li, there is a long-standing chicken-and-egg debate in China. Which came first? And which is more important? Is Confucianism primarily an ethical project focused on humaneness? Or a ritual project aimed at the ritualization of everyday life? On the one hand, we cannot practice rituals properly without being humane already. On the other hand, we become humane only "through self-discipline and observing ritual propriety" (12.1). Sometimes this debate is resolved by describing ren and li as flip sides of the same coin. To switch the metaphor, we might say that these virtues serve as the sand and cement that, when mixed with water, become a firm foundation for both self-cultivation and social harmony.

As this focus on humaneness and ritual propriety suggests, Confucius's teaching was unapologetically thisworldly, focusing on the moral and ritual dimensions of human life here and now. But his attitude toward religion was one of distance rather than disdain. He simply shied away from talk about gods, ghosts, and spirits. Nonetheless, he seems to have respected Shangdi, the personal high god of the ancient Shang dynasty, and *tian*, the less personal heaven of the Zhou. Confucius's own understanding of heaven seems to have been almost entirely impersonal. He regarded heaven as "the author of the virtue that is in me" (7:23) and warned his disciples about contravening its dictates (3:13).[11] But he insisted that heaven, in contrast to the talkative revealer God of the Western mono-theisms, does not speak (17.19). Confucius also cultivated a spirit of silence. "The Master had nothing to say about strange happenings, the use of force, disorder, or the spirits," we learn in the Analects (7.21). When asked about "how to serve the spirits and the gods," Confucius said, "Not yet being able to serve other people, how would you be able to serve the spirits?" When asked about death, he said, "Not yet understanding life, how could you understand death?" (11.12). Confucius was preoccupied not with the gods but with the good—how to live a good life and how to make for a good society.

Mohists and Legalists

As Confucius's life suggests, the Confucian movement was not immediately successful. In fact, for centuries after his death, it was outflanked by competing philosophical schools.

CONFUCIANISM BY THE NUMBERS

The Five Classics

The early scriptures of the Confucian tradition are referred to as the Five Scriptures or the Five Classics (Wujing). Followers of Confucius credit him with writing and editing parts of all of them, but they existed before Confucius in some form and continued to be modified after his death. Early sources refer to a sixth classic (about music), which had been lost by the time the Classics were canonized during the Han dynasty (206 BCE–220 CE). Over time, this canon expanded—to nine and thirteen and so on. According to Tu Weiming, the Five Classics evoke five visions of human life: the metaphysical, the poetic, the social, the historical, and the political:

- Book of Changes (Yijing): a divination manual based on eight trigrams and sixty-four hexagrams and a major source for philosophical speculation throughout Chinese history.

- Book of Poetry (Shijing): an anthology of 305 early poems, all intended to be sung. This collection includes folk songs, court odes, and hymns to gods and spirits.

- Book of Rites (Liji): a ritual manual describing the rites, ceremonies, and customs of Confucius's beloved Zhou dynasty. This classic also includes two chapters, the

Doctrine of the Mean and Great Learning, later separated out and elevated as two of the so-called Four Books.

- Book of History (Shujing): a collection of primary documents, sometimes also called the Book of Documents, regarding the ancient deeds of the culture heroes and sage-kings of Chinese antiquity.

- Spring and Autumn Annals (Chunqiu): the official history of Confucius's home state of Lu, covering events from 722 to around 481 BCE, part of the broader era now known as the Spring and Autumn period.

The largest philosophical school during the Warring States period was the **Mohists**, followers of Mozi (470–391 BCE), who sought harmony through universal love. In their analysis, the value of any action was determined by its usefulness to the state. Does a given activity, such as building housing, boost material wealth and social order? Or, like war, is it useless and unprofitable? Mohists were particularly critical of the Confucians' emphasis on music and ritual, which they saw as a waste of time and money and therefore detrimental to the common good. But the Mohists also rejected what they saw as their unhealthy obsession with filial piety. Far more useful and profitable than partial love for parents and children was universal love—a doctrine that would resound a few centuries later and a continent away in the teachings of Jesus of Nazareth. As the Mohists saw it, universal love was a win-win. If we love ourselves, we are more likely to get what we want. If we love others impartially, we will help them get what they want, and they will help us get what we want, too.

The **Legalists** came to prominence after the Mohists, thanks to the patronage of the Qin dynasty (221–206 BCE), which put an end to the Warring States period by unifying China. Legalists were not interested in the sage-kings of antiquity or in Confucius and the other fuzzy-headed scholars who idealized them. Harsh times called for harsh measures, they argued, including strict laws, ruthless punishments, and a strong centralized government to enforce and enact them. Human beings are wicked. It is foolish to try to elevate them through education or ritual or by appealing to their supposedly innate humaneness when force can do the trick. If rulers want social stability, they need to get their subjects to obey. And to that end, fear is a better motivator than shame.

According to Confucius's early followers, the Mohists were naïve to quest after a love that disregarded relations to kinsmen and countrymen. The human being could never be cut out and removed from the woven cloth of family and community relations, they argued. As for the Legalists, they were wrong to believe that human beings could be perfected by force and fear. Punishments do not actually change us, early Confucians argued. Our innate moral sense is a far better teacher. Early followers of Confucius also took on early Daoists, who, like the early Confucian movement, failed to win imperial favor. Followers of early Daoist thinkers such as Laozi were wrong in their view to imagine that the Dao ("Way") was a path of naturalness, spontaneity, and improvisation. They were wrong as well to glorify the mountain recluse. On this point early Confucians quoted the Analects: "Am I not one among the people of this world? If not them, with whom should I associate?" (18.6).

Mencius, Xunzi, and Classical Confucianism

Like Christianity, Confucianism derives its name from one person. But Christianity as we know it today owes at least as much to Paul (who made it Greek) and Constantine (who made it Roman) as to Jesus. Similarly, Confucianism would not be Confucianism without those who followed Confucius. The first among these great followers—China's "Second Sage"—was Mengzi ("Master Meng"), known in the West as **Mencius**. Another was **Xunzi**. Headliners of the great debate in classical Confucianism, Mencius and Xunzi were China's answer to Hillel and Shammai, the dueling rabbis of rabbinic Judaism. Together with Confucius, they helped create classical Confucianism.

Mencius and Xunzi agreed with Confucius on the importance of learning and on the centrality of humaneness and ritual propriety. They, too, believed that commoners

Mohists
Confucian rivals who criticized the emphasis of Confucius on elaborate rituals and sought social harmony through universal love rather than filial piety

Legalists
law-and-order rivals to Confucians who came to power in the Qin dynasty and argued that social harmony required strong central government and strict laws and punishments

Mencius
China's Second Sage, who argued that human nature is essentially good

Xunzi
key classical Confucian figure who argued that human nature is essentially wicked

Mencius, a Confucian philosopher who lived roughly a century after Confucius, saw human nature as fundamentally good. In this painting from 1922, Mencius studies the classics.

could become sages and profound persons. However, they differed fundamentally in their understandings of the human person. This difference mattered because the Confucian project hung on the possibility of self-cultivation and human betterment. Transform the self, Confucius argued, and political order and social harmony will follow. But what if the self cannot be transformed? And if it can, what techniques will transform it?

Mencius (371–289 BCE), who was born roughly a century after the death of Confucius, argued that human nature was inclined toward goodness as surely as water is inclined to flow downhill. To shift the metaphor, we are hardwired to do good, and when we do otherwise it is because something external to us has short-circuited the good. In a famous story, Mencius evoked the image of a child teetering on the edge of a well, precariously close to falling in. Who among us, he asked, is not immediately alarmed by this situation and touched by compassion for the child? Not to be so moved is not to be human because each of us is born with feelings of compassion. Therefore, to become truly human we do not need to grasp after something beyond us. The germs of our full humanity are within.

Mencius was no fool. He knew that human beings are capable of evil and admitted that our inborn inclinations toward goodness can be frustrated, just as a dam can stop water from flowing downhill. For our goodness to come out, it must be cultivated like sprouts in a garden. Just as we are born with four limbs, he argued, we are born with Four Sprouts: the sprout of commiseration that can grow into humaneness, the sprout of shame that can grow into justice, the sprout of deference that can grow into ritual propriety, and the sprout of the feeling of right versus wrong that can grow into wisdom. If we nurture these Four Sprouts, they will grow into mature virtues, and we will grow into truly human beings.

Xunzi, a third-century BCE thinker who was likely born a bit before his rival Mencius died, was convinced that human nature is evil. Influenced by the Legalist school, he believed that each of us "is born with a fondness for profit," with "feelings of envy and hate," and with "the desires of the eyes and the ears." Consequently, instead of cultivating our true selves, we need to fight our natural inclinations: "Any man who follows his nature and indulges his emotions will inevitably become involved in wrangling and strife, will violate the forms and rules of society, and will end as a criminal."[12] The alternative is to engage in learning and ritual, which bend our rebellious natures toward the good. Whereas Mencius used gentle botanical metaphors to describe the cultivation and growth of sprouts of virtue implanted in us at birth, Xunzi relied on harder metaphors from the workshop—crooked metal shaped by hammering, warped wood bent by steam—to describe the unlikely emergence of a profound person out of a wicked child. Not by cultivation but by force do humans become good, Xunzi argued.

In this debate, Mencius triumphed. Confucianism became a tradition that affirmed not only the possibility of human moral perfection but also the goodness of human nature. In the years following the lives of Confucianism's first three great thinkers, China saw the emergence of a new class of government officials distinguished by learning rather than birth. The elite among these elites—outstanding scholars of high moral character—were called *ru*. This ancient term of derision meaning "weak" had been applied previously to scholars who emphasized life's ritual and ethical dimension. Now it was worn as a badge of honor by the wise and the virtuous. This is why the Confucian tradition is often called the ru tradition, or Ruism.

The Chinese philosopher Xunzi took a less optimistic view of human nature than either Confucius or Mencius. He saw humans as fundamentally evil.

State Confucianism

After classical Confucianism grew up under Confucius and matured under Mencius and Xunzi, its influence rose and fell like a buoy in the sea, as emperors and empires variously pledged (and withdrew) their allegiances to Confucianism, Buddhism, and Daoism. Ultimately, Confucianism emerged as the dominant intellectual impulse in China over the course of more than two millennia.

During his lifetime, Confucius was never able to win many friends or influence many people, and the names of Mencius and Xunzi were mud under the brief but influential Qin dynasty (221–206 BCE) that gave China its name. Qin Shi Huang ("First Emperor of Qin"), who defeated the warring states to become China's first emperor, prophesied that his dynasty would endure ten thousand generations. If you count the massive army of terracotta warriors surrounding his tomb that was unearthed in 1974 in a Chinese field, that estimate might not be far off. But the Qin was one of China's shortest-lived dynasties. Despite ordering his subjects to find an elixir of immortality for him, Qin, too, died young (perhaps by mercury poison from one of the concoctions). Before his death, he centralized government and, in keeping with his grand vision of a unified nation, joined various state walls into the Great Wall of China. He also attempted to unify China ideologically by making Legalism, whose ruthlessness matched his own harsh temperament, the state ideology. To that end, he ordered the burning of the Confucian classics in 213 BCE.

As an imperial ideology, Legalism was similarly short-lived. During China's second imperial dynasty, the Han (206 BCE–220 CE), Confucians ascended from persecuted outsiders to state-sponsored insiders. Just as the Jesus movement developed into Christianity under the sponsorship of the fourth-century CE Roman emperor Constantine, the Confucius movement developed into what we now call Confucianism under the sponsorship of Han emperors.

In 136 BCE, Emperor Wu canonized the Five Classics as the Confucian scriptures and appointed five scholars to specialize in them. In 124 BCE, he established an imperial academy devoted to studying and learning those texts. Early examinations of the graduates of this academy developed into a civil-service examination system in which students with knowledge of Confucian texts were rewarded with jobs in a growing Chinese bureaucracy. But classical Confucianism did not just become the state ideology. It became the state religion. During Emperor Wu's pro-Confucian reign, Daoism and competing ancient Chinese philosophies lost their political favor.

Han emperors turned the home of Confucius in Qufu into a state-sponsored shrine and offered honorary titles, land grants, and tax exemptions to Kong family members. Emperors went to Qufu to offer sacrifices at its Temple of Confucius. In 195 BCE, the founding Han emperor Gaozu visited the Kong family home and offered a "great sacrifice" of ox, sheep, and pig to Confucius. Before the Han era was over, at least a dozen emperors would travel to Qufu to make similar offerings. During that era, the Analects circulated widely, as did commentaries on it.

One Han ruler, Emperor Huan, defied this Confucian wave by persecuting Confucian scholars and lauding the Daoist great Laozi in a quest for his own immortality. After ordering a shrine built to the deified Laozi, he dispatched officials to offer sacrifices before it in 165 CE. The next year, he sacrificed to Laozi and the Buddha at his imperial palace. But none of this alternative piety stopped the long-term ascent of Confucianism

Emperor Ling ordered a fragment of the Five Classics etched into stone in 175 CE. Ling's commission came during the ascendance of Confucianism in the Han dynasty (206 BCE–220 CE).

in the Han, which would also see Emperor Ling order the Five Classics literally etched into stone in 175.

The fall of the Han in 220 ushered in a long period of political disunity that undercut the authority of Confucians and gave Buddhists and Daoists room to maneuver. For a time, the works of Confucius faded from memory. Worship in Qufu collapsed. The Kong family home was neglected. As historian James Flath writes, "The Way, it seemed, had been lost."[13]

Confucians staged sporadic comebacks during the Sui (581–618) and the Tang (618–907) dynasties. Emperors visited Qufu on occasion, conferring upon Confucius the posthumous title of First Sage and then ennobling him as the Exalted King of Culture. But Confucianism continued to lose ground, thanks to the arrival of popular new Buddhist schools, including Pure Land and Chan Buddhism. During the Tang dynasty, Empress Wu, China's only female emperor, responded to Confucian rules against women rulers by favoring Buddhism. Daoism also prospered in fits and starts. In 733, a Tang dynasty emperor included Daoist books alongside the Confucian classics on the reading list for China's civil service exams. Confucianism began its comeback toward the end of the Tang dynasty, when Emperor Wuzong, who favored Daoism, suppressed all "foreign" religions

As Confucianism took hold in imperial China, Confucian texts became the basis for the civil service examinations required for entry into government jobs. This painting from the Song dynasty (960–1279) depicts would-be-bureaucrats taking exams at a palace in Kaifeng, China.

in China, including Zoroastrianism and Christianity. His anti-Buddhist campaign was especially fierce, leading to the destruction of thousands of temples and the forced return to lay life of perhaps hundreds of thousands of monks and nuns.

Neo-Confucianism

The most important development in Confucianism after the classical period was the "Learning of the Way"—known to Westerners as **Neo-Confucianism**—which matured during the Southern Song dynasty (1127–1279) and later spread to Korea, Japan, and Vietnam. In this second epoch of Confucianism, the tradition turned inward. The goal was now to become a sage, and the techniques were close reading, quiet sitting, and other methods of self-cultivation.

Neo-Confucianism began to emerge in the eleventh century under the influence of Northern Song thinkers, including Zhang Zai, whose "Western inscription" is often cited as a major influence on the universal spiritual vision of this emerging tradition:

> Heaven is my father and Earth is my mother, and even such a small creature as I finds an intimate place in their midst. Therefore that which fills the universe I regard as my body and that which directs the universe I consider as my nature. All people are my brothers and sisters and all things are my companions.[14]

The conquest of northern China by non-Chinese tribes in 1127 forced the Song dynasty to relocate to the south and prompted soul searching among Southern Song scholar-officials who feared that the mandate of heaven was being withdrawn before their eyes. In response, Confucians worked to renew their tradition by reverting to its roots. The result was Neo-Confucianism, a reinvention and revival of the Confucian Way—Confucianism 2.0—that creatively combined Buddhist and Daoist influences even as it returned with new vigor to Confucius and other classical sources. This new movement spread amid a new China booming with big cities, far-reaching markets, innovations such as printed books, and a new intellectual class that was rapidly outpacing the old aristocracy. As it became state orthodoxy in the thirteenth century, Neo-Confucianism put an end to roughly seven centuries of Buddhist dominance in China and re-enshrined the Confucian tradition as China's preeminent intellectual lineage.

Four new developments put the "neo" in Neo-Confucianism. First, Neo-Confucians responded creatively to the Buddhist and Daoist traditions, which they criticized as dangerous enemies yet imitated like doting younger siblings. Second, in a move nearly as radical as the Christian reinvention of the Hebrew Bible, they reimagined Confucianism's canon of classical texts. Third, in an effort to revitalize a tradition that in their view had grown stale by rote learning and close textual studies, they directed their gaze away from remaking society to humanizing individuals. Fourth, they shifted the core techniques of the Confucian tradition from morality and ritual to meditative and contemplative practices. In this way, Neo-Confucians made the Confucian tradition more spiritual and more religious—an introspective and experiential tradition of self-cultivation to sagehood.

One key motivation for these changes was a new competitive context. Whereas Confucians in the classical period had developed their beliefs and practices in competition with Legalists and Mohists, now their rivals were Buddhists and Daoists. Standing firmly by Confucius's thisworldliness, Neo-Confucians attacked Buddhist claims that the world is an illusion and kept a healthy distance from both Buddhist theories of reincarnation

Neo-Confucianism
a reinvention and revival of Confucianism that drew on Buddhist and Daoist influences to turn the Confucian tradition inward toward self-cultivation

and Daoist quests for immortality. Neo-Confucians also rejected the Buddhist teaching of emptiness (*sunyata*), which asserts that everything (including the concept of emptiness itself) is empty of unchanging and independent essence. According to Neo-Confucians, there is an eternal and indestructible principle or pattern underlying all things—a sure foundation on which to build not only human lives and societies but also philosophical and religious systems. They called this foundation *li*. Not to be confused with the li that means ritual propriety, this li is usually translated as "principle" or "pattern." Wesleyan professor Stephen Angle helpfully describes it as "coherence": "the valuable, intelligible way that things fit together."[15] This principle of coherence manifests in particular things: the principle of the human being in Michelle Obama, and the principle of a boat in that particular rowboat over there. But there is also an overarching principle, which Neo-Confucians called the "Great Ultimate" (*taiji*), that manifests in *all* things. Those who understand these principles and the ways they interact—how heaven, earth, and humanity fit together—are able to work together harmoniously for the common good.

Neo-Confucians also attacked Buddhism as a foreign religion unfit to guide China, but their most biting critique was that Buddhist monastics and Daoist recluses alike were paragons of selfishness who neglected obligations to parents, children, friends, and rulers in order to pursue their own private nirvanas. Such irresponsible escapism flew in the face of what Confucians had long seen as the undeniably social nature of human beings, who are what we are by virtue of the relationships in which we are forever entwined. "In the final analysis," the great Neo-Confucian thinker Zhu Xi wrote of renouncing society, "this is nothing but self-interest."[16]

This critique of Buddhism and Daoism was far-reaching, extending from philosophy to ethics to politics, but none of the distance Neo-Confucians created between themselves and their rivals eliminated the attraction they felt to Buddhist and Daoist beliefs and practices. And they acted on that attraction by borrowing shamelessly. Neo-Confucianism has been described as a rationalist response to the "superstitions" of Buddhists and Daoists alike—a barring of the door against magical thinking. But one of its key features, and a central reason for its success, was that it presented Confucianism as a religious rival to the other two of China's Three Teachings.

Classical Confucians had kept self-cultivation and social harmony in creative tension. Individual human flourishing depended on social relations and political stability, and social order depended on the virtues of rulers and the ruled. Neo-Confucians continued to reflect on "the king without" and "the sage within," but now, in a development that paralleled the Daoist shift from outer to inner alchemy, the weight of the tradition shifted inward, toward the cultivation of the heart-mind (which in Chinese thought has long been seen as one organ). In the process, Neo-Confucians elevated the importance of the individual in Chinese society and began to supplement the long-standing Confucian focus on social harmony with an equally powerful focus on self-cultivation.

In classical Confucianism, the heroes held up as examples were the sage and the profound person. But sagehood had been reserved almost entirely for the legendary sage-kings of antiquity. In this respect, becoming a sage was an out-of-reach goal for almost everyone, including Confucius himself. In the Analects, Confucius says that he will likely never meet a sage (7:26). In fact, to the surprise of his students, he declares that he would never dare think of himself as one (7:34). Confucius also refuses to reckon himself a profound person (7:33) and implies that he hasn't met one either (7.26). In regard to becoming a profound person, he has "accomplished little" (7.33), adding that he lacks the ease, wisdom, and courage required (14.28).

With the emergence of Neo-Confucianism, these individual goals became more attainable. While Buddhists drew on the notion of our shared buddha nature to argue that everyone can become a buddha, Neo-Confucians spoke of a shared "original principle" or "original nature" that made it possible for every human being to become a sage. Meanwhile, Neo-Confucians perfected a series of techniques for achieving this goal, including "book reading, quiet sitting, ritual practice, physical exercise, calligraphy, arithmetic, and empirical observation."[17] In their textual study, Neo-Confucians downplayed traditional emphases on memorization and commentary in favor of internalizing and acting on what they were reading. They did more than approach the Confucian classics in new ways, however. They rearranged the Confucian canon to support their new ideas.

Neo-Confucians also brought close attention to the spiritual and religious questions Confucius had dodged. However, in their subtle shift from social and moral questions to spiritual ones—from the ideal society and the virtuous person to the quasi-supernatural sage—Neo-Confucians never turned their backs on their tradition's hallmark focus on this world. Religiously, what Neo-Confucians offered China was not a way to transcend the world through something like buddhahood. What they offered was a way to ground the ordinary world in transcendental meaning and purpose—to put heaven underfoot. For this reason, Neo-Confucianism has been described as "religious humanism" or "humanistic religion."

Zhu Xi's "Principle" and Wang Yangming's "Heart-Mind"

The two key figures in the development of Neo-Confucianism were Zhu Xi (1130–1200) and Wang Yangming (1472–1529). Both were disgraced during their lifetimes by rulers fearful of their influence—Zhu was barred from political life for peddling "false learning," and Wang was beaten and banished—but shortly after their deaths each was lionized as a giant of Neo-Confucian thought.

Zhu Xi, a rough contemporary of Wang Zhe, the founder of the Daoist Way of Complete Perfection, was Neo-Confucianism's great synthesizer. Born in Fujian province along China's southeastern coast in 1130, during a Song dynasty that had just lost northern China to non-Chinese invaders, he was said to be a precocious student of philosophy, history, calligraphy, literature, and classical Confucian texts who passed the highest level of the civil service examination while still a teenager.

Though he worked for the government through most of his twenties, Zhu Xi made his mark as a scholar. Deeply indebted to the Buddhist and Daoist traditions, he studied Chan Buddhism under a temple monk and edited a major Daoist text on inner alchemy. His key achievement was quilting a patchwork of Neo-Confucian theories—about li, "vital energy" (**qi**), the heart-mind, "human nature" (*xing*), and the Great Ultimate—into a coherent vision that was simultaneously moral, philosophical, and religious. At the center of that vision stood the drama of human beings perfecting themselves and becoming sages by exploring the mysteries of principle, which he understood to be one and the same with the Great Ultimate. Zhu's method fixed on "the investigation of things," which meant studying Confucian texts and scrutinizing the external world.

The author of some three hundred volumes, Zhu Xi made his mark largely through commentaries on Confucian classics that grounded the Confucian tradition in the past

Zhu Xi
most influential Neo-Confucian thinker and compiler of the Four Books, associated with the rationalistic School of Principle

qi
vital force out of which all things come and to which they all return

Zhu Xi, depicted here in a Chinese paper album leaf painting, was a key figure in the development of Neo-Confucianism. He adapted Buddhist meditation techniques into the Neo-Confucian practice of "quiet sitting."

while directing it toward new intellectual territories. According to Zhu, the long lineage that ran from the ancient sage-kings through Confucius was broken after Mencius. More than a millennium later, this lost Way was rediscovered by pioneering Northern Song Neo-Confucians. Zhu took it as his task to bring their work into a coherent whole. Today, he is often ranked second only to Confucius in terms of his impact on the Confucian tradition.

Zhu Xi put an end to the Mencius/Xunzi debate about human nature by convincing Confucians that Mencius was right: human nature is inherently good. All human beings are made of the same qi, out of which everything in the universe is made. Human beings also possess the same principle, which also serves as the underlying principle of the universe. This principle is perfect, but qi is corruptible, introducing into our bodies and heart-minds all sorts of mental and moral deficiencies. Whether our mixture is muddier (bad) qi or clearer (good) qi determines the set point of our moral character.

Without losing sight of the collective Confucian goal of social harmony, Zhu Xi focused his energies on the individual problem of immorality and the individual goal of sagehood, which he argued could be achieved through self-cultivation. Populate the world with sages, he argued, and we will see that we are all intimately interconnected, not only with one another but also with heaven. In this way, both the Confucian Way and China itself would be renewed. But how to transform oneself through self-cultivation? How to ascend to sagehood?

Zhu practiced many methods, including the quiet sitting that owed much to Chan sitting meditation. In fact, he once counseled a division of the day's activities into close reading and quiet sitting. He also worked to reduce and even eliminate his desire, including sexual desire, by force of will. But his main method was "the investigation of things," which the Great Learning introduces as the culmination of a long chain of causes and effects in which the enlightenment of the world depends on putting states in order, which depends on regulating families, which depends on cultivating selves, which depends on correcting minds, which depends on making thoughts sincere, which depends on extending knowledge, which depends on "the investigation of things." According to Zhu, to investigate things is to look for the principle in everything we encounter—in the natural world, in society, in relationships, in ourselves, and in the writings the great sages of antiquity have left behind. As one engages in this investigation, he argued, one comes to see that principle is one, yet its manifestations are many—a notion echoed by some Hindu thinkers and modern Western perennialists who argue that religion is one yet manifests in various ways.

Zhu Xi may be most significant for reinventing the Confucian canon, replacing a classical curriculum that had expanded far beyond the Five Classics with the Four Books. The **Four Books** included the Analects, in deference to the centrality of Confucius, and the Mencius, because of the crucial role Mencius played in Neo-Confucian commentaries. Also included were two short books, the Great Learning and Doctrine of the Mean, which had previously circulated as chapters in the Book of Rites. One effect of Zhu's new canon was a renewed emphasis on the inner life at the expense of an earlier preoccupation with history, ritual, and politics. Another effect was the reinvigoration of Neo-Confucian spirituality. Zhu himself was a man of prayer who engaged in sacrifices, ancestor veneration, and divination, but from his time forward Neo-Confucianism was marked by an inward-looking contemplative spirituality. In 1313, during the Mongol Yuan dynasty,

Four Books
the fundamental texts for classical Confucianism: Analects, Mencius, Great Learning, and Doctrine of the Mean

the Four Books (and Zhu Xi's interpretation of them) replaced the older classics as the cornerstones of the civil service examination system. They remained the norm until the examination era came to a close at the start of the twentieth century.

Like Confucius, Zhu Xi died, in many respects, a failure. However, a generation after his death in 1200, he was widely honored across China, not least with an ancestral tablet in Qufu's Temple of Confucius in 1241. From the thirteenth century into the twentieth, as China's civil service examinations focused on his critical editions of the Four Books, Zhu Xi became the posthumous gatekeeper for government employment in China. Zhu Xi also had a huge impact on Neo-Confucianism in the Tokugawa shogunate in Japan (1600–1867) and in Korea, where the Four Books and his commentaries became the curriculum for entry into the civil service.

After the Mongol Yuan overtook the Southern Song dynasty in 1279, Neo-Confucianism turned inward with even greater urgency, as thinkers emphasized the cultivation of the heart-mind over Zhu Xi's preoccupation with the investigation of external things. Among them was **Wang Yangming**, Zhu's sharpest critic and the second great figure in the Neo-Confucian tradition. Wang, who lived during the Ming dynasty (1368–1644), challenged Zhu's rationalistic approach with a more idealistic philosophy.

Despite his close association with the School of Mind (or School of Heart-Mind), Wang is best known for his teaching of the unity of knowing and acting. He was a man of action, renowned as a civil servant, teacher, poet, and military man, who from an early age grew weary of scholars who think and think without ever putting their thinking to work. While still a young man, he and a friend put Zhu Xi's practice of the investigation of things to the test by scrutinizing a bamboo grove night and day for a week. This experience taught Wang nothing about bamboo, but it did convince him of the impracticality of the investigation of things. In his early thirties, in a flash of inspiration that overcame him like sudden enlightenment in the Chan Buddhist tradition, Wang found his alternative to Zhu's approach. To become a sage, he realized, it was not necessary to put in the thousands of hours of textual education only elites could afford. Our heart-minds are capable of intuitively and immediately understanding the Confucian Way. That is because, as Wang put it in verse:

Wang Yangming
Neo-Confucian figure associated with the idealistic School of Mind

CONFUCIANISM BY THE NUMBERS

The Four Books

- The Analects (Lunyu): a collection of sayings and stories attributed to Confucius and his followers and one of the most influential books in world history.

- The Mencius (Mengzi): a collection of sayings and stories, including conversations with rulers, attributed to Mencius. This text argues that human nature is basically good.

- The Great Learning: a short portion of the Book of Rites that served for Neo-Confucians as a manual for self-cultivation. Often attributed to Confucius, it is valued for its close attention to a chain of causes and effects that

leads from the investigation of things to knowledge to sincerity to a clear heart-mind to self-cultivation to an orderly family to good government and finally to world peace.

- The Doctrine of the Mean: another short excerpt from the Book of Rites, which, prior to Zhu Xi, was of greater interest to Buddhists than to Confucians because of its clear echoes of the Buddha's doctrine of the Middle Path. This book commends to readers a balanced life that, by avoiding extremes, imitates the equilibrium in the universe.

Everyone has within an unerring compass;
The root and source of the myriad transformations lies in the heart-mind.
I laugh when I think that, earlier, I saw things the other way around;
Following branches and leaves, I searched outside![18]

As he looked to his own "unerring compass," Wang came to understand humaneness as an expression of our connection not only with other people but also with the cosmos. Yes, human beings feel for children walking on the edges of wells. But they also feel compassion for frightened animals, sadness in the face of trampled plants, and regret over shattered floor tiles. Why is that? Because we form "one body" with "Heaven, earth, and the myriad creatures."[19]

Wang's inner turn opened the door to thinkers without much formal education. It also prepared the way for debates about the emotions, which in the logic of the day provided an entry point for women into Neo-Confucian debates. Among these women were three seventeenth-century thinkers, Chang Tong, Tan Ze, and Qian Yi, all married, in turn, to the same man. Their collectively authored *Three Wives Commentary* (1694) challenged Zhu's wariness of the emotions (which in his view were apt to wander away from ritual propriety). As the historian Dorothy Ko argues, these three women made a case for romantic love as "a noble sentiment that gives meaning to human life" and for the emotions as a human universal that does not belong to women alone.[20]

This early modern period also saw the development of an alternative writing system called *Nushu* ("women's script"). Written only by women, this phonetic script developed among peasants in Jiangyong county of Hunan province. It offered women the ability to communicate privately in writing to one another—in letters and in prayers left in temples but also in poetry, folk stories, and autobiographies. "Third day missives" were

Dancers from the National Ballet of China take to the stage in London in 2016 to perform *The Peony Pavilion*, which is based on *Three Wives Commentary*, authored in the seventeenth century by three women married to the same man.

particularly popular in this script. Given to brides on the third day after they were married, these books conveyed advice, encouragement, and condolences from female relatives and friends.

When it came to women's rights, however, Neo-Confucianism as a whole was not progressive. In classical Confucianism, women were almost entirely neglected in discussions of fathers and sons, rulers and subjects, and sages and profound persons (who were widely presumed to be male). In rare occasions when women emerged from the shadows (either as subjects or as topics), they seemed to be summoned simply to be ordered to keep to their place, as in this dispiriting line from the *Classic of History*: "When the hen announces the dawn, it signals the demise of the family." After the demise of the Han, and especially during the Tang dynasty of the seventh through tenth centuries, the teaching and practice of female subservience softened as Buddhists and Daoists gained public power. From the early Song, there are records of women overstepping traditional boundaries by working as midwives or innkeepers or by learning to read or chant Buddhist *sutras*.

As Neo-Confucianism came into vogue, however, gender hierarchies stiffened. In part because of the increasing public visibility of women, Neo-Confucians now wrote explicitly about the roles of women, whom they assigned almost entirely to the home, not least through the excruciating practice of binding the feet of young girls into decorative objects. Zhu Xi's influential *Family Rituals* reaffirmed strict hierarchies in which women and girls owed "Three Obediences" to their fathers, then their husbands, and then their sons. Women were not permitted to study the Confucian classics. Widows were not permitted to remarry. The tradition of foot binding, unknown in Confucius's time, originated and spread alongside Neo-Confucianism, first among nobles in the Northern Song and then among commoners. By the Ming dynasty (1368–1644) there were women from every station and region in China who were barely able to walk.

Today, Zhu Xi and Wang Yangming are remembered as the standard bearers of the two leading Neo-Confucian schools: Zhu's more rationalistic School of Principle and Wang's more idealistic School of Mind. Of the two, the School of Principle has been more successful in China. In Japan, this school was celebrated in the Tokugawa shogunate. The School of Mind made inroads among scholars and politicians influenced by the samurai's "way of the warrior" and among leaders of the Meiji Restoration (1868) that restored imperial rule to Japan even as it aggressively modernized and westernized the nation. Neo-Confucianism also had a profound effect in Korea. It served as the state ideology in the thoroughly Confucianized Joseon dynasty (1392–1910), which gave South Korea its reputation as the most Confucian country on earth.

Anti-Confucianism and the Cultural Revolution

After visiting China during the last three decades of the thirteenth century, the Italian traveler Marco Polo introduced Europeans to China through his book *The Travels of Marco Polo*. As the modern period dawned, China weathered the arrival of Christian missionaries selling Christ in the sixteenth century and European merchants selling everything else in the eighteenth. However, in the mid-nineteenth century it entered into a "century of humiliation" at the hands of a series of European powers who forced China to sign treaties that granted to each of those powers exclusive "spheres of influence" over the China trade. China lost the Opium War to the British in 1842 and then the first Sino-Japanese War to the Japanese in 1895. In the identity crisis that ensued, Chinese intellectuals tried various combinations of Confucian renewal, anti-Confucianism, westernization, and anti-imperialism.

The end of the civil service examination era in 1905, the fall of China's last dynasty in 1911, and the establishment of China as a republic in 1912 turned Confucianism into a scapegoat for almost every loss China was sustaining in the "Great Game" of modernity. After the 1919 Paris Peace Conference, which ended World War I and gave Qufu and the rest of Shangdong province to the Japanese, protesters blamed China's unprecedented global weakness on backward-looking Confucianism. Now is the time, they argued, to "smash Confucius's shop" and to patronize "Mr. Democracy" and "Mr. Science" instead.

Confucius did not lose all his patrons, of course. Chen Huanzhang, the founder of the Confucian Church, which had pushed to make Confucianism China's state religion, lauded Confucius as a national hero and Qufu as "the Jerusalem of Confucianism." "The Confucian religion is the soul of China," he argued. "If the Confucian religion prospers, China prospers."[21] Meanwhile, the Nationalist Party that came to power under Chiang Kai-shek in 1928 worked to marry political liberalism with Neo-Confucianism. Its New Life Movement was shaped by Chiang's Methodist Christianity but took its "four virtues"—ritual propriety, righteousness, honesty, and shame—from the Confucian tradition. In 1934, the Nationalist government turned Confucius's birthday into a national celebration.

A bitter civil war between the Nationalists and the Communists concluded in 1949 with the founding of the People's Republic of China (PRC) and the forced exile of Nationalists to Taiwan. In a climate of fear about how the PRC would mix homegrown Chinese values with imported Marxist-Leninist ideology, the new Communist government named five official religions—Protestantism, Roman Catholicism, Islam, Daoism, and Buddhism—but each was to report to the state via its own patriotic religious association.

Students read Mao's *Little Red Book* in the countryside during China's Cultural Revolution (1966–1976), which denounced Confucius and Confucianism as elitist and oppressive.

The PRC did not name Confucianism, which it sought to destroy rather than merely control.

During the Cultural Revolution (1966–1976), Mao Zedong of the PRC commanded his Red Guards to attack the "Four Olds": old ideas, old culture, old customs, and old habits. The stated purpose was to defend the interests of peasants against entrenched elites. The effect was a frenzy similar to the de-Christianization campaigns that flattened churches and monasteries and sought to erase the memory of Roman Catholicism in the aftermath of the French Revolution. Now zealots for Mao destroyed hundreds of temples and forced religious professionals back into secular work.

"Feudal superstitions" of all sorts were caught in the crosshairs of this new antireligious religion of the messiah of the working people, Chairman Mao, whose *Little Red Book* became China's new scripture. But a special sort of hatred was reserved for Confucianism and for Confucius himself, who became the anti-hero of authoritarianism, nepotism, antimodernism, slavery, capitalism, and feudalism.

During the Cultural Revolution, Red Guards destroyed Confucian artifacts as dangerous remnants of an oppressive age. Here, a Red Guard member smashes a statue at the Confucius Temple in Qufu, China, in 1967.

On November 7, 1966, the Red Guard gathered on Tiananmen Square and issued a scathing manifesto pledging to "Annihilate the Kong Family Business."[22] These threats were not idle. Within days, the Red Guard had massed on Qufu. One leader, Tan Houlan, urged her fellow revolutionaries to move against the "Kong sycophants and reactionary 'authorities' who worship Confucius, and parade them through the streets" of the city. "Pull the 'Uncrowned King' off his horse and smash him to a pulp!" she commanded. "Burn the Confucian scholars [and] flatten the Kongs' graves."[23] Soon they were doing just that. They looted the graves of the descendants of the man they called China's "#1 Hooligan." They smashed tombstones and hung naked corpses from trees. As for Confucius himself, they leveled his burial mound and dynamited his grave, as if to prove that Confucianism itself had become, as one historian of modern China has written, a "wandering soul."[24]

The Red Guards' most fiery attack on Confucian symbols came at Qufu's Temple of Confucius, where their destruction of the Confucius statue appeared to be a crime of passion, complete with a long slit across the throat. As they disemboweled the image, they took coins and silver "organs" secreted away when the statue was constructed in 1730. They then dressed Confucius up in a dunce cap, slathered him with revolutionary slogans, hung him in effigy, and paraded him through the streets on the back of a truck. After dumping what remained of the statue in a ditch, they burned it with copies of the Analects. As the Cultural Revolution expended its fuel, it continued to target Confucius as a super-villain. A popular poster from the 1970s depicted Confucius as a "parasite," a "criminal of the worst type," and a lifelong advocate of the "dictatorship of the slave-owning class."[25]

Contemporary Confucian Revival

The Cultural Revolution expired with Chairman Mao in 1976. Under his successor Deng Xiaoping, who prioritized economic development over Marxist-Leninist purity, the party cast about for a homegrown ideology to legitimize its rule—an alternative to discredited

Drummers play in perfect unison at the Opening Ceremony of the 2008 Beijing Olympics, which began with a quotation, "Isn't it delightful to have friends come from afar?" from the Analects of Confucius.

Marxist-Leninism on the one hand and to unbridled capitalism on the other. That search led to a Confucian revival. Under the slogan "socialism with Chinese characteristics," a flood of articles appeared in Chinese newspapers and magazines in the early 1980s. Conferences and panels followed, along with the restoration of temples and renewed interest in Confucianism in the curricula of Chinese schools. In 1983, the Chinese government appropriated half a million dollars to restore the Confucius statue destroyed in the frenzy in Qufu. The next year, a new "pleasantly benevolent" (and bucktoothed) statue of Confucius was unveiled, and birthday celebrations for Confucius recommenced. By the 1990s, "Confucian fever" was rising, as research centers, scholarship, and popular publications championed a rehabilitated Confucius.

In the early twenty-first century, the Chinese Communist Party began to laud Confucius as a long-lost hero. In 2004, state-sponsored sacrifices to Confucius resumed to great fanfare in Qufu. That same year, the Chinese government began an ambitious program to set up hundreds of Confucian Institutes worldwide to promote the study of Chinese language and culture. At the announcement of that initiative, government officials unveiled a "holy statue" of Confucius in Beijing. All this attention to Confucius served as a search for "usable past," which is to say it was selective—a search for a homegrown ideology in a rapidly changing China and for a Confucius who could act as its ambassador to the modern world. Among Confucian values, party officials stressed education, hard work, deference to authority, social stability, and harmony.

In the mid-2000s, President Hu Jintao made the "harmonious society" a central goal of his administration. The opening ceremonies of the 2008 Beijing Olympics began with drummers chanting a line from the opening verse of the Analects, "Isn't it delightful to have friends come from afar?" China's President Xi Jinping, who came to power in 2012, regularly quoted from the Analects in his speeches, and the CCP described him as a patriarch who treated the Chinese people like family. In 2013, Xi visited Qufu and, after conspicuously purchasing a Confucius biography and a copy of the Analects, promised to read both with care. In 2014, he began promoting Wang Yangming, which resulted almost immediately in a series of tourist attractions in Wang's hometown of Guiyang: a cave shrine where he once lived, a museum, and a theme park in his honor.

Amid this Confucian revival, Confucius got a makeover. The man who, a few years earlier, had been served up as the scapegoat for almost every error in China's past now landed the role of China's savior. One of his biggest promoters, the media studies scholar Yu Dan, sold roughly ten million copies of her blockbuster *Confucius from the Heart* (2006), which presented a feel-good Confucius liberated from political, social, and economic realities. In 2010, a state-backed biopic called *Confucius* opened and flopped (it was up against *Avatar*), but three years later the National Center for the Performing Arts in Beijing premiered a dance drama called *Confucius*, which also toured throughout Australia, Europe, and the United States. Meanwhile, parents sent their children to private Confucian academies that emphasized memorizing the classics, and tourists flocked to Confucian temples. According to the sociologist Anna Sun, who conducted field work on this subject for more than a decade starting in 2000, "ritual worship of Confucius is . . . undergoing a significant and diverse revival in temple settings in contemporary Mainland China."[26]

The strength of this revival has led some to joke that the Chinese Communist Party should be renamed the Chinese Confucian Party. In a startling reversal of the anti-Confucian ardor of the Cultural Revolution, Confucius has been revitalized as a Chinese icon and his birthplace has become a national shrine.

New Confucianism

Some see in this Confucian revival the sprouts of a third wave in Confucian thought—Confucianism 3.0—called New Confucianism. With the rise to power of the PRC and attacks on Confucianism during the Cultural Revolution, many Confucians fled mainland China for Hong Kong, Taiwan, Singapore, and the United States. As they made new lives in this diaspora, they also constructed new understandings of the Confucian tradition.

Like Neo-Confucians, these New Confucians emphasize the inner work of the Confucian tradition, its moral development and self-cultivation. Even more than their predecessors, New Confucians emphasize the spirituality and religiosity of the Confucian tradition. Rejecting the German philosopher Georg Hegel's assertion that Confucius offered "no speculative philosophy," they revel in metaphysics.[27] They praise Confucianism as a "humanistic religion" in which human beings strive to live in harmony with heaven here and now. Not all religions are about the afterlife, New Confucians argue. However, the key characteristic of New Confucians is their commitment to adapting the Confucian tradition to Enlightenment ideas and ideals, even as they criticize the errors and excesses of the modern West.

One key figure in New Confucianism is Tu Weiming (1940–), who was born in China's southwestern province of Yunnan, fled with his family as the Communists came to power, and now works as chair professor of Humanities at Peking University. After earning his PhD at Harvard in East Asian studies in 1968, Tu taught at Princeton and the University of California at Berkeley before spending three decades at Harvard from 1981 to 2010.

Yu Dan (b. 1965)

Yu Dan was a media studies professor at Beijing Normal University when state-owned China Central Television (CCTV) asked her to host a seven-episode series on Confucius on its popular prime-time talk show, *Lecture Room*. The October 2006 series was such a huge hit that it was rushed into print as a book within one month and later translated into English as *Confucius from the Heart*. As "Yu Dan fever" overtook China, that book's author was hailed as China's Oprah.

Confucius from the Heart presents China's greatest sage as a solution to the "spiritual bewilderment" that has come over the Chinese middle class as their country has become an economic powerhouse. "Confucius can teach us the secret of happiness, which is how to find the peace within us," Yu Dan writes. That secret is not supposed to make society harmonious. It is supposed to make us each into "the best possible version of ourselves."[a]

You might think that scholars would be grateful to Yu Dan for convincing a nation to read its classics, but you would be wrong. Whether they were envious of her royalty checks or genuinely concerned for the reputation of Confucius, scholars almost universally decried "the most famous woman in China" as a vulgar popularizer. The Tsinghua University professor Daniel Bell attacked her for turning Confucius into a "feel-good" sage. "By telling people . . . that they should worry first and foremost about their inner happiness," Bell argued, Yu Dan "deflects attention from the economic and political conditions that actually cause people's misery."[b]

While many of these criticisms were principled, others were responses to Yu Dan's gender—efforts to keep the Confucius club exclusively male. In fact, many of the criticisms of Yu Dan's female-friendly approach to Confucius echo the novelist Nathaniel Hawthorne's criticism of popular nineteenth-century women writers as "a damned mob of scribbling women."[c] This gender dynamic was plain in the words of a critic who dismissed her as "an illiterate with a higher degree who takes pleasure in castrating traditional Chinese culture."[d] It was even plainer when she was booed off a stage at Beijing University for wearing a skirt judged to be too short and heels judged to be too high. Some academics have come to Yu Dan's defense, however. One is Yi Zhongtian, who has also appeared on *Lecture Room*. "I don't know if Yu Dan's Confucius is . . . the authentic Confucius," he wrote. "But I do know that this is our Confucius, [the] people's Confucius."[e]

According to Tu, there have been three Confucian epochs, each with different conversation partners. During the first, classical Confucians developed their beliefs and practices in conversation with Mohists, Legalists, and other rivals. During the second, Neo-Confucians reimagined the Confucian tradition in light of the influences of Buddhism and Daoism. In today's third epoch, New Confucians are seeking to incorporate the best influences of the modern West without forgetting their Confucian values.

Convinced that there are multiple modernities rather than just one, Tu praises Enlightenment notions such as "liberty, rationality, due process of law, human rights, [and] the dignity of the individual" for profoundly shaping his life and the lives of many other East Asians.[28] But he is wary of Eurocentric chauvinism, unchecked capitalism, and the decline of Enlightenment values into narcissism. The individualistic and capitalistic values of the modern West need to be constrained by Confucian values of compassion, justice, and harmony, he argues. But the "politicized Confucianism" that has used the words of Confucius as a means of ideological control needs constraining as well. At its worst, the Confucian tradition has served as a naked justification for the authoritarianism and sexism of despots. At its best, that tradition reminds us that with rights come responsibilities, that the self is not an island but part of a network of relations, and that human beings are part of a larger "anthropocosmic unity" that includes heaven, earth, and humanity.[29]

In keeping with their conviction that the Confucian tradition has always evolved, New Confucians are also trying to gestate an authentically Confucian feminism. This is a serious challenge given the long-standing neglect of women in the Confucian tradition, not to mention the dismissal of women as "petty people" in the Analects (17.25). Tu himself is critical of Confucianism's Three Obediences, which have traditionally tied girls and women in China, first, to their fathers, second, to their husbands, and, finally, to their sons. But he views the Five Relationships, including the marital relationship, far more favorably—as relationships of mutuality characterized by affection and respect.

In books such as Chenyang Li's *The Sage and the Second Sex* (2000), Confucian feminists are looking back to the mothers of Confucius and Mencius as exemplars and constructing a new ethic around the egalitarian relationships of friend to friend rather than the hierarchical relationships of ruler and subject. They also observe that while Plato and Aristotle were debating whether women were human beings, early Confucians were affirming that women can become both profound persons and sages. Another key source for Confucian feminists is the early Chinese cosmology of yin and yang, which views the feminine yin and masculine yang as complementary and interdependent principles.

CONFUCIANISM IN THE UNITED STATES

Americans first encountered Confucianism almost entirely through books. Reviews of those books were divided: an eighteenth-century "age of respect" for Confucius and all things China largely yielded around 1840 to what the historian Harold Isaacs has described as an "age of contempt."[30] The respect lingered well after 1840, however, among Ralph Waldo Emerson, Henry David Thoreau, and other Transcendentalists. The Transcendentalists were the first group of American intellectuals to take Asian religions seriously. Though these intellectuals focused largely on Hindu and Buddhist texts, they also read appreciatively in the Analects and other Confucian classics. In 1843, in two issues of the Transcendentalist periodical *The Dial*, Thoreau published translations of sayings from the Four Books. In his unpublished journal, he translated nearly a hundred paragraphs of sayings from a French book on Confucius and Mencius. In *Walden* and *A Week on the Concord and Merrimack Rivers*, he quoted at least ten times from Confucius and other classical Confucians. Recently, scholars have argued that Thoreau's influential writing on civil disobedience was influenced by Mencius's argument for the right to rebel against rulers who, by their immoral actions, have forfeited the mandate of heaven.[31]

One recurring theme among nineteenth-century advocates of Asian religions in the United States was a tendency to applaud ancient texts while condemning modern practices—a move that mimicked the Protestant tendency to applaud ancient Christian scriptures while condemning modern Roman Catholic rituals. Writing in 1824, Emerson denounced the Chinese for bowing down before "crockery Gods which in Europe & America our babies are wise enough to put in baby houses." The "summit of their philosophy & science," he concluded dismissively, "is how to make tea."[32] To his credit, Emerson changed his mind after reading Confucian texts in translation beginning in

1830. Two years later, he was salting and peppering his sermons, lectures, essays, and journals with the sayings of Confucius, and by 1845 he was praising Confucius as "the Washington of philosophy."[33] Emerson—"the American Confucius," according to one scholar—was particularly attracted to Mencius's affirmation of the goodness of human nature and to his belief that the profound person could reach moral perfection through self-cultivation.[34]

Also in the 1840s, Confucianism arrived in person in the United States via Chinese immigrants. After prospectors discovered gold at Sutter's Mill in California in 1848, Chinese miners (almost all men) came to "Gold Mountain," as they called California, and joined the Gold Rush. Other Chinese immigrants to the West Coast worked on farms, in factories, and as railroad workers. The epic Transcontinental Railroad, completed with the driving of the Golden Spike at Promontory Summit in Utah on May 10, 1869, was built to a great extent on the backs (and lives) of Chinese laborers.

Like other immigrants, the Chinese who came to the West Coast brought their gods with them. America's first Chinese temple was built in San Francisco's booming Chinatown in 1853. Before the next century dawned, the West Coast of the United States had at least four hundred similar temples, which mixed Buddhist, Daoist, and Confucian influences with Chinese folk religion. As Chinese immigrants became more visible—in Chinatowns and on job sites—contempt for the "heathen Chinee," as the journalist Bret Harte called them, heated up.[35] Writers denounced the sins of Chinatowns—their brothels and dice games and opium dens—and soon the West Coast was gripped by anxiety over the "Yellow Peril." Popular fears that the United States was in danger of being overrun by "filthy yellow hordes" fueled support for the Chinese Exclusion Act of 1882, which prohibited both immigration from China and citizenship for people of Chinese descent. Confucians did have a presence, however, at the landmark World's Parliament of Religions in 1893 at Chicago's World's Fair, where Pung Kwang Yu presented Confucianism more as a social philosophy than a religion, even as he reflected on the lack of a word for "religion" in Chinese.

Landmark legislation in 1965 reopened immigration from Asia, and in the early 1970s President Nixon's "ping-pong diplomacy" thawed previously icy relations between the United States and the PRC. In this environment of closer relations, New Confucianism spread across East Asia and over into the United States. So did an American offshoot known as the Boston Confucians. Tu Weiming was a key figure in this group, which also included Robert Neville and John Berthrong of Boston University. Together these scholars helped bring Confucianism into dialogue with American pragmatism and the world's religions.

As if to prove the Confucian maxim (also advanced in the Hebrew Bible) that there is nothing new under the sun, Neville and Tu reprised the debate between Mencius and Xunzi about human nature. Neville, a United Methodist minister and self-described Confucian Christian who has served as the president of the American Academy of Religion and the dean of Boston University's School of Theology, echoed Xunzi in his understanding of the inborn sinfulness of human beings. Tu followed Mencius in his affirmation of the essential goodness of human beings. While Neville underscored the key role played by ritual propriety in checking human wickedness, Tu pointed to the key role played by self-cultivation in allowing our inherent humaneness to emerge. What these thinkers shared was their core conviction that Confucian wisdom is universal and therefore need not be confined to its homeland.

LIVED CONFUCIANISM

Lived Confucianism is visible in all sorts of interactions in China, East Asia, and the Chinese diaspora, among those who identify as Confucians and those who do not. It is visible in rituals of bowing to say hello and goodbye, in rituals concerning the giving and receiving of gifts (including the exchange of business cards), and in rituals regarding greeting and taking leave of guests. Relationships between teachers and students are very different where the Confucian tradition has left its mark than in the more egalitarian modern West. In East Asia, these relationships are marked by a certain formality and deference that includes addressing teachers by their proper titles, and never by their first names. But the influence of Confucianism is most visible on the ground in holidays and traditions of ancestor veneration.

Holidays

The only truly distinctive major holiday for Confucians is the birthday of Confucius, which is celebrated on September 28 on mainland China, on the third Sunday of September in Hong Kong, and elsewhere on a date that floats across the lunar calendar between late September and early November. On this holiday, Confucian priests offer sacrifices in Confucian temples. Often lasting for ten days, this celebration includes music and dancing as well as offerings of incense and food.

Confucians also celebrate the Chinese New Year, which typically occurs in early February. In the week of preparation that precedes the Chinese New Year, families engage in an elaborate spring cleaning reminiscent of preparation for Passover in the Jewish tradition. During this preparatory week, the Kitchen God is venerated. Then it is time to start decorating the home for the New Year. Family members return to their ancestral homes. There is eating and drinking and visiting, of course, as well as storytelling and dancing and the lighting of candles. But no Chinese New Year is complete without those most Chinese of contributions to world civilization: fireworks and firecrackers.

One additional Chinese holiday, also practiced by Buddhists, Daoists, and Chinese folk religionists, is particularly dear to Confucians because it is closely tied to ancestor veneration. On Tomb-Sweeping Day, also known as the Pure Brightness Festival, relatives remember their ancestors by cleaning their tombs and decorating them with flowers or fruit. A rite of spring, this holiday occurs on the fifteenth day after the spring equinox, typically in early April. Celebrants pray and burn incense. They burn spirit money to be used by the deceased in the world of the dead, but they also burn paper clothes, paper television sets, paper computers, paper cars, and even paper houses. In another modern spin on this ancient ritual, those who live far away from their homelands can pay cemetery staff to do their tomb sweeping for them while they watch on the Internet.

Tomb-Sweeping Day is an important springtime festival throughout East Asia. Here, family members in Hong Kong visit a cemetery to dust off their relatives' gravesites and to burn incense in their honor.

Ancestor Veneration

Of all Confucian rituals, the most widespread is ancestor veneration, a practice so common it is now seen as simply

Home Shrine

For at least three millennia, since the heyday of the Shang dynasty (1600–1046 BCE), the Chinese have been performing sacrifices to the gods. Today, Confucians continue to perform similar sacrifices in public in Confucian temples, but the more popular rituals take place in the privacy of the home around domestic shrines. These shrines can fill free-standing buildings, but most are confined to a small altar table or shelf. Here, family members make offerings before images of Confucius, buddhas, and Daoist immortals. As important as these offerings is the veneration of ancestors, family members who are remembered and revered in wooden ancestral tablets. The family of the deceased may also burn spirit money, popularly known as "Hell Bank Notes," that can be used by the deceased to pay for afterlife necessities (or luxuries).

The Chinese have long believed that society comprises both the living and the dead. At these home shrines, where ancestors are asked to weigh in on matters of work, travel, and love, the intimate presence of the dead among the living is confirmed. Typically, only a few generations of ancestors are worshiped in this way. As a new generation joins the legions of the dead and their souls migrate from human bodies into ancestral tablets, the tablets of ancestors who have receded from memory are ceremonially burned to make space for the more recently dead.

Chinese or East Asian. Ancestor veneration takes place in the home, in cemeteries, and at temples. Like burial, ancestor veneration is understood in the Confucian world to be an expression of filial piety. Ancestor rites are held on death anniversaries (typically for parents, grandparents, great-grandparents, and great-great grandparents), in each of the four seasons, and on some holidays. Additional rites are held at the gravesite once a year.

Many Confucian families maintain a domestic shrine dedicated to their ancestors, which may occupy a section of a house or apartment or a separate building entirely. This shrine includes a table that holds ancestral tablets traditionally understood to house the spirits of the dead. The ancestral tablets are arranged in rows, with the eldest ancestor at the head of the table. Domestic shrines also include candles, incense burners, platters for food offerings, and perhaps a mat where family members can kneel to pray.

During the Cultural Revolution, the Chinese Communist Party denounced ancestor veneration, but it abided undiminished in Hong Kong, Taiwan, South Korea, Vietnam, Japan, and in Chinatowns worldwide. In recent decades, ancestor veneration has made a comeback in mainland China. The Chinese Spiritual Life Survey of 2007 found that venerating ancestral spirits at gravesides is more popular than attending Christian, Buddhist, or Daoist services or praying, offering incense, or worshiping at Buddhist or Daoist temples. In fact, 72 percent of those surveyed said that they had venerated ancestral spirits at gravesides in the past year.[36] The popularity of this practice, which includes kneeling, burning incense and paper money, and leaving offerings of food, fruits, and wine, led the Chinese government in 2008 to declare Tomb-Sweeping Day a national holiday.

Those who engage in ancestor veneration do not necessarily believe in ancestor spirits. In the 2007 Chinese Spiritual Life Survey, only 20 percent of those who engaged in some sort of ancestor veneration believed that ancestors existed as spirits, and only 4 percent believed that those spirits responded to their descendants' requests. In this regard, people in China seem to be following Confucius in two respects: first, by engaging in ancestral rites, and, second, by doing so without necessarily believing in ancestral spirits. For most people in China today, ancestor veneration is primarily an expression of gratitude and respect to those who brought you into this world.

CONTEMPORARY CONTROVERSY: IS CONFUCIANISM A RELIGION?

In a recurring game on the *Sesame Street* television show, one of the characters sang, "One of these things is not like the others / One of these things just doesn't belong." Before the song was over, the children watching would point to the capital R among three small r's or the upside-down kid among three right-side-up kids. Of all the religions in this book, Confucianism is the one that might not belong. Most people in China see it as a philosophy, not a religion. But virtually every textbook on the world's religions includes Confucianism. Who is right?

When sixteenth-century Jesuits turned Kong Fuzi into "Confucius," they began a long approach-and-avoidance relationship in the West with what came to be called Confucianism. Over the next two centuries, Roman Catholicism's Rites Controversy turned on the religiosity of Confucianism. As Jesuit missionaries won Chinese converts, missionaries from rival orders insisted that those converts should renounce ancestor veneration, which these missionaries saw as an idolatrous practice of a false religion. The Jesuits disagreed. In an effort to harmonize Catholicism and Confucianism, they argued that Confucianism was not a religion because ancestor veneration was a civil custom of respect rather than a religious rite of worship. Beginning in 1704, the Vatican ruled against the Jesuit's policy of accommodation. For the Roman Catholic hierarchy, at least, Confucianism was a religion. In the late nineteenth century, Protestant missionaries and Western scholars agreed. James Legge argued in 1877 that Confucianism was the monotheistic "religion of the Chinese."[37] In 1891, the pioneering German scholar Max Muller included Confucian classics in his *Sacred Books of the East* series.

Chinese intellectuals weighed in after the Republican Revolution of 1911 upended centuries of imperial rule. Some Chinese nationalists argued that their new nation needed a "state religion," and *kongjiao* (or "Confucianity" as Anna Sun helpfully translates this term) was one candidate.[38] After the Communist Revolution of 1949, the question of the religiosity of Confucianism reemerged when the CCP left Confucianism off its list of five official religions.

Today, Chinese intellectuals who argue that Confucianism is a religion fall into two broad camps. Building on the attacks on Confucianism during the Cultural Revolution, one camp argues that Confucianism is a religion in order to disparage it, contending (with Marx) that Confucianism oppressed the Chinese people and (with the sociologist Max Weber) that it held China back economically. "As history has shown us," writes

BIRTH AND DEATH

There are no specifically Confucian birth rites, so Confucians typically follow broader Chinese traditions. Because many Chinese believe that celebrations before birth are bad luck, they hold celebrations for newborns after birth. For the first month, the mother is typically secluded while others focus on the baby's care. On the child's one-month anniversary, friends and family welcome the mother back into the wider world with a bath and a hair wash. They also shower the baby with gifts, often money wrapped in red paper.

Unlike those in the Western monotheisms who see death as unnatural—a punishment inflicted by God on disobedient humans—Confucians in particular and the Chinese more broadly have seen death as a natural part of a broader cycle of change and transformation. When death calls, Confucians have typically buried. Like Jews, who have traditionally argued against cremation as a violation of a body given by God, Confucians view the burning of a corpse as an affront to the filial piety owed to family members.

One popular Chinese belief, also widely shared among adherents of the Three Teachings, is that human beings have two types of souls. Lighter *hun* souls are made of yang qi and heavier *po* souls are made of yin qi. At death, these two souls separate, with the yang souls ascending toward heaven and the yin souls settling into the earth. The death rites that accompany burial combine Confucian, Buddhist,

the Chinese historian Ren Jiyu, "the Confucian religion has brought us only disasters, shackles, and poisonous cancers."[39] The other camp includes those who are trying to revive older efforts to turn Confucianism into China's state religion. Meanwhile, New Confucians insist that Confucianism is religious and that its religiosity is a good thing.

The argument that Confucianism is ethical and philosophical rather than religious is straightforward: when it comes to religion, Confucianism simply lacks the right stuff. Institutionally, it lacks clergy, a creed, and places of worship comparable to synagogues, churches, and mosques. Ritually, it lacks initiation rites and weekly gatherings for worship. Theologically, its orientation is thisworldly, focused on earthly concerns rather than the afterlife, and on relationships among people rather than relationships between humans and gods or spirits. Furthermore, Confucianism has no revelation, at least not

The Scottish Protestant missionary James Legge (left), worked with students at the London Missionary Society's Theological Seminary in Hong Kong during the nineteenth century. Legge defended Confucianism before Western audiences by claiming it was China's monotheistic religion.

in the classical sense of words delivered from a god via a prophet. Confucianism doesn't really have a founder: Confucius came along when the Ru tradition was well under way. Finally, Confucianism may not even have a god, if we understand by that term a personal divinity with agency. "Certainly the idea of a theistic God, not to mention the 'wholly other,'" writes Tu Weiming, "is totally absent from the symbolic resources of the Confucian tradition."[40]

This might seem to be an open-and-shut case until we remember that Hindus have no weekly congregational meetings and Quakers have no clergy. Early Buddhists had no god, and they had no creed until the American Protestant convert Henry Steel Olcott first drafted one in the late nineteenth century. Like Confucians, Jews (who also lack a founder) are also famously uninterested in speculation on the afterlife.

Daoist, and folk traditions and have two main goals: to settle the po soul comfortably into the grave so it is not tempted to linger as a hungry ghost and to settle the hun soul into an ancestral tablet, where it can be worshiped appropriately by descendants.

In keeping with Confucianism's Five Relationships, funerary practices vary depending on the relationship of the mourner to the deceased. Sons typically wear a complete mourning uniform, which consists of cap, coat, leggings, and straw shoes. More distant relations might wear just the cap or no mourning garb at all. The period of mourning also expands as the relationship grows closer, with three years standard for children and one year for a wife, brother, or sister. After death, family members change into mourning clothes and wail to broadcast the death. They wash and dress the corpse and move it to the center of the house. After a last embrace of the body, it is placed in a coffin. The next day, mourners dress in white mourning clothes. Friends come by the house with offerings of the sort you might see on a temple altar: fruit, tea, wine, incense.

The body is not buried until three months after death, though that time can expand if the family cannot find an appropriate gravesite. For centuries, Confucians have taken care to find gravesites via the principles of *feng shui* (literally, "wind and water"). These principles are now in use worldwide in architecture and landscape and interior design, but they were initially used to place graves in spots with an appropriate balance of shady yin and sunny yang.

That said, Confucianism has stood for centuries alongside Daoism and Buddhism as one of China's Three Teachings. For close to two millennia, Confucianism functioned like an established religion, as emperors offered sacrifices to Confucius at state-sponsored Confucian temples. Such stamps of state favor on Confucian rites were disrupted in the early twentieth century by the demise of the imperial system and the rise of Communist China, but they have been revived of late. In addition to official rites at Confucian temples, pious Confucians offer prayers and sacrifices at temples and at homes. To them, Confucius is a wonder-working superhuman being. Though these sacrifices have traditionally been celebrated by men, women and girls are now participating. In fact, women and girls make up more than half of the worshipers who come to revere Confucius at his home temple in Qufu.

Finally, Confucianism is by no means lacking in notions of the transcendent. To be sure, the Chinese (Confucians included) have not traditionally affirmed anything akin to the personal God of the Western monotheisms who directs history and answers prayers. But the creative power of tian ("heaven") is, in the words of the sociologist of religion Peter Berger, "unambiguously religious."[41] So is the notion of the mandate of heaven that has operated from Confucius forward like the medieval Christian notion of the divine right of kings. Others have observed that every key element in Confucianism has a "transcendent focus": the individual looks to the sage, the family to the ancestors, and society to ghosts and gods.[42]

In short, Confucianism has what the Protestant theologian Paul Tillich identified as the essence of religion: an "ultimate concern." At least since the rise of Neo-Confucianism in the medieval period, its ultimate concern has been self-cultivation and self-transcendence. Or, as the East Asianist Rodney Taylor puts it, Confucianism offers a "means of ultimate transformation" with the ultimate goal of sagehood.[43] "Being religious, in the Confucian perspective," Tu Weiming adds, "means being engaged in the process of learning to be fully human."[44]

Confucian temples around the world attract pilgrims and tourists alike. Those who come in search of blessings from Confucius leave offerings of fruit or incense in his honor, as at this shrine in Hanoi, Vietnam.

Given this evidence in favor of Confucian religiosity, some argue that Confucianism is a religion, full stop. Others hedge a bit, locating inside the Confucian tradition a spiritual or religious dimension. Skeptics continue to argue that Confucianism is lacking in too many traditional markers of religion to be considered part of the broader family of religions. Perhaps the most useful synthesis of this debate has been offered by the philosopher Herbert Fingarette, who rejects the binary between religious and secular Confucianism, seeing the Confucian tradition as an example of "the sacred as secular." In his book by that name, Fingarette argues that the Analects is only "apparently secular," given the presence throughout the text of "magic and marvel."[45]

QUESTIONS FOR DISCUSSION

1. How did the chaotic period in which Confucius lived affect his thinking about the human predicament? Why did he admire the ancient sage-kings, and how did this admiration play out in his teachings?

2. Why is counting the number of Confucians in the world so difficult? How do Confucians differ from other religious people when it comes to self-identification?

3. How do the ideals of ren and li create social harmony? How do profound persons exemplify those ideals and cultivate that goal?

4. In the contemporary United States, ritual propriety, filial piety, and ancestor veneration are often degraded as old-fashioned and "empty." Why do you think that is? How might Confucians respond to these assessments?

5. In the twentieth and twenty-first centuries, treatment of Confucianism by the Chinese Communist Party has shifted radically—from Mao's Cultural Revolution to the Confucian revival of today. Why do you suppose the CCP has taken such vastly different approaches, and how has the Confucian tradition changed as a result?

KEY TERMS

Analects, p. 343

Confucius, p. 347

Duke of Zhou, p. 348

filial piety (xiao), p. 354

Five Classics, p. 350

Four Books, p. 372

junzi, p. 354

Legalists, p. 365

li, p. 354

mandate of heaven, p. 349

Mencius, p. 365

Mohists, p. 365

Neo-Confucianism, p. 369

qi, p. 371

ren, p. 354

ru, p. 351

sage (shengren), p. 354

Three Sovereigns, p. 347

Wang Yangming, p. 373

Xunzi, p. 365

Zhu Xi, p. 371

FURTHER READING

Ames, Roger T., and Henry Rosemont Jr. *The Analects of Confucius: A Philosophical Translation*. New York: Ballantine, 1998.

Billioud, Sebastien, and Joel Thoraval. *The Sage and the People: The Confucian Revival in China*. New York: Oxford University Press, 2015.

Fingarette, Herbert. *Confucius: The Secular as Sacred*. Long Grove, IL: Waveland Press, 1998.

Gardner, Daniel K. *Confucianism: A Very Short Introduction*. New York: Oxford University Press, 2014.

Nylan, Michael, and Thomas Wilson. *Lives of Confucius: Civilization's Greatest Sage Through the Ages*. New York: Doubleday, 2010.

Sun, Anna. *Confucianism as a World Religion: Contested Histories and Contemporary Realities*. Princeton, NJ: Princeton University Press, 2013.

Auspicious red ribbons are left by pious and adventurous hikers along the treacherous passages of Mount Hua, one of China's five sacred mountains and home to ancient Daoist shrines and contemporary Daoist hermits.

Daoism

THE WAY OF FLOURISHING

On their way to the temple complex on Crane Call Mountain (Heming Shan) in southwestern China's Sichuan province, visitors enter beneath a stone arch. The top of the arch reads, "Birthplace of Daoism." On the sides of the arch are imprinted the first two lines of the Daoist classic the **Daodejing**:

> The Dao that can be spoken is not the
>   eternal Dao.
> The name that can be named is not the
>   eternal Name.

According to Daoist legends, it was here in 142 CE that the venerable sage **Laozi**, who is traditionally credited with writing the Daodejing, revealed himself to be the divinity **Lord Lao**. The recipient of this revelation, **Zhang Daoling** (34–156), is now widely regarded as a divinity himself.

As they make their way up Crane Call Mountain, visitors pass an ancient tree wrapped in red fabric because of its godlike longevity. Next comes a well of holy water. Drink it, a sign promises, and you will be smarter, better looking, and longer-lived. As a Chinese professor scrambles along the stone stairs marking the path, a Daoist monk-in-training gently tries to slow everyone down. "Not so fast," he says invitingly. "Enjoy the fresh air. The most important thing is to breathe."

Halfway up the mountain, a temple altar is laden with green plants, flowers, peanuts, water, and tea. Pilgrims light incense and bow, their thumbs grasped by their opposing fingers and artfully curved to reproduce the yin/yang symbol of ancient China. Some are asking the gods for a favor, promising to give something back

An ancient tree on Crane Call Mountain is wrapped in red fabric to illustrate its status as a near immortal. The tree's long life and its roots at the site of Zhang Daoling's revelation make it an object of reverence.

Daodejing ("Scripture on the Way and Its Virtue")
the most influential text in Daoist history and one of the world's most frequently translated books, traditionally attributed to Laozi and also called the Laozi

Laozi ("Old Master")
legendary figure credited with writing the Daodejing, revered in his deified forms as Lord Lao and Most High Lord Lao

Lord Lao
Laozi divinized as the personification of the Daodejing, a revealer of Daoist texts, and one of the Three Pure Ones

Zhang Daoling
founder of the first known Daoist organization, the Celestial Masters, and the first in a lineage of Celestial Masters that continues today

in return. Others are returning to make good on a prior promise. Still others are there to take a break from city life, to enjoy a walk up the mountain, or to meet friends for tea.

As you enter this sanctuary, the right side is devoted to the Daoist deity Lord Lao. The left side features a series of five paintings that tell the story of the spiritual cultivation of Zhang Daoling, a scholar, hermit, teacher, and immortal widely regarded as the founder of Daoism as an organized religion. First, Zhang Daoling read and studied the Daodejing. Then he retreated to a cave to meditate. When he was ready, he created a religious institution—on this very site at Crane Call Mountain—and taught in a temple there. In the final painting, he flies on a white crane, a Daoist symbol of longevity.

In the United States and Europe, Daoism is vaguely associated with feminism, environmentalism, alternative medicine, and the freelance spirituality of the "spiritual but not religious." Thanks to hip adaptations of the Daodejing—one of the world's most frequently translated books—and to the bestseller *The Tao of Pooh*, Daoism is also associated with the spontaneity of the Beat Generation and the "go-with-the-flow" spirituality of Winnie-the-Pooh. Here on Crane Call Mountain, Zhang Daoling is lauded for both his spirituality and his religiosity. Yes, he meditates. Yes, he walks through fire and flies through the air. He is also renowned as a healer and exorcist capable of casting out the demons of the possessed. But his real accomplishment is transforming a jumble of Daoist ideas and practices into an organized religion with temples and rituals to call its own. "This mountain is where that happened," the monk-in-training proudly reports.

Other Daoists make similar claims about the Lookout Tower Monastery (Louguan Tai) outside Xian in Shaanxi province. As they tell it, Daoism did not begin in 142 CE with Lord Lao's appearance to Zhang Daoling. It began centuries earlier with Laozi himself, whose life is traditionally dated to the sixth century BCE. As this story goes, Laozi grew bored with his work as a bureaucrat in the collapsing Zhou dynasty. So he quit his job, left society, and wandered west toward the mountains. As he was crossing the western border marking the far reaches of Chinese civilization, he left behind a short text of five thousand characters that came to be known as the Daodejing.

A third sacred place with a claim to be Daoism's birthplace is Green City Mountain (Qingcheng Shan), which, like Crane Call Mountain, sits about an hour and a half by car outside of Chengdu, the capital of Sichuan province. Green City Mountain is reputed to be the place where Zhang Daoling died at the age of 123. Daoists do not use such crude language, however. They say that his physical body became transparent and luminous while he ascended skyward as an immortal in spiritual form.

According to an 895 CE inscription placed in the abbey at the base of Green City Mountain, Zhang Daoling did not just ascend here. Amid the social deterioration of the Han dynasty, the inscription states, "The Most High [Laozi] mandated the Perfected One of True Unity, Lord Zhang of the Three Heavens, to prepare to ride from Chuting and Heming Mountains to this mountain range to carry out the Law of the Awesome

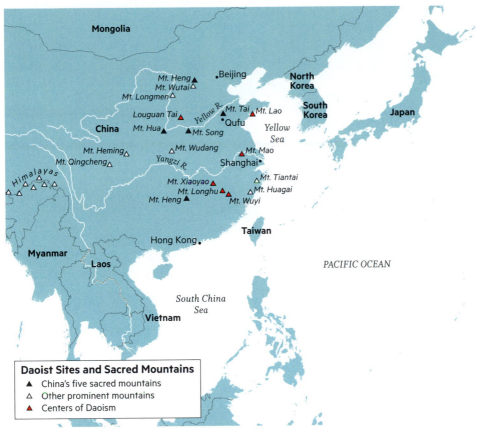

Daoist Sites and Sacred Mountains
- ▲ China's five sacred mountains
- △ Other prominent mountains
- ▲ Centers of Daoism

Mountains are sacred places for Daoists, Buddhists, and other religious groups in China. This map depicts some of China's most sacred mountains, as well as key Daoist sites.

Covenant, cleanse and purify the forests and marshes, and repel the enemy for over [three thousand miles]."[1]

Halfway up Green City Mountain, over stone steps and past huge trees and waterfalls, the Celestial Masters Grotto is said to house the cave where Zhang Daoling meditated. This area includes various altars and an ancient gingko tree laden with handwritten prayers recorded on red wooden tablets. It is overseen by Tang Chengqing, a Daoist master and vice president of the Chinese Taoist Association, whose spiritual practices include painting in a slashing style that recalls Zen Buddhist art. He is dressed in blue robes and a black hat, his long gray hair tied in a topknot.

Photographs of Master Tang posing with Chinese dignitaries ring his studio. A soap opera plays on the television by the door, and a cowboy hat resting atop a coat rack is embroidered with the name of Brazil's soccer superstar Rolandinho. The room is dominated, however, by a large wooden table circled by paintbrushes and marked as sacred by the smoke rising from a single incense stick. Master Tang is busy working his brushes, his robe's oversized sleeves hanging perilously over wet black and red ink as he transforms rice paper scrolls into art.

A short hike down Green City Mountain sits the Palace for Establishing Happiness, and for nature lovers it is a happy-making place. Two massive trees preoccupy the main

Master Tang Chengqing oversees Green City Mountain's Daoist temple complex outside of Chengdu, China. His ink-on-paper painting is part of his contemplative practice.

courtyard, and the verdant walls and roofs of the building also seem to grow out of the mountain itself. Pilgrims and tourists arrive by the busload to light incense, bow, and pray. Just to the right of the main altar, abbot Zhang Mingxin holds court in her outdoor office. An attendant has prepared a table with hot tea, fruits, and nuts. Master Zhang is talking with three Chinese visitors—a Kung Fu master, a businessman, and a Daoist professor—plus (with the help of a translator) a religious studies professor and an environmental journalist from the United States. Zhang seems closer to four feet tall than to five, but her quick wit and wry smile make it plain that she is the largest figure in the room. Dressed in the blue robe, black hat, and topknot that mark her as a Daoist master, she sits stock straight in an oversized chair appointed with red embroidered pillows. Penknife in hand, she slowly peels an apple, cuts it in thin slices, and eats it between sips from a clear glass mug thick with tea leaves. With a mixture of affection and reverence, the Daoist professor calls her "The Big Boss."

As she fields a series of naïve questions about what Daoism is and what Daoists do, she scowls, her brow furrowed, like a stern mother scolding her wayward child for refusing to understand the obvious. Once the conversation turns to more challenging topics, her eyebrows shoot up, she leans back and laughs, and a wide smile breaks across her oval face. It is hard to achieve a human birth, she says. We should cherish it, find ways to keep our physical body healthy and the environment clean. We should eat good food, take herbal medicines, do good deeds, and practice "inner mental cultivation." Throughout this conversation, the abbot, who answers in her monastery to "Older Brother," emphasizes that Daoism affirms the equality of men and women. "If what matters are energies and virtues then everyone is equal," she says. "There is no hierarchy."

Generously, Master Zhang answers the American professor's questions, all intent on uncovering why this place is *the* place. Green City Mountain has "very good qi. Heaven and earth are interconnected here," she explains, adding that this site also lies, like Jerusalem and the Egyptian pyramids, on the globe's 31st Parallel North. She moved to Green City Mountain because she knew it was "a place to get wisdom," she says. And she laments how nature has been sacrificed at the altar of human desire, including the desire to be forever connected to our smartphones. "If we live in that way," she says, "we lose our connection to nature."

The American professor observes that, in the United States, places (such as Lexington and Concord) are revered because something special once happened there (the American Revolution). Not so in China, Master Zhang replies. "Here history does not make the place; it is the place that makes the history." Green City Mountain is overflowing with vital energy. That abundance, which pours out of the ground in the morning, is what makes the mountain holy. It is what drew Zhang Daoling here, and it is what compels her to stay.

OUR STORY

As these three sacred spaces illustrate, to search for the birthplace of Daoism is to search for a mirage in the mountains. If you ask where Daoism began, many Daoists will say it was Crane Call Mountain, observes Professor Jiang Sheng of Sichuan University. But if you ask them where Crane Call Mountain is, they will shrug in silence. The true Crane Call Mountain is located in Daoist lore rather than on road maps or GPS devices. The Crane Call Mountain described previously, outside of Chengdu in Sichuan province, is only one of many possible Crane Call Mountains. Its seemingly ancient temple complex was built in the 1980s, and the temple at the top (which also boasts a tea shop) is just a few years old. The truth of the story of Laozi passing through the lookout tower is also shrouded in the mist that often fogs mountain ranges across China. Early accounts of the transmission of the Daodejing from Laozi to its inquisitive border guard locate the western pass farther east, while designating today's Lookout Tower Monastery merely as the site of the border guard's home.

Even if we could locate the spot where Laozi is said to have transmitted the Daodejing or appeared as Lord Lao to Zhang Daoling, other obstacles to locating the cradle of Daoism remain. Scholars now understand Laozi not as an actual person but as a legendary figure fronting what is most certainly a multiauthored anthology. The historicity of Zhang Daoling is similarly contested. Then there is that knotty problem of the definition of Daoism itself. As Jiang observes, "The origins of Daoism depend on what you think Daoism is." If you see it as a belief system encapsulated in the teachings of the Daodejing, you might focus on the words of Laozi. If you see it as an organized religion, you might focus on the life of Zhang Daoling. If you are not sure how to answer these questions, you might turn to the sacred stories of the Daoist tradition itself, including this composite narrative, drawn from Daoist texts, about the origins of the universe and the ways and means of the mysterious Dao.

One, Two, Three, Ten Thousand

*There was a beginning. There was not a beginning. There was something. There was nothing. Long ago, before heaven and earth, there was only the silent and shapeless, unknowable and unnamable **Dao**: the "Way" as primordial soup and fertile chaos, dark, wet, and deep.*

*Out of this void, the One spontaneously emerged, breathing **qi** ("vital energy") into being. Then the One generated the Two. The vital energy of heaven descended. The vital energy of earth ascended. The competing yet complementary principles of sunny **yin** and shady **yang** began to interact, producing patterns that went on to generate the four seasons, the eight cardinal directions, and the ten thousand things, which is to say everything in the universe, human beings included. In this way, form emerged out of formlessness spontaneously, without God (or gods), plans, or intentions. As the Daodejing puts it:*

> *Dao gave birth to the One.*
> *The One gave birth to the Two.*
> *The Two gave birth to the Three.*
> *And the Three gave birth to the ten thousand things.*
> *The ten thousand things carry yin on their backs and embrace yang.*
> *Through the blending of qi they arrive at a state of harmony.*[2]

Of course, not everything acted in harmony with the Dao, so a new chaos ensued. Humans acted inhumanely, out of balance with their own natures and out of alignment with the patterns and rhythms of the natural world. Families, villages, and dynasties went to war. Sages responded to this chaos by returning to the universal principle of the Dao, seeking to realize it in their own bodies and in their experiences with one another and with the natural world. They believed that rulers who acted in accordance with the Dao could bring harmony back to their domains.

In fact, the story of humanity can be told as a series of efforts to revert to the Dao. This human story includes examples of great sages who have done just that. These sages lived calmly and contentedly by preserving their vital energies and acting naturally and spontaneously. They wandered free from traditional formulations of right and wrong, humaneness and righteousness, wealth and fame. As a result, they flourished in the here and now even as they prepared themselves for immortality.

Dao ("Way")
Ultimate Reality and its manifestations in everyday life, the preexisting source of everything in the cosmos, and the process through which everything in it is transformed

qi
key Chinese concept variously translated as breath, vital energy, life force

yin and yang
ancient Chinese concept in which two complementary principles interact with one another to create individual, societal, and cosmic change

One of these attainers of the Way gestated for eighty-one years in his mother's womb and was born with the wisdom of old age. Because of his white hair, he was called Laozi or "Old Child." A student of the Dao, he worked as a librarian in the dynasty archives. But he grew weary of life in a crumbling Zhou dynasty and of his job as a cog in its bureaucracy, so he decided to leave civilization behind. He quit his job and wandered toward the mountains.

As he was about to cross the western border that marked the far reaches of civilization, the guardian of the pass, a man named Yin Xi, recognized him as a sage of great learning and asked him to share his teachings about the Dao. Laozi agreed. The guardian recorded his words on the ancient Chinese equivalent of the back of a napkin. Then Laozi wandered off, never to be heard from again (at least not in his mortal body).

But Yin Xi saw to it that Laozi's wisdom was widely shared. The text he safeguarded became the five thousand characters we now refer to as the Daodejing. And Yin Xi became Laozi's first disciple and an immortal himself.

More than six centuries later, Laozi reappeared, no longer as a sage but as a divine embodiment of the Dao. The place he chose for his divine descent was Crane Call Mountain. The person to whom he chose to appear was a man by the name of Zhang Daoling. No ordinary man, Zhang Daoling was conceived immaculately in an uncanny encounter between a celestial being and his human mother-to-be. The celestial being flew down from the stars of the Northern Dipper, filled the bedchamber of his mother with the fragrance of wild ginger, and graced her womb with the embryo of a spiritual genius. At birth, Zhang was able to walk. As a young boy, he memorized the Daodejing. As an

In this 1966 wood engraving by Fritz Eichenberg, Laozi sits atop an ox at the mountain pass just before recording the Daodejing and departing China forever.

adult, he withdrew as a hermit to the mountains, where he discovered an elixir that gave him supernatural powers. This elixir empowered him not merely to multitask but also to multi-locate. He could appear and disappear at will.

One day atop Crane Call Mountain, Zhang glanced up and saw a heavenly being descending with a thousand chariots plus golden carriages pulled by dragons and tigers. Revealing himself to be an avatar of Laozi named Lord Lao, this heavenly being charged Zhang with ushering in a new era of Great Peace that would follow the coming demise of the corrupt Han dynasty. Lord Lao also revealed to Zhang a new sacred compact with the gods of the Daoist pantheon that doubled as a blueprint for what he called Orthodox Unity. Zhang and his followers were to turn their backs on the blood sacrifices and priestly payments of local religions. They were to confess their moral failures. If they succeeded, the Great Peace would follow.

Lord Lao equipped Zhang for this mission by proclaiming him the Celestial Master on earth and endowing him with healing powers. He also gave Zhang a series of boons. Some were administrative: a seal of his authority, **registers** of heavenly officials to whom petitions might be addressed, and templates for drafting petitions. Lord Lao also initiated Zhang into secret spiritual techniques, including rituals of exorcism, equipping him with a demon-vanquishing sword and secret talismans to ward off evil spirits.

registers

heavenly records used in Celestial Masters rituals. These documents identify individual Daoists by name and rank and list the supernatural beings to whom they can appeal for grace and favor.

The Celestial Masters founder Zhang Daoling rides a tiger while wielding a demon-defeating sword in one hand and a cup of tea in the other in this eighteenth-century Chinese watercolor.

Zhang Daoling responded by establishing Daoism as an organized religion complete with new rituals and community-based practitioners trained to perform them. He wrote an influential commentary on the Daodejing. He continued to serve as a healer and exorcist who fought with demons and won. At the end of his time on earth, Zhang Daoling drank a portion of an elixir of immortality he had prepared years earlier and gave the rest to his son Zhang Heng. He also gave his son his seal and sword and his talismans and registers, instructing him to pass on the title of Celestial Master to his own son when it came time for him to leave earth. Then, with his wife and some disciples, Zhang Daoling ascended to heaven in the light of day.

DAOISM IN TODAY'S WORLD

Daoism (or Taoism, as it is sometimes spelled) is an indigenous Chinese religion with roots that run deep in ancient China. Its core texts are written in Chinese, its central figures have been Chinese, and its sacred places lie in China. The footprint of the Daoist movement shifted decisively after 1949, when the rise to power of the antireligious Chinese Communist Party prompted many Daoists, including heirs to Zhang Daoling's Celestial Master lineage, to flee to Taiwan. Today, Daoism is influential not only in Hong Kong, Macao, and Taiwan but also in Korea, Japan, and across Southeast Asia. It is active in Chinatowns and the Chinese diaspora worldwide. And it is practiced by convert teachers and communities who have made Daoism multiethnic, multicultural, and multilingual.

In China, Daoism is one of the five religions recognized and regulated by the Communist government (Catholicism, Protestantism, Islam, and Buddhism are the other four). It also stands alongside Confucianism and Buddhism as one of China's venerable Three Teachings. Together, this "Chinese triangle" offers a powerful rebuke to Westerners who imagine that religious traditions are bitter rivals that demand a believer's exclusive allegiance. When it comes to religion, the Chinese have long been polyamorous. According to a widely circulating maxim, they are Confucians on the weekdays, Daoists on the weekends, and Buddhists when they die.

This long-standing insistence on blending rather than separating Confucianism, Daoism, and Buddhism (all English-language terms invented in the modern West) makes it difficult to count accurately the numbers of Confucians, Daoists, or Buddhists. In the

A Quick Lesson on Pinyin and Wade-Giles

Is it Daoism or Taoism? Peking or Beijing? If you are confused, you are not alone. Ancient and modern Chinese are written in characters rather than letters. When translated into English, they must also be transliterated into Roman letters. Until recently, the standard transliteration system was Wade-Giles. In this system, devised in the nineteenth century by one British diplomat and revised in the early twentieth century by another, the subject of this chapter would be Taoism and its most famous book would be referred to as the Tao Te Ching. In 1958, Pinyin became the official method for transliteration in the People's Republic of China because the Chinese government thought it would be easier to use for Chinese minorities and people in foreign countries. Wade-Giles is still used in Taiwan, but Pinyin is now employed in the United Nations and by most scholars of Chinese history and culture. This textbook employs Pinyin as well. Here are a few comparisons:

WADE-GILES	PINYIN	PRONUNCIATION
Tao	Dao	Dow
Tao Te Ching	Daodejing	Dow duh jing
Lao Tzu	Laozi	Lao (as in "Dow") Dzuh
t'ai chi ch'uan	taiji quan	Tie Jee Chwan
Peking	Beijing	Bay Jing
Ch'i	qi	chee

Daoist case, this difficulty is multiplied because of the fact that many Chinese speakers reserve the term "Daoist" for priests and nuns. Moreover, the term for "religion" in China, *zongjiao*, is a relatively recent invention, coined by the Japanese in the late nineteenth century and then taken up by the Chinese. So we should not be surprised that when pollsters ask Chinese adults what their religion is, Daoists are hard to find. In one particularly surprising survey, the Beijing Bureau for Religious Affairs found twenty-five times more Muslims (250,000) in Beijing than Daoists (just 10,000).

When social scientists ask Chinese people whether they engage in Daoist practices, these numbers skyrocket. Nonetheless, it is fair to conclude that Daoism lags behind Confucianism in terms of its influence on Chinese life today, and behind Buddhism in terms of its temples and clerics. The state-sponsored Chinese Taoist Association claims 1,100 temples and shrines in China and 26,000 monks and nuns. The much larger Buddhist Association of China claims 13,000 monasteries and 180,000 monastics. These numbers almost certainly underestimate the power of Daoism in contemporary China, because most Daoists there do not operate within officially recognized organizations.

The World Religion Database finds only 5.7 million Daoists affiliated with official Daoist organizations in China and another 3 million in Taiwan in 2020. A more accurate number of "wider Daoists" combines those figures for card-carrying Daoists with World Religion Database figures for "Chinese folk religionists," who typically practice all Three Teachings together. According to this database, there are 439 million of these wider Daoists in China, 10 million in Taiwan, and 477 million worldwide.

Although the history of Daoism is a story of the rise and fall of many different Daoisms, there are just two main branches in China today: **Orthodox Unity** (Zhengyi), a tradition of householders (as opposed to monastics) that dates to the second century, and **Complete**

Orthodox Unity (Zhengyi) the leading form of householder Daoism and one of the two main Daoist schools today. Orthodox Unity is the successor to the Way of the Celestial Masters and a classic example of ritual-focused "shrine Daoism."

Complete Perfection (Quanzhen) a second major movement of organized Daoism, a monastic tradition founded in the twelfth century by Wang Zhe and now represented largely by its Dragon Gate lineage

Comparison of Religions Worldwide, 2020

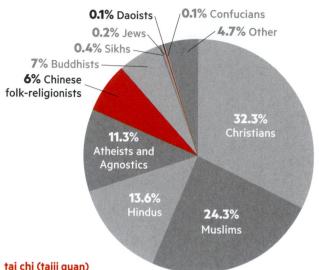

- **0.1%** Daoists
- **0.1%** Confucians
- **0.2%** Jews
- **4.7%** Other
- **0.4%** Sikhs
- **7%** Buddhists
- **6%** Chinese folk-religionists
- **11.3%** Atheists and Agnostics
- **32.3%** Christians
- **13.6%** Hindus
- **24.3%** Muslims

tai chi (taiji quan)
a Chinese martial art that features slow, circular movements. Though widely associated with Daoism, it is a broader Chinese practice.

qigong
umbrella term for energy-based slow exercises and breathing techniques first popularized in China in the 1950s. Falun Gong is an offshoot.

feng shui ("wind and water")
initially a method for determining the best placement of a grave, this method is now used to find sites for homes and to place objects inside homes

Perfection (Quanzhen), a monastic tradition that dates to the twelfth century. In Orthodox Unity, priests marry, have children, and live in the wider world. Complete Perfection masters take vows of celibacy, sobriety, and vegetarianism. With the exception of some hermits, they live in monasteries. As a result, authority passes down in families in Orthodox Unity and from master to disciple in Complete Perfection. Of all the dimensions of religion, Orthodox Unity emphasizes ritual. Complete Perfection emphasizes the experiential dimension, including meditation, visualization, and internal alchemy. In China and beyond, Daoism also flourishes in less institutionalized forms, through a variety of popular practices, including **tai chi** (*taiji quan*) and **qigong**, that are linked in some way to the Daoist tradition.

In recent years, Daoism has been undergoing a state-sponsored revival as the Chinese government has been subtly moving away from Communist ideology and toward indigenous Chinese values. Confucianism and Buddhism have benefited the most from this shift, but Daoism has benefited as well. Daoist temples are being built and restored. Daoist sites are being included on official tourist itineraries. Various Daoist and Daoist-derived practices are spreading, as the Chinese people are searching for deeper meaning than can be provided by their booming consumer culture. Meanwhile, the state-sponsored Chinese Taoist Association has been promoting Daoism as an eco-friendly tradition and Laozi as the "God of Ecology." In Beijing in 2009, at an official summit on "Laozi and Daoist Culture," a representative of the Chinese Taoist Association praised Daoism for promoting "the harmony of human beings and the natural world." According to the Daoist scholar James Miller, who attended the summit, "Daoism is now officially China's green religion."[3]

Globetrotting Chinese teachers and China scholars who every year make new Daoist scriptures available to non-Chinese speakers have also inspired interest in Daoism. But Daoist immortals have circled the globe on the wings of popular culture as well—in books such as *The Tao of Physics*, in blockbuster movies such as *Kung Fu Panda*, in songs by the hip-hop group Wu-Tang Clan, and in popular practices such as **feng shui** design and various martial arts. In this way, Daoist beliefs and practices have gained ground

DAOISM BY THE NUMBERS

Two Daoist Schools

Orthodox Unity (Zhengyi)

"shrine Daoism" led by householder priests

emphasis on communal rituals

more common in Taiwan and southern China

centered in Dragon Tiger Mountain in Jiangxi

said to be founded by Zhang Daoling in second century

Complete Perfection (Quanzhen)

"monastic Daoism" led by celibate monks and nuns

emphasis on self-cultivation

more common in northern China

centered in White Cloud Monastery in Beijing

said to be founded by Wang Zhe in twelfth century

The movement of *qi*, or "vital energy," is vital to the practice of tai chi. Here, a group practices tai chi along the Bund waterfront park, in front of the futuristic skyline of Shanghai, China.

in Australia, Europe, and the United States among people without any familial ties to China. Although the overwhelming majority of Daoists still reside in China and Taiwan, Daoism is slowly becoming a global religion with diasporic communities and converts scattered worldwide.

DAOISM 101

✦ How to live long and flourish?

The term "Daoism" derives not from a founder (like Christianity and Buddhism) or from a people (like Judaism and Hinduism) but from a core concept: the Dao. This term means "path" or "way." So Daoism is the Way of the Way. This root metaphor suggests both movement and change, taking us from one place to another, one state to another, one identity to another.

In the Western monotheisms, worshipers of God, Christ, and Allah respond to the flux and flow of human life by devoting themselves to something that is said to be as permanent and unchanging as a rock. Although the Dao is understood as the unchanging reality behind our changing world, Daoists, like most Chinese thinkers from ancient times to the present, assume that change is inescapable. There is no eternal and unchanging entity whom others call God. The question is how to live with change, how to work with it, and how to find some sort of equilibrium along the way. If you are gazing into a wild river as a Christian or Muslim, your eye might fix on a massive granite boulder seemingly unmoved by the water crashing and surging around it. If you are looking on this same scene as a Daoist, you might revel in the white water instead, or perhaps focus on a kayaker paddling down the river, balanced and joyful amidst the foam and fury.

But Daoism does not just revel in change. It changes itself. Daoism, writes the French scholar Isabelle Robinet, "has never stopped moving, transforming, absorbing."[4] Its practices vary from age to age, lineage to lineage, master to master. The Dao is even said to vary from person to person. The Dao of the butcher, the sage Zhuangzi famously observed, runs through sharp knives, steely concentration, and intimate knowledge of bone and sinew. The Dao of a politician is different (and, alas, duller).

Nevertheless, Daoists have converged on a problem many have identified as the central challenge of religion itself: the mystery of death. For Daoists, death presents itself in multiple dimensions. There is the death that concludes a human life. There is the aging and sickness that precedes it. And there is the lifelessness that besets us along the way. According to the Daoist tradition, plants and animals are naturally connected to the natural rhythms of the Dao. Unfortunately, humans have learned how to live apart from those rhythms. We go our own way, dissipating our qi, sapping our vitality, and stealing years from our lives. Instead of acting in harmony with the Dao, we kick against it. Instead of reveling in naturalness and spontaneity, we insist on the life-sucking norms and conventions of so-called civilization. Thus, we age, grow old, and die too young.

One solution to this problem is immortality. This term can be misleading, however, because Daoists do not necessarily hope for eternal life, and they certainly do not hope for an everlasting afterlife in heaven. In the Daodejing, death is to be accepted alongside life. Around the time of Zhang Daoling and the emergence of organized Daoism, however, the tradition drank deep of older traditions of immortality seekers who viewed death as something to be overcome, perhaps by living forever but more typically by living far longer and far more vital lives.

In the long Daoist history that followed, some Daoists took aim at longevity. Like Hebrew Bible patriarchs who lived for more than a century and died of natural causes, they enjoyed long and healthy lives. Some Daoists went further, hoping for bodily immortality. Other Daoists spoke of yet another possibility: dying without perishing, which is to say moving from physical death through the underworld and then being reborn as immortals.

Others hoped to avoid death entirely by transcending their human bodies and, with them, all constraints of space and time. Together these goals—longevity, physical immortality, "feigning death," and transcendence—amounted to a comprehensive protest against aging and death. But they were also protesting *for* something—for lives that are genuine and vibrant. All of them signified not merely long life but vital life and human flourishing.

This Daoist goal is possible only if we revert to the Dao. Daoists use a variety of verbs to describe this tantalizing possibility: uniting with the Dao, realizing the Dao, aligning with the Dao, and obtaining the Dao. Unfortunately, most of us revert instead to social conventions, moral norms, formal education, and ritual prescriptions. We act intentionally rather than naturally, in accordance with the will rather than the heart.

Bowing to convention doesn't just kill individuals, however. It destroys social harmony. While Confucians see ritual propriety as a solution to the world's ills, Daoists see it as a cause of both human

Daoism at a Glance

Problem: lifelessness

Solution: flourishing

Techniques: various methods designed to allow the practitioner to revert to the Dao, including meditation, visualization, internal alchemy, healthful eating, breathing exercises, and bureaucratic rituals

Exemplars: sages, immortals, and Perfected Persons

In short, Daoism is a tradition in which practitioners seek long life and human flourishing through various techniques designed to align human beings with the Dao.

lifelessness and social chaos. Created things change spontaneously. But the stuff of conventional society—etiquette and ritual, language and thought—molds us, constrains us, deadens us. We build barriers that chop what was once a unified cosmos into smaller and smaller parts, separating us from one another and restricting "the free movement of the Dao." This fragmentation seduces us into seeing ourselves as isolated atoms, distinct from one another and from the Dao. So we become strangers in our own strange lands, frenetic fashioners of civilizations that with every supposed "advance" cut us off from the original harmony of the "pristine Dao."[5] The alternative is reversion to the Dao, which makes all sorts of amazements possible, including escaping the bonds of earthly life, ascending with the wind, and riding the clouds like dragons.

Daoists have never fixed on one or even a few techniques for achieving the goal of human flourishing. Instead they have developed a long list of techniques focused largely on the physical body. More than any other religion, Daoism is preoccupied with the physical body, and with the techniques for flourishing that Daoists have developed over the centuries to preserve and circulate one's qi, to keep one's yin and yang energies in balance, and to otherwise foster the flourishing that comes with reversion to the life-giving Dao. Daoists might visualize deities residing inside their own bodies or far off in the stars. They might engage in dietary disciplines, rituals, moral action, liturgies, breathing exercises, meditation, sexual rites, and wandering. Various physical exercises, such as "bear strides and bird stretches," are modeled not on Indian yogas but on the natural movements of long-lived animals.[6]

Two additional methods for achieving immortality by returning to the Dao stand out. The first is **external alchemy** (*waidan*). Centuries before alchemists in medieval Europe first experimented with turning lead into gold, Daoist alchemists were laboring to refine and compound cinnabar, mercury, lead, and other metals and minerals into elixirs of immortality. In elaborate rituals that combined science, technology, spirituality, and religion, these immortality seekers would retire from society, receive secret alchemical instructions, purify their laboratories, determine an auspicious time for their experiments, and light fires to begin. They would then work to produce in their cauldrons a "golden elixir" consisting of the sort of pure and primordial substance that existed before the emanation of the universe produced yin and yang.

Messing around with mercury, lead, and fire might seem like a dangerous business. It was. In fact, external alchemy claimed the lives of alchemists and rulers alike. Qin Shi Huang, the founding emperor of the Qin dynasty who was buried with his famous terracotta army of soldiers outside modern-day Xian, likely died of elixir poisoning in 210 BCE. Nearly a millennium later, in 1735 CE, so did the Yongzhen Emperor of the Qing dynasty. It should be noted, however, that many Daoists would have interpreted such "deaths" as instances of what the Daoist studies scholar Robert Campany refers to as "escape by means of a simulated corpse."[7]

A related method may have arisen in response to this danger. In **internal alchemy** (*neidan*), earlier alchemical processes were internalized in something akin to meditation. Now the goal was to produce the "golden elixir" inside the alchemist's body, which was imagined to be a cauldron. Internal alchemists aimed to reverse the process in which the void produced the One, the Two, the Three, and the ten thousand things—by reverting back to the duality of yin and yang, then to unity, and finally to the nondual mystery of the Dao. In this way, masters of inner alchemy sought not only to achieve longevity

external alchemy (waidan)
earlier Daoist practice that attempted to create an elixir of immortality out of dangerous metals and minerals

internal alchemy (neidan)
an interiorization of older external alchemical processes in which the elixir of immortality is manufactured inside the human body via meditation and visualization

The yin/yang concept in which complementary "opposites" flow into one another predates Daoism but is nonetheless central to Daoist thinking and practice. The yin side is said to be dark, feminine, passive, and cold while the yang is white, masculine, active, and warm.

Yin and Yang

Yin and yang are complementary forces but, as the yin/yang symbol illustrates, they are also interpenetrating, shading over into one another at their extremes. Yang referred originally to the sunny side of a hill and yin to the shady side, but the associations today are broader:

YIN	YANG
shady	sunny
death	life
slow	fast
heavy	light
feminine	masculine
earth	heaven
night	day
winter	summer
autumn	spring

and immortality but also to return to their original natures and to live in harmony with the Dao.

Daoists use a variety of terms to refer to humans who achieve these goals, including holy persons (*shenren*) and Perfected Persons (*zhenren*). But the most popular term for these exemplars is *xian*, which is sometimes translated as "transcendent" but more typically as "**immortal**." If the Confucian model is the sage, and the Buddhist model is the Buddha, in Daoism it is the immortal. These exemplars are often said to live in the mountains. In fact, the character for *xian* consists of an image of a person and an image of a mountain. Immortals are typically understood to be humans (historical, legendary, or a mix of the two) who have transcended the bounds of earthly existence. Because of their abundant and refined qi, immortals look young. Like Superwoman and other comic book superheroes, they can ride on the wind and fly through the clouds. They can shapeshift into other beings or things. They can control the weather and predict the future. Seemingly ageless, they live on little more than air and dew, unaffected by cold or heat. They can even make themselves invisible (with or without a cloak). Their real claim to fame, however, is defiance of death over the course of unimaginably long lives, including, in some cases, physical immortality.

These immortals remind us that the Daoist goal is not simply to live forever. Who in their right mind would want that without some fundamental transformation? More than eternal life, the goal is a life that soars above ordinary human experience. The goal is flourishing—the sort of life you would want to last forever. For this reason, Robert Campany and some other Daoist studies scholars prefer to translate *xian* as "transcendents," but the term "immortals" is so widely used that it is employed in this chapter as well.[8]

The Dao

The Daoist tradition inherited from ancient China a variety of symbols, including the couplet of yin and yang, which explains (among other things) how change happens. But the overwhelming preoccupation of Daoists is with the concept that lends this tradition its name. Like the Buddha in Buddhism or Christ in Christianity, the Dao is the inescapable concern for Daoists. But this Dao is neither a person nor a god. What is it? And what can it tell us about Daoism?

As has been noted, Dao refers to a path or a way, but unlike those geographical concepts the Dao cannot be contained. It is an everlasting principle. It is an unspeakable mystery. It brings the universe into being and, with it, mortals and immortals alike. It infuses all things. It transcends all things. It directs the transformation of all things. It gathers the wild diversity of the universe into an unpronounceable One. Therefore, it is larger than any single god or religious founder. In the Daoist tradition, the universe emerges out of the Dao. Harmony proceeds from the operations of the Dao. Chaos results from ignorance and neglect of the Dao. Harmony is restored by reverting to the Dao.

When viewed from this perspective, the Dao is the mystery of all mysteries. It is ultimate and therefore unknowable to those who do not know ultimate things. It is formless

immortal (xian) the central exemplar of the Daoist tradition. Also called "transcendents," they enjoy long life and other superpowers achieved through self-cultivation techniques.

and empty of attributes. As such, it is beyond definition. In fact, according to the first line of the Daodejing, it cannot even be named. But this impersonal and ineffable Dao does not remain entirely outside human experience. It manifests as the mother of the ten thousand things—in everything inside and around us, from our kidneys and livers to stars and galaxies. According to Daoists, we can glimpse its patterns (and adapt to them) by paying attention to its workings in the world.

DAOISM: A GENEALOGY

The *Oxford English Dictionary* traces the term "Taoism" to *China Opened* (1838) by the German Charles Gutzlaff, the first Lutheran missionary to China. A commanding Christian presence in China during the first half of the nineteenth century, Gutzlaff used his considerable translation skills both to write Christian tracts and to provide intelligence to the British during the Opium Wars. But "Taouism," as he rendered it, also appears four years earlier in another book by Gutzlaff, *A Sketch of Chinese History* (1834). Though he describes "Taouism" as "a labyrinth of nonsense," Gutzlaff is far friendlier here to the "Taou-tih-king" (Daodejing), which is said to contain "vestiges of unadulterated truth, the Trinity, Logos, immortality."[a]

The very first use of "Taouism," however, seems to have appeared in 1833 in yet another book by Gutzlaff, this time regarding his Chinese travels. Though he criticized "Taou priests" for peddling "idolatry" and "absurdities," he praised them for approximating Christians by affirming "a future state" and "the existence of a Supreme Being." Gutzlaff also found similarities between "their Taou" (which he translated as "reason") and "the *logos* of the Platonic school." The term "Taouism" also appears in a passage criticizing the poor treatment of women, which he lays at the feet of Confucius, "Taouism and Buddhism" alike.[b]

Until recently, many scholars distinguished between early "philosophical Daoism" and later "religious Daoism." This distinction is there in Gutzlaff, but it is plainer in an unsigned book review from 1839 that distinguishes between "the religion of Tao" ("a national superstition") and the humble philosophy of "Laoukeun," a man "of a contemplative mood, who preferred solitude to the turmoils of a wicked world." The "Taoutih king" (Daodejing), this author continues, may include "absurdities and errors," but it also "contains many deep thoughts"— so many that an impartial reader cannot help but "admire the mind of a man, who at such an early stage of the world could make such-like discoveries in natural religion."[c]

The term "Taouism" is absent from *A General Description of China* (1788), an English translation of a 1786 French book by the Roman Catholic Father Jean-Baptist Grosier, but this book has a long section on the "Sect of the Tao-sse" that makes even plainer this imagined distinction between "pure" Daoist philosophy and "degraded" Daoist religion. It recites legends surrounding "a philosopher named *Lao-kiun,* or *Lao-tse.*" It details his profound philosophy, which consists in "endeavoring to live free from grief and pain, and in striving to glide gently down the stream of life, devoid of anxiety and care." It then contrasts his profundity with gross caricatures of the organized Daoism that followed, including the "foolish idea" of concocting a magical "drink that would render mankind immortal." Soon members of this supposedly "contemptible sect" were promoting "every fraud and deceit that cunning can suggest."[d]

In the twentieth century, "Taouism" was shortened to "Taoism" and then, with the recent shift to pinyin in the transliteration of Chinese into English, to "Daoism."

Lu Dongbin

The best known of Daoism's Eight Immortals is Lu Dongbin, a scholar-turned-dropout of the late Tang dynasty (618–907) who was played in more recent memory by Jackie Chan in the film *The Forbidden Kingdom*. Like many college students, Lu was working his way toward employment, marriage, and the success and happiness he thought they would bring, when circumstances upended him.

In a famous story now referred to as the "Yellow Millet Dream," Lu was on his way to a nearby city to take the imperial examination required for civil service work when he stopped at an inn. As the innkeeper was cooking up some yellow millet for him, Lu fell asleep. During his nap, he fast-forwarded to a future in which he had passed the imperial exam and become a rich and respected government official with many children and grandchildren. But this power corrupted him. A scandal erupted, ending his marriage and leaving him a broken man. One day, as he was wandering in exile, a snowstorm stopped him short. He was weak and close to death. Then he woke up, still a young man at the inn with his yellow millet still cooking, but now an intriguing fellow was sitting beside him.

Lu told his dream to the man, who happened to be an immortal. "You have lived a whole life in less time than it took to cook your millet," the immortal said. In that moment, Lu realized that life is a dream. Fortune is fleeting, as is poverty. He decided to change his life. He got out of the rat race and made for the mountains where he could wander free.

Today, Lu is celebrated in Daoist folk tales for his "free and easy wandering." He is also regarded as a patriarch of the Orthodox Unity movement. A frequent object of devotion in Daoist temples, he is often depicted as a handsome scholar who wields a demon-slaying sword and a whisk symbolizing his ability to fly. A Renaissance man who excelled as a poet and calligrapher, Lu is also renowned as a healer, exorcist, alchemist, and master swordsman.

The Gods

Numbers aside, Daoism confounds us in another way. Like Confucianism, it has been described as a "religion without a supreme being" and therefore "neither a polytheism nor a monotheism."[9] That may be right, if by "supreme being" we mean a divinity akin to the God of the Western monotheisms. But the Daoist tradition reveres a long list of immortals and Perfected Persons who seem to act like gods. The tradition also reveres more conventional gods, including some who reside among the stars and others located inside human bodies.

The most popular gods in the Daoist pantheon are the **Three Pure Ones** (*Sanqing*). Widely worshiped from the ninth century forward, these three gods are traditionally depicted together as three old Chinese men:

Three Pure Ones (Sanqing)
the highest and most popular gods in the Daoist pantheon, traditionally depicted together: Celestial Worthy of Primordial Beginning, Celestial Worthy of Numinous Treasure, and Celestial Worthy of the Way and Its Power

- The Celestial Worthy of Primordial Beginning, the highest ranking of these three gods, traditionally depicted in the center of a triptych and therefore as the host. Understood as the creator and a symbol of the Dao itself, this divinity is typically portrayed holding a sphere symbolizing oneness.
- The Celestial Worthy of Numinous Treasure, the second-ranking of these gods, traditionally depicted at the left hand of the Celestial Worthy of Primordial Beginning and therefore as the first guest. Typically portrayed holding a scepter as a symbol of power, this divinity is not eternal, having gestated for 3,700 years before being born as a human incarnation of the Dao.

- The Celestial Worthy of the Way and Its Powers, traditionally depicted at the right hand of the Celestial Worthy of Primordial Beginnings and therefore as the second guest. Wielding a fan as a symbol of immortality and closely associated with Lord Lao, this deity is said to have gestated for eighty-one years before taking on a human body.

Other important divinities include the Jade Emperor and the **Queen Mother of the West**, Daoism's highest god and goddess. The Jade Emperor is a heavenly CEO—an emperor of the cosmic realm who oversees other gods even as he administers the cosmos itself. In Daoist iconography, he is adorned like an emperor, with a black beard and a robe emblazoned with a red dragon. In keeping with his name, he carries a jade tablet. Queen Mother of the West is an ancient Chinese goddess later brought into the Daoist orbit as a symbol of cosmic yin. She, too, is a celestial administrator, though in her case she rules over her fellow goddesses. Since the west is the direction of death in ancient China, she was initially depicted as a terrifying goddess akin to India's Kali, with tiger's teeth, a leopard's tail, and a wild mane of hair. Over time, she evolved into a compassionate mother who, from her western paradise on Mount Kunlun, hands out special peaches—they ripen only once every three thousand years—that ensure immortality for their recipients.

This is only a small sampling of the Daoist pantheon, which extends to three large groups of divine officials (overseeing heaven, earth, and water), who determine human fate, and Five Emperors (overseeing the five directions: north, south, east, west, and center). There is a Dipper Mother associated with the stars of the Big Dipper, and there are gods of thunder and exorcism, literature and culture, war and martial arts. Intriguingly, these gods are not viewed as eternal. Although the offices in the Daoist pantheon are fixed, most of the superbeings who fill them come and go. Only the Dao is eternal.

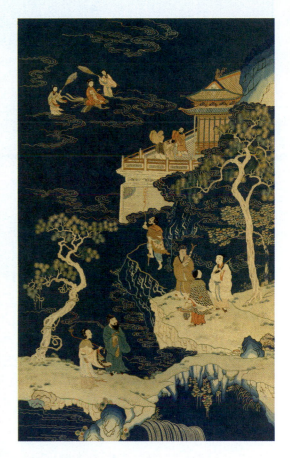

On this embroidered panel from the seventeenth or eighteenth century, the Eight Immortals and the God of Longevity (on the terrace) celebrate the birthday of the Queen Mother of the West, who rides (upper left) atop a mythical bird in the sky.

DAOIST HISTORY

In religions without any clear founder, it can be difficult to fix a birthplace or a birthdate. It can also be difficult to determine just what that religion affirms. Some scholars have tried to resolve this difficulty in Daoist history by distinguishing between the earlier "philosophical Daoism" of Laozi and the later "religious Daoism" of Zhang Daoling. As justification, they point to two ancient Chinese terms that, in their view, suggest a similar distinction between *daojia* ("lineage of the Dao") for philosophical Daoism and *daojiao* ("teachings of the Dao") for religious Daoism. A likelier source of inspiration for this idea was the Protestant assumption, shared by almost all early scholars of religion, that the pure form of any religion is to be found in the ideas articulated in its scriptures, and that later superstitions are desecrations of this original purity. From this perspective, philosophical Daoism was China's version of Protestantism and religious Daoism was its Roman Catholic stepchild, complete with priests and popes and all manner of supposedly superstitious nonsense.

Queen Mother of the West popular ancient Chinese divinity and overseer of her fellow goddesses who predates Daoism but is widely associated with it

This distinction falls apart under scrutiny. There is plenty of philosophy in religious Daoism, not least the philosophy of Laozi, who came to be revered as a god. And there is plenty of religion in philosophical Daoism, both in the Daodejing itself and in what Brown University professor Harold Roth refers to as the early "inner cultivation" lineages of masters and disciples that surrounded the creation and distribution of that text.[10]

Scholars of Hinduism refer to the traditions behind India's ancient Vedic texts as Vedic religion—a tradition not wholly other from Hinduism and yet not quite Hinduism either. Likewise, scholars of Judaism present the sacrificial religion of the Jerusalem Temple as a tradition distinct from the rabbinic Judaism that did not emerge until roughly the time of the early Christian movement. James Miller takes a similar approach with Daoism, referring to the period from antiquity into the second century as an era of "proto-Daoism."[11] Until Zhang Daoling, we don't yet have much evidence of organized Daoist religion, but we cannot ignore this earlier period because it gives us the essential figures and texts of Daoism to come.

Laozi and the Daodejing

The most important figure in the early development of Daoism was Laozi ("Old Master"), the pseudohistorical sage credited with writing the Daodejing. Laozi's life is traditionally dated to the sixth century BCE, making him a contemporary of Confucius, one of many philosophers during the so-called Axial Age who speculated about individual existence.

CHRONOLOGY OF DAOISM

c. 550 BCE Traditional birth year for Laozi

551–479 Traditional dates for Confucius

475–221 Warring States period in China

c. 50 CE Buddhism comes to China

142 Lord Lao appears to Zhang Daoling, who institutionalizes Daoism by founding the Celestial Masters movement

184 Yellow Turban revolt attempts to usher in the "Great Peace"

215 Zhang Daoling's grandson Zhang Lu surrenders to Han dynasty general Cao Cao, putting an end to his thirty-year Daoist theocracy but spreading the Celestial Masters across China

317 Ge Hong completes essays arguing for the legitimacy of the immortality quest and biographies of immortals (or "transcendents")

364–370 CE Spirit medium Yang Xi receives revelations that will form the basis for the Highest Clarity (Shanqing) movement

397–402 CE Transmission of Numinous Treasure (Lingbao) scriptures

456–536 Life of Tao Hongjing, Highest Clarity systematizer and Renaissance man

618–907 Tang dynasty transforms Daoism into China's national religion, turning Laozi's birthday into a national holiday and producing the first Daoist canon

690–705 Reign of Empress Wu, China's only female emperor, who favors Buddhism over Daoism

733 Daodejing is added to the reading list for civil service examinations in China

1101–1125 Reign of Emperor Huizong, who saw Daoist canon into print for the first time and oversaw a period of Daoist flourishing during the Northern Song dynasty

1113–1170 Life of Wang Zhe (aka Wang Chongyang), recluse and founder of the Way of Complete Perfection

1190 Complete Perfection (Quanzhen) emerges as a monastic alternative to the Celestial Masters when it is officially recognized by the Jin dynasty

1222 Complete Perfection leader Qiu Chuji visits Mongol ruler Genghis Khan

During this proto-Daoist period, Laozi remained a mere mortal. But already the ground-work was being laid for devotion to Lord Lao as a god who descends at various moments in world history to set things right. The source for the story about Laozi safeguarding the Daodejing at the border before wandering up into the mountains comes from *Historical Records*, a first-century BCE text by the Chinese historian Sima Qian. Other sources elevate Laozi to more breathtaking heights, describing him as an embodiment of the Dao who "rests in the great beginning, wanders in the great origin" and "has existed since before Heaven and Earth."[12] According to one account, he was swallowed by a queen in India, only to emerge from her armpit one year later as the Buddha. In a parallel tale, his mother's left armpit served as his birth canal.

Unveiled in 2010 in Luoyang, China, this bronze statue, which stands 194 feet tall, is said to be the world's tallest statue of Laozi. In January 2019, Chinese officials deemed it illegal and ordered it to be covered with a massive cloth until it received governmental approval.

The book attributed to Laozi, the Daodejing (also known simply as the Laozi), is a short anthology of sayings by multiple authors written over centuries and likely available in roughly its current form starting in the third century BCE. A millennium later, in 733 CE, a Tang dynasty emperor included it alongside the Confucian classics on the reading list for China's civil service exams. Over the last two millennia, the Daodejing has inspired hundreds of translations and many more commentaries. It is studied today by philosophers and recited piously by the devout. Like any great text, the Daodejing contains multitudes. It has been read as a mystical work and a political treatise, an ethical text and a philosophical reckoning with the paradoxes of language itself. During his 1988 State of the Union address, U.S. president Ronald Reagan quoted the Daodejing in support of his crusade

1445 Ming Daoist canon, the baseline for modern Daoist canons, is compiled and woodblock-printed

1644–1911 Qing dynasty witnesses the flourishing of Complete Perfection Daoism, especially the Dragon Gate lineage centered at Beijing's White Cloud Abbey

1656 Dragon Gate (Longmen) branch of the Way of Complete Perfection is founded

1784 Inauguration of U.S. trade with China

1788 Jesuit missionaries produce (in Latin) the first European translation of the Daodejing

1833 The word "Taoism" first appears in an English-language publication

1868 First English-language translation of the Daodejing

1893 World's Parliament of Religions in Chicago includes an anonymous paper on Daoism

1912–1949 Republic of China inaugurates post-imperial China

1945–1949 Chinese Civil War ends with a Communist victory, and Nationalists flee to Taiwan

1949– People's Republic of China, first led by Mao Zedong

1957 Chinese Taoist Association is established

1966–1976 Cultural Revolution denounces religion and destroys Confucian and Daoist temples, books, and ritual objects

1976 Death of Mao Zedong leads to greater freedom of religion in China

1980s Qigong boom in China

1992 Falun Gong is founded by the qigong practitioner Li Hongzhi

1999 Falun Gong is banned after a major protest in Beijing

2009 China establishes its first research institute devoted to Laozi

2018 President Xi, in 13th National People's Congress speech, praises Laozi and Zhuangzi as "world-renowned great thinkers"

de

power or virtue. Those who attain the Dao are also said to attain this power and this virtue.

wuwei ("nonaction")

sometimes translated as "inaction," but better understood as spontaneous, effortless, or nonintentional action, like water running downhill

for small government: "As an ancient Chinese philosopher, Lao-tzu, said: 'Govern a great nation as you would cook a small fish; do not overdo it.'"[13]

The standard edition of the Daodejing consists of eighty-one chapters divided into two parts: thirty-seven chapters on the Way (*dao*) and forty-four chapters on Virtue (**de**). For this reason, it is called the Daodejing, or "The Scripture on the Way and Its Virtue." Its sayings likely circulated orally before they began to be gathered in written form in the fourth century BCE. We know this because of two archaeological discoveries of Daodejing materials: silk scrolls sealed in 168 BCE in a tomb at Mawangdui in Hunan province and unearthed in the early 1970s, and bamboo slips sealed in a tomb in 300 BCE found near Guodian village in Hubei province in 1993.

The Daodejing emerged out of an era of deep and disruptive change known as the Warring States period, and one of its central concerns is how to wrest order out of chaos, both in society and in individual lives. This text also emerged at the crossroads of a new China—as the Bronze Age was yielding to the Iron Age, and the old feudal order of kings and aristocrats was giving way to a new society of artisans and merchants. At this crossroads, many philosophical schools wrestled with the concept of the Dao in an effort to make sense of the descent of Chinese civilization into unrest and brutality and to put life back on a path toward order and harmony. The Legalist school argued that an emphasis on law and regulations would restore order. Confucians argued that a revival of ritual, etiquette, and propriety would bring back the golden age enjoyed under the Duke of Zhou and other ancient sage-kings.

Like the Analects of Confucius, the Daodejing addressed fundamental human questions about historical change and human agency. How do societies change? How are humans transformed? And how might our answers to these two questions be linked? It answered these questions via axioms and aphorisms that have left many readers scratching their heads. Here we are told to know by not knowing and to act by not acting. We are urged to follow Laozi as he reverts not (as Confucius sought to do) to ancient China but to something more primordial: a community in which individuals act harmoniously in accordance with the Dao.

The core values championed in the Daodejing include spontaneity and naturalness. Confucian preoccupations with ritual are rejected, as are the fine discriminations and differentiations of Confucian thinkers. Readers are urged to work with the Dao rather than against it, to yield to its patterns and rhythms. The key term is **wuwei**, which literally means "nonaction." The point is not to do nothing, however. Neither is it to "go with the flow" like a Beat Generation poet or a Woodstock hippie. It is instead to go with the Way: to act naturally; to act effortlessly without plan, goal, or self-interest. Almost everything in the universe follows its own Dao. Water flows downhill. Pine trees drop pine needles. Cats lick their paws. But humans are different. All too often we lose our way. The way back is to follow the example of the sage who unclenches his grasping fist, letting go of unhealthy desires and living in harmony with the patterns of community life and the ongoing rhythms of the natural world. To act like this is to pave the way toward order and harmony, not only in one's own life but also in society.

It is important to observe what the Daodejing does not teach, including many beliefs and practices that will later become central to classical Daoism. The Daodejing does not contemplate immortality. It accepts death as a given. Moreover, the exemplar in the Daodejing is no world-renouncing hermit. Its exemplar is the socially and politically

The Pleasure of Fishes, a scroll painted by Zhou Dongqing in 1291, depicts a scene from the Daoist classic the Zhuangzi. These fish can be said to represent the Daoist concept of *wuwei* because they follow the Dao naturally and without the intervention of intention.

engaged sage often associated with Confucianism, but with a radically different set of priorities formed in opposition to the way of Confucius.

Zhuangzi

The second most important proto-Daoist figure is the late-fourth-century thinker **Zhuangzi** ("Master Zhuang"). According to pious reports, he earned a living in the artisan economy in his hometown in what is now Henan province. Today, he is remembered as the author of a complicated text also called the Zhuangzi. This remarkable text is longer and more playful than the Daodejing. Instead of pithy aphorisms, it offers stories featuring a goldmine of eccentric characters—animal, human, and divine—who continue to populate Chinese lore. It opens with a story about a massive fish (at least a mile long) who becomes a massive bird who becomes a serious object of scorn among various chattering birds. Later we meet a butcher who attains the Dao by cutting his meat just so, a robber who understands ethics better than Confucius, and an immortal who lives for eight hundred years.

The standard edition of the Zhuangzi is divided into three parts and thirty-three chapters. The seven inner chapters likely date to the fourth century BCE and may well go back to Zhuangzi himself. The outer and miscellaneous chapters were written after his lifetime, likely in the third century BCE, by his followers. This text commends to its readers a radically unconventional life, which begins by distancing oneself from conventional thinking, including distinguishing between good and bad, ugly and beautiful.

The Zhuangzi imagines multiple encounters between Laozi and Confucius. Repeatedly, Laozi comes out on top. When asked what he makes of Laozi (whom he calls "Old Longears"), Confucius says:

> I have finally seen a dragon! . . . Coiled up, his body is complete; extended, his scaly patterns are whole. He rides on the cloudy vapors and is nourished by yin and yang.

Zhuangzi ("Master Zhuang")
Daoist sage credited with writing the humorous and enigmatic book of stories also known as the Zhuangzi

My mouth fell open and I couldn't close it; my tongue arched upward so I couldn't even utter a halting word. How could I have admonished Old Longears?[14]

This giant of a man seems to view Confucius as a pitiful figure, enslaved to moral laws and ritual propriety and all sorts of intellectual distinctions.

In these encounters, we see the emergence of free individuals in rebellion against the many disciplines society inflicts on them. Zhuangzi appears as a man inquiring after the meanings and ends of an individual life and the possibility of radical self-transformation. That possibility is achieved by Perfected Persons who have become one with the Dao and are therefore indifferent to the distinction between life and death. Practitioners of "free and easy wandering," these exemplars act spontaneously and effortlessly in keeping with the values of wuwei. Partial to the wild spaces of the mountains, they see their own bodies as metaphorical mountains graced by the gods. The qi that flows through them offers not only longevity but also transcendence of mundane human life. Thanks to diets of wind and dew, their bodies are almost as light as air. They dance on mountaintops and ride dragons up into the clouds.

When Daoism was institutionalized after 142 BCE under the Way of the Celestial Masters, three key deities emerged: the Three Officials of heaven, earth, and water (left to right).

Organized Daoism and the Celestial Masters

The first real evidence of Daoism as an organized religion comes centuries after the Daodejing, during the second century CE. Organized Daoism was influenced by proto-Daoism and especially by the figure of Laozi who, in this second period of Daoist history, was deified into Lord Lao. Other influences were Buddhism and popular apocalyptic movements that mixed religion, politics, poetry, and war as they anticipated the end of times. But the most important impact on organized Daoism was made by China's imperial courts, with their rituals, hierarchies, and bureaucracies.

Following Lord Lao's revelation to Zhang Daoling atop Crane Call Mountain in 142 BCE, Daoism developed rapidly into the sort of institutionalized religion that makes today's "spiritual but not religious" shudder. In fact, the Way of the **Celestial Masters** featured rituals and liturgies that extended from the inner reaches of the human body to the outer reaches of the universe. Bureaucratically, it organized itself into twenty-four administrative units now likened by historians of China to Catholic parishes overseen by parish priests. It had its own gods, scriptures, officials, and moral precepts. Over time, it would make Zhang Daoling a god, too.

All this began, according to Celestial Masters' lore, when Lord Lao imparted to Zhang Daoling a new sacred compact that emphasized unity and orthodoxy. By drawing sharp lines between "pure" and "deviant" practices, this revelation set Zhang and his followers at odds with many popular practices of their day. The Celestial Masters rejected blood sacrifice and payments to priests. "The gods do not eat or drink," this covenant proclaimed. "The masters do not receive any salary."[15] But the Way of the Celestial Masters did not just dismiss local priests and their sacrifices, it dismissed their gods (without, it should be noted, denying their existence). Of the nine traditional heavens in popular Chinese religion, six were labeled corrupt. Only three gods—the officials of heaven, earth, and water—were said to be worthy of worship. And they were to be approached bureaucratically rather than sacrificially, through carefully drafted petitions to celestial officials.

Those who followed this covenant called their movement the Way of the Celestial Masters, or Tianshi Dao (from *tian*, meaning "heaven"; *shi*, or "master"; and *dao*, or "way"). Outsiders, pointing to its annual tithes of five pecks of rice per year per family (to support priests and the poor), called it the "Way of the Five Pecks of Rice" (or, less graciously, the "rice bandits"). Because of its emphasis on correct doctrine, it also came to be known as Orthodox Unity, a name it continues to go by today.

In a clear departure from the suspicion of traditional ethical and ritual systems in the Daodejing and the Zhuangzi, the Way of the Celestial Masters emphasized the moral dimension of religion. Like the Hebrew Bible prophets, its practitioners disdained sacrificial offerings and demanded moral behavior instead. As they saw it, a vast bureaucracy of celestial officials tracked and recorded our actions. It then punished us for wrongdoing, not least by making us sick and shortening our lives.

Moral and ritual action could lift these punishments and cure these ills. Practitioners would withdraw to a quiet room to contemplate their wrongdoing. They would admit their misdeeds in a ritual many scholars have likened to the Catholic sacrament of confession. The priestlike recipient of this confession was known as a **libationer**, an old title for a village elder who offered sacrifices to local gods. He or she (libationers could be men or women) would not sacrifice to a god, however. Instead, libationers would draft and submit official petitions to the Three Officials of heaven, earth, and water, who were responsible for making wrongdoers sick. These written communications were possible because libationers possessed registers of the names of celestial bureaucrats as well as templates for drafting various petitions. Libationers also knew how to dispatch messengers from their own bodies to convey their petitions to the proper celestial addresses.

Another spiritual technology of the Celestial Masters was the talisman. Libationers would write sacred words and symbols on paper, which could then be burned, mixed with water, and ingested in order to ward off evil spirits or heal. Libationers also collected the annual tithe of rice. They managed bed-and-breakfasts of sorts that supplied free meals and lodging to weary travelers. They also organized three annual assemblies at holy mountains to update family records (of births, marriages, and deaths) and to share a common meal.

When it came to sex, the Celestial Masters were conflicted. On the one hand, they knew sex was necessary for reproduction, and they believed that some forms of sex could increase longevity. On the other hand, they worked hard to regulate and reduce it, insisting that young people should cut back on sexual activity and that people over fifty should abstain entirely. They also rejected as false two popular "arts of the bedchamber" associated with the quest for a longer life: intercourse without ejaculation (intended to conserve one's spiritual essence) and the "borrowing" of qi from a sexual partner (intended to add to the qi stored in one's own body). The Celestial Masters did engage in a choreographed secret sex rite known as "merging breaths." Strictly supervised by a Daoist master, this practice did not take place until after the initiates had engaged in a series of meditations, visualizations, and massages. When intercourse finally occurred, the yang and yin energies of the couple were said to be merged.

The dos and don'ts of the Celestial Masters' moral code were spelled out in Nine Practices to perform and Twenty-Seven Precepts to avoid. In each case, practitioners were

Celestial Masters (Tianshi) first major movement of organized Daoism, a householder tradition emphasizing communal rituals founded in the second century CE by Zhang Daoling and now referred to as Orthodox Unity

libationer Celestial Masters priestly officiant who employs celestial registers to draft petitions to the gods. Unlike the celibate monastics of the Complete Perfection movement, libationers marry.

This 1911 illustration by the French Jesuit missionary Henri Doré depicts the type of talisman hung on the front doors of Daoist homes during the fifth moon in the hope that the year ahead would be peaceful.

promised that, if they followed this list, they could become healthier with longer and more socially harmonious lives.

These moral concerns reflected and contributed to a period of end-of-the-world enthusiasm at the close of the Han dynasty. A series of movements had prophesied coming calamities that would give way to an ideal ruler who would oversee an ideal society known as the "Great Peace" (Taiping). As the Han dynasty began to collapse, the search for this messianic figure became acute. In 184 CE, representatives of Great Peace Daoism worked toward a new golden age of "good government, political harmony, and good health for the masses." Rather than simply waiting for a cosmic reversion to the Dao, they took up arms in an effort to forcibly replace the "blue heaven" of the Han with the "yellow heaven" of their coming kingdom.[16] The Yellow Turbans, as this group was popularly known, lost, but the Celestial Masters movement fared better. After Zhang Daoling's ascension, the Celestial Master role passed to his son Zhang Heng and then to his grandson Zhang Lu.

DAOISM BY THE NUMBERS

Nine Practices of the Celestial Masters[a]

Practice nonaction.

Practice supple weakness.

Practice preserving the feminine; do not act first.

Practice no fame.

Practice pure stillness.

Practice good deeds.

Practice no desire.

Practice knowing to stop at enough.

Practice yielding.

Twenty-Seven Precepts of the Celestial Masters[b]

Do not delight in deviance; delight and anger are the same.

Do not waste essence or pneumas [qi].

Do not harm flourishing pneumas.

Do not eat bloody animals, delighting in their delicious flavor.

Do not long for a meritorious reputation.

Do not practice false arts pointing to shapes and calling them the Dao.

Do not forget the rules of the Dao.

Do not make tentative moves.

Do not lust after jewels and goods.

Do not study deviant texts.

Do not lust after lofty splendor, seeking it by force.

Do not seek fame and renown.

Do not be led into error by ear, eye, or mouth.

Always dwell in humble lowliness.

Do not become irritated easily.

Be deliberate in all matters; do not let the heart become flustered.

Do not indulge yourself in good clothes or fine food.

Do not overindulge.

Do not because of poverty and meanness demand wealth and status.

Do not perform evil acts.

Do not observe many taboos.

Do not pray or sacrifice to the spirits.

Do not be obstinate.

Do not be convinced of your own correctness.

Do not argue with others about who is right; avoid an argument before it arises.

Do not proclaim yourself a sage or claim fame.

Do not delight in weapons.

Drawing on support from local landowners plus a pious peasantry overwhelmed by famine and poverty, Zhang Lu established an independent Daoist state that lasted close to thirty years and covered much of the modern-day Sichuan province. He also oversaw the production of an influential commentary on the Daodejing.

This "Daocracy" collapsed in 215 when Zhang Lu surrendered to the Han general Cao Cao, who would go on to found the Wei dynasty (220–265).[17] But this loss was a surprise win for the Celestial Masters movement, which, because of Cao Cao's forced relocation of its adherents, was cast hither and yon across northern China. As it moved out from its Sichuan homeland into a "Great Diaspora," its teachings spread among a variety of ethnicities and social classes in northern and southern China alike. In the process, it became, according to Daoism scholar Terry Kleeman, "China's first national religion."[18]

Other Organized Daoisms

This migration of Daoists accelerated when Central Asian nomads invaded northern China in the early fourth century and set off a period of unrest now called the Sixteen Kingdoms (317–420). Many Daoists fled south, taking their traditions with them. The result was a division of the Celestial Masters into northern and southern wings. The northerners remained purists, opposed to local deities, to meat and wine sacrifices, and to ancestor worship and trance mediums. The southerners were more open to outside influences, one of which was popular Chinese religion, also known as "folk" religion. The Celestial Masters had for the most part denounced this unofficial yet common religion, but it had thrived in the south. Now beliefs and practices popular in the south—alchemy, meditation, visualization, and various other longevity practices popular among immortality seekers—were increasingly brought under the Daoist umbrella. The second key influence was Buddhism, which came to China via Indian missionaries as early as the first century CE and whose founder was already being creatively confused with Laozi by the second century. Now Daoism took on a wide variety of Buddhist norms and organizational forms, including monasticism, mindfulness meditation, and the philosophical notion of emptiness.

Three important types of Daoist texts and traditions emerged out of this creative ferment. One was called the "Great Clarity" (Taiqing) tradition. Closely tied to pre-Daoist immortality seeker traditions, these texts focused on external alchemy. One important Daoist thinker, Ge Hong (283–343 CE), drew heavily on this tradition. He wrote a key text featuring detailed biographies of immortals (or "transcendents") and another on "how to shun death" through various techniques, including breathing practices, herbal medicines, and elixirs of immortality. He also helped systematize a set of qi circulation practices. According to Robert Campany, Ge Hong described "attaining the Dao" not as "mystical end state" but as "a lifelong process, laborious and agonistic in character."[19]

Rising Moon Over Mt. Nanping: Cao Cao, this 1885 woodblock print by the Japanese artist Tsukioka Yoshitoshi illustrates a scene from a fourteenth-century Chinese novel describing General Cao Cao's battle to establish the third-century Wei dynasty.

Highest Clarity (Shangqing)
also translated as "Supreme Purity," a fourth-century movement that pushed Daoism away from laboratory alchemy toward meditation and other self-cultivation techniques

A second and more consequential development, **Highest Clarity** (Shangqing, sometimes translated as "Supreme Purity"), drew heavily on Ge Hong's insights. In a curious sort of scriptural one-upmanship, this group claimed to be superior to the Taiqing because its revelations came from the Highest Clarity heaven rather than the lower Great Clarity heaven of the Celestial Masters. Also known as the "Mao Shan" movement because of its center on Mount Mao in southeastern China's Jiangsu province, Highest Clarity combined influences from the bureaucratic Celestial Masters with more ecstatic southern folk traditions.

Popular among elites in part because of the literary quality of its texts and the dazzling calligraphy of its scriptures, this movement became the most influential Daoist tradition between the sixth and tenth centuries. Highest Clarity Daoism helped nudge organized Daoism from bureaucracy and rituals toward more private spiritual technologies. It also came to function like a state religion during the first half of the Tang dynasty (618–907), which would also produce the first great collection of Daoist texts, now known as the Daoist canon (Daozang). A collaboration between governmental and religious officials, this "Canon of the Way" helped define Daoist "orthodoxy" (right doctrine), which in turn helped define the proper practice of Daoist rituals.

The Highest Clarity movement is closely associated with Tao Hongjing (456–536), an inventor, author, and Renaissance man whose expertise in painting, calligraphy, pharmacology, and astronomy has led some to liken him to Leonardo da Vinci. But this movement traced its own origins to earlier, fourth-century revelations channeled via a spirit medium named Yang Xi to an aristocratic family who lived near Mount Mao. The sources of these revelations were said to be Perfected Persons from the Highest Clarity heaven who were gracious enough to share their techniques for spirit travel, inner visualization, and alchemy. One of these Perfected Persons was Wei Huacun, a woman who had been a libationer before her death in 334.

Highest Clarity Daoists internalized the Daoist tradition in two ways. First, they taught practitioners to visualize gods that reside inside the human body. This development would pave the way for later efforts to move the site of alchemy into the human body. One technique was to "return to the embryo" in meditation, relive one's time in the womb, and then experience a rebirth to the Primordial Father and the Mysterious Mother. In a second interiorization, Highest Clarity Daoists reconceived of earlier sexual rites, which had been controversial among the Celestial Masters, by characterizing what had been actual physical encounters between male and female practitioners merely as imagined spiritual unions with heavenly beings.

The Highest Clarity movement also distinguished itself from the Celestial Masters by viewing sickness as physiological. Therefore, it healed not through confessions and petitions but through massage and herbs—techniques borrowed from what is now referred to as traditional Chinese medicine. Highest Clarity Daoists also reimagined immortality. Previously, many Daoists were convinced that immortals simply did not die. The Highest Clarity movement conceived of a new path—"regeneration to immortality"—that ran through death and the underworld. According to this new view, which was influenced by Buddhist ideas of reincarnation, practitioners would maneuver after death through a vast afterlife bureaucracy and then either ascend to a post in a celestial bureaucracy or be reborn as immortals.

Another southern development at this time was the Numinous Treasure (Lingbao) movement, which combined Celestial Masters petitioning with Highest Clarity inner visualization. This movement also borrowed heavily from Buddhism. Its scriptures, said to be revealed between 397 and 402, drew heavily on Buddhist teachings. As with Buddhist *sutras*, their recitation was believed to confer merit not only to an individual or a community but also to the entire world.

As the ways of being a Daoist expanded, so did Daoist scriptures. In the fifth century, Daoists organized their sacred texts by dividing them into three parts. Drawing on widespread lore about revelations in caves, this system classified new Daoist texts into "Three Caverns," each of which corresponded to a heaven and a god. Highest Clarity was at the top, followed by Numinous Treasure and then by texts from another tradition known as the Three Sovereigns (Sanhuang).

Daoism versus Buddhism

Organized Daoism took shape around the time Buddhism arrived in China, and for roughly the next millennium these two traditions acted like sibling rivals, cooperating at times, competing fiercely at others, and all the while borrowing unapologetically from one another. Each tradition also attempted to swallow the other, as Daoists interpreted the Buddha as an avatar of Laozi and Buddhists interpreted Laozi as a buddha. Meanwhile, the prospects of Daoists and Buddhists alike rose and fell on the waves of empire. When rulers favored Confucianism or Buddhism, Daoism suffered. When the "Three Teachings, one China" motto was in vogue, Daoism did better. There were also times when Daoism enjoyed imperial favor.

The national status of Daoism was first ratified in 442 when Emperor Taiwu was initiated into the Celestial Masters tradition. Not until the Tang dynasty of the seventh through tenth centuries did Daoism become (for a time) the official religion of China. Daoism ascended in the Tang thanks to the imperial Li family, which claimed bloodlines going back to Laozi. This dynasty canonized Laozi as Sovereign Emperor of Mystery and

The Yuanxuan Daoist Temple in Guangzhou, China, is dedicated to Laozi and features this giant statue of him at its entryway.

Under the Song dynasty emperor Huizong, Daoism experienced a revival. Huizong, who called himself the Lord of the Dao, was a poet, musician, calligrapher, and painter, in addition to the Song's eighth imperial leader.

Primordiality. It built temples dedicated to him. It declared his birthday a national holiday and added the Daodejing to the reading list for the civil service examinations that served as the gateway to government jobs. Tang emperors, in turn, underwent Daoist initiations and sought immortality via external alchemy. After a brief period of Buddhist patronage under Empress Wu Zetian at the end of the seventh century and the start of the eighth, Daoism returned to favor, thanks especially to Emperor Xuanzong (685–762), who composed commentaries on the Daodejing, oversaw the production of the first Daoist canon, and ordered the construction of temples to Laozi on five of China's most sacred mountains.

The collapse of the Tang gave way to the period of the Five Dynasties and the Ten Kingdoms (907–960), which splintered power across China into smaller independent states. However, many of the rulers of these states followed the Tang example of patronizing Daoism in exchange for legitimation of their rule.

The Way of Complete Perfection and Modern Daoism

The reunification of China by the Song dynasty (960–1279) produced rapid changes akin to those that occurred in Europe during the Renaissance and Reformation. A mercantile economy, the proliferation of printing, an explosion of religious texts, and increasing literacy all characterized this period, which also inaugurated modern Daoism. Under the Song dynasty, religious competition swelled among Daoists and between Daoists, Buddhists, and practioners of local religions. New interpretations of Daoism emerged, and with them came new institutions, including monasteries. Increasingly, Daoists emphasized ritual, and especially rituals of exorcizing demons. Earlier in Daoist history, innovations were often supported by revelations from Laozi or Lord Lao. Now Zhang Daoling—depicted as an exorcist, riding a tiger and wielding a sword—was often an inspiration. This was also the golden age of internal alchemy, which began to take shape in the Highest Clarity movement but boomed in the eleventh and twelfth centuries.

Daoism made a comeback in the Song under Emperor Huizong (1082–1135), who wrote Daoist songs, painted Daoist subjects, and called himself Lord of the Dao. Daoist priests taught him alchemical techniques, and he regularly performed Daoist rituals. For a time, he banned Buddhism, and he facilitated the production of the first Daoist canon. Although his bureaucracy remained Confucian, he reigned during a period in the early twelfth century that many scholars now regard as the heyday of Daoism.

The most important new Daoist movement in this period was the Way of Complete Perfection (Quanzhen), which is now the dominant form of monastic Daoism in China and one of Daoism's two most important branches. This "ascetic, eremitic, alchemical and mystical movement," as Daoist scholar Louis Komjathy summarizes it, was established in the twelfth century by **Wang Zhe** (1113–1170), a man variously described as a visionary, renunciant, poet, and lunatic.[20] Complete Perfection Daoism spread through the efforts of his seven disciples and five lay associations, in part because its beautiful literature and compelling stories captured both elite support and the popular imagination. Unlike the Celestial Masters, who emphasized ritual, this monastic movement focused on religion's experiential dimension.

Born to wealth not far from Xian in modern-day Shaanxi province, Wang Zhe was just a boy when the Jurchen Jin dynasty took over the Song capital of Kaifeng. Nonetheless, he received a classical education and worked in the military before taking up drinking

Wang Zhe (1113–1170)
founder of the Complete Perfection movement and one of its patriarchs

full time. The defining moment in his life is said to have come in 1159, when he walked into a tavern in his mid-forties and stumbled upon some Daoist immortals, who initiated him into the secrets of internal alchemy. The next year he encountered another immortal, who asked him, "Why don't you immediately abandon the ocean of the mundane?"[21]

It took him a year, but in 1161 Wang Zhe did just that, abandoning his family for life as a recluse. Now known as Wang Chongyang, he dug a grave and lived in it for three years, composing poetry, disciplining his body, and practicing internal alchemy. "Here Rests Lunatic Wang," read a sign above his home away from home, which he called the "Tomb of the Living Dead."

After abandoning this tomb for a thatched hut, Wang began his life as a teacher in 1167 when, at the age of fifty-four, he set his hut on fire and danced while it burned to the ground. After wandering a thousand miles east to the Shandong peninsula, he took on followers. He instructed them to read across the Three Teachings of Confucianism, Buddhism, and Daoism. He taught renunciation and asceticism, including abstinence from the Four Hindrances: alcohol, sex, wealth, and anger. He also warned against excessive talking and sleeping. His most enthusiastic disciples mortified their bodies in imitation of their teacher. One is said to have lived silent and motionless for six years under a bridge. Another made a cave his home, spending his nights for nine years standing on one foot in order to prevent himself from falling asleep.

In Shandong, a wealthy businessman named Ma Yu offered Wang land on his considerable estate to build a new hut, which he named Complete Perfection—a term he also gave to his religious community. Eventually, Ma Yu became a disciple, but because Wang's way included celibacy he had to separate from his wife, Sun Buer, who became a disciple as well.

Wang Zhe died while traveling in 1170. His disciples took him back to the place where he had razed his hut and buried his corpse there. Today, the founding temple of the Complete Perfection movement marks that spot. Among Wang's many disciples, his followers elevated seven, now known as the Seven Perfected, including his successor Ma Yu and Sun Buer. Today, these disciples are enshrined in Chinese memory thanks to *Seven Daoist Masters*, a folktale that celebrates the lives (and different Daos) of these immortal exemplars.

Two decades after Wang Zhe's death, in 1190, the Complete Perfection order was officially recognized by the Jin dynasty. It got an even bigger boost when the Mongolian warlord Chinggis Khan (aka Genghis Khan), who was on the cusp of extending his empire deep into northern China, summoned Wang's disciple Qiu Chuji to meet him. It was a long journey, but in 1222 Qiu made it to Khan's court. For his efforts, he was rewarded with tax-exempt status for his movement plus a job of his own: overseeing all religious activity under the Mongols.

Like Neo-Confucianism and Chan Buddhism (called Zen in Japan), Complete Perfection is an experiential path. Its followers seek to achieve immortality via internal alchemy

Four Complete Perfection priests stand outside of the White Cloud Temple in Beijing, China, in 1950. This temple now serves as the headquarters of the Chinese Taoist Association.

Sun Buer (1119–1182)

If you walk into a Daoist monastery in China today, you will likely see female and male masters, thanks in part to a twelfth-century woman named Sun Buer, the only woman among the Seven Perfected in the Complete Perfection tradition. Sun Buer was born in Shandong to a landowning family of scholars and received a classical education. As with other immortals, pious stories of her life are shot through with uncanny events. According to one, seven cranes (Daoist symbols of immortality) visited her in a dream and, when one entered her bosom, she knew intuitively that she was with child. When her child grew up, she married Ma Yu, with whom she had three sons. After meeting the Complete Perfection founder Wang Zhe in 1167, she and her husband became his disciples. When he instructed them to swear off family life in order to pursue the rigors of his path, Ma Yu complied. Sun was reluctant to take on an ascetic life.

Here the stories diverge, but they agree that tensions—with her husband, with her teacher, and within herself—abounded in Sun's life. According to one version of a story in which Wang Zhe spent a hundred days alone in his hut on Ma's property, it was Sun who locked him in. A more disturbing story tells of Wang bursting intoxicated into Sun's home and lying down on her bed. Agitated, she raced off to inform her husband of this outrage, only to be told that he had been talking to Wang in the marketplace just minutes earlier.

One year after Ma left his wife and family, Sun became a renouncer, too. She meditated. She achieved complete perfection. She then set herself up in a hermitage of other female recluses. In 1182, on a day and a time of her choosing, she sat down in the lotus position amid her disciples, recited a poem, and passed from death to immortality. Far off in Shandong, Ma Yu glanced up and saw her ascending on a multicolored cloud. "She looked on him and smiled," and he responded "by tearing off his clothes and dancing in celebration of her accomplishment."[a]

Though joined even at death to her former husband and the Seven Perfected, Sun Buer has enjoyed a long afterlife as an immortal and a divinity of her own. In the Yuan dynasty of the thirteenth and fourteenth centuries, she was honored as Primordial Goddess. She may also have helped pave the way for a new form of alchemy, "female alchemy," which seeks to transform menstrual blood into qi (rather than employing sperm as in more traditional inner alchemy). Today, Sun Buer is remembered, in the words of Louis Komjathy, not only as an alchemist but also as "wife, mother, ascetic, hermit, teacher, immortal, and goddess."

and, through meditation, to tame "the apelike mind and the horselike will."[22] Complete Perfection began with hermits like Wang Zhe who lived alone and in isolation, often on mountains. By the thirteenth century it had become monastic, and by 1300 there were four thousand Complete Perfection sites in China and some twenty thousand monastics (about a third of them nuns).

Another significant development during the Song dynasty was the consolidation of various Celestial Masters movements into what is now called Orthodox Unity (Zhengyi). In 1239, Emperor Lizong of the Southern Song declared the thirty-fifth Celestial Master, living on Dragon Tiger Mountain in Jiangxi province, to be overseer of a newly united Daoist tradition to be called by this name. In 1304, the Yuan dynasty that was established when the Mongols defeated the Southern Song declared the thirty-eighth Celestial Master to be the Orthodox Unity Lord in the lineage of Zhang Daoling. Since that time, the Northern and Southern Celestial Masters and the Highest Clarity and Numinous Treasure schools have been largely united under the banner of Orthodox Unity. Sometimes referred to as "shrine Daoism" to distinguish it from the monastic Daoism of Complete Perfection, Orthodox Unity has taken up the mantle of the Celestial Masters in championing a tradition of married priests that emphasizes rituals (and especially rituals of exorcism) to benefit and protect local communities.

The Ming, the Qing, and Dragon Gate Daoism

Modern Daoism continued to change over the seven centuries that spanned the last two Chinese dynasties: indigenous rule under the Ming dynasty (1368–1644) and foreign Manchu rule under the Qing dynasty (1644–1911). It also saw the entry of colonial powers into China, with the opening of U.S. trade in 1784 and after the arrival of the British, Germans, and French following the Opium War (1839–1842) forced China to open to European merchants.

Ming and Qing rulers worked hard to keep the peace by harmonizing the Three Teachings. One strategy was to enforce a religious division of labor in which Confucianism maintained social harmony through moral values while Buddhism and Daoism cultivated inner harmony through meditation and bodily exercises, respectively. During this time, Daoists were forced to choose between two state-approved movements—Orthodox Unity and Complete Perfection—that continue to dominate Daoism today. But emperors also played favorites: Ming rulers preferred Orthodox Unity, and Qing rulers favored Complete Perfection. Meanwhile, simplified and popularized forms of inner alchemy emerged as the clear focus of Daoist belief and practice.

This part of Daoist history is typically told as a tale of decline. The real story is more complicated. In a policy one scholar has referred to as "support and control," Daoist institutions were heavily regulated by government agencies, but Daoism also benefited from imperial support.[23] The popular god Zhenwu ("Perfect Warrior"), adopted by Daoists, saw his star rise in the Ming dynasty under the Yongle Emperor, who credited this Perfect Warrior with his own military success. When the Yongle Emperor moved to the Forbidden City in Beijing in 1421, he installed an image of the Perfect Warrior there. He also ordered his troops to renovate and expand the Perfect Warrior temple complex on Mount Wudang, turning that mountain, which is now the international epicenter for martial arts, into a major Daoist center. Also during the Ming dynasty, a massive Daoist canon was completed in 1455 and then added to in 1607.

This combination of support and control had the unintended effect of bolstering lay associations of non-monks and non-nuns. In addition to elevating local gods, these associations spread popular religious practices such as spirit communication via techniques such as automatic writing. In this practice, which would surface in a different form in nineteenth-century American spiritualism, the medium would enter a trance and become possessed by the spirit of a deity. This deity would then employ the body of the medium to communicate by writing (in this case, characters drawn in a tray of sand).

Participants in these increasingly popular lay associations also refurbished temples devoted to their favorite folk immortals and served as eager audiences for Daoist folktales, including *Seven Daoist Masters*, which first appeared in the Ming dynasty but is still in print today. In the process, they simplified some of Daoism's more esoteric teachings and practices even as they integrated them into Chinese folkways.

The Ming also witnessed a feminization of Daoism. Daoists had for centuries been worshiping the Queen Mother of the West and other goddesses, and men and women had been living side-by-side in Daoist monasteries. In the new lay associations, women played much greater roles. As the China scholar Kristofer Schipper has observed, during the

Under China's Ming dynasty, worship of female deities proliferated. This fifteenth-century bronze statue commemorates Bixia Yuanjun, or the Sovereign of the Clouds of Dawn.

Ming, "women's religion became at last truly emancipated." Worship of female gods and immortals spread rapidly—from the Sovereign of the Clouds of Dawn in northern China to the repurposed Buddhist bodhisattva Guanyin in central China to coastal goddesses in southern China, including the fisherman's daughter Mazu.[24]

China's last imperial dynasty era was the Manchu Qing dynasty, which saw further expansion of the state and increasing control over religious activity. Monasteries remained in many respects captives of government officials, but outside the not-so-all-seeing eyes of the state, lay movements flourished. Toward the end of the Qing, new martial arts such as *taiji quan* proliferated. Known in the West as tai chi, this meditative movement practice consisted of soft, flowing movements of the arms and legs intended to circulate qi through the body.

The key development for Daoism in the Qing was the rapid rise of a monastic movement, the Dragon Gate (*Longmen*) lineage, which since the seventeenth century has been China's main branch of the Complete Perfection school. Dragon Gate Daoists synthesized various internal alchemy traditions. They emphasized asceticism and monastic discipline. They also insisted on balancing the training of body and mind, on the theory that only when both are strong and stable can practitioners advance to the inner alchemical work.

Associated with Wang Zhe's disciple Qiu Chuji, this movement took its name from the Dragon Gate Grotto (*Longmen dong*) in Shaanxi province, where Qiu is said to have practiced for many years. It actually originated earlier, in southeastern China in the Ming dynasty, but it was first institutionalized with monasteries and a proper lineage in the Qing. "Carefully crafted to pass government muster," according to one scholar, it rose to prominence in part because of its leaders' decision to combine Complete Perfection precepts with the Neo-Confucian morality popular among Qing rulers.[25]

Daoism's Dragon Gate (*Longmen*) lineage emerged during the Qing dynasty, taking its name from the Dragon Gate Grotto in Henan, China. These caves, used by monks for meditation, contain thousands of statues of the Buddha and his disciples.

The Robe of the Dao

Unlike Roman Catholic priests with their clerical collars, Orthodox Unity priests are hard to pick out in a crowd because of their preference for ordinary Western clothing. Only when performing rituals do they wear special vestments. By contrast, Complete Perfection monks and nuns wear their identities on their sleeves. In fact, they wear them on their entire bodies, in the form of a plain, dark blue or black garment known as the "robe of the Dao." Typically made of cotton or hemp, this oversized robe features extra-wide "cloud sleeves" that overflow the hands, evoking the free-flowing and larger-than-life existence of immortals who have attained the Dao.

This robe can fall all the way to the ankles, or it can stop just above the knees. Under it, monks and nuns wear either dark or white pants. If the robe is short, they might wear tall white socks. The footwear of choice is a pair of comfortable flat "cloud shoes," again black or dark blue, made of cloth and soled with rubber. In this outfit, Daoist monastics are said to feel free to move at ease through their day-to-day lives, whether they are sitting and meditating or wandering up into cloud-topped mountains.

Complete Perfection monks and nuns let their hair grow long and wind it up tight into a topknot secured by a wooden hairpin. Their caps, also black or dark blue, vary from monastery to monastery but feature a hole that allows the topknot to poke through. One popular model, the Hat of Primal Chaos, features a flat top and wide brim encircling the forehead.

Although it is not unusual to see Complete Perfection monastics sporting white garments to ease their way through scorching summers, the black or dark blue robe carries considerable significance. Ancient Chinese thinkers divided the natural world into five elements or phases: wood, fire, earth, metal, and water. Black and dark blue signals the wood phase, which is also associated with birth, growth, the east, and spring. But most important, these colors are associated with darkness and mystery, in this case the darkness and mystery of the ineffable Dao itself. To wear this robe is to associate with the Dao. It is also literally to clothe oneself in what one scholar has described as "the colorless color of the Dao."[a]

Given these associations, it should not be surprising that Complete Perfection monastics treat these garments with respect. They typically have two sets of clothing, and after they clean the one they are not using, they fold it up and tuck it away with care. When it wears out and grows old, they reverently burn it.

This Dragon Gate lineage ensured its place in Chinese society thanks to a former wandering monk named Wang Changyue (d. 1680), who served as abbot of White Cloud Temple in Beijing for nearly a quarter of a century beginning in 1656. Wang centralized ordinations at White Cloud, transforming Dragon Gate into the gatekeeper for monastic Daoism and securing its place as the dominant form of Daoism on the mainland. Today, the White Cloud Temple houses the only surviving copy of the 1445 Daoist canon. It is also the headquarters of the Chinese Daoist Association and the Dragon Gate lineage. Many Daoist pilgrimage destinations in China are run by Dragon Gate masters. Masters Zhang Mingxin and Tang Chengqing of Green City Mountain both have Dragon Gate lineages. The Lookout Tower Monastery outside of Xian is also a Dragon Gate site.

Among the self-cultivation practices popularized under the Qing was female alchemy (nüdan), which, as its name implies, was designed to help women achieve immortality. This practice aimed to "behead the red dragon" by avoiding menstruation. But it tried to do more than simply preserve vital bodily fluids. Whereas internal alchemy for men aimed to transform semen into qi, female alchemy aimed to do the same for menstrual blood. Techniques for this transformation included "breathing exercises, internal visualizations, self-massage, mental concentration, and the suppression of emotions." The ultimate goal was to help women revert to the primordial state of union with the Dao. As the Daoist scholar Elena Valussi has observed, texts in this tradition asked intriguing questions about the differences and similarities between men and women and the physical and ritual transformation of women into men. "The Dao does not differentiate between men and women. Why do they have differences (in practice?)"[26]

Daoism after Empire

For roughly two millennia, the fortunes of Daoists were hitched to the fortunes of empires, as various Daoist groups fell into and out of dynastic favor. In 1912, that imperial system came to an end. The period that followed—under Nationalists and then Communists—was disastrous for Daoists, who suffered under regimes that viewed religion as ancient nonsense, a barrier that needed to be blown up for China to emerge as a global power in the modern world.

In 1911, Nationalists revolted against the Qing dynasty. One year later they forged the Republic of China. Mindful of their country's long history of political patronage of religion, Orthodox Unity and Complete Perfection Daoists organized official associations promising loyalty to the new government as well as various reforms. However, Nationalists had come to power promising to modernize China by westernizing it, and to them that meant siding with science against "superstition." They seized Daoist temples, turning some into schools and others into government offices. In an effort to curry government favor, Daoists worked hard to remake themselves in the image of a proper "world religion," which at the time meant subtracting anything that might look like superstition, emphasizing the philosophy of Laozi over ritual objects, and adding Christian elements such as "an identifiable clergy, a church as the location of its practice, and a set canon of sacred scriptures articulating its belief system."[27] In this contest to become a proper religion, Complete Perfection Daoists came out ahead by marketing Daoism as China's oldest homegrown religion.

Things got worse after World War II ended in 1945 and the People's Republic of China (PRC) emerged in 1949. One of the aftereffects of World War II had been a civil war in China between the Nationalists in power and their Communist rivals. When the Communists triumphed in 1949 under the leadership of Mao Zedong (1893–1976), the Nationalists fled to Taiwan, which under the terms of surrender that had ended World War II had been transferred from the Japanese to the Nationalists. On the mainland, the PRC then brutally suppressed religion as illusion, an agent of oppression, an obstacle to progress, and a relic of the old feudal order of lords and peasants. According to Mao's new Communist dogma, which saw religion as "the opium of the people," in Karl Marx's words, monasteries were dangerously dreamy escapes from the real world of class conflict, scriptures were repositories of ancient foolishness, and the only coming utopia was a purely secular state in which religion had withered away.[28] In response to this persecution, Orthodox Unity Daoists fled, establishing their de facto headquarters in Taiwan's capital of Taipei under the direction of the 63rd Celestial Master. Complete Perfection Daoists stayed on the mainland, casting their lot with the new Communist government.

The PRC did recognize five religions—Protestantism, Catholicism, Buddhism, Daoism, and Islam—but their activities were strictly controlled through official religious associations, including the Chinese Taoist Association, which was established in 1957. The

PRC did not stop at control, however. It closed down religious organizations. It attacked temples, churches, and mosques. It burned books, smashed icons, and forced monks and nuns to return to secular life.

During the Cultural Revolution (1966–1976), the so-called Red Guards tracked down and destroyed what had been desecrated before. In the process, China came to resemble France immediately following the French Revolution, when a widespread "de-Christianization" campaign seized church property, exiled priests, and otherwise replaced Roman Catholicism with its own secular Cult of Reason. This time it was Communism that was crushing religion and installing itself as a new secular faith.

Things began to improve for religious folks after Mao's death in 1976 and particularly after his successor, Deng Xiaoping (1904–1997), launched a series of economic reforms in 1978. One year later, the ban on religion was lifted, and churches, mosques, and temples started to reopen. In 1989, the Dragon Gate ordination ceremonies that the Nationalists had shut down resumed at White Cloud Temple in Beijing. In 1995, Orthodox Unity resumed ceremonies at Dragon Tiger Mountain.

Much attention has been paid to a state-sponsored Confucian revival in twenty-first-century China, but recent decades have also seen a revival of Daoism, another indigenous antidote to imported Marxism. Daoism continues to be strictly controlled in China. Daoist activities are run through the Chinese Taoist Association. Daoist temples and monasteries are owned by the state. Monastics are paid by the state. Daoism has benefited, however, from Communist Party efforts to stimulate tourism by restoring temples and monasteries and promoting pilgrimages to them.

Thanks to support from China's Bureau of Tourism, there are now massive Laozi statues across the country, including at the Lookout Tower Monastery outside Xian. Though denounced by some as spiritual and aesthetic monstrosities, these statues draw tourists

Located near Qingdao on the East China Sea, Mount Lao includes a monastery for Daoism's Complete Perfection school. The approach to the Laozi statue on the site contains hundreds of cloth banners, which together contain the entire Daodejing.

who come from afar for the privilege of having Laozi photobomb their selfies. But pious pilgrims come, too. While some visitors race up hundreds of stairs at Mount Lao (Laoshan) in China's eastern Shandong province in order to take a quick photo at the base of a huge bronze statue of Laozi, others go slowly. On a recent afternoon, a group of a few dozen proceeded deliberately up the steps, quietly reciting the Daodejing as they went. Each would take one step and then lie down on the stone stairs in a full-body prostration, then get up and take one step more.

DAOISM IN THE UNITED STATES

Daoist ideas arrived in the United States later and with less force than Confucian, Buddhist, and Hindu ideas. Transcendentalists and Theosophists, two early groups that promoted Asian religions as alternatives to Christianity, were relatively uninterested in what we now call Daoism. Some Americans read pioneering English-language translations of the Daodejing by the Scottish Protestant missionary John Chambers (1868) and by James Legge (1891), another Scottish Protestant missionary who worked alongside Max Muller to produce the *Sacred Books of the East* series. No Daoists appeared at the World's Parliament of Religions in Chicago in 1893, but Daoism did, via an anonymous paper. Though awarded a prize, this strange paper interpreted Daoism through a Protestant lens and largely in a negative light—as a decline from "the true learning of the worthies . . . of the past" into a magical and superstitious "genii-religion." Alas, the unnamed author lamented, "Taoists only practice charms, read prayers, play on stringed or reed instruments, and select famous mountains to rest in." The "fundamental doctrines" of real Daoism had "utterly disappeared."[29]

Daoism worked its way onto the radar of American intellectuals after the Chicago-based German American author and editor Paul Carus (who had attended the World's Parliament) published *Lao-Tze's Tao-Teh-King* through his Open Court Publishing Company in 1898. Dwight Goddard's *The Buddhist Bible* (1932), which launched the Beat Generation writer Jack Kerouac on his own Buddhist pilgrimage after he picked it up in a library in 1954, included discussion of the Daoist tradition. But Goddard lamented how Laozi's visionary philosophy had been "buried under the burden of self-induced trance and vision and revelation as a guide for the attainment of success and good luck."[30]

Daoist ideas were also in play in the 1970s television series *Kung Fu* and in blockbuster films such as *The Karate Kid* (1984) and *Crouching Tiger, Hidden Dragon* (2000). Some have even argued that *Mary Poppins* is a Daoist movie, starring an immortal who descends from on high to open the film and ascends at the end to complete it. It takes no arguing at all to make the same point about the Star Wars series with its Jedi masters and their admonitions to "use the force." Nor is there doubt about a 1990 television episode of *The Simpsons*, in which Lisa helps her brother, Bart, improve his mini-golf skills by filling him up with a mocktail of Zen and Daoist wisdom. "Embrace nothingness, become like an uncarved stone," says this forever young eight-year-old sage. "The most important book of all [is] the Tao Te Ching by Lao-tzu."[31]

In recent decades, Daoism has moved into American popular culture through books that popularize this tradition even as they reimagine (or, according to some critics, bastardize) it. This genre includes bestsellers such as Fritjof Capra's *The Tao of Physics* and a seemingly endless catalog of similar titles for readers of all tastes. For sports lovers, there is *The Tao of the Jump Shot*, plus additional tomes on the Tao of surfing, golf, baseball, chess, and poker. For movie lovers, there is *The Dao of the Dude* (about the cult hero in the film *The Big Lebowski*). There are biographical projects on the Taos of Bill Murray, Muhammad Ali, Warren Buffett, and Willie Nelson. More religious options include *The Tao of Islam*, *The Tao of Zen*, *The Tao of Jesus*, and a book on the Jewish mystic Martin Buber called *I and Tao*. One popular subgenre focuses on household pets—from *The Tao of Meow* to *The Tao of Bow Wow*. Other "Tao of" titles cover dating, beauty, nutrition, leadership, management, Twitter, motherhood, womanhood, architecture, travel, psychology, happiness, stress, massage, love, sex, and war.

Adherents and Sympathizers

But what about actual American Daoists? To answer that question, it is useful to follow the religious studies scholar Thomas Tweed in distinguishing between "adherents" with a relatively high level of commitment and "sympathizers" who engage in Daoist practices or read Daoist books without joining a Daoist community or even thinking of themselves as Daoists.

The number of Daoist adherents in the United States is low, likely in the tens of thousands. If you factor in sympathizers who view their tai chi practice as Daoist or turn to the Daodejing for inspiration, however, that figure is certainly in the millions. In fact, the most important distribution centers for Daoist ideas and practices in the United States are doubtless the thousands of martial arts schools scattered across the nation. Scholars of Daoism observe that concepts such as qi and practices such as tai chi are generically Chinese rather than specifically Daoist. Yet for many Americans, these concepts and practices are gateways into Daoism.

It is also useful to distinguish between birthright Daoists, usually Chinese or Chinese Americans who were born into the religion, and convert Daoists, usually European Americans who switched to it as adults. Birthright Daoists are more likely to be interested in the communal part of their tradition, including its rituals. Convert Daoists are more likely to be ignorant or hostile to those rituals while focusing inward on self-cultivation.

The story of birthright Daoists in the United States begins with Chinese laborers who immigrated after the discovery of gold in 1848 in California. The 1860 Census found 34,933 Chinese immigrants living in the United States, and that figure rose sharply after the construction of the Transcontinental Railroad began in 1863. Unlike many other immigrant groups, the Chinese did not bring religious professionals with them, so religious work fell largely to local mutual aid associations referred to as "companies." The first Chinese temple in the United States was built in San Francisco's Chinatown in 1853 by the Sze Yap Company. Similar temples, widely described as "joss houses" (from *deus*, the Portuguese word for god), mixed elements of the Three Teachings with Chinese popular religion, and before the century was over there were about four hundred of them in western states.

The Chinese Exclusion Act of 1882 severely restricted but did not entirely stop Chinese immigration. A few immigrants arrived around the time of the Communist victory in China in 1949, either directly from the mainland or via Taiwan and Hong Kong. Share Lew (1918–2012), the first Daoist priest in the United States, spent time in China as a wandering ascetic and a Daoist monk before fleeing to San Francisco in 1948.

When Chinese miners came to the United States during the gold rush of the mid-1800s, they brought their gods with them. This altar is located in the oldest of those temples still standing today: the Weaverville Joss House in Weaverville, California.

Also among these early immigrants were martial arts instructors. One of the most celebrated was Da Liu, who moved to New York City in 1955 and began teaching a short form (about twenty minutes) of tai chi for busy Americans. Liu worked in the China section at the United Nations, so perhaps that is how he was able to immigrate. He taught at the UN's China Institute and New York City's Central YMCA, and by the early 1960s he had become a celebrity, profiled in *Black Belt* magazine and *Vogue* and attracting celebrity students such as the New York Yankees slugger Reggie Jackson. Da Liu explicitly identified as a Daoist. In a 1962 *New Yorker* profile, he said that tai chi was "invented by Taoist monks." This "consummate embodiment of softness and firmness, retreat and advance," he added, promoted health, youthfulness, and longevity.[32]

Though *Newsweek* called him the founder of tai chi in the United States, Da Liu had plenty of competition in that department. Sophia Delza was an American dancer who lived in Shanghai and taught modern dance there from 1948 until 1951. She also studied tai chi. When she returned to the United States, she started teaching it, including at the UN, Actors Studio, and Carnegie Hall. In 1954, she offered the first public performance of tai chi in the United States at the Museum of Modern Art. She also wrote what appears to be the first book published in the United States on the topic: *T'ai Chi Ch'uan: Body and Mind in Harmony* (1961).

Tai chi arrived much earlier on the West Coast, when the Chinese Consolidated Benevolent Association brought Choy Hok Peng from Hong Kong to San Francisco's Chinatown in 1939 to teach tai chi to Chinese Americans. Choy established a tai chi club in San Francisco—likely America's first—and during his travels around the United States he established two more, in New York City and Los Angeles, before returning to Hong Kong in 1947. A later arrival was Cheng Man-Ching (1902–1975), who came to New York City

The American modern dancer Sophia Delza demonstrates tai chi postures for the cover of her book, *T'ai Chi Ch'uan: Body and Mind in Harmony*. Delza played a significant role in introducing tai chi to the United States in the 1950s and 1960s.

via Taiwan in 1964. Though he set up shop in Chinatown, his school attracted European Americans who called their teacher "The Professor." Cheng's short form reduced the traditional 108 postures of tai chi to a more manageable 37 and in the process cut the time for the practice to just ten minutes.

More explicitly Daoist institutions started to proliferate in the 1970s. Two factors, one on the supply side and one on the demand side, were crucial. First, immigration legislation in 1965 resumed immigration from Asia, opening the door to Daoist teachers. Second, the emergence of the counterculture meant that there was a hungry audience for new spiritual teachings and techniques.

The Taoist Sanctuary, America's first official Daoist organization, was established in North Hollywood, California, in 1970 by Share Lew and an Anglo-Egyptian-Sudanese man named Khigh Dhiegh. This pioneering organization, now known as the Taoist Institute, offers martial arts instruction and classes on books such as the Daodejing and the Yijing (Book of Changes). Though Dhiegh was not from China—he was born Kenneth Dickerson in Spring Lake, New Jersey—he played an evil Chinese spy on the television show *Hawaii Five-0*. He may also have been America's first homegrown Daoist convert.

In 1976, Taoist Sanctuary members brought a man named Hua-Ching Ni from Taiwan to Los Angeles to teach them about traditional Chinese medicine. Ni opened The Shrine of the Eternal Breath of Tao in Malibu and an associated instructional institution called the College of Tao. He also maintained a shrine in his home dedicated to the Three Pure Ones. Later offshoots included the Union of Tao and Man acupuncture clinic, the Yo San University of Traditional Chinese Medicine, and the Universal Society of the Integral Way. The two key sources of Ni's authority are a medical lineage said to go back thirty-eight generations and a religious lineage said to run to seventy-five.

Not all Daoist institutions in the United States were run by immigrants, however. One European American who exerted a strong pull over American Daoism was Liu Ming, who was born Charles Belyea in Boston in 1947. In the mid-sixties, while still a teenager, he began studying meditation with various teachers before training for twelve years in a Tibetan Buddhist lineage. After his ordination as a Buddhist monk in Taiwan, he began to work with Daoist masters and was ordained in that tradition as well. Returning to the United States, he joined what had become an established circuit of seminars and retreats in California. In 1986 he founded Orthodox Daoism in America. Keenly interested in bringing Daoist monasticism to the United States, he developed a curriculum and began training monks. His organization is critical of Western efforts to reduce Daoism to the Daodejing or to self-cultivation only. Its newsletter describes Daoism as "a personal and collective religious practice, not merely a group of philosophical ideas or yogas." [33]

Perhaps the most successful Daoist group in the United States is the Healing Tao, an inner alchemy tradition that focuses on meditation and visualization. This group was founded by the well-traveled Mantak Chia (b. 1944), a Chinese man who was born in Thailand and studied Daoism in Hong Kong. In 1974, he arrived in New York City and opened the Taoist Esoteric Yoga Center (later the Healing Tao Center) in Chinatown. Trained in both Western and traditional Chinese medicine, he taught the scientific side of the Daoist tradition. Fame came to Chia with the publication of his *Taoist Secrets of Love: Cultivating Male Sexual Energy* (1984), which arrived as the "family values" of the conservative Reagan era were straining to put an end to the sexual experimentation of the counterculture. With the assistance of well-placed followers, Chia's empire expanded into a national and then international network of instructors and classes.

Chia's American operation, Healing Tao USA, is now run by Michael Winn. The curriculum taught by Chia's thousand-plus certified instructors includes "sexual cultivation," but the broader appeal is a "spiritual but not religious" approach, which Winn explained in an interview with College of Charleston professor Elijah Siegler:

> Daoism is taking a different form, not necessarily a religious form, than it is taking in China, with temples and uniforms, and the state religion and all that stuff, that's its history. In the West it's taking more of the form of personal belief and identification with the Dao and the structures of the Dao, kind of like getting back to early Daoism, before all that existed in China. [34]

Not all American Daoist groups cater to European Americans. One of the most venerable Chinese American Daoist organizations is an American outpost of the Hong Kong–based Ching Chung Taoist Association (CCTA). With Complete Perfection temples in Singapore, Australia, Vancouver, and San Francisco, this may be the world's largest nonmonastic Daoist organization. The story of this group's San Francisco community begins in Hong Kong in 1978 with a divination rite in which a medium possessed by the popular Daoist deity Lu Dongbin instructed the Hong Kong Ching Chung community to send an emissary to the United States to establish a temple there. The temple they later established in San Francisco is devoted to popular Complete Perfection figures, including founder Wang Zhe and his disciple Qiu Chuji. Foregoing the experiential focus of many European American Daoists, the CCTA is a classic example of "shrine Daoism." Here the emphasis is on the community rather than the individual, and on priestly rites rather than individual self-cultivation.

But Is It Daoism?

Some scholars claim that Daoism in the United States has almost nothing to do with Daoism in China. In fact, Elijah Siegler uses the term "American Daoism" to refer to what he sees as a new religious movement born in the United States in the 1970s and 1980s. This new American religion is, in his view, almost entirely divorced from Daoism in China. According to Siegler, it has eight characteristics:

1. It is nonexclusive and nondogmatic.
2. It recognizes Laozi as its founder and the Daodejing as its scripture.
3. It is not tied to any one place, China included.
4. It is "historically unreflective" and therefore disconnected from prior Daoist traditions.
5. It is unconcerned with scriptures (other than the Daodejing).
6. It is apolitical.
7. It is unconcerned with and critical of both social ethics and religious ritual.
8. It is nonsectarian and nondenominational.[35]

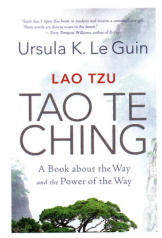

Science-fiction writer Ursula Le Guin's 1998 translation of the Daodejing has been both praised and criticized for attempting to turn this ancient text into something modern.

In other words, American Daoism is a "cafeteria tradition" where you go through the line and pick whatever you feel like eating that day. And the main entrée left behind on the warming trays is Daoist religion. Or, as Solala Towler boasts in *Embarking on the Way: A Guide to Western Taoism*: "There is nothing to join, no vows to take, no special naming, clothing style or diet to follow. It is strictly up to the individual to apply whatever aspect of the tradition he or she wishes."[36]

The story that animates American Daoists of this sort is an old one. In its simplest version, it follows the conventions of what novelist Kurt Vonnegut has called the "man in the hole" story: Things were just fine (the man was walking along) but then something bad happened (he fell in the hole) but then someone came along and made everything right (by rescuing him). In the case of Daoism (or so this story goes), things were going along fine as long as its original essence was understood to lie in the philosophical heights of the Daodejing. Then it fell in the hole of later religious Daoism, which muddied it up with all sorts of liturgies, rituals, and superstitions. American Daoists say they are now pulling Daoism out of that hole, cleaning it up, and returning it to its pristine purity.

Religious traditions are amorphous and shifting things, so religious studies scholars generally refuse to get into the business of patrolling the boundaries of any particular religious orthodoxy. But scholars do generally view as misguided any purported "return" to the Daodejing as the pristine source of Daoism. According to their criticisms, such revitalization efforts are by-products of Protestant anti-Catholic prejudices and colonial fantasies. Curiously, these critics offer their own "man in the hole" stories. In their narratives, the original pristine Daoism of Zhang Daoling and the Celestial Masters has fallen into the hole of American Daoism. It is the job of real Daoist scholars to pull it out of that hole, clean it up, and send it on its way. University of Georgia professor Russell Kirkland, after dismissing "the fatuous fluff" of popular books such as *The Tao of Pooh* and "the narcissistic new pseudo-translation" of the Daodejing by the science-fiction writer Ursula Le Guin, concludes that "what passes for 'Taoism'" in such books "has <u>nothing</u> to do with <u>real Taoism</u>." To think otherwise is to engage in "spiritual colonialism."[37] Taking Kirkland to his logical extreme, Terry Kleeman has said that "there are no Daoists in

America."[38] The real Daoists, from this perspective, are the religious Daoists, and the more religion the better.

In response to a query from the Daoism scholar Jonathan Herman, Le Guin admitted that she worried about "cheapening and trivializing Daoism" while she was writing her Daodejing adaptation. But the practice of translation is "inevitably transgressive," she wrote, and "compromise is also inevitable." There is no way that Daoist studies scholars can restrict the interpretation of popular Daoists texts to their library carrels and offices, she continued. The Daodejing and the Zhuangzi are, among other things, "great works of art." As such, all human beings (novelists included) have the right to try to make sense of their profundities as best as they can.[39]

LIVED DAOISM

All religious traditions are internally diverse and change over time, but Daoism is unusually multiform. Daoists have never settled on a single activity, such as the Mass in Roman Catholicism or daily prayer in Islam, that draws the entire community together. Individual Daoists have not felt constrained to employ any single practice. A typical practitioner might combine a dietary regimen with the observation of moral precepts, breathing exercises, meditation, calligraphy, wandering in the wilderness, and ingesting qi-rich energy. As a result, the everyday activities of Daoists differ from school to school, lineage to lineage, and person to person. While many Daoists seek the ultimate goal of flourishing (perhaps forever) by reverting to the Dao, others seek simply to act in greater harmony with the Dao and its rhythms—to live healthier and more energetic lives that embody such Daoist values as spontaneity and naturalness. Nonetheless, Daoist practices can be divided into two main types, each aimed at aligning with the Dao: individual practices of self-cultivation—such as meditation, internal alchemy, and "nourishing life" (*yang-sheng*)—and communal rituals such as offerings and festivals.

Meditation

Cross-culturally, scholars have observed at least three broad types of meditation: concentration, insight, and visualization. Meditators can concentrate on a single object, they can observe more broadly what is happening inside the practitioner or outside in the wider world, or they can bring gods or other objects of contemplation into their mind's eye. Daoist meditators engage in all three of these types in an effort to return to their original nature, before it deviated from the Dao.

There are many Daoist forms of concentration meditation, including "fasting the heart-mind," "sitting in forgetfulness," and "guarding the One." Today, the most popular is called "quiet sitting." All these techniques begin with an emptying of some sort. Practitioners seek to withdraw from the ordinary world of sight and sound. Then they empty the "heart-mind" (*xin*) of day-to-day thoughts, emotions, discriminations, and judgments, moving past distinctions between positive and negative, good and bad. Once the state of stillness that accompanies this nondualistic "empty mind" is achieved, the practitioner is open to mystical union with the Dao.

During insight meditation, which was adapted from Buddhist mindfulness techniques, practitioners might observe their breathing, following it in and out of their abdomen and

One popular form of Daoist meditation is "quiet sitting." This photograph from 2015 depicts Wang Zhixia at eighty-three years old sitting in meditation at Zhongnan Mountain in Baoji, China, where she lived in a hut for almost forty years with no electricity.

more specifically in and out of the still center point of their lower abdomen, just below the navel and in front of the spine. Another approach is to focus one's nonjudgmental awareness on the qi moving through one's organs.

Inner observations of this sort can shade over into visualization. According to broader Chinese ideas, the body is a microcosm of the cosmos, which is in turn a macrocosm of the body. As meditators visualize the inner workings of their bodies, including the deities residing in their organs, they are also visualizing the inner workings of the cosmos and the deities in the heavens above. Other forms of Daoist visualization include ecstatic journeys to faraway constellations and to parts of the body, which are variously described as halls, chambers, towers, courts, and palaces. During these journeys, adept meditators learn to imitate the rhythms of the sun and the moon. They absorb qi and light. They interact with gods and immortals and return anew.

One popular form of visualization locates the Three Pure Ones, the most popular gods in the Daoist pantheon, in the Big Dipper. Typically portrayed as old men, these deities are said to be the three primordial emanations of the Dao. During this visualization, practitioners conjure up the Three Pure Ones in their mind's eye. They then take a deep breath as these gods enter their mouth and then their organs. In this way, what has been visualized is actualized inside the body, as the Three Pure Ones take up residence inside the practitioner.

Internal Alchemy

Another technique for immortality and union with the Dao, internal alchemy, shares much with meditation and visualization. Internal alchemy became the leading self-cultivation technique during the Northern Song dynasty and remains so today. Underlying this practice is a theory of the self in which everyone is born with a fixed storehouse of vital essence called *jing*. We waste this energy in many ways, including sexual activity. As this jing runs down, we grow old. When it runs out, we die. Internal alchemy begins with basic conservation of energy strategies, including avoiding ejaculation in men ("subduing the white tiger"). But such conservation is not enough. Also needed is an alchemical process in which this bodily energy can be refined (like turning lead into gold) into a more ethereal qi energy, which can then be deployed to create inside the body an "immortal embryo" made of an even more ethereal form of spirit energy called *shen*. Through various techniques of qi circulation, this embryo then gestates inside the body for many years until it comes to consist entirely of pure yang. It is then ready to emerge out of the "heavenly gate" at the crown of the head as an immortal who has attained the Dao.

"Nourishing Life"

The term *yangsheng* ("nourishing life") encompasses a variety of body practices designed to cultivate health, vitality, and long life by preserving and circulating one's vital energies and by keeping the physical body active through various postures and movement sequences. Many of these are rooted in broader Chinese medicine concepts, but Daoists adopted and adapted them and according to the Daoist studies pioneer Isabelle Robinet they "remain a foundation of all Taoist practices" today.[40] Daoist studies scholar Thomas Michael, who finds hints of yangsheng in the Daodejing, isolates four key practices in this broad "program of physical cultivation: qi circulation . . . dietetics . . . sexual arts" and a form of calisthenics called *daoyin* ("to guide and pull").[41] The latter term refers to postures and movements that often imitate the postures and movement of animals. Contemporary qi circulation techniques include both tai chi and qigong.

Offerings

Daoists who practice self-cultivation techniques typically seek to reach their religious goals through strenuous self-effort. No god gives immortality to them as a gift. If they are able to revert to the Dao and win immortality, they will have done so through their own hard work. Not all Daoists are adept at self-cultivation, however. For many Daoists, the Way of the Way leads through communal rituals performed on their behalf by priestly officials.

Offerings are the most important Daoist rituals. These rites of renewal, not unlike the renewal of marriage vows, are meant to reaffirm and restore the relationship of a community with its gods. More broadly, offerings aim, in the words of James Miller, "to restore the world to the state of the primordial Dao in which heaven, earth and humanity flourished together in creative harmony."[42] The community making this offering might be as large as an empire or a nation-state. It might be as small as a village, family, or individual. Classically, the most elaborate of these offerings was the Grand Offering, addressed to thousands of deities with the intention of renewing cosmos and society and ensuring the peace and harmony of civilization. In 1993, a Grand Offering at the White Cloud Temple in Beijing brought together Orthodox Unity and Complete Perfection Daoists from China, Taiwan, and Hong Kong.

Grand Offerings can be performed in cycles that run anywhere from one to sixty years, but they are also done on an as-needed basis. They last from one day to several weeks and include public and private activities. After much preparation, an offering begins when a priest marks and consecrates the place where it will occur. A temporary altar is built, often in the area where a temple's grounds meet the surrounding city or village. Next the appropriate gods are invited, both in writing and orally. Neighboring communities might bring icons from their temples to the festivities. After the gods arrive, incense is offered. Additional offerings of candles, fresh flowers, fresh fruit, tea, and wine are made. Surrounding this ritual activity is a community festival that typically includes singing, dancing, elaborate costumes, and boisterous parades in which gods are marched through the streets in ceremonies intended not only to purify and protect the community but also to entertain.

On the night before the last day, ghosts of the dead are invited to attend the festivities, and lanterns are lit to lead the way. This final day focuses on Buddhist-inspired offerings intended both to alleviate the ghosts' suffering and to cajole them into leaving members of the community alone. Finally, the priest who invited the gods to attend thanks them for coming and asks them to leave. The temporary altars are struck like so many theater sets, and life goes back to a renewed normal.

The private portion of the offering takes place inside a temple. The door to the temple is closed and patrolled by guards. The only people allowed inside are priests and community elders. To prepare for these rituals, the statues of the gods are taken down and replaced with sacred scrolls. Priests read from these scrolls. They perform various hand gestures and liturgical dances. Accompanying these acts are meditations in which masters seek to align with the Dao individually much as the broader offering is intended to align

Daoist priests sacrifice to the kitchen god in Xian, China, in 2009. Offerings to this deity are undertaken as part of Chinese New Year celebrations.

BIRTH AND DEATH

Like Daoist holidays, Daoist birth ceremonies typically follow Chinese folk customs, beginning with prayers for the pregnant mother and child. But for Daoists, the most important birth ritual takes place when the baby is thirty days old. On this "full moon day," priests beseech the gods to protect and favor the newborn. Friends and family members offer the child gifts, often wrapped in red paper, as red symbolizes happiness. Parents offer gifts, such as red eggs, in return. This is also an important day for the mother, as it brings to an end thirty days of ritual confinement at home. She takes her first bath since giving birth, washes her hair for the first time, and reemerges into the ordinary world.

Like practitioners of Chinese popular religion, Daoists affirm that human beings have two kinds of souls: *hun* or "cloud" souls that are made of yang qi and are therefore more spiritual, and *po* or "white" souls that are made of yin qi and are therefore more material. Death separates these souls. The lighter yang souls ascend into the air, and the heavier yin souls descend into the ground. According to many Daoists, another hun soul takes a more circuitous route after death—through a vast celestial bureaucracy, where it is eventually reincarnated. Another *po* soul goes down into the underworld, where it is judged via institutions and processes that mimic those of ancient imperial courts.

After death, Daoists wash and dress the corpse and place it in a coffin. Attendants may adorn the clothes of the deceased with cranes, peaches, or other symbols of long life. They may place in the coffin items the deceased might use in the afterlife, including food, drink, and money. At an altar near the coffin, mourners light candles and burn incense. Dressed in simple mourning clothes—traditionally homespun sackcloth but nowadays more likely loose white garments—they may

the community with the Dao collectively, so that heaven, earth, and humanity can live together once again in harmony.

Holidays and Festivals

Many holidays celebrated by Daoists are generic Chinese holidays. Because the Chinese follow a combination of the lunar and solar calendars, the dates for these holidays move across the Western calendar. The Chinese New Year, the most important festival in China, usually falls in February. Family members exchange gifts and make offerings to their ancestors. Daoists put their own spin on this holiday by making offerings to the Three Pure Ones. Other Chinese holidays also celebrated by Daoists include the summer solstice, the longest day of the year, when yang energy is at its peak, and the winter solstice, the shortest day of the year, when yin energy is uppermost. Daoists also throw festivals for their major gods and immortals, including the Jade Emperor, Queen Mother of the West, Zhang Daoling, Lu Dongbin, and Lord Lao.

CONTEMPORARY CONTROVERSY: FALUN GONG

Like many other body exercises now widely associated with Daoism, qigong ("breath practice") has old roots in China (particularly in the yangsheng techniques for "nourishing life"), but qigong as we know it today surfaced in the 1950s. Combining breathing

also burn "Hell Bank Notes" and credit cards as well as elaborate paper creations of televisions, cars, and even houses, all intended to make the afterlives of the deceased easier. Traditionally, these rites took place at home. They are now often performed in temples.

Daoist death rites are a mixture of Confucian, Buddhist, and folk traditions with some singularly Daoist elements. In fact, it is not unusual for Buddhist priests to chant Daoist liturgies, and vice versa. These rites consume an odd number of days (even numbers are inauspicious), typically three, five, or seven, though now in more secularized urban areas they might take just half a day. To the accompaniment of drums and other musical instruments, priests labor to make a happy home for a hun soul in a wooden ancestral tablet, to safeguard mourners from hungry ghosts, to secure forgiveness for the dead, and to equip them for their afterlife journeys. It is possible for afterlife bureaucrats to be paid off or to look the other

way. It is also possible for them to make mistakes, sending good people to bad places or bad people to good places, as in the snafu that begins the television series *The Good Place*. In rituals that go back to the early Celestial Masters, Daoist priests may also draft and deliver documents regarding the deceased to underworld bureaucrats to make sure things go smoothly.

One place where Daoists diverge from Buddhists is their preference for burial over cremation. The placement of the coffin in the cemetery is often determined by feng shui principles, which are now used in home architecture and design but were originally intended to find sites for graves on hillsides. Mourning can conclude at the end of the death rites, but classically it extends to forty-nine days, in keeping with Buddhist beliefs that it takes that many days for the hun soul to be reborn. At the end of this period, mourners burn their clothes and return as best as they can to day-to-day life.

exercises, mental concentration, and body movements, this qi cultivation practice was initially promoted by the PRC as a form of traditional Chinese medicine. It was then banned as a feudal superstition, only to reappear in public parks in the 1970s. By the 1980s, China was undergoing a "qigong fever" that saw the proliferation of qigong teachers and organizations. According to official government data, those organizations boasted sixty million members in 1990.

The most controversial of these organizations is Falun Gong ("Practice of the Dharma Wheel"), an extraordinarily successful new religious movement that creatively combines Daoist and Buddhist influences. Falun Gong practice includes breathing, meditation, and slow exercise. It also has a very strong moral component. It emphasizes three virtues—"truthfulness, compassion, and forbearance"—and it insists that efforts to increase one's qi will not bear fruit unless practitioners also cultivate their inner moral nature. Practically speaking, this means avoiding alcohol, smoking, homosexuality, and extramarital sex.

Also known as Falun Dafa, Falun Gong was founded in 1992 by Li Hongzhi, a qigong practitioner who had studied under Daoist and Buddhist teachers. Operating outside the official oversight of the Chinese Taoist Association and the Buddhist Association of China, it exploded during the 1990s as a response to the spiritual vacuum created by the official atheism of the Communist regime. As its numbers swelled to as many as one hundred million members (mostly urban and older), the Chinese government grew wary, and coverage in official media became frosty and then hostile. On April 25, 1999, about ten thousand members gathered for a major protest just outside Beijing's Forbidden City—the largest since the 1989 Tiananmen Square uprising. Increasingly fearful of a Falun Gong membership that rivaled that of the CCP itself, the Chinese government banned the organization

Falun Gong members staged a peaceful protest before a United Nations vote on China's human rights record in Hong Kong in July 2011. Demonstrators read books, meditated, and stood in formations in order to draw attention to alleged governmental persecution of Falun Gong members.

on July 22, 1999, as "a cult" that, according to a spokesperson for the Chinese Embassy to the United States was "trying to spread superstition" and "disrupt social stability."[43] The Chinese government also arrested thousands of members of what it now saw as not only a cult but also a political movement. Falun Gong members responded by doubling down on their protests, accusing the Chinese government of censorship, torture, organ harvesting, and murder. According to one scholar, Falun Gong morphed over the course of a few decades from a form of therapeutic exercise into a spiritual movement and then into "a transnational political organization aimed at toppling the CCP."[44]

Falun Gong encapsulates many of the themes in the long story of Daoism in China and beyond: the interpenetration of Daoism and Buddhism, the inseparability of religion and politics, and the expansion of Daoism beyond its Chinese homeland. Today, Falun Gong continues to operate under the radar in China and worldwide, still directed by Li Hongzhi, who has lived in the United States since 1998. It is, according to many scholars, one of the fastest-growing new religious movements in the world.

QUESTIONS FOR DISCUSSION

1. What is the Dao? What are some ways that Daoists have historically tried to "revert to the Dao"?

2. What is the role of nature in Daoism? How do Daoists distinguish between what is natural and what is unnatural?

3. What does wuwei mean? Is it a mindset? A way of behaving? How do Daoists try to cultivate wuwei?

4. What do Daoists mean by "immortality"? What are some of the ways that different Daoists have attempted to achieve this goal?

5. What aspects of Daoist belief and practice have been adopted and adapted by contemporary Americans? What elements do Americans tend to ignore? What do you suppose accounts for this selectivity?

KEY TERMS

Celestial Masters (Tianshi), p. 412

Complete Perfection (Quanzhen), p. 399

Dao ("Way"), p. 396

Daodejing ("Scripture on the Way and Its Virtue"), p. 391

de, p. 410

external alchemy (waidan), p. 403

feng shui ("wind and water"), p. 400

Highest Clarity (Shangqing), p. 416

immortal (xian), p. 404

internal alchemy (neidan), p. 403

Laozi ("Old Master"), p. 391

libationer, p. 413

Lord Lao, p. 391

Orthodox Unity (Zhengyi), p. 399

qi, p. 396

qigong, p. 400

Queen Mother of the West, p. 407

registers, p. 397

tai chi (taiji quan), p. 400

Three Pure Ones (Sanqing), p. 406

Wang Zhe, p. 418

wuwei ("nonaction"), p. 410

yin and yang, p. 396

Zhang Daoling, p. 391

Zhuangzi ("Master Zhuang"), p. 411

FURTHER READING

Kleeman, Terry F. *Celestial Masters: History and Ritual in Early Daoist Communities.* Cambridge, MA: Harvard University Press, 2016.

Kohn, Livia. *Daoism and Chinese Culture.* Cambridge, MA: Three Pines Press, 2001.

Laozi. *The Daodejing of Laozi.* Translated by Philip J. Ivanhoe. Cambridge, MA: Hackett Publishing, 2003.

Mair, Victor H. *Wandering on the Way: Early Taoist Tales and Parables of Chuang Tzu.* Honolulu: University of Hawaii Press, 1998.

Miller, James. *Daoism: A Beginner's Guide.* London: OneWorld Publications, 2008.

Palmer, David A., and Elijah Siegler. *Dream Trippers: Global Daoism and the Predicament of Modern Spirituality.* Chicago: The University of Chicago Press, 2017.

The 1,600-foot tall Shiprock monolith, known to the Diné as "the Winged Rock," is part of the sacred Navajo landscape located in the volcanic fields of New Mexico.

10

Navajo Religion

THE WAY OF BEAUTY

It's mid-May and the last weekend of skiing at the Arizona Snowbowl north of Flagstaff, Arizona. The Snowbowl isn't as fancy as Colorado's Vail or Utah's Snowbird, but there's plenty of parking and it's sunny and in the high 40s with a clear view of the mountain-top. Everybody seems happy to get in a few last runs before the season ends. At the Agassiz Lodge, skiers and snowboarders who are taking a break from the action sit at picnic tables with chipped green paint. The mood is festive. A bearded guy is walking around in an Abominable Snowman costume. Rock music is playing over the loudspeakers. An American flag flies overhead.

When the Snowbowl opened for the season on November 18, 2018, the Save the Peaks Coalition, including members of the Navajo Nation (who refer to themselves as the Diné, or "The People") lined the road that winds up the mountain to protest snowmaking with reclaimed sewer water piped up from Flagstaff to the San Francisco Peaks. Along with environmentalists, who protested injuries to the mountain's ecology, Navajos and other indigenous nations objected to the defiling of their sacred mountain. On opening day, protesters gathered at the base of the mountain to pray. They drove halfway up and marched the rest of the way, chanting, "No desecration for recreation." Later, the Flagstaff-based Diné activist Klee Benally, who helped organize the protest, reflected on the bind he and other members of the Navajo Nation are in as they try to go about their daily lives in Flagstaff: "Every time we flush a toilet we are compelled to violate our religious freedom," he said.

Diné ("The People")
the Navajo people

Holy People (Diyin Dine'é)
superbeings who are the subjects of Navajo stories and the recipients of prayers and ceremonies

Diné Bikéyah
the Navajo homeland; set amid the four sacred mountains, also known as Navajo-land, as distinct from the legal boundaries of the Navajo reservation

inner form
wind-animated life force inside the outer form of a living thing. Ceremonies are addressed to the inner forms of Holy People, whose outer forms are no longer in this world.

At least thirteen indigenous nations regard the San Francisco Peaks as sacred. The Hopi believe that ancestral spirits known as *kachinas* live for half the year on this mountain, which they call "The Place of Snow on the Very Top." The Havasupai believe that life began here—that "the Peaks are the origin of the human race . . . [and] the point of their creation."[1] Some Apache believe that the mountain—"White Mountain Seated in the Direction of the Big Dipper"—is home to supernatural beings called the Gaan.

The **Diné** do not regard this mountain as an inanimate mass. Dook'o'oosliid, "Shining On Top," as they call it, is to them a living being. In Navajo creation stories, the first human beings emerged out of the earth in what is now the U.S. Southwest. One of their **Holy People (Diyin Dine'é)**, First Man, used soil he brought from one of the underworlds to form the four sacred mountains: Colorado's Blanca Peak (Sisnaajiní) in the east, New Mexico's Mount Taylor (Tsoodził) in the south, Arizona's San Francisco Peaks (Dook'o'oosliid) in the west, and Colorado's Hesperus Peak (Dibé Nitsaa) in the north. There are two other holy mountains—Gobernador Knob and Huérfano Mountain in New Mexico—but the four mountains listed above are particularly important insofar as they have formed the boundary of the Navajo homeland (**Diné Bikéyah**) since the time the Diné emerged from the underworld.

Each of the four sacred mountains has a spiritual "**inner form**"—some have likened this key Diné concept to Western notions of the "soul"—that gives breath, life, and knowledge to living things.[2] According to the former Navajo Nation president Joe Shirley Jr., these mountains "were placed on Mother Earth by the Holy People who made them repositories of the herbs, plants, stones, and soil that go into the medicine bundles used to cure our people of illness and restore their lives to harmony."[3]

Regarding the San Francisco Peaks, Shirley continues, "The Navajo people believe Dook'o'oosliid to be the residence of the Holy People who have influenced, guided, and supported Diné from time immemorial."[4] Along with other sacred mountains, Navajos appeal to the San Francisco Peaks "to render aid in healing the sick, protecting the people and their goods, bringing rain for crops and livestock, and insuring tranquility in life."[5]

NAVAJO RELIGION BY THE NUMBERS

Four Sacred Mountains

Four is the most important number in Navajo thought, storytelling, and ritual. There are four colors (white, blue, yellow, black) and four sacred plants (corn, beans, squash, tobacco). There are also four sacred mountains, each associated with one of the four cardinal directions:

East	Blanca Peak, Colorado	white	white shell
South	Mount Taylor, New Mexico	blue	turquoise
West	San Francisco Peaks, Arizona	yellow	abalone
North	Hesperus Peak, Colorado	black	jet

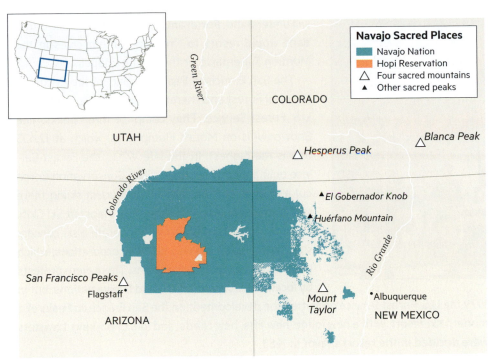

The Diné's sacred lands span close to 30,000 square miles within four important mountain peaks in the Four Corners region of the United States. This map also depicts the narrower boundaries of the Navajo Nation, as defined by the federal government. This reservation encircles the federally defined home of the Hopi Nation.

Many sacred places draw devotees to them, but some keep devotees away. Muslims are drawn to Mecca in Saudi Arabia and Roman Catholics to St. Peter's Basilica in Vatican City. The holiness of those places beckons the faithful near. In contrast, the "Holy of Holies" in the Jerusalem Temple could be approached only once a year, and then only by the high priest and only after he had been ritually purified. The San Francisco Peaks is a holy place of the latter sort. "We don't go up there just to play around," Klee Benally explains. The Diné go only when they have a sacred purpose—to make an offering or to gather soil or herbs for ceremonies. "You cannot just voluntarily go up on this mountain at any time," says Shirley. "You have to sacrifice. You have to sing certain songs before you even dwell for a little bit to gather herbs, to do offerings."[6]

The Diné have come to this mountain for centuries to gather herbs, stones, soil, and water for the **medicine bundles** (*jish*) they use in their ceremonies. The songs in those ceremonies speak of the activities of the Holy People here from the beginning of time. The Diné call the San Francisco Peaks "Mother." On this mountain, they commune with the Holy People by conducting ceremonies, making offerings, and praying. But this sacred land has, in their view, been desecrated by the Snowbowl, which is carved out of this mountain. To explain this desecration to religious studies scholars, federal judges, and other outsiders, they resort to analogies from Christianity they hope non-Navajos

medicine bundle (jish)
pouch containing powerful objects (stones, herbs, feathers, animal parts) wrapped together and used by a medicine person

Demonstrators march through Flagstaff, Arizona, on January 18, 2018, to protest the use of treated wastewater to make artificial snow on a mountain the Navajo consider to be sacred land.

will understand. For example, they ask whether Christians would resort to "'relieving' themselves in the Mormon Tabernacle or the Sistine Chapel."[7]

The San Francisco Peaks are part of the Coconino National Forest and therefore under the control of the U.S. Forest Service. They comprise three peaks. The Snowbowl is on Mount Humphreys, which at 12,633 feet is the highest. In the late 1930s, the Forest Service built a lodge and the Civilian Conservation Corps cut a road up the mountain. The modest skiing there was long managed by the nonprofit Flagstaff Ski Club. During the 1970s, the permit to operate a ski concession on the mountain was held by corporations, which pushed for a series of expansions. There were protests by locals, environmentalists, and Native nations, but in 1979 the U.S. Forest Service permitted the development on the San Francisco Peaks of a modern ski resort, with a new lodge, new lifts, new roads, and lots of parking. Lawsuits were decided in the resort's favor in 1983.

In 2002, the Arizona Snowbowl Resort Limited Partnership (ASR), which had bought the ski area a decade earlier and operated it under a Special Use Permit, proposed to purchase treated wastewater from the City of Flagstaff and pump it up the mountain to create artificial snow. They also proposed a major expansion. Again, protests followed. In 2005, the Forest Service announced that it would allow most of the proposed expansion, including artificial snowmaking with treated wastewater.

Environmental organizations and six Native nations filed suit against the Forest Service, arguing that its decision violated environmental laws and the religious liberty rights of Native Americans. These plaintiffs lost in a lower court but prevailed by a 2-1 vote in the Ninth Circuit Court of Appeals. In his majority decision, Judge William Fletcher wrote:

> The record in this case establishes the religious importance of the Peaks to the appellate tribes who live around it. From time immemorial, they have relied on the Peaks, and the purity of the Peaks' water, as an integral part of their religious beliefs. The Forest Service and the Snowbowl now propose to put treated sewage effluent on the Peaks. To get some sense of equivalence, it may be useful to imagine the effect on Christian beliefs and practices—and the imposition that Christians would experience—if the government were to require that baptisms be carried out with "reclaimed water."[8]

The ASR corporation then secured an "en banc" rehearing before nine Ninth Circuit judges. The court records included testimony by elders of the Navajo and other Native nations that the proposal threatened their religions and their ways of life. Nonetheless, these judges found no "substantial burden" on anyone's religious liberties. Native nations were outraged. "How is it," asked Vincent Randall, a councilman of the Yavapai-Apache Nation, "that the federal government can promote the interests of a handful of skiers and businessmen over the deeply held religious beliefs of over 250,000 Tribal People?"[9]

In 2011, the work began with the clear-cutting of trees and the laying of nearly fifteen miles of wastewater pipes. The next year, snowmaking machines started firing artificial snow made from nonpotable reclaimed sewer water across the mountain. Signs warned skiers not to consume the snow.

Back at the Snowbowl today, the opinions of skiers and snowboarders obviously incline toward snowmaking. They are here after all. However, some express concerns about how clean the water is, and many seem conflicted about the controversy. "I see both sides," says a middle-aged white man from Flagstaff, "but selfishly I like the idea of having snow." A thirty-something white man from Phoenix who is just strapping on his ski boots is similarly conflicted. "I honestly do not know what you do about it. On the one hand they were here first," he says of the Diné. "On the other hand, this place has been here a long time." Another white man in his thirties sporting a tattoo of a mechanistic tree of life also says he sees both sides. "I take advantage of the side that is doing the snowmaking," he admits, "but I absolutely have a deep respect for the other side."

The only person who unequivocally takes the Navajo side isn't a skier. He's an Anglo guy in his fifties who is there with a friend. "I agree with the tribes. It's pollution. Nasty," he says. "I feel for them.... It makes me pissed off."

Other skiers criticize the Native nations. A twenty-something white man with a long-sleeve black Harley-Davidson T-shirt and a green camouflage cap says, "I like skiing," when asked about the controversy. "There's reclaimed wastewater on every golf course in Phoenix." When asked about the Navajo's religious liberty claims, he compares that controversy to the controversy over slave reparations: "It's over and done with. Put it to rest."

A college professor from Phoenix and his wife are more amused than annoyed. "I like the snow," he says. "I know the Indians made a stink about it," but "snow has been filled with dinosaur poop for millions of years, so why are they griping about it?... [It's] mass hysteria."

How to make sense of this controversy, and of Diné religion today? One place to begin is with the local nature of Diné religion. As the religious studies scholar Suzanne Crawford O'Brien observes, "Native religious practices are not portable; they are place-bound and dependent on access to specific locations."[10] The Israelite religion that centered around the Jerusalem Temple was a place-based religion, but after that sacred center was destroyed in the sixth century BCE, Jews gradually developed a portable religion that could be practiced anywhere its rabbis could read and interpret its texts. Christianity, which developed out of Judaism, was equally portable. Because the overwhelming majority of judges in the United States were raised in Jewish or Christian homes, the U.S. legal system struggles to make sense of the role that sacred places play in Native religious traditions. When judges are looking for religion, they look for it in scriptures and churches.

The religious studies scholar Charles Long defined religion as "orientation." He meant that metaphorically: religion helps one come to terms with "one's place in the

Klee Benally (1975–)

Klee Benally is a filmmaker and activist who has performed as a traditional Navajo dancer and a guitarist and lead singer in a punk rock band. His life demonstrates the inseparability in Navajo life of religion, politics, art, dance, voice, and land.

Benally was born in 1975 on Black Mesa in the Navajo Nation. His grandmother, Roberta Blackgoat, was an indigenous rights activist who protested the partition of her ancestral lands by the Navajo-Hopi Indian Land Settlement Act of 1974. Passed in part to facilitate strip-mining of coal in Black Mesa, this law redrew Hopi and Navajo borders and forced the relocation of thousands. It also ran barbed wire through Benally's family land. As a child, Benally accompanied family members to protests and court proceedings. He went to ceremonies with his father, the medicine man Jones Benally, and learned traditional songs and dances.

In 1989, Benally formed the punk rock band Blackfire with his sister Jeneda, who played bass, and his brother Clayson, who played drums. They toured across the United States and in Canada, Mexico, Europe, and Africa. In 2002, Blackfire won best pop/rock album at the Native American Music Awards (NAMA) for their first LP, *One Nation Under*. In 2008, their *Silence Is a Weapon* won NAMA's album of the year. One CD on this two-disc album featured punk rock. The other featured Navajo songs performed by the traditional music and dance group the Jones Benally Family, which also includes their father, Jones Benally. Blackfire's music incorporated Navajo elements into the punk rock tradition and, according to their website, addressed "government oppression, relocation of indigenous people, eco-cide, genocide, domestic violence and human rights."[a]

Active in political protests focused on protecting indigenous lands and the environment, Klee Benally produced a coming-of-age feature film called *Power Lines* (2016) about a young Diné poet who runs away to find her real home. He also made a series of documentary films, including *The Snowbowl Effect* (2005), which documents protests against wastewater snowmaking on the San Francisco Peaks. About judicial decisions to allow that snowmaking, Benally said, "The deeply held religious beliefs of hundreds of thousands of citizens of this country have been trumped by a single for-profit private business operating on public lands. What I keep wondering is 'How is that considered justice?'"[b]

world."[11] Michael McNally, an expert in Native American religions, means it literally when he says that the San Francisco Peaks "orient disciplines of Navajo prayer and daily life alike."[12] To cut the ties of Navajos to their sacred places is to disorient them, as surely as cutting the ties of Muslims to Mecca would disorient every Muslim who bends down to pray.

One further thing to consider: It is common in the modern West to think of religion as preoccupied with some otherworldly prize. Christians, for example, see themselves as wandering through this world on a journey toward their true home in heaven. However, there are religions, such as Daoism and Confucianism, whose practitioners are thoroughly at home in this world. Navajo religion is similar. Like practitioners of China's religions of reversion, Diné traditionalists are indifferent to speculation about the afterlife. Instead of salvation in the next world, they focus on healing and harmony in this world. For them, this world is Diné Bikéyah—the homeland, given to the Diné by the Holy People, that is located not by looking down at a GPS but by looking up at a sacred mountain and finding oneself at home.

OUR STORY

Because the term "Navajo" originated with Spanish settler-colonialists, who derived it from Tewa-speaking Pueblo peoples, members of the Navajo Nation are increasingly referring to themselves in public as Diné. They refer to their creation story as Diné Bah-ane', which means "story of the people." According to Paul Zolbrod, the author of *Diné Bahane': The Navajo Creation Story*, this oral tradition constitutes "the soul of a distinct Navajo identity."[13] But there is not just one creation story; there are many. And though they converge on key moments and key themes, they are told in different ways in different ceremonies and songs. The Diné believe that these stories were given to them by the Holy People, and they continue to be transmitted orally today.

These Diné creation stories can be divided into two categories:

- emergence stories about the journey of the Holy People up from four lower worlds to the earth world the Diné inhabit today
- origin stories describing how the things that matter to the Diné—Navajoland, the Blessingway and other ceremonies, Earth Surface People, medicine bundles, Changing Woman, the Pueblo, the hogan, clans, sacred mountains—came to be

The story that follows tells of the emergence. This story is long and complex, and only a small portion of it can be presented here. This version is necessarily selective and incomplete, but it offers a sense of how the Diné tell their emergence story.

Like emergence stories of other Native nations, this narrative begins not at the origin of the universe but in the middle of things. The Holy People and many other beings are in one of the underworlds. Various difficulties, including a great flood, force them to move up out of each underworld until they break through the earth's surface. The central figures in this story are First Man and First Woman. The story that follows also tells of the origins of the sacred mountains. Taken as a whole, Diné emergence and origin stories arc from chaos to order, from quarreling to peace, from disharmony to harmony, from the monochromatic ugliness of the underworlds to the polychromatic beauty of Changeable Earth. Whenever disharmony reemerges, images of this primordial world provide a model for efforts to restore that original harmony.

The version of the emergence story that follows was passed down through a Navajo leader named Sandoval, who was worried about his people's oral stories fading from memory in a world of alphabets and books. In November 1928, he tracked down Aileen O'Bryan, who lived at the time at Mesa Verde National Park, and asked her to write down what he told her in a book. His stories were translated into English over seventeen days by his nephew, Sam Ahkeah, and published, O'Bryan reports, largely "without interpolation."[14]

The Emergence

The First World was black as black wool. It had four corners, and over these appeared four clouds. These four clouds were in color, black, white, blue, and yellow.

The Black Cloud represented the Female Being or Substance. The White Cloud represented the Male Being or Substance.

This nineteenth-century woven blanket depicts an important scene from the Diné creation story in which two Holy People stand on a rainbow beside the maize plant that they gave to the Earth Surface People.

In the East, at the place where the Black Cloud and the White Cloud met, First Man was formed; and with him was formed the white corn, perfect in shape, with kernels covering the whole ear.

The First World was small in size, a floating island in mist or water. On it there grew one tree, a pine tree, which was later brought to the present world for firewood.

The creatures of the First World are thought of as the Mist People; they had no definite form, but were to change to men, beasts, birds, and reptiles of this world.

Now on the western side of the First World, in a place that later was to become the Land of Sunset, there appeared the Blue Cloud, and opposite it there appeared the Yellow Cloud. Where they came together First Woman was formed, and with her the yellow corn. This ear of corn was also perfect.

First Man burned a crystal for a fire. First Woman burned turquoise for a fire. They saw each other's lights in the distance. When the Black Cloud and the White Cloud rose higher in the sky First Man set out to find the turquoise light. He went twice without success, and again a third time. The fourth time he walked to it and found smoke coming from a home.

"Here is the home I could not find," First Man said.

First Woman answered: "Oh, it is you. I saw you walking around and I wondered why you did not come."

Again the same thing happened when the Blue Cloud and the Yellow Cloud rose higher in the sky. First Woman saw a light and she went out to find it. Three times she was unsuccessful, but the fourth time she saw the smoke and she found the home of First Man.

"I wondered what this thing could be," she said.

"I saw you walking and I wondered why you did not come to me," First Man answered.

As First Woman was thinking, First Man spoke to her. "Why do you not come with your fire and we will live together." The woman agreed to this. So instead of the man going to the woman, as is the custom now, the woman went to the man.

About this time there came another person, the Great-Coyote-Who-Was-Formed-in-the-Water, and he was in the form of a male being. He told the two that he had been hatched from an egg. He knew all that was under the water and all that was in the skies. First Man placed this person ahead of himself in all things. The three began to plan what was to come to pass; and while they were thus occupied another being came to them. He also had the form of a man, but he wore a hairy coat, lined with white fur, that fell to his knees and was belted in at the waist. His name was First Angry or Coyote. He said to the three: "You believe that you were the first persons. You are mistaken. I was living when you were formed."

Then four beings came together. They were yellow in color and were called the wasp people. They knew the secret of shooting evil and could harm others. They were very powerful.

This made eight people.

Four more beings came. They were small in size and wore red shirts and had little black eyes. They were the spider ants. They knew how to sting, and were a great people.

After these came a whole crowd of beings. They were the black ants. They also knew the secret of shooting evil and were powerful; but they killed each other steadily.

And after the wasps and the different ant people there came the beetles, dragonflies, bat people, the Spider Man and Woman, and the Salt Man and Woman, and others. And this world, being small in size, became crowded, and the people quarreled and fought among themselves, and in all ways made living very unhappy.

The Second World

Because of the strife in the First World, they all climbed up from the World of Darkness and Dampness to the Second or Blue World.

They found a number of people already living there: blue birds, blue hawks, blue jays, blue herons, and all the blue-feathered beings. The powerful swallow people lived there also, and these people made the Second World unpleasant for those who had come from the First World. There was fighting and killing.

The First Four found an opening in the World of Blue Haze; and they climbed through this and led the people up into the Third or Yellow World.

The Third World

A great river crossed this land from north to south. It was the Female River. There was another river crossing it from east to west; it was the Male River. This Male River flowed through the Female River and on; and the name of this place is the Crossing of the Waters.

There were six mountains in the Third World. In the East was the Standing Black Sash. Its ceremonial name is the Dawn or White Shell Mountain. In the South stood the Great Mountain, also called Mountain Tongue. Its ceremonial name is the Blue Bead or Turquoise Mountain. In the West stood the Abalone Shell Mountain. In the North stood Many Sheep Mountain. Its ceremonial name is Obsidian Mountain. Then there was the Upper Mountain. It was very sacred; and its name means also the Center Place, and the people moved around it. Its ceremonial name is Precious Stone or Banded Rock Mountain. There was still another mountain and it was also a sacred mountain.

There was no sun in this land, only the two rivers and the six mountains. And these rivers and mountains were not in their present form but rather the substance of mountains and rivers as were First Man, First Woman, and the others.

Now beyond White Shell Mountain in the east, there lived the Turquoise Hermaphrodite also known as the Turquoise Boy. And near this person grew the male reed. In the West there lived the White Shell Hermaphrodite or Girl, and with her was the big female reed which grew at the water's edge.

Now the plan was to plant.

First Man called the people together. He brought forth the white corn which had been formed with him. First Woman brought the yellow corn. They laid the perfect ears side by side; then they asked one person from among the many to come and help them.

They planted the seeds, and their harvest was great.

It was the custom when the black cloud rose in the morning for First Man to come out of his dwelling and speak to the people. But after First Man found his wife with another he would not come out to speak to the people. For four days, First Man remained silent, and would not touch food or water.

At this time the Great-Coyote-Who-Was-Formed-in-the-Water came to First Man and told him to cross the river. They made a big raft and crossed at the place where the Male River followed through the Female River. And all the male beings left the female beings on the riverbank.

In the beginning the women did not mind being alone. They cleared and planted a small field. On the other side of the river First Man and the chiefs hunted and planted their seeds. They had a good harvest. Four seasons passed. The men continued to have plenty and were happy; but the women became lazy, and only weeds grew on their land. The women wanted fresh meat. Some of them tried to join the men and were drowned in the river.

First Woman made a plan. As the women had no way to satisfy their passions, some fashioned long narrow rocks, some used the feathers of the turkey, and some used strange plants. First Woman told them to use these things. One woman brought forth a big stone. This stone-child was later the Great Stone that rolled over the earth killing men. Another woman brought forth the Big Birds; and others gave birth to the giants and monsters who later destroyed many people.

On the opposite side of the river the same condition existed. The men, wishing to satisfy their passions, killed the females of mountain sheep, lion, and antelope. Lightning struck these men. When First Man learned of this he warned his men that they would all be killed. He told them that they were indulging in a dangerous practice. Then a chief spoke: he said that life was hard and that it was a pity to see women drowned. He asked why they should not bring the women across the river and all live together again.

"Now we can see for ourselves what comes from our wrong doing," he said. "We will know how to act in the future." The three other chiefs agreed with him, so First Man told them to go and bring the women.

After the women had been brought over the river First Man spoke: "We must be purified," he said. "Everyone must bathe. The men must dry themselves with white corn meal, and the women, with yellow."

This they did, living apart for 4 days. After the fourth day First Woman came and threw her right arm around her husband. She spoke to the others and said that she could see her mistakes, but with her husband's help she would henceforth lead a good life. Then all the male and female beings came and lived with each other again.

The people moved to different parts of the land. Some time passed; then First Woman became troubled by the monotony of life. She made a plan. She went to the Coyote called First Angry, and giving him the rainbow she said: "Take the rainbow and go to the place where the rivers cross. Bring me the two pretty children of the Water Buffalo, a boy and a girl."

The Coyote agreed to do this. He walked over the rainbow. He entered the home of the Water Buffalo and stole the two children; and these he hid in his big skin coat with the white fur lining. And when he returned he refused to take off his coat but pulled it around himself and looked very wise.

After this happened the people saw white light in the East and in the South and West and North. One of the deer people ran to the East, and returning, said that the white light was a great sheet of water. The sparrow hawk flew to the South, the great hawk to the West, and the kingfisher to the North. They returned and said that a flood was coming.

And all this happened because the Coyote had stolen the two children of the Water Buffalo, and only First Woman and the Coyote knew the truth.

When First Man learned of the coming of the water he sent word to all the people, and he told them to come to the mountain in the east. He told them to bring with them all of the seeds of the plants used for food. All living beings were to gather on the top of the mountain in the east. First Man traveled to the six sacred mountains, and, gathering earth from them, he put it in his medicine bag.

The water rose steadily.

When all the people were halfway up the mountain in the east, First Man discovered that he had forgotten his medicine bag. Now this bag contained not only the earth from the six sacred mountains but his magic, the medicine he used to call the rain down upon the earth and to make things grow. He could not live without his medicine bag, and he wished to jump into the rising water; but the others begged him not to do this. They went to the kingfisher and asked him to dive into the water and recover the bag. This the bird did. When First Man had his medicine bag again in his possession he breathed on it four times and thanked his people.

When they had all arrived it was found that the Turquoise Boy had brought with him the big Male Reed; and the White Shell Girl had brought with her the big Female Reed. They tried to blow inside the reed, but it was solid. They asked the woodpecker to drill out the hard heart. Soon they were able to peek through the opening, but they had to blow and blow before it was large enough to climb through. They climbed up inside the big male reed, and after them the water continued to rise.

The Fourth World

When the people reached the Fourth World they saw that it was not a very large place. Some say that it was called the White World; but not all medicine men agree that this is so.

The female Water Buffalo pushed her head through the opening in the reed. She had a great quantity of curly hair which floated on the water, and she had two horns, half black and half yellow. From the tips of the horns the lightning flashed.

First Man asked the Water Buffalo why she had come and why she had sent the flood. She said nothing. Then the Coyote drew the two babies from his coat and said that it was, perhaps, because of them.

The Turquoise Boy took a basket and filled it with turquoise. On top of the turquoise he placed the blue pollen from the blue flowers, and the yellow pollen from the corn; and on top of these he placed the pollen from the water flags; and again on top of these he placed the crystal, which is river pollen. This basket he gave to the Coyote who put it between the horns of the Water Buffalo. The Coyote said that with this sacred offering he would give back the male child. He said that the male child would be known as the Black Cloud or Male Rain, and that he would bring the thunder and lightning. The female child he would keep. She would be known as the Blue, Yellow, and White Clouds or Female Rain. She would be the gentle rain that would moisten the earth and help them to live. So he kept the female child, and he placed the male child on the sacred basket between the horns of the Water Buffalo. And the Water Buffalo disappeared, and the waters with her.

The Fifth World

First Man was not satisfied with the Fourth World. It was a small barren land; and the great water had soaked the earth and made the sowing of seeds impossible. He planted the big Female Reed, and it grew up to the vaulted roof of this Fourth World. First Man sent the badger to the upper world, and he returned covered with mud, terrible mud. First Man gathered chips of turquoise which he offered to the five Chiefs of the Winds who lived in the uppermost world of all. They were pleased with the gift, and they sent down the winds and dried the Fifth World.

First Man and his people again sent the badger up the reed. This time when the badger returned he said that he had come out on solid earth. So First Man and First Woman led the people to the Fifth World, which some call the Many Colored Earth and some the Changeable Earth. They emerged through a lake surrounded by four mountains.

Now after all the people had emerged from the lower worlds, First Man and First Woman dressed the Mountain Lion with yellow, black, white, and grayish corn and placed him on one side. They dressed the Wolf with white tail feathers and placed him on the other side. They divided the people into two groups. The people who had the Mountain Lion for their chief turned out to be the people of the Earth. They were to plant seeds and harvest corn. The followers of the Wolf chief became the animals and birds; they turned into all the creatures that fly and crawl and run and swim.

And after all the beings were divided, and each had his own form, they went their ways.

This is the story of the Four Dark Worlds and the Fifth, the World we live in.

After emergence, the earth's surface was nothing more than dried mud. First Man and First Woman and others planned a new world that included day and night and the four seasons. They then built a scale model of the world they had thought into being. As they prayed, that scale model swelled into the earth world now set beneath sun, moon, and stars. The Holy Wind blew life and breath into everyone and everything, including the sacred mountains. It endowed living things with inner forms to match their outer forms. In so doing, it gave them thought and speech and

The Diné creation story speaks of Navajoland as an area bound between four sacred mountains in what is roughly the Four Corners region of the Southwest. Here, a young Diné girl sits in Monument Valley, Utah, selling hand-beaded wares.

set them in motion. All was in order. Then chaos came. First Man went out for a walk and ran into Changing Woman, whom he and First Woman raised as their own. When Changing Woman came of age, they did a ceremony for her. They made a copy of their medicine bundle and gave the original to her. They then receded from the world of outer forms. Changing Woman and Sun had two sons, Monster Slayer and Child of the Water, who killed the earth's demons and made the world harmonious. On the surface of this world, Changing Woman created the Diné, also known as the Earth Surface People. After teaching the Earth Surface People what they need to know to restore beauty and harmony whenever ugliness and disharmony overtook them, the Holy People withdrew. But their inner forms remained, ready and able to communicate with and act on behalf of the people who call on their names.

NAVAJO RELIGION IN TODAY'S WORLD

There are now 573 federally recognized tribal nations. Textbooks on the world's religions often attempt to collapse these nations into one chapter on Native American religion or indigenous religion, but their religions are in many cases at least as distinct as Hinduism is from Islam. Therefore, this chapter focuses on just one of those federally recognized tribal nations: the Diné.

Daisy Taugelchee, pictured during the 1970s with her loom, was a renowned Navajo weaver. Her work received top prizes at ceremonial competitions for over fifty years and was featured on a 2004 U.S. Postal Service stamp.

Why this choice? The Diné are the largest Native American nation in terms of territory and the second largest (after the Cherokee) in terms of population. Moreover, their reservation is located, unlike those of most indigenous nations within U.S. borders, inside their traditional boundaries. The Diné are widely regarded not only for their fine arts, including Navajo rugs and silver and turquoise jewelry, but also for their extraordinarily complicated religious stories, beliefs, and rituals. Today, the Diné economy is driven by mining, animal husbandry, weaving, and silversmithing. The Navajo Nation steered clear of the gambling business for many years, but in 2008 they opened their first casino, the Fire Rock Casino in Church Rock, New Mexico.

Navajo art and religion are inseparable. In fact, virtually all Navajos are artists because of the place of honor given to creativity and movement in Diné life and thought. Many Navajos are well-known artists, including Daisy Taugelchee and R. C. Gorman. Taugelchee is widely regarded as the greatest Navajo weaver ever, and her work was featured on a U.S. Postal Service stamp in 2004. Gorman was celebrated in the *New York Times* as an American Picasso for his paintings and prints of Native American women.

The Diné are also understandably proud of their Code Talkers, who during World War II turned the Navajo language, which had never been written down, into an unbreakable code for the U.S. Marines. In the spring of 1942 at Camp Pendleton in California, the twenty-nine Navajo recruits who developed that code used Navajo words for birds to refer to particular kinds of planes and Navajo words for fish to refer to particular kinds of ships. They also used Navajo words for letters in the English alphabet. For example, the Navajo term for cat (*mósí*) and dog (*łééchąąʼí*) stood in for C and D. At the battle of Iwo Jima, Code Talkers handled more than eight hundred messages. Although the contributions of the four hundred Navajos who used this code remained classified and therefore secret until 1968, Code Talkers were publicly honored in a ceremony held at the Pentagon in Washington, DC, in 1992. In 2001, President George W. Bush presented the Congressional Gold Medal to four of the twenty-nine surviving Navajos who created the code.

Navajo Code Talkers in the U.S. Marine Corps use an "unbreakable code" based on the Diné language to transmit a secret message during World War II.

The Diné are governed by the Navajo Nation, which manages the Navajo reservation in the Four Corners area of the Southwest where Arizona, Utah, New Mexico, and Colorado meet. Since its establishment in 1868, that reservation has changed in size and shape many times, but it now comprises some 27,425 square miles, or roughly the size of Massachusetts, New Hampshire, and Vermont combined. Today, the Navajo Nation claims 300,000 officially enrolled members. The 2010 U.S. Census found 332,129 people living in the United States who claim Diné ancestry, and a total population in the Navajo Nation of 173,667.[15]

Of course, not all of these people practice traditional Diné religion. Many attend Christian churches, and many participate in a new religious movement called Peyotism because of its reverence for and ingestion of a small, spineless cactus plant called peyote. About half of all Navajos are peyote practitioners and, according to a 2011 survey, 30 percent practice Christianity exclusively.[16] Although some Diné Christians insist on the exclusive truth of Christianity, most Navajos approach traditional Diné religion, Peyotism, and Christianity the way people in China approach the "Three Teachings" of Confucianism, Daoism, and Buddhism. They see the benefits of each and feel free to mix and match them as they go about their daily lives.

A 2014 study of Native Americans in the Southwest, where the Diné tradition is strong, found that 54 percent of the people surveyed reported that their "aboriginal" traditions were "very important" to them, while 36 percent and 34 percent, respectively, said that their Christian and Native American Church (NAC) beliefs were very important. This same study found a considerable amount of overlap, with 29 percent saying that both aboriginal and NAC beliefs were very important to them and 17 percent saying that both aboriginal and Christian beliefs were very important. Ten percent considered all three to be very important.[17]

NAVAJO RELIGION 101

➔ How to restore beauty?

Traditional Diné religion, which is the primary subject of this chapter, includes stories upon stories, each with multiple interpretations, each attached to myriad rituals and beliefs, and none separated from the "real world" of farming, animal husbandry, wage labor, humor, art, and medicine. Studying Navajo religion is further complicated by the fact that the Navajo have shown little interest in systematizing their religious thought or creating an orthodoxy, or "right doctrine," that could be used to expel dissenters as heretics.

The Navajo documented important events through cave paintings. This one, depicting a nineteenth-century Spanish missionary expedition into Navajo lands, is located on the walls of the Canyon de Chelly Monument in Arizona.

Like other religions, traditional Navajo religion has changed over time and is internally diverse. Colonizers and missionaries who credit themselves with discovering the "New World" inflicted all sorts of horrors on Navajos. There are no precise numbers for the Navajo death toll, but the historian D. E. Stannard has estimated that 100 million Native people perished in what he calls the "American Holocaust." "The destruction of the Indians of the Americas was, far and away, the most massive act of genocide in the world," he wrote.[18] However, Native peoples have survived and thrived. Scholars who study the Navajo underscore their tremendous resilience, documenting how they have preserved their traditions through creative adaptation. The Diné's adaptability enabled them to respond creatively to centuries of broken treaties, foreign missions, suppression of religious traditions, forced assimilation, economic depressions, stereotyping in popular media, cultural and capitalistic appropriation of their cultural treasures, war, forced marches, and assaults on their population by infectious disease epidemics. In recent years, this resilience has enabled the Diné to adapt to American society and law, including the predominance of Christianity and the religious liberty clause of the First Amendment.

Scholarship on Native American religions is also rapidly developing. In the wake of the Red Power movement of the 1970s and the subsequent emergence of postcolonial studies, there is now appropriate skepticism about using Western concepts (such as religion) and Western academic disciplines (such as archaeology and anthropology) to interpret Native American cultures. Non-Native scholars are increasingly aware of the dangers of slipping into stereotypes about the "vanishing Indian" or into related romantic assumptions that the real native cultures can be found only in the pristine past. These scholars are also cognizant of the dangers of continuing to colonize by other means, including teaching and scholarship. Many attempt to draw on experts from indigenous nations and to quote from those experts as much as possible. But doing so can be difficult. Because many Diné beliefs and practices are revealed only to the initiated, those who hold these secrets are understandably unwilling to divulge them. One way to respond to this difficulty is to draw on Diné courtroom testimony about the things they hold dear, including the San Francisco Peaks and other sacred places.

One further point: this book is written from the perspective, shared by the Diné, that understandings of religion as private and set apart from more public aspects of human life are inadequate. From the San Francisco Peaks to Mecca to Bodh Gaya, religion is embedded in and inseparable from other forms of culture. With this holism in mind, Michael McNally has argued that the traditions of Navajos and other Native nations may be "better described as *lifeways* rather than as *religions*."[19] In referring here to Diné religion, we are referring to that diverse complex of beliefs, practices, symbols, stories, sacred places, ceremonies, ceremonial practitioners, and ritual instruments that inform the Diné way of life. Another synonym for this complex is "the corn pollen path," so called because of the emphasis in the Diné lifeway on corn as a source and symbol of life.

THE NAVAJO: A GENEALOGY

Writing about Navajo religion is complicated by the fact that many Navajos do not believe that Navajo religion exists. There is no word for religion in the Navajo language and, like many Hindus, the Diné mostly prefer to refer instead to their "way of life." Navajos correctly observe that the concept of religion is an invention of the modern West. They understand that term to presume an all-too-simple split between the sacred and the secular and the private and the public. They also understand it to encode a problematic understanding of human life as something you can cut up into separate realms of religion, society, economy, politics, art, language, medicine, and land. This segmenting does violence to more holistic Diné understandings of the inseparability of their stories and ceremonies from other arenas of human life.

There is no English word similar to "Buddhism" or "Christianity" to describe Navajo religion. The term "Navajo" itself comes into English via early seventeenth-century Spanish speakers, who used variations of the Tewa word *Navahu*—from *nava*, meaning field, and *hu*, meaning wide arroyo—to describe a cultivated arroyo. The Spanish then applied variations of this word to describe the *indios* who occupied such places.

In the English language, there is an obscure reference in a book called *Modern Geography* (1811) to a mountain chain in the western United States called "Nabajo." A plainer reference can be found in a March 8, 1822, journal entry by Jacob Fowler, a soldier and surveyor who fought repeated battles against Native Americans. "The Spanierds Have Sent 700 men against the nabeho Indeans," Fowler wrote. In 1834, the lawyer and newspaperman Albert Pike referenced "an Indian girl with her Nabajo blanket" in a volume of prose and poetry he wrote after traveling along the Santa Fe Trail.[a]

An 1836 book reprints an 1824 newspaper article from Missouri that praises at length "a people heretofore unknown to us," namely, "a nation of Indians called the *Nabijos*." "Their skill in manufacturing, and their excellence in some of the useful and ornamental arts, show a decided superiority of genius over all the other tribes of the western continent," the article observes. Drawing on the stereotype of the "noble savage" uncorrupted by civilization, it describes this tribe as a people "whose customs have never been altered, and whose arts and mode of living have never been adulterated by an intercourse with civilized society." It also praises "their power and bravery" as "proverbial among the Spaniards" and provides details about their way of life, including how they live outside villages as farmers, growing corn, tobacco, and peaches, and husbanding "fine flocks of sheep."[b]

hocho

ugliness, disharmony, chaos; often paired with its contrasting term *hozho*. Hocho characterizes the lower worlds of death.

Earth Surface People

human beings, so named because they were created and live on the surface of the earth

hozho

beauty, harmony, and the central value in Navajo life, often paired with its contrasting term *hocho*. Upon its creation, the upper world was characterized by hozho.

Sa'a Nághaí Bik'e Hózhó (SNBH)

Navajo goal of life, often expressed in stories, songs, prayers, and everyday conversations; translations include "in old age walking, his trail beautiful"

Hocho and Hozho

According to Diné oral traditions, the world is an interrelated whole in which human beings find themselves in relationships not only with one another and with the Holy People but also with plants, animals, natural forces such as thunder and lightning, and places such as mountains and rivers. Good and evil are present throughout this world and in almost everything. Evil is not an independent power or force, however. It is part of a good-to-bad spectrum. Therefore, the goal is not to eradicate evil. It is to balance it so that the original harmony of the universe (itself a mix of positive and negative forces) can be restored. This reversion to original harmony finds echoes in Daoism and Confucianism, which are also religions of reversion. However, instead of reverting to the naturalness of the Dao or to the beloved sage-kings of Confucius, the Diné revert to the original harmony that was present at the creation of the world.

According to the Navajo way, the central problem of human life is **hocho**, which refers to disease, disharmony, ugliness, chaos, misfortune, conflict, and evil. This "state of worthless, evil conditions" is neither original nor inevitable.[20] It is produced by some action or inaction that causes an individual or the community (or both) to fall ill or otherwise depart from original beauty. The cause can be Coyote, a key figure of the Navajo tradition, who revels in creating chaos. Hocho can also be brought on by Holy People, **Earth Surface People** (the Diné), or other human beings.

The solution to this problem is to revert to **hozho** by restoring the individual and the community to beauty, harmony, and balance. This difficult-to-translate word is the central concept in the Navajo way—"the grand metaphor by which the Navajo understand the world and their place in it."[21] Hozho is often rendered in English as beauty or harmony, but it also refers to "good, happiness, and everything that is positive"—"a state of balance and proper relations with all aspects of the natural and supernatural worlds."[22] Hozho can be used as a noun, a verb, and an adverb—to say that beauty is restored, that something has become beautiful, or that something has been done beautifully. It is a holistic ideal that simultaneously conjures up "the intellectual concept of order, the emotional state of happiness, the moral value of the good, the biological condition of health and well-being and the aesthetic charm of balance, harmony and beauty."[23]

Hozho is also a recurring theme in Navajo creation stories. It is invoked repeatedly in prayers and in the popular Blessingway ceremony, whose Navajo-language name is *hozhooji*. It describes the indescribable condition that existed right after the world was created—when the inner forms of dawn and twilight flew up the sacred mountains and looked out over the world and saw beauty wherever they looked. It is this longing for and pursuit of hozho that marks Navajo religion as a way of beauty.

When asked to describe the goal of Navajo life, Navajos do not typically respond with hozho alone. They respond with a saying that includes that term: **Sa'a Nághaí Bik'e Hózhó** (SNBH). This phrase, which appears widely in Navajo stories, songs, and prayers, has been described as the master key to unlocking the mysteries of the Diné way of life. The pioneering Irish American ethnographer Washington Matthews translated the first two words in this phrase literally as "in old age walking" and the final two words as "his trail beautiful." He also rendered the entire phrase as "long life and happiness." The American linguist Gladys Reichard translated it, less literally, as, "According to the ideal may restoration be achieved." Others have whittled it down to "long life and happiness into old age" or, simply, "walking in beauty." The Navajo poet Rex Lee Jim has rendered it into a prayer of sorts: "May I walk, being the omnipresent beauty created by the one that moves beyond old."[24] In its less lofty uses, the phrase can point, more simply, to the health and well-being that comes from proper relationships.

Together these four words also evoke a recurring cycle of agricultural life that moves from beginning to end and then reverts to the beginning again in the planting and harvesting of crops. A similar cycle is evident in the motion of Changing Woman's life from birth to puberty to maturity to old age and back again. Another interpretation of this rich phrase sees masculine energy (and thought) in the first two words and feminine energy (and speech) in the third and fourth. SNBH also represents the coming together of Changing Woman's parents: Long Life Boy and Happiness Girl.[25] SNBH thus evokes both reproduction (human fertility, livestock vitality, and abundant crops) and complementarity. It represents an orderly world "in which the inner and outer forms are in balance—east complements west, north complements south, men complement women."[26]

Central to this all-important phrase is a sense of movement. In Diné life and thought, everything is in flux. The Native American artist Trudy Griffin-Pierce sees this imperative to move in sand paintings, which "are full of symbolically expressed motion: swirling snakes, rotating logs, streaming head plumes, whirling rainbows." The heroes of the Diné's creation stories are often on the move. This emphasis on movement is particularly plain in the Holy Wind, which not only animates all living things but gets them up and moving. To balance is not to be static, Griffin-Pierce argues, it is to be in motion. The order evoked by the word *hozho* is a "dynamic order."[27] The restoration of this dynamic order is evoked in the Blessingway, in which the patient's body, mind, and voice are symbolically identified with the earth and then with SNBH itself as the singer sings:

> *Saah Naaghaii Bikeh Hozho I shall be,*
> *Before me it will be hozho as I live on,*
> *Behind me it will be hozho as I live on,*
> *Below me it will be hozho as I live on,*
> *Above me it will be hozho as I live on.*[28]

Ceremonies and Holy People

The main technique for restoring this way of beauty is the ceremony—a one- to nine-day event that aims to revert things to their original beauty by reestablishing right relationships among the Diné, between the Diné and the natural and social worlds, and between the Diné and the Holy People. Because illness is viewed as a symptom of a wider disorder, ceremonies aim to restore the health and harmony of not only an individual but also a community and the wider cosmos.

Many religious people, including Jews, Christians, and the Navajo's Pueblo neighbors, observe holy days in keeping with a calendar. The very term "holy days" implies as

---

Navajo Religion at a Glance

Problem: hocho, or ugliness, chaos, disequilibrium, and all that is bad

Solution: hozho, or harmony, beauty, balance, and all that is good

Techniques: prayers, offerings, and ceremonies meant to restore individuals and the community to health and harmony

Exemplar: Changing Woman and other creation story heroes who turn ugliness into beauty and sickness into health

In short, Navajo religion is a way of beauty in which medicine people and their patients work together to cultivate health and harmony through various ceremonies.

Hastin-Acani-Badanie, a Navajo singer, conducts a Shooting Chant in St. Michaels, Arizona, to improve the health of a mother and her baby. Shooting Chants are used to expel evil spirits from people.

hogan ("place home")
domestic and religious structure that opens to the east and is used for ceremonies

singer (hataalii)
medicine person, also known as a chanter, who organizes and conducts ceremonies in order to restore individual health and community harmony

Changing Woman
the epitome of goodness in the Navajo Way, she brought the Diné into being and embodies the cycle from birth to puberty to maturity to happy old age

First Man and First Woman
the first male/female pair, they planned, modeled, and brought into being the Earth Surface World after emerging from the lower worlds

much. In contrast, Navajo ceremonies occur whenever someone needs protection or healing. They take place not in a church or synagogue but in a home, which Navajos call a **hogan** ("place home"). These ceremonies typically originate with a request from a particular individual who is suffering from an illness or whose life is otherwise out of balance.

Singing is so central to these ceremonies that they are often called chantways. The medicine person who performs them is called a **singer (hataalii)**. Traditionally, there were dozens of ceremonies. Nowadays, seven or eight are still widely performed. Some of these ceremonies are curative and aim to restore hozho. Others are preventive and aim to maintain hozho.

Diné ceremonies are addressed to the Diyin Dine'é, who are the exemplars of the Navajo way. The most common translation for this phrase is "Holy People." That translation is not ideal because Holy People are not holy, at least not in the sense of always being well behaved. It is a common misperception in the West that to be a god is to be good. But gods who are good—"big gods" who exemplify goodness and punish evil, in the words of the social psychologist Ara Norenzayan—are actually quite rare in the world's religions.[29] In this respect, the Holy People are like most gods. An intriguing mix of good and bad, they are perfectly capable of helping and hurting humans, of restoring order and stirring up chaos (though some tend more toward evil and others toward good). What distinguishes Holy People from Earth Surface People is not their morality but their superpower. For this reason, "superbeings" is a better translation.[30] However, the translation "Holy People" is nevertheless widespread.

Changing Woman The most beloved Holy Person is **Changing Woman**. According to the Diné author Rose Mitchell, of all the Holy People, "only Changing Woman is totally dependable and without a side that will bring you harm."[31] A key character in Navajo creation stories and in the Blessingway, Changing Woman is the daughter of Long Life Boy and Happiness Girl. She is the mother (with Sun) of the hero twins, Monster Slayer and Born for Water (also known as Child of the Water), who, by slaying the demons that came up from the underworlds, prepared the way for harmony on earth. She then used the powers of the medicine bundle given to her by **First Man and First Woman** to make **corn** and the first Diné. Like the Hindu goddess Parvati, who used the dried skin from her own body to create her son Ganesha, Changing Woman mixed her dry skin with four types of corn and minerals of four colors to make four couples who would form the first Navajo clans. For this reason, the Diné widely describe Changing Woman as "our Mother."

A symbol of creation and renewal, Changing Woman also was the first girl to undergo the puberty ritual for girls now known as *kinaalda*. She is said to cycle from season to season and from birth to puberty to maturity to old age, appearing in the spring as a fertile woman, and in the fall as old and barren. Because she also cycles from white to blue to yellow to black dresses, she is also known as White Shell Woman, Turquoise Woman, Abalone Woman, and Jet Woman.

Father Sky and Mother Earth Complementarity is a central value in the Navajo way, beginning with the first male/female pair, First Man and First Woman, who raised Changing Woman and played such a central role in the emergence story. Father Sky and Mother Earth also embody the harmony and balance of the sexes that characterizes hozho. Father Sky is associated with the Sun, Moon, and stars and Mother Earth with corn, tobacco, squash, and beans. The Diné also gender and pair their four sacred mountains: joining their male mountain in the east (Blanca Peak) with their female mountain in the west (San Francisco Peaks) and their female mountain in the south (Mount Taylor) with their male mountain in the north (Hesperus Peak). They also understand human beings to have two complementary winds, one from the mother and another from the father.

Coyote Coyote, another major character in the emergence story, has been likened to trickster figures in other literature and folklores. A creature of chaos, his lying, lust, and gluttony lead him to disrupt whatever harmony he might encounter. In one story that illustrates Coyote's impulsive nature, Black God is carefully taking the stars from a blanket at his feet and forming them into constellations. Coyote comes along, picks up the blanket, and shakes all the stars randomly up into the sky.

Forever in motion, Coyote is a homeless wanderer who can rapidly change his appearance. He is also fearless, likely because if he dies he can spring back to life as surely as Wile E. Coyote in the Looney Tunes cartoons. Like all living beings, however, this fearsome yet entertaining character is not all bad. His foolishness makes him an unwitting teacher, and on occasion he exhibits wisdom, such as the time he argued successfully for death to be permanent in order to save the world from overcrowding.

Holy Wind The subtle force undergirding the movement and change so highly prized in Navajo thinking is **Holy Wind (Nilchi)**. This life force, reminiscent of *qi* (vital energy) in Chinese thinking, was present at creation and is present today. After Changing Woman shaped the first Diné, the Holy Wind brought her creations alive by entering their bodies through the fingers and toes before exiting through the ears and the tops of the head. It left them with whirls on their fingertips, toes, and hands. As it moves, the Holy Wind gives strength and protection to plants, animals, humans, rivers, mountains, and clouds, which are all interconnected by this shared life force. To lose this wind is to grow sick and die.

Holy Wind does more than animate and sustain, however. It also acts as a guide and a messenger. It led the Holy People up through the underworlds and guides Earth Surface People today. The Holy Wind also enables the Diné to think and communicate, making language, speech, and wisdom possible. As such, it also functions as a messenger between the Earth Surface People and the Holy People. Today, it exists inside all forms of life, which are in turn capable of imparting wisdom to anyone who interacts with them.

corn
traditional Diné food staple and the food of the Holy People, a crucial element (as pollen or cornmeal) in ceremonies, a symbol of fertility, and a repository of the powers of creation

Coyote
a key figure in Diné stories; a dangerously entertaining wanderer known for stirring up chaos through his lies, lust, greed, gluttony, and impatience

Holy Wind (Nilchi)
animating life force and a source of movement for all living things, associated with breath, speech, thought, and action

Members of a Diné family gather in a field in White Cone, Arizona, in 1979 for the *kinaalda* puberty ceremony of a young girl (right, wrapped in a blanket). An older woman cuts a cornmeal cake that was baked overnight in the ground outside of a *hogan*.

NAVAJO RELIGIOUS HISTORY

Navajos and non-Navajo academics have different understandings of the history of the Diné way of life. Academics typically trace the origins of all Native Americans to humans who crossed from Asia into the Americas around twenty thousand years ago. Navajos instead trace their origins to their emergence from the underworlds in the place they call Navajoland. There are also Navajo oral traditions of interactions with ancestral Puebloans (once referred to as the Anasazi), with whom the Navajo feel intimately connected. Historians and Navajos agree, however, on two things: that the Navajo have endured almost unimaginable suffering since the first contact with Europeans, and that they have shown creativity and resilience in adapting to these horrors.

After the arrival of the Spanish in the Southwest in the sixteenth century, Navajos suffered and died from epidemics of infectious diseases that cut short the lives of millions of native people in the Americas. They were killed by soldiers, imprisoned and executed by settlers, enslaved, confined to reservations, taxed beyond capacity, beset by economic depressions, missionized by Christians, and in many cases forced to convert. Their ceremonies were outlawed, their ritual experts punished, and their ritual instruments were destroyed, stolen, or auctioned off. Yet the Diné survived, retaining their cultural and religious traditions through creative adaptation.

Precontact Navajo History

The Diné speak a language that is part of the Athabaskan language family still prevalent in eastern Alaska, western Canada, and parts of the northwestern United States. Most scholars believe that the Navajo migrated into the Southwest from Athabaskan-speaking regions to the north. Navajo oral traditions also attest to a similar migration. The timing of this arrival is disputed. There is little doubt that the Diné arrived before the Europeans, and many anthropologists and archaeologists date that arrival to a time between 1400 and 1525. However, there is some archaeological evidence, including tree-ring dates from hogan-like structures, that could push that arrival date back to 1100.

Initially, the Navajo were hunter-gatherers and they remained seminomadic into the twentieth century. They may have learned techniques for farming corn and squash from Plains groups as they traveled south. In the Southwest, they settled into more sedentary lives as agriculturalists. Diné oral traditions speak of long-standing interactions with the Pueblo and of various adaptations of Pueblo culture. During the seventeenth century or earlier, the Navajo learned farming methods from the Pueblo and shaped them to their own purposes. The Pueblo also influenced Navajo art, including the rugs for which Navajos are internationally regarded. One must be careful with these lists of influences, however, lest they "doom the Navajos to second-class citizenship" as a people who needed to be taught how to survive.[32] Surely the Diné had survival skills long before they started farming and weaving, and like all peoples they likely lent as much as they borrowed. They used those survival skills in interacting with other tribes and then Europeans.

The Pueblo Revolt

In 1493, Pope Alexander VI issued a papal proclamation commanding Roman Catholics to conquer and colonize new lands in the Americas. That project did not affect the Diné

The clay pottery of ancestral Puebloans (formerly known as the Anasazi) is celebrated for its geometric designs and white and gray color schemes. It differs from other ancient Mesoamerican pottery, which tended to be molded from brown clay. This vase dates to approximately 1000 CE.

until Spaniards started to show up in the Southwest in the sixteenth century. The most notorious colonizer was Governor Juan de Oñate, who claimed New Mexico for Spain in 1598 and set the stage for the Pueblo Revolt of 1680. Oñate is remembered today for the 1599 Acoma Massacre, which claimed the lives of several hundred residents of the Acoma Pueblo, still active west of Albuquerque, New Mexico. Many of those who were not killed were taken as slaves and had a foot cut off.

In French territories in North America, missionaries from Roman Catholicism's Jesuit order employed a strategy of accommodation and inclusion, attempting to integrate Catholic beliefs and practices into native cultures (and vice versa). By contrast, the missionaries from the Franciscan order who dominated in the Southwest employed a strategy of confrontation and exclusion, demanding that converts turn their backs on their native cultures, languages, and kinship groups.

The first Franciscans arrived in Navajoland in 1627 but had little success converting the *Apaches de Navajo*, as they called the Diné. In fact, Navajos managed largely to avoid the Spanish for roughly a century after the Franciscans arrived. The Pueblo were not so lucky. Franciscans, as part of a confrontational missions strategy, destroyed Pueblo objects and the kivas, or ceremonial rooms, where Pueblo rituals took place. They forced the Pueblo to go to church and prohibited traditional religious gatherings. The Pueblo who refused to comply were beaten in public. The Pueblo were also victimized by a system that forced them to pay a portion of their crops every year to the Spanish government and to work in Spanish households for free. Meanwhile, the Pueblo died in massive numbers from European diseases to which they had no immunity. When Spaniards entered their region in the late sixteenth century, there were an estimated one hundred thousand Pueblo in the Southwest. A century later there were roughly thirty thousand.

This wall painting at the Museum of Northern Arizona is one panel of a forty-eight-foot mural called "Journey of the Human Spirit" (2001) by Hopi artists Michael Kabotie and Delbridge Honanie. It depicts the Pueblo fight against the encroachment of the Spanish into their lands during the Pueblo Revolt of 1680.

During the middle of the seventeenth century, the Pueblo launched a series of unsuccessful revolts against Spanish rule. Their determination stiffened in 1675 after the Spanish arrested forty-seven of their medicine men and convicted them of sorcery. Three died by hanging. The rest were flogged and released. One of those religious leaders was Popé (or, Popay), who spent the next five years trying to convince Pueblo communities from Taos in the north to Isleta in the southwest to work together to overthrow Spanish rule and restore the balance to Pueblo life.

The Pueblo Revolt, which has also been labeled the "first American Revolution," began on August 10, 1680. Popay's men quickly captured the Spaniards' Santa Fe capital. Before a month had passed, the Spanish retreated, leaving behind four hundred dead, including twenty-one Franciscan missionaries. The Pueblo celebrated their victory by striking out at the religious symbols of their colonizers. According to a Pueblo witness named Pedro Naranjo, they smashed church bells, burned crosses and images of the Virgin Mary, nullified Catholic marriages, and renounced their Catholic names. In this way, Naranjo reported, these revolutionaries "returned to the state of their antiquity."[33]

Efforts to create a revitalized society in keeping with the traditions of their ancestors were frustrated by persistent droughts and ongoing raids from rival tribes. When the Spanish returned and retook their lands after twelve years of Pueblo self-rule, they were somewhat more accommodating of native religions and more open to multiple religious affiliations.

Livestock, which are typically overseen by Navajo women, have played a key role in the economy and culture of the Navajo Nation for centuries. Here, a family tends to its flock in Monument Valley, Utah, during the 1980s.

The Navajo interacted minimally with the Spanish, perhaps because they were still seminomadic. But Spaniards brought horses and sheep, and the Diné traded to acquire them. In the process, the Diné became pastoralists as well as agriculturalists. They also became raiders of livestock and warriors who defended their livestock from other raiders, especially the Apache. Raiding became an even more important part of Navajo culture after the Spaniards brought the horse to North America, but Mexicans and Spaniards raided, too, as did other tribes. Traditionally, women owned both the livestock and the land, and Navajo society was matrilineal. After getting married, men would move in with their bride's mother's family. The children they produced would trace their descent through their mothers, and daughters would inherit property from their mothers.

Just as the Diné initially benefited from their distance from the Spanish in the 1500s and 1600s, they benefited from the short hiatus from Spanish rule after the Pueblo Revolt. During the 1700s, they raised sheep and produced weavings for trade with Europeans and Mexicans. But they couldn't escape the fact that they were living in an enclave surrounded by foreigners. In 1805, more than a hundred Diné men, women, and children died in a massacre at Canyon de Chelly in modern-day Arizona. Things got much worse after the United States took over large tracts of the Southwest in the 1840s.

The Long Walk and the Navajo Nation Treaty

Through the Louisiana Purchase of 1803, the United States had already roughly doubled its land mass, which stretched west into modern-day Texas, New Mexico, and Colorado. Animated by the spirit of "manifest destiny" that saw the West as a gift from God, Americans claimed much of western North America in the 1840s. They annexed Texas in 1845. After defeating Mexico in the Mexican-American War, they gained control of much of the Southwest in the Treaty of Guadalupe Hidalgo of 1848. Life was hard for the Diné for the next two decades, as war broke out periodically with American settler colonialists, but it got much worse during the "Fearing Time" of the early 1860s. During this era, the Diné were increasingly dominated by federal, state, and local governments that suppressed their religious traditions and their language, forced children to enroll in boarding schools, killed livestock, seized and exploited lands, and otherwise sought to control Diné affairs.

As this era opened, General James H. Carleton was appointed in 1862 to oversee the New Mexico Territory. As historian Peter Iverson observes, U.S. policy toward Native Americans and immigrants alike was split between the impulses to assimilate, to segregate, and to subdue. When it came to the Diné, federal efforts focused on two strategies: getting the Diné, who were still seminomadic, to "change from their present roving habits to the pursuit of agriculture," and getting them to abandon their traditional ceremonies for proper Christian worship.[34] But Carleton was not an assimilationist, and under other circumstances he might have tried to subdue the Diné militarily. But the Civil War, which would run from 1861 to 1865, had drawn troops back east and left settlers vulnerable to Navajo and Apache raids. So Carleton chose a policy of segregation. He decided to move the Navajo to a reservation at Bosque Redondo in New Mexico outside of Fort Sumner, and he was willing to do whatever it took to make that happen.

In 1863, Carleton sent orders to the frontiersman Kit Carson to round up the Navajo and take them there. "Say to them—'Go to Bosque Redondo, or we will pursue and destroy you,'" Carleton wrote. "This war shall be pursued against you if it takes years, now that we have begun, until you cease to exist or move."[35] Initially, very few Navajos surrendered,

This U.S. Department of Defense photograph was originally captioned "Fort Sumner, New Mexico. Guadeloupe County at the Bosque Redondo on Pecos River. Counting Indians." It depicts the gruesome conditions that Diné prisoners were subjected to by the U.S. government during the Long Walk of the 1860s.

so Carson and his troops transitioned quickly to subduing. Cutting a deadly path across Navajo lands, they killed and captured the Diné and destroyed their homes. They filled Diné watering holes with dirt, killed Diné livestock, and destroyed Diné crops, fields, and orchards. Some Diné, determined to remain on their own land, continued to resist. A group led by the headman Manuelito held out for years, but when faced with a choice between starvation and surrender, most surrendered.

Between 1863 and 1868, some fifty-three groups of Navajo prisoners—perhaps as many as ten thousand—were forced to walk more than three hundred miles through the desert to a hastily constructed Bosque Redondo Indian Reservation at Fort Sumner, New Mexico. This forced march of suffering and death—the Long Walk, in Diné memory—was similar to the Trail of Tears walked by the Cherokee as they were exiled from their homelands in the Southeast in the late 1830s to Indian Territory in modern-day Oklahoma. Pregnant women, the sick, and the elderly who could not keep up were shot and killed. "It was horrible the way they treated our people," a Navajo named Curly Tso reported. "Some old handicapped people, and children who couldn't make the journey, were shot on the spot, and their bodies were left behind for crows and coyotes to eat."[36]

The years survivors spent at Fort Sumner were catastrophic for the Diné. The land was overworked and the facilities, designed for four to five thousand people, were dangerously overcrowded. Anglo settlers and local tribes repeatedly raided the reservation. Religious ceremonies were banned, as were songs and prayers in the Navajo language. Efforts to raise crops were thwarted by drought. Food was rationed. Diseases spread. Nearly one thousand Navajos escaped, but roughly fifteen hundred captives died of illness and malnutrition.

Eventually, the U.S. government recognized that this experiment had failed. In 1868, the U.S. government and the Diné entered into a treaty that would allow the five to seven thousand Navajo survivors at Bosque Redondo to go free.

General William Tecumseh Sherman initially planned to relocate them to an Indian Territory in Oklahoma, but Diné women appealed to him to allow them to take a "Long Walk Home" to Navajoland. The Navajo leader and ceremonial singer Barboncito, who traveled to Washington, DC, to negotiate the terms of the treaty, told Sherman:

> When the Navajos were first created, four mountains and four rivers were pointed out to us, inside of which we should live, that was to be our country, and was given to us by the first woman of the Navajo tribe. . . . I hope to God you will not ask me to go to any other country than my own.[37]

Sherman agreed to allow the Diné to return home. The treaty established a Diné reservation of about 3.5 million acres inside the four sacred mountains and recognized the sovereignty of the Diné people over their nation. The boundaries of that reservation expanded in 1878 and on various later occasions, and it now totals more than 17 million acres in northeastern Arizona, southeastern Utah, and northwestern New Mexico.

The Diné today view the "Old Paper," as they call the Navajo Treaty, as a sacred artifact not only of their sovereignty but also of their survival at a time when their numbers had been reduced to about ten thousand and they were threatened with extinction. They understand that agreement as a compact with the United States as well as the Holy People, who put an end to the suffering and death of the Long Walk and set them on a course back home.

The seven or eight thousand Navajo survivors who were able to return home brought with them new silversmithing techniques, which made use of turquoise, and new ceremonies, including the Chiricahua Windway. For the most part, they returned to subsistence shepherding and farming. They also returned to find Christian missionaries, who got a boost from a new so-called Peace Policy introduced in 1868 by President Ulysses S. Grant's administration. This policy handed control over Indian affairs to Christian missionaries supervised by a newly created Board of Indian Commissioners (BIC). It was strengthened by U.S. Indian court judges who in 1883 began imprisoning Diné medicine people for conducting "evil" ceremonies.

The BIC gave the Navajo franchise to Presbyterians, who quickly established two missions on the reservation but made few converts. Mormons baptized their first converts

A Christian church built by the Blackgoat family sits at the entrance to their property on Navajo Nation land. Many Diné Christians also practice some combination of Peyotism and traditional Diné religion.

Peyotism
pan-tribal religious tradition
that uses the mildly hallucinogenic cactus peyote in its
meetings

Native American Church
pan-tribal Peyotist organization established in 1918 and
now called the Native American Church of North America

in the 1870s, and Methodists, Episcopalians, and Catholics arrived in the last decade of the nineteenth century. These Christian groups might have capitalized on federal laws in the 1880s that outlawed traditional religious ceremonies among Native groups, but the soul-winning was meager. Not until the 1950s would Christianity make any real headway among the Navajo.

The Native American Church

Long before Europeans arrived in the Americas, the Huichol people of northern Mexico were partaking of peyote, a mildly hallucinogenic plant that grows in northern Mexico and southern Texas. Peyote (from the Aztec term *peyotl*), contains round buttons that are typically dried for ritual use. Practitioners chew these buttons or boil them in water to make a tea. Peyote's bitter taste often produces nausea, which can then yield to feelings of well-being and euphoria. Like the moment of "sacred seeing" in which the Hindu devotees look into the eyes of their gods and are seen in return, this is a key moment in peyote ritual.

Peyotism spread from Mexico to Oklahoma in the 1870s and 1880s, as the federal government was forcing more and more tribes onto reservations. One reason for this rapid and widespread diffusion was intertribal connectivity, which helped turn Peyotism into a pan-Indian movement. Also fostering these connections were new and improved roads and railroads, boarding schools, and Wild West shows and rodeos. A second reason for the popularity of Peyotism was the ability of traveling roadmen to capitalize on these connections. Not unlike the circuit riders who spread Methodism across the United States in the 1830s and 1840s, these roadmen spread the story and practice of their religion.

Local, state, and federal officials tried to suppress or outlaw Peyotism as a drug cult. In 1918, the U.S. House of Representatives held hearings on antipeyote legislation supported by Christian groups and temperance organizations such as the Anti-Saloon League. The Native nations and their allies who testified did their best to convince the politicians and the press that Peyotism was a religion. Because of the dominance of Christianity in the American imagination, they did so largely by comparing it with Christian symbols, beliefs, and practices.

Earlier, in a letter to the Bureau of Indian Affairs commissioner, the pioneering Winnebago Peyotist Albert Hensley had referred to the "medicine" of peyote as "a portion of the body of Christ even as the communion bread is believed to be a portion of Christ's body by other Christian denominations."[38] At the congressional hearings, the ethnologist James Mooney testified that peyote was not dangerous, did not foster immoral behavior, and deserved religious liberty protections. He did so by analogy, arguing that Peyotism was "as close an approximation to Christianity and as efficient a leading up to Christianity as the Indian, speaking generally, is now capable of."[39]

In 1918, representatives from various tribes came together to charter the **Native American Church** of Oklahoma, which they hoped would help win for them the religious liberty protections of the First Amendment. Its purpose, as stated in its articles of incorporation, was "to foster and promote . . . the Christian religion with the practice of the Peyote Sacrament as commonly understood and used . . . and to teach the Christian religion with morality, sobriety, industry, kindly charity and right living and to cultivate a spirit of self-respect and brotherly union among the members of the Native Race of Indians." As similar organizations were incorporated, and roadmen spread the good news

The peyote plant is native to parts of northern Mexico and southern Texas. A spineless cactus, it grows in clumps low to the ground and flowers from March through May. The term "peyote" is Spanish and derives from the Aztec word for "glistening" or "divine messenger."

of Peyotism across Native American communities. Peyotism developed, in the words of anthropologist Omer Stewart, into "one of the strongest pan-Indian movements in the United States."[40]

The key figure in early Peyotism in what is now the United States was the Comanche leader Quanah Parker (c. 1845–1911). It is unclear how Parker, who was born in modern-day Oklahoma or Texas to a Comanche headman and a white woman captive, was introduced to peyote. According to one widely told story, he developed a life-threatening infection after he was gored by a bull in Mexico. A white doctor was no help, but a local medicine man administered a peyote tea that saved his life. Parker then attended an all-night ceremony where he consumed peyote. He learned oral traditions concerning peyote's healing powers. Eventually, he became a roadman himself who took peyote back to the Comanche in Oklahoma.

Parker presented the "Peyote Road," as he called it, as a more direct route to Jesus than traditional Christianity. "The white man goes into his church house and talks *about* Jesus," he said, "but the Indian goes into his tipi and talks *to* Jesus."[41] This approach looked to peyote for healing and guidance. It also emphasized ethics, opposing alcohol use and adultery and promoting compassion and nonviolence.

This new religious movement was called the Quanah Parker Way and the Comanche Way, but it is now known as the Half Moon Way because of its use of an altar made of soil curving around a fire pit in the shape of a half crescent. Atop and in the middle of that altar, which opened to the east, was a large peyote button referred to as Grandfather Peyote. The movement spread among the Comanche and then out to other Native nations in the western United States. Today, most Peyotists in North America follow this Half Moon Way.

The second most popular form of Peyotism also developed in the late nineteenth century. The Big Moon or Cross Fire Way, as it is called, is traced to John Wilson, a mixed-race man (Delaware, Caddo, and French) of the Caddo tribe. It is said that, during his peyote experiments, he was blessed with a vision that led from the empty tomb of Jesus to the Moon in the Sky. He was then instructed how to conduct his peyote ceremony.

Parker had integrated Christian elements into his ceremony, but Wilson was more explicit about depicting the Peyote Road as a road to the Son of God. His Cross Fire altar, which was shaped like a horseshoe, included two intersecting lines that simultaneously marked the four directions and formed a cross. His meetings, where tobacco use was not allowed, freely employed Christian language and symbols, including the Bible. The Lord's Prayer was recited and the name of Jesus was sung.

Altars notwithstanding, the Cross Fire community was not all that different from the Half Moon community. Practitioners in both groups saw peyote as a medicine and a sacrament—a physical and a spiritual gift. The point of going to a meeting was not to experience visions but to heal, to learn, and to grow from peyote. Both communities stressed the curative function of peyote, particularly its ability to cure the disease of alcoholism that was ravaging reservations at the time. The communities grew in part because their practices seemed to do just that.

Initially, both meetings were patronized almost entirely by men, though women who were sick and in need of healing could also participate. Gradually, women and children began joining their husbands, fathers, and grandfathers, and women's participation ramped up substantially in the 1950s and 1960s. It was not unknown for women to run peyote meetings. A practitioner named Dog Woman, whose husband was a roadman, is

This peyote rattle was made by the Peyotism innovator John Wilson circa 1885 in Oklahoma. It is crafted from a dried gourd, wood, animal hide, glass beads, brass bells, and feathers. Rattles are used alongside water drums in all-night Native American Church ceremonies.

said to have become the first Cheyenne woman to run meetings after she was given peyote ritual equipment, complete with a Grandfather Peyote, a staff, a drum, and a gourd, by Quanah Parker himself.[42]

Within a few years of the NAC's founding in 1918 in Oklahoma, peyote churches were established in surrounding states and among other Native nations. In 1944, the NAC renamed itself the Native American Church of the United States, which became the Native American Church of North America in 1955. The Native American Church of Navajoland was founded in 1966 and was recently renamed Azee' Bee Nahagha of Diné Nation ("Peyote Ceremony of Diné Nation").

The history of the suppression of Peyotism is almost as long as that of Peyotism itself. In 1620, the Spanish Inquisition denounced its use as an "act of superstition condemned as opposed to the purity and integrity of our Holy Catholic Faith."[43] When Peyotism moved up to Oklahoma, nineteenth-century Christian missionaries tried to outlaw it. The U.S. government also tried to suppress Peyotism. In 1890, the Bureau of Indian Affairs issued an order "to seize and destroy the mescal bean," as it called the peyote button, and to criminalize its use and distribution.[44] In 1899, the Oklahoma Territory outlawed its possession and distribution. Between 1917 and 1937, most western states did the same. John Collier, who was appointed commissioner of Indian Affairs by President Franklin D. Roosevelt, promoted an "Indian New Deal" that promised to replace old federal policies of assimilation and Christian missionizing with a new policy of "cultural pluralism" that would put an end to the suppression of Native American religions. Nonetheless, a federal law banned peyote in 1965, and in 1970 Congress listed it as a Schedule 1 drug.

CHRONOLOGY OF NAVAJO RELIGION

1100–1525 CE Navajo culture emerges on what is now known as the Colorado Plateau near today's Four Corners region of the American Southwest

1493 Pope Alexander VI issues papal bull to conquer and colonize new lands in the Americas

1598–1599 Spanish conquistador Juan de Oñate claims New Mexico on behalf of Spain and leads a massacre at Acoma Pueblo that takes several hundred lives

1627 The first Franciscans arrive in Navajoland in a failed effort to convert the *Apaches de Navajo*

1680 Pueblo Revolt drives the Spanish out of modern-day New Mexico

1805 The Spanish kill more than one hundred Diné men, women, and children in the Canyon de Chelly massacre

1838–1839 Trail of Tears; forced march of some seventeen thousand Cherokee from their southeastern homelands to Indian Territory in modern-day Oklahoma

1863–1868 The Long Walk; forced march of thousands of Diné to incarceration at Bosque Redondo outside Fort Sumner in New Mexico

1868 Navajo Treaty ends their captivity at Bosque Redondo and allows the Diné to return from exile to a newly formed Navajo reservation in their homeland

1883 U.S. Indian court judges begin sending Diné medicine people to prison for engaging in "evil" ceremonies

1890 Bureau of Indian Affairs orders the seizure and destruction of peyote and criminalizes its use and distribution

1918 Native American Church is founded

1924 Indian Citizenship Act grants citizenship to all Native Americans born in the United States; they are not yet allowed to vote

1934 Indian Reorganization Act adopts "Indian New Deal" policies, including a new principle of noninterference in Native American religion

The Diné were relatively slow to take up Peyotism. Diné Christians opposed it, as did traditional Diné, who saw it as a threat to the Navajo way. In 1940, the Navajo Tribal Council passed a resolution prohibiting peyote use, which it described as "harmful and foreign to our traditional way of life."[45] In 1958, three Navajo Peyotists were arrested and later found guilty and sentenced by the Navajo tribal court. Peyote was legalized in the Navajo Nation in 1967, and Navajo territories in Arizona and New Mexico quickly became a stronghold for the NAC.

There are many reasons for the popularity of Peyotism among Native Americans in general and Navajos in particular.[46] First is its widespread reputation for healing, which Peyotists trace to the divine power of Grandfather Peyote. The Navajo word for peyote is *azee'* ("medicine"), and when the anthropologist David Aberle interviewed Navajos for a 1966 book, he found that roughly four out of five of his interviewees first used peyote in hopes of being cured.[47]

Peyote also gained in popularity because it was viewed as ancient and local rather than modern and imported. The Diné in particular gravitated to Peyotism as a healing ceremony that was in many ways consistent with the traditional Navajo religion. It, too, placed individual illness and wellness inside a broader holistic system of disharmony and harmony. It, too, was a sung religion whose ceremonies took place around a sacred circle. Some Diné even viewed Peyotism as yet another traditional healing ceremony, lauding its ability to cure alcoholism. Peyotism also spread because it offered an ethical way of life, which included not gambling, not drinking, not lying, and faithfulness in marriage.

1929–1939 Great Depression decimates Navajo economy

1934 Federal livestock reduction policy further cripples Navajo economy while also threatening traditional Navajo religion

1940 Navajo Tribal Council bans peyote use as "harmful and foreign"

1942–1945 Diné Code Talkers in the Marines employ Navajo language as an unbreakable code in World War II

1966 Native American Church of Navajoland is founded

1967 Navajo Tribal Council lifts ban on peyote use in the name of religious freedom

1969 Navajos declare themselves to be the Navajo Nation

1978 American Indian Religious Freedom Act (AIRFA) affirms religious liberty for Native Americans, including possession of sacred objects and access to sacred sites

1990 Supreme Court rules in *Oregon v. Smith* that Peyotism is not constitutionally protected

1993 Religious Freedom Restoration Act (RFRA) instructs Supreme Court to weigh the "substantial burdens" of religious practitioners against the "compelling state interest" of government

1994 American Indian Religious Freedom Act (AIRFA) amendments legalize ritual peyote use by Native American Church members

2001 President George W. Bush presents Congressional Gold Medals to World War II Code Talkers

2008 Ninth District Court of Appeals rules against Native tribes in *Navajo Nation v. U.S. Forest Service,* allowing snowmaking with treated wastewater to go forward on the San Francisco Peaks

Another reason for Peyotism's success was its leaders' openness to multiple religious affiliations. Peyotists typically felt free to participate not only in peyote meetings but also in traditional ceremonies and church services. Although some Christians insisted on religious exclusivity, many viewed these three options as different paths up the same mountain. As the historian Thomas C. Maroukis observes, visitors to NAC cemeteries today can see "a sacred pipe or eagle feathers (traditional), a Peyote drum or teepee (NAC), and a cross (Christian), all on the same headstone."[48]

One final factor contributed to Peyotism's popularity: consuming peyote in a small group around a fire from dusk to dawn created not only intense experiences of social solidarity but also direct access to what participants understood to be the divine. People felt a mysterious presence as they sat with each other and with Grandfather Peyote, and after they went home in the morning they wanted to return again.

The only major roadblock to Peyotism's growth now seems to be a dwindling supply of peyote. Serious strains on that supply have been caused by a combination of the popularity of Peyotism, Mexican laws banning the export of peyote to the United States, growing development in peyote-growing regions of the United States, increased droughts brought on by climate change, recreational use in non-Native populations, and lawsuits by non-Natives demanding that they be granted equal access to peyote buttons for sacramental use. In 2017, the Diné and members of other Native nations worked through a nonprofit called the Indigenous Peyote Conservation Initiative to purchase 605 acres in South Texas to reforest as peyote habitat.

LIVED RELIGION IN NAVAJOLAND

Today, many Diné rise with the sun to pray at dawn, noon, and at evening time. During the intervening day, they may participate in traditional ceremonies, NAC meetings, Christian worship services, or some combination of all three.

Ceremonies

Ceremonies are the central practices in traditional Navajo religion. Unlike Saturday synagogue services or Sunday church services, they are held on an as-needed basis. Whereas Pueblo ceremonies are generally paid for and performed on behalf of a social group, Navajo ceremonies are for individuals and are held in homes. Their stated purpose is to restore the health and harmony to a patient, who is called the **one-sung-over**. The ceremony is also believed to restore hozho to the community and the wider world.

Ceremonies bring the one-sung-over into contact with the Holy People. They aim to convince (or coerce) those superbeings to restore the sick to well-being. During a ceremony, the Holy People are invited into the hogan via prayers and offerings. The one-sung-over is encouraged to identify with a hero in a creation story who was able to turn ugliness into beauty, chaos into order. Each ceremony has an origin story that explains when it was first used and how it was transmitted from the Holy People to the Earth Surface People.

The ceremony must be performed properly in order to compel the Holy People to help. Intriguingly, the Navajo see ceremonies as contracts in which the Holy People are

one-sung-over
patient in a Navajo ceremony

Jones Benally, a Diné medicine man, stands in front of his office at the Winslow Indian Health Center in Winslow, Arizona. He is known for using traditional Diné chanting techniques in combination with Western medical treatment for healing.

obliged by the Diné ethic of reciprocity to act as requested and restore the one-sung-over to health and harmony: "Correct performance equals healed patient."[49] In this way, the patient is not only healed but also reconnected to Diné stories and the Diné way of life and restored to right relationships with Diné land, family members, community members, and the Holy People.[50]

This work is done largely through song. In traditional Diné religion, the key utterance is not a sermon or a scripture reading. It is not even a prayer or a dance, though prayers and dances are part of many ceremonies. The central utterance of Navajo religion is the song, the central act is singing, and the central ritual actors are the singer and the one-sung-over.

Almost every scholar who has studied Diné ceremonies from the nineteenth century forward has tried to devise a scheme to classify them.[51] The only thing these efforts prove is that these ceremonies may not be classifiable. Nonetheless, there is some consensus that they can be divided into three broad types:

- Holyway, which restores health by attracting what is good to the patient. This is the largest category.
- Evilway, which restores health by repelling what is harmful to the patient.
- Lifeway, which restores health by treating injuries caused in accidents.

Two types of specialists officiate in Navajo ceremonies, a diagnostician and a singer. The **diagnostician** or diviner uses various means to determine the cause of the problem. This diagnosis is holistic, taking account of the whole person who is ill as well as the status of the surrounding community. The diagnostician then recommends a particular technique to attack the root cause of the problem. In some cases these prescribed cures

diagnostician
ceremonial practitioner who diagnoses the illness of a particular individual and recommends an appropriate course of healing (often a ceremony)

The Hogan

Traditional Navajo hogans are both domestic and ceremonial sites. Made of wood and covered in mud, they open to the east, and their four main supports symbolize the four sacred mountains. Hogans are of two gendered types: male hogans are shaped like a pointed cone; female hogans are circular and round. Today few Navajos live in traditional hogans, which are now used largely for ceremonial purposes. A Blessingway song recounts the construction of the first hogan by Coyote with assistance from First Man, First Woman, and others. The Navajo author Rose Mitchell refers to the hogan as "the center of the family, and the mother, the heart."[a]

In recent years, hogans have begun to attract tourism to the Navajo Nation. The northern Arizona hogan pictured here is a popular rental on Airbnb. Located at the Shash Diné Eco-Retreat, it is advertised as "a traditional earth and log Navajo Hogan," ideal for "glamping" near Lake Powell.[b] The owners note that their family history on their off-the-grid sheep ranch extends to fifteen generations on land that "dates back to ancient times." They call their B&B a "5 billion star hotel."[c]

are relatively simple: purification or prayer or herbal remedy. In many cases, a stronger cure may be needed, and that is where ceremonies come in. The ceremony the patient and his or her family decide to hold is then performed by a singer who specializes in that particular ceremony. This singer organizes the ceremony, engages in various purification rituals in advance of it, and then oversees it.

There are many women diagnosticians, and women also gather ceremonial herbs. Singing women are rarer, but women do take on this role, particularly after menopause. In her research for *Blood and Voice: Navajo Women Ceremonial Practitioners* (2003), Maureen Trudelle Schwarz interviewed seventeen ceremonial practitioners and five apprentices who were women.

Neither diagnosticians nor singers are priests. To become a singer, an initiate must learn a ceremony. This learning is accomplished through a long and detailed apprenticeship that can take many years, so most singers specialize in just one or two. As an apprentice, the student learns the stories behind the ceremonies. He or she also learns how to create the ritual objects used in a ceremony and how to sing the songs and say the prayers. All must be memorized precisely and performed without errors. If the ceremony is not done right, it will not work. Each ceremony lasts one to nine nights, and in some cases the diagnostician may recommend more than one ceremony.

Ceremonies include a variety of ritual activities, including sweat purification, consuming herbs and corn pollen, bathing with yucca soap, sand painting, offerings, prayers, and lots of singing accompanied by drums, rattles, whistles, and other instruments. Men are assigned to the south side of the hogan and women to the north. The singer sits to the southwest facing the patient, who occupies the northwest side.

Ceremonies often conclude at dawn with a ritual called Breathing In. The one-sung-over faces the sun, stretches out her arms with her palms to the sky, pulls the power of the sun's rays toward her mouth with cupped hands, and then breathes it in. She does this four times to express her hope that the ceremony will accomplish what it is intended to do (and her determination to do what she can to make it so).

The Blessingway

Blessingway (hozhooji)
the most popular and important Navajo ceremony; a preventive ritual that aims at health, good fortune, and long life

The **Blessingway (hozhooji)**, which has been likened to the backbone of the Diné body and to the main stalk of a corn plant, is the most popular Diné ceremony and often the first one a singer learns. In keeping with the Diné emphasis on reversion to original harmony, the Blessingway recalls and reenacts the creation in an effort to re-create its beauty, harmony, and blessings. It tells of the origin of Changing Woman and her twin sons, of women's puberty rites, of Diné clans, and of the Blessingway itself. Unlike most Navajo ceremonies, the Blessingway is preventive rather than curative. Blessingways are conducted for childbirth, puberty, weddings, and long life. They are also performed to bless medicine bundles and new houses.

The received wisdom among anthropologists is that this ceremony developed after European contact and was shaped by Navajo-Pueblo interactions during the late seventeenth and early eighteenth centuries. Navajo oral traditions say the Blessingway was inaugurated shortly after the emergence. Diné scholar Harry Walters agrees, arguing that "the absence of extended references to livestock in the core ceremonial tales and the emphasis on corn and corn pollen speak to an aboriginal origin."[52] Shorter than more complicated ceremonies, the Blessingway typically consumes part of a night, the next morning, and all of the next night. It is, according to former Navajo Nation president Joe Shirley Jr., "the main ceremony that ties . . . all ceremonies together."[53]

Blessingways are relatively modest affairs, typically attended by family members and rarely by more than a dozen people. The Blessingway singer Frank Mitchell reports that, on the morning of this ceremony, the one-sung-over is ritually washed with soap and water

Sheila Goldtooth is a Blessingway singer in Canyon de Chelly, Arizona.

Frank and Rose Mitchell (1881–1967) (c. 1874–1977)

Frank and Rose Mitchell may have the best-documented lives in Navajo history. Each is the subject of an extensive autobiography edited by the anthropologist Charlotte Frisbie. *Navajo Blessingway Singer: The Autobiography of Frank Mitchell* (1977) is an excellent written source of information about the Blessingway, and *Tall Woman: The Life Story of Rose Mitchell* (2001) is the only full-length biographical treatment of the life of a Diné woman. These books describe a couple with twelve children who, despite their difficulties, continued to revert back to the Diné goal of "long life and happiness." Their lives also represent the gender complementarity highly prized in the Diné way.

Frank Mitchell worked in the wage economy that took so many Diné away from farming and raising livestock in the early twentieth century. After learning English at a boarding school in Fort Defiance, Arizona, he worked for a nearby Franciscan mission. He also hauled things to and from trading posts in a wagon. Later he worked as a politician, judge, and Blessingway singer. When the Navajo Tribal Council was formed in 1923, he was elected to represent Chinle, Arizona. In that role, he helped win Navajo women the right to vote. In his late forties he became a judge. Mitchell is largely remembered as a Blessingway singer, an occupation he learned from his father-in-law. After retiring, he worked with the Franciscan priest Berard Haile to produce recordings of the Blessingway and other ceremonies now held at the National Archives in Washington, DC. When asked why he put so much work into that project, he said, "When there is no more Blessingway, there will be no more Navajo people."[a]

Rose Mitchell was a mother, midwife, and weaver who took care of her family's farm and livestock. She did not go to school, she did not speak English, and she did not ever leave the reservation. In her biography, however, she left behind an extraordinarily lively and detailed account of a long life that would stretch beyond the century mark. Rose is far more candid than Frank, attending to both the blessings of her life and the difficulties presented by a marriage to a husband who was rarely home and not always faithful. "Making a living with someone" is how she refers to married life, and she has a clear understanding of the division of labor. "I was in charge of the hogan and everything concerned with it," she says. "With other things, like [the children's] schooling or what singers to get when someone needed a ceremony, he was in charge." Mitchell concludes her book with "words to the future generations" on, among other things, marriage. "I think if men and women ... treat each other with respect, talk with each other, learn to plan together, help each other, work together, and if they show affection ... then it's possible to stay together for many, many years."[b]

and then dried and sprinkled with corn pollen, all to the accompaniment of bathing songs and then drying songs. "Everything is washed out of you, and then the drying puts it back into you again, sacred and renewed," Mitchell explains.[54] The singer uses the medicine bundle to bless the one-sung-over. Prayer songs then invoke the sacred mountains and ask the Holy People for protection and blessing. During prayers, the one-sung-over may hold a prayer stick prepared out of reeds and decorated (or stuffed) with feathers, jewels, and pollen. Around eleven or noon, there is a time to eat and a break until evening.

In the evening, the hogan is blessed to the accompaniment of hogan songs. The Twelve-Word song of the Blessingway (which actually has twelve *verses*) concludes the first part of the evening rituals, typically around midnight. The songs that follow include songs about the sacred mountains. Eventually the dawn songs come, followed by another concluding Twelve-Word song at the end.

As the festivities conclude, the one-sung-over leaves the hogan with some corn pollen, sprinkling it toward the dawn and from north to south. "Then you inhale the dawn four times and give a prayer to yourself, the dawn, and everything that exists," Mitchell explains. "Everything is to be made holy again."[55] When the one-sung-over reenters the hogan, more pollen is passed around and the ceremony is finished.

Other Traditional Ceremonies

Other ceremonies include Enemyway, Mountainway, and Nightway. Enemyway is an antidote to the ill effects of contact with non-Navajos. It was inaugurated after Changing Woman's twins restored the earth to harmony by killing human-eating monsters. That first Enemyway ceremony helped purify the twins and the earth itself from the contamination of enemy ghosts. Today, the Enemyway is used to restore the bodies and minds of Navajo soldiers after tours of duty overseas. This ceremony is also called the Squaw Dance (though some consider that term derogatory) because it includes a rare public element in these usually private ceremonies: a dance that closes out the ceremony. Years after his Enemyway ceremony, John Brown Jr., a Navajo Code Talker, described that experience in an interview with the National Museum of the American Indian:

> I had nightmares thinking about the blood. The Japanese and the smell of the dead. Rotting Japanese and they probably got into my mind. And they had a Squaw Dance for me. . . . And I imagine they killed that evil spirit that was in my mind. That's what it's about. . . . It works.[56]

While Enemyway restores right relationships between the patient and non-Navajos, Mountainway restores right relationships between the patient and animals and therefore serves as an antidote to the ill effects of contact with bears and other creatures. Nightway restores right relationships between the patient and a subset of the Holy People known as *yé'ii*, or the Fail-to-Speak People, who, as their name implies, can call to one another but do not use speech. Nightway ceremonies may be appropriate when the patient suffers from blindness, deafness, or paralysis. On their final night, these ceremonies also feature public dances, in this case of masked and costumed ye'ii.

Sand Paintings

Sand paintings are an important part of many Navajo ceremonies. The Navajo term for this work of art and for the ritual that employs it—*iikaah*, or "enter and go"—suggests an image of the Holy People arriving at the ceremony through the sand painting and then leaving through it after their jobs are done.

Sand paintings are made of colored sands and ground minerals. Singers compose them on the floor in the middle of the hogan during a ceremony. Sand paintings, which are blessed with corn pollen or cornmeal, typically depict the four directions, the four mountains, and Holy People. During the ceremony, the one-sung-over walks into and sits down inside the sand painting. The singer applies its sand to the one-sung-over's feet, legs, body, and head so that the one-sung-over can identify more fully with the hero in the story that is being sung. After the ceremony, the one-sung-over stands up and leaves restored and renewed, literally enacting the "enter and go" imperative of this ceremonial art. Like Tibetan Buddhist sand paintings, which are typically cast into a body of water after

sand painting
Diné ceremonial tool made of sand and ground minerals that serves as a portal for Holy People to enter and exit a ceremony

A sand painter draws an image of water deities in Arizona during the 1980s. During healing ceremonies that use this spiritual technology, a medicine person invites the one-sung-over to identify with Holy People depicted in the sand painting.

BIRTH AND DEATH

The Diné have traditionally affirmed that life comes when the Holy Wind enters the body through the ears, and death comes when the Holy Wind exits the body through the fingers. The Diné have also observed many taboos regarding birth and death. There are things that should not be eaten and things that should not be said or seen.

The Blessingway ceremony is often performed before birth to ensure a safe pregnancy and a healthy child. Births used to take place in the hogan, but now they almost always occur in hospitals. After birth, traditional Navajos bury the umbilical cord in a special place that is said to anchor newborns to their family home and connect them to a future job or vocation—inside a corral if it is hoped the child will grow up to tend livestock, for example, or in a field if it is hoped the child will become a farmer.

The Diné also hold a First Laugh ceremony, traditionally hosted by the first person to make a baby laugh out loud. In this ceremony, salt is placed in the child's right hand and then given away to friends and family in attendance. The baby's first laugh is seen as a first step into language and social life. Giving the salt away is a similar first step into the Diné system of reciprocity.

The Diné accept death as a fact of life—a truism taught by Coyote in Navajo creation stories—but their death rites are marked by "strict avoidance of contact with the dead in order to prevent illness or unnatural death."[a] In order to minimize the ritual pollution that comes from such contact, the Diné have typically buried simply, quickly, and privately, with very few people involved (often just four mourners) and little to no speculation about any afterlife.

Traditionally, mourners would untie their hair and then bathe and dress the corpse, placing the shoes on the wrong feet. If the deceased died in a hogan, it was customary to take the corpse out through a hole cut in the north side. The family would then abandon the hogan. If it was winter and the ground was frozen, the hogan might even be collapsed on top of the body for burial. Otherwise, the family would carry the body to a burial site far away and bury it with the deceased's possessions. At a traditional burial, the Diné do not sing or offer eulogies. Their graves are unmarked and

they have accomplished their ritual tasks, Diné sand paintings are gathered up from the floor, taken outside, and scattered to the winds.

Medicine Bundles

Singers use a medicine bundle (*jish*), which they prepare and periodically renew (typically every four years) from a variety of sacred objects. A ceremony cannot go forward without this crucial ritual object, which recalls and harnesses the powers of creation. The sacred mountains were made from soil brought up from the underworld in First Man's medicine bundle, and soil and other materials from those same mountains is used in medicine bundles today. Many Navajos also keep a medicine bundle in their home. John Holiday, a medicine person from Monument Valley, says that "these bundles hold wisdom, sound language, sacred songs, and prayers—everything that makes up your life. It is to keep things in order, at peace, and prosperous."[57] Steven Begay of the Navajo National Historic Preservation Department explains that the Diné use these bundles to "pray the prayers of the mountains." Because "the soil from the mountain is in there, we are speaking directly to the mountain. And that prayer is taken back to the top of these mountains."[58]

mountain soil bundle
the best-known Navajo medicine bundle and the Blessingway's central ritual object; it includes soil and jewels from the four sacred mountains

The **mountain soil bundle** of the medicine man Frank Mitchell took years to prepare. He gathered soil from each of the four sacred mountains. He and his companions made offerings and prayed at each. They bathed in waterholes and dried themselves with

largely unvisited. As one Diné woman put it, "They don't have a Sing at a burial.... They don't talk when they bury a person.... They bury people in a certain direction with the head to the North, with their faces up and their arms outstretched."[b]

After the burial, mourners smooth out their footprints and return home by a different route, skipping and hopping to avoid detection by the ghost of the dead. After burial, four days of mourning follow, in which mourners do not work or travel and speak as little as possible. Mourning ends with ritual purification followed by a communal meal. The bereaved are then urged to "forget the dead and turn toward life and the living."[c]

Today, most Navajo deaths take place in hospitals or in modern homes, and funeral directors often handle the arrangements. Christians usually have public funerals in churches with hymn singing and eulogies followed by burial in a Christian cemetery. Death taboos are fading somewhat, perhaps because in the modern wage economy so many jobs (in the military and as police officers, ambulance drivers, nurses and doctors) require contact with the dead, but often

A proud mother holds her baby in a traditional cradle board in Window Rock, Arizona.

a few traditional practices endure among Christians. Meanwhile, death rituals of Navajo Peyotists, which often include a through-the-night peyote meeting with prayers for the dead, combine Christian and traditional practices.

cornmeal. They dressed as sacred dancers and went to the top of each mountain. They left jewels behind "as a gift to Mother Earth for what [they] were going to take from her."[59] Then they took a little soil, went back down each mountain, blessed themselves with corn pollen, and put their ordinary clothes back on.

In preparing his bundle, Frank Mitchell began with a mirage stone (aragonite) at the center. He arranged small sacks of earth from the four sacred mountains around it, each in the appropriate cardinal direction. He placed "a perfect white shell from the ocean" underneath these materials like a basket. Around the mirage stone, he arranged more stones and jewels and "bits of various types of vegetation that grow on the earth and all kinds of herbs" and fur or hair or hide from "all kinds of animals living on earth," plus some corn pollen. He wrapped it all in unwounded buckskin from a deer killed by human hands without arrows or bullets. He then tied it together into a bundle just the right size for his hand.

Native American Church Meetings

Today, the Half Moon and Cross Fire ceremonies are quite similar. The primary differences are the shapes of their altars and their relative emphasis on Christian themes. Preparations for a Native American Church ceremony begin when an individual sponsor approaches a roadman with a request. Someone may be sick, or perhaps there is a funeral to observe or a birth, graduation, or wedding to celebrate. Peyotists also hold scheduled meetings each year on holidays such as New Year's Day, Easter, Memorial Day, the Fourth of July, and Christmas. Meetings typically begin on Saturday evening and go into Sunday morning.

On the afternoon before the ceremony, a tipi is constructed. A fire hole is dug and the altar is constructed from soil around it. A line is drawn on the altar symbolizing the "Peyote Road."

The roadman organizes and leads the meeting, which goes from dusk to dawn. In his peyote box he brings his ritual tools, including a staff of life; a fan, often made of eagle feathers, used to dispatch prayer to the Creator; and a drum with water and coals inside it. During the meeting, the roadman sits on the west side of the tipi set up for the service, facing the fire altar in the center. On his right is the chief drummer. On his left is the cedar man, who stokes the fire with purifying cedar chips. Across from this trio, on the north side of the door that opens out to the east, is the fireman who tends the fire. Participants fill out the circle inside the tipi, facing one another and the sacred fire.

Like the Vedic rituals of ancient India, which also involved a sacred fire, these ceremonies begin with a statement of intention. That intention is often to cure an illness with the "medicine" of peyote, but if the meeting is held to bless a holiday or as a rite of passage, that purpose will be noted. As the peyote is passed around the circle, participants consume it. The roadman holds his tools and sings the opening song to the accompaniment of the drum chief. His staff and the other ritual items are passed to the drum chief and then to the cedar chief and around the circle as participants take turns singing. There are prayers for the person needing healing.

Around midnight, Cross Fire services feature a sermon that draws on a biblical text and uses the Bible as a ritual tool. Half Moon meetings feature a water ritual. The fireman brings a bucket of water to the roadman, who touches the water with an eagle-bone whistle and uses the feather fan to splash water in all four directions, on the ritual items, and on everyone who is there, including Grandfather Peyote. He then passes the water around for everyone to drink.

After midnight, more songs are sung and more peyote is consumed. At dawn, the roadman leaves the tipi and blows a whistle to summon Morning Water Woman. In many peyote legends, a woman, sometimes called Peyote Woman, is said to have discovered this medicine, and here Morning Water Woman (who is often the roadman's wife) plays that revered role. As her name suggests, she brings water to drink. After she enters the tipi, the roadman sings four songs, and she says a few things about the intention of the meeting. She rolls a cigarette and smokes it (again, only in the Half Moon tradition). She then prays, and the water is passed around the circle.

As the sun rises, participants take a ritual meal of four sacred foods: water, corn, fruit, and meat. The Half Moon roadman may give a concluding speech, and participants in Cross Fire services finish with the Lord's Prayer. Everyone exits the tipi and, after some informal conversation, joins in a celebratory feast.

Christian Worship Services

Christian worship is also part of lived religion in Navajoland today. The strong growth of Mormonism, evangelicalism, and Pentecostalism that began in the 1950s during the postwar revival of Christianity in the United States turned the Diné into "the most missionaried people in the world."[60] As the postwar economy boomed, more and more Navajos traded in traditional occupations on the reservation for jobs in the wage economy. The social dislocation that resulted, combined with increased interactions with outsiders brought on by new roads and the availability of automobiles, opened up younger Navajos to all sorts of new influences, Christianity included.

The Church of Jesus Christ of Latter-day Saints, or Mormons, grew rapidly in the 1950s through the work of its Southwest Indian Mission, which worked to evangelize both Navajos and Zunis. Evangelical and fundamentalist Protestantism boomed in that same decade, and today Pentecostalism is growing even faster. Although many of the earliest churches established among the Navajo were mainline Protestant congregations that were relatively open to traditional Navajo religion, many, though not all, Pentecostals today view traditional Navajo singers and Native American Church roadmen as enemies to be defeated.

One source of the Pentecostals' success is their Navajo pastors, who often use both English and Navajo in their worship services. Another factor—and a key to Pentecostalism's worldwide growth—is its emphasis on the experiential dimension of religion and on religious ecstasy in particular. The Holy Spirit, like the Holy Wind, causes some to speak in foreign tongues and others to burst out in prophecy. Navajo Pentecostalism is marked by many of the techniques that sparked revivals on the frontier during the Second Great Awakening of the mid-nineteenth century, including camp meetings, tent revivals, emotional preaching, and ecstatic displays of the power of God. In keeping with the long-standing emphasis in the Navajo way on curing illness, Pentecostal services also stress spiritual healing.

Writing in 1990, Charlotte Frisbie concluded that Pentecostalism represented "the strongest challenge to the future of traditional religion" in Navajoland.[61] That remains

Florence Barker of the Manuelito Church of God preaches at the 23rd Annual Navajo Nation Camp Meeting in Fort Defiance, Arizona, in 2012. One reason for the success of evangelical Christianity in the Navajo Nation is its use of Diné preachers.

the case today, though it should be noted that many Pentecostal churches led by Navajo pastors do not see themselves as engaged in spiritual warfare with medicine men and roadmen. Many are open to their parishioners attending traditional ceremonies and Peyotist meetings. In this way, most Navajos continue to display multiple religious affiliations. They may go to a Bible group on Wednesday night, an NAC meeting on Saturday night, and see to it that their daughter has a proper *kinaalda* ceremony when she comes of age.

CONTEMPORARY CONTROVERSY: NAVAJO RELIGION AND THE LAW

All religious people operate inside legal regimes that affect how they think and act religiously, but the law is particularly powerful in the case of Native American religious practitioners. From first contact with Europeans, they have encountered efforts to change, suppress, and outlaw their religious activities by conquerors, missionaries, agents, judges, and other officials of foreign governments.

The American legal system might seem to be friendly to the religious liberty rights of Navajos and other Native Americans. The First Amendment instructs the U.S. Congress to "make no law respecting an establishment, or prohibiting the free exercise thereof," and the Supreme Court now understands those two clauses to apply to state governments as well. Moreover, the American Indian Religious Freedom Act (AIRFA) of 1978 affirmed the religious liberty rights of Native Americans, including access to sacred sites. But when it comes to Native American religion and the law, things are seldom as they seem. Howard Shanker, who represented the Navajo in the lawsuit that attempted to prevent treated sewer water from being used on the San Francisco Peaks, says that in cases of this sort it is rarely enough to have the Constitution on your side. "I tell my clients we have the facts on our side and the law on our side," he says, "so we have about a twenty percent chance of winning."[62]

Lawsuits over sacred lands would seem to be quite different from lawsuits over sacred plants, but they are actually closely connected. Both provide insights into the continuing struggles of Navajo religious practitioners with the coercive powers of the U.S. government, even as they reveal information about Diné practices often shielded from the public view. These legal proceedings demonstrate that the U.S. judiciary continues to view Navajo religion largely through the lens of Protestant Christianity, which privileges texts over places and individual faith over collective rituals. The blind spot that results leaves many judges unable to see Navajo religion as religion. At the same time, it leaves the Diné and their sacred lands almost entirely unprotected from state and federal actions that prevent them from sharing the religious liberties enjoyed by most other U.S. citizens.

Oregon v. Smith

The strongest recent challenge to Peyotism came in the form of a U.S. Supreme Court ruling in *Oregon v. Smith* (1990). Alfred Smith was a recovering alcoholic active in Alcoholics Anonymous. He was also a member of the Native American Church who worked in a drug and alcohol rehabilitation program for Native Americans for the State of Oregon, where possession of peyote was a felony. His employers, after learning that Smith and a coworker had been attending NAC services, confronted them. Smith argued that peyote was not a drug but a religious sacrament. Still, Smith and his coworker were fired in 1984. They filed for unemployment compensation, which the state denied, so they sued the Employment Division of Oregon's Department of Human Services. The case arrived at the Supreme Court in 1989, and the next year its justices ruled against Smith and his coworker by a 6–3 margin, upholding Oregon's right to refuse religious exemptions to their antipeyote law. In a landmark decision, Justice Antonin Scalia argued that the plaintiffs' constitutionally protected religious liberty was not violated. Because the Oregon antipeyote law did not target religious use but aimed at peyote use broadly, the injury to Smith's religious liberty was incidental and therefore constitutional. Or, as Scalia put it, "We have never held that an individual's religious beliefs excuse him from compliance with [a] . . . neutral, generally applicable regulatory law."[63]

This Supreme Court decision further narrowed the scope of religious liberty by radically restricting the kinds of cases in which a long-standing balancing test would apply. This so-called Sherbert test—established by the Supreme Court in *Sherbert v. Verner* (1963)—set up a procedure for weighing the religious liberty rights of an individual against the interests of the federal and state governments. More specifically, that three-part test called on the courts to balance a "substantial burden" on an individual's practice against a "compelling state interest" and then to ensure that the state was using the "least restrictive means" to safeguard that interest.

This decision produced an outcry from Native nations, religious groups, and civil libertarians. Congress responded surprisingly quickly and nearly unanimously, with two pieces of legislation protecting religious liberty. In 1993, it passed the Religious Freedom Restoration Act (RFRA), which directed the Supreme Court to "restore the compelling interest test . . . and to guarantee its application in all cases where free exercise of religion is substantially burdened." That test would apply even in cases of generally applicable laws. In 1994, it passed an amendment to the American Indian Religious Freedom Act that specifically legalized ritual peyote use by Native American Church members. There were two catches, however: the peyote had to be consumed for "bona fide traditional ceremonial purposes," and the user had to be a member of a federally recognized Native American tribe.

The Navajo Nation v. U.S. Forest Service

As the Snowbowl's appeal came a second time before the Ninth District Court of Appeals in December 2007, the Navajo Nation and the other plaintiffs seemed to have a lot going for them. Although their lawsuit to stop snowmaking with nonpotable treated wastewater on the San Francisco Peaks was now being heard by nine justices sitting "en banc" on the Ninth District Court of Appeals, they had previously prevailed before a smaller three-judge panel of that same court in March 2007. In his majority opinion in that Diné victory, which was decided 2–1, Judge Fletcher had most emphatically found a "substantial burden" on the free exercise of religion of the Navajo and the Hopi. In fact, he found that part of the case open and shut.

The Final Environmental Impact Statement (FEIS) prepared by the Forest Service in 2005 had also included language that seemed to make the case for a "substantial burden" on the Native nations by itself. "The San Francisco Peaks are sacred to at least 13 formally recognized tribes that are still actively using the Peaks in cultural, historic, and religious contexts," the FEIS stated:

- They are the abode of deities and other spirit beings.
- They are the focus of prayers and songs whereby humans communicate with the supernatural.
- They contain shrines and other places where ceremonies and prayers are performed. . . .
- They are the source of soil, plant, and animal resources that are used for ceremonial and traditional purposes. . . .
- They contain places that relate to legends and stories concerning the origins, clans, traditions, and ceremonies of various Southwestern tribes.[64]

Regarding the Diné specifically, the FEIS offered an extensive survey of Navajo beliefs about their four sacred mountains in general and the San Francisco Peaks in particular. It noted that "medicine men collect soil for their medicine bundles and herbs for healing ceremonies" there, that Navajo traditions identify it as the home of three Holy People,

Pictured here in Window Rock, Arizona, in 2007, Joe Shirley Jr. served as president of the Navajo Nation from 2003 to 2011. He testified in federal court about the threats to religious liberty presented by the Arizona Snowbowl's use of treated wastewater to create artificial snow on sacred Diné land.

that owls and other sacred animals live there, that Navajos conduct ceremonies there, and that it is a "source of curing powers" and a site of "numerous sacred places," including "offering places, plant gathering areas, and mineral gathering areas."[65]

When their case appeared before district court in Arizona in October 2005, elders from other Native nations had offered extensive testimony about the burden that treated wastewater snowmaking would place on their religions. The proposed project, Vincent Randall of the Apache said, "would make the holy place impotent. Once something is desecrated and . . . God leaves that holy place," he explained, "then it is no longer powerful as an intermediary to God himself."[66]

So much for the facts. As for the law, Supreme Court justices had declared RFRA unconstitutional in 1997 as applied to the states, but it continued to apply to the federal government and therefore to the Forest Service. So it was up to the Ninth District to see whether the religious liberty rights of the Navajos and other tribes had been "substantially burdened" by the decision to go forward with treated wastewater snowmaking and, if so, to see whether the Forest Service had a "compelling state interest" in seeing that expansion go forward, and whether the proposed project pursued that interest by the "least restrictive means."

In 2008, the Ninth Circuit Court said yes to the Snowbowl and wastewater snowmaking on the Peaks. In fact, it reversed the prior decision in almost every particular. Drawing on *Lyng v. Northwest Indian Cemetery Protective Association*, a 1988 case in which the Supreme Court stated that a "substantial burden" on religious exercise could exist only when the government "coerce[s] individuals into acting contrary to their religious beliefs," it found no "substantial burden" on the religious liberties of any tribe or tribal member in this case. In its 6–3 decision, it admitted that "the presence of the artificial snow on the Peaks is offensive to the Plaintiffs' feelings about their religion and will decrease the spiritual fulfillment Plaintiffs get from practicing their religion on the mountain." However, it concluded that these "mere damaged feelings" did not rise to the level of a "substantial burden." Neither did the plaintiffs' "subjective spiritual experience."[67]

Why? In her trial testimony, a Forest Service archaeologist named Judith G. Propper said that none of the impacts on any Native American nations or individuals met the "legal threshold for 'substantial burden.'" Invoking the *Lyng* case, she argued that the Forest Service's action "did not prohibit the exercise of religion. It didn't penalize the tribes for their practice of religion. It didn't coerce anyone into violating their religious beliefs."[68] In its decision, the Ninth Circuit adopted Propper's argument (and *Lyng*) almost point for point. Because "there is no showing the government has coerced the Plaintiffs to act contrary to their religious beliefs under the threat of sanctions, conditioned a governmental benefit upon conduct that would violate the Plaintiffs' religious beliefs," the majority concluded, "there is no 'substantial burden' on the exercise of their religion."

It is tempting to object to this line of argument by exclaiming that all religion is subjective. That is where Judge Fletcher went with his Ninth Circuit Court dissent. Quoting from the definition of religion by the philosopher William James, he argued that "religious exercise invariably, and centrally, involves a 'subjective religious experience.'"

That is true to a point. But it is not quite on point. It obscures the fact that Navajo religion is far less subjective than the modern American Protestantism Judge Fletcher's dissent conjures up. Practitioners of Diné and other indigenous religions did describe the government's actions as offensive at a number of points in the 2005 trial. President Shirley, for example, said it was like being forced as a child to watch the rape of your mother. "That hurts me just watching," he said. "It affects the mind."[69]

However, the more urgent objection was that the wastewater on the mountain would make Diné prayers and ceremonies ineffective. When a practitioner gathers soil from the four sacred mountains for a medicine bundle, he uses a shell or a stone to pick it up. "It can't touch human hands," the Navajo singer Steven Begay explains.[70] If it does, it will be contaminated and will not work. The same goes for soil that is contaminated by wastewater: it can't be used to make or renew a medicine bundle.

Norriz Nez, another singer, also goes to the San Francisco Peaks to gather medicine. In court, he testified that the wastewater snowmaking "will ruin the medicine . . . it will ruin the plants, and water and the earth" that medicine people gather from the mountain to make their medicine bundles.[71] Without these bundles, singers can't do their ceremonies. And without those ceremonies, the Navajo way of life would fall into chaos. The desecration of the Peaks "would throw our whole culture out of balance," testified Larry Foster, who assists medicine persons in traditional ceremonies. "We would lose our culture, our identity. We would lose our songs, our ceremonies. . . . We just wouldn't be able to exist."[72]

Government lawyers repeatedly pointed out that the ski area took up a tiny portion of the mountain. Couldn't the Navajo gather the materials they needed for their medicine

The San Francisco Peaks, one of the Diné's four sacred mountains, as seen from Wupatki National Monument in Arizona.

bundles elsewhere on the mountain? Navajo witnesses repeatedly replied that they didn't carve their mountain up into parts. They described the Peaks as a living entity and likened its outer form to a human body. Foster likened the existing ski area to a scrape that leaves a scar and compared pouring treated sewage water on it to an injection with a "contaminated needle." "I can live with a scar," but making snow out of sewage "would be like injecting me and my mother, my grandmother, the Peaks, with impurities."[73]

Under the Constitution and in laws such as RFRA, all religions are supposed to be protected. But throughout the history of religious liberty cases involving Native nations, members of those nations have had to resort to a strategy of legitimating their religions by likening them to Christianity. The Peyote movement, for example, "had to represent itself as Christian, and in order to do so it had to adjust itself to fit into white settler models for what counted as Christianity," as the historian Tisa Wenger observes.[74] In the 2005 bench trial for *Navajo Religion v. U.S. Forest Service*, Diné witnesses similarly drew analogies to Christianity. They also referred to other Western religions in a bid to be considered alongside Jews and Muslims as legitimate practitioners of a real religion.

Foster called the medicine bundle "our Bible." He called Changing Woman "our Virgin Mary" and the coming-of-age ceremony she inaugurated "a confirmation" or "a bar mitzvah." His pilgrimages to the four sacred mountains to renew his medicine bundle were "similar to Muslims going to Mecca." The Peaks was "like our tabernacle, our altar to the west."[75] Echoing Foster, Roberta Blackgoat said, "Between these four Sacred Mountains is a room for the Diné people, where it has been made like a church, and way out on the west side, by the San Francisco Peaks, inside the room is our altar."[76] In his spirited dissent in 2008, Judge Fletcher also drew on a Christian analogy when he suggested that his Ninth Circuit colleagues would be sure to see a "substantial burden" on religion "if the government permitted only treated sewage effluent for use as baptismal water."[77]

These sorts of analogies have two purposes. The first is to present the Navajo way as a religion that deserves religious liberty protections as surely as Christianity, Judaism, and Islam do. The second purpose is to make judges, who are almost always more familiar with Christianity (and the Western monotheisms) than with Native American religions, feel the emotional weight of the facts before them—to walk for a moment in the shoes of the plaintiffs, to imagine how it would feel to watch more than a million gallons of treated wastewater effluent sprayed over your mother's body.

Imagine you are a Christian and the U.S. Forest Service is coming into your church every day for weeks on end each winter and spraying the sanctuary with treated wastewater. You could still go to the church. You could still pray there. But would you? And would your God still be there to hear your prayers? The first of these questions speaks to injured feelings and subjective spiritual experience. Would you choose to go to such a church? Would it diminish your spiritual experiences there? The second line of questioning is more to the point: Would your God still be there to hear your prayers? Would your religion still work? Most Christians would say that God would not abandon such a church—that Jesus would still be there amidst his people. If they felt otherwise, they could just go to another church. But this is where the analogy breaks down, because many Navajos are not sure that the Holy People will continue to reside on the Peaks if their mountaintops are routinely injected with contaminated wastewater. And if they are sure that their deities have abandoned that place, they have nowhere else to go.

Michael McNally has made every effort to consider the Diné's objections to wastewater snowmaking on the Peaks on their own terms. What he sees is yet another example of a profound misunderstanding of Native American religions by U.S. courts. What is at stake in this case is not individual spirituality, he argues. It is not the spiritual diminishment of a few Diné seekers after some subjective experience of what the Ninth District decision referred to as the "integration of man and mountain into one." What is at stake is more communal and objective. The majority's rhetorical shift from "religion" to "spirituality"— from the endangerment of a long list of Diné rituals tied to the mountain to the diminishment of a romanticized and individualized "search for spiritual fulfillment"—obscures the fact that what the Navajo and others are talking about here "is not principally an individual matter of interior states, but a collective matter of duties, ceremonies, peoplehood."[78]

Judge Fletcher, in his majority decision in the three-judge appeal, wrote, "If Appellants do not have a valid RFRA claim in this case, we are unable to see how any Native American plaintiff can ever have a successful RFRA claim based on beliefs and practices tied to land that they hold sacred."[79] Klee Benally, who has compared the Snowbowl's wastewater snowmaking to "destroying part of the Vatican and converting it to a skateboard park," put it more succinctly: "What part of sacred don't you understand?"[80]

QUESTIONS FOR DISCUSSION

1. What is the significance of referring to Navajo religion as a "place-based" tradition? What is the religious significance of the land for the Diné?

2. Why do you suppose that some Diné prefer to refer to their "way of life" rather than their "religion"? How is the term "religion" useful in this case, and how is it reductive or misleading?

3. How do the concepts of hocho and hozho interact with each other in Diné life and thought? Are they opposites? What practices do the Diné use to move from disharmony to harmony?

4. What roles do the Holy People play in Diné creation stories and ceremonies? Why does this chapter refer to them as "superbeings" rather than "gods"?

5. The First Amendment is said to secure the right to religious liberty for U.S. citizens. Why does this constitutional right seem to fail so often when it comes to lands held sacred by Native nations? Why did the courts rule against the Navajo in the controversial Snowbowl case?

KEY TERMS

Blessingway (hozhooji), p. 475

Changing Woman, p. 460

corn, p. 460

Coyote, p. 461

diagnostician, p. 473

Diné ("The People"), p. 442

Diné Bikéyah, p. 442

Earth Surface People, p. 458

First Man and First Woman, p. 460

hocho, p. 458

hogan ("place home"), p. 460

Holy People (Diyin Dine'é), p. 442

Holy Wind (Nilchi), p. 461

hozho, p. 458

inner form, p. 442

medicine bundle (jish), p. 443

mountain soil bundle, p. 478

Native American Church, p. 468

one-sung-over, p. 472

Peyotism, p. 468

Sa'a Nághaí Bik'e Hózhó (SNBH), p. 458

sand painting, p. 477

singer (hataalii), p. 460

FURTHER READING

Diné traditions are oral, and many Diné are skeptical of the value of written texts. When asked to suggest books on Diné religion, one informant replied, "The books are the ones in our elders' heads."[81] With that criticism in mind, here are a few reading suggestions:

Iverson, Peter. *Diné: A History of the Navajos*. Albuquerque: University of New Mexico Press, 2002.

Maroukis, Thomas C. *The Peyote Road: Religious Freedom and the Native American Church*. Norman: University of Oklahoma Press, 2010.

Mitchell, Frank. *Navajo Blessingway Singer: The Autobiography of Frank Mitchell*. Edited by Charlotte J. Frisbie. Tucson: University of Arizona Press, 1977.

Mitchell, Rose. *Tall Woman: The Life Story of Rose Mitchell*. Edited by Charlotte J. Frisbie. Albuquerque: University of New Mexico Press, 2001.

Witherspoon, Gary. *Language and Art in the Navajo Universe*. Ann Arbor: University of Michigan Press, 1977.

Zolbrod, Paul G. *Diné bahane': The Navajo Creation Story*. Albuquerque: New Mexico University Press, 1984.

REJECTING RELIGION

For religious folk from the time of Vedic and Israelite priests to today, religious beliefs and practices have been a solution to the human predicament. However, for many nonreligious folk, religion itself is the problem.

Strictly speaking, agnosticism and atheism are about nonbelief in God alone. As a practical matter, however, these nonbelievers reject as well the authority of priests, the usefulness of ritual, supernaturalism, the afterlife, the soul, and other "trappings" of the religious life. Of course, some agnostics and atheists today view the stuff of religion with indifference rather than antipathy. They don't affirm belief in God but they don't worry about it either. However, many nonbelievers view religion as one of the contagious diseases of human civilization and irreligion as its cure.

In this way, the family of atheists stands apart from religious practitioners from India who seek release from this world; religious practitioners of the Middle East who seek to repair it; and practitioners of the Confucian, Daoist, and Navajo religions who seek to revert to a way of life before human civilization lost its original harmony. The release these nonbelievers seek is not from this world but from religion itself. The repairs they seek aim to counteract the destruction brought on by belief in and submission to "God." And instead of looking backward to a supposed golden age, they look forward in the name of progress, science, logic, and reason to better times to come.

In recent decades, nonbelievers have struggled to define themselves not by what they deny but by what they affirm, gravitating toward labels such as "humanists" and "freethinkers." But the specter of religion continues to linger over how they think and what they do. This book therefore regards the family of atheists and agnostics as rejecters of religion.

The Milky Way galaxy, home to planet Earth. Atheists and agnostics typically point not to God but to scientific theories of the Big Bang to explain the universe's creation.

Atheism

THE WAY OF NO WAY

It is 11:00 a.m. on Sunday morning at Conway Hall in central London, and the congregation is on its feet singing and dancing. If you wandered in and thought you had stumbled upon a Protestant megachurch, you are forgiven. There is a live band—electric guitar, bass, saxophone, piano, drums, singer—and the lyrics are projected onto a huge screen. The hall is packed with young, urban twenty- and thirty-somethings, designer coffees in hand, casually dressed in denim, leather, and the occasional rumpled skirt or sportcoat. On the stage, the minister/emcee, with his hands up high and his head tilted back, looks like pictures of the "Laughing Jesus" popular in born-again Christian circles.

Just above the screen is a quote from Shakespeare's *Hamlet* that doubles as Conway Hall's motto (and a motto of atheists in general): "To Thine Own Self Be True." One of the T-shirts for sale reads, "Good is Great." The pop songs here—one is Jefferson Starship's "We Built This City"—are actually pop songs. The minister/emcee, Sanderson Jones, describes himself as a "recovering professional comedian" whose accomplishments include breaking the record for the world's longest hug. And the poems read instead of a sermon come not from the Word of God but from the mouth of a tattooed anarchist sporting black leather chaps.

Today at the Sunday Assembly, as this congregation is called, there is no mention of God—or, for that matter, of atheism either. In fact, it's hard to figure out why two or three hundred Londoners have given up a couple of hours this Sunday morning to assemble. What is going on here?

Congregants gather at the Sunday Assembly led by comedians Sanderson Jones (right) and Pippa Evans (center), at Conway Hall in London.

For a British society, Conway Hall has an oddly American past. It began in 1793 as a Universalist congregation under the direction of New Englander Elhanan Winchester, who brought with him on his transatlantic voyage to London the good news that everyone was destined for salvation. From that point forward, this congregation was a home for radical religious dissent. By the time it moved into South Place Chapel in London in 1824, it had rejected the divinity of Jesus and become Unitarian. Under the ministry of Moncure Conway, an American abolitionist and social reformer who became its minister in 1864, it moved even further to the left theologically, becoming a society with "no theological creed . . . that could fetter its members."[1]

Conway had a storied life. He began his career as a horseback-riding Methodist revivalist but moved quickly in the direction of **freethought**, a tradition of critical inquiry that called religious truth claims into question by subjecting them to the light of reason. He subsequently sauntered around Walden Pond with the Transcendentalist Henry David Thoreau, visited the poet Walt Whitman in Brooklyn, met with President Abraham Lincoln, called on the champion of evolution Charles Darwin, and was eulogized by the steel magnate Andrew Carnegie. More anthropologist than theologian, Conway introduced his theology-free congregation to new trends in science. He invited them to join him on both his "earthward pilgrimage" (from obsession with the next world to life here and now) and his "pilgrimage to the wise men of the East."[2] During his quarter century at South Place, Conway replaced prayers with meditation and Bible readings with selections from Asian scriptures. Under Conway's successor, Stanton Coit (also an

freethought
an intellectual tradition of independent inquiry based on logic, reason, and science rather than religious authority

American), the society reinvented itself as an *ethical* society explicitly devoted to virtue rather than faith. Now known as the Conway Hall Ethical Society, this group moved in 1929 into its current site at Conway Hall on Red Lion Square (which also boasts a memorial bust of the famously skeptical British philosopher Bertrand Russell). Today it serves as "a home for humanism" and a home for the Sunday Assembly.

The Sunday Assembly was founded in 2013 by Sanderson Jones and fellow comedian Pippa Evans. On their way to a gig, Evans told Jones that she didn't believe the Christian doctrines she had learned growing up as an evangelical, but she missed church. Soon they were organizing "something like church but without God." Initially they billed it as an "atheist church," but over time they dropped that label, which they had come to see as unnecessarily negative. Now, according to their website, they focus on "the things that we do believe in, rather than the things we don't."[3]

Widespread publicity about the Sunday Assembly prompted criticism by religious folks who saw it as sacrilegious and by atheists who saw it as too religious. It even underwent its own schism, when a New York City faction broke off to form a more militantly atheistic group—the Godless Revival—over the Sunday Assembly's refusal to get tough with God.

Today, the Sunday Assembly, which describes itself as "radically inclusive," claims seventy chapters in eight countries. Its charter begins with three defining features. The Sunday Assembly, it affirms,

1. Is 100% celebration of life. We are born from nothing and go to nothing. Let's enjoy it together.
2. Has no doctrine. We have no set texts, so we can make use of wisdom from all sources.
3. Has no deity. We don't do supernatural but we also won't tell you you're wrong if you do.[4]

In addition to its weekly or monthly meetings, this secular community sponsors weekend events it bills as "retreats to the future." It also engages in volunteer community work through an outreach arm called Action Heroes. Its motto is "Live better, help often, and wonder more."[5]

OUR STORY

In affirming that human beings are "born from nothing and go to nothing," members of the Sunday Assembly are drawing on a long lineage of atheists, agnostics, and secular humanists who have crafted their own creation story of human life on this planet (and of this planet in the universe). Instead of the biblical book of Genesis that inspires the stories of Christians and Jews, this lineage draws on science: the works of geologists such as Charles Lyell, evolutionary biologists such as Charles Darwin, birth control advocates such as Margaret Sanger, and astrophysicists such as Stephen Hawking. This is one way they might tell their creation story.

The Big Bang

In the beginning was the Big Bang. Roughly 13.8 billion years ago, all the matter that now fills the universe was compressed into a tiny dot of unimaginable heat and density. We do not know how all that stuff got there. And technically it was neither stuff (since matter did not yet exist) nor there (since space did not yet exist either). We do not even know what physical laws governed what was happening, because the laws of the universe as we now know them did not yet apply. But somehow, mysteriously, came the explosion of all explosions. Out of this First Event (which is by definition beyond explanation) came not only our expanding universe but also time and space, matter and antimatter.

As time moved forward and space expanded away from this violent beginning, the universe cooled and became less dense. After one second, there were protons, neutrons, and electrons, and the temperature of the universe fell to ten thousand million degrees (about a thousand times as hot as the center of the sun). The four forces that now govern the universe—gravity, electromagnetism, and the weak and strong forces—had also come into being. After a few minutes the nuclei of helium and heavy hydrogen and lithium formed.

The temperature of the universe gradually fell to a few thousand degrees. But it was still dark. No stars had formed. This Dark Age came to an end roughly 250 million years after the Big Bang, when the universe cooled and expanded enough for gravity to pull some of its gases into galaxies and stars. Those stars then began to convert the lighter elements that formed them into heavier elements that became planets and comets and asteroids.

Flash forward to 4.5 billion years ago and steer toward the Milky Way galaxy and our solar system, where our sun formed out of the gaseous debris of exploding supernovas. The universe had cooled considerably from its white-hot start, but Earth was still too hot to sustain life. Three or four billion years ago, it finally cooled enough to form a solid crust. Next came an atmosphere, albeit an unbreathable one, poor in oxygen and choked with acids; oceans that harbored microscopic living cells and bacteria; and algae that, through photosynthesis, produced oxygen, changing the atmosphere from toxic to tonic.

The first complex, multicelled animals developed roughly 700 million years ago. A huge leap forward in the number and complexity of these animals came during the Cambrian outburst, a short but wildly productive spurt that began roughly 540 million years ago, when evolution ran wild. "Name a creature, from a nematode worm to Cameron Diaz," writes the popular science writer Bill Bryson, "and they all use architecture first created in the Cambrian party."[6]

About 500 million years ago, the first land plants developed, and roughly 50 million years later the first land animals. Dinosaurs ruled Earth until they were extinguished, likely by a massive asteroid that crashed about 65 million years ago into the Yucatan Peninsula and whipped up earthquakes, fires, and tsunamis before wrapping the planet in a cold shroud and wiping out more than half of all species.

Flash forward again to the land mass we now call Africa around seven million years ago, where some of our earliest ancestors, humanlike primates, walked on two feet out of a tropical forest into the savannah. These primates had evolved from apes, which had evolved from earlier mammals, which had evolved from amphibians, which had evolved from fish, which had evolved from multicellular organisms, which had evolved from single-cell organisms. Over time their descendants would learn to make and use tools, to cook with fire, to speak, and to communicate complex ideas with one another. As their brains and bodies grew larger, roughly 300,000 years ago they evolved into homo sapiens.

According to evolutionary theory, humanlike creatures evolved from primates in Africa seven million years ago. For atheists, this theory discredits biblical accounts of human creation.

Contrary to popular opinion, human beings do not stand at center stage in the drama of creation. We are literally stardust: water and oxygen and carbon brought to Earth by time and chance. Or, as the British philosopher Bertrand Russell once put it, "Man is part of Nature, not something contrasted with Nature. His thoughts and his bodily movements follow the same laws that describe the motions of stars and atoms."[7]

As a species, we human beings spent most of our existence foraging for food as hunter-gatherers in Africa. Roughly 90,000 years ago, we migrated north onto the Arabian Peninsula, and 40,000 years after that we had reached southeast Asia and Australia. The agricultural revolution that started after 10,000 BCE fostered settlements and then homes and cities in Mesopotamia, China, Egypt, and the Indus River Valley. Empires followed, including the Roman Empire, which spread to the British Isles in 43 CE and controlled them until the fifth century. In 50, the Romans built London, which by the end of the first century was Britain's largest city.

Londoners were pagans first, worshipers of Roman deities such as Mars, the god of war. Then they became Roman Catholics. During the Reformation of the sixteenth century, they became Protestants—members of Henry VIII's divorce-friendly Church of England. But England, and London especially, became a hotbed for religious dissenters beginning in the eighteenth century. And in 1793, some of them banded together to form the dissenting congregation that would later build Conway Hall. In the nineteenth century, London became the Mecca of atheists and agnostics, home to Darwin and Russell as well as the philosopher John Stuart Mill, the revolutionary Karl Marx, the politician Charles Bradlaugh, the novelist Virginia Woolf, the psychoanalyst Sigmund Freud, the cryptologist Alan Turing, the actor Ricky Gervais, and the evolutionary biologist Richard Dawkins. The remains of Darwin, a self-described "agnostic" who may have done more than anyone else in the modern West to undermine Christian orthodoxy, lie in London's Westminister Abbey, the personal church of the Queen of England. There, one of the men who replaced the ancient superstitions of the church with the experimental truths of modern science is buried in plain sight. He lives on in the only way human beings can—in the legacy he left behind, which in his case was one of empirical observation, radical doubt, and a life of intellectual adventure.

ATHEISM IN TODAY'S WORLD

The overwhelming majority of *homo sapiens* who have walked the earth have been religious folk, so **atheism** has always been a minority report, perhaps even a footnote. Moreover, it has always attracted more elites than ordinary folks. But those elites have carried weight, particularly in the modern period. Many of the most influential philosophers, psychologists, and political theorists of the last two hundred years—think Friedrich Nietzsche, Jean-Paul Sartre, Sigmund Freud, Karl Marx—were atheists. So were many of modernity's most brutal dictators: Mao Zedong, Joseph Stalin, Vladimir Lenin, Pol Pot, Slobodan Milosevic.

It is extraordinarily difficult to determine how many nonbelievers there are in the world because they are typically not organized, and their numbers are small in many countries. Even in the presence of official data, it is almost impossible to distinguish "organic atheism," which is chosen, from "coerced atheism," which is mandated by a nation-state. Given these difficulties, it should not be surprising that estimates of total nonbelievers vary wildly—anywhere from 2 to 13 percent worldwide.

China, with a population approaching 1.5 billion (or close to one out of every five *homo sapiens*), is the wildcard here. The Chinese Communist Party (CCP), which has ruled China since 1949, is officially atheistic, and under its founding chairman Mao Zedong, who led the country until his death in 1976, it brutally suppressed religious activity. Just how deeply this opposition to theism has permeated the Chinese population is difficult to assess. Also elusive is the extent to which religious belief and practice have revived in recent years as a result of CCP leaders' friendlier attitudes toward religion.

Another obstacle to determining the relative global strength of atheism is the stigma associated with calling yourself an atheist in areas where religious adherence is strong. Western antagonism to atheism is ancient, but it intensified in response to the bloodletting of the French Revolution of the late eighteenth century, when, in the name of progress, the guillotine fell especially heavily on Roman Catholic clergy. The Cold War of the 1940s to the 1990s pitted the "atheistic communism" of the Chinese and the Soviets against the "Judeo-Christianity" of the post–World War II United States. Today in the United States, atheism is more visible, yet the stigma of calling oneself an atheist remains. Globally, there are at least a dozen countries in which atheism is illegal, and many more where nonbelievers are persecuted. Given this stigma, it should not be surprising that, in many surveys of religious belief, there is a wide gap between participants who report that they do not believe in God or a higher power and those who are willing to self-identify as atheists.[8]

That said, the World Religion Database (WRD) ranks **agnosticism**—with 9.4 percent of the world's population in 2020—as the world's fifth-largest religious affiliation. Atheists fall further down the list, but still well ahead of Sikhs and Jews, with a share of 1.9 percent. A recent worldwide Gallup poll arrived at a much higher number, with 11 percent of respondents calling themselves "convinced atheists." The top four atheist populations in this poll were in China (where 61 percent of those surveyed were "convinced atheists"), Hong Kong (34 percent), Japan (31 percent), and the Czech Republic (30 percent). The most religious

This Ten Commandments monument was erected at the Texas State Capitol in Austin in 1961. Critics of similar monuments argued that they violated constitutional guarantees of the separation of church and state, but in 2005 the U.S. Supreme Court decided they were lawful because they fulfilled a secular purpose.

country surveyed was Thailand, where 94 percent described themselves as religious.[9] It is not surprising that there are more nonreligious people in China—over half a million, again according to the WRD—than in any other country. The number two country in this category is more of a surprise: the United States, with over 66 million nonreligious.[10]

The atheist demographic has not been carefully surveyed worldwide, but in Europe and the United States, atheists tend to be young, well educated, urban, and white. They also tend to be men. Whereas almost all religious groups skew toward women, most atheist groups are led by men and many panels at atheist conferences feature only white male speakers. Some women in Europe and the United States have criticized atheist organizations not only as male preserves but also as boys' clubs in which sexism and misogyny are rife. In 2014, the atheist author Sam Harris drew fire from women's groups for referring to atheism's "critical posture" as "intrinsically male."[11]

Discussions regarding nonbelief are complicated by "nones," who, according to a 2016 poll by the Public Religion Research Institute, now account for 25 percent of U.S. adults.[12] This rapidly growing cohort of people who affiliate with no particular religious tradition seems to provide new evidence for the old **secularization theory**, which argued that as societies modernized they would abandon religion. However, this evidence is complicated by two factors: Many nones are quite religious, and many more describe themselves as spiritual.

Some people refuse to affiliate with religious organizations not because they do not believe in God but because they believe in God so fervently that they cannot imagine any human institution adequately capturing the mysteries of the divine. In the U.S. Religious Landscape Survey conducted in 2014 by the Pew Research Center, 23 percent of the more than 35,000 people interviewed were religiously unaffiliated, and that percentage was well over a third among 18- to 49-year-olds. However, less than a third of these nones called themselves atheists (3 percent) or agnostics (4 percent).[13] In other surveys, about half of the religiously unaffiliated affirmed the divinity of Jesus.

Other nones fall into the increasingly popular **spiritual but not religious (SBNR)** category. They do not affiliate with any religion, and, in many cases, they have strong

atheism
the belief that God does not exist

agnosticism
the belief that humans cannot know whether God exists, or the position of particular individuals that they themselves do know whether God exists

secularization theory
the sociological theory that as the world becomes more modern it will become less religious

spiritual but not religious (SBNR)
an identity and social category signaling a negative view of organized religion and a positive view of individual spiritual practices

Comparison of Religions Worldwide, 2020

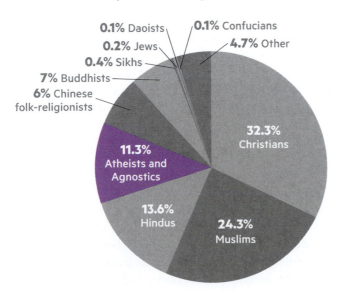

- **0.1%** Daoists
- **0.2%** Jews
- **0.4%** Sikhs
- **7%** Buddhists
- **6%** Chinese folk-religionists
- **0.1%** Confucians
- **4.7%** Other
- **32.3%** Christians
- **11.3%** Atheists and Agnostics
- **13.6%** Hindus
- **24.3%** Muslims

Types of the Religiously Unaffiliated, 2020

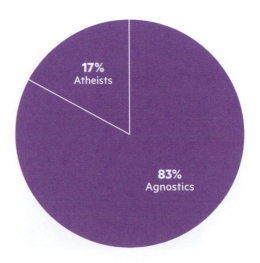

- **17%** Atheists
- **83%** Agnostics

criticisms of religious dogmas, which they typically view as antiquated and false, and religious rituals, which they see as shallow and empty. SBNRs are particularly critical of the trappings of "organized religion," which they see as irredeemably hierarchical and complicit in sexism, racism, and homophobia. Nonetheless, this cohort floods into yoga centers and eagerly engages in mindfulness meditation. With their emphasis on religious tolerance and spiritual individualism, SBNRs stand in a long line of critics of "secondhand religion" who have found comfort and wisdom not in scriptures but in nature and in their own hearts and minds.

Two related factors seem to be at play in the rise of the nones. The first is a decline in the stigma of being a religious free agent. The second is an increase in the stigma of being a church member. According to sociologists who study the religious "marketplace," Americans have long "overconsumed" religion because social norms favored religious activity. You used to be considered a bad citizen, a bad marriage prospect, and a bad employee if you didn't show a little faith in faith. And it is still necessary for almost all American politicians to pledge their allegiance to God as well as flag. In January 2007, Representative Pete Stark of California became the first U.S. congressperson to self-identify as a nonbeliever. The only other member of Congress who has followed in his footsteps is Arizona's Kyrsten Sinema, who was elected to the House in 2012 and to the Senate in 2018. However, she identifies simply as religiously unaffiliated.

One reason Americans outside of Capitol Hill have felt free to take tentative first steps out of the atheist and agnostic closet is the visible moral failure in recent years of religious leaders, including televangelists and Catholic priests. As the not-so-almighty have fallen, many of those who were raised in religious households have felt empowered to stand up and question whether religious beliefs and practices really do produce moral behavior. What is so moral, they ask, about affiliating with homophobic evangelists or pedophilic priests? Meanwhile, more parents are deciding to raise their kids without any religion, and more of those children are staying unaffiliated as adults. All this is happening because the status gap between nones and believers has never been narrower.

Politics is a second factor in the rise of the nones. The Republican Party began to gain ground in the late 1970s by attaching itself to family, morality, and God, even as the Democratic Party insisted on the strict separation of church and state. In the process, the GOP became the GOD party, and Democrats became the party of secularism—not a good strategy in a country where roughly nine out of ten voters believed in the divine.

Like religious folks, nonbelievers assert their identities on billboards, bumper stickers, T-shirts, and jewelry. This bumper sticker features the "Darwin fish," which reimagines the "Jesus fish" symbol by adding evolved legs and the name of the evolutionary theorist Charles Darwin.

In recent years, Barack Obama, Hillary Clinton, and other Democratic leaders took pains to realign their party with prayer and piety. Even so, "Christian" and "conservative" are now widely seen as identities that are linked at the hip. Some liberal voters who used to describe themselves as Christians now deny that affiliation lest they be allying in the process with conservative policies and the GOP. These are basically the same reasons so many Europeans have divorced themselves from their country's established churches: because the marriage of a given church with a particular political regime is never eternal, and when it ends it leaves angry children in its wake. The irony here is rich: the efforts in recent decades by the Religious Right to make

ATHEISM AND AGNOSTICISM: A GENEALOGY

The English word "atheism" derives from the Greek term *atheos*, which means "without God" or "god-less." It first appears in English in the early modern period, beginning with *A VVoorke Concerning the Trewnesse of the Christian Religion* (1587), a translation of a French book that grouped atheists alongside "Iewes, Mahumetists, and other infidels" and defined "Atheisme" as "utter Godlesnes." The term "atheist" (also spelled athyst and athist) comes a few years earlier, with a 1571 reference to "Atheistes which say . . . there is no God" and a 1577 reference to "Atheists, or godlesse men." The term "agnostic" arrived on the scene nearly three centuries later and is widely attributed to Thomas Huxley, an English biologist and close friend of Charles Darwin. Huxley unveiled his coinage at a Metaphysical Society meeting one evening in London in 1869. Within a few months, the British weekly *The Spectator* was describing "Pope Huxley" as "a great and even severe Agnostic—who goes about exhorting all men to know how little they know." Much later, in an 1899 essay, Huxley explained why he rejected for himself such labels as atheist, theist, pantheist, materialist, idealist, and freethinker before settling on this new term, which "came into [his] head as antithetic to the 'gnostic' of Church history."[a]

Huxley did not confine his "not-knowing" solely to the God question. What he called "the region of the uncertain" extended for him to many philosophical questions, including the contest between idealism (which assumes that ideas precede matter) and materialism (which assumes that matter precedes ideas).[b] Rather quickly, the term was employed far outside philosophy and theology—for example, to economists "agnostic" about where the bond market is trending or undergraduates "agnostic" about whether animals have emotions.

America more Christian have done just the opposite, pushing younger Americans out of the pews in droves. Some of those who have left churches are now building their own institutions, crafting new sorts of moral and spiritual communities and making meaning in new ways.

ATHEISM 101

➜ Who needs God?

The world's religious diversity is matched by its nonreligious diversity. Within the wide spectrum of nonbelievers in things religious, there are people who do not believe in God or a higher power who call themselves atheists. There are also people who do not believe in God or a higher power who refuse that label. Nica Lalli, a writer and self-described "pink atheist," observes that "atheists don't speak with just one voice."[14] Like the religions of the world, the atheisms of the world are internally diverse and change over time. Nonetheless, it is possible to hazard some generalizations about the atheist family, and to make some distinctions among its members.

The prefix *a-* in English and other Indo-European languages signals a denial or a loss. In the case of atheists and agnostics, what is being denied is belief in or knowledge of God.

This Freedom From Religion Foundation billboard criticizes President Trump's push for a southern border wall even as it endorses President Jefferson's 1802 support for a "wall of separation between Church & State."

But nonbelievers do more than reject theism. They typically also reject religion and the religions, including their doctrines, which they classify as superstition, and their rituals, which they characterize as "blind" and "empty." Refusing the authority of clergy and sacred books, many claim to rely on reason alone. They see no need for faith, especially if it requires a leap into irrationalism. They regard miracles as impossible violations of the laws of science. They prefer empirical observation over magical thinking. They focus their energies on life before death. Finally, many nonbelievers regard religion as not only false but also dangerous. According to the Freedom From Religion Foundation, religion "has been used to justify war, slavery, sexism, racism, homophobia, mutilations, intolerance, and oppression of minorities. The totalitarianism of religious absolutes chokes progress."[15] According to many New Atheists, members of a controversial fraternity of recent thinkers who tend toward angry anti-theism, "religion is man-made" and murderous—a hazard to your health and a pox on society.[16] The solution is to flush this poison out of your system.

Long before Darwin traveled to South America on his research vessel the *Beagle* or Conway sailed from America to England, nonbelievers were arguing over what to call themselves. Today, the term "atheist" refers most simply to a non-theist, someone who does not believe in the existence of God or the gods. The term "agnostic" refers to a non-knower, someone who does not know whether God or the gods exist. Among nonbelievers, however, many refuse both of these identities. Some call themselves "secular humanists" or simply "humanists." Others prefer "freethinkers" or "rationalists" or "materialists" or "skeptics." Each of these alternatives carries with it slightly different shades of meaning, but even about the core terms—atheist and agnostic—there is considerable disagreement within what we will refer to here as the "atheist family."

If at its root atheism refers to non-theism, an atheist is literally "godless." Technically this godlessness could signal something passive: an absence of theism. In practice, however, it typically signals the active rejection of theism—a denial of the existence of God or the gods. In an attempt to sort out this ambiguity, philosophers

Atheism at a Glance

Problem: ignorance

Solution: knowledge

Techniques: reason, science, skepticism, and critical inquiry

Exemplars: freethinkers who think for themselves rather than follow the secondhand teachings of prophets, messiahs, priests, and other authorities

In short, atheism (and agnosticism) are part of a skeptical tradition that pursues human flourishing in a godless universe by rejecting religion as false and harmful.

sometimes distinguish between negative atheism and positive atheism, where a **negative atheist** is anyone (agnostics included) who does not affirm theism and a **positive atheist** is someone who believes theism is false.

A distinction can also be made between overt and covert atheism. For much of recorded human history, those who turned their backs on the gods have been seen as morally suspect and socially dangerous. How is social order to be preserved if some in our midst do not believe in a Supreme Being who lays down the law and enforces it with eternal rewards and punishments? The broad-mindedness of the English philosopher John Locke in his *Letter Concerning Toleration* (1689) did not extend to atheists, and atheism today is still punishable by death in more than a dozen countries.

Although the term "atheist" formally attends only to the existence of God, as a practical matter most atheists also deny a host of related doctrines, including the afterlife, the immortality of the soul, miracles, reincarnation, hell, and providence. The ancient Greek philosopher Plato refers in *Laws* to three types of atheists: those who do not believe in the existence of gods, those who believe the gods stand aloof from human affairs, and those who believe the gods are unresponsive to prayers and sacrifice.

Some analytic philosophers constitute another type of atheist: nonbelievers in God who refuse to call themselves atheists on the grounds that the theistic proposition makes no sense. According to the logical positivism of the British philosopher A. J. Ayer, statements are meaningful only insofar as they can be verified. Because we cannot either prove or disprove that God exists by experiment, logic, or observation, the proposition that God does not exist must be said to be neither true nor false but simply nonsensical.

The term "atheism" has for most of human history served as an accusation rather than an identity—something to decry in others rather than to find in oneself. As an accusation, it has only sometimes meant someone who does not believe in God. More often it has stood in for a charge of heresy, signaling that the accused believes in the *wrong* God rather than none at all. Of the Protestant reformer John Calvin, Thomas Jefferson wrote, "He was indeed an Atheist . . . If ever man worshipped a false god, he did."[17] Jefferson's friend, the Deist and firebrand for liberty Thomas Paine, described Christianity in general as "a species of atheism," protesting, "It professes to believe in a man rather than in God."[18] Even Joseph Smith Jr., the founder of Mormonism, was labeled "this Atheist Smith"—"as ignorant and as impudent a knave as ever wrote a book."[19]

There is a spectrum of agnosticisms as well. **Weak agnosticism** says, "I don't know whether God exists," while **strong agnosticism** makes a bolder claim: "Whether God exists is not knowable." Some atheists criticize agnostics for trying to be neutral in a war in which neutrality is not possible. Dawkins's *The God Delusion* (2006) calls agnostics "namby-pamby, mushy pap, weak-tea, weedy, pallid fence-sitters."[20] But agnostics can sneer at atheists, too—for pretending to know something that cannot be known. "The atheist claims to know that there is no God; the agnostic admits that he is uncertain," writes the sociologist of religion Peter Berger, a practicing Lutheran. "Put differently, an atheist is someone directly told by God that God does not exist."[21]

Another term on this spectrum, **anti-theism**, signals a more militant viewpoint that, unsatisfied with merely denying the existence of God, insists on aggressively opposing organized religion and proselytizing for atheism along the way. Many of today's New Atheists are anti-theists.

The terms **humanism** and **secularism** and the hybrid **secular humanism** all point to efforts akin to those of the Sunday Assembly to say what nonbelievers affirm

negative atheist
someone who does not affirm theism

positive atheist
someone who affirms that theism is false

weak agnosticism
the position of a particular individual that he or she does not know whether God exists

strong agnosticism
the position that it is not possible for anyone to know whether God exists

anti-theism
strong rejection of God belief often marked by intense opposition to theists

humanism
a worldview affirming the supreme importance of human beings, human agency, and human life here and now

secularism
a worldview that emphasizes life on earth as opposed to transcendent realities, with an emphasis on strictly separating church and state

secular humanism
a worldview that rejects religion and supernaturalism in order to emphasize and celebrate human life here and now

Adopted by the British Humanist Association in 1965, this symbol of the "Happy Human" is now widely used as a humanist icon.

rather than what they oppose. Humanism refers most basically to a point of view that emphasizes human rather than divine things. Humanists tend to be non-theistic and anti-supernaturalist, taking science and reason as their guides. Many also affirm that human beings are basically good, insisting that we can live lives that are not only ethical but also meaningful without God. Secularism directs our attention toward sociology rather than anthropology, and more specifically to whether a society should be religious or secular (from the Latin word *saeculum*, or "of this age," which is to say pertaining to worldly things). Secularists often focus on political questions, such as keeping religion out of public schools and governments out of the religion business. This term was coined in 1851 by the English writer and labor activist George Jacob Holyoake, who used it to refer to "a code of duty pertaining to this life, founded on considerations purely human."[22] But it has carried different connotations over time and across the globe. Nonetheless, secularists typically do favor not only the strict separation of church and state but also a public square empty of religious influence. In recent years, Talal Asad and other religious studies scholars have argued that secularism and religion are not really opposites—that the forms of "the secular" and the forms of "religion" in any given society take their cues from one another.[23] In this regard, they are more like feuding siblings than faraway strangers.

In his book *Seven Types of Atheism*, John Gray makes a point that is worth stressing: there is no *one* atheism any more than there is any *one* religion. Of Gray's seven types, the most intriguing is mystical atheism, which includes various "negative theologians" whose divinity is so distant from the world and so inscrutable that it makes no sense to call them theists. This category helpfully blurs the boundaries between belief and nonbelief—by placing practitioners of this "atheism of silence" squarely inside the bounds of the world's religions.[24]

One final introductory point about this family of atheists: though in theory atheists deny and agnostics doubt the existence of all gods, as a practical matter they are able to say "no" only to the gods they know. When Freud theorized about the Oedipal complex and the Father God, he was obviously not talking about the Hindu goddess Kali. Neither was he talking about divinity in general, or even about the god in the Greek tragedy *Oedipus the King*. He was talking about the God of the Jews and Christians he knew in late-nineteenth-century Europe. Most of today's New Atheists know little about the divinities of India and China, so when they labor to yank down the idols they find so odious, they are pulling almost entirely against the weight of the Christian, Jewish, and Islamic traditions.

ATHEISM BY THE NUMBERS

Seven Types of Atheism

- the New Atheism
- secular humanism
- various religions of science
- various political religions, including communism and Nazism
- the anti-theism of "god-haters" such as the Marquis de Sade
- the thoroughgoing atheism of philosopher George Santayana and others, which denies not only divinity but also the piety of human progress
- mystical atheism

ATHEIST HISTORY

To many in the modern West, atheism seems to be a relatively recent creation, gestated in the Renaissance of the fourteenth to seventeenth centuries, born in the Enlightenment that followed, and matured in the work of Karl Marx and other nineteenth-century revolutionaries. But atheism is an ancient idea. It is also a religious idea developed and spread by religious people inside religious traditions.

You can find atheism in the Hebrew Bible, which refers (twice) to those who say in their heart, "There is no God" (Psalms 14:1; 53:1). You can find it in the Quran, which refers to those who claim, "There is nothing but our present life; we die, and we live, and nothing but Time destroys us" (45:25). You can also find it today among observant yet secular Jews who deny God but go to weekly Jewish services and eat only kosher food.

Non-theism in Ancient India

The roots of religious atheism run deeper and farther east than early Judaism and early Islam, however, into the bedrock of the religious traditions (and secularisms) of India. There, in ancient Sanskrit, the "argumentative Indian" was born and, with it, according to philosopher Amartya Sen, "a larger volume of agnostic or atheistic writings than in any other classical language."[25] Because the concept of religion is a modern invention, these ancient agnostics and atheists did not attack "organized religion" as contemporary nonbelievers typically do. Their nonbelief focused instead on the gods and on priests and philosophers who presumed to act and speak on their behalf.

Hinduism In ancient Indian writings, skeptics rejected received notions of divinity as creator, moral order, personal divinity, and overseer of human history. They said yes to **naturalism** and no to supernaturalism, yes to thisworldly pleasure and no to otherworldly asceticism. They also rejected karma, reincarnation, the immortal soul, and the afterlife. Turning their backs on the philosophy that sees earthly life as an illusion, they insisted that the only reality was here and now. They also made fun of those who thought that India's ancient scriptures made sense or that fire sacrifices had actual effects.

Two of the six orthodox schools of ancient Indian philosophy denied the existence of an eternal and personal god active in the affairs of this world. And all three of the heterodox schools of roughly the sixth century BCE—Buddhists, Jains, and Lokayatas—rejected the authority of the ancient scriptures known as the Vedas. The Lokayatas ("Thisworldly Ones") called these revered texts "the prattling of knaves, characterized by the three faults of untruthfulness, internal contradiction, and useless repetition." Members of this school also denied both the goal of Hinduism (spiritual liberation) and its analysis of the human problem (captivity inside the cycle of life, death, and rebirth). "There is no world other than this; there is no heaven and no hell," reads a fourteenth-century work on the Lokayatas' founder Charvaka. "The realm of Shiva and like regions are invented by stupid imposters."[26]

Various shades of doubt and nonbelief also find voice in the Hindu scriptures themselves. In the Rig Veda, the oldest of the Vedic texts, India offers the world one of its great expressions of agnosticism—a shrug in the face of the question that has preoccupied modern Western physicists and astronomers: What happened at the beginning of the universe?

naturalism
the view that everything is caused by and composed of natural entities that can be studied scientifically

Who really knows? Who will here proclaim it? Whence was it produced? Whence is this creation? The gods came afterwards, with the creation of this universe. Who then knows whence it has arisen? Whence this creation has arisen—perhaps it formed itself, or perhaps it did not—the one who looks down on it, in the highest heaven, only he knows—or perhaps he does not know" (Rig Veda 10.129).[27]

The Ramayana epic, which follows the tumultuous love story of the god Rama and his wife Sita, is a deeply devotional text, but it allows space for the counterargument that afterlife beliefs are nothing more than political tools. "Accept the idea once and for all, high-minded prince, that there exists no world to come," the skeptic Javali says to Rama. "Address yourself to what can be perceived and turn your back on what cannot."[28]

Buddhism Buddhism is a popular test case in the study of religion because it seems to have been founded by a man who had little use for divinity and even less for faith. But almost every Buddhist who came after the Buddha occupied a supernatural world filled with gods and ghosts to worship or ignore. Nonetheless, release from suffering is said—in early Buddhism, at least—to be achieved by self-effort, without the intervention of any supernatural power. The Buddha's instructions for living called into question not only the soul but also any entity (divinity included) said to be permanent and unchanging. Everything is impermanent and in motion, taught the Buddha. Nothing stands outside of the flux and flow of human life.

Later Buddhist philosophers developed sophisticated critiques of popular ideas of God circulating in India and Tibet. In one *sutra*, a skeptic takes a swipe at virtually every dogma of ancient Indian philosophers, from sacrifice to karma to reincarnation: "There is nothing bestowed, offered in sacrifice, there is no fruit or result of good or bad deeds, there is not this world or the next. . . . [T]he talk of those who preach a doctrine of survival is vain and false. Fools and wise, at the breaking up of the body, are destroyed and perish, they do not exist after death."[29]

CHRONOLOGY OF ATHEISM

c. 2000 BCE The Gilgamesh epic, the world's oldest recorded story, first begins to circulate

c. 6th century BCE Buddhism and Jainism emerge as religious movements without gods

551–479 BCE Life of Confucius

1770 Baron d'Holbach's *The System of Nature* becomes the first unambiguously atheistic book published in Europe

1789–1799 Revolutionaries in France confiscate church property, force monks and nuns into secular occupations, and abolish Christian holidays

1791 The First Amendment of the Bill of Rights of the U.S. Constitution enshrines religious liberty as a basic right and forbids merging church and state

1844 Karl Marx describes religion as "the opium of the people"

1851 George Holyoake, English writer and labor activist, coins the term "secularism"

1859 Charles Darwin authors *The Origin of Species*

1866 Charles Bradlaugh, the first atheist elected to UK Parliament, establishes the National Secular Society

1869 Thomas Huxley coins the term "agnostic"

1882 Nietzsche, in *The Gay Science*, declares, "God is dead"

Buddhism challenges traditional definitions of religion by its relative disinterest in gods. Located in Macha Bucha Memorial Park in Bangkok, Thailand, this statue depicts the Buddha (standing) addressing disciples who have achieved enlightenment without any supernatural assistance.

Jainism Another form of religious atheism, Jainism, is best known today for its teaching of *ahimsa* (noninjury), which influenced the nonviolent civil disobedience of Mohandas Gandhi and the Reverend Martin Luther King Jr. This tradition emerged in ancient India around the time of the Buddha. Its founding figure, Mahavira (599–527 BCE), who is viewed by his followers as the last in a line of great teachers, embraced key Hindu concepts,

1917 The Russian Revolution prompts church seizures, seminary closures, murders of priests and bishops, and bans on religious books

1925 The Scopes "Monkey Trial" upholds a ban on teaching evolution in Tennessee public schools

1927 Freud authors *The Future of an Illusion*

1933 *Humanist Manifesto* is published

1949 Communists take over China and establish the officially atheistic People's Republic of China

1963 American Atheists is founded and the U.S. Supreme Court rules against school-sponsored prayer and devotional Bible reading in public schools

1966 *Time* magazine cover asks, "Is God Dead?"

2004 The *End of Faith* by Sam Harris announces the arrival of the New Atheism

2009 Barack Obama calls the United States "a nation of Christians and Muslims, Jews and Hindus, and nonbelievers" in his 2009 inaugural address

2016 The Public Religion Research Institute reports that 25 percent of American adults are religiously unaffiliated

including karma, but rejected ritual sacrifice, the caste system, and the authority of the Vedas. He also rejected Hindu polytheism and its personal deities. Whereas Hindus claim that the gods create, sustain, and destroy the world, Jains insist that no god does any such thing. There is no god who creates the universe because the universe is eternal and uncreated. There is no god who maintains the universe because that is the job of karma, whose laws in this tradition are ironclad. In fact, the idea of a god who would create and sustain a world as full of suffering as ours to Jains is as repulsive as it is nonsensical.

Like early Buddhism, Jainism began with renouncers who sought to escape from the painful cycle of life, death, and rebirth. In this quest, renouncers were on their own. There were no gods to help humans escape from karmic bonds. Only through fasting, meditation, and other ascetic techniques could humans burn off the karma that attaches our souls to matter and achieve the life of bliss and wisdom that comes from separating from the material world. This goal is possible thanks to the teachings of *Jinas* ("Spiritual Victors"), liberated souls who have achieved this goal through their own efforts and then shared their insights with the world.

Jains do use words such as "God" to refer to these Jinas, whom they worship in temples that seem to operate very much like their Hindu counterparts. But these beings do not play the active roles played by Greco-Roman gods and the Christian God. The Jina, writes anthropologist Lawrence Babb, is an "Absent Lord": "He responds to no prayers or petitions, and dispenses no saving grace."[30] For this reason, anthropologist Anne Vallely refers to Jainism as "God-saturated atheism."[31]

Non-theism in Ancient China

In ancient China, a humanist affirmation of the supreme value of life on earth was the mainstream position of both Confucians and Daoists. Even the elusive term *tian* ("heaven") pointed not to existence in another realm but to an impersonal force that orders life here on earth. When asked about gods and other supernatural beings that populated Chinese popular piety, Confucius (551–479 BCE), the founder of Confucianism, typically responded with a yawn. Though he participated in prayers and sacrifices, he refused to speculate about ghosts and spirits. He also sidestepped questions about the afterlife, asking one inquirer, "Not yet understanding life, how could you understand death?" (Analects 11:12).[32]

Confucius's successor Mencius took Confucianism in a more spiritual direction, but other early Confucians made it more strictly materialistic. Xunzi affirmed the importance of sacrifice and divination on social grounds—because religious rituals fostered community—but he scoffed at the notion that these rituals did anything at all to influence supernatural beings. "You pray for rain and it rains. Why?" wrote the ever-practical Xunzi. "For no particular reason, I say. It is just as though you had not prayed for rain and it rained anyway."[33]

A later Chinese critic of popular gods, goddesses, and ghosts was the first-century CE thinker Wang Chong, who offered materialist explanations for everything from the origin of the universe to thunder and lightning. Wang Chong rejected efforts to turn "heaven" into a personal deity who rewarded and punished human beings, tracing the origins of this view to rulers seeking supernatural sanction for their policies. Today, the Chinese typically refer to Confucianism as a philosophy rather than a religion. It has no gods, and it focuses on social order, which, according to Confucius, is secured by learning, etiquette, and proper relationships.

Though Confucianism's sister tradition of Daoism would eventually develop all the hallmarks of religion, including belief in immortals and various meditation techniques, early Daoist texts such as the Daodejing and the Zhuangzi were at best indifferent to gods and the afterlife. Their goal was human flourishing, which unfolded here on earth wherever spontaneous sages followed the Dao ("Way"). For Confucians, you followed that Way by adhering to social norms, performing rituals, and observing rules of etiquette. For their early Daoist critics, you flourished instead by acting naturally and spontaneously, unrestrained by social expectations, like water running downhill. You aimed not at life after death but at health, longevity, and flourishing here on earth. And God was not necessary for any of that.

Non-theism in Ancient Greece and Rome

Religious skepticism can also be glimpsed in ancient Western civilizations—in the Gilgamesh epic from ancient Mesopotamia, for example, where Gilgamesh, king of Uruk, goes in search of the secret of immortality after the death of his friend Enkidu. During his wanderings, Gilgamesh encounters a series of characters who tell him that this world is all there is. "There is only death. There is no light beyond," says the Scorpion. "The gods gave death to man and kept life for themselves," says the barmaid Siduri. "That is the only way it is."[34] And right after Gilgamesh finds the plant that promises immortality, a serpent snatches it from his hand.

But the ancient Greeks are typically remembered in the West as the founders of the atheism family. In Greek mythology and the Greek epics, the gods act in the world and on our emotions. Aphrodite employs her famous aphrodisiacs to make us fall in love. Ares, god of war, comes to the aid of the Trojans in Homer's *Iliad*. Philosophers in ancient Greece called this providential worldview into question, offering explanations of human and natural events without conjuring up the supernatural. Like Wang Chong of China, the Greek philosopher Democritus explained thunder and lightning in terms of natural forces. In *The History of the Peloponnesian War*, Thucydides explained military maneuvers in entirely human terms.

Later Greek-speaking thinkers also helped lay the foundation for modern atheism by criticizing popular understandings of the gods. Carneades, who ran Plato's Academy in the second century BCE, cited poisonous snakes as an example of something that no just god would intentionally create. Later, Darwin would be similarly troubled by parasitic wasps that take up residence inside living caterpillars in order to eat them alive from inside. What intelligent (and loving) designer, he asked, would create such things? Such arguments anticipated those of Christopher Hitchens, the New Atheist who attempted to rebut the "intelligent design" argument by pointing to the vestigial appendix and "the many caprices of our urinogenital arrangements."[35]

The Sophists, who influenced Socrates' most famous line—"All I know is that I know nothing"—were the agnostics *par excellence* of the ancient world. Gorgias reportedly claimed that nothing exists and even if it did we could neither know nor communicate it. Another pre-Socratic skeptic, Protagoras, announced his agnosticism in the opening lines of "Concerning the Gods": "Concerning the gods I am unable to discover whether they

The ancient Greek thinker Democritus, also known as the "laughing philosopher," posited natural rather than divine causes for phenomena such as thunder and lightning.

Xenophanes (c. 570–475 BCE)

The world is indebted to atheists and other nonbelievers for a variety of nonreligious theories of religion—explanations of the origin and function of religion that do not reference God or gods. These secular theories of religion include the views that religion originated in wish fulfillment, that the gods are the personification of natural forces, and that religious practices express economic facts. Epicurus, "the atheist philosopher *par excellence*" according to Marx, is best known for his "Epicurean" emphasis on pursuing pleasure, but he was also a theorist of what we now call religion who believed that god belief originated in fear.[a] Another popular theory of the gods propounded in Greek antiquity was euhemerism, named after Euhemerus, who argued that divine beings are deified humans—great kings elevated to divine status by the enthusiasms of their followers.

Among the pre-Socratic philosophers, Xenophanes may have been the staunchest skeptic. He scoffed at divination and criticized popular poets for depicting the gods as thieves, adulterers, and dissemblers. But he was also a progenitor of comparative religion. Centuries before the twentieth-century humanitarian Albert Schweitzer accused historical Jesus scholars of looking into a well and seeing themselves, Xenophanes observed that human beings make gods in their own image. If oxen, horses, and lions could draw, they would draw gods that look like oxen, horses, and lions, he reasoned. Human beings are no different: "Ethiopians say that their gods are flat-nosed and dark, Thracians that theirs are blue-eyed and red-haired."[b] But Xenophanes was no atheist. He described God as one, eternal, unchanging, unmoving, and, oddly enough, spherical (in other words, nothing whatsoever like a human being).

exist or not, or what they are like in form; for there are many hindrances to knowledge, the obscurity of the subject and the brevity of human life."[36]

Religious dissenters in the Roman Empire, which circled the Mediterranean and blanketed much of Western Europe beginning in the first century BCE, advanced many of these Greek arguments. "All religions are equally sublime to the ignorant, useful to the politician, and ridiculous to the philosopher," wrote the Epicurean poet Lucretius.[37] Lucian, in his satires, took on naïve belief in the gods, including Zeus, who is ridiculed in *Lover of Lies* as "hearing prayers as they come up through tubes, and granting or rejecting them, then settling some auguries, and finally arranging the weather."[38]

As for atheism proper, it existed in Greek and Roman antiquity principally as a slur. While ancient Western philosophers did progressively strip the gods of their traditional jobs, they did not deny their existence. But "atheism" and "impiety" were also legal charges, which typically focused not so much on religious belief as on religious practice—the failure to worship the gods of the state. Still, Athenian authorities banished Protagoras for his claim that "man is the measure of all things" and Anaxagoras was banished for his theory that the sun was a rock, not a god. Most famously, Socrates (469–399 BCE) was tried and executed for failing to revere the gods of Athens and for the related charge of corrupting the youth. Early Christians were similarly charged with being atheists for refusing to bow down before Roman gods. "Hence we are called atheists," said the second-century Christian apologist Justin Martyr. "And we confess that we are atheists with reference to gods such as these, but not with reference to the most true God."[39] Some Jesus followers returned the favor by charging their antagonists with atheism. All told, it is far easier to find accusations of godlessness in ancient Greece and Rome than actual atheists.

The Middle Ages, Renaissance, and Reformation

The Middle Ages in Europe were dominated by religious thought—Jewish, Christian, and Muslim—with nary an atheist to be found. There were thinkers who rejected revelation, creation, or the immortality of the soul. And believers wrote mock debates against imagined nonbelievers. But according to one historian of the period, "none of the medieval polemics ever actively denied the existence of God or even claimed an agnostic position."[40] Nonetheless, theologians in this period did some heavy lifting for atheists to follow. By advancing his proofs for the existence of God as an abstract and impersonal Unmoved Mover and First Cause, the Catholic theologian Thomas Aquinas (1225–1274) did an end-run around the more personal biblical God. "Fideists" such as Duns Scotus, by distinguishing sharply between faith and reason and conceding that revelation could not be confirmed by reason alone, left the domain of science to others.

Another influential medieval thinker, the Spaniard Averroes (1126–1198), did similar work within the Islamic tradition, rejecting both the bodily resurrection and literal interpretations of the afterlife as described in the Quran. Via extensive commentaries on Plato and Aristotle, Averroes also dismissed traditional views of God expressed in the leading Islamic schools. Because the universe is eternal, he argued, God cannot be its creator.

The Renaissance, the fourteenth-to-seventeenth-century effort to understand human life in human terms, saw a revival of the classics of ancient Greece and Rome and a renewed interest in ancient skepticism. The French historian Lucien Febvre has argued,

The Spanish-born Muslim rationalist philosopher Averroes was widely criticized for using reason to undercut human free will and God's providence. In this 1867 engraving from a book on medieval scholars by the French writer Louis Figuier, Averroes (right) is declared a heretic and banished to Spain by the caliph Yaqub al-Mansur in 1195.

however, that atheism was literally unthinkable during the Renaissance. In a world in which the church played such a massive part in explaining everything from why the sun came up in the morning to why suffering exists, the ideas necessary to sustain non-theism were simply not available. According to Febvre, it was possible to act as if there were no God, to treat God as irrelevant to human history or to the drama of your own life, but it was impossible to truly believe that God had left the stage.[41]

Those who want to challenge this view often turn to Niccolo Machiavelli (1469–1527), who was denounced as a follower of the devil following the publication of his master-piece in amoral statecraft, *The Prince* (1532). Anticipating the later German philosopher Friedrich Nietzsche, Machiavelli argued that popular Christianity made followers meek and weak, lacking in the virility required in the take-no-prisoners politics for which he remains notorious. Machiavelli also seemed to inhabit a moral universe lacking in fear of divine judgment. But was he an atheist?

In *The Prince*, Machiavelli wrote, "There is nothing more important than appearing to be religious," so it is not surprising that scholars today are confused about whether he was a believer or just dressed himself up as one. Some have called him an "arch-atheist," but at least one biographer has concluded that "Niccolo's God is the creator, master deity, providential, real, universal, . . . a judge, just and forgiving, rewarding and punishing, awesome, a force transcendent, separate from but operative in the world."[42] Either way, Machiavelli bequeathed to the atheist family two powerful ideas: the notion that religion is a means rather than an end and the notion that political theory can go forward without reference to God.

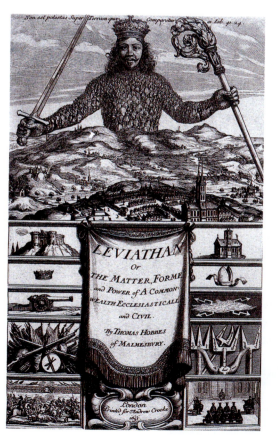

Title page to *Leviathan* (1651) by the English philosopher Thomas Hobbes, who traced human government not to God but to human beings who entered into a contract to keep at bay a chaotic "State of Nature" in which life was "nasty, brutish, and short."

We tend to think of the leaders of the sixteenth-century Protestant Reformation as knights of faith, and they were believers, of course, but the door to atheism was nudged further open by the likes of Martin Luther. The Protestant Reformation was, of course, a religious movement—an effort to reform Roman Catholicism that ended up gestating Protestantism, but many of the criticisms Luther and his fellow reformers advanced against the "priestcraft" and "popery" of Catholicism would be used later, almost verbatim, by atheists and agnostics against religion in general (Protestantism included). Whereas Protestants rejected the authority of popes and priests and denounced many sacraments as hocus pocus, later non-believers rejected the authority of all clergy and judged all ritual to be empty. The spillover of the theological battles of the Reformation into actual war—between Protestants and Catholics and among Protestants themselves—also provided ammunition for the argument of later atheists that religion literally had blood on its hands. ("The philosopher has never killed any priests," wrote the French philosophe Denis Diderot, "whereas the priest has killed a great many philosophers.")[43]

One witness to these wars of religion, England's political philosopher, Thomas Hobbes (1588–1679), began his political philosophy by describing life in the state of nature as "nasty, brutish, and short." To buffer themselves from these natural dangers, people banded together—no God required—to create society and government. Hobbes did pay the homage to Christianity required in his time, but when he sat down to list the four sources of the origin of religion in his classic *Leviathan* (1651), all were, in essence, errors: "opinion of ghosts, ignorance of second causes, devotion towards what men fear, and taking of things casual for prognostics."[44] In time, "Hobbism" would become a synonym for atheism and debauchery.

The Enlightenment

The **Enlightenment** or "Age of Reason" of the late seventeenth and early eighteenth centuries is remembered for making freethinking mainstream. It began with two philosophers, Rene Descartes in France and John Locke in England, who started with skepticism and then worked to establish a firm foundation for knowledge (including knowledge of God). As a rationalist, Descartes (1596–1650) believed that reason is the main source of human knowledge. He is best known for searching for first principles in philosophy and finding one in his famous *cogito*: "I think, therefore I am." Of this we can be certain, he argued: we possess innate ideas quite independent from sensation, and we can prove their reality—including the reality of God and the immortality of the soul—through rational arguments alone. Disagreeing with Descartes, Locke (1632–1704) and other empiricists were convinced that we begin life with a "blank slate" and come to truth via empirical observation alone. Both Descartes and Locke have been described as defenders of Christian faith, but each began with radical doubt and attempted to build a foundation for knowledge of God on secular grounds alone. By opening the philosophical conversation with doubt rather than faith and by shifting that conversation's sources from revelation to reason (or sensation), each pushed open the door to stronger forms of skepticism.

One of those forms was the **pantheism** of the controversial philosopher from Holland Baruch Spinoza (1632–1677). Born in 1632 in Amsterdam into a family that had escaped Portugal in order to practice Judaism, Spinoza was banned from his synagogue in 1656 at the age of twenty-three for doubting biblical revelation and the immortality of the soul. Though "Spinozism" came to be identified with atheism, Spinoza was no atheist. In fact, according to the poet Novalis, he was "God-intoxicated."[45] However, Spinoza did deny to God the supernatural activities typically assigned to divinity in the Western monotheisms. He also denied to human beings any conventional understanding of free will. According to Spinoza's most famous dictum, there was no distinction between God and nature. There is only one substance in the universe, he argued, and that substance is *Deus sive natura* ("God or nature").

Today, Spinoza is claimed by many Jews who are proud to point to one of their own among the world's greatest philosophers. In a Jewish folk tale, a man complains to his rabbi about Spinoza's outrageous view that there is no essential difference between humans and animals. The rabbi replies, "In that case, why have animals never produced a Spinoza?"[46] To which, one imagines Darwin (and perhaps Spinoza) retorting, "They have!"

Historians disagree about precisely when self-identified atheists finally appear in the modern West, but there is no doubting the presence of atheists during the Enlightenment, that period of intellectual "light" after the "Dark Ages" in which reason, progress, and toleration served as an alternative Holy Trinity and philosophes spoke of moving beyond the childhood of the mind to true intellectual maturity. "Gone," the Georgetown professor Jacques Berlinerblau wrote of Victorian England, were "the ventriloquists, misdirection, and sock puppets of the pre-revolutionary French theatre. An infidel could now declare one's infidelities in broad daylight" (though he might get a few years in prison for the pleasure).[47]

Enlightenment
wide-ranging European intellectual movement of the seventeenth and eighteenth centuries that affirmed human progress and religious tolerance even as it elevated science and reason over religious superstition

pantheism
the belief that God and the natural world are identical—that divinity and the universe are one

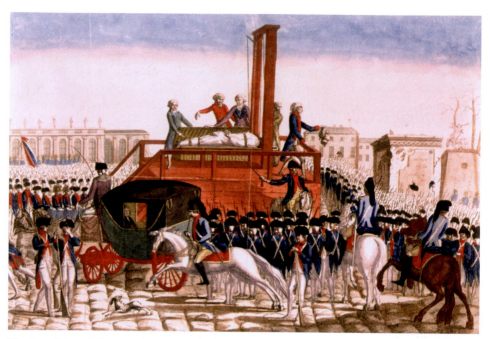

The French Revolution overthrew not only the monarchy and Roman Catholicism but also the doctrine that kings ruled by divine right. This image depicts the execution by guillotine of King Louis XVI in Paris in 1793.

Atheism was most powerful in eighteenth-century France, where the Enlightenment's revolt against authority and tradition was especially strong. In France, the firebrand Voltaire translated the angry anticlericalism of his compatriots into the famous motto, "*Écrasez l'infame!*" ("Crush the infamous thing!"). There, on the eve of the French Revolution, "atheist" finally became an identity rather than a slur, and even Catholic clerics (in this case, Jean Meslier) could fantasize about hanging royals with "the guts of priests."[48]

Denis Diderot (1713–1784) was the chief architect of the greatest intellectual achievement of the French Enlightenment: the twenty-eight-volume *Encyclopédie* (1751–), which aimed to set down the world's wisdom solely on the basis of reason and evidence and, in so doing, to dispel the forces of ignorance and tradition propping up both church and state. This plainly political encyclopedia defined the philosophe as someone who, "trampling on prejudice, tradition, universal consent, authority, in a word, all that enslaves most minds, dares to think for himself."[49] So we should not be surprised that Diderot himself trampled on organized religion with glee.

While other skeptics grieved over the loss of God, looking back wistfully on earlier times of innocent faith, Diderot looked back with fury. Anticipating today's angry atheists, Diderot criticized Islam (and Christianity for good measure) as warmongering religions: "There is not a Musselman alive who would not imagine that he was performing an action pleasing to God and his Holy Prophet by exterminating every Christian on earth, while the Christians are scarcely more tolerant on their side."[50] Recalling Xenophanes, he objected to religion on moral grounds. Once upon a time, he wrote, there was a man who, destroyed by an unfaithful family and unscrupulous business partners, withdrew to a cave to plot his revenge. What could he do to punish them—to turn them against one another and against even life in this world? Rushing out of his cave, he shouted, "God!

God!" And as God's name echoed from village to village and city to city, people "argued with each other, became bitter, cursed each other, [and] cut each other's throats."[51]

That allegory and the bulk of Diderot's critical commentary on religion were not published until after his death. His friend Baron d'Holbach (1723–1789) took a different tack, publishing during his lifetime both anonymously and under the names of dead friends. The Western world's first real evangelist for atheism, d'Holbach hosted an infamous salon of skeptics in Paris. One evening at that salon, after the Scottish philosopher David Hume said that he had never had the pleasure of meeting an atheist, d'Holbach remarked that he was dining with seventeen.

In books such as *Christianity Unveiled* (c. 1766) and *Good Sense* (1772), d'Holbach gave voice to the religious radicalism of the French Revolution. He attacked Christianity and other religions on political and moral as well as philosophical grounds. God is a phantom, "known only by the ravages, the disputes, and the follies which he has caused upon the earth," he wrote. Christianity turns its followers into slaves. And religion in general is a barrier to progress, a roadblock to enlightenment, a manufacturer of intolerance and death.

D'Holbach's most widely read book, *The System of Nature* (1770), has been described as "the Atheist's Bible," a status secured by calls for its public burning by Roman Catholic officials. The first unambiguously atheistic book published in Europe, it distilled the firewater of freethinking France into its most potent form. It was doggedly anti-theistic, deterministic, and materialistic—no God, no free will, and not a whiff of the supernatural. "If we go back to the beginning of things," D'Holbach wrote in a line that managed to criticize religion on scientific, moral, *and* political grounds, "we shall always find that ignorance and fear created the gods; that imagination, rapture, and deception embellished or distorted them; that weakness worships them; that credulity nourishes them; that custom spares them; and that tyranny favors them in order to profit from the blindness of men."[52]

Radical doubt turned the philosophes and their friends against not only the Roman Catholic Church but also the ancient regime it had long supported. The French Revolution of 1789 produced a democratic French Republic as well as a Reign of Terror that saw mass executions of enemies of the revolution, including priests and nuns. A part of a far-reaching de-Christianization campaign that sought to create a purely secular public square, the French Republic seized church lands and destroyed church property.

The French Revolution did not just de-Christianize French society, however. Revolutionaries promoted civil religions celebrating their new republic. They crafted a new revolutionary calendar that got rid of the Sabbath and saints' days and dated world history not from the birth of Jesus but from the birth of the French republic. A Cult of Reason worshiped "one God only, the People." At its inaugural Festival of Reason in 1793, its secular priests turned the cathedral of Notre Dame into the Temple of Reason and the Virgin Mary into the Goddess of Liberty. This short-lived atheistic religion was quickly replaced by a more god-friendly Cult of the Supreme Being, which burned atheism in effigy in its own Festival of the Supreme Being in 1794.

Amidst the furor of the French Revolution, revolutionaries destroyed churches and executed priests, but new religions emerged, too. In this engraving of the "Festival of Reason," held in 1793 in Notre Dame, a "Queen of Reason" personifies the rational ideals of the new republic.

The Enlightenment was more moderate in Germany, England, and America. In Germany, the key figure was Immanuel Kant (1724–1804). Though he equated "enlightenment" with "emancipation from superstition," Kant labored to find a place for God in his philosophy.[53] Or, as he put it, he "den[ied] knowledge in order to make room for faith."[54] As he worked to synthesize and critique the thinking of Descartes and Locke, Kant observed that we are caught in a bind. The innate ideas championed by rationalists cannot get us anywhere without taking sensations into consideration. But our experiences of these sensations are always shaped by innate ideas. As a result, what Kant called things-in-themselves ("noumena") are veiled from us. We can never know them; all we can know are how things appear to our senses ("phenomena").

To put Kant's point in theological terms, all we can know is how God *seems* to us. We cannot prove the existence of God, nor can we disprove it. Those who choose to believe in God are free to do so as a matter of faith. Here, Kant is trying to reestablish a basis for religion on moral terms, bringing God back in by the back door. Observing that we all recognize a "categorical imperative" to do good, Kant worked to establish free will, the immorality of the soul, and the existence of God, not by legal proofs but as "practical postulates" that we must affirm if we hope to live by the "moral law within."[55]

In the British Isles, the Enlightenment produced at least one leading agnostic in the form of Scotsman David Hume (1711–1776). Like Locke, Hume was an empiricist, but he found no room in empiricism for knowledge of the divine. In his *Dialogues Concerning Natural Religion* (1779), he examined all the leading arguments for the existence of God and found them wanting.

Deism, which saw moral action as the core religious act, was the forward edge of the breaking wave of the Enlightenment in England. Deists did not deny God. They just denied that God had anything to do with them. From their perspective, God was like a watchmaker who created the world and then wound it up tight and observed its operations without interfering. Though Deists affirmed afterlife rewards and punishments, they denied miracles. So while God was operative at the beginning (as creator) and the end of time (as judge), he was, for all intents and purposes, absent from the remainder of human history.

The Modern Western Pantheon

Atheism's heyday in the West came in the nineteenth century, when a series of social shifts (industrialization, immigration, urbanization) and intellectual developments (Bible criticism, evolutionary theory, and comparative religion) undercut the traditional authority of religion and transformed faith into a choice rather than an inheritance. In Europe, these "acids of modernity" produced the original "Four Horsemen" of atheism—Ludwig Feuerbach, Karl Marx, Friedrich Nietzsche, and Sigmund Freud—who understood religion as projection, class ideology, will-to-power, and wish fulfillment. God did not create humans, they argued. Humans created God.

The nineteenth-century German philosopher Ludwig Feuerbach famously asserted that humans made God in their image, not the other way around.

Feuerbach   As a follower of the German idealist philosopher Georg Wilhelm Friedrich Hegel, Ludwig Feuerbach (1804–1872) was one of Germany's "Young Hegelians." But in *The Essence of Christianity* (1841), Feuerbach turned Hegel upside down. Hegel had seen nature and history as outgrowths of the Absolute—"objectifications" of an idea. Feuerbach, by contrast, saw the Absolute as a projection of perfect human attributes. To be a

Christian was to worship the best in human nature—our love, our reason, our will—as if it belonged to someone else. And *God* is the word we use to describe that someone else. In reality, however, "the belief in God is nothing but the belief in human dignity."[56] In other words, theology is anthropology: when we say "God" we mean "Us."

Like d'Holbach, who argued that the notion of God alienates us from the natural world, Feuerbach claimed that religion alienates us from human nature—from our selves. Feuerbach did self-identify as an atheist, but he also referred to himself as a believer in anthropotheism. "I deny God," he wrote. "But that means that for me I deny the negation of man."[57] Instead of worshiping some abstract Absolute, he argued, let us stand in awe before the "divinity of human nature."[58]

Karl Marx, the nineteenth-century German theorist best known for his communist philosophy, criticized religion as the "opium of the people."

Marx Another Young Hegelian, Karl Marx (1818–1883), labored to translate Feuerbach's critique of religion into action. Yes, religion is a human product. Yes, God is a projection of human desires. But Marx analyzed these desires in rigorously materialistic terms and with an emphasis on the socioeconomic production of individual religious sentiment. Marx is remembered for describing religion as a narcotic—"the opium of the people"—that compensates believers for suffering in this world with promises of afterlife rewards. However, his analysis of religion offered a surprisingly positive appraisal of its social role. "Religious suffering is at one and the same time the expression of real suffering and a protest against real suffering," he wrote. "Religion is the sigh of the oppressed creature, the heart of a heartless world and the soul of soulless conditions."[59] But why be satisfied with an ideology whose reason for being is the sigh? Why continue simply to protest economic exploitation? Why not rise up and do something about it?

Marx wrote his doctoral dissertation on the ancient philosophers Democritus and Epicurus, and he prefaced it with this succinct creed from the Greek playwright Aeschylus: "In one word, I hate all the gods."[60] As a social and economic theorist, however, Marx did not believe that religion was the problem. The problem was capitalism. It is capitalism that alienates us from our true humanity. Christianity simply serves to mask that alienation, by turning the untold suffering it causes into something the working class could endure. "Long enough have the instructors of the people fixed their eyes on heaven; let them at last bring them back to earth," wrote d'Holbach, whose **materialism** Marx also studied keenly.[61] Marx argued, similarly, that Christianity directed our collective gaze away from the real problems of this world to fantasies in the next. It offered the working class rituals that allowed them to sigh together over their economic exploitation. It instructed the faithful to obey their masters. It told a story of by-and-by salvation that compensated for hardships in this life with the promise of eternal life to come. In doing so, it provided divine sanction for medieval serfdom and modern capitalism alike. In short, it was a form of "inverted consciousness" and top-down social control.

Like Darwin, who believed that natural history was driven by the life-and-death conflicts of natural selection, Marx believed that human history was driven by class conflict. Economic struggles produced ideas. The dominant religious ideas in any epoch would therefore reflect and serve the interests of the dominant class. If the interests of the working class were to triumph over the interests of their capitalist overlords, the fuel of religion would be spent and religion itself would sputter and come to an end. "The abolition of religion as the illusory happiness of the people is the demand for their real happiness," Marx argued. "To call on them to give up their illusions about their condition is to call on them to give up a condition that requires illusions."[62]

materialism
the view that everything originates in matter and is caused by material forces that can be studied scientifically

The nineteenth-century German theorist Friedrich Nietzsche is best known for his statement "God is dead."

Nietzsche   The history of atheism includes not only gleeful atheists, dancing like Diderot on God's grave, but also solemn atheists, nostalgic for times of naïve faith and troubled over what modernity has wrought. The German critic Friedrich Nietzsche (1844–1900) was in the latter group, fretting over a world with God's blood on its hands.

In a parable in Nietzsche's *Gay Science* (1882), a madman runs into a marketplace shouting, "I seek God, I seek God!" The shoppers only laugh. So he asks and answers his own question: "'Whither is God?' he cried; 'I will tell you. *We have killed him*—you and I. All of us are his murderers. . . . God is dead.'" The madman then proceeds into nearby churches singing a requiem for the not-so-eternal God. "What after all are these churches now," he asks, "if they are not the tombs and sepulchers of God?"[63]

Nietzsche saw the threat God's funeral posed not only to religion but also to truth, ethics, civilization, and science. He responded to that threat with a "transvaluation of values." Christian morality was slave morality, he argued—a revolt of the weak against the strong. Its core values (humility, passivity, dependence) were efforts to overturn the natural order of things by elevating the mediocre over the great. Its emphasis on sacrifice and self-denial betrayed our physical desires, our animal instincts, our freedom. This slave morality was also a herd morality, hostile to individual creativity and rooted in envy of elites.

Far better was the "master morality" of the aristocrat, the warrior, and the hero, whose lives were marked not by godliness or even goodness but by beauty, strength, courage, pride, and authenticity. Nietzsche's heroes were virile men who stood up straight in a godless world moving quickly "beyond good and evil." In the end, Nietzsche prophesied the coming of a new messiah called the *Ubermensch* (Overman), who would embody this life-affirming "will to power" in all its glory.

Freud   Sigmund Freud (1856–1939), the Austrian founder of psychoanalysis, offered a more psychological critique of religion. "Religious teachings," he wrote in *The Future of an Illusion* (1927), "are illusions, fulfillments of the oldest, strongest, and most urgent wishes of mankind." The task of religion was to deploy those illusions toward three ends: to "exorcize the terrors of nature, . . . reconcile men to cruelty of Fate, particularly as it is shown in death, and . . . compensate them for the sufferings and the privations [of] civilized life."[64] As children, Freud explains, we are helpless. Initially, we look to our mothers to protect us. Later we turn for that protection to the father, who has more power. And eventually we transform that father into the divine "Father," whom we simultaneously love and fear.

The founder of psychoanalysis, Sigmund Freud, criticized religions as illusions, rooted not in reason but in wish fulfillment and other subconscious desires. Here, Freud works in his London study on a manuscript.

Of all these nineteenth-century atheists, the most politically influential was Marx. His writings inspired the rise of communism in China and the Soviet Union and, with it, political religions—militant anti-theisms that saw religions of any sort as rivals to the sacredness of the state. Marx also inspired killers—from Mao in China to Lenin and Stalin in Russia to Pol Pot in Cambodia—who were as eager to murder in the name of atheistic communism as many Christians and Muslims during the Crusades were eager to kill in the name of their God.

The Russian Revolution of 1917 and the Communist takeover of China in 1949 led to regimes that sought to realize Marx's prophecy that religion was destined to wither away along with capitalism. In both countries, churches, temples, and monastic institutions were seized and religious professionals were forcibly secularized—in some cases, murdered—all in an effort to institute communism as an antireligious state religion. As communism spread during the Cold War, state atheism moved into Eastern Europe, Vietnam, and Cuba. With the fall of the Berlin Wall in 1989 and the collapse of the Soviet Union two years later, both communism and atheism seemed to be in retreat.

Organized Atheism

Modern Western atheism has largely been the work of individuals rather than groups. But freethinkers have organized. The secular religions in revolutionary France were one notorious example. Later, during the mid-nineteenth century, the French founder of sociology, Auguste Comte, organized the Religion of Humanity, complete with its own seven sacraments, its own priests, its own Holy Trinity (Humanity, Earth, Destiny), and its own calendar, with months named after Dante, Homer, Aristotle, and Descartes.

During the Russian Revolution, religious buildings and leaders were forcibly secularized to make room for a new regime committed to both atheism and communism. In this 1919 painting by Ivan Vladimirov, clergy are forced to muck out barrack stables as a Russian soldier looks on.

In the United Kingdom, the utopian socialist Robert Owen (1771–1858) founded Halls of Science, which held secular services on Sundays, complete with sermons and hymns. Owen later immigrated to the United States, where he established a short-lived utopian community in New Harmony, Indiana, that took on a "trinity of evils": private property, irrational religion, and traditional marriage.

Beginning in the late nineteenth century, members of the atheist family formed a variety of organizations focused on ensuring the separation of church and state, defending atheists' rights, engaging in social service, and combating the stigmas associated with nonbelief. Many were also social reformers who saw parallels between chattel slavery, on the one hand, and enslaving the mind, women, and the working class, on the other. In the United Kingdom, the pioneering group was the National Secular Society, established in 1866 by Charles Bradlaugh, who is remembered today as the first atheist elected to Parliament. Other early UK groups included the Rationalist Press Association (est. 1885), and the Union of Ethical Societies (est. 1896).

These British efforts inspired discussions of humanism in the early twentieth century in the United States, particularly in Unitarian circles. In 1927, scholars from the University of Chicago and nearby Unitarian congregations established the Humanist Fellowship, which began publishing *The New Humanist* one year later. American humanists also produced *A Humanist Manifesto*, which appeared in *The New Humanist* in 1933. Signed by thirty-four leading American intellectuals, including the philosopher John Dewey and many Unitarian ministers, this document championed fifteen points of a non-theistic yet nonetheless "religious humanism." It described "the universe as self-existing and not created," and it affirmed that human beings are "a part of nature" that "emerged as a result of a continuous process." Sounding a note now widespread among theorists of religion, it also proclaimed that "the distinction between the sacred and the secular can no longer be maintained."[65]

Pastafarianism originated in protest and parody. Here, Ian Harris sports a colander on his head in 2015 as he protests the refusal of the Driver and Vehicle Licensing Agency in Brighton, United Kingdom, to allow members of minority religions to wear religious garb in driver's license photographs.

Today, other humanist groups include the British Humanist Association, also known as Humanists UK. There are organized atheist groups such as American Atheists (1963) and organized groups of secularists such as the London-based National Secular Society. Other groups are more explicitly political in nature, such as the Freedom From Religion Foundation, which advocates in the United States for the strict separation of church and state.

Finally, there are organizations that parody religious beliefs and institutions, including Pastafarianism, also known as the Church of the Flying Spaghetti Monster. This group began with a 2005 letter by a "concerned citizen" named Bobby Henderson protesting a Kansas State Board of Education policy of teaching intelligent design and evolution as competing theories. Why stop at the Christian theory that God designed the universe, Henderson asked? Why not include Flying Spaghetti Monsterism? Although this "religion" began as a parody, it has taken on serious causes, including advocating in courts ~~wide~~ for strict church/state separation.

~~I~~EISM IN THE UNITED STATES

~~the~~ United States has more Christians than any country on earth. Many U.S. ~~be~~lieve their country was founded as a Christian nation. However, according ~~histo~~rian Amanda Porterfield, the United States was also "conceived in doubt."[66] ~~colonies~~ that would later become the United States were largely run on the European ~~model, with A~~nglicanism serving as the established church of Virginia, for example, and ~~Congregationa~~lism as the established church of Massachusetts. With the exception of ~~Rhode Island an~~d Pennsylvania, which were relatively safe havens for religious dissenters, each colony favored one Protestant denomination over the others and paid for churches and ministers with tax revenues. The Constitution's First Amendment changed all that—by enshrining religious liberty and separating church and state.

In the late eighteenth century, Deism enjoyed a vogue. In fact, America's first two presidents—George Washington and John Adams—were Deists. But as political parties emerged, and with them the bitter partisanship of the elections of 1796 and 1800, the nation turned toward evangelical Protestantism. During the Second Great Awakening of the early 1800s, revivalists used fear and loathing of Jefferson and other "infidels" to drive Americans into the arms of Jesus. In this way, the stories of freethought and Christianity in the United States became closely intertwined.

Thomas Paine and Thomas Jefferson

As in Europe, it is difficult to determine precisely when atheism emerged in the United States, but its roots go back at least to the early national period and to the controversial Deist Thomas Paine (1737–1809). Paine was the author of *Common Sense* (1776), a pamphlet that helped to turn America's colonists into revolutionaries, but he was not just a political revolutionary. He was a religious revolutionary whose antireligion manifesto, *The Age of Reason* (1794, 1807), took on the Western religions ("human inventions set up to terrify and enslave mankind"), the Bible ("the word of a demon"), and Christian theology ("the study of nothing").[67] Apart from the fallout from his books, Paine lived an amazing life. Banned from England for sedition, he fled to France, where he was elected to the French National Convention and then jailed. He wrote *The Age of Reason* from prison and then returned in 1802 to the United States. By that time, there was no place in American

In this 1895 cartoon in *Truth Seeker* by the atheist illustrator Watson Heston, Lady Liberty joins George Washington, Thomas Jefferson, and Benjamin Franklin in lauding Thomas Paine as an "author-hero and patriot."

hearts for Paine. Jefferson, who was elected president in 1800, had made common cause with Baptists and Methodist revivalists, who as religious minorities favored the separation of church and state. So Paine died "the best-hated man in America"—a "filthy little atheist" in the words of Theodore Roosevelt.[68]

History dealt a kinder fate to Thomas Jefferson who, among other things, was the author of an 1802 letter to the Baptists of Danbury, Connecticut, describing a constitutional "wall of separation between Church & State." Although a slaveholder himself, Jefferson was a fervent believer in religious liberty. In his only book, *Notes on the State of Virginia* (1785), Jefferson wrote, "It does me no injury for my neighbour to say there are twenty gods, or no god. It neither picks my pocket nor breaks my leg." During the bitterly partisan election of 1800, which pitted Jefferson against President John Adams of the Federalist Party, pious partisans of Adams attacked Jefferson as the "great arch priest of Jacobinism and infidelity." Pointing to Jefferson's book as proof of his disqualifying nonbelief, the Presbyterian minister William Linn fumed, "Let my neighbour once persuade himself that there is no God, and he will soon pick my pocket, and break not only my *leg* but my *neck*. If there be no God, there is no law." The *Connecticut Courant* joined the fray, suggesting that Jefferson might be a secret Jew or Muslim. No one seems to know, it wrote, "whether Mr. Jefferson believes in the heathen mythology or the alcoran [Quran]; whether he is a Jew or a Christian; whether he believes in one God, or in many; or in none at all."[69]

Jefferson's actual religious views were complicated. Over the last two centuries, many have lumped him with Paine as a partisan of Deism. Others have described him as an atheist, a Unitarian, an Anglican, an Epicurean, and a secular humanist. By any name, Jefferson was a critic of Christianity who had no use for either its creeds ("mere Abracadabra") or its Calvinist theologians ("mere Usurpers of the Christian name"). But Jefferson was also a deeply religious man who, according to one of his biographers, was "the most self-consciously theological of all America's presidents."[70]

During his time in the White House, Jefferson cut-and-pasted his own version of the New Testament—the "Jefferson Bible"—which excised from the Gospels every whiff of a miracle, including the resurrection itself. He did this not to bury Jesus but to praise him. Earlier, Paine had imagined Jesus as a Deist made in his own image, "a virtuous and an amiable man" and a "revolutionist" like himself who "had in contemplation the delivery of the Jewish nation from the bondage of the Romans."[71] Jefferson, too, looked back on the life of Jesus and saw a character quite like himself—an enlightened sage whose moral teachings were as self-evident as the truth that all "men are created equal."

African American and Women Freethinkers

Abolitionist Frederick Douglass protested in his autobiography the wide gap between "the impartial Christianity of Christ" and "the partial and hypocritical Christianity of this land." Here he appears in the frontispiece of that book, *Narrative of the Life of Frederick Douglass, an American Slave* (1845).

One of Jefferson's contributions to American religion was the sharp distinction he drew between the religion of Jesus and the religion of the churches. In *Narrative of the Life of Frederick Douglass, an American Slave* (1845), Jefferson's contemporary, the slave-turned-abolitionist orator Frederick Douglass, made a similar move, laying down the boldest of lines between the holy "Christianity of Christ" and the wicked "Christianity of this land." It was his Christian duty, Douglass argued, to "hate the corrupt, slaveholding, women-whipping, cradle-plundering, partial and hypocritical Christianity of this land." To refer to that so-called religion as Christianity, he wrote, was "the boldest of all frauds, and the grossest of all libels." Then he went on to accuse America's so-called

Christians—its ministers, missionaries, and church members—of the grossest hypocrisy for preaching purity and marriage while selling slaves into prostitution and breaking up families on the auction block.[72]

Other slave narratives came closer to professing atheism. Like Jews who found it difficult to find God amidst the horrors of the Holocaust, authors of these accounts found reasons to doubt the existence of God amidst the horrors they experienced on slave ships and slave plantations. For example, Austin Steward's *Twenty-Two Years a Slave* (1857) argues that the hypocrisy of the slaveholder who whipped a slave one minute and then walked into church the next led slaves to doubt both "the sincerity of every white man's religion" and the existence of God. "Can it be a matter of astonishment, that slaves often feel that there is no just God for the poor African?"[73]

Pioneering women contemporaries of Steward also connected the dots between Christianity and slavery, even as they added women's oppression to the growing list of Christendom's sins. Two of the most intriguing of these pioneers of feminism—Frances Wright and Ernestine Rose—were foreign-born activists who drank deep of the more radical streams of the Enlightenment in Europe. Because women were considered at the time to be more naturally religious than men, women like Wright and Rose were viewed by Christian ministers as even more dangerous than male freethinkers.

Frances Wright (1795–1852) was born to money in Scotland in 1795 and visited the United States in 1818 to see a play she had written into production in New York City. She made a name for herself with a travel book called *Views of Society & Manners in America* (1821) and achieved renown beginning in 1828 as the first woman to speak to large mixed-gender audiences in the United States. She spoke against slavery and for the rights of the working classes. She established a short-lived utopian community for freed slaves outside modern-day Memphis, Tennessee. She was particularly controversial for her views on religion.

As revivalists of the Second Great Awakening were converting Americans by the millions to evangelical Protestantism, Wright preached reason and science instead. Observing that revivalists were targeting women, she condemned the awakening as a sort of sleepiness—an "odious experiment on human credulity."[74] Wright denounced "the clerical hierarchy" and "the clerical craft" as "the two deadliest evils which ever cursed society."[75] "Turn [your] churches into halls of science, and exchange [your] teachers of faith for expounders of nature," she said.[76] She herself did just that, buying a dilapidated church in Lower Manhattan in New York City and calling it the Hall of Science. With Robert Owen's son, Robert Dale Owen, she established a freethought weekly newspaper, the *Free Enquirer*. New York City's mayor Philip Hone responded to her provocations by denouncing her as the "female Tom Paine."[77] Evangelical ministers, calling her "The Red Harlot of Infidelity," employed popular fears of "Fanny Wrightism" to draw more and more Americans to their revivals and into their Bible-believing churches.[78]

Though largely forgotten today, the pioneering women's rights advocate Ernestine Rose (1810–1892) was, in her heyday, one of the most talked about women in the United States. At the age of seventeen, she left her rabbi father and her Polish homeland. After sojourns in Berlin, Paris, and London, she arrived in the United States in 1836. An intersectional thinker over a century and a half before that term came into vogue in the early twenty-first century, Rose argued for the liberation of "slaves of race, slaves of faith, slaves of sex," and saw the causes of abolitionism, freethought, and women's rights as intimately intertwined.[79] In 1858, she argued, "As long as woman was forced to pay taxes without the

The suffragette Ernestine Rose rejected religion, including her rabbi father's Judaism, on the theory that religions were irrational and oppressed women. In this 1872 drawing from *The Graphic*, Rose appears third from the left, looking at the standing speaker, Rhoda Garrett, who is addressing a women's rights meeting in London.

right to representation—as long as the colored man is transformed into a piece of chattel because his face is darker than his owner—as long as an honest, conscientious avowal of a disbelief in the fashionable superstition called religion is a crime," the Declaration of Independence was "a dead letter."[80]

"A minority of one," in her own words, Rose was a cosmopolitan foreigner of Jewish origins and a rare woman orator in an age in which the public sphere was almost universally understood to be for men alone.[81] She was one of the only women in the freethought movement and one of the only atheists agitating for the abolition of slavery and women's rights. During an address at a Thomas Paine birthday celebration in New York City in 1848, she argued that "superstition keeps women ignorant, dependent, and enslaved beings.... The churches have been built upon their necks."[82] In an 1861 lecture later published as *A Defence of Atheism*, she lamented the "monstrous crimes" perpetrated by believers "on account of difference of belief." "Sweep all belief in the supernatural from the globe," she wrote, and "you would cleanse and purify the heart of . . . hypocrisy, bigotry, and intolerance."[83]

As with Frances Wright, ministers seemed more horrified by Rose's sex than her arguments. On the eve of a speech she was to give in Bangor, Maine, the Congregationalist minister G. B. Little fumed that a woman atheist was worse than a prostitute. "We know of no object more deserving of contempt, loathing, and abhorrence than a female Atheist," he wrote. "We hold the vilest strumpet from the stews to be by comparison respectable."[84] Thanks to Little's words, Rose packed the two-thousand-seat venue. But fear of Rose and her ilk continued to pack Americans into Bible-believing churches as well.

The Golden Age of Freethought

Despite all this pioneering work, members of the atheist family operated largely behind the scenes for most of the nineteenth century. Their nonbelief was the secret that dared not speak its name, except among daredevils such as Steward, Wright, and Rose. Then the golden age of freethought in the last few decades of the nineteenth century produced a series of great orators and new publications and organizations.

The most prominent orator was the "Great Agnostic" Robert Ingersoll (1833–1899), who did more than anyone else to spread the gospel of freethinking in the United States after the horrors of the Civil War. A lawyer, a Republican, and the son of a preacher, Ingersoll ("Robert Injuresoul" to his enemies) made a name for himself via a famous speech at the 1876 Republican National Convention, but he made his life as an agnostic. For roughly three decades until his death in 1899, he captivated huge crowds in towns and cities across the country with his shocking attacks on the Bible and his unyielding support for evolution. Ingersoll's real passion, however, was for secular government. He also worked hard to rehabilitate the reputation of Thomas Paine, whom he regarded as an American hero. Rejecting the view that the United States was a Christian nation, he repeatedly turned the attention of his listeners back to American heroes who crafted "the first secular government that was ever founded in this world." They "knew that to put God in the Constitution was to put man out," Ingersoll said. They "intended that all should have the right to worship, or not to worship; that our laws should make no distinction on account of creed."[85]

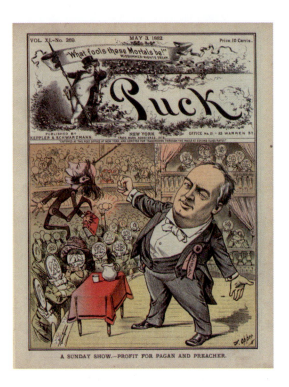

The "Great Agnostic" Robert Ingersoll barnstormed across the United States after the Civil War, attacking religion and promoting secular government. This 1882 *Puck* magazine cartoon—"A Sunday Show.–Profit for Pagan and Preacher"—makes Ingersoll out to be a slimy salesman, just in it for the money.

Ingersoll was a large man who loomed even larger in freethought cartoons. In one cartoon that ran in 1895 in the *Truth Seeker*, the atheist Watson Heston depicted Ingersoll, properly dressed in a vest and tie, in a bowling alley. As he sends a massive ball down a "line of argument" and scatters pins labeled "miracles," "prayer," and "God myth," Ingersoll strikes fear into his disheveled Christian onlookers. A critical cartoon, "A Sunday Show—Profit for Pagan and Preacher," ran thirteen years earlier in *Puck* magazine. It depicted Ingersoll winking knowingly at the reader while lecturing to a packed house of coins, a reference to the handsome living Ingersoll made from his lectures.

Ingersoll's heyday also witnessed women activists who championed votes for women alongside free love and freethought. In a book called *Woman, Church and State* (1895), the suffragist Matilda Joslyn Gage denounced the view that Eve brought sin into the world and that sex was sinful. *The Woman's Bible* (1895–1898) is typically associated with the Christian women's rights leader Elizabeth Cady Stanton, but it was produced by a committee of twenty-six additional women, Gage included. This multiyear commentary decried the misogyny its authors saw in the Bible. "The canon and civil law; church and state; priests and legislators; all political parties and religious denominations have alike taught that woman was made after man, of man, and for man," it read. "Creeds, codes, Scriptures and statutes, are all based on this idea." But *The Woman's Bible* also advanced a series of more positive proposals, such as addressing prayers to a "Heavenly Mother."[86]

From the "Monkey Trial" to Madalyn O'Hair

The most dramatic event in the American history of atheism was the Scopes "Monkey Trial" of 1925. At issue was a substitute biology teacher named John Scopes, who was arrested for flouting a Tennessee law banning the teaching of evolution in the public schools. In the summer of 1925, the nation's eyes turned to a courtroom in Dayton, Tennessee, that would later become the subject of dozens of books and films, including the 1960 feature *Inherit the Wind*. Representing the state of Tennessee was William Jennings Bryan, "The Great Commoner," who in a long career as a progressive had represented his Democratic Party three times as its presidential candidate. (He lost to William McKinley twice and then to William Howard Taft.) But Bryan also represented fundamentalism, a new type of militantly antimodern, Bible-believing Protestantism that objected strongly to evolutionary thought. Taking the other side in *The State of Tennessee v. John Thomas Scopes* was Clarence Darrow, an agnostic and American Civil Liberties Union leader who believed that "doubt was the beginning of wisdom, and the fear of God was the end of wisdom."[87]

The facts were not at issue: Scopes had violated the law. But was the law constitutional? Darrow said no. The First Amendment prohibits "the establishment of religion," and in this case, Darrow argued, Tennessee was establishing Christianity as its state religion by siding with Christian thinkers against evolutionary science. In the dramatic climax of this extraordinary trial, which was covered by newspapers around the world, Darrow called Bryan to the stand and quizzed him on the Bible, forcing Bryan to admit that even he did not read it literally.

Bryan won the case, but the newspaper reporters in the room declared Darrow the winner in a runaway decision. Among them, H. L. Mencken was the one who dubbed this display of "simian imbecility" the "Monkey Trial." In his syndicated column, he opined that the trial had served notice "on the country that Neanderthal man is organizing in these forlorn backwaters of the land, led by a fanatic, devoid of sense and devoid of conscience."[88] Scopes called the trial "the beginning of the decline of fundamentalism," although that wasn't quite accurate.[89] Many fundamentalists did scurry to the sidelines of the public square after 1925, reevaluating their strategies and building up their own institutions. But they reemerged as a powerful political force in the late 1970s under the direction of the Reverend Jerry Falwell of the Moral Majority.

While Darrow publicized freethought from Dayton, Tennessee, secularism was also rising in New York City in the Harlem Renaissance of the 1920s and 1930s, thanks in large part to the influence of the radical writer, orator, and activist Hubert Harrison (1883–1927). Like Ernestine Rose, Harrison was an internationalist and an equal opportunity critic who left his homeland—in his case, the West Indies—as a teenager. He opposed capitalism and embraced socialism only to leave the Socialist Party after seeing that its leaders put whiteness before class. Thomas Paine's writing led him to doubt the Bible, which led him to doubt God. In a 1908 letter to a friend he later transcribed into his diary, he reported finding "a new belief." "Now I am an Agnostic," he wrote, "because I prefer . . . to go to the grave with my eyes open."[90]

Like Rose, Harrison has been largely forgotten, but his "race first" writings were a major influence on the Pan-Africanism movement of the Caribbean-born Marcus Garvey and the Black Power movement of the 1960s. Harrison also influenced such Harlem

Renaissance writers as Langston Hughes, Richard Wright, and Zora Neal Hurston. One of their most provocative works was the Langston Hughes poem "Goodbye, Christ" (1932):

> Goodbye,
> Christ Jesus Lord God Jehova,
> Beat is on away from here now.
> Make way for a new guy with no religion at all—
> A real guy named
> Marx Communist Lenin Peasant Stalin Worker ME—[91]

Perhaps the most notorious figure in the American story of nonbelievers was Madalyn Murray O'Hair, who came to public prominence in the early 1960s after suing to stop Baltimore's public schools from subjecting her son William to mandatory prayers and Bible readings. In a 1963 decision that continues to upset cultural conservatives today, the U.S. Supreme Court took her side, banning both devotional Bible reading and school-sponsored prayers in the public schools. That same year she founded American Atheists. Soon, *Life* magazine was profiling O'Hair as "the most hated woman in America"—a reputation she encouraged by (among other things) suing to remove "In God We Trust" from U.S. currency and debating evangelists on *The Phil Donahue Show*. In 1966, *Time* magazine asked, in a bold, black and red cover, "IS GOD DEAD?" Though prompted by O'Hair, the cover article featured Protestant and Jewish "death of God" theologians. These radicals represented, according to *Time*, an oddly "reverent agnosticism" and for a brief period they flashed across magazine covers and television screens, where they were eagerly hissed and booed. But they did not replace O'Hair, who remained the nonbeliever American believers loved to hate.

O'Hair, who had her two sons out of wedlock and never seemed to meet a friend she could not alienate, was an imperfect vessel for the atheist cause. She was, by her own admission, an "offensive, unlovable, bull-headed, defiant, aggressive slob," but for better or worse she served as America's standard bearer for nonbelief and the strict separation of church and state during the 1960s and 1970s.[92] A magnet for controversy, O'Hair watched her son William become a born-again Christian in 1977, leading her to repudiate him. In 1995, she mysteriously disappeared along with her granddaughter and her other son Jon. Their bodies were found buried on a Texas ranch in 2001.

New Atheists

Throughout U.S. history, there has been a strong presumption that religion is a private matter and should not be debated in the public square. Of course, that public square has never been absent of religious beliefs and practices. The U.S. Congress opens its sessions with prayers, and presidents swear their oaths on Bibles. But, from George Washington forward, when politicians invoked God, they typically did so generically, up to and including President-elect Dwight D. Eisenhower, who remarked in 1952 that his country made "no sense unless it is founded in a deeply held religious faith, and I don't care what it is."[93] In the late 1970s and early 1980s, however, this gentlemen's agreement began to break down, as Democrat Jimmy Carter and Republican Ronald Reagan repeatedly invoked God and quoted from the Bible. It collapsed during the faith-based presidency of President George W. Bush, who invoked Jesus as his favorite political philosopher.

"Good without God" Advertising

It is common to think of atheism as an affair of the mind alone, but it, too, has its material culture. In 2008, in the *Guardian*, the comedian Ariane Sherine vented about a new Christian bus advertising campaign. As an afterthought she suggested, at least half in jest, that her atheist readers should donate five pounds each so they could put an ad of their own on a bus. With the support of the British Humanist Association and the New Atheist Richard Dawkins, the campaign quickly raised more than two hundred thousand pounds. Before the end of the year, buses were rolling across London proclaiming, "There's probably no god. Now stop worrying and enjoy your life." Copycat efforts followed in at least fifteen other countries, from Brazil to Australia. Christian opposition shut down a "No God, no master" campaign in Croatia after one day, but in the United States the American Humanist Association and the Freedom From Religion Foundation were able to launch parallel bus campaigns in Washington, DC, and other U.S. cities with slogans such as "You can be good without God" and "Don't believe in a Supreme Being? You are not alone." Most of these advertisements were text only, but they made atheists visible across London and other cities worldwide. They also transported atheism from the privacy of individual minds into the public square.

As conservative Republicans argued that the United States was a "Christian nation" and justified their public policies with Bible quotations and professions of faith, secularists felt compelled to respond. When the New Atheism announced itself via the publication of *The End of Faith* (2004) by Sam Harris, it was undoubtedly reacting to 9/11 and to the rise of violent Islamicism. But it was also a response to the collapse of the old gentlemen's agreement to keep governmental proclamations of religion at least somewhat generic. Pushing back against the "Christian nation" ideal, Harris, Christopher Hitchens, and cognitive scientist Daniel Dennett all published bestsellers and garnered massive media coverage in the first decade of the twenty-first century. They were joined by British and French thinkers such as Richard Dawkins and Michel Onfray, as well as novelists (Salman Rushdie and Philip Pullman) and TV hosts (Bill Maher).

There was not much that was new in the "New Atheism," however. Like atheists before them, New Atheists put their trust in science rather than dogma, reason rather than faith. They said religion was a human construction. They argued that belief in God was foolish and childish, driven by fear and built on illusions. Hitchens characterized the Western monotheisms as "a plagiarism of a plagiarism of a hearsay of a hearsay," adding that religion East and West derives from "the bawling and fearful infancy of our species."[94] This is an old complaint, itself a plagiarism of Freud, who got it from Marx, who got it from Feuerbach, updated only by the New Atheists' trademark indignation.

But there was some novelty in the New Atheism. New Atheists focused more than their predecessors on the evils of organized religion, which Hitchens characterized as "violent, irrational, intolerant, allied to racism and tribalism and bigotry, invested in ignorance and hostile to free inquiry, contemptuous of women and coercive toward children."[95]

Instead of focusing on the crimes and misdemeanors of Judaism and Christianity, as earlier atheists had done, they sharply criticized Islam, which Dawkins called the "greatest force for evil today" and Harris termed "a thoroughgoing cult of death."[96] New Atheists also questioned the value of religious tolerance. Before 9/11, Hitchens argued, it made sense to view religion as "harmless nonsense," but the horrors of that day made that view untenable. Echoing Hitchens, Dawkins argued that religion is "dangerous because we have all bought into a weird respect, which uniquely protects religion from normal criticism. Let's now stop being so damned respectful!"[97] Harris also labeled religious tolerance "one of the principal forces driving us toward the abyss."[98]

More than their predecessors, the New Atheists also emphasized what Hitchens referred to as the "poison" of religion. Many earlier nonbelievers had conceded that religion was a social good, useful for inculcating morals and maintaining social order. The New Atheists insisted that religion was hazardous to your health and a pox on society. "Religion has caused innumerable people not just to conduct themselves no better than others," wrote Hitchens, "but to award themselves permission to behave in ways that would make a brothel-keeper or an ethnic cleanser raise an eyebrow."[99]

Another distinguishing feature of the New Atheists was their anger. They weren't just atheists, they were anti-theistic zealots in a take-no-prisoners war on faith, which Dawkins described as "one of the world's great evils, comparable to the smallpox virus but harder to eradicate."[100] Their enemies in this war were not only religious fanatics but also so-called moderates who, by making religion appear to be rational and harmless, issued every day "an open invitation to extremism."[101]

This anger led some nonbelievers to seek out kinder and gentler atheists, including Hemant Mehta, who has a major presence online as "The Friendly Atheist." Meanwhile, the New Atheist Sam Harris has distinguished himself from some of his peers by taking a keen interest in mindfulness meditation and other avenues to spiritual experience. In *Waking Up: A Guide to Spirituality Without Religion* (2014), he argues for "a rational approach to spirituality." In a similar vein, the Swiss-born British philosopher Alain De Botton has contended for a new form of atheism—"Atheism 2.0," he calls it—that moves beyond the secular fundamentalism of the New Atheists by taking seriously the benefits of communal singing and communal meals and even of prayers, rituals, and pilgrimages to sacred places. "The most boring and unproductive question one can ask of any religion is whether or not it is true," he writes in *Religion for Atheists* (2012). "Religions are in the end too complex, interesting and on occasion wise to be abandoned simply to those who believe in them."

The journalist Ta-Nehisi Coates is not typically classed among the New Atheists, but his bestseller *Between the World and Me*, an open letter to his son about the dangers presented to black bodies by the American Dream, is resolutely godless. In his searing prose, Coates refuses to comfort his son and his other readers—black, brown, white, and otherwise—with traditional pieties about God bending the arc of history toward justice. In this book, there is neither grace nor glory—no God to pick you up when you fall down and no Promised Land to which you are marching. "My understanding of the universe was physical," Coates writes, "and its moral arc bent toward chaos then concluded in a box."[102]

Beyond the World and Me serves as a reminder that the stereotype that African Americans are especially religious is just that: a stereotype. The civil rights movement of the 1950s and 1960s was, of course, a religious demonstration. But among the marchers were members of the Student Nonviolent Coordinating Committee, which evolved into a

Jennifer Hecht (1964–)

Jennifer Hecht is a poet and a historian. She is also an atheist and the author of the bestselling *Doubt: A History* (2003), which surveys skeptics of all stripes, from Socrates to Emily Dickinson. Raised Jewish on Long Island in New York, Hecht has jokingly referred to her earlier self as an "atreeist" who sulked over not being allowed to set up a Christmas tree in her home. Colored eggs were allowed, but not at Easter. "Thus, I was raised against the calendar and the population," she says.[a]

While working on *Doubt*, Hecht reports, she did not believe in God, but she did not identify as an atheist either. She now refers to herself as a proud atheist who puts her faith in humanity. Regarding the term "agnostic," she says, its half-life is up. "If people want to retain it with the meaning 'I personally have not yet made up my mind' that seems okay," she writes, but the argument that "you can't prove a negative so we have to allow for the possibility of God and Superman… seems philosophically silly to me."[b]

After two of her close friends—both fellow poets whom she met in graduate school at Columbia University—took their own lives, she wrote a Facebook post against suicide, which became an article in the *Boston Globe*, which became a book called *Stay: A History of Suicides and the Philosophies Against It* (2013). Most arguments against suicide are religious. Hecht's is not. It is historical and philosophical, and it has two key turns. The first is that suicide does harm far beyond the harm it does to the body of the deceased. It damages the community. And because of the phenomenon of "suicide contagion," one suicide makes it far more likely that friends and family members will commit suicide, too. "That means that every suicide may be a delayed homicide," Hecht writes.[c] The book's second turn is more philosophical. Each of us is made up of multiple selves, both past and future, Hecht argues. The self who is considering suicide should also consider his or her future selves and decide to "stay" on their behalf.

younger, more radical, and more secular alternative to the pastoral pieties of the Reverend Martin Luther King Jr. and many civil rights leaders. The Black Lives Matter movement, born in 2013 in response to police killings of African American men, is similarly youthful, radical, and largely secular, with many LGBTQ leaders in its midst and open hostility toward Christianity among many in its rank and file.

Out of the Closet

The New Atheism may be keeping some atheists in the closet by putting an angry face on nonbelief. But it is calling other atheists out of the closet—by making atheism a point of view that finally dares to speak its name. The Internet, and social media in particular, are likely doing the same, by creating and sustaining online communities for nonbelievers.

It is unclear what effect these efforts are having on the identities of those who do not believe in God. Likely those effects are mixed. Globally, the stigma of nonbelief remains. In the United States, recent surveys have found that only about half of American citizens say they would be willing to vote for an otherwise qualified atheist for president.[103] Forty-eight percent said they would not want their children to marry an atheist.[104] However, atheists are more vocal and more visible worldwide than they once were. Barack Obama, in his 2009 inaugural address, described the United States as "a nation of Christians and Muslims, Jews and Hindus, and nonbelievers." And many college campuses in the United States now have humanist chaplains.

CONTEMPORARY CONTROVERSY: BUT IS IT A RELIGION?

One intriguing contemporary debate concerns the religious status of ardent nonbelief. New Atheists are surely responding to the rise of fundamentalism. But are they also manifestations of it? Is atheism, as novelist David Foster Wallace wrote, an "anti-religious religion"?[105]

Most atheists today scoff at the notion that they are in any way *religious*. "Our belief is not a belief. Our principles are not a faith," wrote Hitchens. "We do not hold our convictions dogmatically."[106] But irreligion today boasts the same sort of frothing evangelists that religion does. Many atheists are certain they have found all the answers. Many are certain that their opponents are lost and in need of saving. New Atheists, according to the journal *First Things*, have banished skepticism from their ranks, exhibiting instead "the sort of boorish arrogance that might make a man believe himself a great strategist because his tanks overwhelmed a town of unarmed peasants, or a great lover because he can afford the price of admission to a brothel."[107] The journalist Chris Hedges calls them "secular fundamentalists" spewing "the same kind of bigotry and chauvinism and intolerance that marks the radical Christian right."[108] Michel Onfray, the French philosopher and author of *The Atheist Manifesto* (2011) who is often counted among the New Atheists, detects the stench of religion in much contemporary atheism and wishes for a stiff breeze to blow it away. "The tactics of some secular figures seem contaminated by the enemy's ideology: many militants in the secular cause look astonishingly like clergy," he writes. "They act like clergy, too."[109]

Whether any "ism" qualifies as a religion turns on two hinges: a definition of religion, and facts about the "ism" at hand. If we follow the nineteenth-century anthropologist E. B. Tylor in defining religion as "belief in Spiritual Beings," atheism does not qualify. But no serious scholar of religion nowadays follows Tylor. His definition is too focused on belief, which is only a part of any religion, and too focused on spiritual beings. All sorts of religious people deny God, including many Jews, Buddhists, Daoists, and Confucians.

Moreover, the history of atheism has featured all sorts of secular religions, including the Cult of the Reason and the Cult of the Supreme Being in revolutionary France. In the twentieth century, communists in the Soviet Union and China continued to demonstrate that secular religions are by no means exempt from fanaticism. Their acolytes have bowed at least as low to Stalin and Mao as Christians have to Christ. As many scholars have observed, "the secular" and "the religious," are not the polar opposites we often imagine them to be. Their varieties are intimately tied up with one another and with the social and cultural worlds around them. In a 1961 case brought by a Maryland man who had lost his appointment as a notary public because of his refusal to declare his belief in God, the U.S. Supreme Court swung its considerable weight toward this idea that the "secular" can also be "religious," concluding in a widely debated footnote that, because secular humanism walks like a religion and talks like a religion, the courts should treat it like one.[110]

Today, few scholars of religion offer substantive definitions of religion that focus on belief in God or gods. Functional definitions, which focus on what religion *does* rather than what religion *is*, are more popular. But most scholars are now gravitating toward an understanding of religion that borrows from the early-twentieth-century philosopher

BIRTH AND DEATH

Members of the atheist family are divided about the need for rituals. Most are happy to relegate them to the dustbin of religions past and to proceed with their births, lives, and deaths with minimal pomp and circumstance. "I believe that when I die I shall rot, and nothing of my ego will survive," wrote the British atheist Bertrand Russell, and his equally unsentimental followers have concluded that there is no reason to ritualize our entry into the world or our exit from it.[a]

Some nonbelievers, however, are convinced that rites of passage are a human need that needn't be hijacked by religious dogma. According to Greta Christina, writing in *Free Inquiry*, rituals and traditions "provide structure, a skeleton for our lives." Rather than reject them altogether, nonbelievers should recognize them as "basic human needs" and accommodate them as best as they can. In a piece called "Why Nonbelievers Need Ritual Too," Suzanne Moore argues that nonbelievers deserve beautiful rituals, too. "For me, not believing in God does not mean one has to forgo poetry, magic, the chaos of ritual, the remaking of shared bonds."[b]

To that end, "secular celebrants" and "humanist celebrants" have emerged in recent years to conduct baby-naming ceremonies, weddings, and funerals. One common feature of these ceremonies is personalization. A website called Humanist Ceremonies that serves as a network for a few hundred humanist celebrants across the United Kingdom emphasizes this

Ludwig Wittgenstein's understanding of "family resemblances." Some terms, such as "games," he observed, do not share a common essence. They cohere more like a family does, through a variety of overlapping similarities. According to one common (yet admittedly incomplete) formula advanced by the University of California, Santa Barbara, religious studies professor Catherine Albanese, members of the family of religions typically exhibit "Four C's":

- creed (or statement of beliefs and values)
- cultus (ritual activities)
- code (standards for ethical conduct)
- community (institutions)

Atheists have a short creed but a creed nonetheless: "I do not believe in God." One's standing as an atheist almost always hangs on this factor alone. In this respect, atheism is no less doctrinal than any of the world's religions. And it is, in one respect, at least as dogmatic. It is possible to be a Jew and either believe or disbelieve in God. To be an atheist one must affirm the dogma that there is no god.

Cultus is more complicated. Atheists do not typically engage in ritual activities. They do not typically gather to celebrate the birthdays of Thomas Paine or Charles Darwin. The Sunday Assembly is a striking example because it is so unusual. And though similar groups are now popping up, including an American group called the Oasis Network with nonreligious congregations who meet weekly on Sundays, atheists are far more likely to watch football on Sundays than to gather (as Oasis members do) to "celebrate the human experience."[111]

Atheists are divided when it comes to a code of ethical conduct. The overwhelming consensus among atheists today is that you do not have to believe in God to be moral. In 2009, a subway advertisement campaign in New York City asked, "A million New Yorkers are good without God. Are you?" Around the same time, the Harvard University humanist chaplain Greg Epstein released a book also called *Good Without God*. There are dissenters, however. Onfray, who describes himself as a proud hedonist, believes

personal touch. "There is no set script for a humanist naming ceremony—it's too personal an occasion for that," it reads. "Instead, every naming is tailored to meet the particular family's requirements."[c] In this way, humanist naming ceremonies follow the Conway Hall motto: "To thine own self be true."

Many nonbelievers choose to donate their bodies to science. This choice makes plain one's preference for scientific learning over dogma even as it provides a convenient end run around traditional death rites centered on the corpse. For those who do not donate their cadavers, there is a strong preference for cremation over burial. One reason nonbelievers in Europe and the United States prefer cremation is that burial is associated with Judaism, Christianity, and Islam. Another reason is that cremation is widely perceived as quick, easy, and inexpensive—it just seems to be the simplest way to go.

But in death, too, some nonbelievers are finding new ways to ritualize. Secular memorial services roughly follow the forms of the Christian funerals they are rejecting. So there are talks rather than sermons, songs rather than hymns, and often a moment of silence rather than prayers. One common feature is an emphasis on celebration over mourning, life over death. The focus on celebrating life and on customizing the farewell is also flowing over into religious funerals and memorial services. In all types of services, religious or secular, it is now common for families of the deceased to personalize the ritual and to begin with a proclamation that the intention is not to mourn in the face of a death but to celebrate a life.

that Anglo-American atheists are still captive to the dos and don'ts of their Christian training. It is time, he argues, to convert from "Christian atheism" to his "atheistic atheism"—from an ethic of self-denial to an ethic of pleasures. "To enjoy and make others enjoy without doing ill to yourself or to others, this is the foundation of all morality," he writes.[112] In advancing this plea for a more atheistic atheism, however, he is not dispensing with a code of ethical conduct. He is merely urging his fellow atheists to adopt a new one.

When it comes to the fourth *C*, few atheists join atheistic communities. As has been noted, there are all sorts of organizations for atheists and agnostics and humanists. By one account, there are 1,390 nonbeliever organizations in the United States.[113] However, one of the largest, American Atheists, claims only a few thousand members. And the total members of local nonbeliever groups—perhaps 50,000 to 100,000—pales in comparison to church members even in a small U.S. city. Over the last decade or so, many nonbelievers have joined online communities, which have empowered some of them to come out of the closet and claim their identities more publicly. But according to a book called *Organized Secularism in the United States* (2017), the tendency of most atheists is to go it alone. When it comes to organizing these opponents of organized religion, "There is still a proverbial mountain to climb."[114]

In the end, whether atheism is a religion is too complicated a question for any simple answer. It depends on the facts of any given case. It varies from person to person, from group to group. Many members of the atheist family simply are not religious. They take their atheist creed with a shrug and would never think of joining any gathering of nonbelievers that would have them as a member. For others, atheism is their *life*. It defines who they are, how they think, how they speak, and with whom they associate. They would

This ad in the "Good without God" campaign by the Center for Inquiry urges passersby to set aside the stereotype that nonbelievers cannot be moral citizens.

A million New Yorkers are good without God.

Are you?

BigAppleCoR.org
COALITION OF REASON

never consider marrying someone who believes in God. To borrow from the definition of religion by the Protestant theologian Paul Tillich, atheism is their "ultimate concern."[115]

There is evidence, however, that religious atheists of this sort are in relatively short supply in the broader atheist family. A recent review of psychological literature on nonbelievers has challenged stereotypes of atheists as deviants, concluding that "atheists show themselves to be less authoritarian and suggestible, less dogmatic, less prejudiced, more tolerant of others, law-abiding, [and] compassionate."[116]

QUESTIONS FOR DISCUSSION

1. What are the different types of atheism and agnosticism, and how do those two categories differ from each other?

2. Why has there been a documented rise in recent years in the religiously unaffiliated ("nones") and those who identify as "spiritual but not religious"? What are some of the religious, political, and social factors driving this trend in the United States?

3. What do you make of religious atheism? Why do some scriptures refer surprisingly positively to atheism and agnosticism? How is it possible to be a member of certain religious communities and not believe in God or the gods?

4. What historical developments in the modern period led to the breakdown of the widespread religiosity that characterized Europe in the Middle Ages? Which were most significant and why?

5. Many atheists are blasé about religion, but others are more overtly hostile. What accounts for the hostility to religion of Karl Marx and the New Atheists? What are their arguments against religion? Do you find those arguments persuasive? Why or why not?

KEY TERMS

agnosticism, p. 498

anti-theism, p. 503

atheism, p. 498

Deism, p. 516

Enlightenment, p. 513

freethought, p. 494

humanism, p. 503

materialism, p. 517

naturalism, p. 505

negative atheist, p. 503

pantheism, p. 513

positive atheist, p. 503

secular humanism, p. 503

secularism, p. 503

secularization theory, p. 499

spiritual but not religious (SBNR), p. 499

strong agnosticism, p. 503

weak agnosticism, p. 503

FURTHER READING

Baggini, Julian. *Atheism: A Very Short Introduction.* New York: Oxford University Press, 2003.

Hecht, Jennifer Michael. *Doubt: A History: The Great Doubters and Their Legacy of Innovation from Socrates and Jesus to Thomas Jefferson and Emily Dickinson.* New York: HarperOne, 2003.

Jacoby, Susan. *Freethinkers: A History of American Secularism.* New York: Metropolitan Books, 2004.

Schmidt, Leigh Eric. *Village Atheists: How America's Unbelievers Made Their Way in a Godly Nation.* Princeton, NJ: Princeton University Press, 2016.

Turner, James. *Without God, Without Creed: The Origins of Unbelief in America.* Baltimore: The Johns Hopkins University Press, 1985.

Endnotes

Chapter 1

1. Joan Didion, *The White Album* (New York: Farrar, Straus & Giroux), 11.
2. Pew Research Center, "U.S. Religious Knowledge Survey," September 28, 2010, https://www.pewforum.org/2010/09/28/u-s-religious-knowledge-survey; Pew Research Center, "What Americans Know about Religion," July 23, 2019, http://www.pewforum.org/2019/07/23/what-americans-know-about-religion.
3. Huston Smith, *The World's Religions* (New York: HarperOne, 2009), 5.
4. Friedrich Max Muller, *Introduction to the Science of Religion* (London: Longmans, Green, 1873), 16.
5. W. B. Yeats, "He wishes for the Cloths of Heaven," in *Yeats's Poetry, Drama, and Prose*, ed. James Pethica (W. W. Norton & Company, Inc., 2000), 29.
6. Religious Literacy Project, "Four Principles," https://rlp.hds.harvard.edu/our-approach/four-principles.
7. Jonathan Z. Smith, *Imagining Religion: From Babylon to Jonestown* (Chicago: The University of Chicago Press, 1982), xi.
8. Alfred Korzybski, *Science and Sanity: An Introduction to Non-Aristotelian Systems and General Semantics* (n.p.; International Non-Aristotelian Library Publishing Company, 1933), 476.
9. Lewis Carroll, *Through the Looking-Glass, and What Alice Found There* (New York: Macmillan, 1875), 124.
10. Robert A. Orsi, *Between Heaven and Earth: The Religious Worlds People Make and the Scholars Who Study Them* (Princeton, NJ: Princeton University Press, 2005), 2.
11. E. B. Tylor, *Primitive Culture*, vol. 1 (London: John Murray, 1871), 384.
12. Friedrich Schleiermacher, *The Christian Faith*, trans. H. R. Mackintosh and J. S. Stewart (Edinburgh: T & T Clark, 1928), 17.
13. Karl Marx, "Critique of Hegel's Philosophy of Right" (1844), in *Marx on Religion,* ed. John Raines (Philadelphia: Temple University Press, 2002), 171.
14. William James, *The Varieties of Religious Experience* (New York: Longmans, Green, 1902), 31.
15. Emile Durkheim, *The Elementary Forms of the Religious Life,* trans. Joseph Ward Swain (London: George Allen & Unwin, 1915), 47.
16. Sigmund Freud, *The Future of an Illusion*, trans. W. D. Robson-Scott (London: Hogarth Press, 1928), 43.
17. Paul Tillich, *Systematic Theology, Volume Three* (Chicago: University of Chicago Press, 1963), 130.
18. Mary Daly, *Beyond God the Father: Toward a Philosophy of Women's Liberation* (Boston: Beacon Press, 1973), 19.
19. Charles H. Long, *Significations: Signs, Symbols, and Images in the Interpretation of Religion* (Philadelphia: Fortress Press, 1986), 7.
20. Talal Asad, *Genealogies of Religion: Discipline and Reasons of Power in Christianity and Islam* (Baltimore, MD: Johns Hopkins University Press, 1993), 29.
21. Ninian Smart, *The World's Religions* (New York: Cambridge University Press, 1989), 12–21.
22. Catherine Albanese, *America: Religions and Religion* (Belmont, CA: Wadsworth, 1981), 8–9. Another formula, "the 3B Framework," developed by Benjamin Marcus at the Religious Freedom Center in Washington, DC, focuses more on identity. It includes belief (including "theological, doctrinal, scriptural and ethical" claims), behavior (acting via "rituals, holidays or daily devotional practices . . . both inside and outside of strictly religious settings"), and belonging (including membership in religious communities as well as broader communities of value). See Religious Freedom Center, "Religious Identity Formation: The 3B Framework," http://www.religiousfreedomcenter.org/grounding/identity.
23. Thomas A. Tweed, *Crossing and Dwelling: A Theory of Religion* (Cambridge, MA: Harvard University Press, 2006), 30.
24. Smith, *The World's Religions*, 73.
25. Kristofer Schipper, *The Daoist Body*, trans. Karen C. Duval (Berkeley: University of California Press, 1993), 158.
26. Smith, *The World's Religions*, 73.

Chapter 2

1. Henry D. Thoreau, *Cape Cod* (Boston: Ticknor and Fields, 1865), 116.
2. Jonathan P. Parry, *Death in Banaras* (Cambridge: Cambridge University Press, 1994), 13.
3. "The Virtues of Varanasi," in *The Norton Anthology of World Religions: Volume 1,* ed. Jack Miles (New York: Norton, 2015), 271–272.

4. Amartya Sen, *The Argumentative Indian: Writings on Indian History, Culture and Identity* (New York: Farrar, Straus & Giroux, 2006).

5. Wendy Doniger, *The Hindus: An Alternative History* (New York: Penguin, 2009), 248.

6. Wendy Doniger, *On Hinduism* (New York: Oxford University Press, 2014), 92, 94.

7. Wendy Doniger O'Flaherty, *Siva: The Erotic Ascetic* (New York: Oxford University Press, 1981).

8. Diana L. Eck, *Encountering God: A Spiritual Journey from Bozeman to Banares* (Boston: Beacon Press, 1993), 137.

9. The Bhagavad Gita, trans. Laurie L. Patton (New York: Penguin, 2008), 51. Unless otherwise noted, all Gita quotations in this chapter are from this translation.

10. Wendy Doniger attributes this distinction to A. K. Ramanujan in her *The Hindus: An Alternative History*, 390.

11. Wendy Doniger, "Humans, Animals, and Gods in the Rig Veda: 1500–1000 BCE," in *Norton Anthology of World Religions: Volume 1*, 88.

12. Patrick Olivelle, *The Early Upaniṣads: Annotated Text and Translation* (New York: Oxford University Press, 1998), 24.

13. Aldous Huxley, *The Perennial Philosophy* (New York: Harper & Brothers, 1945), 4.

14. Patrick Olivelle, alternately, renders *tat tvam asi* as "that's how you are." See his *The Early Upanishads*, 253, 560–561.

15. Olivelle, *The Early Upaniṣads*, 225.

16. Ralph Waldo Emerson, *Journals of Ralph Waldo Emerson*, vol. 7, ed. Edward Waldo Emerson and Waldo Emerson Forbes (Boston: Houghton Mifflin, 1913), 511; T. S. Eliot, "Dante," in *Selected Essays* (London: Faber & Faber, 1951), 258; Kai Bird and Martin J. Sherwin, *American Prometheus: The Triumph and Tragedy of J. Robert Oppenheimer* (New York: Knopf, 2005), 309.

17. Doniger, *The Hindus: An Alternative History*, 284.

18. Wendy Doniger, "Vernacular Hinduism in South India, 800–1800 CE," in *Norton Anthology of World Religions: Volume 1*, 306.

19. A. K. Ramanujan, "On Women Saints," in *The Divine Consort: Radha and the Goddesses of India*, ed. John Stratton Hawley and Donna Marie Wulff (Delhi: Motilal Banarsidass, 1982), 316; A. K. Ramanujan, *The Collected Essays of A. K. Ramanujan*, ed. Vinay Dharwadker (New York: Oxford University Press 2004), 277.

20. *The Upanishads*, trans. Patrick Olivelle (New York: Oxford University Press, 2008), 265.

21. Wendy Doniger, "The Zen Diagram of Hinduism," in *Norton Anthology of World Religions: Volume 1*, 65.

22. "The Gods—and a Goddess—in the Puranas: 400–1200 CE," in *Norton Anthology of World Religions: Volume 1*, 233.

23. C. Mackenzie Brown, *The Triumph of the Goddess: The Canonical Models and Theological Visions of the Devi-Bhagavata Purana* (Albany: State University of New York Press, 1990), 60.

24. Mirabai, "Life Without Hari," in *Norton Anthology of World Religions: Volume 1*, 430.

25. Diana L. Eck, *India: A Sacred Geography* (New York: Harmony, 2012), 456.

26. Mohandas Gandhi, *Autobiography: The Story of My Experiments with Truth* (New York: Dover, 1983), 233.

27. Henry David Thoreau to Harrison Blake, November 20, 1849, in Henry D. Thoreau, *The Correspondence of Henry D. Thoreau*, vol. 2: 1849–1856, ed. Robert N. Hudspeth et al. (Princeton: Princeton University Press, 2018), 43.

28. "Aims and Ideals of Self-Realization Fellowship," Self-Reliance Fellowship, https://yogananda.org/aims-and-ideals.

29. Paramhansa Yogananda, *Autobiography of a Yogi* (New York: Philosophical Library, 1946), 370, 270.

30. "A TM Catechism," in Thomas A. Tweed and Stephen Prothero, *Asian Religions in America: A Documentary History* (New York: Oxford University Press, 1999), 242.

31. A. C. Bhaktivedanta Swami Prabhupada and John Lennon, *Search for Liberation* (Los Angeles: Bhaktivedanta Book Trust, 1981), 1–21.

32. International Society for Krishna Consciousness, Inc. v. Lee, 505 US 672 (1992), https://www.law.cornell.edu/supremecourt/text/505/672.

33. Nat Hentoff, *Jazz Is* (New York: Random House, 1976), 205.

34. Joanne Punzo Waghorne, "The Hindu Gods in a Split-level World: The Sri Siva-Vishnu Temple in Suburban Washington, DC," in *Gods of the City*, ed. Robert Orsi (Bloomington: Indiana University Press, 1999), 103–130.

35. Mark Twain, *Following the Equator: A Journey Around the World* (Hartford: American Publishing, 1897), 504.

36. Diana Eck, *Darsan: Seeing the Divine Image in India* (New York: Columbia University Press, 1998).

37. McKim Marriott, "The Feast of Love," in *Krishna: Myths, Rites, and Attitudes*, ed. Milton Singer (Honolulu, HI: East-West Center Press, 1966), 204.

38. "Central Provinces," in *Encyclopaedia of Religion and Ethics*, vol. 3, ed. James Hastings (New York: Charles Scribner's Sons, 1911), 314.

39. Eck, *India: A Sacred Geography*, 55.

40. Kancha Ilaiah with Yoginder Sikand, "Hindutva Is Nothing But Brahminism," *Outlook*, April 5, 2002,

https://www.outlookindia.com/website/story/hindutva-is-nothing-but-brahminism/215089.

41. Amrit Wilson, "India Is a 'Republic of Fear,'" *The Guardian*, April 18, 2018, https://www.theguardian.com/commentisfree/2018/apr/18/india-republic-fear-narendra-modi-britain.

42. Basharat Peer, *A Question of Order: India, Turkey, and the Return of Strongmen* (New York: Columbia Global Reports, 2017), 15.

HINDUISM: A Genealogy

a. Adam Olearius, *The Voyages and Travels of the Ambassadors From the Duke of Holstein* (London: Thomas Dring and John Starkey, 1662), 74, 77.

b. J. Ovington, *A Voyage to Suratt* (London: Jacob Tonson, 1696), 375.

c. John Marshal, "A Letter from the East Indies, of Mr John Marshal to Dr Coga, Giving an Account of the Religion, Rites, Notions, Customs, Manners of the Heathen Priests Commonly Called Bramines," *Philosophical Transactions* 22 (1700–1701): 734.

d. Henry Barkley Henderson, *The Bengalee: Or, Sketches of Society and Manners in the East* (London: Smith, Elder, 1829), 46.

e. "Priestley's Comparison of Jewish and Hindoo Religion," *The Monthly Magazine and American Review* 2, no. 6 (June 1800): 426.

f. Michael Symes, *An Account of an Embassy to the Kingdom of Ava*, vol. 1, 2nd ed. (London: J. Debrett, 1800), 233.

g. Rammohun Roy, *Translation of the Ishopanishad, One of the Chapters of the Yajur Veda* (Calcutta: Philip Pereira, 1816), iii.

h. "Baptist Mission in India: Letter from Mr. Ward to Mr. Morris," March 24, 1801, *The New-York Missionary Magazine, and Repository of Religious Intelligence* 3 (1802): 316; Mr. Gerike letter, January 18, 1803, in *Glad Tidings: Or an Account of the State of Religion within the Bounds of the General Assembly of the Presbyterian Church* (Philadelphia: R. Aitken, 1804), 28; "Review of Considerations on Christianity in India," *The Christian Observer* 7, no. 4 (April 1808): 262.

HINDUISM BY THE NUMBERS: Four Vedic Gods

a. John Y. Fenton et al., *Religions of Asia* (New York: St. Martin's Press, 1999), 72.

PROFILES IN HINDUISM: Kabir

a. Kabir, "His Death in Banares," trans. Arvind Krishna Mehrotra, *Poetry*, March 2011, https://www.poetryfoundation.org/poetrymagazine/poems/54391/his-death-in-benares.

PROFILES IN HINDUISM: Indra Nooyi

a. Lavina Melwani, "She Met Pepsi's Challenge," *Hinduism Today*, June 1998, https://www.hinduismtoday.com/modules/smartsection/item.php?itemid=4636.

Chapter 3

1. "The Mahabodhi Temple Complex at Bodh Gaya," UNESCO, https://whc.unesco.org/en/list/1056; "Statistics of Domestic and Foreign Tourist Visit to the State of Bihar," Bihar Tourism, http://www.bihartourism.gov.in/data/tourist_data/2010%20&%202011&2012.pdf.

2. David Geary, *The Rebirth of Bodh Gaya: Buddhism and the Making of a World Heritage Site* (Seattle: University of Washington Press, 2017), 47.

3. Xuanzang, "The Great Tang Dynasty Record of the Western World," in *The Norton Anthology of World Religions: Volume 1*, ed. Jack Miles (New York: Norton, 2015), 1196.

4. Xuanzang, "Great Tang Dynasty Record," 1193.

5. Hajime Nakamura, *Gotama Buddha: A Biography Based on the Most Reliable Texts* (Tokyo: Kosei, 2000), 181.

6. "The Buddha's Final Days," in *The Norton Anthology of World Religions: Volume 1*, 841, 852.

7. This population data here is for "wider Buddhism," a new category developed by Todd Johnson at the World Religion Database (WRD). Most surveys of the world's religions assign only one religion per person. Because Chinese folk-religionists tend to follow a combination of the "Three Teachings" of Buddhism, Daoism, and Confucianism, they are rarely counted among the world's Buddhist, Daoist, or Confucian practitioners. In this chapter, "wider Buddhism" includes the core Buddhists the WRD has typically counted as Buddhists, plus all Chinese folk-religionists. In other chapters, "wider Confucianism" includes all Chinese folk-religionists and "wider Daoism" includes all Chinese folk-religionists (who, for this purpose, are each counted three times). For an earlier version of this category, which also included the nonreligious in China as "wider Buddhists," see Todd M. Johnson and Brian J. Grim, *The World's Religions in Figures: An Introduction* (Malden, MA: Wiley-Blackwell, 2013), 36, 130.

8. "Los Angeles," The Pluralism Project, http://pluralism.org/landscape/los-angeles/.

9. Donald Lopez, personal communication, April 4, 2019.

10. Henry Clarke Warren, *Buddhism in Translations* (Cambridge: Harvard University, 1896), 117–22.

11. "Wander Solitary as a Rhinoceros Horn," in *The Norton Anthology of World Religions: Volume 1*, 910–11.

12. Walpola Rahula, *What the Buddha Taught*, rev. ed. (New York: Grove, 1974), 57.

13. Ananya Vajpeyi, *Righteous Republic: The Political Foundations of Modern India* (Cambridge: Harvard University Press, 2012), 41.

14. "The Bodhisattva Who Bestows Children," in *The Norton Anthology of World Religions: Volume 1*, 1253.

15. "Ever in the Female Form," in *The Norton Anthology of World Religions: Volume 1*, 1169.

16. "The Lotus Sutra," in *The Norton Anthology of World Religions: Volume 1*, 961–62.

17. "The Heart Sutra," in *The Norton Anthology of World Religions: Volume 1*, 1045.

18. Donald S. Lopez Jr., *The Lotus Sūtra: A Biography* (Princeton: Princeton University Press, 2016).

19. "On the Origins of Zen," in *The Norton Anthology of World Religions: Volume 1*, 1214.

20. The first two koans can be found in Steven Heine and Dale S. Wright, *Zen Classics: Formative Texts in the History of Zen Buddhism* (New York: Oxford University Press, 2006), 206. For the remaining koans, see Ekai, called Mumon, *The Gateless Gate*, trans. Nyogen Senzaki and Paul Reps (Los Angeles: John Murray, 1934), http://www.sacred-texts.com/bud/glg/index.htm.

21. Masao Abe, *A Study of Doge: His Philosophy and Religion*, ed. Steven Heine (Albany: State University of New York Press, 1992), 29.

22. "The Martin Luther of Japan," *National Geographic* 16, no. 3 (March 1905): 96.

23. Noah Brannen, "False Religions, Forced Conversions, Iconoclasm," *Contemporary Religions in Japan* 5, no. 3 (Sept 1964): 237.

24. "Tantric Masters," in *The Norton Anthology of World Religions: Volume 1*, 1160.

25. Guy Newland, *The Two Truths in the Madhyamika Philosophy of the Ge-luk-ba Order of Tibetan Buddhism* (Ithaca, NY: Snow Lion, 1992), 49.

26. Donald S. Lopez Jr., introduction to *Buddhism in Practice*, ed. Donald S. Lopez Jr., abridged ed. (Princeton: Princeton University Press, 2007), 7.

27. Stephen Prothero, "Henry Steel Olcott and 'Protestant Buddhism,'" *Journal of the American Academy of Religion* 63, no. 2 (Summer 1995): 299.

28. Stephen Prothero, *The White Buddhist: The Asian Odyssey of Henry Steel Olcott* (Bloomington: Indiana University Press, 1996).

29. John Malkin, "In Engaged Buddhism, Peace Begins with You," interview with Thich Nhat Hanh, *Lion's Roar*, July 1, 2003, https://www.lionsroar.com/in-engaged-buddhism-peace-begins-with-you;

Thich Nhah Hanh, *Peace Is Every Step: The Path of Mindfulness in Everyday Life* (New York: Bantam, 1991), 91.

30. Helen Tworkov, "Interbeing with Thich Nhat Hanh: An Interview," *Tricycle*, Summer 1995, https://tricycle.org/magazine/interbeing-thich-nhat-hanh-interview/.

31. Malkin, "In Engaged Buddhism," https://www.lionsroar.com/in-engaged-buddhism-peace-begins-with-you.

32. Sallie King, *Socially Engaged Buddhism* (Honolulu: University of Hawaii, 2009), 1.

33. Henry David Thoreau, *A Week on the Concord and Merrimack Rivers* (Boston: Ticknor and Field, 1867), 75.

34. Ralph Waldo Emerson to Elizabeth Hoar, 17 June 1845, in *The Letters of Ralph Waldo Emerson*, ed. Ralph L. Rusk, vol. 3 (New York: Columbia University Press, 1939), 290.

35. "Zen: Beat & Square," *Time*, July 21, 1958, 49.

36. Alan Watts, "Beginning a Counterculture," in *Asian Religions in America: A Documentary History*, ed. Thomas A. Tweed and Stephen Prothero (New York: Oxford University Press, 1999), 229.

37. United States v. Seeger, 380 US 163 (1965).

38. Sandy Boucher, *Turning the Wheel: American Women Creating the New Buddhism*, updated ed. (Boston: Beacon Press, 1993), 138.

39. Secular Buddhism, "No Robes. No Ritual. No Religion," https://secularbuddhism.wordpress.com.

40. Robert Wuthnow and Wendy Cadge, "Buddhists and Buddhism in the United States: The Scope of Influence," *Journal for the Scientific Study of Religion* 43, no. 3 (2004): 363–380.

41. Jack Kornfield, "Meditation on Lovingkindness," https://jackkornfield.com/meditation-on-lovingkindness/.

42. Edward Conze et al., eds., *Buddhist Texts Through the Ages* (Oxford, England: Bruno Cassirer, 1954), 253.

43. Matsuo Basho, *Narrow Road to the Interior: And Other Writings*, trans. Sam Hamill (Boston: Shambhala, 1998), 3.

44. Charles Allen, *Ashoka: The Search for India's Lost Emperor* (London: Little, Brown, 2012), 412–413.

45. Narada, *The Buddha and His Teachings* (Mumbai, India: Jaico, 2006), 198.

46. Mikael S. Adolphson, *The Teeth and Claws of the Buddha: Monastic Warriors and Sohei in Japanese History* (Honolulu: University of Hawaii Press, 2007).

47. Xue Yu, "Buddhists in China during the Korean War (1951–1953)," in *Buddhist Warfare*, eds. Michael Jerryson and Mark Juergensmeyer (New York: Oxford University Press, 2010), 145.

BUDDHISM: A Genealogy

a. Eva Pascal, "Buddhist Monks and Christian Friars: Religious and Cultural Exchange in the Making of Buddhism," *Studies in World Christianity* 22, no. 1 (March 2016): 6; Urs App, *The Birth of Orientalism* (Philadelphia: University of Pennsylvania Press, 2010), 185.

b. Robert Knox, *An Historical Relation of the Land Ceylon* (London: Richard Chiswell, 1681), 72.

c. William Chambers, "Some Account of the Sculptures and Ruins at Mavalipuram," *Asiatick Researches* 1 (1788): 162, 164; Francis Buchanan, "On the Religion and Literature of the Burmas," *Asiatick Researches* 6 (1801): 262.

d. C. F. Volney, *Lectures on History* (London: J. Ridgway, 1800), 148.

PROFILES IN BUDDHISM: B. R. Ambedkar

a. Dr. B. R. Ambedkar, "What Path Freedom," in *Untouchable!: Voices of the Dalit Liberation Movement*, ed. Barbara R. Joshi, trans. Vasant W. Moon (New York: Zed, 1986), 30.

MATERIAL BUDDHISM: Manzanar Monument

a. Melissa Hung, "Walking in Their Footsteps at a Former Japanese Internment Camp," *Code Switch* (blog), NPR, April 29, 2017, https://www.npr.org/sections/codeswitch/2017/04/29/485574562/walking-in-their-footsteps-at-a-former-japanese-internment-camp.

b. "Teakettle and Paper Cranes," Museum Management Program, National Park Service, https://www.nps.gov/museum/exhibits/manz/exb/Remembering/Cemetery/MANZ5157_teakettle_origami.html.

BIRTH AND DEATH

a. Paul Gwynne, *World Religions in Practice: A Comparative Approach*, 2nd ed. (Hoboken, NJ: Wiley, 2018), 114.

b. Guru Rinpoche, *The Tibetan Book of the Dead*, trans. Francesca Fremantle and Chogyam Trungpa (Boston: Shambhala, 2003), 56, 62.

PROFILES IN BUDDHISM: Aung San Suu Kyi

a. Aung San Suu Kyi, *The Voice of Hope: Conversations with Alan Clements* (New York: Seven Stories Press, 1997), 51, 200–201.

b. "Myanmar Treatment of Rohingya Looks Like 'Textbook Ethnic Cleansing', says UN," *The Guardian*, September 11, 2017, https://www.theguardian.com/world/2017/sep/11/un-myanmars-treatment-of-rohingya-textbook-example-of-ethnic-cleansing.

Chapter 4

1. Khushwant Singh, *History of the Sikhs, vol. 1, 1469–1839*, 2nd ed. (New York: Oxford University Press, 2005), 93.

2. Jasjit Singh, "Lost in Translation? The Emergence of the Digital Guru Granth Sahib," *Sikh Formations* 14, nos. 3-4 (2018): 339–51

3. Unless otherwise noted, English translations from the Guru Granth here are from https://www.sikhitothemax.org. The translation used on this popular site is by Sant Singh Khalsa, an Arizona pediatrician and follower of the Sikh teacher Yogi Bhajan. Because of its status as a first mover into the digital space, this is now the dominant English translation worldwide. There is not yet any contemporary scholarly translation.

4. Nikky-Guninder Kaur Singh, *Sikhism: An Introduction* (New York: I. B. Taurus, 2011), 1.

5. Gurinder Singh Mann, "Baba Nanak and the Founding of the Sikh *Panth*," in *Brill's Encyclopedia of Sikhism*, vol. 1, ed. Knut A. Jacobsen et al. (Leiden, Netherlands: Brill, 2017), 3.

6. Kaur Singh, *Sikhism*, 59.

7. Singh, *A History of the Sikhs*, vol. 1, 30.

8. Singh, *A History of the Sikhs*, vol. 1, 30. Singh's source is a collection of birth stories entitled *Puratan Janam Sakhi*, ed. Bhai Vir Singh (Amritsar: Bhai Vir Singh, 1948), http://sikhbookclub.com/Book/Puratan-Janam-Sakhi-Shri-Guru-Nanak-Dev-Ji.

9. Mann, "Baba Nanak and the Founding of the Sikh *Panth*," 4, 10.

10. Kaur Singh, *Sikhism*, 11.

11. Singh, *A History of the Sikhs*, vol. 1, 34.

12. *Hymns of Guru Nanak*, trans. Khushwant Singh (Hyderabad, India: Orient Longman, 1969), 12.

13. Richard Fox, *Lions of the Punjab: Culture in the Making* (Berkeley: University of California Press, 1985), 112.

14. Government of India, *Census of 1891*, Imperial Series, vol. 9, Burma Report, vol. 1 (Rangoon, Burma: Government Printing, 1891), 82.

15. Mann, "Baba Nanak and the Founding of the Sikh *Panth*," 7.

16. Kaur Singh, *Sikhism*, 71.

17. Singh, *A History of the Sikhs*, vol. 1, 41.

18. Kaur Singh, *Sikhism*, 59.

19. Pashaura Singh, "Gurmat: The Teachings of the Gurus," in *The Oxford Handbook of Sikh Studies*, ed. Pashaura Singh and Louis E. Frenech (New York: Oxford University Press, 2014), 238.

20. Anne Murphy, "Objects, Ethics, and the Gendering of Sikh Memory," *Early Modern Women* 4 (Fall 2009): 161–68.

21. Pashaura Singh, "Understanding the Martyrdom of Guru Arjan," *Journal of Punjab Studies* 12, no. 1 (2005): 29.

22. Louis E. Fenech and W. H. McLeod, *Historical Dictionary of Sikhism*, 3rd ed. (Lanham, MD: Rowman & Littlefield, 2014), 179.

23. Max Arthur Macauliffe, *The Sikh Religion: Its Gurus, Sacred Writings and Authors*, vol. 5 (Oxford, England: Clarendon Press, 1909), 96.

24. Singh, *A History of the Sikhs*, vol. 1, 75.

25. Purnima Dhavan, *When Sparrows Became Hawks: The Making of the Sikh Warrior Tradition, 1699–1799* (New York: Oxford University Press, 2011).

26. Major J. Browne, *India Tracts . . . also An History and of the Origin and Progress of the Sikhs* (London: Logographic Press, 1788), x–xi.

27. Harjot Oberoi, "From Ritual to Counter-Ritual: Rethinking the Hindu-Sikh Question, 1884–1915," in *Sikh History and Religion in the Twentieth Century*, ed. Joseph T. O'Connell et al. (Toronto: University of Toronto, Centre for Sikh Studies, 1988), 154.

28. Michael Hawley, "Sikh Institutions," in *The Oxford Handbook of Sikh Studies*, ed. Singh and Fenech, 324.

29. W. H. McLeod, ed. and trans., *Textual Sources for the Study of Sikhism* (Dover, NH: Manchester University Press), 79.

30. Andrew Roberts, *Churchill: Walking with Destiny* (New York: Viking, 2018), 272.

31. National Sikh Campaign (website), http://www.sikhcampaign.org/

32. "Kirpan Is Not a Weapon," SikhiWiki, http://www.sikhiwiki.org/index.php/Kirpan_is_not_a_weapon.

33. James Lochtefeld, personal communication, March 21, 2019.

34. Hew McLeod, "Sikh Hymns to the Divine Nature," in *Religions of India in Practice*, ed. Donald S. Lopez Jr. (Princeton, NJ: Princeton University Press, 1995), 129.

35. GG translation in Kaur Singh, *Sikhism*, 69.

36. Singh, "Gurmat," in *The Oxford Handbook of Sikh Studies*, ed. Singh and Frenech, 235.

37. Mary Daly, *Beyond God the Father* (Boston: Houghton Mifflin, 1973), 19.

38. Nikky-Guninder Kaur Singh, "A Feminist Interpretation of Sikh Scripture," in *The Oxford Handbook of Sikh Studies*, ed. Singh and Frenech, 612.

39. "Sex Ratio in India," Population Census 2011, https://www.census2011.co.in/sexratio.php; and "Amritsar District: Census 2011–2019 Data," https://www.census2011.co.in/census/district/602-amritsar.html.

40. Amardeep Singh, "Women in Sikhism: A Promising Reform," August 11, 2005, https://www.lehigh.edu/~amsp/2005/08/women-in-sikhism-promising-reform.html.

41. Nikky-Guninder Kaur Singh, "Why Did I Not Light the Fire? The Refeminization of Ritual in Sikhism," *Journal of Feminist Studies in Religion* 16, no. 1 (Spring 2000): 70, 79, 82.

42. Louis E. Fenech, review of *The Feminine Principle in the Sikh Vision of the Transcendent*, by Nikky-Guninder Kaur Singh, *The Journal of Asian Studies* 55, no. 1 (February 1996): 200.

SIKHISM: A Genealogy

a. Charles Wilkins letter to the Secretary of the Asiatick Society, March 1, 1781, plus an attached account of his visit to "the College of the Seeks," in *Asiatick Researches* 1 (1788): 288–94.

b. Alexander Dow, *The History of Hindostan*, vol. 2 (London: T. Becket and P. A. De Hondt, 1768), Appendix, 82.

c. Major J. Browne, *India Tracts . . . also An History and of the Origin and Progress of the Sicks* (London: Logographic Press, 1788), i–v.

d. Joseph Davey Cunningham, *A History of the Sikhs* (London: John Murray, 1849), 341.

SIKHISM BY THE NUMBERS: The Ten Gurus

a. Anne Murphy, "Objects, Ethics, and the Gendering of Sikh Memory," *Early Modern Women* 4 (Fall 2009): 163

MATERIAL SIKHISM: The Turban

a. "Sikh Soldier First Guardsman to Parade Outside Buckingham Palace Wearing Turban," *The Telegraph*, December 11, 2012, https://www.telegraph.co.uk/news/religion/9737480/Sikh-soldier-first-guardsman-to-parade-outside-Buckingham-palace-wearing-turban.html.

PART II

1. Ara Norenzayan, *Big Gods: How Religion Transformed Cooperation and Conflict* (Princeton, NJ: Princeton University Press, 2013).

Chapter 5

1. Sidra DeKoven Ezrahi, "Women of the Wall Is a Diversion from the Real Issue: The Occupation," *Haaretz*, June 22, 2016, https://www.haaretz.com/opinion/.premium-omwen-of-the-wall-misses-the-real-issue-occupation-1.5399782.

2. Unless otherwise noted, all biblical quotations in this chapter come from Adele Berlin et al., *The Jewish Study Bible* (New York: Oxford University Press, 2004), which features a translation by the Jewish Publication Society.

3. Simon Goldhill, *Jerusalem: City of Longing* (Cambridge: Harvard University Press, 2010), 74.

4. Goldhill, *Jerusalem: City of Longing*, 77.

5. David Biale, personal communication, July 6, 2019; Yair Lior, personal communication, June 26, 2019.

6. Herman Melville, *White-Jacket*, in *Herman Melville: Redburn, White-Jacket, Moby-Dick* (New York: Library of America, 1983), 506.

7. Einstein does not appear to have ever said or written these exact words about God as a dice player. However, as a part of an ongoing conversation about quantum mechanics, he did write in a letter dated December 4, 1926, to his friend, the physicist and mathematician Max Born, "I, at any rate, am convinced that He is not playing at dice." See Albert Einstein, Hedwig Born, and Max Born, *The Born-Einstein Letters; Correspondence between Albert Einstein and Max and Hedwig Born from 1916 to 1955 with Commentaries by Max Born* (New York: Walker, 1971), 91.

8. "Muslim-Western Tensions Persist," Pew Research Center, July 21, 2011, https://www.pewresearch.org/global/2011/07/21/muslim-western-tensions-persist.

9. Michael Lipka, "Unlike U.S., Few Jews in Israel Identify as Reform or Conservative," *Fact Tank* (blog), Pew Research Center, March 15, 2016, https://www.pewresearch.org/fact-tank/2016/03/15/unlike-u-s-few-jews-in-israel-identify-as-reform-or-conservative/.

10. Jacob Neusner, "Judaism," in *Our Religions*, ed. Arvind Sharma (New York: HarperOne, 1994), 314.

11. Stephen M. Wylen, *Settings of Silver: An Introduction to Judaism* (Mahway, NJ: Paulist Press, 2000), 40.

12. Elie Wiesel, *Wise Men and Their Tales* (New York: Schocken, 2003), 278.

13. Arno Mayer, *Why Did the Heavens Not Darken? The "Final Solution" in History* (New York: Pantheon, 1988), 25.

14. Martin Luther, *On the Jews and Their Lies*, in *Luther's Works*, vol. 47, ed. Franklin Sherman (Philadelphia: Fortress Press, 1971), 275.

15. Melila Hellner-Eshed, *A River Flows from Eden: The Language of Mystical Experience in the Zohar*, trans. Nathan Wolski (Stanford, CA: Stanford University Press, 2009), 1.

16. Yaacob Dweck, *The Scandal of Kabbalah: Leon Modena, Jewish Mysticism, Early Modern Venice* (Princeton, NJ: Princeton University Press, 2011), 2.

17. Harold Bloom, *The American Religion* (New York: Simon & Schuster, 1992), 99.

18. Leora Batnitzky, *How Judaism Became a Religion: An Introduction to Modern Jewish Thought* (Princeton, NJ: Princeton University Press, 2013).

19. Simon Sebag Montefiore, *Jerusalem: The Biography* (New York: Knopf, 2011), 398.

20. Theodor Herzl, *A Jewish State*, trans. Sylvie Avigdor and Jacob de Haas (New York: Federation of American Zionists, 1917), 10, 44.

21. Balfour Declaration, November 2, 1917, The Avalon Project, Lillian Goldman Law Library, Yale Law School, https://avalon.law.yale.edu/20th_century/balfour.asp.

22. Anne Frank, *The Diary of a Young Girl: The Definitive Edition*, ed. Otto H. Frank and Mirjam Pressler, trans. Susan Massotty (New York: Doubleday, 1995), 333.

23. Elie Wiesel, *Night*, trans. Marion Wiesel (New York: Hill and Wang, 2017), 64, 34.

24. A. M. Dalbray, "*Les Juifs des Silence*," *Amif* (November 1967): 1771, quoted in Ellen S. Fine, *Legacy of Night: The Literary Universe of Elie Wiesel* (Albany: State University of New York Press, 1982), 30; Seymour Bolten quoted in Edward T. Linenthal, *Preserving Memory: The Struggle to Create America's Holocaust Museum* (New York: Columbia University Press, 2001), 43.

25. "Declaration of Establishment of State of Israel," May 14, 1948, Israel Ministry of Foreign Affairs, https://mfa.gov.il/mfa/foreignpolicy/peace/guide/pages/declaration%20of%20establishment%20of%20state%20of%20israel.aspx.

26. Kaufmann Kohler, *Jesus of Nazareth from a Jewish Point of View* (New York: Funk & Wagnalls, 1899), 2–3; "Christ as Ethical Light: Rabbi Gup, Agreeing with Dr. Wise, Denies Jews Crucified Jesus," *New York Times*, December 26, 1925, 3.

27. Leon A. Jick, *The Americanization of the Synagogue, 1820–1870* (Hanover, NH: University Press of New England, 1976), 84.

28. Shari Rabin, "The First Egalitarian Minyan?" *Jewish Book Council*, March 27, 2018, https://www.jewishbookcouncil.org/pb-daily/the-first-egalitarian-minyan.

29. The Pittsburgh Platform, https://www.ccarnet.org/rabbinic-voice/platforms/article-declaration-principles/

30. "A Portrait of Jewish Americans," Pew Research Center, October 1, 2013, https://www.pewresearch.org/wp-content/uploads/sites/7/2013/10/jewish-american-full-report-for-web.pdf.

31. Daniel B. Schwartz, "An Icon for Iconoclasts: Spinoza and the Faith of Jewish Secularism," *AJS Perspectives* (Spring 2011), perspectives.ajsnet.org/the-secular-issue-spring-2011/an-icon-for-iconoclasts-spinoza-and-the-faith-of-jewish-secularism.

32. "Society for Humanistic Judaism Supports Proclamation of the International Federation of Secular Humanistic Jews," Society for Humanistic Judaism, https://www.shj.org/humanistic-jewish-life/issues-and-resolutions/proclamation.

33. Martin Kavka, "American Jews: From Holocaust to New Age Hasidism?" *Religion Dispatches*, May 23, 2013, http://religiondispatches.org/american-jews-from-holocaust-to-new-age-hasidism.

34. Bruce Bashford, *Oscar Wilde: The Critic as Humanist* (Cranbury, NJ: Associated University Presses, 1999), 68.

35. "American and Israeli Jews: Twin Portraits from Pew Research Center Surveys," Pew Research Center, January 24, 2017, https://www.pewforum.org/essay/american-and-israeli-jews-twin-portraits-from-pew-research-center-surveys; "A Portrait of Jewish Americans," Pew Research Center, October 1, 2013, https://www.pewresearch.org/wp-content/uploads/sites/7/2013/10/jewish-american-full-report-for-web.pdf.

36. *Sefer Hasidim* 13C, quoted in Joseph L. Baron, *A Treasury of Jewish Quotations* (Lanham, MD: Rowman & Littlefield, 2004), 14.

37. Wiesel, *Wise Men and Their Tales*, 298.

38. Rachel Adler, "The Jew Who Wasn't There: Halacha and the Jewish Woman," *Response: A Contemporary Jewish Review* 7, no. 2 (Summer 1973): 77–78, 81.

39. Judith Plaskow, *The Coming of Lilith: Essays on Feminism, Judaism, and Sexual Ethics, 1972–2003* (Boston: Beacon Press, 2005), 59, 63; Mary Daly, *Beyond God the Father: Toward a Philosophy of Women's Liberation* (Boston: Beacon Press, 1973), 19.

40. Jeffrey S. Gurock, *Orthodox Jews in America* (Bloomington: Indiana University Press, 2009), 285.

JUDAISM: A Genealogy

a. Shaye J. D. Cohen, *The Beginnings of Jewishness: Boundaries, Varieties, Uncertainties* (Berkeley: University of California Press, 1999), 106.

b. "Judaism, n.,"*OED Online*, Oxford University Press, https://www-oed-com.ezproxy.bu.edu/view/Entry/101869.

c. "A Genealogy for Judaism: Daniel Boyarin's 2015 Bampton Lectures in America," Biblical Studies Online, June 21, 2015, https://biblicalstudiesonline.wordpress.com/2015/06/21/a-genealogy-for-judaism-daniel-boyarin. See also Daniel Boyarin, *Judaism: The Genealogy of a Modern Notion* (New Brunswick, NJ: Rutgers University Press, 2018).

d. Jonathan Klawans, "Judaism Was a Civilization: Toward a Reconstruction of Ancient Jewish Peoplehood," *Religion Compass* 12, no. 10 (October 2018). See also Adele Reinhartz, "The Vanishing Jews of Antiquity," *Marginalia*, June 24, 2014, https://marginalia.lareviewofbooks.org/vanishing-jews-antiquity-adele-reinhartz.

JUDAISM BY THE NUMBERS: Thirteen Principles by Maimonides (1160)

a. "Maimonides: The 13 Principles and the Resurrection of the Dead," Medieval Sourcebook, https://sourcebooks.fordham.edu/source/rambam13.asp.

PROFILES IN JUDAISM: Ruth Bader Ginsburg

a. Michelle Boorstein, "Ruth Bader Ginsburg Calls for the Equal Rights Amendment to the Constitution," *Washington Post*, February 2, 2018, https://www.washingtonpost.com/news/acts-of-faith/wp/2018/02/02/carrying-an-i-dissent-tote-bag-on-stage-ruth-bader-ginsburg-tells-d-c-crowd-shes-still-going-full-steam.

BIRTH AND DEATH

a. Jack Riemer, ed., *Jewish Reflections on Death* (New York: Schocken, 1975), 23.

Chapter 6

1. Mark Twain, *The Innocents Abroad* (Hartford, CT: American Publishing, 1869), 573.

2. Paula Fredriksen, *From Jesus to Christ: The Origins of the New Testament Images of Jesus* (New Haven: Yale University Press, 1988).

3. Thomas Jefferson to Ezra Stiles Ely, June 25, 1819, and Jefferson to William Short, April 13, 1820, in *The Writings of Thomas Jefferson*, vol. 7, ed. H. A. Washington (New York: Derby & Jackson, 1859), 128, 156.

4. Candida Moss, *The Myth of Persecution: How Early Christians Invented a Story of Martyrdom* (New York: HarperOne, 2013).

5. Eusebius, *Life of Constantine*, in *A Select Library of Nicene and Post-Nicene Fathers of the Christian Church*, vol. 1, eds. Henry Wace and Philip Schaff (New York: Christian Literature Company, 1890), 490.

6. In his fourth-century *Life of Anthony*, the Egyptian theologian Athanasius said this of the early monastic hero Anthony the Great. See Lawrence S. Cunningham, *A Brief History of Saints* (Malden, MA: Blackwell, 2005), 19–20.

7. "Medieval Sourcebook: Urban II (1088–1099): Speech at Council of Clermont, 1095, Five Versions of the Speech," Fordham University, https://sourcebooks.fordham.edu/source/urban2-5vers.asp.

8. Pope Innocent III in James Brundage, *The Crusades: A Documentary History* (Milwaukee, WI: Marquette University Press, 1962), 208–209.

9. Gerhart B. Ladner, *Images and Ideas in the Middle Ages*, vol. 2 (Rome: Edizioni di Storia e Letteratura, 1983), 893.

10. St. Athanasius, *On the Incarnation*, trans. John Behr (Yonkers, NY: Saint Vladimir's Seminary Press, 1993), 60.

11. Roland Herbert Bainton, *Here I Stand: A Life of Martin Luther* (Peabody, MA: Hendrickson Publishers, 2015), 180.

12. Thomas Carlyle, *On Heroes, Hero-Worship, and the Heroic in History* (London: Longmans, Green & Co., 1908), 131.

13. Andrew Pettegree, *Brand Luther* (New York: Penguin, 2016), 81.

14. Martin Luther, *A Commentary on Saint Paul's Epistle to the Galatians* (London: Blake, 1833), 421.

15. Martin Luther, *D. Martin Luthers Werke: Kriitische Gesamtausgabe*, vol. 38 (Weimar, Germany: Hermann Bohlau, 1883), 143, quoted in Mark U. Edwards, *Luther's Last Battles: Politics and Polemics, 1531–46* (Minneapolis, MN: Fortress, 2004), 63.

16. Martin Luther, *Luther's Works: Lectures on Galatians, 1535, Chapters 1–4* (St. Louis, MO: Concordia Publishing, 1986), 386.

17. Otto Clemen, ed., *Luthers Werke in Auswahl*, vol. 4, 6th ed. (Berlin: de Gruyter, 1967), 421–428, https://sourcebooks.fordham.edu/mod/1519luther-tower.asp.

18. Martin Luther, "Preface to the Letter of St. Paul to the Romans," http://www.ccel.org/l/luther/romans/pref_romans.html.

19. Pope Leo X, *Exsurge Domine*, 1520, Papal Encyclicals Online, http://www.papalencyclicals.net/leo10/l10exdom.htm.

20. Bainton, *Here I Stand*, 185–86.

21. Max Weber, *The Protestant Ethic and the Spirit of Capitalism: and Other Writings*, ed. and trans. Peter Baehr and Gordon C. Wells (New York: Penguin, 2002), 93.

22. Abraham Lincoln, "Second Inaugural Address," March 4, 1865, Lillian Goldman Law Library, Yale Law School, http://avalon.law.yale.edu/19th_century/lincoln2.asp.

23. Neville Williams, *Henry VIII and His Court* (New York: Macmillan, 1971), 131.

24. Grant Wacker, "Searching for Eden with a Satellite Dish: Primitivism, Pragmatism, and the Pentecostal Character," in *Religion and American Culture*, ed. David Hackett (New York: Routledge, 1995), 437–458.

25. Pope Pius IX, *The Syllabus of Errors*, 1864, Papal Encyclicals Online, http://www.papalencyclicals.net/pius09/p9syll.htm. All subsequent quotations from this encyclical are from this source.

26. "The Vatican Council, Fourth Session—Chapter 4," http://www.piustheninth.com/apps2/app14.htm.

27. Voltaire to Pope Benedict XIV, August 17, 1745, in *Life of Voltaire*, vol. 1, James Parton (Boston: Houghton, Mifflin, 1892), 502; Arthur Hertzberg, *The French Enlightenment and the Jews* (New York: Columbia University Press, 1968), 301.

28. Thomas Paine, *The Age of Reason* (Philadelphia: James Carey, 1797), 6, 12, 15, 145.

29. Ralph Waldo Emerson, "Divinity School Address," in his *Nature; Addresses, and Lectures* (Boston: James Munroe, 1849), 141.

30. Thomas Jefferson to Benjamin Waterhouse, June 26, 1822, National Archives, https://founders.archives.gov/documents/Jefferson/98-01-02-2905.

31. David Bebbington, *Evangelicalism in Modern Britain: A History from the 1730s to the 1980s* (Grand Rapids: Baker: 1989), 2–3.

32. Jonathan Edwards, "A Faithful Narrative of the Surprising Work of God," in *Jonathan Edwards: The Great Awakening, The Works of Jonathan Edwards, Vol. 4*, ed. C. C. Goen (New Haven: Yale University Press, 1972), 128–211.

33. Ronald C. White, *The Eloquent President: A Portrait of Lincoln through His Words* (New York: Random House, 2005), 163.

34. Nathan O. Hatch, *The Democratization of American Christianity* (New Haven: Yale University Press, 1989), 9.

35. Abel Stevens, *History of the Methodist Episcopal Church in the United States of America* (New York: Carlton & Porter, 1864), 174.

36. Stephen Prothero, *Religious Literacy: What Every American Needs to Know—and Doesn't* (New York: HarperOne, 2007), 90.

37. John R. Mott, *The Evangelization of the World in this Generation* (New York: Student Volunteer Movement for Foreign Missions, 1900).

38. Jon Butler, *Awash in a Sea of Faith: Christianizing the American People* (Cambridge: Harvard University Press, 1990), 225.

39. "Joseph Smith—History," in *Pearl of Great Price*, https://www.lds.org/scriptures/pgp/js-h/1.10,18.

40. "Joseph Smith—History," in *Pearl of Great Price*, https://www.lds.org/scriptures/pgp/js-h/1.10,18.

41. R. Laurence Moore, *Religious Outsiders and the Making of Americans* (New York: Oxford University Press, 1986), 44.

42. Friedrich Schleiermacher, *On Religion: Speeches to Its Cultured Despisers*, trans. John Oman (London: Kegan, Paul, Trench, Trubner & Co., 1893), 14, 106.

43. Gary Dorrien, *The Making of American Liberal Theology: Imagining Progressive Religion, 1805–1900* (Louisville: Westminster John Knox Press, 2001), xxii.

44. Walter Lippman, *A Preface to Morals* (New Brunswick: Transaction Publishers, 1982), 51.

45. Mark Noll, *The Civil War as a Theological Crisis* (Chapel Hill: The University of North Carolina Press, 2006).

46. Walter Rauschenbusch, *Christianity and the Social Crisis* (New York: Macmillan, 1913), 3, 29, 28, 207, 7.

47. John Ireland, *The Church and Modern Society: Lectures and Addresses* (New York: McBride, 1896), 73; Patrick Henry Ahern, *The Life of John J. Keane, Educator and Archbishop, 1839–1918* (Milwaukee, WI: Bruce Publishing, 1955), 94.

48. George M. Marsden, *Fundamentalism and American Culture: The Shaping of the Twentieth Century Evangelicalism, 1870–1925* (New York: Oxford University Press, 1980), 122.

49. J. Gresham Machen, *Christianity and Liberalism* (New York: William B. Eerdmans Publishing Co., 1923), 6.

50. George M. Marsden, *Fundamentalism and American Culture* (New York: Oxford University Press, 2006), 236.

51. Harry Emerson Fosdick, "Shall the Fundamentalists Win?" History Matters, http://historymatters.gmu.edu/d/5070/.

52. H. Richard Niebuhr, *The Kingdom of God in America* (New York: Harper, 1937), 193.

53. David Brooks, "Obama, Gospel and Verse," *New York Times*, April 26, 2007, https://www.nytimes.com/2007/04/26/opinion/26brooks.html.

54. Frederick Douglass, *Narrative of an American Slave* (Boston: Anti-Slavery Office, 1845), http://utc.iath.virginia.edu/abolitn/abaufda14t.html.

55. Albert Cleage, *The Black Messiah* (New York: Sheed and Ward, 1968), 8, 33.

56. James H. Cone, *Black Theology and Black Power* (Maryknoll, NY: Orbis, 1997), 151.

57. Mary Daly, "The Women's Movement: An Exodus Community," *Religious Education* 67 (Sept.–Oct. 1972): 327–335.

58. Mary Daly, *After the Death of God the Father: Toward a Philosophy of Women's Liberation* (Boston: Beacon Press, 1974), 19.

59. Alice Walker, *In Search of Our Mothers' Gardens: Womanist Prose* (New York: Harcourt, Brace Jovanovich, 1983), xi.

60. Grant Wacker, *Heaven Below: Early Pentecostals and American Culture* (Cambridge: Harvard University Press, 2001), 266.

61. Douglas J. Nelson, "For Such a Time as This: The Story of Bishop William J. Seymour and the Azusa Street Revival," (PhD diss., University of Birmingham, 1981), 234.

62. *The Apostolic Faith*, February–March, 1907, 7, quoted in Gaston Espinosa, "Ordinary Prophet: William J. Seymour and the Azusa Street Revival," in *The Asuza Street Revival and its Legacy*, eds. Harold D. Hunter and Cecil M. Robeck Jr. (Eugene, OR: Wipf & Stock, 2006), 49.

63. "Azusa Street Revival," in *Encyclopedia of American Religious History*, vol. 1, ed. Edward L. Queen II et al. (New York: Facts on File, 2001), 50.

64. Wacker, *Heaven Below*, 205.

65. Joel Robbins, "The Globalization of Pentecostal and Charismatic Christianity," *Annual Review of Anthropology* 33 (2004): 121.

66. Wacker, *Heaven Below*, 268.

67. Jeff Sharlet, "Donald Trump, American Preacher," *New York Times Magazine*, April 12, 2016, https://www.nytimes.com/2016/04/17/magazine/donald-trump-american-preacher.html.

68. Madonna, *Material Girl* (New York: Sire Records, 1984).

69. Dana Robert, "Shifting Southward: Global Christianity since 1945," *International Bulletin of Missionary Research* 24, no. 2 (2000): 50–58.

70. Mark A. Noll, *The New Shape of World Christianity: How American Experience Reflects Global Faith* (Downers Grove, IL: IVP Academic, 2009), 111.

CHRISTIANITY: A Genealogy

a. Geoffrey Chaucer, *The Canterbury Tales*, http://www.librarius.com/canttran/manlawtr/manlawtale533-581.htm; W. Bonde, *Pylgrimage of Perfection* (1526), cited in "Christian, adj. and n.," OED Online, Oxford University Press, March 2019, www.oed.com/view/Entry/32448; Sebastian Münster, *A Treatyse of the Newe India*, trans. Richard Eden (London: E .Sutton, 1553), title page; Richard Hooker, *Of the Lawes of Ecclesiasticall Politie*, vol. 5 (London: John Windet, 1597), 139.

b. William Shakespeare, *The Two Gentlemen of Verona*, ed. W. G. Boswell-Stone (New York: Duffield, 1908), 38.

PROFILES IN CHRISTIANITY: Augustine of Hippo

a. Saint Augustine, *Confessions*, trans. Henry Chadwick (New York: Oxford University Press, 2009), 145.

b. Saint Augustine, *Confessions*, 207–208.

PROFILES IN CHRISTIANITY: Aimee Semple McPherson

a. Sarah Comstock, "Aimee Semple McPherson: Prima Donna of Revivalism," *Harper's Magazine* (December 1, 1927): 12.

MATERIAL CHRISTIANITY: The Ground Zero Cross

a. "World Trade Center Cross," Wallbuilders, https://wallbuilders.com/world-trade-center-cross/.

Chapter 7

1. All quotations from the Quran in this chapter are from Seyyed Hossein Nasr et al., eds., *The Study Quran: A New Translation and Commentary* (New York: HarperOne, 2015).
2. Malcolm X, *The Autobiography of Malcolm X as Told to Alex Haley* (New York: Ballantine, 1999), 369, 348.
3. Asra Q. Nomani, *Standing Alone in Mecca: An American Woman's Struggle for the Soul of Islam* (New York: HarperOne, 2005), 68.
4. William C. Chittick, *The Sufi Doctrine of Rumi* (Bloomington, IN: World Wisdom, 2005), 82.
5. Department of Islamic Art, "Calligraphy in Islamic Art," in *Heilbrunn Timeline of Art History* (New York: The Metropolitan Museum of Art, 2000), http://www.metmuseum.org/toah/hd/cali/hd_cali.htm.
6. Jurgen Wasim Fremgen, *The Aura of Aliph: The Art of Writing in Islam* (New York: Prestel, 2010).
7. Jonathan E. Brockopp, "Interpreting Material Evidence: Religion at the 'Origins of Islam,'" *History of Religions* 55, no. 2 (November 2015): 136.
8. Aisha Lemu and Fatima Hereen, *Woman in Islam* (London: Islamic Council of Europe, 1976), 25.
9. Michael Cook, *Muhammad* (New York: Oxford University Press, 1996), 78.
10. Fred M. Donner, *Muhammad and the Believers: At the Origins of Islam* (Cambridge: Harvard University Press, 2010), 195, 58, 197.
11. Brockopp, "Interpreting Material Evidence," 129.
12. Annemarie Schimmel, *Islam: An Introduction* (Albany: State University of New York Press, 1992), 104.
13. Schimmel, *Islam*, 105.
14. Carl W. Ernst, *The Shambhala Guide to Sufism* (Boston: Shambhala, 1997), 117.
15. Annemarie Schimmel, *Mystical Dimensions of Islam* (Chapel Hill: University of North Carolina Press, 2011), 72.
16. Ernst, *The Shambhala Guide to Sufism*, xii.
17. Sepoy, "XQs I: A Conversation with Teena Purohit," June 7, 2013, http://www.chapatimystery.com/archives/univercity/xqs/xqs_i_a_conversation_with_teena_purohit.html.
18. W. C. Smith, *Modern Islam in India: A Social Analysis* (London: Gollanez, 1946), 105.
19. Muhammad Iqbal, *The Reconstruction of Religious Thought in Islam* (London: Oxford University Press, 1934), 92.
20. Jane Dammen McAuliffe, "The Classical Synthesis Encounters Modernity," in *The Norton Anthology of World Religions: Volume 2*, ed. Jack Miles (New York: Norton, 2015), 1843.
21. Sayyid Qutb, *Milestones*, trans. Ahmad Zaki Hmmad (Indianapolis: American Trust Publications, 1990), 7.
22. Carl W. Ernst, *Following Muhammad: Rethinking Islam in the Contemporary World* (Chapel Hill: University of North Carolina Press, 2004), 68; Guilain Deneoux, "The Forgotten Swamp: Navigating Political Islam," *Middle East Policy* 9, no. 2 (June 2002): 61.
23. Martyn Oliver, "'A Thousand and One Nights' and the Construction of Islam in the Western Imagination" (PhD, Boston University, 2009).
24. Thomas Bluett, *Some Memoirs of the Life of Job* (London: Richard Ford, 1734), 21–22.
25. Michael A. Koszegi and J. Gordon Melton, *Islam in North America: A Sourcebook* (New York: Routledge, 2017), 158.
26. *Nashville Tennessean*, "Rule Switch Allows Whites as Muslims," June 19, 1975, in Lawrence H. Mamiya, "Minister Louis Farrakhan and the Final Call: Schism in the Muslim Movement," in *The Muslim Community in North America*, eds. Earl H. Waugh et al. (Edmonton: University of Alberta Press, 1983), 249.
27. Pew Research Center, "U.S. Muslims Concerned About Their Place in Society, but Continue to Believe in the American Dream," July 26, 2017, 35, 22.
28. Jenna Johnson, "Trump Calls for 'Total and Complete Shutdown of Muslims Entering the United States,'" *Washington Post*, December 7, 2015, https://www.washingtonpost.com/news/post-politics/wp/2015/12/07/donald-trump-calls-for-total-and-complete-shutdown-of-muslims-entering-the-united-states/?utm_term=.eae19cc588d9.
29. Charles Kurzman, *The Missing Martyrs: Why There Are So Few Muslim Terrorists* (New York: Oxford University Press, 2011), 7, 11, 27–28. Survey data is from Pew Research Center, "Muslims and Islam: Key Findings in the U.S. and Around the World," August 9, 2017, http://www.pewresearch.org/fact-tank/2017/08/09/muslims-and-islam-key-findings-in-the-u-s-and-around-the-world.
30. Samuel P. Huntington, "The Clash of Civilizations?" *Foreign Affairs* 72, no. 3 (Summer 1999): 22–49.
31. Pew Research Center, "Concerns about Islamic Extremism on the Rise in Middle East," July 1, 2014, http://www.pewglobal.org/2014/07/01/concerns-about-islamic-extremism-on-the-rise-in-middle-east.
32. Richard Dawkins, "Islam Is One Of The Great Evils In The World," https://www.youtube.com/watch?v=yyNv8kvd2H8.

PROFILES IN ISLAM: Rumi

a. Jalan al-din Rumi, *The Masnavi: Book One*, trans. Jawed Mojaddedi (New York: Oxford University Press, 2004), 4.

ISLAM: A Genealogy

a. William, Archbishop of Tyre, *Godeffroy of Boloyne* (1481; London: Early English Text Society, 1893), 1, 274.

b. 1500s quotations are from James A. H. Murray, *A New English Dictionary on Historical Principles*, vol. 6 (Oxford Clarendon Press, 1908).

c. On the 1613 date for Islam's first appearance in English, see David R. Blanks, "Western Views of Islam in the Premodern Period," in *Western Views of Islam in Medieval and Early Modern Europe*, eds. David R. Blanks and Michael Frassetto (New York: St. Martin's Press, 1999), 14.

PROFILES IN ISLAM: Muhammad Ali

a. Thomas Hauser, *Muhammad Ali: His Life and Times* (New York: Simon and Schuster, 1991), 82.

b. "Scorecard," *Sports Illustrated*, March 16, 1964, https://www.si.com/vault/1964/03/16/608418/scorecard.

c. Bob Orkand, "I Ain't Got No Quarrel With Them Vietcong," *New York Times*, June 27, 2017, https://www.nytimes.com/2017/06/27/opinion/muhammad-ali-vietnam-war.html.

MATERIAL ISLAM: Mihrab

a. "Unlikely Mosque Designer Wows with Reverent Stunner," *Hurriyet Daily News*, May 23, 2009, http://www.hurriyet.com.tr/gundem/unlikely-mosque-designer-wows-with-reverent-stunner-11707701.

PART III

1. Keping Wang, *Reading the Dao: A Thematic Inquiry* (New York: Continuum, 2011), 18.

Chapter 8

1. Sebastian Veg, "Wang Xiaobo and the No Longer Silent Majority," in *The Impact of China's 1989 Tiannanmen Massacre*, ed. Jean-Philippe Beja (New York: Routledge, 2011), 89.

2. Liang Cai, "When the Founder Is Not a Creator: Confucius and Confucianism Reconsidered," in *Varieties of Religious Invention: Founders and Their Functions in History*, ed. Patrick Gray (New York: Oxford University Press, 2015), 65.

3. M. Fournier De Flaix, "Development of Statistics of Religion," *Publications of the American Statistical Association* 3, no. 17 (1892): 32; and Louis Henry Jordan, *Comparative Religion: Its Genesis and Growth* (New York: Charles Scribner's Sons, 1905), unnumbered page facing title page, both cited in Anna Sun, *Confucianism as a World Religion: Contested Histories and Contemporary Realities* (Princeton, NJ: Princeton University Press, 2013), 111–112.

4. A. S. Cua, "Junzi (Chun-tzu): The Moral Person," in *Encyclopedia of Chinese Philosophy*, ed. Antonio S. Cua (New York: Routledge, 2003), 331.

5. *The Analects of Confucius: A Philosophical Translation*, trans. Roger T. Ames and Henry Rosemont Jr. (New York: Ballantine, 1998), 76. Unless otherwise noted, all future translations from the Analects in this chapter will be from this source.

6. Yuan Li and Wen Haiming, "Confucius," in *The Oxford Handbook of Process Philosophy and Organizational Studies*, ed. Jenny Helin et al. (New York: Oxford University Press, 2014), 53.

7. Confucius, *Analects with Selections from Traditional Commentaries*, trans. Edward Slingerland (Indianapolis, IN: Hackett, 2003), 88.

8. James Legge, *The Chinese Classics*, vol. 1 (London: Trubner, 1861), 88.

9. Martin Luther King Jr., "Letter from Birmingham Jail," in *American Bible: How Our Words Unite, Divide, and Define a Nation*, ed. Stephen Prothero (New York: HarperOne, 2012), 467.

10. Herbert Fingarette, "The Music of Humanity in the Conversations of Confucius," *Journal of Chinese Philosophy* 10, no. 4 (1983): 217.

11. Confucius, *The Analects*, trans. D. C. Lau (New York: Penguin, 1979), 89.

12. *Xunzi: Basic Writings*, trans. Burton Watson (New York: Columbia University Press, 2003), 161.

13. James A. Flath, *Traces of the Sage: Monument, Materiality, and the First Temple of Confucius* (Honolulu: University of Hawai'i Press, 2016), 58.

14. Wing-tsit Chan, ed. and trans., *A Source Book in Chinese Philosophy* (Princeton, NJ: Princeton University Press, 1963), 497.

15. Stephen C. Angle, *Sagehood: The Contemporary Significance of Neo-Confucian Philosophy* (New York: Oxford University Press, 2009), 35.

16. Wing-tsit Chan, *A Source Book in Chinese Philosophy*, 555.

17. Tu Wei-ming, "The Confucian Tradition in Chinese History," in *Heritage of China*, ed. Paul S. Ropp (Berkeley: University of California Press, 1990), 131.

18. Philip J. Ivanhoe, *Readings from the Lu-Wang School of Neo-Confucianism* (Indianapolis, IN: Hackett, 2009), 181.

19. Ivanhoe, *Readings from the Lu-Wang School of Neo-Confucianism*, 162.

20. Dorothy Ko, *Teachers of the Inner Chambers: Women and Culture in Seventeenth-Century China* (Stanford, CA: Stanford University Press, 1995), 84.

21. Yong Chen, "On the Rhetoric of Defining Confucianism as 'a Religion'" (PhD diss., Vanderbilt University, 2005), 86.

22. Sang Ye and Geremie R. Barme, "Commemorating Confucius in 1966–67," *China Heritage Quarterly*, December 2009, http://www.chinaheritagequarterly. org/scholarship.php?searchterm=020_confucius. inc&issue=020.

23. Michael Schuman, *Confucius: And the World He Created* (New York: Basic Books, 2015), 94.

24. Yu Ying-shih, quoted in *Neo-Confucianism: A Philosophical Introduction*, ed. Stephen C. Angle and Justin Tiwald (Malden, MA: Polity Press, 2017), 210.

25. "'The Evil Life of Confucius': An Anti-Confucius Poster from the Cultural Revolution," Reed College, http://people.reed.edu/~brashiek/syllabi/Poster/ running.html.

26. Anna Sun, *Confucianism as a World Religion*, 153.

27. G. W. F. Hegel, "Oriental Philosophy," in *Hegel's Lectures on the History of Philosophy*, trans. E. S. Haldane and Frances H. Simson (London: Routledge and Kegan Paul, 1955), 121.

28. Tu Wei-ming, "Expectations and Vision for the Confucius Institute," Confucius Institute, January 2011, http://www.cim.chinesecio.com/hbcms/f/article/ info?id=cc8cf600ad2a4c06907575c1cb33ea5f.

29. Tu Wei-ming, *Centrality and Commonality: An Essay on Confucian Religiousness* (Albany: State University of New York Press, 1989), 9.

30. Harold Isaacs, *Scratches on Our Minds: American Images of China* (New York: John Day, 1958), 15.

31. Matthew A. Foust, *Confucianism and American Philosophy* (Albany: State University of New York Press, 2017), 41–60.

32. Ralph Waldo Emerson, *The Letters of Ralph Waldo Emerson*, vol. 7, ed. Eleanor Tilton and Ralph Rusk (New York: Columbia University Press, 1990), 127.

33. Ralph Waldo Emerson, *Journals of Ralph Waldo Emerson with Annotations*, vol. 7, ed. Edward Waldo Emerson and Waldo Emerson Forbes (Boston: Houghton Mifflin, 1913), 126.

34. Kyle Bryant Simmons, "Emerson, the American Confucius: An Exploration of Confucian Motifs in the Early Writings (1830–1843) of Ralph Waldo Emerson" (PhD diss., University of Texas at Dallas, 2013).

35. Bret Harte, "Plain Language from Truthful James," *The Overland Monthly Magazine*, September 1870, twain.lib.virginia.edu/roughingit/map/chiharte.html.

36. "Spiritual Life Study of Chinese Residents" (2007), The Association of Religion Data Archives (ARDA), www.thearda.com/Archive/Files/Descriptions/ SPRTCHNA.asp.

37. James Legge, *Confucianism in Relation to Christianity* (London: Trubner, 1877), 4.

38. Sun, *Confucianism as a World Religion*, 10.

39. Sun, *Confucianism as a World Religion*, 81.

40. Tu Wei-ming, *Centrality and Commonality*, 116.

41. Peter Berger, "Is Confucianism a Religion?" *The American Interest*, February 15, 2012, https://www.the-american-interest.com/2012/02/15/is-confucianism-a-religion.

42. Joseph A. Adler, "Divination and Sacrifice in Song Neo-Confucianism," in *Teaching Confucianism*, ed. Jeffrey L. Richey (New York: Oxford University Press, 2008), 74.

43. Rodney L. Taylor, *The Religious Dimensions of Confucianism* (Albany: State University of New York, 1990), 3.

44. Tu Wei-ming, *Centrality and Commonality*, 94.

45. Herbert Fingarette, *Confucius: The Sacred as Secular* (Prospect Heights, IL: Waveland, 1989), 3, 5.

CONFUCIANISM: A Genealogy

a. John Francis Davis, *The Chinese*, vol. 2 (London: Charles Knight, 1836), 74.

b. Robert Morrison, "Remarks on the Language, History, Religions, and Government of China," *The Evangelical Magazine and Missionary Chronicle* 3 (November 1825): 456.

c. Richard Hakluyt, *The Principal Navigations Voyages Traffiques & Discoveries of the English Nation*, vol. 6 (New York: Macmillan, 1904), 372, 370.

PROFILES IN CONFUCIANISM: Yu Dan

a. Yu Dan, *Confucius from the Heart: Ancient Wisdom for Today's World* (New York: Atria Books, 2009), 15, 20, 81.

b. Daniel A. Bell, *China's New Confucianism: Politics and Everyday Life in a Changing Society* (Princeton, NJ: Princeton University Press, 2010), 174.

c. Frank L. Mott, *Golden Multitudes* (New York: Macmillan, 1947), 122.

d. Sun Shuyun, "Chicken Brother for the Soul? No Thanks," *The Guardian*, May 16, 2009, https://www. theguardian.com/books/2009/may/17/confucius-from-the-heart-yu-dan.

e. Sun, *Confucianism as a World Religion*, 143.

Chapter 9

1. Du Guangting, "Recorded for the Ritual of Merit and Virtue for Repairing the Various Observatories of Qingchang Mountain," in *Norton Anthology of World Religions: Volume 1*, ed. Jack Miles (New York: Norton, 2015), 1861.

2. Thomas Michael, *The Pristine Dao: Metaphysics in Early Daoist Discourse* (Albany: State University of New York Press, 2005), 56.

3. James Miller, "China's Green Religion," https://www.jamesmiller.ca/chinas-green-religion-2-2/.

4. Isabelle Robinet, *Taoism: Growth of a Religion*, trans. Phyllis Brooks (Stanford, CA: Stanford University Press, 1997), 2.

5. Michael, *The Pristine Dao*, 74, 77.

6. Victor H. Mair, *Wandering on the Way: Early Taoist Tales and Parables of Chuang Tzu* (Honolulu: University of Hawaii Press, 1994), 145.

7. Robert Ford Campany, *To Live as Long as Heaven and Earth: A Translation and Study of Ge Hong's Traditions of Divine Transcendents* (Berkeley: University of California Press, 2002), 53.

8. Robert Ford Campany, *Making Transcendents: Ascetics and Social Memory in Early Medieval China* (Honolulu: University of Hawaii Press, 2009).

9. Kristofer Schipper, "Taoism: The Story of the Way," in *Taoism and the Arts of China*, ed. Stephen Little and Shawn Eichman (Berkeley: University of California Press, 2000), 34.

10. Harold D. Roth, *Original Tao* (New York: Columbia University Press, 1999), 8.

11. James Miller, *Daoism: A Short Introduction* (Oxford, England: OneWorld, 2005), 1–2.

12. Livia Kohn, ed., *Readings in Daoist Mysticism* (Magdalena, NM: Three Pines Press, 2009), 143.

13. Ronald Reagan, "Address Before a Joint Session of Congress on the State of the Union," January 25, 1988, https://www.presidency.ucsb.edu/documents/address-before-joint-session-congress-the-state-the-union-0#axzz1xnQLFdLi.

14. Mair, *Wandering on the Way*, 140.

15. Schipper, "Taoism: The Story of the Way," 41.

16. *Norton Anthology of World Religions: Volume 1*, A20.

17. James Robson, "Classical Daoism Takes Shape," in *Norton Anthology of World Religions: Volume 1*, 1592.

18. Terry F. Kleeman, *Celestial Masters: History and Ritual in Early Daoist Communities* (Cambridge, MA: Harvard University Press, 2016).

19. Campany, *To Live as Long as Heaven and Earth*, 11, 8–9.

20. Louis Komjathy, *Cultivating Perfection: Mysticism and Self-Transformation in Early Quanzhen Daoism* (Leiden: Brill, 2007).

21. Louis Komjathy, *The Way of Complete Perfection: A Quanzhen Daoist Anthology* (Albany: State University of New York Press, 2013), 278.

22. John Lagerway, "Daoism: The Daoist Religious Community," in *Encyclopedia of Religion*, ed. Lindsay Jones (Detroit: Macmillan, 2005), 2200.

23. Stephen R. Bokenkamp, "Daoism: An Overview," in Jones, *Encyclopedia of Religion*, 2187.

24. Schipper, "Taoism: The Story of the Way," 51–52.

25. Russell Kirkland, *Taoism: The Enduring Tradition* (New York: Routledge, 2004), 110.

26. Elena Valussi, "Female Alchemy and Paratext: How To Read *nüdan* in a Historical Context," *Asia Major* 21, no. 2 (2008): 158, 167.

27. *Norton Anthology of World Religions: Volume 1*, 2070–2071.

28. Karl Marx, "Critique of Hegel's Philosophy of Right," in *Marx on Religion*, ed. John Raines (Philadelphia: Temple University Press, 2002), 171.

29. Anonymous, "Taoism, a Prize Essay," in *The Dawn of Religious Pluralism: Voices from the World's Parliament of Religions, 1893*, ed. Richard Seager (La Salle, IL: Open Court, 1993), 362–333.

30. Dwight Goddard, *A Buddhist Bible: The Favorite Scriptures of the Zen Sect* (Thetford, VT: Dwight Goddard, 1932), 19.

31. "Dead Putting Society," http://www.simpsonsworld.com/video/260539459670?related=260539459670.

32. Constance Feeley and Brendan Gill, "T'ai Chi Ch'uan," *New Yorker*, December 15, 1962, 32.

33. Newsletter quoted in Louis Komjathy, "Tracing the Contours of Daoism in North America," *Nova Religio* 8, no. 2 (November 2004): 22.

34. David A. Palmer and Elijah Siegler, *Dream Trippers: Global Daoism and the Predicament of Modern Spirituality* (Chicago: The University of Chicago Press, 2017), 94.

35. Elijah Siegler, "The Dao of America: The History and Practice of American Daoism" (PhD diss., University of California, Santa Barbara, 2003), 17.

36. Solala Towler, *Embarking on the Way: A Guide to Western Taoism* (Eugene, OR: Abode of the Eternal Tao, 1997).

37. Russell Kirkland, "The Taoism of the Western Imagination and the Taoism of China: De-Colonializing the Exotic Teachings of the East" (paper presented at the University of Tennessee, October 20, 1997), https://faculty.franklin.uga.edu/kirkland/sites/faculty.franklin.uga.edu.kirkland/files/TENN97.pdf.

38. Kleeman quoted in Louis Komjathy, "Tracing the Contours of Daoism in North America," *Nova Religio* 8, no. 2 (November 2004): 22.

39. Ursula K. Le Guin, "Epilogue: Dao Song," in *Daoism and Ecology: Ways Within a Cosmic Landscape*, ed. N. J. Girardot et al. (Cambridge, MA: Harvard University Press, 2001), 411–413.

40. Robinet, *Taoism*, 91.

41. Thomas Michael, *In the Shadows of the Dao: Laozi, the Sage, and the Daodejing* (Albany: SUNY Press, 2016), 103.

42. James Miller, *Daoism: A Beginner's Guide* (Oxford, England: OneWorld Publications, 2008), 64.

43. Carlyle Murphy, "Chinese Crackdown Protested: Falun Gong Backers Say Movement Shouldn't Be Banned," *Washington Post*, July 22, 1999, A25.

44. Stephen Noakes, "Falun Gong, Ten Years On: Review Article," *Pacific Affairs* 83, no. 2 (2010): 354.

DAOISM: A Genealogy

a. Charles Gutzlaff, *A Sketch of Chinese History*, vol. 1 (London: Smith, Elder and Co., 1834), 308, 69.

b. Charles Gutzlaff, *The Journal of Two Voyages Along the Coast of China* (New York: John P. Haven, 1833), 307–311.

c. A Correspondent, "Review of the Shin Seen Tung Keen," *Chinese Repository* 7, no. 10 (February 1839): 505, 514, 523.

d. Abbe Grosier, *A General Description of China*, vol. 2 (London: G. G. J. and J. Robinson, 1788), 203, 205, 206, 211, 208.

DAOISM BY THE NUMBERS: Nine Practices and Twenty-Seven Precepts of the Celestial Masters

a. Kleeman, *Celestial Masters*, 91–92.

b. Kleeman, *Celestial Masters*, 92–93.

PROFILES IN DAOISM: Sun Buer

a. Louis Komjathy, "Sun Buer: Early Quanzhen Matriarch and the Beginnings of Female Alchemy," in *Nan Nü* 16, no. 2 (December 2014): 171–238.

MATERIAL DAOISM: The Robe of the Dao

a. Louis Komjathy, *The Daoist Tradition: An Introduction* (New York: Bloomsbury, 2013), 292.

Chapter 10

1. Havasupai elder quoted in Plaintiffs'/Appellants' Opening Brief, Navajo Nation v. U.S. Forest Service, 535 F.3d 1058 (9th Cir. 2008), 37.

2. Berard Haile, *Soul Concepts of the Navajo* (St. Michaels, AZ: St. Michaels Press, 1975).

3. Navajo Nation President Joe Shirley Jr., "Signed Statement to UNESCO," Plaintiffs'/Appellants' Opening Brief, Exhibit 3, *Navajo Nation*.

4. Navajo Nation President Joe Shirley Jr., "Signed Statement to UNESCO," Plaintiffs'/Appellants' Opening Brief, Exhibit 3, *Navajo Nation*.

5. Robert S. McPherson, *Sacred Land, Sacred View: Navajo Perceptions of the Four Corners Region* (Salt Lake City, UT: Signature, 1992), 18–19.

6. Joe Shirley Jr. testimony, "Reporter's Transcript of Proceedings," *Navajo Nation*, 804.

7. Isaac H. Salay, "Hózhó: Balance and Beauty in the Navajo World" (bachelor's thesis, Colorado College, 2016), 2, https://digitalccbeta.coloradocollege.edu/pid/coccc:26350/datastream/OBJ

8. Navajo Nation v. U.S. Forest Service, 479 F.3d 1024 (9th Cir. 2007).

9. "Declaration of Vincent Randall," Plaintiffs'/Appellants' Opening Brief, Exhibit 2, *Navajo Nation*, 2.

10. Suzanne J. Crawford, *Native American Religious Traditions* (New York: Routledge, 2016), 124.

11. Charles H. Long, *Significations: Signs, Symbols, and Images in the Interpretation of Religion* (Philadelphia: Fortress Press, 1986), 7.

12. Michael McNally, "From Substantial Burden on Religion to Diminished Spiritual Fulfillment: The San Francisco Peaks Case and the Misunderstanding of Native American Religion," *Journal of Law and Religion* 30, no. 1 (February 2015): 39.

13. Paul G. Zolbrod, *Diné bahane': The Navajo Creation Story* (Albuquerque: New Mexico University Press, 1984), 19.

14. Aileen O'Bryan, *The Diné: Origin Myths of the Navaho Indians* (Washington, DC: U.S. Government Printing Office, 1956). This document is in the public domain because it is a U.S. government publication. The original text has been abridged here and lightly edited for clarification.

15. Navajo Division of Health Navajo Epidemiology Center, *Navajo Population Profile: 2010 U.S. Census*, December 2013, www.nec.navajo-nsn.gov/Portals/0/Reports/NN2010PopulationProfile.pdf.

16. Derek Milne, "Diyin God Bizaad: Tradition, Change and Pentecostal Christianity among the Navajo" (PhD diss., University of California, Los Angeles, 2001), 527.

17. Eva Marie Garrouette, et al., "Religio-Spiritual Participation in Two American Indian Populations," *Journal for the Scientific Study of Religion* 53, no. 1 (March 2014): 17–37.

18. David Stannard, *American Holocaust: Columbus and the Conquest of the New World* (New York: Oxford University Press, 1992), x.

19. Michael D. McNally, "The Practice of Native American Christianity," *Church History* 69, no. 2 (December 2000): 849.

20. Trudy Griffin-Pierce, "The Continuous Renewal of Sacred Relations: Navajo Religion," in *Native Religions and Cultures of North America*, ed. Lawrence E. Sullivan (New York: Continuum, 2000), 131.

21. Gary Witherspoon and Glen Peterson, *Dynamic Symmetry and Holistic Asymmetry in Navajo and Western Art and Cosmology* (New York: Lang, 1995), 15.

22. Gary Witherspoon, *Language and Art in the Navajo Universe* (Ann Arbor: University of Michigan Press, 1977), 24; Griffin-Pierce, "The Continuous Renewal of Sacred Relations," 131.

23. Klaus Mainzer, *Symmetries of Nature: A Handbook for Philosophy of Nature and Science* (New York: Walter de Gruyter, 1996), 17–18. On hozho as both moral and aesthetic (the good and the beautiful), see Clyde Kluckhohn, "The Philosophy of the Navaho Indians," in *Readings in Anthropology*, 2nd ed., ed. Morton H. Fried (New York: Crowell, 1968), 686.

24. Washington Matthews, *Navaho Legends* (Boston: Houghton, Mifflin, 1897), 266; Gladys A. Reichard, *Navaho Religion: A Study of Symbolism* (Tucson: University of Arizona Press, 1983), 47; John A. Grim, "Cosmology and Native North American Mystical Traditions," *Théologiques* 9, no. 1 (2001): 134; Rex Lee Jim, "A Moment in My Life," in *Here First: Autobiographical Essays by Native American Writers,* ed. Arnold Krupat and Brian Swann (New York: Modern Library, 2000), 232.

25. John R. Farella, *The Main Stalk: A Synthesis of Navajo Philosophy* (Tucson: University of Arizona Press, 1984), 170–71. A similar interpretation sees this phrase as a coming together of the inner forms of Mother Earth and Father Sky. See Griffin-Pierce, "The Continuous Renewal of Sacred Relations," 134–140.

26. Sam D. Gill and Irene F. Sullivan, *Dictionary of Native American Mythology* (New York: Oxford University Press, 1994), 128.

27. Griffin-Pierce, "The Continuous Renewal of Sacred Relations," 123.

28. Witherspoon, *Language and Art in the Navajo Universe,* 26.

29. Ara Norenzayan, *Big Gods: How Religion Transformed Cooperation and Conflict* (Princeton, NJ: Princeton University Press, 2015).

30. David F. Aberle, "The Navajo Singer's Fee: Payment or Presentation," in *Studies in Southwestern Ethnolinguistics*, ed. D. H. Hymes and W. E. Bittle (The Hague: Mouton, 1967), 16.

31. Rose Mitchell, *The Life Story of Rose Mitchell, a Navajo Woman*, ed. Charlotte J. Frisbie (Albuquerque: University of New Mexico Press, 2001), 297.

32. Peter Iverson, *Diné: A History of the Navajos* (Albuquerque: University of New Mexico Press, 2002), 14.

33. Charles Wilson Hackett, *Revolt of the Pueblo Indians of New Mexico and Otermín's Reconquest, 1680–1682,* vol. 9 (Albuquerque: University of New Mexico Press, 1942), 248, http://www.digitalhistory.uh.edu/disp_textbook.cfm?smtid=3&psid=651.

34. John Macrae Washington to Adjutant General Jones, 3 February 1849, in Iverson, *Diné: A History of the Navajos,* 40.

35. James H. Carleton to Kit Carson, 19 September 1863, in *Condition of the Indian Tribes: Report of the Joint Special Committee* (Washington, DC: Government Printing Office, 1867), 139.

36. Ruth Roessel and Broderick H. Johnson, "Curly Tso," in *Navajo Stories of the Long Walk Period* (Tsaile, AZ: Navajo Community College Press, 1973), 103.

37. Iverson, *Diné: A History of the Navajos,* 63–64.

38. Thomas Constantine Maroukis, *The Peyote Road: Religious Freedom and the Native American Church* (Norman: University of Oklahoma Press, 2010), 37.

39. L. G. Moses, *Indian Man: A Biography of James Mooney* (London: University of Nebraska Press, 2002), 191–192.

40. Omer Stewart, *Peyote Religion: A History* (Norman: University of Oklahoma Press, 1987), 224, xiii.

41. William T. Hagan, *Quanah Parker: Comanche Chief* (Norman: University of Oklahoma Press, 1993), 57.

42. "Nelson Turtle," Carlos Sauer (website), www.carlossauer.net/novosite/?page_id=1949.

43. Irving A. Leonard, "Decree against Peyote, Mexican Inquisition, 1620," *American Anthropologist* 44 (1942): 324–336.

44. Omer C. Stewart, *Peyote Religion: A History* (Norman: University of Oklahoma Press, 1987), 129.

45. Stewart, *Peyote Religion,* 296.

46. On reasons for Peyotism's popularity, see Maroukis, *The Peyote Road,* 59–92.

47. David F. Aberle, *Peyote Religion among the Navajo* (Chicago: Aldine, 1966), 183.

48. Maroukis, *The Peyote Road,* 91.

49. McPherson, *Sacred Land, Sacred View,* 126.

50. See Elizabeth L. Lewton and Victoria Bydone, "Identity and Healing in Three Navajo Religious Traditions: Są'áh Naagháí Bik'eh Hózhóó," *Medical Anthropology Quarterly* 14, no. 4 (December 2000): 476–497. These authors see this reconnection as therapeutic.

51. Fifty-eight ceremonies are listed in Leland C. Wyman and Clyde Kluckhohn, "Navajo Classification of Their Song Ceremonials," *Memoirs of the American Anthropological Association* 50, no. 24 (1938): 3–38.

52. Iverson, *Diné: A History of the Navajos*, 12.

53. Joe Shirley Jr. testimony, "Reporter's Transcript of Proceedings," *Navajo Nation*, 799.

54. Frank Mitchell, *Navajo Blessingway Singer: The Autobiography of Frank Mitchell*, ed. Charlotte J. Frisbie (Tucson: University of Arizona Press, 1977), 213.

55. Mitchell, *Navajo Blessingway Singer*, 218.

56. "Native Words Native Warriors," National Museum of the American Indian, https://americanindian.si.edu/education/codetalkers/html/chapter5.html.

57. McPherson, *Sacred Land, Sacred View*, 74.

58. Steven Begay, "Reporter's Transcript of Proceedings," *Navajo Nation*, 744.

59. Mitchell, *Navajo Blessingway Singer*, 202.

60. David Kucharsky, "Toward a Red Theology?" *Christianity Today*, May 1975, 46.

61. Charlotte J. Frisbie, "Temporal Change in Navajo Religion: 1868–1990," *Journal of the Southwest* 34, no. 4 (Winter 1992): 492.

62. Howard Shanker, interview by Stephen Prothero, May 15, 2019.

63. Oregon v. Smith, 494 US 872 (1990), https://www.oyez.org/cases/1989/88-1213.

64. U.S. Forest Service, *Final Environmental Impact Statement for Arizona Snowbowl Facilities Improvements*, Volume 1, February 2005, 3-8.

65. U.S. Forest Service, *Final Environmental Impact Statement for Arizona Snowbowl Facilities Improvements*, Volume 1, 3-11 to 3-12.

66. Vincent Randall testimony, "Reporter's Transcript of Proceedings," *Navajo Nation*, 700–701.

67. Lyng v. Northwest Indian Cemetery Protective Association, 485 U.S. 439 (1988); Navajo Nation v. U.S. Forest Service 535 f.3d 1058 (9th Cir. 2008) at 10041, 10042.

68. Judith G. Propper testimony, "Reporter's Transcript of Proceedings," *Navajo Nation*, 1582.

69. Joe Shirley, Jr. testimony, "Reporter's Transcript of Proceedings," *Navajo Nation*, 802–803.

70. Steven Begay testimony, "Reporter's Transcript of Proceedings," *Navajo Nation*, 744.

71. Norris Nez testimony, "Reporter's Transcript of Proceedings," *Navajo Nation*, 890.

72. Larry Foster testimony, "Reporter's Transcript of Proceedings," *Navajo Nation*, 208, 206.

73. Larry Foster testimony, "Reporter's Transcript of Proceedings," *Navajo Nation*, 214, 205.

74. Tisa Wenger, *Religious Freedom: The Contested History of an American Ideal* (Chapel Hill: University of North Carolina Press, 2017), 128.

75. Larry Foster testimony, "Reporter's Transcript of Proceedings," *Navajo Nation*, 194, 197, 198, 205–206, 218.

76. Vincent Schilling, *Native Defenders of the Environment* (Summertown, TN: 7th Generation, 2011), 107–8.

77. Navajo Nation v. U.S. Forest Service, 535 F.3d (2008) at 10105.

78. Michael McNally, "From Substantial Burden on Religion to Diminished Spiritual Fulfillment," 53, 56.

79. Navajo Nation v. U.S. Forest Service, 479 F.3d 1024 (2007), https://caselaw.findlaw.com/us-9th-circuit/1003582.html.

80. Schilling, *Native Defenders of the Environment*, 110; Klee Benally, interview by Stephen Prothero, May 17, 2019.

81. Benally, interview.

PROFILES IN NAVAJO RELIGION: Klee Benally

a. "About," Blackfire, https://www.blackfire.net/about.

b. Jeff Berglund, "Blackfire's Land-Based Ethics: The Benally Family and the Protection of Shi Keyah Hozhoni," in *Indigenous Pop: Native American Music from Jazz to Hip Hop*, ed. Jeff Berglund et al. (Tucson: University of Arizona Press, 2016), 186.

THE NAVAJO: A Genealogy

a. John Pinkerton, *Modern Geography* (London: T. Cadell, 1811); Jacob Fowler, *The Journal of Jacob Fowler*, ed. Elliott Coues (New York: Harper, 1898), 123; Albert Pike, *Prose Sketches and Poems, Written in the Western Country* (Boston: Light & Horton, 1834), 99.

b. G. Turner, *Traits of Indian Character*, vol. 1 (Philadelphia: Key & Biddle, 1836), 202–204.

MATERIAL NAVAJO RELIGION: The Hogan

a. Rose Mitchell, *The Life Story of Rose Mitchell, a Navajo Woman*, ed. Charlotte J. Frisbie (Albuquerque, NM: University of New Mexico Press, 2001), 294.

b. "Hogan 2 Glamping on Navajoland," Airbnb, https://www.airbnb.com/rooms/15389211?source_impression_id=p3_1567711741_1v6LHyaLYhVxjJ+0.

c. "History," Shash Diné, http://www.shashdine.com/history.

PROFILES IN NAVAJO RELIGION: Frank and Rose Mitchell

a. Frank Mitchell, *Navajo Blessingway Singer: The Autobiography of Frank Mitchell*, ed. Charlotte J. Frisbie (Tucson: University of Arizona Press, 1977), 337.

b. Rose Mitchell, *The Life Story of Rose Mitchell*, 296, 298.

BIRTH AND DEATH

a. Charlotte J. Frisbie, "Introduction" to a Special Symposium on Navajo Mortuary Practices and Beliefs, *American Indian Quarterly* 4, no. 4 (November 1978): 303.

b. A woman from Navajo Mountain, quoted in Mary Shepardson, "Changes in Navajo Mortuary Practices and Beliefs," *American Indian Quarterly* 4, no. 4 (November 1978): 385.

c. Shepardson, "Changes in Navajo Mortuary Practices and Beliefs," *American Indian Quarterly* 4, no. 4, (November 1978): 387–88.

Chapter 11

1. Moncure D. Conway, *Centenary History of the South Place Society* (London: Williams and Norgate, 1894), xi.

2. Moncure Daniel Conway, *My Pilgrimage to the Wise Men of the East* (Boston: Houghton, Mifflin, 1906), 113.

3. "FAQ," Sunday Assembly, https://www.sundayassembly.com/faq.

4. "Our Story," Sunday Assembly, https://www.sundayassembly.com/story.

5. "FAQ," Sunday Assembly, https://www.sundayassembly.com/faq.

6. Bill Bryson, *A Short History of Nearly Everything* (New York: Broadway Books, 2003), 327.

7. Bertrand Russell, *What I Believe* (New York: E. P. Dutton, 1925), 1.

8. Daniel Cox, "Way More Americans May Be Atheists Than We Thought," FiveThirtyEight, May 18, 2017, https://fivethirtyeight.com/features/way-more-americans-may-be-atheists-than-we-thought. On this "anti-atheist sentiment," see also Penny Edgell et al., "Atheists and Other Cultural Outsiders: Moral Boundaries and the Non-Religious in the United States," *Social Forces* 95, no. 2 (December 2016): 607–638.

9. "Losing Our Religion? Two Thirds of People Still Claim to Be Religious," Gallup International, 2015, http://gallup-international.bg/en/Publications/2015/223-Losing-Our-Religion-Two-Thirds-of-People-Still-Claim-to-Be-Religious.

10. Todd M. Johnson and Brian J. Grim, eds., *World Religion Database* (Leiden/Boston: Brill, 2019).

11. Sam Harris, "I'm Not the Sexist Pig You're Looking For," September 15, 2014, https://samharris.org/im-not-the-sexist-pig-youre-looking-for/.

12. Betsy Cooper et al., "Exodus: Why Americans Are Leaving Religion—and Why They're Unlikely to Come Back," PRRI, September 22, 2016, https://www.prri.org/research/prri-rns-poll-nones-atheist-leaving-religion.

13. "Religious Landscape Study," Pew Religious Center, https://www.pewforum.org/religious-landscape-study/#religions.

14. Nica Lalli, "Atheists Don't Speak With Just One Voice," *HuffPost Contributors*, October 10, 2007, https://www.huffpost.com/entry/atheists-dont-just-speak_b_67955.

15. "What Is a Freethinker?," Freedom From Religion Forum, https://ffrf.org/faq/feeds/item/18391-what-is-a-freethinker.

16. Christopher Hitchens, "Religion Poisons Everything," *Slate*, April 25, 2007, https://slate.com/news-and-politics/2007/04/religion-poisons-everything.html.

17. Thomas Jefferson to John Adams, April 11, 1823, National Archives, https://founders.archives.gov/documents/Jefferson/98-01-02-3446.

18. Thomas Paine, *The Age of Reason* (Philadelphia: James Carey, 1797), 27.

19. Alexander Campbell, *Delusions: An Analysis of the Book of Mormon* (Boston: Benjamin H. Greene, 1832), 15, 11.

20. Richard Dawkins, *The God Delusion* (New York: Mariner Books, 2008), 69.

21. Peter L. Berger, "Pilgrims," *The American Interest*, August 14, 2014, https://www.the-american-interest.com/2014/08/13/pilgrims/.

22. George Jacob Holyoake, *The Origin and Nature of Secularism* (London: Watts, 1896), 79.

23. Talal Asad, *Formations of the Secular: Christianity, Islam, Modernity* (Palo Alto, CA: Stanford University Press, 2003).

24. John Gray, *Seven Types of Atheism* (New York: Farrar, Straus & Giroux, 2018).

25. Amartya Sen, *The Argumentative Indian: Writings on Indian History, Culture and Identity* (New York: Farrar, Straus & Giroux, 2005), 23.

26. Wendy Doniger, *The Hindus: An Alternative History* (New York: Penguin, 2009), 185; Ray Billington, *Understanding Eastern Philosophy* (New York: Routledge, 1997), 44.

27. *The Rig Veda*, trans. Wendy Doniger O'Flaherty (New York: Penguin, 2005), 25.

28. *The Ramayana of Valmiki: An Epic of Ancient India, Volume II*, ed. Robert P. Goldman, trans. Sheldon I. Pollock (Princeton, NJ: Princeton University Press, 2016), 300.

29. Jake H. Davis, ed., *A Mirror Is for Reflection: Understanding Buddhist Ethics* (New York: Oxford University Press, 2013), 148.

30. Lawrence A. Babb, *Absent Lord: Ascetics and Kings in a Jain Ritual Culture* (Berkeley: University of California Press, 1996), 92.

31. Stephen Bullivant and Michael Ruse, eds., *The Oxford Handbook of Atheism* (New York: Oxford University Press, 2013), 356.

32. *The Analects of Confucius: A Philosophical Translation*, trans. Roger T. Ames and Henry Rosemont Jr. (New York: Ballantine, 1998), 144.

33. T. C. Kline III and Justin Tiwald, eds., *Ritual and Religion in the Xunzi* (New York: SUNY Press, 2014), 25.

34. *Gilgamesh: A Verse Narrative*, trans. Herbert Mason (New York: Mariner Books, 2003), 57.

35. Christopher Hitchens, *God Is Not Great* (New York: Twelve, 2007), 85.

36. W. K. C. Guthrie, *The Sophists* (New York: Cambridge University Press, 1971), 234.

37. Eric Maisel, *The Atheist's Way: Living Well Without Gods* (Novato, CA: New World Library, 2009), 14.

38. James Thrower, *Western Atheism: A Short History* (New York: Prometheus Books, 1999), 47.

39. Justin Martyr, *The First and Second Apologies*, trans. Leslie William Barnard (New York: Paulist Press, 1997), 26.

40. Dorothea Weltecke, "The Medieval Period," in *The Oxford Handbook of Atheism*, eds. Stephen Bullivant and Michael Ruse (New York: Oxford University Press, 2013), 167.

41. Lucien Febvre, *The Problem of Unbelief in the Sixteenth Century* (Cambridge: Harvard University Press, 1985).

42. Sebastian De Grazia, *Macchiavelli in Hell* (New York: Vintage, 1994), 58.

43. Denis Diderot, *Observations on the Drawing Up of Laws*, in *The Age of Enlightenment*, ed. Lester G. Crocker (New York: Macmillan, 1969), 256.

44. Thomas Hobbes, *Leviathan*, ed. Michael Oakeshott (New York: Touchstone, 2008), 83.

45. Rebecca Goldstein, *Betraying Spinoza: The Renegade Jew Who Gave Us Modernity* (New York: Random House, 2006), 12.

46. Louis Jacobs, *The Jewish Religion: A Companion* (New York: Oxford University Press, 1995), 482.

47. Jacques Berlinblau, "Jewish Atheism," in *The Oxford Handbook of Atheism*, eds. Stephen Bullivant and Michael Ruse (New York: Oxford University Press, 2013), 330.

48. Jean Meslier, *Testament: Memoir of the Thoughts and Sentiments of Jean Meslier* (Amherst, NY: Prometheus, 2009), 37.

49. Roy Porter, *The Enlightenment* (London: Macmillan, 1990), 3–4.

50. *Diderot's Selected Writings*, ed. Lester G. Crocker, trans. Derek Coltman (New York: Macmillan, 1966), 256.

51. Raymond Tallis, *In Defence of Wonder and Other Philosophical Reflections* (New York: Routledge, 2014), 222–223.

52. Corliss Lamont, *The Philosophy of Humanism*, 8th ed. (Amherst, NY: Humanist Press, 1997), 45.

53. Immanuel Kant, *Critique of Judgement*, trans. James Creed Meredith (New York: Oxford University Press, 2007), 124.

54. Immanuel Kant, *Critique of Pure Reason*, trans. Paul Guyer and Allen W. Wood (New York: Cambridge University Press, 1998), 117.

55. Immanuel Kant, *Critique of Practical Reason*, trans. Werner S. Pluhar (Indianapolis, IN: Hackett, 2002), 65, 203.

56. Ludwig Feuerbach, *The Essence of Christianity*, trans. George Eliot (New York: Harper & Row, 1957), 105.

57. Sidney Hook, *From Hegel to Marx: Studies in the Intellectual Development of Karl Marx* (New York: Columbia University Press, 1994), 222.

58. Feuerbach, *The Essence of Christianity*, xxxvi.

59. John Raines, ed., *Marx on Religion* (Philadelphia: Temple University Press, 2002), 248, 5.

60. Hook, *From Hegel to Marx*, 18.

61. Baron d'Holbach, "Common Sense," in *The Enlightenment: a Sourcebook and Reader*, ed. Paul Hyland et al. (New York: Routledge, 2003), 90.

62. Karl Marx, "Critique of Hegel's Philosophy of Right," in *Marx on Religion*, ed. John Raines (Philadelphia: Temple University Press, 2002), 171.

63. Friedrich Nietzsche, *The Gay Science*, trans. Walter Kaufmann (New York: Vintage, 1974), 181–182.

64. Sigmund Freud, *The Future of an Illusion*, trans. James Strachey (New York: Norton, 1961), 29, 18.

65. William F. Schultz, *Making the Manifesto: The Birth of Religious Humanism* (Boston: Skinner, 2002), xxvi.

66. Amanda Porterfield, *Conceived in Doubt: Religion and Politics in the New American Nation* (Chicago: University of Chicago Press, 2012).

67. Paine, *The Age of Reason*, 6, 15, 145.

68. Dixon Wecter, "Hero in Reverse," *Virginia Quarterly Review* 18, no. 2 (Spring 1942): 251; Theodore Roosevelt, *Gouverneur Morris* (Boston: Houghton Mifflin, 1888), 289.

69. "Jefferson's Letter to the Danbury Baptists," Library of Congress, https://www.loc.gov/loc/lcib/9806/danpre.html; Thomas Jefferson, *Notes on the State of Virginia* (London: John Stockdale, 1787), 265; Theophilus Parsons to John Jay, May 5, 1880, in *The Correspondence and Public Papers of John Jay*, vol. 4, ed. Henry P. Johnson (New York: G. P. Putnam's Sons, 1893), 270; William Linn, *Serious Considerations on the Election of a President* (New York: John Furman, 1800), 19; *Connecticut Courant*, August 18, 1800, quoted in Susan Dunn, *Jefferson's Second Revolution: The Election Crisis of 1800 and the Triumph of Republicanism* (Boston: Houghton Mifflin, 2004), 148.

70. Edwin S. Gaustad, *Sworn on the Altar of God: A Religious Biography of Thomas Jefferson* (Grand Rapids, MI: Eerdmans, 1996), xiii.

71. Paine, *The Age of Reason*, 12, 10.

72. Frederick Douglass, *Life of an American Slave* (Boston: Anti-Slavery Office, 1845), http://utc.iath.virginia.edu/abolitn/abaufda14t.html.

73. Austin Steward, *Twenty-Two Years a Slave, and Forty Years a Freeman* (Rochester, NY: William Alling, 1857), 98.

74. Frances Wright, *Life, Letters and Lectures, 1834/1844* (New York: Arno, 1972), viii.

75. Frances Wright, *Address on the State of the Public Mind* (New York: Free Inquirer, 1829), 9.

76. Frances Wright, *Course of Popular Lectures* (New York: Free Enquirer, 1829), 103.

77. Philip Hone, *The Diary of Philip Hone, 1828–1851*, vol. 1, ed. Allan Nevins (New York: Dodd, Mead, 1927), 9–10.

78. Lori D. Ginsberg, "'The Heart of Your Readers Will Shudder': Fanny Wright, Infidelity, and American Freethought," *American Quarterly* 46, no. 2 (June 1994): 195.

79. Sara A. Francis Underwood, *Heroines of Freethought* (New York: Somerby, 1876), 268.

80. Bonnie S. Anderson, *The Rabbi's Atheist Daughter: Ernestine Rose, International Feminist Pioneer* (New York: Oxford University Press, 2017), 116.

81. *Proceedings of the Meeting of the Loyal Women of the Republic* (New York: Phair, 1863), 21.

82. Anderson, *The Rabbi's Atheist Daughter*, 99, 70.

83. Ernestine L. Rose, *A Defence of Atheism* (Boston: J. P. Mendum, 1881), 21, 18.

84. Leigh Eric Schmidt, *Village Atheists: How America's Unbelievers Made Their Way in a Godly Nation* (Princeton, NJ: Princeton University Press, 2016), 8.

85. Robert G. Ingersoll, *The Works of Robert Ingersoll*, vol. 9 (New York: Dresden, 1902), 74; and Robert G. Ingersoll, *The Works of Robert Ingersoll*, vol. 1 (New York: Dresden, 1909), 201.

86. *The Woman's Bible*, vol. 1 (New York: European Publishing, 1895), 7, 29.

87. Clarence Darrow, *The Story of My Life* (New York: Charles Scribner's Sons, 1932), 32.

88. H. L. Mencken, *On Religion* (Amherst, NY: Prometheus, 2002), 202–203.

89. John T. Scopes, *Center of the Storm: Memoirs of John T. Scopes* (New York: Holt, Rinehart, & Winston, 1967), 31.

90. Hubert Harrison to Frances Reynolds Keyser, May 20, 1908, in *A Hubert Harrison Reader*, ed. Jeffrey B. Perry (Middletown, CT: Wesleyan University Press, 2001), 37, 39.

91. Langston Hughes, *The Collected Poems of Langston Hughes*, ed. Arnold Rampersad (New York: Knopf, 1994), 166–167.

92. Bryan F. Le Beau, *The Atheist: Madalyn Murray O'Hair* (New York: New York University Press, 2003), 113.

93. Patrick Henry, "'And I Don't Care What It Is': The Tradition-History of a Civil Religion Proof Text," *Journal of the American Academy of Religion* 49, no. 1 (Mar 1981): 41.

94. Hitchens, *God Is Not Great*, 280.

95. Hitchens, *God Is Not Great*, 56.

96. Richard Dawkins (@RichardDawkins), Twitter post, March 1, 2013; Sam Harris, *Letter to a Christian Nation* (New York: Norton, 2004), 123.

97. Richard Dawkins, in "Has the world changed?—Part two," *The Guardian*, October 11, 2001, https://www.theguardian.com/world/2001/oct/11/afghanistan.terrorism2.

98. Sam Harris, *The End of Faith: Religion, Terror, and the Future of Reason* (New York: Norton, 2004), 15.

99. Hitchens, *God Is Not Great*, 6.

100. Richard Dawkins, "Is Science a Religion?" *The Humanist* 57, no. 1 (January/February 1997), http://www.2think.org/Richard_Dawkins_Is_Science_A_Religion.shtml.

101. Richard Dawkins, *The God Delusion* (Boston: Houghton Mifflin, 2006), 346.

102. Ta-Nehisi Coates, *Between the World and Me* (New York: Spiegel & Grau, 2015), 28.

103. In a 2012 Gallup poll, only 54 percent of American adults said they would vote for an atheist for president. See Jeffrey M. Jones, "Atheists, Muslims See Most Bias as Presidential Candidates," Gallup, June 21, 2012, https://news.gallup.com/poll/155285/atheists-muslims-bias-presidential-candidates.aspx. That figure rose to 58 percent in 2015. See Lydia Saad, "Support for Nontraditional Candidates Varies by Religion," Gallup, June 24, 2015, https://news.gallup.com/poll/183791/support-nontraditional-candidates-varies-religion.aspx.

104. Penny Edgell et al., "Atheists as 'Other': Moral Boundaries and Cultural Membership in American Society," *American Sociological Review* 71, no. 2 (April 2006): 218.

105. David Foster Wallace, "All That," *The New Yorker*, December 6, 2009, https://www.newyorker.com/magazine/2009/12/14/all-that-2.

106. Hitchens, *God Is Not Great*, 5.

107. David Bentley Hart, "Believe It or Not," *First Things*, May 2010, https://www.firstthings.com/article/2010/05/believe-it-or-not.

108. Charly Wilder, "I Don't Believe in Atheists," *Salon*, March 13, 2008, https://www.salon.com/2008/03/13/chris_hedges/.

109. Michael Onfray, *Atheist Manifesto: The Case Against Christianity, Judaism, and Islam* (New York: Arcade, 2011), 10.

110. Torcaso v. Watkins, 367 U.S. 488 (1961), https://caselaw.findlaw.com/us-supreme-court/367/488.html. This footnote listed secular humanism among the "religions in this country which do not teach what would generally [be] considered a belief in the existence of God."

111. "About the Oasis Network," Oasis Network, https://www.networkoasis.org/about-oasis.

112. Greg M. Epstein, *Good Without God: What a Billion Nonreligious People Do Believe* (New York: William Morrow, 2009).

113. Alfredo Garcia and Joseph Blankholm, "The Social Context of Organized Unbelief: County-Level Predictors of Nonbeliever Organizations in the United States," *Journal for the Scientific Study of Religion* 55, no. 1 (March 2016): 70–90.

114. Ryan Cragun and Christel Manning, introduction to *Organized Secularism in the United States*, ed. Ryan T. Cragun et al. (Boston: de Gruyter, 2017), 5.

115. Paul Tillich, *Dynamics of Faith* (New York: Harper & Row, 1957), 1.

116. Benjamin Beit-Hallahmi, "Atheists: A Psychological Profile," in *The Cambridge Companion to Atheism,* ed. Michael Martin (New York: Cambridge University Press, 2007), 313.

ATHEISM AND AGNOSTICISM: A Genealogy

a. Philip of Mornay, *A VVoorke Concerning the Trewnesse of the Christian Religion, Written in French: Against Atheists, Epicures, Paynims, Jewes, Mahumetists, and Other Infidels,* trans. Philip Sidney and Arthur Golding (London, 1587), 349, https://quod.lib.umich.edu/e/eebo/A07769.0001.001/1:6.20?rgn=div2;view=fulltext; "atheist, n. and adj.," *OED Online,* http://www.oed.com.ezproxy.bu.edu/view/Entry/12450?redirectedFrom=atheist#eid; R. H.

Hutton, "Pope Huxley," *The Spectator,* January 29, 1870, https://mathcs.clarku.edu/huxley/comm/Hutton/PopeH.html; Thomas H. Huxley, "Agnosticism," in *Christianity and Agnosticism: A Controversy,* ed. Henry Wace et al. (New York: Appleton, 1889), 38.

b. Huxley, "Agnosticism and Christianity," 196.

PROFILES IN ATHEISM: Xenophanes

a. Karl Marx, *The German Ideology* (New York: Prometheus Books, 1976), 154.

b. Christopher Shields, ed., *The Blackwell Guide to Ancient Philosophy* (Hoboken, NJ: Wiley-Blackwell, 2003), 9.

PROFILES IN ATHEISM: Jennifer Hecht

a. Jennifer Michael Hecht, interview by TheBestSchools.org, https://thebestschools.org/features/jennifer-michael-hecht-interview/.

b. Jennifer Michael Hecht, "Down with Agnosticism," *Patheos,* November 21, 2011, https://www.patheos.com/blogs/secularoutpost/2011/11/21/down-with-agnosticism; Jennifer Michael Hecht, interview by TheBestSchools.org.

c. Jennifer Michael Hecht, "Stay," *Boston Globe,* February 7, 2010, http://archive.boston.com/bostonglobe/ideas/articles/2010/02/07/stay/.

BIRTH AND DEATH

a. Bertrand Russell, *What I Believe* (New York: E. P. Dutton, 1925), 13.

b. Suzanne Moore, "Why Non-believers Need Rituals Too," *The Guardian,* December 27, 2013, https://www.theguardian.com/commentisfree/2013/dec/27/why-non-believers-need-rituals-atheists; Greta Christina, "Rituals and Traditions," *Free Inquiry* 36, no. 6 (October/November 2016): 13.

c. "Humanist Ceremonies," Humanists UK, https://humanism.org.uk/ceremonies/humanist-namings/.

Credits

Text

CHAPTER 1: "Ceremony" from *Ceremony* by Leslie Marmon Silko, copyright © 1977, 2006 by Leslie Marmon Silko. Used by permission of Viking Books, an imprint of Penguin Publishing Group, a division of Penguin Random House LLC. All rights reserved.

CHAPTER 2: "His Death in Benares" by Kabir, translated by Arvind Krishna Mehrotra. Published by New York Review Books. Copyright © 2011 by Arvind Krishna Mehrotra. Reprinted by permission of New York Review Books. All rights reserved.

CHAPTER 3: Excerpt from *The Art of Forgiveness, Lovingkindness, and Peace* by Jack Kornfield, copyright © 2002 by Jack Kornfield. Published by Rider. Used by permission of Random House Group Limited and Bantam Books, an imprint of Random House, a division of Penguin Random House LLC. All rights reserved.

CHAPTER 4: Passage from the *Sukhmani* from *Textual Sources for the Study of Sikhism* (Manchester University Press, 1984), translated and edited by W. H. McLeod. Reprinted by permission of the W. H. McLeod Estate.

CHAPTER 6: "Crusades, 1096–1204" map, from *World History: Patterns of Interaction*, Student Edition. Copyright © 2009 by Houghton Mifflin Harcourt Publishing Company. All rights reserved. Used by permission of the publisher. Any further duplication is strictly prohibited unless written permission is obtained from Houghton Mifflin Harcourt Publishing Company. "Changes in Global Christianity's Center of Gravity (33 CE–2050 CE)" map, from Todd Johnson and Sun Young Chun, "Tracking Global Christianity's Statistical Centre of Gravity, AD 33–AD 2100," *International Review of Mission 93*(369): 166–181, 2004. Reprinted with permission from Todd Johnson.

CHAPTER 8: Excerpt from "Four Verses on Pure Knowing Written for My Students," from Yangming, Wang, Philip J. Ivanhoe ed. *Readings from the Lu-Wang School of Neo-Confucianism*, p. 181. Copyright © 2009 by Hackett Publishing Company, Inc. Reprinted by permission of Hackett Publishing Company, Inc. All rights reserved.

CHAPTER 9: "Nine Practices of the Celestial Masters" and "Twenty-Seven Precepts of the Celestial Masters" from *Celestial Masters: History and Ritual in Early Daoist Communities* by Terry F. Kleeman, pp. 92–94. Reprinted with permission from the Harvard University Asia Center.

CHAPTER 10: Blessingway song lyrics republished with permission of Walter De Gruyter and Company, from "The Central Concepts of Navajo World View I," *Linguistics*, by Gary Witherspoon, Vol. 119, 1974; permission conveyed through Copyright Clearance Center, Inc.

CHAPTER 11: Excerpt from "Goodbye Christ" from *The Collected Poems of Langston Hughes* by Langston Hughes, edited by Arnold Rampersad with David Roessel, Associate Editor, copyright © 1994 by the Estate of Langston Hughes. Reprinted by permission of Harold Ober Associates and Alfred A. Knopf, an imprint of the Knopf Doubleday Publishing Group, a division of Penguin Random House LLC. All rights reserved.

Photographs

FRONT MATTER: Page xxvii: Meera Subramanian

CHAPTER 1: Pages 2–3: Meera Subramanian; p. 5: Meera Subramanian; p. 6: Shannon Stapleton/Reuters/Newscom; p. 9: Judith Bicking/Alamy Stock Photo; p. 10: Eric Nathan/Alamy Stock Photo; p. 12: Michael Brooks/Alamy Stock Photo; p. 13: Universal Education/Universal Images Group via Getty Images; p. 15: Demelza Cloke/Alamy Stock Photo; p. 18: © SZ Photo/Scherl/Bridgeman Images; p. 19: Radek Hofman/Alamy Stock Photo; p. 21: Meera Subramanian; p. 22: ZUMA Press, Inc./Alamy Stock Photo; p. 24: LOOK Die Bildagentur der Fotografen GmbH/Alamy Stock Photo.

CHAPTER 2: Pages 28–29: Indranil Aditya/Alamy Stock Photo; p. 31: Meera Subramanian; p. 33: Agencja Fotograficzna Caro/Alamy Stock Photo; p. 37: Pictures from History/Bridgeman Images; p. 38: Majority World/UIG/Bridgeman Images; p. 39: Dinodia Photos/Alamy Stock Photo; p. 40: imageBROKER/Alamy Stock Photo; p. 41: Yawar Nazir/Getty Images; p. 43: Pictures from History/Bridgeman Images; p. 47: National Geographic Image Collection/Alamy Stock Photo; p. 48: Pictures from History/Rainer Krack/Bridgeman Images; p. 49: ©The British Library Board/Leemage/Bridgeman Images; p. 51: Putu Artana/Alamy Stock Photo; p. 52: Nina Paley; p. 54: Heritage Image Partnership Ltd/Alamy Stock Photo; p. 57: age fotostock/Alamy Stock Photo; p. 59: Roland et Sabrine Michaud/akg-images; p. 60: akg-images/Fototeca Gilardi; p. 62: PVDE/Bridgeman Images; p. 64: Pictures from History/Bridgeman Images; p. 65: Pictorial Press Ltd/Alamy Stock Photo; p. 66: ZUMA Press, Inc./Alamy Stock Photo; p. 67: Sean Pavone/Alamy Stock Photo; p. 70: Meera Subramanian; p. 71: Angela Bellas/Alamy Stock Photo; p. 73: Azrin Ahmad; p. 75: Xinhua/Alamy Stock Photo.

CHAPTER 3: Pages 78–79: narvikk/Getty Images; p. 80: Meera Subramanian; p. 81: Chetchai Ngampattaravorakul/Alamy Stock Photo; p. 82: Meera Subramanian; p. 83: Mireille Vautier/Alamy Stock Photo; p. 84: robertharding/Alamy Stock Photo; p. 88: robertharding/Alamy Stock Photo; p. 91: Art Directors & TRIP/Alamy Stock Photo; p. 92: Pictures from History/Bridgeman Images; p. 94: Pictures from History/Bridgeman Images; p. 95: © Losang Gyatso; p. 98: Nikreates/Alamy Stock Photo; p. 99: Prisma by Dukas Presseagentur GmbH/Alamy Stock Photo; p. 100: Meera Subramanian; p. 101: Karen Cowled/Alamy Stock Photo; p. 104: Photo © Costa/Bridgeman Images; p. 105: Pictures from History/Bridgeman Images; p. 108: Photo © Chinch Gryniewicz/Bridgeman Images; p. 110: don jon red/Alamy Stock Photo; p. 111: UtCon Collection/Alamy Stock Photo; p. 113: San Francisco History Center, San Francisco Public Library; p. 114: David Litschel/Alamy Stock Photo; p. 116: Dee Jolie/Alamy Stock Photo; p. 118: Craig Lovell/Eagle Visions Photography/Alamy Stock Photo; p. 120: robertharding/Alamy Stock Photo; p. 123: Leonid Plotkin/Alamy Stock Photo; p. 124: theodore liasi/Alamy Stock Photo.

CHAPTER 4: Pages 128–29: PS-I/Alamy Stock Photo; p. 130: Sameer Sehgal/Hindustan Times via Getty Images; p. 133: Blaine Harrington III/Alamy Stock Photo; p. 135: Pacific Press/Alamy Stock Photo; p. 138: Jim West/Alamy Stock Photo; p. 140: Gabriela Rosell/Shutterstock; p.

Index

Page numbers in italics refer to illustrations and tables.